BELIEF AND CULT

Belief and Cult

RETHINKING ROMAN RELIGION

JACOB L. MACKEY

PRINCETON UNIVERSITY PRESS
PRINCETON & OXFORD

Copyright © 2022 by Princeton University Press

Princeton University Press is committed to the protection of copyright and the intellectual property our authors entrust to us. Copyright promotes the progress and integrity of knowledge. Thank you for supporting free speech and the global exchange of ideas by purchasing an authorized edition of this book. If you wish to reproduce or distribute any part of it in any form, please obtain permission.

Requests for permission to reproduce material from this work should be sent to permissions@press.princeton.edu

Published by Princeton University Press
41 William Street, Princeton, New Jersey 08540
99 Banbury Road, Oxford OX2 6JX

press.princeton.edu

All Rights Reserved

First paperback printing, 2025
Paper ISBN 9780691236537

The Library of Congress has cataloged the cloth edition as follows:

Names: Mackey, Jacob Louis, 1971– author.
Title: Belief and cult : rethinking Roman religion / Jacob L. Mackey.
Description: Princeton : Princeton University Press, [2022] | Includes bibliographical references and index.
Identifiers: LCCN 2021049285 (print) | LCCN 2021049286 (ebook) | ISBN 9780691165080 (acid-free paper) | ISBN 9780691233147 (ebook)
Subjects: LCSH: Rome—Religion. | Belief and doubt. | BISAC: HISTORY / Ancient / Rome | LITERARY CRITICISM / Ancient & Classical
Classification: LCC BL803 .M326 2022 (print) | LCC BL803 (ebook) | DDC 292.07—dc23/eng/20220103
LC record available at https://lccn.loc.gov/2021049285
LC ebook record available at https://lccn.loc.gov/2021049286

British Library Cataloging-in-Publication Data is available

Editorial: Rob Tempio, Chloe Coy
Production Editorial: Terri O'Prey
Production: Erin Suydam
Publicity: Alyssa Sanford, Charlotte Coyne
Copyeditor: Kathleen Kageff

Jacket/Cover art: Mosaic of a sacred choir, 3rd century CE, from the Temple of Diana Tifatina (now site of Abbey of St. Angelo in Formis), near the ancient city of Capua, Italy. Photo: I. Shurygin

This book has been composed in Arno

For Luke and Greta
paterna cum caritate

BRIEF CONTENTS

Detailed Contents ix
Preface xv
Acknowledgments xix
Abbreviations xxi

Introduction: Roman Religion, from Intuitions to Institutions   1

PART I. THEORETICAL FOUNDATIONS

1   Losing Belief   27

2   Recovering Belief   59

3   Belief and Emotion, Belief and Action   98

4   Shared Belief, Shared Agency, Social Norms   136

5   Shared Belief, Social Ontology, Power   172

PART II. CASE STUDIES

6   Belief and Cult: Lucretius's Roman Theory   209

7   *Ad incunabula*: Children's Cult as Cognitive Apprenticeship   244

8   The "Folk Theology" of Roman Prayer: Content, Context, and Commitment   291

9   *Inauguratio*: Belief, Ritual, and Religious Power   337

    Epilog: Comparison, Explanation, and Belief   371

Glossary 395
References 399
Index Locorum 447
General Index 459

DETAILED CONTENTS

Preface xv
Acknowledgments xix
Abbreviations xxi

Introduction: Roman Religion, from Intuitions to Institutions 1
   0.1. Roman Cult and the Question of Belief 1
   0.2. From Roman Intuitions to Roman Institutions 5
   0.3. HADD and Social Cognition 9
   0.4. Intentionality and Belief 17

PART I. THEORETICAL FOUNDATIONS

Chapter 1. Losing Belief 27
   1.1. *Introduction* 27
   1.2. *A History of Belief-Denial and the Belief-Action Dichotomy* 27
   1.3. *An Anatomy of Belief-Denial and the Belief-Action Dichotomy* 44
      1.3.1. Belief Is Christian 44
      1.3.2. Belief Is a Concept 46
      1.3.3. Belief Is a Linguistic Practice 49
      1.3.4. Beliefs Are Unknowable 53
   1.4. *Conclusion: Historical Empathy and Other Minds* 55

Chapter 2. Recovering Belief 59
   2.1. *Introduction* 59
   2.2. *The Intentionality of Belief* 60
      2.2.1. Belief Requires a *Subject* in Order to Exist 63
      2.2.2. Beliefs Are about *Objects* 64

	2.2.3. Beliefs Have *Content*	65
	2.2.4. Belief Is a Distinctive *Psychological Mode*	68
	2.2.5. Belief Has a Mind-to-World *Direction of Fit*	69
	2.2.6. Beliefs Define Their Own *Conditions of Satisfaction*	72
	2.2.7. Summary Thus Far	75
2.3.	*Discursive Intentionality: Extending the Analysis to Language*	75
2.4.	*Belief-in*	77
2.5.	*Belief Intensity*	79
2.6.	*Intuition and Inference Produce Nonreflective and Reflective Beliefs*	82
	2.6.1. The Two Systems and "Theological Incorrectness"	83
	2.6.2. Intuition and Roman Religious Culture	87
	2.6.3. Inference and Agency	91
2.7.	*Conclusion*	95

Chapter 3. Belief and Emotion, Belief and Action — 98

3.1.	*Introduction*	98
3.2.	*Belief and Emotion*	99
	3.2.1. What Is Emotion?	101
	3.2.2. Belief and Emotion in Apuleius and Livy	106
3.3.	*Belief and Action*	109
	3.3.1. A Simple Belief-Desire Model of Action	113
	3.3.2. Deontology: Desire-Independent Reasons for Action	116
	3.3.3. *Pietas* as a Deontology	126
	3.3.4. An Enriched Model of Action	130
3.4.	*Action Theory and Folk Psychology*	133

Chapter 4. Shared Belief, Shared Agency, Social Norms — 136

4.1.	*Introduction*	136
4.2.	*Roman Consensus*	139
4.3.	*Shared Intentionality and Shared Agency*	143
	4.3.1. Shared Intentionality	144
	4.3.2. Shared Agency and Joint Action	145
	4.3.3. Mutual Belief	147

DETAILED CONTENTS xi

   4.3.4. Aggregate versus Collective versus Joint Intentionality   149
   4.3.5. Jointly Sharing Beliefs and Agency in Sacrifice   153
  4.4. *Norms, Collective Intentionality, Communal Common Ground, and Large-Scale Cooperation*   159
  4.5. *Conclusion*   165
  4.6. *Coda: Durkheim among the Ruins*   166

Chapter 5. Shared Belief, Social Ontology, Power   172
  5.1. *Introduction*   172
  5.2. *Objective and Exterior or Subjective and Interior?*   173
  5.3. *A Social Ontology*   177
   5.3.1. Imposition of Function   178
   5.3.2. Constitutive Rules   180
   5.3.3. Shared Intentionality and Social Ontology   192
   5.3.4. *Societas* versus "Emergent Social Entity"   194
  5.4. *Concluding Caveats and Possible Objections*   201

PART II: CASE STUDIES

Chapter 6. Belief and Cult: Lucretius's Roman Theory   209
  6.1. *Introduction*   209
  6.2. *Why Lucretius?*   210
  6.3. *Epicurean Action*   213
  6.4. *A Lucretian Archaeology of Religious Belief*   214
  6.5. *Excursus: Roman Epiphanies*   220
  6.6. *False Beliefs*   227
   6.6.1. Philodemus on Religious Inference   231
  6.7. *A Lucretian Aetiology of Cult*   233
  6.8. *A Cognitive Theory?*   235
  6.9. *Action Theory and Cult in Lucretius*   236
  6.10. *A Prescription for Cult Practice*   239
  6.11. *Conclusion*   242

xii DETAILED CONTENTS

Chapter 7. *Ad incunabula*: Children's Cult as Cognitive Apprenticeship ... 244
    7.1. Introduction ... 244
    7.2. Ontogeny of Social Cognition ... 248
    7.3. Learning to Pray: Imitation and Individual Agency ... 251
    7.4. Religious Participation: From Joint Attention to Cultural Cognition ... 264
        7.4.1. Ritual Norms, Overimitation, and Orthopraxy ... 271
        7.4.2. Joint Commitments ... 279
        7.4.3. Shared Beliefs ... 281
    7.5. Religious Instruction: Beyond Apprenticeship ... 282
    7.6. Conclusion ... 290

Chapter 8. The "Folk Theology" of Roman Prayer: Content, Context, and Commitment ... 291
    8.1. Introduction ... 291
    8.2. Some Guiding Theoretical Principles ... 294
    8.3. Roman Prayer ... 303
    8.4. Prayer Form ... 307
    8.5. The Force of Prayer ... 311
    8.6. Counterintuitive Content ... 319
    8.7. Context and Commitment ... 330
    8.8. Conclusion ... 335

Chapter 9. *Inauguratio*: Belief, Ritual, and Religious Power ... 337
    9.1. Introduction ... 337
    9.2. Cognition and Ritual Form ... 339
    9.3. Auspicia ... 344
    9.4. Cognition-about-Practice: Antony's *Flaminate* ... 347
    9.5. Cognition-in-Practice ... 361
    9.6. Constitutive versus Nonconstitutive Beliefs ... 362
        9.6.1. Constitutive Beliefs ... 362
        9.6.2. Nonconstitutive Beliefs ... 367
    9.7. Conclusion: Belief, Religious Reality, and Power at Rome ... 369

Epilog: Comparison, Explanation, and Belief — 371
   10.1. Introduction — 371
   10.2. Prescendi's Model of Roman Sacrifice — 372
   10.3. Roman Sacrifice in Dionysius of Halicarnassus's Antiquitates Romanae — 373
   10.4. Roman Sacrifice in Arnobius of Sicca's Adversus Nationes — 376
   10.5. Human Sacrifice in Caesar's De bello Gallico — 381
   10.6. Comparison, Explanation, and Belief in Dionysius, Arnobius, and Caesar — 385
   10.7. Believing in Belief — 392

Glossary 395
References 399
Index Locorum 447
General Index 459

PREFACE

THIS IS A BOOK about Roman religion. This is a theoretical book. If Roman religion interests you, but theory does not, this book may not be for you. However, the book doesn't do theory for theory's sake. Rather, it offers theoretical solutions to problems posed by the study of Roman religion in the hopes of inspiring new ways of thinking about it and, indeed, any religion, ancient or otherwise. The book is not only for my fellow classicists and ancient historians but also for anyone interested in religions and in theoretical approaches to their study, especially those based in cognitive theory.

The central problem in the book is that of belief. For some time, scholars doubted whether belief was relevant to Roman religion. Recently, they have begun revisiting belief. This book's contention is that it is not sufficient merely to reintroduce talk of belief; we also need to understand exactly how belief works in Roman religion. Belief did not manifest in Roman religion as *faith*, through which the believer is saved (as in, e.g., Paul's Epistle to the Romans). However, it did manifest in other ways and, in so doing, enabled the entire panoply of traditional Roman religious actions, practices, and ways of thinking and feeling. In these chapters, I explain how, in Roman religion, belief underlay religious emotions, and played a causal role in individual cult action. I show that when shared intersubjectively, belief facilitated the sharing of agency in coordinated joint ritual actions. Such shared belief also granted religious norms their coercive power. Norms are but a part of what I shall call social ontology, and Roman social ontology depended on the Romans' shared beliefs. That is, shared belief played a central role in the creation and maintenance of all Roman socioreligious reality, replete with festival days, priestly statuses, ritual practices, and the various rules and normative powers of permission, obligation, and restriction that these social realities embodied and exerted.

To conjoin "Roman" and "religion" as I do in this book may be thought to require a defense, so we must get one little bit of theorizing out of the way here once and for all. Some scholars are concerned that "religion" may not be a term applicable to the Romans.¹ I want to insist that it is. This doubt springs from concerns both etic and emic. On the etic side, it arises from a kind of positivism. The reasoning appears to go like this: "religion" names a concept that is defined by a clear set of historically determined criteria. If there were no Roman phenomena that precisely met all these supposed criteria, then the Romans did not have religion.² But surely this is too unsupple a stance. Romans engaged in a variety of practices that they themselves conceived as directed toward gods. These god-directed activities would seem to fall most naturally within the category of practices that our (really rather loose) concept of *religion* covers, and thus within the extension of our term "religion."

On the emic side, scholars worry that the Romans might not have had a discrete concept of "religion,"³ and if they did not have the concept, they could not have had the thing. On these grounds we may equally doubt whether they had an economy or even tuberculosis.⁴ This worry reflects a confusion about social ontology. While a community requires a concept of, say, *tribunatus plebis*, "plebeian tribuneship," in order to have plebeian tribunes, it need not have an explicit concept of economy in order to have an economy, in other words, the systematic—and discoverable—consequences of producing, consuming, trading, loaning, buying, selling, and so on. By the same token, a society need not have an explicit concept of religion to have religion, that is, to have practices that involve doing things to, for, with, directed toward, or significantly involving gods, spirits, and other nonhuman entities. Thus, roughly, we may distinguish between social things such as plebeian tribuneships and plebeian tribunes that are, in a sense, created by the very concept of them (and by the practices undertaken in light of the concept), and social things that arise as a result of various more or less (often less) systematic attitudes and practices, like producing and consuming, for which organizing and clarifying concepts, etic or emic, such as "economy" may subsequently be invented. Religion belongs to this latter group.

1. E.g., Henig 1995: 68; Bremmer 1998: 10; Gradel 2002: 4–5; Ando 2003: 2–3; Rüpke 2007c: 6; Nongbri 2008; Barton and Boyarin 2016.

2. I owe this observation mutatis mutandis to John R. Searle's 1983b and 1994 articles about literary theory.

3. However, see Casadio 2010: 310 on this: "In an age of cultural encounter and cosmopolitanism, when the old local character of the cults was vanishing, and in an age of philosophic-religious syncretism . . . a word was wanted to gather up and express all the religious aspects of human existence: it had to be a word not equivalent to any definite technical notion, 'and such word was *religio*'" (citing Fowler 1908).

4. For doubts about the ancient economy, see Morley 2004: 33–50. For doubts about tuberculosis in ancient Egypt, see Latour 1998, and cf. his more recent *retractatio*, Latour 2004.

Concepts and terms such as "economy" or "religion" confer all sorts of cognitive and practical powers on their possessors, even when they don't create their objects ex nihilo, and thus one must attend to the semantic fields of the lexemes in a given language and to the conceptual resources of a given linguistic community.[5] As sketchy as their understanding of the economy may have been, Romans like the pontifex Cotta in Cicero's *De natura deorum* could nonetheless array activities such as praying to gods and performing rituals involving gods under the catchall phrase *omnis populi Romani religio*, "the entire religion of the Roman people" (3.5). That Cotta could then refer to the constituent parts of *religio* as *religiones* does no harm to the singular's usage as an umbrella term. Compare how we might speak both of particular "sports" and also of "sport" in general (*OED* s.v. 4a). Moreover, Cicero could say, propria voce, things like this: *sua cuique civitati religio ... est, nostra nobis*,[6] "each city-state has its own religion; we have ours" (*Flacc.* 69). This book is about the *religio* of Cicero's city-state, in the republican period. I use the term "religion" in a sense that I think he and the pontifex Cotta would have recognized: to refer to Rome's *sacra et auspicia*, "rituals of sacrifice and of the auspices," and their associated gods, priests, prayers, ritual practices, and norms.[7]

I hope that Cotta would approve, as well, of my undertaking, which is to challenge the commonplace that belief is not a category of much relevance to the study of Roman religion. After all, Cotta claimed that he himself accepted traditional Roman beliefs, *opiniones*, about the gods and their cult (*N.D.* 3.5). Belief, I argue here, is a human universal. It is the *contents* of beliefs and the beliefs *about* belief that vary. Everyone knows that Italians kiss, Japanese bow, and Americans shake hands.[8] All these practices are local expressions of the universal act of greeting. I endeavor in this book to keep one eye always on the universal, that is, on belief as a human capacity, and another on particulars such as Cotta's *opiniones* about the gods of Rome and their cult. I seek to show how the Romans recruited a cognitive faculty common to our species in order to create a unique and distinctive religious world of their own.

---

5. For some Roman concepts expressible by "*religio*" and "*religiones*," see Rüpke 2007c; and Casadio 2010.

6. Unless otherwise noted, throughout this book ellipses will indicate that material from the original text has been omitted.

7. In this book, mainly for reasons of space, I include no formal discussion of the third branch of Roman religion mentioned by Cotta, which comprised the workings of the Etruscan haruspices and the *quindecemviri sacris faciundis* (Cic. N. D. 3.5): *cumque omnis populi Romani religio in sacra et in auspicia divisa sit, tertium adiunctum sit si quid praedictionis causa ex portentis et monstris Sibyllae interpretes haruspicesve monuerunt*.

8. Morrison and Conaway 2006: 2.

ACKNOWLEDGMENTS

THIS BOOK STARTED as a 2009 dissertation in Princeton University's Department of Classics and has been a long time—too long, really—in the making. It benefitted immensely from the attentions of my readers, Denis Feeney and Harriet Flower, and especially my adviser, Robert Kaster. At my defense, James Rives asked me a question about power that I could not answer then but have endeavored to answer here. He also provided pages of extraordinarily helpful written comments on the dissertation after I had defended it.

Rob Tempio, my editor at Princeton University Press, was an early believer in the project and stood by me steadfastly even as five cross-country moves and four local moves ate up my summers and made me, but thankfully not him, despair of ever seeing a finished manuscript. The fact that you are holding this book is owed in large part to his quiet faith that I could and would finish it, and that it would be worth the wait. Jennifer Larson, a reader for the press, provided extraordinarily incisive comments on almost every page of the manuscript. She improved the book incalculably. A second reader for the press, who remained anonymous, also made a great many improving suggestions.

Between 2009 and now, I have been fortunate to have had numerous opportunities to hone my ideas before audiences at a variety of conferences and talks at the Center for Advanced Study in the Behavioral Sciences at Stanford University, Columbia University, City University of New York Graduate College, Notre Dame Institute for Advanced Study, Notre Dame Classics, New York University, Princeton University, University of Reading, Rutgers University, Society for Classical Studies, University of St. Andrews, Stanford University, Theoretical Roman Archaeology Conference 2014, University of California–Los Angeles, University of California–San Francisco, University of Southern California, University of British Columbia, and University of Oslo.

I have also shared my writing, the occasional email exchange, and in-person conversations with many scholars in the fields of classics, the cognitive sciences, and philosophy. I owe debts of gratitude that this brief note cannot express to Leonardo Ambasciano, Clifford Ando, David Armstrong, Robert Audi, Andreas Bendlin, Keith Bradley, Jan Bremmer, Jennifer Devereaux, the late Garrett Fagan, Denis Feeney (again), Dana Fields, Jeff Fish, Jay Fisher,

Harriet Flower, the late Thomas Habinek, Tom Harrison, Brooke Holmes, Bob Kaster (again), Joshua Katz, Christian Kaesser, Jennifer Larson, Josipa Lulic, Jake MacPhail, Jon Master, Michael McOsker, Peter Meineck, Blanka Misic, Malek Moazzam-Doulat, Henrike Moll, Jason Nethercut, Ryan Nichols, Andrej Petrovic, Ivana Petrovic, Verity Platt, Erica and Ryan Preston-Roedder, Andrew Riggsby, Meredith Safran, Michael Schmitz, Andrew Shtulman, Rob Sobak, Damian Stocking, Joseph Streeter, Georg Theiner, Anna Uhlig, Jyri Vaahtera, Henk Versnel, and Andrew Young. I apologize to all my friends and acquaintances who helped me with this project but whose names I have omitted.

I thank Lydia Herring-Harrington for her beautiful photographs and Kate Stanchak for the elegant figures she created. This book would have turned out much messier than it did without the excellent editing services, at various stages of its production, of Ellen Douglas, Jake McPhail, Louise Chapman, and the amazing Kathleen Kageff.

None of these readers, audiences, scholars, photographers, illustrators, or editors is responsible for any error, misprision, or solecism of mine.

Most of all, I thank my wife, Gina Greene, whom I was so very fortunate to meet in graduate school. She has supported this project from dissertation to book and has endured summer after summer and break after break as I worked in my plodding way on this seemingly interminable project. Finally, I dedicate this book to my dear children, Luke and Greta: it bears witness to the time I spent researching and writing instead of being present for them.

ABBREVIATIONS

Abbreviations of ancient authors and works follow those in the
Oxford Classical Dictionary or *Lewis and Short:
A Latin Dictionary*.

Abbreviations of journal titles follow the conventions of
L'Année philologique or ISO 4.

BELIEF AND CULT

Introduction

ROMAN RELIGION, FROM INTUITIONS
TO INSTITUTIONS

nullum est animal praeter hominem quod habeat notitiam aliquam dei, ipsisque in hominibus nulla gens est neque tam mansueta neque tam fera, quae non, etiamsi ignoret qualem haberi deum deceat, tamen habendum sciat.

There is no living being except man that has any conception of god, and among men themselves there is no race so mild or so wild that it does not know that one must believe god to exist, even if it does not know what sort of being one ought to believe god to be.

CICERO, DE LEGIBUS, 1.24

0.1. Roman Cult and the Question of Belief

Rome, 176 BCE. Gnaeus Cornelius Scipio Hispallus ("Cornelius") and Quintus Petilius Spurinus ("Petilius") have won election to the consulship, Rome's chief executive magistracy, held jointly by two men for a term of one year. Before Cornelius and Petilius can assume office, each must sacrifice an ox to the gods on the Capitoline Hill, at the Temple of Jupiter, in order to ascertain divine approval of his consulship. When Petilius's ox, upon examination by his sacrificial assistants, turns out to have a deformed liver, a very bad omen, the senate instructs him to keep sacrificing oxen until he receives *litatio*, a positive sign.

Cornelius, meanwhile, has no better luck. His face registering distress [*confuso vultu*], he reports to the senate that the liver of the ox he sacrificed had dissolved when his assistants were preparing it for examination. He himself can hardly believe his assistants' announcement of this fact [*parum credentem ipsum*], yet upon inspection he finds it to be true. The senators are terrified [*territi*] by this prodigy [*prodigium*].

Their concern [*cura*] only grows when Petilius returns with news that after sacrificing three more oxen, he has still not been able to obtain *litatio*. They order him to keep sacrificing until the gods accept one of his victims. The story goes that he eventually obtained acceptance from all the gods except for Salus, the goddess of health and safety, who persisted in rebuffing his offerings.

Later that year, Cornelius presides over the Feriae Latinae or Latin Festival, at which the Latin cities of central Italy come together on the Alban Mount, some miles south of Rome, to offer joint sacrifice to Jupiter. The festival is marred, and anxieties arise, as a result of a flaw in the ritual. The college of Roman priests prescribes that the entire festival be repeated (a remedy known as *instauratio*). Before this can happen, Cornelius falls from his horse as he descends the Alban Mount. He is paralyzed and soon dies. Not long after, while leading a battle against Rome's enemies in northwestern Italy, Petilius, who, recall, never could obtain a positive sign from the goddess Salus, is killed by a javelin strike.[1]

I summarize this story from the Roman historian Livy, who records these incidents in his sweeping history of Rome from its origins to his own day. Livy, a masterful storyteller, builds tension by interspersing the ominous details of failed sacrifice with mundane reports of the senate's ho-hum deliberations about state business and other daily affairs. I have had to leave most such details out, but the effect of Livy's full original is to cultivate a growing sense of dread that culminates in the deaths, one after the other, of the ill-fated consuls. For reasons not entirely discernible, the gods reject the leaders that the Roman people have chosen by ballot, despite the fact that the Roman senate and priests apply every ritual resource at their disposal in response to the gods' omens, seeking reconciliation with them. The consuls, for their part, are anxious to adhere to traditional cult practice and distressed when doing so fails to produce the anticipated results. It is a story of cult institutions, of their failure, of the inscrutability of the divine mind, of omens that beggar belief, of emotions such as anxiety and terror, and—so the narrative insinuates but does not assert—of almost inevitable deaths.

It is an oversimplification, but not a very egregious one, to say that in the past, scholars told us that the sort of ritual action described by Livy, and Roman cult as a whole, amounted to compulsory and obsessively precise, but

---

1. Liv. 41.14–18.

ultimately rather mindless, ritual performances. An emphasis on ritual is of course understandable, given the primacy of ritual in the texts and other relics of Roman culture that survive. Yet even when ritual performances have been construed as rather more than mindless, when they have been seen, as over the past four decades or so, to have done cultural-ideological work by reflecting, reinforcing, and reifying social hierarchies and material relations, nonetheless the tendency has been to discount affective dimensions of cult and, most relevant to this book, to discount belief as central or even important to the Roman ritual tradition.

Nineteenth-century scholarship informed us that Roman religious beliefs, especially in comparison to Christian beliefs, were pretty unimpressive. Twentieth-century scholarship often said that the Romans did not have religious beliefs or even *belief* at all, a claim that was sometimes extended to the ancient Greeks. We were asked to accept, as I detail in chapter 1, that Romans had ritual *instead of* belief. On this "ritual thesis," through hundreds of years of their history, Romans like Petilius and Cornelius just *did stuff* because that was the stuff they were supposed to do. Roman religion was a matter of objective institutions that prescribed physical gestures. To look for emotion or cognition, especially belief, was to import "Christianizing" prejudices about what religion was supposed to be and to ignore the empirical realities of Roman practice.

This book joins other recent works of scholarship dedicated to offering an alternative to the outline just sketched. Specifically, beginning at around the turn of the century, we have seen the appearance of compelling defenses of Roman (and of ancient Greek) belief. Today, many books and articles on Roman (and Greek) religion happily talk about "belief" or "beliefs and practices." This is all to the good. However, this book arises out of the conviction that more is needed. We need to do more than merely go from not using the word "belief" to using it once again. This introduction exposes the overall shape of the book and provides the essential theoretical resources that readers will need in order to get the most out of the chapters that follow.

I shall argue in these chapters that Roman belief was crucial to just about everything in Livy's narrative and, more broadly, to just about everything that we might care to describe as "Roman religion." We should not, of course, look to Roman religion for a creed, of the sort that Christianities were to develop. Nor should we imagine that we shall find any Romans obsessing about orthodoxy, or "correct belief," nor that we shall find them construing belief as a requirement for salvation. However, none of this entails that the Romans did not have belief. Indeed, I make the case in chapter 1 that these obvious differences between traditional Roman and later Christian religious cognition—differences that have led some historians to relativize belief itself to a particular time, place, and religious culture—owe not to Christians having belief and polytheists lacking it. Rather, both engaged in the kind of cognition we call believing, which is merely, at a first approximation, mentally representing how matters stand in the world. Where they differed was not in their human capacities for cognition but in their cultural traditions of *metacognition*, that is, their ways of thinking about their own thinking, including their belief. Christians, unlike polytheists, "believed in belief."[2] They believed that their own beliefs and indeed their own capacity to believe possessed a religious value. It is not that traditional Romans could not sometimes "believe in belief"; it is merely that they believed in it rather differently.

Belief may be, as noted, a matter of mentally representing how matters stand in the world. But there is plenty more to say about it, and chapter 2 is dedicated to gaining clarity on what exactly belief is. The discussion there prepares us to investigate, in the remaining chapters, the ways in which Roman belief, properly understood, was central to (1) emotions, such as the perturbation of Cornelius and the terror of Livy's senators; (2) action, such as the consuls' ritual acts; (3) norms, that is, the sort of rules—often unwritten and unspoken—that specified the gestures in the consuls' sacrificial performances, the terms of *litatio*, and the prescriptions for ritual failure and ritual error offered by the senate and the college of priests; (4) cooperation, as in the consuls' group acts of cult involving collaboration among various ritual specialists, the senate's collective deliberations over omens, and the communal celebration of the Feriae Latinae; and even (5) social reality, such as the sacral status of Jupiter's temple or the determinate and determinative religious powers of priests. For I shall defend the perhaps startling claim that the shared beliefs of the Romans played a central role in creating and sustaining all Roman socioreligious reality and all Roman socioreligious power.

Presumably, no one would deny that the Romans experienced emotions, undertook actions, adhered to and endorsed cultural norms, cooperated in collective cult, or inhabited a "world," a uniquely Roman socioreligious reality, made up of temples, priests, and rituals, all with distinctive social properties and powers. Yet if we do not understand the role that Roman belief played in causing, creating, and sustaining all these phenomena, then we have understood neither the phenomena nor indeed Roman belief. And if we do not understand these phenomena and the Roman beliefs that underlay, produced, and sustained them, then in an important sense we do not understand Roman cult.

2. Dennett 2006: 200ff.

This book thus seeks to understand pre-Christian Roman cult by way of understanding belief. Its core thesis is that Roman religious emotions, actions, rituals, norms, institutions, and socioreligious realities depended for their very existence on Roman beliefs. These features of Roman cult are thus unintelligible and inexplicable without reference to belief. Throughout the book, I try to show that this thesis holds not only from an etic or "outsider's/observer's" perspective, but also from an emic or "insider's/participant's" perspective.

The book consists of two parts: chapters 1 through 5 are theoretical, treating of the denial about belief that appears in the scholarship (chapter 1), belief as it is in fact (chapter 2), belief's role in emotion and action (chapter 3), belief and norms (chapters 3 and 4), collective belief (chapter 4), and belief's contribution to creating and sustaining socioreligious reality and power (chapter 5). Chapters 6 through 9 present case studies, treating of Lucretius's Roman theory of belief and cult (chapter 6), Roman children's acquisition of religious beliefs in ritual practice (chapter 7), belief in contexts of praying (chapter 8), and belief, power, and religious reality in the ritual of inauguration (chapter 9). An epilog concludes the book by looking at three ancient attempts to account for alien sacrifice. It asks what role the ancients assigned—and what role we should assign—to belief in attempts to explain the cult practices of other peoples. At stake in every one of these chapters is the fate of a commitment that has enjoyed wide acceptance and even now informs some scholarship on Roman and other ancient religions, to wit, the notion that in non-Christian religious traditions only ritual behavior, not belief, plays any essential role. We must overcome this venerable dichotomization between cognition and action, for it impoverishes our understanding of Roman belief and in so doing hollows out our conception of Roman cult practice.

0.2. From Roman Intuitions to Roman Institutions

This book offers an account of Roman belief and cult from intuitions to institutions. For present purposes, the intuitions in question will be Roman intuitions of divine agency, that is, an immediate *impression* rather than a reflectively arrived-at judgment about a more-than-human agent or that agent's handiwork. Later chapters explore intuition's role in the formation of Roman religious beliefs (chapter 2) and intuitions about ritual form and efficacy, that is, the impression that a given act of cult was successful (or not) and has created an effect (or not) in the religious world (chapter 9). All these types of intuitions are produced, as we shall see, by our faculties of social cognition.

Let us define at the outset "agent" and "intuition." An agent or, frequently in the literature but somewhat redundantly, intentional agent, is any entity possessing agency, which is the capacity to *act*, or to move on purpose, in order to accomplish a goal, even if that goal is merely the action itself. As to intuition, about which we shall have more to say at section 2.6, we may note that the lexeme is ubiquitous in the cognitive science of religion (CSR), on which this book draws, and is subject to competing accounts.[3] Some cognitive scientists hold that intuition is the output of inferences that take place below the level of conscious accessibility.[4] Some philosophers, by contrast, offer an account of intuition as a noninferential process.[5]

We need not resolve such questions for our purposes in this book; however, we should note that the term "intuition" is ambiguous between process and product. One can speak of the cognitive process of intuition or of the cognitive products of the process, that is, intuitions. I shall endeavor to use the term in such a way as to make it clear whether I intend by it the process or its product. When I use "intuition" in the sense of "process," what I am referring to is the cognitive process that results in new thoughts (i.e., intuitions) carrying a degree of self-evidence that simply appear in consciousness, with no trace of any reasoning process that may have led to them, just as in perception certain features of the world simply become sensibly present. This definition implies the phenomenology of the cognitive product: "When we have an intuition, we experience it as something our mind produced but without having any experience of the process of its production."[6] Because of the immediacy with which intuition (process) puts intuitions (products) in our heads, we may think of the process as a kind of "intellectual perception"[7] that delivers, as product, cognitive "seemings." Some parallels and contrasts with perception are as follows: in "perception, the seeming is perceptual and the awareness sensory." (It perceptually *seems* that an object is in front of me and I am sensorily *aware* of the object.) In contrast, in "intuition, the seeming is intuitive and the awareness intellectual."[8] (It intuitively *seems* to me that gods are involved in this or that event, and my *awareness* of this proposition is mental, not sensory.)

Our faculties for social-cognitive intuition populate the world with (for this is social cognition's special domain) *agents*, not only visible and mundane, but also sometimes invisible and divine. Among such intuitions, the theological ones may settle, given the right support, into theological beliefs. In turn, out of intuitions and beliefs about more-than-human agents, religious institutions

---

3. On intuition in CSR, see Horst 2013. For philosophical accounts, see Pust 2019.
4. E.g., Mercier and Sperber 2017: 64–67.
5. E.g., Audi 2013: 83–96.
6. Mercier and Sperber 2017: 65.
7. Chudnoff 2013: 1 ("intellectual perception") and 41 ("seemings").
8. Chudnoff 2011: 641.

may arise. For as soon as intuition has settled into belief, people may engage with the believed divine agent, and those engagements may coalesce into a more or less determinate practice, and a discourse may develop around that practice, further elaborating or fixing it, and before long religious institutions—god-centered human constructs, such as ritual prescriptions, festivals, priesthoods, priestly functions, and so forth—may arise.

Or so a plausible causal story—aetiology with an "a"—might go. The Romans had their own ways of doing this sort of explanatory work. A case in point may be found in Vergil's narrative of Aeneas's visit to the future site of Jupiter's great temple on the Capitoline Hill, in what would one day be Rome. Aeneas, Rome's primordial founding figure, gets a guided tour of the future site of Rome from King Evander, a transplant to Italy from Greek Arcadia. Natives of the area, aboriginal Romans, as it were, had already apprehended something numinous on the Capitoline Hill (*Aen.* 8.349–50):

> *iam tum religio pavidos terrebat agrestis*
> *dira loci, iam tum silvam saxumque tremebant.*

> Even then the forbidding sanctity of the place used to frighten
> the timorous rustics, even then they trembled at its forest and rock.

If we ask what the early inhabitants *saw* on the Capitoline Hill that caused them such awe, Vergil's unsatisfying answer must be "forest and rock" (*silvam saxumque*). Their arousal, then, derived not from what they *saw* but from what they *intuited* beyond or within the trees and stones, to wit, *religio dira*, "forbidding sanctity." So I have translated it, but bear in mind that the word *religio* often denotes simply—and fittingly, if we are to see here the first stirrings of a distinctive, local *Roman* religion[9]—"cult."

This episode reflects the Roman world's repletion with gods. Apart from their images, they were only rarely seen with the eyes, but their presence was regularly felt or intuited in just this way. Certain places just *seemed* haunted by them. Reports of such intuitive rather than perceptual epiphanies—that is, divine manifestations—permeate Latin literature. Natural settings, especially groves, seem regularly to inspire them. For example, the first poem of Ovid's third book of love elegy, *Amores*, begins thus (*Am.* 3.1.1–4):

> *Stat vetus et multos incaedua silva per annos;*
>   *credibile est illi numen inesse loco.*

> A wood stands, ancient and unhewn through many years;
>   it is credible that a divine presence is in that grove.

---

9. So Hardie 1986: 217–18.

Ovid uses the adjective *credibile*, "credible," not to suggest a settled theological belief, still less a sensory perception of a god, but rather, something conducive to belief, a theological *seeming* or intuition.[10]

Seneca the Younger describes how such intuitions—cognitive seemings or intellectual perceptions—arise and pass quickly into belief. When you enter a grove (*lucus*), the right conditions—"the high growth of the woods" (*proceritas silvae*), "the solitude of the place" (*secretum loci*), and your own "wonder at the shade" interspersed with clearings—may combine to "produce for you a credence of a divine presence" (*fidem tibi numinis faciet*).[11] I translate Seneca's *fides* as "credence," by which I intend to capture what I take to be his meaning: a kind of intuitive sense of divine presence.

Belief may also be inspired not by a peaceful grove but by violent storms, as in our Vergilian passage, to which we now return. Aeneas's guide Evander continues his tour with these words (*Aen.* 8.351–54):

"hoc nemus, hunc" inquit "frondoso vertice collem
(quis deus incertum est) habitat deus; Arcades ipsum
credunt se vidisse Iovem, cum saepe nigrantem
aegida concuteret dextra nimbosque cieret."

"This grove, this hill with its leafy crown, a god inhabits,
though which god is uncertain," he said. "My Arcadians
believe that they have seen Jupiter in person,
when, as so often, he shakes his darkening aegis
in his right hand and rouses the storm clouds."

A profound interplay among cognitive processes of perception, intuition, inference, and belief is at work here. The aboriginal natives were struck, recall, by their intuition of the *religio* of the place. Evander believes that a god, though he knows not which, abides there. His Arcadians have seen—something—on the hill's heights, and they have come to believe, perhaps through inference from the buffeting storms, that it was Jupiter himself.

What we have here amounts to an aetiology for the origin of religious belief, more specifically, of belief about the god of the Capitoline Hill, the religious center of the Roman world. Indeed, the passage adumbrates a three-stage aetiology: the rustic natives represent primitive intuition, the more civilized Evander, belief mixed with uncertainty (on which, see section 0.4), and his Arcadians, settled belief. These three cognitive responses represent not merely

---

10. See Hunt 2016: 185.
11. Sen. *Ep.* 41.3.

successive stages in the human response to the numinous, but enduring and coterminous possibilities of Roman religious experience as well.

So much for Roman discourses of intuition and belief. Distinctively Roman modes of explaining the origins of institutions existed as well. A typical move is to ascribe an institution to the action of a founder, who is often (semi)divine. Once numinous intuitions have passed into a belief in the presence of divine agents, it is no surprise if practices are evolved for making contact and negotiating with them. Thus, as we shall see in chapter 9, Romulus founded at once Rome and the Roman practice of augury when he and his brother Remus, standing on hills that neighbor the Capitoline, ritually consulted the local gods for approval of their plan to establish a city.[12] On one Roman theory, surveyed in chapter 7, such authoritative ritual performances may spread from individual to individual through imitation and eventually settle into practices—become institutions—through repetition, habit, and *consensus,* that is, collective agreement.

This book endeavors to rethink the role of cognition in Roman cult from numinous intuitions to cult institutions. Such intuitions arise from developmentally natural mental processes (see section 0.3 and chapter 2). Cult institutions depend on our species-specific skills of "shared Intentionality,"[13] our capacity to share such mental states as intentions, desires, and beliefs (see chapter 4). We explore relationships among (in various combinations) intuition, inference, epiphany, and belief in chapters 2, 6, and 8. In chapter 6, we reconstruct a Roman aetiology of cult institutions. Chapters 5 and 9 apply to the case of cult a modern theory about the role played by collective belief—a form of shared Intentionality—in the ontology of institutions.

For now, it remains to introduce, in the next section, some theses about human social cognition and its relevance to theological belief that are central to this book. In the section after that, we do the same for the theory of Intentionality. Theories about our developmentally natural ways of cognizing other agents as well as the picture of belief offered by the theory of Intentionality underlie every chapter in this book.

0.3. HADD and Social Cognition

Belief really has only five possible etiologies (without the "a": "causal origin"), which may work their effects alone or in combination. These are: sensory perception, memory, testimony, inference, and intuition. This book touches on

---

12. See Liv. 1.6.4.
13. Tomasello, Carpenter, et al. 2005.

all but memory.[14] Chapter 6 explores how (apparent) sensory perceptions may lead to religious belief, as they did in the cases of Livy's Cornelius and Vergil's Arcadians. The latter, recall, saw something that they took to be Jupiter, while the former needed to see his ox's dissolved liver for himself in order to accept the omen. "Testimony" I construe broadly to include any cultural representation of the divine. This includes the reports of Livy's consuls to the senate and ranges from explicit pedagogy (chapter 7) to prayer (chapter 8). Intuition, such as the numinous intuitions of Vergil's aboriginal Romans, as well as processes of theological inference are dealt with in chapters 2, 6, and 9. It will be useful, now, to say some introductory words about the intuitions that derive from our faculties of *social cognition*.[15] For we return repeatedly in these chapters to social cognition and the intuitions it delivers.

This book operates on the premise that social cognition and social-cognitive intuitions contribute to theological belief and cult practice. Social cognition may be defined, for our purposes, as the suite of developmentally natural, species-specific human cognitive faculties that give rise to intuitions of *agency*, intuitions about the mental states of *agents*, and intuitions about how agents' mental states inform their *action*.[16] It is, in a sense, the human skillset for seeing conspecifics as "Others" (in Levinas's sense) with whom the Self may engage and interact. Precisely because it populates the world with agents, social cognition is central—according to the interdisciplinary field of CSR—to the generation and maintenance of theological beliefs and ritual practices for engaging with gods.[17]

---

14. For which, see, e.g., Cusumano et al. 2013.

15. For a full but concise discussion of social cognition, see Frith and Frith 2012. I am concerned in this section primarily with the social-cognitive faculty that is often called "folk psychology." For present purposes, we need take no position on whether folk psychology is a "Theory of Mind Module" (Leslie 1994), an "Intentional stance" (Dennett 1987), a "simulation" (Goldman 2006), an "embodied simulation" (Gallese and Sinigaglia 2011), "narrative practice" (Hutto 2008), or "direct perception" (Gallagher 2008a).

16. For cross-cultural evidence regarding the core faculties of social cognition, see especially the analysis of the components of social cognition and an assessment of their universality in Malle 2008; For cross-cultural testing of basic social-cognitive capacities, see, e.g., Callaghan, Rochat, et al. 2005; Callaghan, Moll, et al. 2011; Shahaeian et al. 2011. Given basic social-cognitive capacities, nothing prevents and everything conduces to the elaboration of local folk-models of mind: for a Roman one, see Short 2012.

17. See now Larson 2016 for a CSR approach to Greek religion and an expert overview of the CSR field.

A core, and no doubt primitive, task of social cognition is to help us distinguish animate agents from inanimate objects. Cicero conceptualizes the distinction (*Rep.* 6.28):

> *inanimum est enim omne, quod pulsu agitatur externo; quod autem est animal, id motu cietur interno et suo.*
>
> *Inanimate* is anything that is moved by external force; *animate* is anything that is driven by an internal impulse of its own.

Inanimate nonagents move only with the application of external force, while animate agents move on their own, as a result of internal forces. These, for Cicero, come from the mind or soul, *anima* (hence "animate"), whose "property and power," *natura et vis*, it is to move bodies. An agent is thus any animate, minded entity capable of purposefully *acting*.

This distinction comes naturally to the neurotypical mind.[18] That is, neurotypical social cognition automatically distinguishes agents from nonagents. Social cognition also provides us with a set of pretheoretical, intuitive expectations about different entity types.[19] Even young infants intuitively expect inanimate objects to be bounded, solid, and impenetrable by other objects, to fall downward if not supported, to move continuously along inertial paths rather than to jump from place to place, and to require outside physical contact in order to get moving in the first place, among various other properties.[20] By contrast, even infants expect that animate entities and especially human agents initiate their own movement, which is not restricted to inertial paths, and that their movement is purposeful or teleological, that is, that their movement is *action* that is directed toward a *goal*.[21] Infants also expect agents to interact with one another and to exert not merely contact causation, but also

---

18. Neuro-atypical development and neuropathology may affect cognition about animacy and agency. Autism reduces detection of animacy (Congiu et al. 2009) and of agency or biological motion (Blake et al. 2003). Frontotemporal dementia also reduces detection of both (Fong et al. 2017).

19. For brief summaries of research into several "core systems" or domains of "core knowledge," about objects, agents, number, the layout of space, and so forth, see, respectively, Kinzler and Spelke 2007 and Spelke and Kinzler 2007. For "core social cognition," see Spelke, Bernier, and Skerry 2013. Cf. Barrett 2011a: 58–68 for developmentally natural cognition regarding objects, space, biological entities, and so on.

20. See Baillargeon 2004 for a succinct account and Baillargeon, Gertner, and Wu 2011 for a more expansive account of children's understanding of objects and object events.

21. On animacy and especially human agency, see Carpenter 2011; Meltzoff 2011a; Opfer and Gelman 2011.

causation-at-a-distance, or "social causation," on one another, through gestures and vocalizations.[22]

Social cognition inclines us to intuit agency, and to construe objects and events in agentive terms, on the basis even of exiguous cues.[23] Cognitive science of religion researchers speak of the mind's "Hypersensitive Agency Detection Device" (HADD), a "mental tool" (to use a figurative expression often found in CSR) that attributes, and is prone to overattribute, agency.[24] This mental tool, HADD, delivers intuitions of the presence, sometimes in their actual absence, of agents. To be clear: our social-cognitive faculties need stimuli to produce intuitions of agency, but it would be wrong to say that it is the *behavior* of agents that produces intuitions of agency. Rather, the *agent* and its *behavior* are themselves intuitions produced for us by our social-cognitive faculties in response to stimuli. Agency and behavior are not simply "given" in any sensory percept but must rather be interpreted in.[25] A sensitivity to agency has clear advantages, even if it may yield "false positives." As Simon Baron-Cohen notes, "in evolutionary terms, it is better to spot a potential agent ... than to ignore it."[26] Obliviousness to agents is death. Overidentification of agents is, in most cases, a modest inconvenience. In other cases, it may play a role in the etiology of theological belief.

The workings of HADD and its relevance to theological belief may perhaps be discerned in some verses of the republican satirist Lucilius and in Lactantius's commentary on them. The Christian polemicist attacks what he regards as the superstitious adherents of traditional Roman cult by quoting the poet, prefacing his quotation with the words, "in the following verses, Lucilius scoffs at the stupidity of those who suppose that cult images are gods":[27]

ut pueri infantes credunt signa omnia aena
vivere et esse homines, sic isti somnia ficta
vera putant, credunt signis cor inesse in aenis.

---

22. See Schlottmann and Surian 1999; Rochat et al. 2004; Schlottmann et al. 2009.

23. Heider and Simmel 1944, in "An Experimental Study of Apparent Behavior," initiated the empirical study of this cognitive phenomenon. Michotte 1963 details further such experiments. See Scholl and Tremoulet 2000 for an overview of research in this field. Cf. the experiment reported in Barrett and Johnson 2003.

24. HADD was coined in Barrett 2000. For updates on HADD research, see Andersen 2019 and Van Leeuwen and van Elk 2019.

25. I hope it is obvious that I am not asserting that agents and their behavior do not exist apart from our cognizing of them. Of course they do.

26. Baron-Cohen 1995: 35.

27. Lact. *Inst.* 1.22.13: *nam Lucilius eorum stultitiam, qui simulacra deos putant esse, deridet his versibus.* The verses quoted are Lucil. 15.526–28.

Just as infant children believe all bronze statues live and are human
   beings,
so those [i.e., the superstitious] suppose that imagined dreams
are true, they believe that a heart lies within bronze statues.

For Lactantius, the adults are in a sorrier state than the children, "for the children suppose statues are people, but the adults suppose they are gods."[28]

Lucilius's verses and Lactantius's discussion provide a testament to HADD's power to inspire religious belief by generating intuitions of animacy and agency. Researchers usually discuss HADD in relation to motion, which HADD may interpret as the goal-directed behavior of an agent, but we must recognize that the mere "visual form" of a statue may "trigger agency-intuitions" as well.[29] When Lucilius's children encounter statues, they believe (*credunt*) them to be alive (*vivere*) and human (*esse homines*). Certainly no one *teaches* them this, nor do they appear, on Lucilius's account, to work through a process of *inference* to get to it. The mind's Hypersensitive Agency Detection Device causes them simply to *intuit* it: the statues just *seem*, immediately and self-evidently, to be living people. In their innocent minds, these intuitions—agential seemings—easily settle into beliefs that the statues are agents.

Roman adults, too, could experience such agential intuitions in their encounters with naturalistic representations, as suggested by the common observation that statues seem to breathe, *spirantia signa*, or live.[30] However, whereas most Roman adults knew that some intuitions of animacy were not to be trusted, and therefore declined to *believe* that statues were alive, Lucilius's credulous man follows his intuitions and comes to believe that the statue contains a living heart (*credunt signis cor inesse in aenis*). Lactantius extends this class of people to include superstitious pagans "who suppose that cult images are gods" (*qui simulacra deos putant esse*). Notice how both Lucilius and Lactantius, though separated by centuries and by religious culture, agree in taking it for granted that their contemporaries could believe that statues were gods. Presumably, HADD's intuitions of agency played a role in conducing to such

---

28. Lact. *Inst.* 1.22.14: *illi enim simulacra homines putant esse, hi deos.*

29. Van Leeuwen and van Elk 2019: 241.

30. Verg. *G.* 3.34. Cf. Verg. *Aen.* 6.847–48: *spirantia . . . aera; vivos . . . de marmore vultus*; Apul. *Met.*, 11.17: *simulacra spirantia*; Plin. *Ep.* 3.6.2: *etiam ut spirantis*; Petr. *Sat.* 52.1 sends up the trope: *pueri mortui iacent sic ut vivere putes*; cf. Ov. *Met.* 10.250–51: *virginis est verae facies, quam vivere credas, et, si non obstet reverentia, velle moveri.* Plin. *H.N.* 35.95 notes that even animals can be fooled, as by a picture of Apelles: *picturas inductis equis ostendit: Apellis tantum equo adhinnivere, idque et postea semper evenit.*

beliefs. (We explore some further implications of Lactantius's response to Lucilius's verses at section 2.6.2.)

Our agent-sensitive minds may even lead us to *treat* as agents objects that we could not possibly *believe* to be agents. Augustine notes, for example, that people may become angry at inanimate objects (*rebus inanimis irascatur*), such as a malfunctioning pen, and smash it as if exacting vengeance on an agent who has wronged them.[31] Augustine's smasher of pens surely does not *believe* that this object of wrath is a malicious agent. However, as this example suggests, we need neither naturalistic representations, such as bronze statues, nor any other agency cue, such as self-propelled motion, in order to invest an inanimate object with agency and treat it accordingly.

If HADD's intuitions that an agent (or for that matter, the handiwork of an agent, i.e., an artifact) is present are not dismissed as false positives, other social-cognitive resources, especially "folk psychology" (roughly equivalent to "Theory of Mind" or "ToM" and sometimes also called "mindreading"),[32] kick in to tell us what might be going on in the agent's head, so that we can both predict and explain the agent's behavior. Theory of Mind is a set of social-cognitive skills that permits us both implicit and explicit reasoning about others' emotions, desires, goals, intentions, and beliefs. It permits us to see others' behavior as teleological, spontaneously generating for us (quite fallible) understandings about the *desires* and *intentions* on which they are acting, about the *goals* they are pursuing, and about the *sensory perceptions* and *beliefs* about the world that are guiding them. It allows us to see bodily gestures as "trying," "avoiding," "chasing," "hesitating," and so on.

Romans had their own ways of talking about all of this, of course. When theorizing about matters philosophical or rhetorical, for example, they could remark on the intersubjective transparency of one person's psychological states to another. Take, for example, two texts of Cicero, one from *De legibus* and the other from *De oratore*:[33]

---

31. Aug. *Civ.* 14.15: *nam et ipsam iram nihil aliud esse quam ulciscendi libidinem veteres definierunt; quamvis nonnumquam homo, ubi vindictae nullus est sensus, etiam rebus inanimis irascatur, et male scribentem stilum conlidat vel calamum frangat iratus.* Cf. Sen. *Ira.* 2.26.2–3 for anger at books and clothing.

32. The term "mindreading" as used in the psychological literature usually refers in the first place to our indispensable social-cognitive *faculty* of intuiting, inferring, and reasoning about others' mental states, not to the cognitive *distortion* of making unfounded assumptions about others' thinking.

33. Cf. Cic. *De Or.* 3.221: *imago animi vultus, indices oculi: nam haec est una pars corporis, quae, quot animi motus sunt, tot significationes et commutationes possit efficere.* Cf., e.g., *De Or.* 3.222; Cic. *Pis.* 1.1.

Leg. 1.26–27: *speciem ita* [sc. *natura*] *formavit oris, ut in ea penitus reconditos mores effingeret.* [27] *nam et oculi nimis argute quem ad modum animo affecti simus loquuntur et is qui appellatur vultus, qui nullo in animante esse praeter hominem potest, indicat mores.*

Nature has so shaped the appearance of the face that it has portrayed on it the character hidden deep inside. [27] For the eyes tell all too clearly how we have been affected in our mind, and that which is called the expression, which can exist in no living thing except the human being, reveals our character.

De Or. 3.223: *isdem enim omnium animi motibus concitantur et eos isdem notis et in aliis agnoscunt et in se ipsi indicant.*

The minds of all people are excited by the same emotions and people recognize these emotions by the same signs in others as they reveal them in themselves.

For Cicero, human beings are united by and made intelligible to one another, even without a common language, by deep cognitive, affective, expressive, and bodily commonalities.[34] He proposes that we perceive in the eyes and the expression of others what is going on in their minds as well as the nature of their *mores*, or character.[35]

Quintilian extends the Ciceronian analysis to include the expression of emotion in animals: animals' minds "are grasped through their eyes and through certain other signals of the body" (*oculis et quibusdam aliis corporis signis*). Thus, although they lack language, the anger, joy, and other dispositions of beasts are apparent to us.[36] We see in Quintilian's thesis social cognition at work. For he sees even animals as minded agents, not wholly unlike ourselves, with affective and cognitive episodes similar to our own.

Needless to say, if the Romans could extend their social-cognitive intuitions to animals, they could extend them to gods. For this reason, we return to social cognition throughout these chapters and address its ontogeny (i.e., its

---

34. Cf. Fantham 2004: 296. See Fögen 2009b on the universal language of gesture, *vultus*, and nonverbal vocalization in Roman thought.

35. Paul Ekman has famously posited and tested for a few "basic" emotions (1999a) that are universally recognized in facial expressions (1999b). On cross-cultural continuity in emotion recognition, see also Scherer et al. 2011.

36. Quint. *Inst.* 11.3.66: *quippe non manus solum sed nutus etiam declarant nostram voluntatem, et in mutis pro sermone sunt, et saltatio frequenter sine voce intellegitur atque adficit, et ex vultu ingressuque perspicitur habitus animorum, et animalium quoque sermone carentium ira, laetitia, adulatio et oculis et quibusdam aliis corporis signis deprenditur.*

development and maturation) in chapter 7, where we discuss the contributions of Roman children's maturing powers of social cognition to their religious learning. For now, it is worth mentioning one cognitive milestone: false belief understanding. By age four or five, children begin to manifest full-blown ToM.[37] At age three, children understand and use only desire-talk, attributing wants and desires to others and recognizing that these wants and desires affect their behavior. However, a year or so later, children begin to "theorize" about the beliefs of others. Under the age of four or five, children do not understand that if mom did not see dad remove the milk from the fridge, she should believe—wrongly—that it is still there. At this young age, children mistakenly assume that mom's beliefs track the same reality to which they themselves have perceptual access. To grasp that mom can have false beliefs due to her limited perceptual access to relevant information is a cognitive achievement of the kindergarten year.

Social cognition begins, then, in cognition *about* other agents, about mom, for example, and her desires and (possibly false) beliefs.[38] But social cognition also has a collective dimension, to wit, cognition *with* other agents.[39] Cognition *with* others enables us to share mental episodes—attention, perception, desires, emotions, intentions, goals, and beliefs—with others in mutual recognition that we are so sharing, and even that a plural subject "we"—not just individuals, an "I" and a "you"—is the collective bearer of the mental episode. Chapters 4, 5, and 7 show how this capacity for cognitive sharing—shared Intentionality—allowed Romans to collaborate in joint activities, engage in cultural learning, and thus create and maintain their social reality, that is, the unique world of cult practices, priests, institutions, and associated socioreligious powers and obligations that they inhabited.

Let us now sum this section up. The connection between social cognition and Roman religion is this. The faculty of HADD tuned ancient minds, as it does our own, in favor of believing that agents are or have been present, at work in the world around us. And ToM made it possible for Romans to conceive of, hold beliefs about, reason about, and communicate about the workings of the minds of gods. To be clear: HADD's intuitive sensitivity to agency and ToM's intuitive expectations about agents are not themselves beliefs, but

---

37. The term "Theory of Mind" (ToM) was coined by the psychologists D. Premack and G. Woodruff (1978). See Wellman 2014 for a comprehensive treatment of ToM. See Barrett 2011a: 74–77 for a brief discussion of ToM from a CSR perspective. For a history of ToM research, see Boden 2006: 1.486–92. Cross-cultural studies of ToM include, for Chinese children, Tardif and Wellman 2000; Wellman et al. 2006; D. Liu et al. 2008; for Iranian children, Shahaeian et al. 2011; for Micronesian children, Oberle 2009.

38. Carpenter 2011: 106–10.

39. Carpenter 2011: 106, 110–17; Tomasello, Carpenter et al. 2005.

they lead to intuitions about agents that can in turn lead to beliefs. Because social cognition predisposes the mind to see agency everywhere and to interpret even nonagential phenomena in agential terms, it is an anthropomorphizing cognitive faculty. This predicts that gods across cultures will be represented as agents—more-than-human agents, but agents nonetheless—and thus as deeply anthropomorphic where it really counts: in their psychologies.

Thus, the Romans reasoned about gods much as they reasoned about one other, that is, as psychologically anthropomorphic agents intelligible by means of the mundane mental tools in the social-cognitive toolbox. As two cognitive scientists have stated, human beings' "intuitive assumptions about the psychology of agents purchase them vast amounts of knowledge about [gods] for free."[40] When this intuitive knowledge about divine agents is coupled with cultural representations of divine beings, the result is what I shall call in chapters 2 and 8 (and throughout) "folk theology."[41] Folk theology differs from the abstruse doctrinal theology of Aquinas's *Summa theologiae* or even of Cicero's *De natura deorum* in that it is a matter not of formal study and disciplined philosophical reflection but of the interaction of informal social learning and social-cognitive intuition.

In this section and previous sections, we have spoken about beliefs—about acquiring them, having them, and attributing them to others—and also about mental episodes such as perceptions, intuitions, desires, intentions, and emotions. All these mental phenomena share a single property, called "Intentionality," which relates them to one another systematically. I would maintain that it is innocence of belief's place in the economy of the mental, as one Intentional state among others, with its own discrete and indispensable cognitive task to perform, that has allowed some scholars to suppose it to be a modular, detachable, optional, or historically contingent feature, to be denied or attributed to this or that culture, society, or epoch at will. So, let us now introduce this other central theoretical commitment of this book, to wit, the theory of Intentionality.

0.4. Intentionality and Belief

Cognition is famously embodied, embedded, enacted, and extended (hence "4E cognition").[42] On the 4E account, the mind and its cognitive processes do not reside in the brain alone. Instead, cognition is *extended* insofar as at least

---

40. McCauley and Lawson 2007: 227.
41. I borrow the term from Barrett 2004a: 10.
42. For a handy overview of 4E cognition (which is sometimes a synonym for and at other times distinct from both "situated cognition" and "distributed cognition"), especially in its relevance to humanistic study and classics in particular, see Anderson, Cairns, and Sprevak 2019.

some cognitive processes include manipulations the cognizer performs on features of the environment. It is *enacted* insofar as some cognitive processes are constituted by causal couplings or actional transactions between a cognizer and its environment. It is *embedded* insofar as some cognitive processes depend for their occurrence on scaffolding to be found out in the world, external to the cognizer. And it is *embodied* insofar as cognitive processes include some of the cognizer's own nonneural bodily operations.

The excitement justly generated by 4E cognitive theory should not obscure the fact that cognition is also *Intentional*. *Intentionalism* is the thesis that a defining feature of mind is *Intentionality*, which is the property of being *about* or *directed at* objects in the world.[43] That is, unlike anything else in nature, the mind's episodes and states—its fears, sorrows, hopes, desires, intentions, beliefs—*represent* the world and its objects. If I believe that Jupiter is the god of the Capitoline, I bear a mental state that is *about* Jupiter, a mental state that takes Jupiter as its object. My belief *represents* its object in a certain way, from a perspective, in this case, as god of the Capitoline. This perspectival representation constitutes my belief's *content*.

No book can do it all. Here, I largely leave out of consideration 4E approaches, which I take not so much to replace as to supplement Intentionalism.[44] I focus on Intentionalism in the conviction that it provides the strongest theoretical grip on the question of belief, for if belief is anything at all, it is an Intentional state.[45] (It is impossible to imagine a belief that is not *about* anything!) Moreover, it strikes me that only Intentionalism can fully account for cognition about non-existent objects, such as gods. To think and talk about gods—to believe or assert, for instance, that Jupiter is the god of the Capitoline—one has to be able to think and talk about an object that is a feature of *no* environment. This is not to say that Roman religion and Roman religious cognition were not deeply embodied, embedded, enacted, and

---

43. Crane 2001a: 4–8. See Searle 1983a: 1–4.

44. Cf. Andy Clark 2016: 291–94. Hutto and Myin 2017 represents a radical enactive attempt to see how far one can get with content-free "basic minds" before one must introduce the notion of content.

45. One cannot be all things to all people. I also do not offer a diachronic account of religious change at Rome or a history of republican religion (see now Rüpke 2012), or any account of the interactions of religious and other institutions in a given period, for example, divination and politics at the end of the republic (Santangelo 2013), or an account of religious individualization (Rüpke 2019). What I try to do is offer a way to think productively about belief, and Intentionality more generally, in Roman religion. The framework I offer here is meant to complement other cognitive (such as 4E), theoretical, and indeed straightforward historical accounts of Roman religion.

extended in natural and artificial environments of groves, gardens, street corners, temples, and households that were replete with statues, images, sights, sounds, smells, and activity. It is simply that this is not the subject of this book. This book deals with Intentionality: belief, its objects, their representation, and the implications of these things for Roman cult.

In order to avoid confusion, it will be crucial to distinguish the everyday and narrower sense of intentionality from the technical but broader sense. The term "intentional" and related lexemes are ambiguous between the *aboutness* I have described and *purposiveness*. In everyday usage, we speak of *intentions* to act (that is, plans) or actions done *intentionally* (on purpose). However, to say that cognition is Intentional is *not* to say that it is *purposeful*, though of course it may be that, too. I use "Intentionality," with an uppercase *I*, to refer not to purposiveness but to that property of a mental episode, and indeed of a speech act or public representation, by virtue of which it is *about, of, directed at*, or *represents* some object. Both intentions and even actions are Intentional in this sense (see chapters 2 and 3). Plans to act, that is, intentions, are a class of Intentional mental phenomena. To say that our intentions are Intentional is to say that they share with our beliefs, desires, hopes, fears, and other mental episodes the property of being *representational*, of being *about* their objects. Beliefs, for example, represent as their objects states of affairs in the world, while intentions represent as their objects our action *plans* and *goals* in acting. For clarity, I capitalize the first letter of "Intentionality" and related terms when I refer to Intentionality in this broader, technical sense.[46] I shall put the first letter of all terms related to "intention," as in "a plan to act," in lowercase.

The term "mental episode" introduces another terminological matter to clear up. By "mental episodes," I mean to capture properly "episodic" mental phenomena, such as *emotions*, which arise and tail off, as well as mental *events*, like the sudden appearance to consciousness of an intuition, mental *acts*, like adding up two numbers in one's head, and, finally, mental *states*, like beliefs and desires, which may perdure indefinitely. All such episodes are Intentional.

Intentionality (uppercase *I*) was of theoretical interest to ancient philosophers, on whose work the modern study of Intentionality is founded.[47] Franz Brentano is credited with initiating the modern study of Intentionality in the

---

46. I also capitalize the "I" in *Intentionality* and related terms when those terms appear in my quotations from other authors.

47. For Intentionality from Aristotle to Brentano, see Sorabji 1991. For ancient philosophy of Intentionality, see Sorabji 1992; V. Caston 1993, 1998, 2002, and 2008; essays in Perler 2001, especially V. Caston 2001. See Crane 2001a: 8–13 for a very brief history of research on Intentionality.

late nineteenth century. Inspired by Aristotle and the Scholastics, he posited that Intentionality was the "mark of the mental," the feature that distinguished mind from everything else in nature. He famously wrote (1874: 68):

> Every mental phenomenon is characterized by what the Scholastics of the Middle Ages called the Intentional (or mental) inexistence[48] of an object, and what we might call, though not wholly unambiguously, reference to a content, direction toward an object (which is not to be understood here as meaning a thing), or immanent objectivity. Every mental phenomenon includes something as object within itself, although they do not all do so in the same way. In presentation something is presented, in judgement something is affirmed or denied, in love loved, in hate hated, in desire desired and so on.

Mental phenomena differ from physical phenomena in that they *contain*—or as we have already put it, they are *about* or *directed on*—objects: "in presentation something is presented . . . in desire desired." Brentano thought *all* mental phenomena and *only* mental phenomena were Intentional. Intentionality, on this view, defines the mental—everything that exhibits Intentionality is mental—and thus gives the science of psychology its own discrete object of study. We need not decide whether Brentano was right in order to accept that at least some mental phenomena, such as belief, clearly are Intentional.

From the standpoint of Intentionality, mental phenomena fall into clear classes. I have already distinguished a variety of mental episodes: emotions, mental events, mental acts, and mental states, like belief. Further distinctions are possible. Belief, for example, is a member of a class of Intentional states sometimes called "representational," "theoretical," "cognitive," or "doxastic," which is the term I use in this book. Such states aim to represent the way the world *is*. They may be positive, such as *belief, knowledge, conjecture, assumption, presupposition,* and *acceptance,* all of which represent how matters stand. They may be negative, such as *doubt, denial, rejection,* and *disbelief,* all of which represent how matters do *not* stand. And they may be neutral, as in the case of *uncertainty*.[49] These Intentional states are "doxastic" because they seek to represent, fit, match, or be adequate to matters as they stand, to the world as it is. Thus, one can believe, accept, reject, doubt, or be uncertain *that* some state of affairs obtains.

---

48. Brentano 1874 wrote not of "nonexistence" but of "*Inexistenz*," that is, "existence-in," which means that a mental state or episode contains within itself an object, which "exists-in" it.

49. See Mulligan 2013.

Permit me here a brief aside. If knowledge, like belief, is a doxastic state, why not just speak of religious "knowledge"?[50] I have several reasons to prefer "belief." First, knowledge is a kind of belief. For, according to a definition that goes back to Plato's *Theaetetus*, knowledge is a belief (a) that is true and (b) that the believer can justify with an account. Thus, if one knows something, one believes it, but if one believes something, one does not necessarily know it.[51] So, belief is the higher-order category: it is, in fact, "the *generic*, least-marked term for a *cognitive* [i.e., doxastic] state."[52] For this reason, knowledge does not appear to offer an especially useful alternative to belief.

Now, it may be that "knowledge" has greater emic resonance in some contexts than "belief." After all, Cicero could speak of *scientia colendorum deorum*, "knowledge of how to worship the gods" (*N.D.* 1.116). However, this fact does not delegitimize the use of "belief" as an etic term. As Henk Versnel reminds us, "Scholarly discourse is always etic and should therefore be conducted in etic terms."[53] Moreover, "knowledge" is not even the appropriate emic term in every context. The same Cicero that spoke of *scientia*, could also speak of adhering to the "beliefs" about the gods, the *opiniones*, of the ancestors (*N.D.* 3.5). And his contemporary, the scholar of Roman tradition Marcus Terentius Varro, theorized—or so Augustine tells us—the difference between divine and merely human cognition thus: "it is characteristic of man to believe, of god to know" (*hominis est enim haec opinari, dei scire*; *Civ.* 7.17).

Indeed, the Romans could even institutionalize *not* knowing. Aulus Gellius's *Attic Nights* records an example. In centuries past, he writes, when an earthquake had occurred, the Romans used to dedicate a festival to the god that had caused it. Yet they declined to name the god to whom the festival was dedicated, in pious recognition of their ignorance of which one it was. Gellius reports on a finding of Varro's research into Roman cult traditions. If pressed to identify the deity, they eschewed names, substituting instead a formula that encoded lack of religious knowledge: the rituals were dedicated "to the god or goddess," *si deo si deae* (*N.A.* 2.28.2–3).[54] These early Romans *believed* gods caused earthquakes, but they did not *know* which gods, and they institutionalized their belief-cum-ignorance in the resulting cult tradition. In light of such

---

50. With Ando 2008, and Rüpke 2016: 44.

51. See Saler 2001: 50.

52. Dennett 1998: 324, emphasis in the original, cited by Saler 2001: 57, in an excellent defense of "belief" in the study of religion.

53. Versnel 2011: 548.

54. On the ancient formula *si(ve) deus si(ve) dea*, "whether god or goddess" for invoking an unknown god, see Alvar 1985.

examples and arguments, this book constitutes a defense of belief's legitimacy as a category of both etic and emic validity.

So much for knowledge and its place among doxastic mental states. Representing states of affairs in the world is but one property of the mind. A complementary property is to represent it as we would that it were. Thus, in addition to the doxastic we have what I shall call *practical* mental states. These are often denoted by other terms, like "motivational," "volitive," and "conative." The practical class includes desires, which represent how we wish the world were, and intentions, which represent our goals, that is, how we would like to cause the world to be, and our plans of action for achieving them. Note that practical states, just like doxastic states, are representational, which is just to say, Intentional. However, while doxastic states seek to represent the way the world is, practical states represent the world as we would have it be or plan to make it.

These distinctions will be important when we explore the Intentionality of beliefs, desires, and intentions in chapter 2, of emotions and actions in chapter 3, and of collective cognition and collective action in chapter 4. Most broadly, I hope to convey a holistic conception of the mental. For belief must be understood in its cognitive context, where the doxastic and the practical components of mind have their proper place and relationships. For without practical mental episodes, we could not picture our interventions in the world. But without doxastic episodes, we could not picture a world in which to intervene. If the Romans had had no belief, they could hardly have represented the world as a religious space in which to act. In chapter 1, we trace two scholarly positions: first, that the Romans had belief but that it was not central to their religious life and, second, that the Romans did not even have the capacity for belief. I hope that the holistic Intentionalist understanding of belief presented in this book will persuade those in each camp both that the Romans *did* have the capacity for belief and that this central doxastic mental state *did* occupy a central place in Roman cult.

I situate my Intentionalist account of belief in Roman cult within broader cognitive science and philosophy research contexts, not only CSR and developmental psychology, which we have already touched on,[55] but also speech act theory, shared (or collective) intentionality, and social ontology. These latter three intimately interconnected theoretical programs take Intentionalism for granted. Thus, this is a theoretical book. If you dislike theory, this book may not please you. Yet I do not do theory for theory's sake here. Rather, I attempt to offer a clear application of theory to problems posed by Roman cult in the hope of inspiring new ways of thinking about this or any religion. And

---

55. For Roman "developmental psychologies," see Mackey 2019.

I should say up front: I present everything here in the spirit not of planting a flag to defend to the death but rather in a spirit of science, that is, of openness to better arguments and new evidence. Moreover, I do not pretend to have teased out every or even the most important implications for the study of Roman religion of the various theories that I have presented and employed here. Thus, I intend this book as a contribution to conversation rather than its closure.

The task before us is no small one. We must analyze what it means to believe; how having religious emotions derives from having religious beliefs; how belief guides individual action; and how the capacity, possessed by individuals, for sharing beliefs and other cognitive episodes collectively with others—shared Intentionality—enabled the performance of group cult acts. Finally, we shall have to investigate how it was that shared Intentionality, and especially shared belief, created and maintained Roman socioreligious reality and socioreligious power. For shared Intentionality and shared belief allowed the Romans to live in not only a natural world of earth, water, sky, flora, and other living things, but also a sociocultural world of religious institutions, festivals, cult practices, priestly statuses, and all the very real, very consequential coercive social norms and causal social powers that attended these things. The task is not small, but if we succeed, we shall have rethought Roman belief and cult, from intuitions to institutions.

PART I

Theoretical Foundations

1

Losing Belief

1.1. Introduction

This chapter has critical aims. It clears ground for the constructive chapters that follow. In the first section, I sketch a history of the loss of belief in scholarship on Roman religion. I show how a dichotomy between belief and action accompanied by a denial of belief had sprung up by the early twentieth century and had come to prevail by the century's end. The origins of the dichotomy lie in early Christian antipagan polemic, while belief-denial was encouraged by developments in late twentieth-century anthropology. In the second, final section, I expose some of the flaws of the central premises and arguments offered in support of the belief-action dichotomy and belief-denial.

This chapter and the next four attempt to show that belief is not nearly as fraught as has often been assumed. As we shall see, some scholars have taken "belief" to name a distinctively Christian attitude, not available to traditional Romans. Instead, I will be arguing, "belief" is just the English word for a very basic sort of cognitive state, which is characteristic of all neurotypical human beings, whose job is to represent the way things stand in the world. It will turn out that belief, under this deflationary description, plays a central role in our cognitive and practical lives. It underlies emotion, individual and collective action, and even socioreligious reality. Before we deal with these contentions, however, we must address in the present chapter the question of how belief came to be divorced from action and then denied altogether in scholarship on Roman religion.

1.2. A History of Belief-Denial and the Belief-Action Dichotomy

An important survey of Roman religion by John North closes by recapitulating its aim "to summarize and report on some fundamental changes in our way of looking at the religious life of Roman pagans." North notes that "the understanding of" Roman religion had been "blocked in the past by expectations inappropriate to the Romans' time and place." One of these inappropriate expectations consisted of attributing too much importance to "any question of the participants' belief or disbelief in the efficacy of ritual actions." In contrast, scholars had concluded in recent decades that they had "good reason to suspect that the whole problem [sc. of belief] derives from later not pagan preoccupations." Belief was now to be seen as largely anachronistic to Roman religion and reference to it usually a solecism. Evaluation of the new approach was welcomed "by the progress that may be made, or not made, in the future" under its auspices.[1]

Now, there can be no doubt that the past several decades, and especially the years since the publication of North's survey, have witnessed unprecedented growth in novel, productive, theoretically sophisticated, and self-reflexive approaches to Roman religion. And yet I would plead that a tendency in evidence throughout this period, the tendency to assert that belief is not a category of much relevance to the Romans, has impeded our appreciation of the cognitive aspects of Roman cult. Despite some notable recent attempts to challenge this attitude, antibelief convictions persist among some classicists. In certain respects, such convictions are quite traditional, rooted in early Christian polemics against pagans that were appropriated into Protestant disparagement of Catholic ritualism. In other respects, antibelief sentiments are new, stemming from late twentieth-century anthropological theorizing. So let us begin by briefly reviewing the fate of belief in scholarship on Roman religion. For we must see whence we have come in order to grasp where we are and to decide where we wish to go.

Once upon a time, researching Roman religion meant, in part, reconstructing its "original" state from the evidence of necessarily later sources. This pursuit occupied scholars such as Johann Adam Hartung, who helped found the field with his *Die Religion der Römer* in 1836. In the striking image of his "Vorrede," Hartung describes authentic Roman religion as "an ancient temple" (*ein alter Tempel*) on which a later structure (*Überbau*), assembled of Greek and other alien materials, had been imposed. Both of these structures collapsed, leaving to the scholar the task of excavating the remains (*die Trümmer*) of the first structure from under the rubble of the later one.[2] Hartung's image

---

1. North 2000a: 84–85. A version of this and the following two chapters appeared as Mackey 2017.

2. Hartung 1836: 1.ix. The sketch offered here makes no claim to being exhaustive. On Hartung, Mommsen, Wissowa, Cumont, and the history of the study of Roman religion, see Scheid 1987; Bendlin 2000; Stroumsa 2002; Bendlin 2006; Phillips 2007; Ando 2008: ix–xvii; Rives 2010: 244–51, esp. 247ff.; and Scheid 2016: 5–11.

of architectural supersession and collapse proved canonical: Preller, Aust, and Wissowa, among others, cited it approvingly.[3] Guided by Hartung's conceit, with its tragic motif of "das Erlöschen des alten Glaubens"[4] (the dying out of the old belief), scholars could not but disparage the religion of the historical republic as contaminated or degenerate.[5]

This thesis sat well with Theodor Mommsen, for whom "the old national religion was visibly on the decline" in the age of Cato and Ennius, undermined by Hellenism and other eastern influences.[6] However, for Mommsen, Roman religion qua religion had always fallen short.[7] At its best, it had served as a system of ritual marked by a practical legalism,[8] but by the late republic it was merely a tool with which the elite cynically exploited "the principles of the popular belief, which were recognized as irrational [*als irrationell erkannten Sätze des Volksglaubens*], for reasons of outward convenience."[9] Mommsen's view of republican religion as a means of manipulation or social control has ancient authority, for example, that of Polybius (6.56), whom he cites.[10] More importantly, it is surely no coincidence that this scholar, with his particular interests and expertise, should have identified a legalistic paradigm at the heart of Roman religion.

Mommsen's legalistic paradigm proved influential; Georg Wissowa absorbed its lessons. He dedicated the first edition of his still fundamental *Religion und Kultus der Römer* to the elder scholar, asserting that without Mommsen's Lebenswerk—especially *Römisches Staatsrecht* (1871–88) and his

---

3. Preller 1858: 41–42n2; Aust 1899: 1; Wissowa 1902: 1; and Wissowa 1912: 1. See further Bendlin 2006: 235–36.

4. Hartung 1836: 1.244.

5. See, e.g., Fowler 1911: 428–29, admiring by contrast the "revival of the State religion by Augustus."

6. Mommsen 1862–66: 2.402. "So ging es mit der alten Landesreligion zusehends auf Neige" (Mommsen 1856: 844).

7. Mommsen 1856: 152: "den geheimnisvollen Schauer, nach dem das Menschenherz doch auch sich sehnt, vermag sie [sc. *römische Religion*] nicht zu erregen." Mommsen may have been "agnostic," but we can see his "education in the Lutheran tradition" (Scheid 2016: 10) reflected in this quotation. See below, text accompanying nn. 23–25.

8. See the discussion at Mommsen 1862–66: 1.222–27, which concludes (227): "Thus the whole criminal law rested as to its ultimate basis on the religious idea of expiation. But religion performed no higher service in Latium than the furtherance of civil order and morality by means such as these."

9. Mommsen 1862–66: 2.433, cited in Fowler 1911: 2. German: Mommsen 1857: 417.

10. The manipulation thesis reaches an apex in L. Taylor 1949, chapter 4. See Champion 2017: 1–22 for a critique of this "elite-instrumentalist" view.

contributions on the *Fasti* to *CIL* I, *pars prior* (1893²)—his own work would not exist.[11] In the "Vorwort" to his book's second edition, Wissowa responded to the charge that his account lacked "Religiosität."[12] Defending his "juristische" perspective, that is, the "Gesichtspunkt des *ius pontificium*" (point of view of the priestly law) he explicitly aligned himself with Mommsen and his paradigm.[13] It was for another scholar, Franz Cumont, to discover a source of the "religiosity" that Wissowa had neglected: the "Oriental religions."[14] Cumont adduced dry Roman legalism to explain the appeal of these foreign cults. Roman religion was "froide" (cold) and "prosaïque" (prosaic), its priests comparable to jurists,[15] its observances comparable to legal practice.[16]

Cumont's cold legalism stopped one step short of empty formalism. Arthur Darby Nock, an otherwise extraordinarily sensitive scholar, took that step. In his essay for the tenth volume of *The Cambridge Ancient History* (1934), Nock asserted that Roman religion was "in its essence a matter of cult acts" (465). It was a "religion made up of traditional practice"; "it was not a matter of belief" (469); it was, in a word, "jejune" (467). In Nock's appraisal, we see quite clearly the dichotomy between belief and practice that came to inform even the most rigorous scholarship: Roman religion was strictly "a matter of cult acts"; "it was not a matter of belief." Where Hartung had traced a "dying out" of belief, and where Mommsen had derided "irrational" belief, Nock saw no

---

11. Wissowa 1902: x: "kein Kapitel dieses Buches hätte geschrieben werden können." See Scheid 1987: 309; and Bendlin 2006: 236ff. On the epistolary relationship between these men, see Scheid and Wirbelauer 2008.

12. The charge reflects a Protestant notion of true religion as, in Schleiermacher's famous words, "Frömmigkeit," "piety," that is, a "feeling of absolute dependence on God" (das Gefühl schlechthiniger Abhängikeit von Gott): Schleiermacher 2003: 32, 38, 44, 67, 265, 283, etc. See Bendlin 2000: 120; and Bendlin 2006: 229.

13. Wissowa 1912: viii. On this moment in Wissowa's intellectual career and its import, contrast Bendlin 2006 and Scheid 2016: 7–21.

14. Cumont 1906: 37: "Les religions Orientales, qui ne s'imposent pas avec l'autorité reconnue d'une religion officielle, doivent pour s'attirer des prosélytes, émouvoir les sentiments de l'individu."

15. Cumont 1906: 36: "Ses pontifes, qui sont aussi des magistrats, ont réglé les manifestations du culte avec une précision exacte de juristes." This is cited in Fowler 1911: 2–3, in the course of the author's acknowledgment of and departure from Mommsen and Wissowa's legalistic paradigm.

16. Cumont 1906: 37, cited in Fowler 1911: 2–3: "Sa liturgie rappelle par la minutie de ses prescriptions l'ancien droit civil." None of this is to say, of course, that the Romans' was not a religion of law: in addition to Wissowa 1912, see Watson 1992 and 1993; Meyer 2004; Ando and Rüpke 2006; Tellegen-Couperus 2012.

real role for belief at all, only empty cult.[17] This is not to say that Nock had taken the step that later scholars would take and denied that Romans could *believe*. It was merely that Roman belief was not a relevant component of Roman cult. A dichotomy between belief and practice, as well as denial about belief, had entered the scholarly discourse on Roman religion.[18]

According to the view whose development we have sketched thus far, Roman religion had always been preoccupied with ritual action. Regarding belief, however, we may discern a bifurcation into two schools of thought. If we back up a couple centuries, we see that Bernard de Fontenelle, in his *Histoire des Oracles* of 1687, had surveyed Cicero's remarks on religion and opined that "among the pagans religion was only a practice, for which speculation was unimportant. Do as the others do and believe whatever you like."[19] Fontenelle's thesis, though not intended as a compliment, does have certain merits. For the norm "believe whatever you like" makes Roman polytheism a culture without a norm of *cognitive conformity* in the domain of theology. This distinguishes it from those Christian and other traditions that do endorse such a norm.[20] To his credit, Fontenelle had declined to declare the beliefs of the Romans inadequate, as one later school of thought was to do, nor had he denied beliefs to the Romans, as a second, still later school would to do.[21] Instead, he had merely noted the Romans' relative *cognitive autonomy*. (This is a term to which we return throughout the book.)

According to the first of these two later schools of thought, into which, as we have seen, Mommsen fell, Roman cult had beliefs associated with it, but they were nugatory. This view may be found expressed repeatedly, as for

---

17. A similar framework, motivated by a teleological view of Christian religiosity, had already been posited by W. R. Smith for ancient Semitic religions: "ritual and practical usage were, strictly speaking, the sum total of ancient religions"; such religion "was not a system of belief with practical applications; it was a body of fixed traditional practices" (1889: 21). On Smith, see Harrison 2015a.

18. Kindt 2012: 30–32 and Harrison 2015a diagnose an analogous dichotomy in the study of Greek religion.

19. Fontenelle 1687: 64: "Il y a lieu de croire que chez les Payens la Religion n'estoit qu'une pratique, dont la speculation estoit indifferente. Faites commes les autres, et croyez ce qu'il vous plaira." On this passage and recent "neo-Fontenellian" approaches, see Parker 2011: 31–39.

20. Indeed, the Jesuit Jean-François Baltus attacked as impious Fontenelle's treatise and the work of Antonie van Dale (1683) on which it was based (Baltus 1707). Following Antonie van Dale, Fontenelle argued that the pagan oracles had been merely human frauds, not the work of demons. This thesis clashed with the received theory that Christ's incarnation had silenced antiquity's demonic pagan oracles. See Ossa-Richardson 2013.

21. Cf. Parker 2011: 32–33.

example with considerable vehemence by Stephen Gaselee in the *Edinburgh Review* (1913: 89):

> The indigenous Roman religion seems indeed to have been one of the least satisfying forms of belief ever possessed by any nation. It consisted of a large number of ritual observances, closely bound up with the routine of the household and of the State, in combination with a host of gods that can only be described as the palest and most bloodless personifications of ordinary and extraordinary actions.

The second school of thought, that of Nock, held that Roman religion was simply "not a matter of belief," nugatory or otherwise.

The two schools of thought represented by Mommsen, on the one hand, and by Nock, on the other, both articulate in their respective ways what had become by the late nineteenth century a ubiquitous dichotomy between belief and ritual. However, this dichotomy hardly had its origins in the disinterested findings of secular scholarship. Instead, it was rooted in Protestant anti-Catholic polemic. If the religious beliefs of the Romans fared badly in this ideologically fraught scholarship, their religious practices hardly fared better. Here is Mommsen again (1862–66: 1.222–23):

> the Latin religion sank into an incredible insipidity and dullness, and early became shrivelled into an anxious and dreary round of ceremonies.

Lest the reader fail to draw the parallel between ancient Romans and modern Catholics, Mommsen obligingly draws it himself: these unfortunate traits of Roman religion were "no less distinctly apparent in the saint worship of the modern inhabitants of Italy."[22]

The approach to Roman religion common to these scholars of the nineteenth and early twentieth centuries, with its opposition of belief to action, was not new, as the example of Fontenelle shows. Indeed, it was older than Fontenelle. It was situated within and structured by a polemic that dated back to the Reformation, when Martin Luther had elevated *fides* and "der Glaube des Herzens" (the faith of the heart) of "der innere Mensch" (the inner man) over a supposed Catholic formalism that relied on "gute Werke" (good works) performed by what Luther termed "der äußere Mensch" (the outer man).[23] And, if "faith" (*fides*, "Glaube") was a Protestant byword from Luther on, it is

---

22. Mommsen 1862–66: 1.223. It is hard to know whether Jew or Roman fares worse in Mommsen's comparisons, as at 2.400: "The catalogue of the duties and privileges of the priest of Jupiter . . . might well have a place in the Talmud."

23. Luther 1520. On the inner man / outer man distinction, see Rieger 2007: 8off. and 234ff.

perhaps telling that the first attested use of "ritual" appears in the *Acts and Monuments* of the English Protestant polemicist John Foxe, who faults an epistle of Pope Zephyrinus to the bishops of Egypt for "contayning no maner of doctrine ... but onely certayn ritual decrees to no purpose."[24] Here, in the sixteenth century, we can already discern the opposition that will come to determine the assumptions of so much scholarship on Roman religion, the opposition of insufficiently excogitated beliefs ("no maner of doctrine") to meaningless practices ("ritual decrees to no purpose").[25]

Indeed, this Reformation rhetoric, which casts Catholics as pagans[26] and Protestants as late antique Christians, drew from ancient wellsprings, such as Lactantius, who in a characteristically polemical passage proposed a dichotomy between action and cognition, body and soul, which tracks and informs his distinction between pagan and Christian (Lact. *Div. Inst.* 4.3.1):

> *nec habet* [sc. *deorum cultus*] *inquisitionem aliquam veritatis, sed tantummodo ritum colendi, qui non officio mentis, sed ministerio corporis constat.*
>
> Nor does the cult of the gods amount to any search for truth but merely a ritual of worshipping, which consists not in a function of the mind, but in employment of the body.

Here we see already, *in ovo*, not only Luther's doctrine of "inner man" versus "outer man" and his castigation of Catholic work righteousness, but also Foxe's polemical dichotomization of doctrine and ritual.

Now, scholars in recent years have shown themselves sensitive to the influence that ideological and confessional elements exert on the putatively objective narratives and judgments of historiography. They have not hesitated to expose and reject tendentious categories implicit in the paradigms of the nineteenth and early twentieth centuries. Notions of an early, authentic Roman religiosity beset by contaminating external influences or degenerating internally from neglect, for example, have been rightly discarded; the manipulation thesis no longer exerts quite the explanatory allure it once did; and the

---

24. Foxe 1570: 1.83, cited in *OED* s.v. ritual, which is cited in turn by J. Z. Smith (1987: 102), whose chapter (96–103) on Protestant construal of the emptiness of Catholic ritual is especially instructive. J. Z. Smith 1990 studies the context of Protestant anti-Catholic polemic in which modern religious studies—especially comparative studies of early Christianity and late antique religions—are situated. See Wiebe 1999 for more on the nineteenth-century Protestant context of the origins of the academic study of religion.

25. For a host of examples of the "empty ritual" thesis in classical scholarship, see the citations in Phillips 1986: 2697n56.

26. See Conyers Middleton 1729 for one of the most florid examples.

legalistic aspects of Roman religion are no longer seen as failings of authentic sentiment. Progress, indeed, dramatic progress, has been made.[27]

As part and parcel of that progress, we have already seen scholars such as North questioning whether non-Christian religions should be judged and evaluated in terms of belief. Surely both schools—the one that found the beliefs of the Romans wanting and the one that found the Romans wanting beliefs—were wrong to measure the ancients against a modern, Christian yardstick? Perhaps belief is not a necessary or even intelligible category of analysis in the study of non-Christian religions? The voicing of such doubts was intended to dislodge Christianity, with its focus on *faith*, as the normative or exemplary religion, the standard against which all others must be judged. In so doing, this move meant to expose the judgments of a Mommsen or a Gaselee for what they were, to wit, condescending, Christianizing censures of Roman religion's inadequate or "irrational" beliefs. This relativism about belief was also intended to disarm the evaluations of a Hartung or a Nock. For how can we speak of "the dying out of the old belief" or chide the Romans for lacking belief if belief was simply never relevant to their tradition of worship? This stance, which was meant to be charitable, derived in part from developments in twentieth-century anthropology, where the hazards of assessing other traditions in light of Western concepts and norms had come vividly into view.

The signal anthropological study that encouraged scholars of Roman religion to cast off outmoded ideas about belief was Rodney Needham's *Belief, Language, and Experience*, which appeared in 1972. Needham takes *belief* in its standard usage to refer to "inner states of individuals." On the everyday understanding, these inner states amount to "a common human capacity which can immediately be ascribed to all men."[28] Against this pedestrian understanding of the term, he concluded, on the basis of his attempt to locate belief among the Penan of Borneo and the Nuer of the Sudan, that it was a mistake for the Western researcher to attribute beliefs to individuals of other cultures. As we shall see, Needham is often misinterpreted as asserting that belief is an inherently Western, Christian mental state not shared by non-Western, non-Christian peoples. However, his true thesis is much stronger and much more

---

27. For overviews of this progress with rather different emphases, see Phillips 2007; Rives 2010; and "Translator's Foreword" by Clifford Ando in Scheid 2016: xi–xvii. An exhaustive history of scholarship on Roman religion, attentive to the various intellectual contexts that have shaped its study, is a desideratum.

28. Needham 1972: 5 and 3.

radical, to wit, that *no one* has ever believed.[29] He writes, for example, as follows (1972: 188):

> The notion of belief is not appropriate to an empirical philosophy of mind or to an exact account of human motives and conduct. Belief is not a discriminable experience, it does not constitute a natural resemblance among men, and it does not belong to "the common behaviour of mankind."

On this view, reference to belief in the anthropological study of religion should be eschewed as misguided and misguiding. However, this is not because belief is properly Western or Christian. Rather, it is because belief is an incoherent category even within Western, Christian culture. "Belief" refers to no psychological state of which we can speak meaningfully at all. Needham's views have done a great deal of harm to the study of ancient religion. I shall attempt to show what is wrong with some of his most pernicious arguments later in this chapter.[30] For now I would only note that if we should accept Needham's conclusions, we might well throw up our hands with him: "I am not saying that human life is senseless, but that we cannot make sense of it."[31]

Scholars of ancient religion did not delay in drawing inspiration from Needham's skepticism about belief,[32] even if they have usually missed his most radical conclusion. Simon Price, in his *Rituals and Power: The Roman Imperial Cult in Asia Minor* (1984), stands at the vanguard of and typifies the flawed reception of Needham, from whom he draws a relativist rather than a universalist lesson about the problem of belief. Price helped to establish, and asserted perhaps most vehemently, the new approach to belief that we have seen heralded by North, according to which belief is a Christian, not pagan phenomenon. It is worth quoting Price at modest length (1984: 10–11):

> Indeed the centrality of "religious belief" in our culture has sometimes led to the feeling that belief is a distinct and natural capacity which is shared by all human beings. This of course is nonsense. [Here Price footnotes, without comment, Needham 1972.] "Belief" as a religious term is profoundly Christian in its implications; it was forged out of the experience which the Apostles and Saint Paul had of the Risen Lord. The emphasis which

---

29. I thank Joseph Streeter for helping me see, *per litteras*, the full implications of Needham's arguments.

30. See, too, Streeter 2020, which neatly defeats Needham's arguments using resources internal to them.

31. Needham 1972: 244.

32. In turn, Needham could comment on the work of ancient historians, as in a 1990 review faulting Veyne 1988 for a lack of rigor in discussing the beliefs of the Greeks and Romans.

"belief" gives to spiritual commitment has no necessary place in the analysis of other cultures. That is, the question about the "real beliefs" of the Greeks is again implicitly Christianizing.

For the ancients, he continues, "Ritual is what there was." Price's animadversions have proved influential,[33] as has his appeal to Needham's study, as we shall see.

First, I would note in passing here a virtue of Price's book that is often overlooked. The disproportionate influence of Price's antibelief rhetoric has obscured his conception of "ritual as a public cognitive system."[34] If what he meant by this was that Roman ritual amounted to a mechanism for distributing representations widely, this is an excellent idea. It may fairly be said to inform this entire book: in a sense, chapters 4–9 are dedicated to this idea. For now, suffice it to say that if Roman ritual was a public cognitive system, then presumably it depended causally on and played a causal role in forming Roman *beliefs*, among other cognitive states and processes.

Whatever the virtues of Price's study may be, we must focus here on the canonical status it granted Needham's book among classicists. Two years after the appearance of *Rituals and Power*, for example, C. R. Phillips III cited Needham in an article entitled "The Sociology of Religious Knowledge in the Roman Empire." He rightly took exception to the view expressed by Nock, recognizing that "Roman religion . . . by its very postulation of superhuman beings and rituals for dealing with them cannot be mere actions."[35] Yet he nonetheless declined to allow that the "postulation of superhuman beings" might constitute anything resembling belief: "The very word 'belief' represents far too slippery a category to help investigators, while considerable doubt may be cast on contemporary models for mental life."[36] Although Phillips expressed ambivalence about Needham's work,[37] we can still see the latter's influence reflected in the former's skepticism as to whether the ancients

---

33. From Bowersock 1989: 206, to Collar 2013: 63–64, the influence of Price's denial continues to be felt.

34. S. Price 1984: 9, and cf. 8.

35. Phillips 1986: 2710.

36. Phillips 1986: 2702.

37. Phillips 1986: 2689: Needham "offers a thorough and thought-provoking study of the problem" of belief, and his "enterprise has utility," but "the logic of Needham's analytic position produces paralysis." More recently, Phillips has accepted the relevance of belief, e.g., 2007: 13 (and cf. 26): "most specialists nowadays reject the idea that Roman religion constituted 'cult acts without belief.'"

entertained anything like what we call "beliefs." Needham's book continues to be cited as definitive by classicists. Jason Davies, to take just one example, wrote: "'Belief' is ... deeply problematic: it may be that this paradoxical concept is one peculiar to the Christianized West."[38]

These latter quotations are addressed to *Roman* religion, but Price, it will be noted, was writing not about Romans per se, but about Greeks under Roman rule. The dichotomy of belief and ritual with which he operated may accordingly be found echoed in scholarship on Greek religion. In 1985 for example Paul Cartledge wrote that "classical Greek religion was at bottom a question of doing not of believing, of behaviour rather than faith."[39] Much more recently we have been told, "Ancient Greek religion had little to do with belief, and a great deal to do with practice and observance of common ancestral customs."[40] Andreas Bendlin, analyzing trends in the study of Roman religion, and Thomas Harrison, performing the same office for Greek religion, diagnosed in this resurrected dichotomy between belief and action what both called an "orthodoxy."[41] This orthodoxy was part and parcel of what we have seen North, writing in the same year as Bendlin and Harrison, herald as a new approach.

Statements of this orthodoxy dating from the decades that straddle the millennium are not far to find. A relatively unobjectionable example: "In the case of polytheistic religions, action, not belief, is primary."[42] More tendentiously: "One of the hardest features of ancient religion for the modern student is the sheer unimportance of belief"; what was important was "correct observance of rituals."[43] Similar, but boiled down: "For the Romans, religion was not a belief . . . : it was purely utilitarian practice."[44] Now expanded: "For the

---

38. J. Davies 2004, citing Needham 1972 at 5n15; cf. J. Davies 2011, citing Needham at 398 and elsewhere. On the Greek side, see, e.g., Giordano-Zecharya 2005, citing Needham at 330n19 and 343; and Gagné 2013, citing Needham at 7n17.

39. Cartledge 1985: 98. Cf., much earlier, Burnet 1924: 5: "Athenian religion was a matter of practice, not of belief."

40. N. Evans 2010: 7. Many more such remarks about Greek religion cited in Harrison 2000: 18–23; Harrison 2007: 382–84; Versnel 2011: 539–59, esp. 544–45; Harrison 2015a; Petrovic and Petrovic 2016: 1–37.

41. Bendlin 2000: 115 (cf. 2001); Harrison 2000: 18. Petrovic and Petrovic 2016: 2 speaks of "a long tradition which peaked in the latter part of the twentieth century" of denial about belief in Greek religion.

42. Rüpke 2007d: 86.

43. Dowden 1992: 8.

44. Turcan 2000: 2.

Romans, *religio* was not a matter of faith or belief, of doctrine or creed, but rather of worship—of divination, prayer, and sacrifice."[45] More expansively still: "For the Romans, *religio* especially denoted ritual precision. Being religious, 'having religion,' did not mean believing correctly, but performing acts such as sacrifice or oracles (*sacra et auspicia*) at the right point in time and in the right series of parts."[46] Most authoritatively: in Roman religious life, "experiences, beliefs and disbeliefs had no particularly privileged role in defining an individual's actions, behaviour or sense of identity."[47] And, quite briefly, in a very recent formulation: Roman cult "was a religion of doing, not believing."[48] All these dicta, which derive for the most part from introductory texts,[49] are but recent statements of the old dichotomy that opposes belief to action and of the old denial of belief's relevance to Roman cult. As in Price, these recent statements of the dichotomy and of denial appear as theoretical sophistication and sympathetic appreciation of Roman alterity rather than as denominational rancor and Christian sanctimony. Nor is the dichotomy or the denial limited to classics; both continue to inform the study of religion in a variety of disciplines.[50]

Of course, it would be wrong to say that dichotomy and denial have been the only theorizations of Roman belief ever proposed. For example, Mommsen's contemporary Henry Nettleship posited an intimate link between Roman belief and religious action: "public religion was the outward representation of the belief that a Providence governed the progress of the Roman empire."[51] Much more recently, John Scheid discerned "a faith within Roman religion," which "took for granted the existence of gods and proposed the necessity and efficacy of ritual commerce with them."[52] Additionally, Denis Feeney has observed that the Romans did not just *have* religious beliefs,

---

45. Warrior 2006: xv.

46. Auffarth and Mohr 2006: 1608–9.

47. Beard et al. 1998: 1.42.

48. Beard 2015: 103.

49. Similarly, Scheid 2003a: 18–22. For the privileging of practice in more specialized literature, see, e.g., North 1976: 1ff.; Feil 1986: 1.42 (citing Muth 1978); Levene 1993: 10–13, 79, 229, etc.; Gargola 1995: 5; Stewart 1998: 2; Gradel 2002: 4–5; Rasmussen 2002: 169.

50. Recognition of the dichotomy: Bell 1992: 19–20. A plea to rethink it: J. Z. Smith 2002. Review and assessment of belief-denial: Bell 2002 and 2008. A recent reassertion of belief-denial: Lindquist and Coleman 2008. Streeter n.d. analyzes and dismantles the most recent anthropological arguments against belief.

51. Nettleship 1885: 133.

52. Linder and Scheid 1993: 55: "une foi dans la religion romaine"; "elle donnait pour acquise l'existence des dieux et posait la nécessité et l'efficacité du commerce rituelle avec eux." Cf.

they also had *discourses* about them.⁵³ On the Greek side, Albert Henrichs (to present just one example) wrote that "the rituals [the Greeks] performed were mere corollaries of their belief in the existence and power of the gods."⁵⁴ Despite such interventions, it remains too common to see Roman and often Greek cult as paradigmatic cases of religious *doing* rather than religious *believing*.

However, here we should pause. After all, is there not *something* to these views that I have just rehearsed? Western scholars such as I need to take care not to privilege Christianity, with its focus on *faith*, as the norm against which all other traditions must be judged. In the study of ancient religion, which is always at least implicitly a comparative endeavor, one must attend carefully to divergences between pagan modes of religiosity and modes perhaps more familiar in the West. I observed that Fontenelle's formulation of the Roman "way of believing"—*faites commes les autres, et croyez ce qu'il vous plaira*—has its merits. And there are indeed divergences among pagan, modern, and premodern Christian "cultures of belief."⁵⁵ Let us consider four points.

First, Roman religious culture was inclusive and agglutinative, Christianity exclusive. The Romans happily adopted new gods and practices, and, I would argue, new beliefs along with them. In contrast, most Christianities, from antiquity to the present day, have exclusivity baked in. For example, monotheism is of the very essence of Christianity, in just about all its manifestations. As such, it has always insisted on some sort of belief or believing with respect to Christ as the means to salvation. Such exclusivity requires renunciation of previous or extraneous commitments in a way that is alien to traditional Roman religiosity. Only under an exclusive regime does belief, its confession, and its policing become salient.

The remaining three points derive from or expand on this first one. The second point is that many Christianities have been organized around a definitive and obligatory set of explicit doctrines while Roman religion was not organized thus. Third, one of these doctrines was that believing as such (not just the content of a particular belief) was efficacious of the soul's salvation, as seen in, for example, Paul's Letter to the Romans. Such ideas were alien to traditional Roman religion. Fourth, Roman pagans neither foregrounded overt profession of approved beliefs nor fretted over such self-reflexive

---

Mueller 2002: 19: "the emotions (as well as terms like 'belief') should not be neglected"; Rives 2007: 48: "we must be careful not to throw out the baby with the bathwater."

53. Feeney 1998: 11: "This is not to say that language of belief is never an issue when we are discussing the 'ancient' religions. It certainly is, as we shall see in detail."

54. Henrichs 2010: 26.

55. For a proposal that we study differing "cultures of belief," see Mair 2013.

epistemological attitudes as have gone under the names of πίcτιc, *fides*, or faith. In other words, pagan *metacognition*, that is, their "thinking about their own thinking" (see at section 1.3.2, below), with respect to belief differed from Christian metacognition in being less obligatorily self-conscious. Pagans could just believe without meditating overmuch on *what* or *the fact that* they believed. These four considerations, which are surely part of the point of the various antibelief positions that we have discussed, rightly inform the contrast scholars have drawn between Roman religion and those religions in which "believing as such" is "a central element in the system."[56]

However, a note of caution and a brief digression are in order here. Just because "believing as such" was not central to Roman cult does not entail that the Romans could not engage in metacognition, and perhaps even "believe in belief."[57] Seneca, for example, held that *believing* that there are gods (*deos credere*) was the primary "veneration of the gods," *deorum cultus*.[58] And in *De natura deorum*, Cicero's Cotta affirms, against Balbus's insinuations, his endorsement of "the beliefs (*opiniones*) that we have received from our ancestors concerning the immortal gods."[59] In *De legibus*, speaking propria voce, Marcus could assert his belief in the utility of such *opiniones* for communal life and the keeping of faith among human beings.[60] Then there is Livy, who expected his readers to believe that belief in the divinity of Romulus soothed the grief of his followers after his mysterious disappearance.[61] Or, again, Livy and Cicero both attest a tradition that the liturgical reforms of Numa had a salutary effect on the minds, *animi*, of the warlike Romans. They hold that he made his reforms acceptable by causing his citizens to believe that the nymph Egeria had guided him in formulating them.[62] These examples amount to nothing if not instances of belief in the power of belief.

Cicero, in his *De republica*, takes a dimmer view of such a proclivity to believe. He depicts Scipio worrying over beliefs such as those promulgated about Romulus and Egeria. How could the *maiores*, living in their cultured age, have believed myths such as the apotheosis of Romulus? Their belief and

---

56. Beard et al. 1998: 1.43.

57. In the happy expression of Dennett 2006: 200ff. For "belief in belief" in Ptolemaic Egypt, see Roubekas 2015.

58. Sen. *Ep.* 95.50: *primus est deorum cultus deos credere*. Cf. Cic. *Dom.* 107: *nec est ulla erga deos pietas nisi honesta de numine eorum ac mente opinio*.

59. Cic. *N.D.* 3.5: *opiniones quas a maioribus accepimus de dis immortalibus*.

60. Cic. *Leg.* 2.16: *utilis esse autem has opiniones quis neget . . . ?*

61. Liv. 1.16.8: *mirum, quantum illi viro nuntianti haec fidei fuerit quamque desiderium Romuli apud plebem exercitumque facta fide inmortalitatis lenitum sit*.

62. Cic. *Rep.* 2.26: *animos . . . religionum caerimoniis mitigavit*; cf. Liv. 1.19.4–5.

proclivity to believe were problems to be explained.[63] Cicero could divide even his own contemporaries into those who believed such myths and those who did not.[64] So, perhaps because their polytheistic culture did not enforce cognitive conformity with respect to theological attitudes, the Romans could and did freely discuss beliefs, entertain beliefs about belief, and even believe or disbelieve in the value of this or that belief or of the proclivity to believe itself.

The texts I have alluded to in the previous paragraphs are shot through with the Latin lexicon of *belief* terms: *credere, putare, opinio, fides*, and many more. Those who deny the relevance of belief rarely engage with such passages and their vocabulary. When they do, the results are telling, for they tend to suppose that they can discredit the Latin terms as evidence for Roman belief, when in fact they only demonstrate belief's indispensability. For example, Jason Davies comments on the word *credo* as it appears in a funerary inscription cited by Charles King. In King's translation, the inscription reads, "I believe [*credo*] that some deity or another was jealous of [my daughter]" (*quam nei esset credo nesci[o qui] inveidit deus*).[65] King wants to take *credo* here as evidence for a belief about the gods, but Davies warns that we should not take the term as "positive evidence for one particular frame of mind." After all, "elsewhere *credo* is used of accepting an inference from visible evidence." He suggests accordingly that we should translate it not *I believe* but "I suppose/I conclude/ I accept/I realise/I deduce/I cannot avoid what seems evident."[66]

Davies is right to suggest that we need to consider nuances of context carefully when thinking about the frame of mind of Latin speakers, dead for two millennia, and when thinking about our translations of their terms. However, nothing in his proposed alternatives tells against belief. For the cognitive product of "accepting an inference from visible evidence" is a belief. Similarly, the mental states referred to by the alternative verbs he proposes are all beliefs, or more broadly what I called in the book's introduction and shall call in chapter 2 "doxastic" states: mental states whose job is to represent how things stand in the world. Thus, "I suppose" implies that one entertains the doxastic state of "supposition," in which one imagines a state of affairs as obtaining. When we "conclude," the resulting conclusion becomes our belief. When we "accept," "realize," or "deduce," *what* we accept, realize, or deduce is that a given state of

---

63. Cic. *Rep.* 2.17–20. The language of belief and disbelief runs throughout this passage. In order: *putaretur, opinionem, ad credendum, recepit, respuit, creditum, crederetur, credidissent.*

64. Cic. *Leg.* 1.4: *nec dubito quin idem et cum Egeria conlocutum Numam et ab aquila Tarquinio apicem impositum putent.*

65. C. King 2003: 278–79, citing Warmington 1940: 22.

66. J. Davies 2011: 402.

affairs obtains. The cognitive product of these processes of accepting, realizing, or deducing is nothing but *belief* that a given state of affairs obtains. Finally, when we "cannot avoid what seems evident," we come to *believe* what seems evident. Davies's proposed alternatives amount, in the main, to verbs describing cognitive processes that lead to belief as cognitive product.

To return now from our digression, I would happily tender the four points I offered on the differences between Christian and pagan cognitive culture as charitable, if nonliteral, interpretations of the belief-denial position and of the quotations in its support that we have reviewed. The points, to restate them, were as follows: First, Roman religion was open rather than exclusive. Second, it was not distinguished by a set of core tenets, even if it did manifest what might be called "faith" with respect to gods and cult. Third, Romans did not accord believing much intrinsic religious value, and certainly no inherent salvific efficacy, although this does not mean that they could not have beliefs, including beliefs about salvation of one sort or another, here or in the afterlife.[67] Finally, as a result of these three factors, Roman religion did not accord a central place to confessions of belief, although this does not mean that Romans could not be reflective about what they believed and about belief itself.

I have found, especially in the "oral tradition" of the classroom, the conference, and the lecture series, that many scholars hold views no more radical than these. Yet a great many published statements, of the sort we have reviewed, militate against such charity and seem to demand a literal reading. And I have found in the oral tradition, too, that many scholars insist on just such a literal reading and refuse to countenance any reference whatsoever to belief. We have been asked to agree with Needham that belief is not a "natural capacity which is shared by all human beings,"[68] that "beliefs ... had no particularly privileged role in defining an individual's actions,"[69] and that the Romans had no beliefs one way or the other about "the efficacy" of the "ritual actions"[70] that they performed at the cost of so much time, trouble, and material expenditure. The result of such pronouncements has been, as Andreas Bendlin has

---

67. Consider, for example, the gold leaves found in Italian and Sicilian graves bearing witness to a belief that one may find favorable or unfavorable reception in the afterlife, depending on one's possession of privileged knowledge of what to do and say upon arrival in the underworld: see, in the edition of Graf and Johnston 2007, tablets 1–9, the latter from Rome.
68. S. Price 1984: 10.
69. Beard et al. 1998: 1.42.
70. North 2000a: 84.

noted, a focus on "the ritual dimension of the Roman religious experience rather than a possible cognitive dimension."[71]

So, a rethinking of the dichotomy between belief and action and of the denial of belief was clearly due. Just such a rethinking commenced at the turn of the millennium. Scholars of classical antiquity have reopened the question of belief and have been looking afresh at it and at cognition more generally as necessary components in any holistic picture of ancient religious life.[72] This book joins and seeks to contribute to these efforts. I argue that on both theoretical and evidentiary grounds the consensus about belief and its relationship to action that was in place at the beginning of this century stands in need of reconsideration, however valuable much of the work conducted under its auspices. I concur, mutatis mutandis, with Thomas Harrison when he writes of Greek religion, "Rather than dismissing 'belief' . . . , we need to reclaim it."[73]

This book represents an attempt at reclamation. Yet it will not suffice merely to affirm of the Romans that they had beliefs. We must understand belief as what I called in the book's introduction an "Intentional state," see how it underpinned religious emotion, investigate its role in the etiology of cult action, and finally consider its collective dimensions. When shared collectively, belief made it possible for individuals to share agency and cooperate in group cult acts, allowed for cult norms and conventions, and contributed to the creation of Roman religious reality and its attendant social powers. In other words, we must go well beyond debating whether the Romans entertained beliefs. And we must also go beyond merely reintroducing talk of belief.

The remainder of this chapter points out some flaws in the main antibelief arguments. The rest of the book illustrates the many ways in which belief was implicated in Roman cult.

---

71. Bendlin 2001: 193. Cf. Phillips 2007: 26: "Perhaps it is time for specialists in Roman religion to renew contact with their erstwhile colleagues in religious studies and anthropology—those fields are rife with promising approaches such as the cognitive."

72. For the emerging approach to belief in Greek and Roman religion, see Bendlin 2000; Harrison 2000; C. King 2003; Harrison 2007; Phillips 2007; Parker 2011; Versnel 2011; Kindt 2012; Harrison 2015a; and Petrovic and Petrovic 2016. Cognitive theory, broadly construed, now informs many studies of the Greco-Roman world. For a fully committed, rather than piecemeal, cognitive approach to Greek religion, see now Larson 2016. Other cognitive theorizations of ancient religion may be found in Whitehouse and Martin 2004; Beck 2006; Bowden 2010. For cognitive theory in Greco-Roman literary, cultural, and historical studies, see, e.g., Fagan 2011; Meineck 2011 and 2018.

73. Harrison 2000: 22. Cf. Kindt 2012: 31, on scholarship on Greek religion: "The neglect of religious beliefs came at a high price."

1.3. An Anatomy of Belief-Denial and the Belief-Action Dichotomy

We have seen that an understanding of what belief amounts to has proved elusive. The word "belief" is often used idiosyncratically in the study of religion, especially ancient ones. Scholarly usage often does not correspond to the way belief is understood in the cognitive sciences, philosophy, the social sciences, or even daily life. The effect of this idiosyncrasy is to preclude certain interdisciplinary conversations. Even more basically: not all understandings of belief are equally adequate to the phenomenon itself. Why retain inaccurate ones?

I offer in the four subsections that follow a brief anatomy of some misleading propositions about belief, especially those that contribute to scholarly denial about belief. I address in turn the notions that belief is inherently Christian, that it is a concept, that it is a linguistic practice, and finally that the beliefs of others are unknowable. This anatomy does not profess to answer every objection raised against the propriety of belief to the study of ancient religions. Instead, I prefer to keep the anatomy brief and to focus, in the remainder of the book, on my positive theory of belief. The cumulative effect should be to dissolve the dichotomy between belief and action. I hope, too, that the cogency of the positive position I put forth in the following chapters will disarm any arguments in favor of belief-denial that I may have ignored in the following anatomy.

1.3.1. Belief Is Christian

The first proposition to address is that both the phenomenon and the term "belief" are uniquely Christian. This is simply not true.[74] We saw this view expressed by Simon Price, whose gambit was to historicize the phenomenon and lexeme and thereby assert their contingency. He condemns the word in his admonition that "'belief' as a religious term is profoundly Christian in its implications."[75] And he posits that the phenomenon of believing is the result of a unique religious experience undergone by particular individuals (the

---

74. Cf. C. King 2003: 279: "Far from being 'implicitly Christianizing,' belief is not even intrinsically connected with religion or religious concepts."

75. S. Price 1984: 10. More recently Gagné 2013 imagines that "belief" cannot escape its "fundamental ties to conviction and devotion and so many other heirs of the Christian *credo*" (7).

Apostles) at particular moments in time (a postresurrection meeting with Christ) and is thus inextricably entangled with Christian origins.

The historical claim that not beliefs with certain contents but rather belief *itself*, as a kind of cognitive state, "was forged out of the experience which the Apostles and Saint Paul had of the Risen Lord" is hard to accept at face value.[76] Indeed, it is a claim that participates in the very Christianizing that Price expressly wishes to avoid. Jonathan Z. Smith has laid bare the implications for the comparative study of religion of such allegations of Christian uniqueness:[77]

> The centre, the fabled Pauline seizure by the "Christ-event" or some other construction of an originary moment, has been declared, *a priori*, to be unique, to be *sui generis*, and hence by definition, incomparable.

Thus, as for scholars of previous centuries, so for Price, a commitment, perhaps merely tacit, to Christian exceptionalism underpins his verdict of belief's inapplicability to ancient religions.[78]

In attempting to extirpate Christianizing categories of analysis, Price and scholars of a similar persuasion have allowed those very categories to inform their first principles. They imagine that the word "belief" of necessity refers baldly to or connotes covertly "the Christian virtue of faith."[79] Just as bachelors are unmarried, so belief, on this misprision, is just analytically or by definition Christian.[80] But surely the word gets used in non-Christian ways with non-Christian import all the time, even when it is used "as a religious term." I hope that this becomes clear in the remainder of this chapter and in those that follow.

For now, merely note that Price's position exhibits the genetic fallacy, that is, the mistake of supposing that some moment in a thing's history discredits,

---

76. Cf. D. M. Johnson 1987, contending, in what is best read as a prank, "that no one believed anything, strictly speaking, until Greek thinkers of the sixth century B.C. showed people how to do this" (323).

77. J. Z. Smith 1990: 143. Cf. esp. 36–53.

78. Cf. Harrison 2000: 20: "Ironically," Price's "position falls into exactly the trap that it seeks to avoid" and C. King 2003: 276: "the product of a Christianizing bias in favor of Christian uniqueness."

79. A definition marked as *arch.* or *Obs.* in OED^2 (1989) s.v. 1.b, but curiously elevated in OED^3 (2011) to I.1.a. It appears that scholars of religion have got to the lexicographers!

80. Further examples: J. Davies 2004: 5 (quoted above and just below) and mutatis mutandis J. Davies 2011: 411: "if we were to say that 'group X believed in Y/believed Y' then we would be concluding that a group in antiquity took up a position comparable to a modern religious group." This holds only if we take for granted the troubled premise that belief is inherently a "modern religious" cognitive state.

authenticates, or mechanically determines the current significance of the thing.[81] Because Christians once used or even still use the English word "belief" to refer to Christian faith, the word is supposed to be hopelessly tied to Christianity. Should we generalize this genetic method, we would have to stop speaking of *atoms* on the grounds that the word is linked to theories of Leucippus and his successors that are incommensurable with modern physics. We would have to quit speaking of the *cosmos*, given the term's redolence of pre-Copernican astronomy. Finally, we would have to wonder how early Christians managed to cleanse words like *fides* and *credo* of their pagan overtones. Were they not, so to speak, "profoundly *polytheistic* in their implications"? Fides, after all, had a temple on the Capitol.[82] Obviously, we can use all these terms in their current, secular senses and still talk about *Christian* (or *Roman*) belief, *Epicurean* atoms, and the *Ptolemaic* cosmos. We shall see that Price's Christianizing assumptions do not hold and that belief is not an anachronism.

1.3.2. Belief Is a Concept

Our second proposition maintains that belief is first and foremost a *concept*. If the concept of belief is not found in a given culture, then belief will not be found there, either. This misprision is closely related to or perhaps a more ecumenical version of the idea that belief is inherently Christian. We have already seen the belief-as-concept line expressed thus: "'Belief' is . . . deeply problematic: it may be that this *paradoxical concept* is one peculiar to the Christianized West."[83] A similar notion informed Needham's study and an oft-cited article by Jean Pouillon.[84]

Indeed, confusion of belief as a *type* of mental state realized in human brains with more or less reflective *concepts* of belief continues unabated. Thus, Ethan H. Shagan, in his recent book *The Birth of Modern Belief*, proposes to treat of "the history of belief itself."[85] Yet within a few pages it becomes clear

---

81. Cf. Versnel 2011: 548, emphasis in the original: "The argument . . . that 'believing' *originally* meant 'having faith' or even 'to pledge allegiance to' (and that our word 'belief' still betrays traces of those connotations) is *in this respect* irrelevant."

82. Ziółkowski 1992: 28–31.

83. J. Davies 2004: 5, emphasis added.

84. Needham 1972, emphasis added: "The *concept* of belief is an historical product" (41); "the English *concept* of belief has been formed by a Christian tradition" (44). Cf. Pouillon 1982: 8, emphasis added: "this *notion* [sc. religious belief] does not have universal value." Appeal to Pouillon 1982 in classical scholarship: e.g., Giordano-Zecharya 2005: 330–47 passim; J. Davies 2004: 5n15; Gagné 2013: 7n17; in anthropology: e.g., Lindquist and Coleman 2008: 5–6; and Dein 2013.

85. Shagan 2018: ix.

that what really interests him is "the notion of belief."[86] This slippage from the mental state to conceptualizations of the mental state is not an accident. For scholarly interest in "the concept of X" often rests on the unstated premise that X is concept relative, which is to say, "socially constructed," in some more or less well-specified sense.[87] Thus, like many historians of belief, Shagan believes that belief is nothing but its conceptualization, one of any number of "supposedly natural categories" ripe for "historicizing" and thus for relativizing to a time and place.[88]

It is true, of course, that one may or may not have an explicit, theoretical concept of "belief," just as one may or may not possess the concept of "tubercle bacillus." Yet to be bereft of a well-articulated concept of belief is no more to be free of beliefs than to lack the concept of tubercle bacillus is to be insusceptible, as Latour permitted himself to be interpreted,[89] to tuberculosis. Equally, the ways in which belief has been discussed and conceptualized are susceptible to historical analysis. However, the very possibility of a *concept* of belief, and of a *history* of such concepts, depends on a human cognitive skill that has hitherto not been sufficiently appreciated by belief's historicizers: *metacognition*.[90]

Metacognition is our ability to cognize our own cognition, to take our own thought as an object of thought, to think and talk about our own thinking (and recursively, to think about our own thinking about our own thinking). Metacognition allows us to monitor, assess, and exert control over our own thought processes, including our individual beliefs and our faculty of believing. In this way, metacognition allows us to develop and to transmit via language concepts of belief. These concepts of belief are really nothing more than distinct sets of *beliefs about belief*. To have a concept of belief thus presupposes two prior capacities, to wit, the capacity to believe and the capacity to metacognize one's own belief.

Mere linguistic competence granted native speakers of Latin rich metacognitive resources. Belief and related doxastic states could be denoted, with varying metacognitive perspectives on the cognition in question, by *opinio* and *opinor*, "belief" and "believe"; *credo*, also "believe," but sometimes "trust"; *fides*, "trust," but sometimes "faith," "credence," or "belief"; *scientia* and *scio*, "knowledge" and "know"; *cognitio* and *cognosco*, "acquaintance" and "become acquainted

---

86. Shagan 2018: 13.

87. I try to specify a responsible theory of "social construction" in chapter 5.

88. Shagan 2018: 12. See Streeter n.d. for a well-developed argument against the possibility of a "history of belief."

89. Doubts about tuberculosis in ancient Egypt: Latour 1998. Cf. his *retractatio*: Latour 2004.

90. For metacognition, see Frith 2012 and Proust 2013.

with"; *coniectura*, "a guess"; *sententia*, "opinion"; *arbitror*, "think"; and *puto*, "suppose." These and numerous other lexemes permitted Romans to think about their own thinking and make fine-grained distinctions among their own doxastic cognitive processes and products.

A lexicon for mental phenomena, such as that of Latin, permits the development of metacognitive discourses and traditions of metacognitive discourse about cognition. I propose that it is in different traditions of metacognition about belief that the true differences between Roman and Christian belief reside. Many early and late antique Christians "believed in belief."[91] They believed that belief was crucial for the individual's salvation. And not just any old belief: they believed that only the "right" beliefs conduced to the desired effect. Hence, orthodoxy and an investment in creeds. Hence, the sort of creedal self-monitoring familiar from, say, Augustine's *Confessions*. Traditional Romans did not believe this way about belief. They did not, on the whole, "believe in belief" as a source of religious value, in and of itself, for the individual. As a result, they did not metacognitively scrutinize their own religious beliefs for orthodoxy, in the manner of an Augustine. This is not to say that they did not reflect on and fret over their own beliefs. Nor is it to say that they could not sometimes assert that the right kind of theological belief was, in and of itself, beneficial not so much to the individual as to society.[92] We saw that they could do both these things in section 1.2, above. Yet on no construal of the differences between Roman and Christian metacognitive traditions can we say that the Romans *lacked* belief. They had belief and beliefs but believed differently about them than later Christians did.

So, while concepts of belief can have histories, and while these histories are made possible by our metacognitive ability to take belief as an object of belief, belief itself, as a type of mental state, cannot be said to have a history,[93] except perhaps a biological, evolutionary one. For the capacity to believe—to represent mentally how matters stand in the world—is a core feature of the human mind. And it just so happens that English speakers have for some time been (metacognitively) calling this feature of the mind "belief," not only in everyday use, but in technical usages, too.

The larger lesson is that conceptual relativity, at least in this particular domain, does not entail ontological relativity.[94] Belief, unlike *auspicatio* (the Roman practice of taking the auspices) or the *tribunatus plebis* (the plebeian

---

91. The formulation of Dennett 2006: 200ff.
92. E.g., Cic. *Leg.* 2.15–16, discussed at section 8.6.
93. Streeter n.d.
94. See further, Searle 1995: 160–67.

tribuneship), does not depend for its existence on how it is implicitly or explicitly conceptualized. Believing, that is, representing such and such as being the case, is simply what minds do, as we shall see in detail in chapter 2. Indeed, as already mentioned, it is in part the mind's capacity to believe that allows us to form and entertain concepts, such as the mistaken concepts of belief promulgated by Needham, Price, Davies, and others. If they did not believe a number of inaccurate things about belief, they would not have the concepts of belief that they do. So, while their *concepts* of belief exist only insofar as they have *beliefs* about belief, belief *as such* does not exist relative to any concept of or belief about it.

I would hazard that confusion to the contrary has arisen because there *are* some entities that really *do* depend on our beliefs and concepts, and therefore exist only relative to certain beliefs and conceptual schemes, such as the previously mentioned *auspicatio* and *tribunatus plebis*. There can be no *auspicatio* absent a reasonably determinate concept of what taking the auspices entails and likewise for the office of *tribunus plebis*. In fact, this book is in large part about the cognitive creation and maintenance, in the Roman religious world, of such concept-dependent entities and their very real social power. However, belief was not such a concept-dependent entity, not even in ancient Rome. Instead, it played a role in the creation and maintenance of concept-dependent entities in ancient Rome. But these are matters to be explored in chapter 5.

1.3.3. Belief Is a Linguistic Practice

There is a linguistic version of the conceptual-relativity thesis. It holds that in order to attribute beliefs to people of other cultures, we must at a minimum (1) find a word in their language that translates exactly as "belief" or "believe" and then (2) observe them making first-person affirmations of belief using that word. These premises underwrite the projects of Needham and Jean Pouillon and as might be expected in a philological discipline may be found among classicists.[95] Needham put it thus (1972: 108):

> Where, then, do we get the notion of belief from? From the verb "believe," and its inflected forms, in everyday English usage. Statements of belief are the only evidence for the phenomenon; but the phenomenon itself appears to be no more than the custom of making such statements.

---

95. See, e.g., J. Davies 2011: 401–2 (worrying about the word *credo*), and cf. 404n32 and 406–7. An example from the oral tradition: I was once admonished by a senior Latinist for attributing religious beliefs to the Romans. He could not imagine any Roman pagan saying *"credo in deum/deos."* This consideration, which he regarded as decisive, is irrelevant, as we shall see.

Not only do we get our "notion of belief" from the verb "believe," but, what is more, "statements of belief are the only evidence" for belief. Finally, believing is "no more than the custom" of using the verb "believe."

On his first page, Needham describes the epistemological crisis, occasioned by a concern about language, that inspired his book. Although "it was certain that the Penan spoke of the existence of a spiritual personage named Peselong" and although "his attributes were well agreed," nonetheless, the Western anthropologist "had no linguistic evidence at all" about the beliefs of the Penan. This is because the Penan have "no formal creed, and ... no other conventional means for expressing belief in their god."[96] Needham spends many pages studying the etymology of the English belief/believe lexeme and surveying words in the tongues of the Penan, Nuer, and others that might translate as "belief" or "believe."[97] These are worthy endeavors in their own right. Yet one cannot help but wonder if the fact that "the Penan spoke of the existence of" their god might not have counted as the "linguistic evidence" of belief that Needham was seeking.

Before continuing with Needham, let us first turn to Jean Pouillon to see structuralism's contribution to this mistaken notion of belief. Pouillon's ethnographic problem is the Dangaléat people. He wonders, "how can one tell whether they believe [*croire*] and in what way? What question can one ask them, using what word of their language, in what context?"[98] His linguistic question is this: "is a translation of the verb [sc. *croire*] in all its senses possible in other languages, using a single term?"[99] Pouillon's structuralism leads him, after he has spent some pages identifying the semantic range of *croire* in its various constructions, to determine that all possible "meanings" of the verb *croire*, "even the contradictory ones, are intrinsically linked."[100] He finds that although "we can translate all aspects of the verb 'to believe,'" we cannot translate "the verb itself" into Dangaléat.[101] The presupposition that *croire* expresses all its possible meanings whenever it is used, along with the finding that the

---

96. Needham 1972: 1.

97. Needham 1972: 32–50.

98. Pouillon 1982: 4.

99. Pouillon 1982: 1.

100. Pouillon 1982: 5 (for "linked" the text reads "liked"). Cf. 8: "All the meanings of the verb 'to believe' should then come together." Pouillon's mistake continues to damage the study of ancient religion, e.g., Giordano-Zecharya 2005: 331: "the Christian and modern use of the word ... subsumes three senses, inextricably." Similarly, for Gagné 2013 the "vast semantic range of the word 'belief'" (7) and "the force of its connotations" (8) prove intellectually insurmountable and thus apotropaic.

101. Pouillon 1982: 5.

Dangaléat have no comparable verb, motivate Pouillon's conclusion that a vast gulf separates Christian and Dangaléat modes of cognition.[102]

We shall take these claims in the order of presentation, but let us start with a fact about cultural cognition. There is no question that the lexicon of words for mental states in any given language plays an important role in a speaker's reasoning about the mental states of self and other. That is, any such lexicon affects a speaker's folk-psychological and metacognitive abilities.[103] However, we should not suppose that *believing itself* depends on any specific lexicon or linguistic practice, or that "statements of belief are the only evidence" we have for belief. Far from it. Needham could have saved himself the trouble of writing his book based solely on the evidence that he presents on page 1. For all he required in order to attribute belief to the Penan was the fact that, as he admits, they speak of and agree about their god and his attributes. No linguistic construction for "expressing belief" is needed beyond the simple speech act of *assertion*.[104] If the Penan make assertions about their god, those assertions are prima facie evidence for their beliefs about their god.

The same answer may be given to Pouillon's series of questions about the Dangaléat: "how can one tell whether they believe . . . ? What question can one ask them, using what word of their language . . . ?" Here again, Dangaléat assertions would typically count as evidence of Dangaléat beliefs, regardless of whether there is any "word of their language" for "croire." Pouillon would no doubt have rejected this, because he assumed that belief was a Christian mental state whose unique quality could be captured and expressed only by *croire*, as understood in all its conceivable meanings taken at once. As he says, "it seems impossible to overcome the polysemy of the word."[105] However, this assumption that the entire semantic potential of a term is gratuitously deployed in each use of the term is unfounded.[106] As lexicographers know, a term's meaning differs pragmatically from use to use and from context to context: this is why dictionaries offer multiple, distinct definitions of words. Pouillon's quest for a single Dangaléat word whose semantic range maps precisely onto that of *croire* is a red herring, for *croire* does not express its entire semantic

---

102. Pouillon 1982: 5–8.

103. See, e.g., Wellman 2014: 25–26 and 160–67; Zufferey 2010: 27–51. Needham 1972: 25–28 has a useful discussion of this point.

104. As forcefully argued against Needham from Needham's own Wittgensteinian perspective in Streeter 2020. For assertion and belief, see Searle 1979a: 12–13; Searle and Vanderveken 1985: 18–19, 54–55, and 59–60; Jary 2010: 32–51; MacFarlane 2011; Goldberg 2015: 144–203.

105. Pouillon 1982: 4.

106. Barr 1961: 219 identified this tendency in biblical scholarship as "illegitimate totality transfer."

potential each time and in every context that it is used.[107] Moreover, his quest reflects an emic/etic confusion. For when we speak of "belief" we use an etic term. Whether the Dangaléat had a corresponding emic term is as irrelevant as whether they had a term for tubercle bacillus: they still had the thing named.

In sum, we can attribute beliefs to agents on the basis of their assertive speech acts. An assertion need not be embedded as a sentential clause dependent on a verb of believing ("I believe that . . .") because the primary point of assertion, whatever its other pragmatic purposes in any given context, is to express or make explicit a speaker's belief regarding a state of affairs. All other uses of assertion—to lie, to write fiction, and so on—are predicated on this primary pragmatic function.[108] I know of no language of which the speakers do not make assertions. This point about speech acts is important. I shall argue in chapter 8 that beliefs can be attributed on the basis of other types of speech acts and, indeed, on the basis of nonlinguistic behavior.

For now, the most telling result of our discussion, and the greatest refutation of the theories of Needham and Pouillon, is the deduction that we could attribute beliefs to people who speak a language with no mental-state lexicon at all, simply because we do not require speakers to use first-person verbs of believing in order to attribute beliefs to them. Indeed, young children get by on a lexicon of practical states ("she wants") before they mature into a lexicon of doxastic states ("she thinks"). Presumably, then, a culture in which tracking and discussing doxastic states such as belief was of minimal relevance to its members could thrive without ever developing a vocabulary for doxastic states.[109] But this would not entail that its members had no beliefs.

Unlike these hypothetical scenarios, Latin lexicalized all sorts of psychological episodes and had a rich thesaurus of words for doxastic states of differing intensities, for example, as we saw in section 1.3.2, above, *opinio* and *opinor*, "belief" and "believe"; *credo*, also "believe," but sometimes "trust"; *fides*, "trust, but sometimes "faith" or "belief"; and so on. Any language with a lexicon of mental-state words grants its users resources for explicitly attributing mental states to others and for metacognition, that is, for thinking about one's own

---

107. Cairns and Fulkerson 2015b, section 2, vividly argues a thesis complementary to my own here, using the example of αἰδώϲ/αἰδέομαι.

108. For more on assertions, see section 2.3 and chapter 8. Assertive speech acts can, as mentioned, be used to lie or write fiction, or indeed to act a role in a drama, or even with the perlocutionary intention of getting another to believe something regarding which one has no settled belief oneself. In these cases, the aesthetic, dramatic, deceptive, or persuasive effects of assertions *depend on* the fact that their illocutionary point is to tell how the world is and, thus, express a psychological state of belief regardless of whether one *really has* the expressed belief.

109. I thank Andrew Shtulman for this observation.

thinking. Yet even if Latin had no terms whatsoever for any mental episode, still, Camillus's Roman auditors would have understood him to be expressing his beliefs when, in Livy's telling, he asserts "we have a city founded through auspication and inauguration; no place in it is not filled with cult practices and with gods."[110] Any rhetorical and pragmatic power these assertions had derived from the fact that they purported, qua assertions, to make explicit and public Camillus's beliefs.

1.3.4. Beliefs Are Unknowable

There is a diffidence in some recent literature concerning our ability to divine anything about the Romans' cognitive and affective states and, indeed, most broadly speaking, their *experience*.[111] This final section addresses the study of ancient experience as well as of ancient belief. Regarding belief, we have been warned that "it is a mistake to overemphasize any question of participants' belief or disbelief in the efficacy of ritual actions, *when we have no access to their private thoughts*."[112] As to experience, we are admonished:[113]

> We can never know what any Roman "felt," at any period, when he decided to use his wealth to build a temple to a particular god; still less how Romans might have felt when entering, walking past or simply gazing at the religious monuments of their city.

Note the scare quotes around *felt*. If these passages advise us that we can never know what the Romans might have thought or experienced in the privacy of their hearts, other passages go further, suggesting that we cannot know whether the Romans even had psychological states that we could recognize, for "considerable doubt may be cast on contemporary models for mental life."[114] Indeed, preemptory surrender has been enjoined as a methodological

---

110. Liv. 5.50.2: *urbem auspicato inauguratoque conditam habemus; nullus locus in ea non religionum deorumque est plenus*. See Ando 2015a: 17–24. On this occasion, Camillus urges his fellow Romans not to move to Veii after the Gallic sack of Rome of 390. Even if this *diligentissimus religionum cultor* (Liv. 5.50.1) is in his heart of hearts a thoroughgoing Polybian, cynically manipulating a credulous audience, his project still involves publicly expressing beliefs through assertion, and thereby appealing to, activating, and eliciting beliefs in his audience.

111. Experience as such has been gaining attention in scholarship on ancient religion: see Rüpke 2013: 20–22 for references and reflections; see also the collection of papers in Driediger-Murphy and Eidinow 2019.

112. North 2000a: 84, emphasis added.

113. Beard et al. 1998: 1.125.

114. Phillips 1986: 2702.

principle, for even if we could locate and accurately interpret ancient religious beliefs,[115]

> we would be quite wrong to believe that we could then understand these "beliefs" in the same way that we understand the "beliefs" of modern religions.

On this hypothesis, even if we could work out the Romans' religious beliefs, we *still* could not hope truly to understand them.

The premise informing these proposals is that ancient texts, artifacts, and behaviors that have survived to us or for which we have evidence do not necessarily constitute any "index" of any "experience,"[116] thoughts, or feelings the Romans may have had. What is more, even when ancient materials may licitly be taken, albeit with all due caution, as indexes of Roman experiences, feelings, or beliefs, we still cannot understand these Roman mental episodes because of the irreducible alterity, the "sheer difference"[117] of these ancients. Of course, we hardly want to come to our encounters with the Romans assuming that we already know them, that they do *not* differ from us, that their relics are self-interpreting. But whence this extreme of epistemological reserve?

We may look again to Needham for an answer. Skepticism about the psychological states of his ethnographic informants, and thus about the entire *Verstehen* project, permeates his whole book. In the first chapter, titled "Problem," he had found fault with the practice of his colleagues (1972: 2):

> If... an ethnographer said that people believed something when he did not actually know what was going on inside them,... then surely his account of them must... be very defective in quite fundamental regards.

Even when informed by a Nuer man that several Nuer verbs readily translate as "to believe" in religious contexts,[118] Needham persisted in maintaining that "we remain completely ignorant of what is the interior state of the Nuer toward their god."[119]

---

115. My translation of North 2003: 344: "même si nous pouvions déduire de telles croyances religieuses et les interpreter correctement, nous aurions bien tort de croire que nous pourrions alors comprendre ces 'croyances' de la meme manière que nous comprenons les 'croyances' des religions modernes."

116. Beard et al. 1998: 1.125.

117. Beard et al. 1998: 1.x. Cf. Versnel 2011: 10–18, criticizing this radical alterity thesis vis-à-vis the Greeks.

118. Needham 1972: 30n13 and accompanying text.

119. Needham 1972: 31.

In one very specific sense, Needham and the classicists who follow his lead are quite right that we are "completely ignorant" about the inner lives of cultural (or any) others. We do "not actually know what was going on inside" of the Romans. Consider: sensory perceptions, bodily feelings, emotions, and beliefs are first-person episodes. This entails that one has no *immediate* access to *anyone's* sensory, cognitive, or affective experience but one's own, whatever the cultural similarities or differences between self and other. Yet this hardly justifies solipsism.[120] Others obviously have inner states, even if our only evidence for those states is their outward behavior, including their speech.

So, we must always be on guard against our own failures of historical empathy. Such failures surely account for at least some antibelief statements. Historical empathy requires that we set aside our own standards in judging past cultures and people, as for example when we assume that philosophical sophistication is inconsistent with devotion to ritual. Mary Beard once wrote, in a passage redolent with Protestantizing bias:[121]

> How can we possibly imagine sophisticated intellectuals like Cicero or sceptical poets like Ovid leaping through bonfires in a ritual concerned with the purification of flocks and herds?

I am in a position to recommend that we imagine exactly that. I was raised in a tiny village in south India on an ashram at the feet of a guru who was deeply schooled in the traditions of both Vedanta and British education, who effortlessly quoted Plato, Shakespeare, and Keats, but who also conducted daily rituals of ancestor worship in which he lit incense and burned camphor on a bed of carbonized cow dung at a shrine housing the cremated remains of his father, who had been his guru. We need to cultivate the historical empathy to imagine Romans like Cicero and Ovid in scenarios not unlike this one. And sometimes we just need to accept what they tell us about themselves, their activities, experiences, and yes, even their beliefs.

1.4. Conclusion: Historical Empathy and Other Minds

As we close this chapter, we may test our historical empathy by examining a story told by Augustine of the pain, emotion, and belief of Innocentius, a prominent Carthaginian. Innocentius had undergone surgery for fistulas "in

---

120. Versions of cultural solipsism continue to be regarded as paradigm-subverting methodological interventions among some anthropologists, e.g., Robbins and Rumsey 2008.

121. Beard 1987: 2.

the hinder and lowest part of his body."[122] In surgery, he had suffered horrific pains (*dolores*).[123] Unfortunately, his surgeons had missed a fistula, so deeply was it tucked away. The wretched man anticipated a second surgery with great fear (*tantus ... metus*), because he believed (*non dubitare*) that he would not survive it.[124] His entire household, in sympathy with its master, wept "like the lamentation at a funeral."[125] Yet in the end, after much pitiable prayer, Innocentius was miraculously cured by a "merciful and omnipotent God," to the great joy (*laetitia*) of the man and his relations, who immediately offered prayers of thanks amid tearful rejoicing (*lacrimantia gaudia*).[126]

Now, none of us is Innocentius, and no one, not his household or Augustine, has experienced precisely his fistulas, his pains in surgery, his beliefs and fears anticipating a second surgery, or his joy at his miraculous cure. Innocentius's bodily pains, his belief that he would die, and his successive emotions of fear and joy had a first-person, private existence rather than a third-person, public existence. Thus, Innocentius alone was *directly* acquainted with them, no matter how empathetic, tuned-in, and close to him his household and friends like Augustine may have been. It is worth remarking that all of this holds as much for us and our own closest kin as for the Romans, the Penan, or the Nuer.

However, these facts about the subjectivity of the psychological episodes occasioned by Innocentius's fistulas hardly sponsor Needhamian cultural solipsism, that is, doubt as to whether minds enculturated differently from one's own possess underlying cognitive structures anything like one's own, such as the varieties of Intentionality that Innocentius experienced: bodily pain, belief, emotion.[127] The *content* of those episodes as well as the *individual episodes themselves* were unique to Innocentius and were, of course, determined by his life history, including his cultural situatedness. However, the episode *types*—bodily pain, belief, and emotion—are universal to Homo sapiens as a

---

122. Aug. *Civ.* 22.8.7: *curabatur a medicis fistulas, quas numerosas atque perplexas habuit in posteriore atque ima corporis parte. iam secuerant eum et artis suae cetera medicamentis agebant.*

123. Aug. *Civ.* 22.8.8: *passus autem fuerat in sectione illa et diuturnos et acerbos dolores.*

124. Aug. *Civ.* 22.8.16: *tantus enim eum metus ex prioribus invaserat poenis, ut se inter medicorum manus non dubitaret esse moriturum.*

125. Aug. *Civ.* 22.8.14: *ex maerore nimio domini tantus est in domo illa exortus dolor ut tamquam funeris planctus.*

126. Aug. *Civ.* 22.8.21. The telling of this miracle is not incidental to Augustine's motivations: *Civ.* 22.8.1: "for even now, miracles take place in His name" (*nam etiam nunc fiunt miracula in eius nomine*).

127. For the Intentionality of beliefs and emotions, see chapters 2 and 3, below. For the Intentionality of bodily feelings, see Goldie 2002.

species of minded being. On this universality, psychology and cognitive science are built.[128]

Moreover, the fact that Innocentius's psychological episodes and experiences were personal (or *ontologically subjective*, that is, dependent on a minded subject for their very existence) does not entail that we can make no claims or have no knowledge about them that is factual (or *epistemically objective*).[129] What we or Augustine think, say, or write about Innocentius's pain is either accurate or inaccurate. In principle, if not always in practice, we can *really know* that Innocentius felt pain "in the hinder and lowest part of his body" and thus be far from ignorant about "what was going on inside" of him. This holds for any Roman about whom we have the requisite data. Of course, we must never forget that any ancient experience that we can study "is always something which is already told, spoken about, and thus constructed."[130] The surviving tellings and constructions are the only indexes to the experience we have. And, indeed, we ourselves reconstruct from these constructions, as I have reconstructed Innocentius's experience from Augustine's construction of it, retold it from his telling, and turned it to my own use, as Augustine turned it to his. We can neither capture nor recapture the intrinsic first-person subjectivity of ancient experience, in all its ineffability, but we can surely glean some factual *understanding* of it.[131]

Now, how can I possibly justify such a claim about the "knowability" of other minds, the epistemic objectivity of the ontologically subjective? Rather than attempt such a whimsical project, I shall limit myself to a point about the condition of the possibility of disciplines such as classics and the social sciences. When we treat Roman behavior *as behavior* we implicitly treat it differently than we treat electrons, dimethyl sulfoxide, the circulation of blood, or the seasonal abscission of deciduous trees. We treat it as the purposeful activity of *agents* who *act* for *reasons* explicable in terms of what we really have no choice but to see as their physical sensations, perceptions, perspectives, emotions, desires, intentions, and beliefs. For example, when we treat Roman linguistic artifacts as such—as purposeful, meaningful uses of language, as questions, commands, assertions, *vota, carmina, orationes*, or epitaphs—we thereby *necessarily* ascribe to the ancients Intentional states appropriate to these speech

---

128. Or are only just beginning to be built: see J. Henrich 2020 on the dangers of inference to universal human psychology from experiments run on WEIRD (Western, Educated, Industrialized, Rich, and Democratic) subjects.

129. More on ontological subjectivity and epistemic objectivity (for which, see Searle 1995: 7–13; and Searle 2010: 17–18) at section 5.2, below.

130. Vuolanto 2016: 16.

131. Cf. Rüpke 2016: 62–63.

acts. If we did not take this "Intentional stance,"[132] we would fail to see these linguistic artifacts as *artifacts* at all—as questions, commands, assertions, *vota*, *carmina*, *orationes*, or epitaphs—but merely register them, if at all, as mindless marks, like patterns in the sand.[133]

As human beings, we have no choice but to see the linguistic products of our fellows as driven by their intentions and other mental episodes, *if we are to see them as linguistic products at all*. Similarly, as historians, we are simply *in the business* of taking Roman behaviors as indexes of Roman psychological states. We must not be naive about this project, but equally we must not reckon some version of solipsism the *ne plus ultra* of methodological circumspection. It is easy to overlook the foregoing considerations because they are the half-buried foundations on which not only history but also textual criticism, literary study, anthropology, cultural psychology,[134] and indeed any *social* endeavor whatsoever stands, the unconscious background and unstated condition of the possibility of approaching others, of any time or place, *as others* akin to oneself. Indeed, even those scholars who pointedly eschew the belief/believe lexeme nonetheless covertly ascribe beliefs to the subjects of their study, as we saw above when we examined Jason Davies's treatment of the verb *credo*, in section 1.2.[135] Such scholars appear not to recognize their own practice for what it is and beliefs for what they are. In the next chapter, I begin a new conversation about the nature of belief and how we as historians of religion should treat both the cognitive phenomenon and the relevant lexemes in our necessarily etic discourse.[136]

---

132. The term comes from Dennett 1987. For the necessity of appealing to Intentionality in the social sciences, see Searle 1991.

133. In the famous image of Knapp and Michaels 1982: 727–28.

134. I take the term "cultural psychology" from Kaster 2005: 3. For Greek cultural psychology, see, e.g., Cairns 1993 and Halliwell 2008.

135. Two further examples from J. Davies 2011: 403: "the Romans would have vigorously contested the claim that they had no evidence for religious deductions"; 422: "it was almost universally axiomatic that one could influence gods through ritual." The troublesome lexeme *belief* is avoided even as the psychological state of belief is attributed. See Versnel 2011: 548 for a similar observation regarding scholarship on Greek religion.

136. Versnel 2011: 548: "Scholarly discourse is always etic and should therefore be conducted in etic terms."

2

Recovering Belief

2.1. Introduction

We saw in the previous chapter that over the course of the last two centuries a dichotomy between belief and action arose in scholarship on Roman religion. This dichotomy led first to derogation of Roman religious beliefs as risible and of Roman cult action as empty, and later to denial that belief played any significant role in Roman cult. These views militate in favor of setting to one side any question of Roman religion's psychological dimensions and focusing instead on its behavioral dimensions. We saw, however, that these antibelief positions are untenable and that psychology is not off limits to the historian. We saw, in fact, that it's not even optional. In this chapter, I offer a positive theory of belief as a so-called Intentional cognitive state. I point to some implications for Roman religion of understanding belief in this way and attempt thereby to show its historiographical value.

In section 2.2, I explore the Intentionality (a term explained in the introduction, in section 0.4, and again below) distinctive to belief, and I show that because of its systematic relationships with other Intentional episodes such as desire and intention (i.e., a *plan* to act), belief is a vital part of any historical research project with aspirations beyond behavioral description. Section 2.3 extends the account of *cognitive* Intentionality to the *discursive* Intentionality of speech acts. In section 2.4, I distinguish between *belief-in* and *belief-that*, two cognitive states that are distinct but sometimes conflated. This book, it should be noted, deals with *belief-that*. Two sections discuss two psychological aspects of belief relevant to historians: degrees of intensity of belief (2.5) and the distinction between nonreflective and reflective beliefs (2.6).

My hope in the present chapter is to shed some light on belief, a cognitive state that as chapter 1 attests has sometimes been found mysterious, to paint a holistic picture of belief's place in human cognition, and to suggest its relevance to the study of religion.[1]

2.2. The Intentionality of Belief

Let us build from the ground up. Human beings, our minds, and our consciousness are in the world and part of the world. The consciousness that we as minded beings possess grants us a *perspective* on the world that the mindless entities with which we share the world lack.[2] To have a conscious perspective, that is, for there to be a way the world appears to us, means that our minds possess the property of *Intentionality*, that is, "directedness upon the world."[3] Another way to explain Intentionality is to say that it is the capacity of our minds to *represent* (and thus to be *directed on* or to be *about*) objects and states of affairs in the world.

Recall from the introduction that the term "intentionality" is ambiguous. In an everyday but narrow sense, it means "purposiveness," as when we speak of *intentions* to act (plans) or actions done *intentionally* (on purpose). But in its technical and also broadest sense, "Intentionality" (always spelled in this book with an uppercase *I* to distinguish it from intentionality as purposiveness, with a lowercase *i*) amounts to the *directedness, aboutness,* or *representationality* of many if not most mental episodes, including not only plans and purposes but also beliefs, desires, fears, loves, hopes, and so on. To say that mental episodes possess "directedness" is to say that they *represent* or are "about" their objects. The Intentionality that is a feature of mental *episodes*—a term that includes properly "episodic" mental phenomena, such as emotions, which arise and tail off, as well as mental *events*, such as perceptions, mental *acts*, such as calculating a figure in one's head, and mental *states*, such as memories, beliefs, desires, and intentions—relates us *to* the world in various ways that we shall now explore.

Now, concerning the Intentional state that is belief, we must establish two things at the outset. First, despite what Needham and like-minded scholars might say, belief is a perfectly normal, mundane cognitive state. Second, there is no special cognitive state of "religious belief" over and above mundane belief.[4] Religious beliefs are normal, mundane cognitive states that may be

---

1. It is important to note that my goal here is not to synthesize all the latest developments in the cognitive science of belief but merely to make clear what belief is.

2. See Chalmers 1995 for the "hard problem" (200) of consciousness, that is, the problem of *experience*: Why exactly are there some entities for which it is *like something* to be that entity?

3. Crane 2001a: 4–8. See also Searle 1983a: 1–4.

4. Cf. Barrett 2004a: 21.

about nonnormal, extramundane, or divine states of affairs (and may for that reason be especially freighted with emotion or conviction). So, what is it about belief, religious or otherwise, that makes it the distinctive Intentional state that it is? The short answer is that belief relates us to the world by representing *how things are.* (Note that it is one thing merely to represent something and another thing to represent it, as we do when we believe, as *being the case.*) This holds whether you think the mind is a spiritual substance breathed into you by God or the result of a biological brain in a body evolved through natural selection.

In what follows, I begin by discussing six logically interrelated features of belief that give it its distinctive Intentionality: subject, object, content, psychological mode, direction of fit, and conditions of satisfaction.[5] I then survey two psychological aspects of belief.[6] First, beliefs vary in their degree of intensity. Second, beliefs fall on a continuum from automatic and unreflective to effortful and reflective. Some consequences for the study of ancient religion will emerge as we go. The discussion will be technical but will, I hope, pay for itself in the coin of clarity about belief as an Intentional state. I must emphasize that I am not "redefining" belief to suit an agenda. Rather, I am trying to explain the cognitive state that we just so happen to call belief and to elucidate some of its non-obvious logical and psychological features. If we aspire to engage in an informed conversation about belief in ancient religion that goes beyond appeal to the gut or misplaced reverence for books like Needham's *Belief, Language, and Experience*, then, I submit, we must take account of the considerations offered below, even if only to reject or revise some subset of them as the conversation about belief progresses.

Let us ease our way into our discussion with a brief survey of three relevant definitions of belief. Those outside the scholarly study of Roman religion, such as the editors of the second edition of the *Oxford English Dictionary*, often take "belief" to mean roughly "mental acceptance of a proposition, statement, or fact, as true."[7] While this definition is handy, it may be a bit misleading. It

---

5. I rely primarily on Searle 1983a: 1–36; Crane 2001a: 1–33; Crane 2013: 89–117. Very brief overview of roughly the same material: Tollefsen 2015: 8–10; less briefly: Searle 2010: 25–41. For phenomenological takes on Intentionality, see Gallagher and Zahavi 2008: 107–28; and Drummond 2012.

6. As noted in the introduction, I omit discussion of those *epistemological* aspects of belief of greatest interest to ancient (and most modern) philosophers, such as Plato, whose Theaetetus distinguishes false belief, true belief, and true belief with an account, i.e., "justified true belief" or knowledge.

7. OED^2 s.v. belief 2: "Mental acceptance of a proposition, statement, or fact, as true, on the ground of authority or evidence; assent of the mind to a statement, or to the truth of a fact

gives the impression that believing is a matter of mulling over and deciding whether one approves of a proposition. We shall see that from a psychological point of view, this is not usually the case.

Before we go there, however, let us consider a well-known definition offered in defense of the word's deployment in the study of Roman religion: belief is "a conviction that an individual (or group of individuals) holds independently of the need for empirical support."[8] Two points: First, defining belief as "conviction" risks circularity. Lexicographic circularity is not vicious per se,[9] but I would submit that the logical properties of belief outlined below provide greater theoretical grip than does "conviction." Second and more important is the question of empirical support. It is true that empirical support is not *necessary* for belief, but we must not therefore suppose that belief is distinguished by a lack of *any* support. For the testimony of others adequately warrants many beliefs. A great deal of what the Romans believed about the gods was supported by such social rather than empirical factors. However, we shall also see that Roman beliefs could have empirical, inferential, and other sources and supports.[10]

In fact, the sources of belief are these: sensory perception, memory, testimony, intuition, and inference. Here, I shall discuss intuition and inference. Much of this book is, in a sense, about the many guises of testimony through which most cultural learning takes place. That is, we shall see that Roman beliefs derived primarily from intersubjective and social sources, not empirical ones. After all, it is typically in intersubjective and social contexts, not in contexts of empirical observation, that we form beliefs about such entities as oxygen and the soul,[11] germs and angels,[12] Jupiter and *auspicia*. So, one rather oblique upshot of this book is that Romans were non-empirically epistemically entitled to their religious beliefs. Their beliefs were the result of natural

---

beyond observation, on the testimony of another, or to a fact or truth on the evidence of consciousness; the mental condition involved in this assent." For *OED*² s.v. belief 1, see section 2.4, below. In *OED*³, the entry quoted here roughly overlaps with s.v. belief I.1, 4, 6, and especially 7. For *OED*³ s.v. belief I.1.a, 2, and 5.b, see section 2.4, below.

8. C. King 2003: 278.

9. Cf. *OED*³ s.v. belief I: "mental conviction."

10. Cf. especially Ando 2008: 13–17 on the "empiricist epistemology" of Roman religion, and see at sections 9.2 and 9.6.1, below.

11. Guerrero et al. 2010.

12. P. Harris et al. 2006. On our psychological predisposition to trust in testimony, see P. Harris 2012. On why we believe those whom we believe, see Mercier 2020.

human cognition situated and functioning in normal social and cultural contexts.[13]

Returning to definitions of "belief," we find a much more promising one, informed by decades of work in the philosophy of mind, proffered by cognitive scientists of religion Justin Barrett and Jonathan Lanman. In their formulation, belief is "the state of a cognitive system holding information (not necessarily in propositional or explicit form) as true in the generation of further thought and behavior."[14] A deflationary definition of belief such as this has much to recommend it. To "hold information as true" just means to treat some information as an accurate representation of states of affairs. Moreover, as the definition helpfully specifies, beliefs need not be held in the form of explicit linguistic propositions (although the content of the belief will have, logically, a propositional structure: see section 2.2.3, below). The definition also captures succinctly the connections between belief and other cognitions and between belief and action. Beliefs may, for example, serve as premises for reflection and inference (section 2.6, below) or as the bases of emotions (section 3.2). Beliefs also play an important role in the etiology of action (section 3.3). We shall explore these contentions in due course, but first let us situate belief as one Intentional state among others in order to grasp its distinctive nature.

2.2.1. *Belief Requires a* Subject *in Order to Exist*

Like any mental episode, a belief's existence depends on a subject with some sort of mind to own or have or bear it. Compare the pain of Innocentius, as described at the end of chapter 1. That pain existed only insofar as it was experienced by Innocentius, a minded subject. It was thus *ontologically subjective*, that is, dependent on a minded subject for its very existence. For there can be no pain without a subject to bear it. Beliefs, too, are ontologically subjective, but unlike pain, one need not be conscious of having a given belief at a given moment in order to have that belief. You were probably not consciously thinking that Cicero was consul in 63 BCE until you read this, but if you know anything about Roman history, you already believed it. We are not consciously aware of most of the things we believe most of the time. These beliefs are in principle accessible but not currently being accessed. Such beliefs are called

---

13. We return to the role of social factors in promoting belief below, at chapters 4, 6, 7, and 8. On non-empirical epistemic entitlement to beliefs based on social interaction, see Burge 1993, esp. 458–59 and 466–67. For more on "social epistemology," see Audi 2015: 217–57. On the roles of social and cognitive factors in the acquisition of religious beliefs, see Thagard 2005; Bergstrom et al. 2006; P. Harris and Koenig 2006; Barrett 2011a: 41ff.

14. Barrett and Lanman 2008: 110; so too Lanman 2008: 54.

"dispositional." Beliefs that one has accessed and of which one is at a given moment conscious are distinguished as "occurrent."[15]

Insofar as the existence of beliefs, dispositional or occurrent, depends on a minded subject, beliefs differ from ontologically objective entities, such as carbon, oak trees, and stars, which exist independently of subjects or minds. Note, incidentally, that belief's subject-dependence provides grounds for questioning the oft-encountered observation that Romans had no "interiorized belief"[16] or that they did not believe in our "internalised sense."[17] Beliefs can, of course, be "externalized," in the form of public representations. For example, they can be *expressed* through the speech act of assertion. And yet belief qua belief is intrinsically internal. Beliefs do not arise or subsist anywhere but in the minds of subjects, even if they can be expressed in public representations.

The fact that beliefs, desires, intentions, and so on, belong to minded subjects also imposes limits on our attribution of these Intentional episodes. It is common to speak of group entities as having Intentionality, as when we say, "Britain plans to leave the EU." However, this is merely a shorthand way of attributing intentions to Britons, because Britain itself does not have a mind. Nor do societies, cultures, and other collective entities have minds; so, it is wrong to attribute beliefs and Intentionality to them literally, as Durkheim and others have done. We return to these issues in chapter 4.

2.2.2. Beliefs Are about Objects

That is, beliefs are *about* or *directed at* (*on, toward*) or *represent* "stuff," where *stuff* amounts to states of affairs, objects, events, situations, processes, properties, relations, and so on.[18] The stuff a belief is about is called, technically, its *Intentional object*.[19] *Intentionality* is just the quality of directedness toward an Intentional object shared by belief and other Intentional episodes. Examples of Intentional episodes that have Intentional objects include perception, attention, desire, fear, and intentions to act (which as we've seen are Intentional but should not be confused with Intentionality or "aboutness" per se). Beliefs are about states of affairs that one *takes* to exist. In contrast, desires are about states of affairs one wishes *did* exist, while intentions are about states of affairs

---

15. For more details, see Searle 1992: 155–62.
16. Scheid 2016: 113, and cf. 18.
17. Beard 2015: 103.
18. Searle 1983a: 16–19; Crane 2001a: 13–18; Crane 2013: 90–96, esp. 92.
19. Crane 2001a: 15–16; Crane 2013: 4.

one plans to *cause* to exist. More on these distinctions at sections 2.2.4 through 2.2.6, below.

For now, just consider the tremendous significance of the *object* of an Intentional episode in Livy's account of the end of the regal period in Rome. Arruns and Titus, the sons of the Roman king Tarquin, and Brutus, who is the king's nephew and presumed to be simpleminded, visit the Delphic oracle and learn that the first of them to kiss his mother will rule Rome. All three men leave Delphi planning to be the first to kiss his mother. Yet only Brutus succeeds when he kisses the earth, "the mother of all." Soon he will expel Tarquin and found the Roman republic.[20] The brothers had mistaken the *Intentional object* of the oracle's cryptic words, and so kissed their female parent. Only Brutus discerned correctly the Intentional object of the oracle's riddle.

2.2.3. *Beliefs Have* Content

As cognitive states *directed toward* objects, beliefs have *content*. A belief's content (technically, *Intentional content*) is the perspective from which, the aspect under which, or the way in which it represents its object. Just as one cannot gaze on the Campidoglio from no particular vantage point, so Intentional episodes cannot neutrally represent their Intentional objects in a view from nowhere. All Intentional episodes present or represent their objects under some aspect, from some perspective, from one point of view rather than another.[21] Thus, as we just saw, the Pythia represented the earth (an Intentional object) under the riddling aspect of *mother*.

The aspectual or perspectival feature of Intentional episodes determines the *content* that each one has. The perspectival nature of content entails that two beliefs can be about the same *object* but have different *contents*, that is, represent the same object under different aspects.[22] Gaius can believe that *the eagle is never killed by lightning*, and Julia can believe that *the eagle is the shield bearer of Jupiter*.[23] Both beliefs share an object, the eagle, but they differ in content, that is, in the way they represent the same object. Intentional content is immensely consequential. Oedipus wanted to marry *the woman* he believed *was the queen of Thebes* (content) but not *the woman* he believed *was his mother*

---

20. Liv. 1.56.10–12.

21. Searle 1983a: 4–22 passim; Searle 1992: 130–31 and 156–59; Crane 2001a: 18–21 and 28–30; Crane 2013: 96–102.

22. See Crane 2001b: 345 and 348; Crane 2013: 97.

23. Examples derived from Plin. *N.H.* 10.6.15.

(content). The Intentional content of Oedipus's belief about Jocasta, the way he represented this Intentional object, undid him.

An aspect of cognition deeply relevant to the study of religion comes to light when we characterize beliefs in terms of Intentional objects and Intentional contents. Robert Brandom elaborates on an insight of Brentano,[24] noting that Brentano saw that extramental, material stuff "can only stand in physical or causal relations to actually existing facts, events, and objects." However, "Intentional states can 'refer to contents' that are not true (do not express actual facts) and be 'directed upon objects' that do not exist." So, the *content* of Oedipus's belief about his mother may be wrong, even though his mother (the *object* of his belief) does exist. Or one may entertain beliefs that are directed on an object, such as Jupiter, that does not exist. Cognition is unique in this way: "I can only kick the can if it exists, but I can think about unicorns even if they do not."[25]

The examples of the beliefs of Gaius, Julia, and Oedipus show that the contents of beliefs have a propositional structure, though this structure need not be realized in explicit linguistic form in the believer's mind. For clarity, I italicized the words that express the propositional contents of the beliefs, above. The content of the belief is never simply *the eagle* or *the woman*. Beliefs represent whole states of affairs, for example, that *the eagle is the shield bearer of Jupiter*. In ordinary English, propositions are statements, plans, proposals, or items put forward for consideration. I use "proposition" in its logically more basic sense, as a term for the structure of the *content* of a perceptual experience, a belief, a desire, or a speech act.[26] So Julia may see, believe, doubt, wish, fear, or assert that *the eagle is the shield bearer of Jupiter*. The content's propositional structure remains the same in all these cases.

Note, however, that it would be a fatal mistake in the study of religion to suppose that beliefs are *about* propositions or that beliefs take propositions, especially linguistically realized propositions, as their *objects*.[27] If beliefs were *about* propositions, then only religions with codified creeds would feature beliefs: the beliefs would be about the creed. We observe this confusion when we read of, for example, "a *credo*, a group of statements which become the *direct object* of belief."[28] I want to emphasize that the credo's statements are not

---

24. For Brentano and Intentionality, see introduction, section 0.4.

25. Brandom 2014: 348. See below, section 2.2.5.

26. See Searle 1983a: 6; Searle 2008b; Searle 2015: 39–41.

27. Cf. Searle 1983a: 16–19; Crane 2013: 91. One can of course have beliefs about propositions *as such*: e.g., I believe that propositions are the contents of many types of mental states.

28. Pouillon 1982: 3, emphasis added on *direct object*.

the *objects* of belief; rather, they give the *content* of belief.[29] The objects of belief, and the objects of belief's linguistic expression in the credo, are just God, Jesus Christ, and so on; actual *stuff*, in other words, not statements *about* stuff. In contrast, the content of belief, like the linguistic content of the credo, amounts to the *way* in which these Intentional objects, this stuff, are represented. So, in the Nicene Creed, God is represented *as* omnipotent father, Jesus Christ is represented *as* incarnated for our salvation, and so forth.[30] Similarly, Gaius represents the eagle *as* never killed by lightning, while Julia represents it *as* Jupiter's shield bearer. Gaius and Julia have beliefs about *the eagle*, not about propositions. Yet the contents of their beliefs about the eagle are propositional in structure.

Note, finally, that not all Intentional states have propositional content the way belief typically does.[31] For example, one may love and fear the gods,[32] where the *objects* of one's Intentional states of love and fear are just *the gods*, and the *content* of these Intentional states is not propositional but *objectual*.[33] That is, you can love and fear not only states of affairs but also an entity (or class of entities).

I close with a final reason, perhaps the most important reason, that historians of religion should care about the distinction between *Intentional object* and *Intentional content*. Imagine that a Roman has a pig. At various times, she believes this pig to be, or otherwise represents this pig as, *animal*, "living being"; *sus*, "pig"; *caro*, "meat"; *porcina*, "pork"; and *victima*, "sacrificial victim." In each case a single organism, a single mass of tissue, blood, and bone, is the *object* of our Roman's belief. But the *content* of each belief, the aspect under which each belief represents the same object, differs in ways that have tremendous cognitive, cultural, and practical significance. For the *content* of each of our Roman's beliefs plays an important role in determining the status of her pig. That is, the

---

29. The Latin creeds use the locution *credo in*, on which, see section 2.4, below.

30. An atheist might say that beliefs about God have *content* but no *object* (see Searle 1983a: 16–18) or that they do have an object (they *really are* about something) but that the object is non-existent (see Crane 2013). This atheist might also say that the beliefs about Jesus expressed in the credo do have an *object* that once existed (the historical Jesus) but inaccurate *content* (he was incarnated for our salvation).

31. See Crane 2001a: 112–14; Crane 2013: 102–12. For nonpropositional, "objectual" belief, see section 2.4, below.

32. Plaut. *Poen*. 282: *deos . . . et amo et metuo*.

33. Montague 2007. Cf. Grzankowski 2015. No Intentional state occurs in isolation: love and fear of the gods arise against a background of beliefs and other attitudes about the gods: see at section 3.2, on emotion.

content of a given belief affects whether the pig is to count that day as livestock, supper, or an offering to the gods.

It is tempting to say that our Roman *just knows* that her pig is, for example, a *victima*. It just is a *victima*, so she represents it as such. This point is true but limited. It may be an *epistemologically objective* fact that the pig is a *victima*, but that fact itself depends on subjects: it is *ontologically subjective*. For in a world devoid of subjects holding beliefs about *victimae*, the pig would be mere pig. Nothing in the pig's biological constitution made it a *victima*. Stated baldly, some things exist only because they are believed to exist. This is true of Roman social reality, which featured *victimae* only because Romans represented in the Intentional contents of their cognitions certain objects as *victimae*. The implications of this for Roman social ontology extend far beyond pigs to social statuses, cult practices, and religious institutions as well as the normative powers these things exerted. The details, which cannot be spelled out here (but see section 2.2.5, below), of cognition's causal role in creating Roman religious reality will occupy us in chapters 5 and 9.

2.2.4. Belief Is a Distinctive Psychological Mode

We have seen that all Intentional states represent their objects from a perspective and this perspective constitutes the Intentional state's content. But what makes a given Intentional state a *belief*? The determinant of belief lies neither in an Intentional state's object nor in its content, but in the subject's *attitude* toward the object as it is represented in the state's content. *Psychological mode* is a technical term for *attitude*.[34] "Belief" names a basic psychological mode, as do "desire," "intention," "fear," "hope," and so on.

Psychological mode and content vary independently. Thus, Gaius may believe, desire, intend, fear, or hope that *the eagle is never killed by lightning*. The content (*how* the eagle is represented) remains the same in each case. *The eagle is never killed by lightning* remains constant. What does change is Gaius's attitude toward this state of affairs: he can believe it, or doubt it, or desire it, or fear it, or hope it, and so on.

As we saw in the introduction (section 0.4) and shall see in the next section, attitudes may be "doxastic" or "practical." Belief is the central "doxastic" psychological mode. We may characterize it thus:

- In *belief*, the Intentional content is a state of affairs (a fact) that one takes to be the case.

---

34. Searle 1983a: 15–16; Crane 2001a: 31–32; Searle 2004: 166–67. Sometimes psychological mode is also called *Intentional mode*.

Desire and intention are central "practical" psychological modes:

- In *desire*, the Intentional content is a state of affairs (a desideratum) that one wishes were the case.
- In *intention*, there is typically a double Intentional content, that is, a *goal* and a *means*: the *goal* is a representation of a state of affairs in the world that one plans to cause to be the case; the *means* is a representation of the action(s) one plans to execute in order to *achieve* the goal. (Of course, sometimes the goal and means are identical, as in for example dancing.)

2.2.5. *Belief Has a Mind-to-World* Direction of Fit

For all Intentional states, direction of fit follows directly from psychological mode.[35] When one *believes* that a state of affairs obtains, one's representation "aims," in the traditional metaphor,[36] to fit or be adequate to the world. It is simply a basic feature of mind that it can represent, match, conform to, or *fit* states of affairs in the world. Obvious benefits accrue to organisms able to represent states of affairs not only in the immediate perceptual environment but also outside of it, through memory,[37] belief, thought, reflection, imagination, and so on. Intentional states with the mind-to-world direction of fit are often called "representational," "theoretical," "cognitive," or as I prefer, "doxastic." Such states may be positive, such as *belief, knowledge, assumption, presupposition,* and *acceptance*, or negative, such as *doubt, denial, rejection,* and *disbelief,* or neutral, such as *uncertainty*.[38] These Intentional states are distinguished as doxastic by the fact that they seek to fit, match, or be adequate to the way things stand in the world. Thus, one can believe, accept, reject, doubt, or be uncertain *that* some state of affairs, in fact, obtains. All such states are doxastic in that they try to fit the world.

Conversely, some Intentional states have the opposite direction of fit: *world-to-mind*. If the pontifex maximus desires that the *res publica* be preserved for five more years,[39] he wants something about the world to conform to the content of his Intentional state. World-to-mind states are often called

---

35. Searle 1983a: 7–9 and 15–16; Searle 2004: 167–69.

36. See Chan 2014: 1.

37. Memory's mutability is one of its *psychological* rather than *logical* features. Memory, however changeable and "constructive" (e.g., Schacter 2012), remains an Intentional state with mind-to-world direction of fit, like belief.

38. See, e.g., Mulligan 2013.

39. Liv. 22.10.2.

"motivational," "volitive," "conative," or as I prefer, "practical." They include desires and intentions. This terminological variety should not cause us to miss the fact that mind-to-world and world-to-mind states are both representational. It is only that one seeks to represent the world as it *is* while the other represents the world as we would have it *be*.

Some (but far from all) of our doxastic and practical attitudes represent something in the world in a certain way and, by virtue of representing it that way, contribute to *making* it that way. *Representing* X (say, Cicero) as Y (say, augur) involves mind-to-world Intentionality, because the representation "fits" a state of affairs taken to exist. We represent Cicero as augur because that is, in actual fact, what he was. But insofar as the representation also plays a role in *making* X into Y, it seems to involve world-to-mind Intentionality, because in such cases the world (the X term, here, Cicero) comes to match the representation (the Y term, here, augur). For this reason, these attitudes, whether beliefs, intentions, or any other state, have sometimes been said to have a "double direction of fit."[40] Romans represented Cicero as and believed him to be an augur (mind-to-world). In so doing, they, in a sense, *created* a bit of social reality, that is, in *recognizing* him as an augur they thereby *made* him an augur and *maintained* him in that role (world-to-mind). If no one believed or otherwise represented that Cicero was an augur, and therefore did not treat him as an augur in relevant practical contexts, he would not have *been* an augur. I call such social-reality-creating-and-maintaining attitudes, whether doxastic or practical, *constitutive attitudes*, because in representing X as Y, they help *constitute* X as Y.[41]

Of course, there are limitations on these reality-constituting powers of our Intentional states. We can represent a pig, X, as a *victima*, Y, as in section 2.2.3, above, and thereby contribute to *making* it a *victima*, but we cannot represent it as, say, a fish, and thereby contribute to making it a fish. Unlike fish, many of the entities in the social world are what they are, Y, because we believe or otherwise represent them as Y. Why, ultimately, can a line of stones count as a boundary, Cicero as an augur, or a gesture as a cult action? Because we represent the line of stones *as* a boundary, and Cicero *as* an augur, and the gesture *as* a cult action, and we therefore behave accordingly. We shall return to this topic of the ontology of the social world, to constitutive attitudes, and to constitutive belief in particular in chapters 5 and 9.

---

40. E.g., Searle 2010: 170: For person X to be president, people "have to be able to think something. For example, they typically think 'He is President,' and such thoughts are sufficient to [create and maintain X as president] . . . and thus have the double direction of fit." Laitinen 2014 offers arguments against double direction of fit, while nonetheless accepting the constitutive role of our representations in creating social reality.

41. See further at section 5.3.2.

For now, we must finish up with direction of fit. At elementary levels of Intentionality, direction of fit has its complement in *direction of causation*.[42] Perceptual experience, for example, *fits* the world but, conversely, the world *causes* the perceptual experience (barring hallucination).[43] Likewise, intentions, if satisfied in purposive action, *cause* change in the world (including in our own action) and thereby *cause* the world to fit the intention. Indeed, we typically *experience* our perceptions as caused by their objects and our actions and their effects as caused by our intentions.[44]

Belief may but need not have this world-to-mind direction of causation, and for this reason it is a less elementary level of Intentionality. For beliefs, unlike perceptions, need not be caused by their objects. True, beliefs may be caused relatively directly, by sensory perception and intuition, but they may also be caused indirectly, by inference, for example, as well as by all sorts of *testimony*, such as assertion, interlocution, less direct social interactions and communications,[45] and artifactual and graphic representations of all sorts, or by these factors in combination. In other words, our beliefs about object or state of affairs X are often caused not by X itself (if it even exists) but by what people communicate, directly or indirectly, about it.

We shall see Roman religious examples of many of these belief-inducing factors throughout this book. For now, speaking of social causes of belief, simply consider Julia's belief about Jupiter's eagle. Her belief has a mind-to-world direction of fit, but not a world-to-mind direction of causation, because nothing about the eagle (or Jupiter) per se caused her to believe it to be Jupiter's shield bearer. Instead, she acquired this belief via testimony, that is, in interaction with others who evinced such a belief or made such linguistic representations, or from cultural representations such as cult images, rituals, prayers, poems, and other forms of discourse that represented or presupposed such a role for the eagle. Thus, beliefs and religious beliefs especially tend rather often to be caused by cultural and social learning. They need not be caused by their objects and indeed need not and very frequently do not even have objects—such as gods and spirits—that exist.[46]

These theses about the differences in direction of causation for perception and for belief are ancient, even if the terminology is not. I limit substantiation of this claim to a telling passage from Cicero's *De legibus*. Marcus notes that the variety and discrepancy among people's beliefs (*opinionum varietas*

---

42. For more on direction of causation, see at section 3.3.4.

43. More on perception from a biological perspective that is relevant here: Burge 2010: 376–96.

44. Searle 1983a: 83–100 and 117–26; Searle 2001: 40–47; Searle 2015: 58–63.

45. See nn. 12–13, above.

46. For non-existent objects of Intentionality, see Crane 2013.

hominumque dissensio) causes us confusion, especially in light of the commonality of everyone's sensory perceptions (*Leg.* 1.47):[47]

> *Nam sensus nostros non parens, non nutrix, non magister, non poeta, non scaena depravat, non multitudinis consensus abducit a vero; animis omnes tenduntur insidiae, vel ab iis quos modo enumeravi qui teneros et rudes quom acceperunt, inficiunt et flectunt ut volunt, vel ab ea quae penitus in omni sensu implicata insidet, imitatrix boni voluptas, malorum autem mater omnium.*

> No parent, no nurse, no teacher, no poet, no theater scene, corrupts *our senses*, no consensus of the crowd seduces them from the truth. All the snares are laid out *for our minds*, either by those people whom I just mentioned who, when they get hold of young and untaught minds, taint them and bend them as they wish, or by that which sits deep inside, tangled up with every sense, pleasure the imitator of good but mother of all evils.

I wish to draw attention to just two features of this passage: first, it expresses the truism and ancient *topos* that we tend to derive our beliefs, especially false ones, from social and cultural sources; second, it contrasts the diversity and fallibility of these socioculturally acquired beliefs with the consistency and relative adequacy to their objects of sensory perceptions.[48] So perception and belief may differ in their causes and fundamentality, but the fact that both have mind-to-world directions of fit makes both evaluable by norms of accuracy, and thus, especially in the case of beliefs of the religious sort, of abiding interest to ancient philosophers, from the pre-Socratics to Augustine. More on this in chapter 6, where we see what Lucretius had to say about beliefs and Roman cult.

2.2.6. Beliefs Define Their Own Conditions of Satisfaction

An Intentional state's "conditions of satisfaction"[49] are represented in its *content*. Thus, the *desire* of the pontifex maximus that the res publica be preserved for five more years is *satisfied* on the *condition* that the res publica actually is so preserved. The desire's own content represents what it would take to satisfy that very desire, that is, the *conditions* that satisfy it. Analogously, the *belief* that the altar of Jupiter Soter is on the Capitoline is *satisfied* (i.e., true, accurate,

---

47. For textual notes, brief discussion, and some parallel passages, see Dyck 2004: 196–98. Cicero here expresses a Stoic view, but it could be shared by other schools, e.g., the Garden (C. Taylor 1980; Everson 1990).

48. Cf. Cic. *Leg.* 1.30: *nam et sensibus eadem omnium conprehenduntur, et ea quae movent sensus, itidem movent omnium.* See the textual note and comments of Dyck 2004: 148–49.

49. Searle 1983a: 10–13 and 19–21; Searle 1992: 175–77; Searle 2004: 169.

correct) on the *condition* that the altar really is on the Capitoline.[50] Like the desire, the belief represents the conditions of its own satisfaction. The critical difference between a practical state with world-to-mind direction of fit, such as desire, and a doxastic state with mind-to-world direction of fit, such as belief, is as follows. If the desire is not satisfied, something in the world turned out not to conform to the mind. However, if the belief is not satisfied, something in the mind failed to conform to the world.[51] So, *satisfaction* is a broad and useful concept in the study of Intentionality. Desires may be *fulfilled* or not, beliefs may be *true* or not, and intentions may be *acted on* and *achieved* or not. The term *satisfaction* encompasses all of these: *fulfillment, truth,* and so on.

These notions of direction of fit and conditions of satisfaction expose the fundamental natural *normativity* of Intentionality. Human cognition is normative from bottom to top. We shall discuss some natural norms of the emotions at section 3.2 and of shared Intentionality and agency at sections 4.3.5 and 4.4 (see also at section 7.4.1). The natural normativity of cognition, of which we are typically unaware,[52] is what makes possible higher-level social or conventional forms of normativity, of which we are often exquisitely aware.

We shall consider how conventional, social norms may inform action at section 3.3 and throughout this book more generally. For now, it seems worthwhile to note that even basic cognition is characterized by natural *constitutive* norms.[53] By "constitutive" I mean that part of what *logically constitutes* belief, part of *what it is* for a mental state to be a belief, is that it has an "aim," an internal norm, of representing states of affairs accurately. As our discussion of conditions of satisfaction suggests, "accuracy" should not be taken to imply "Truth," communion with transcendent Platonic forms, or the fathoming of hidden essences. It merely implies picturing the world and being epistemically responsive to our experience of the world with enough fidelity that we can make our way through it. Nor should the fact that belief aims for accuracy be

---

50. Serv. *ad Aen.* 8.652: *ara in Capitolio est Iovis Soteris.*

51. Anscombe 1957: 56 first presented this idea by contrasting two lists, one used by a shopper to buy groceries (cf. desire) and the other made by a detective recording the shopper's actions (cf. belief).

52. Cf. Burge 2010: 311–12 on the natural (or internal) norms of perception and belief (emphasis in the original): "Some norms are *natural norms*"; "the applicability of natural norms is independent of any individual's setting or acceding to them ... natural norms are also independent of any individual's appreciating them."

53. See the biologically grounded arguments in Burge 2010: 308–15 and 338–41. "There are ... representational natural norms for belief and belief-formation. ... Such norms are associated with believers whether or not they know or care about them. They are norms constitutively associated with the nature and basic function of belief" (Burge 2010, 312). See also Gregory 2012. For debate, see the essays in Chan 2014.

taken to imply that we do not harbor all sorts of ludicrous beliefs, or that we do not believe things because we *want* to believe them, under the influence of confirmation bias and motivated reasoning,[54] or that all our beliefs are mutually consistent.[55] Indeed, sometimes we believe one thing in one context and another inconsistent thing in another. On the beach in the evening, we may intuitively believe the sun is setting. In astronomy class the next morning, we may reflectively believe the earth revolves. All these *psychological* features of believing do no violence to the *logic* of believing, that is, that its aim is to picture the world as it is.

This natural norm of belief—accurate representation—is not a contingent, conventional, or socially constructed fact about belief but rather constitutes what it is to be belief.[56] It is easiest to see this when beliefs fail. If Gaius believes that the *taberna* on the corner serves his favorite wine, but when he gets there it turns out that it does not, then Gaius's belief has failed to meet a natural norm of belief. It fails of mind-to-world fit and so is not satisfied. Obviously, it is better for Gaius and his projects that his beliefs be satisfied, that is, accurate.[57] Similarly revealing of belief's internal norm of accuracy is the absurdity of an assertion like, "The *taberna* is out of wine, but *I* believe it's not."[58] Despite motivated reasoning and confirmation bias, we generally do not simply select beliefs that we feel it would be nice to have. Gaius does not believe the *taberna* has his wine just because it would be nice to think so. This holds for a huge share of our beliefs. In a great many cases, our beliefs follow from what appears to us to be the case based on our perceptions, intuitions, inferences, interlocutions, and other sources of information. Thus, Gaius revises his belief about the *taberna*'s wine once he's arrived.

54. On motivated reasoning, see Kunda 1990. On confirmation bias, see Oswald and Grosjean 2004; and Kahneman 2011: 79–88.

55. We do not have space here to address in detail all these psychological (rather than logical features) of belief. On inconsistency, see Feeney 1998: 14–21, reflecting on what he translates as the "brain-balkanisation" thesis of Veyne 1988 (chapter 4, in Veyne's original French, speaks of "balkanisation des cerveaux"). See, more extensively, Versnel 1990, on cognitive dissonance in Greco-Roman religion. On cognitive dissonance and related phenomena, see, e.g., Cherniak 1981; Harmon-Jones 2000; Egan 2008; M. Davies and Egan 2013, esp. 705ff.

56. Burge 2010: 339: "Some basic norms or standards associated with an enterprise—natural norms—are set by the nature of the enterprise itself, not by choice or convention."

57. Belief can, of course, be rarified away from its basic reality-representing function, as in Wallace Stevens's *Adagia* (Stevens and Bates 1990: 189): "The final belief is to believe in a fiction, which you know to be a fiction, there being nothing else. The exquisite truth is to know that it is a fiction and that you believe in it willingly." Even here, the logical primacy of belief's reality-representing function is what grants Stevens's statement its power.

58. Moore's paradox.

A similar analysis holds for other Intentional states. Part of what constitutes a desire is its norm of fulfillment, and part of what constitutes an intention is its norm of effective action. It is their normative nature that allows Intentional states such as beliefs, desires, emotions, and intentions to relate us to the world. As organisms, we need beliefs to navigate the world, desires to tell us where we want to go, emotions to tell us what matters to us, and intentions to get us moving (more on this below). Because, as scholars, we always begin our ruminations about belief at the top, at the level of the complex religious beliefs of people in a distant society, it is easy for us to miss this bedrock feature of cognition, its natural normativity. The theme of normativity in several of its manifestations runs throughout this book, from natural norms internal to basic cognition and action to the conventional or social norms that underlie *pietas* and cult.

2.2.7. Summary Thus Far

Let us now summarize how these six features of belief fit together. Belief requires a minded *subject*. The subject's *Intentional* states, such as belief, are about or directed toward *objects*, that is, features of the world. An Intentional state's *content* is the way the Intentional state represents the object that it is about, its perspective on the object. There are several *psychological modes* or *attitudes* through which subjects may relate to such contents. In *belief*, a subject relates to a content by taking it to be the case (rather than hoping, wishing, or fearing it to be the case). Belief's distinctive psychological mode determines that it has a mind-to-world *direction of fit*. That is, belief is an Intentional state whose content ideally conforms to or matches up with states of affairs. The content of a belief defines its *conditions of satisfaction*. If states of affairs really *are* as represented in the content of a belief, then the belief is satisfied, that is, accurate. A natural norm of accurate representation is thus constitutive of belief. The foregoing features are not discovered by investigating a society's discourse about belief. They are, rather, logical properties of belief. If the foregoing six features do not pertain to a candidate type of mental state, then that type of mental state is not belief but something else. Belief is but one among many Intentional episodes by which embodied subjects relate to the natural, social, and cultural world in which they are embedded as agents.

2.3. Discursive Intentionality: Extending the Analysis to Language

We saw that the propositional content of an Intentional state need not be expressed linguistically. Yet this is the place to note an important parallel between psychological Intentionality and linguistic or discursive Intentionality, which owes to the fact that speech acts derive their Intentionality from the intrinsic Intentionality of speakers.[59] (This point will become especially important in chapter 8.) Both cognitive states and speech acts are Intentional; that is, they both are *about* or *represent* states of affairs. As a result, both are susceptible to the six-point logical analysis just provided for cognitive states. Speech acts must be produced by a minded *subject*, they are directed on or about *objects*, and they are *contentful*, which is to say they represent their objects under a particular aspect. Speech acts express the uttering subject's *psychological attitude* toward the content of the utterance. They also have *direction of fit*, either *word*-to-world or world-to-*word*, and they represent their own *conditions of satisfaction*. If Gaius states, "The eagle is never killed by lightning," his speech act is *satisfied* (i.e., true) if his words match the facts about the eagle.[60] Analogously, if Gaius prays, "May the eagle not be killed by lightning," his speech act is satisfied (i.e., fulfilled) if the world comes to match his words and the eagle escapes such a death.

Speech acts fall into five classes: Assertive, Commissive, Directive, Expressive, and Declaration.[61] This list captures the five basic *illocutionary forces* speech acts can have. A speech act is a linguistic act in which a speaker applies one of the five illocutionary forces F to a propositional content p. Thus, every speech act has the form $F(p)$. One upshot of this analysis is the discovery that force and content vary independently. Different illocutionary forces (F) may be applied to the same propositional content (p). So, for example, one may assert, request, or promise (F) that *the eagle is never killed by lightning* (p).

Each illocutionary force entails a direction of fit. Assertives represent in words how things stand in the world, so they have the *word*-to-world direction of fit. As we saw at section 1.3.3, they tend to express, and thus are the most direct evidence for, a speaker's beliefs, which have a *mind*-to-world direction of fit. Commissives commit speakers to change the world to match their words, so they have world-to-*word* direction of fit. Commissives ideally reflect a speaker's intentions, with world-to-*mind* direction of fit. Like Commissives, Directives have world-to-*word* direction of fit. They reflect a speaker's desire to get an addressee to change the world to match his or her words. Desires, of course, have world-to-*mind* direction of fit. Expressives report how a speaker *feels* about a state of affairs whose existence he or she takes for granted. We

---

59. Searle 1983a: 4–13. Cf. Brandom 2014: 349–51. Aristotle would have agreed: see *Int.* 1.

60. For more on "satisfaction" in speech act theory, see Vanderveken 2004.

61. Searle 1969; Searle 1979a; Searle and Vanderveken 1985; Vanderveken 1990. For earlier speech-act theories, see Austin 1962 and, on the work of Adolf Reinach, the essays in Mulligan 1987. Historical overview of speech-act theorizing in B. Smith 1990.

shall return to Declarations in chapter 5, but for now we may note that they are unique among speech acts in having a *double direction of fit*, in parallel with what I called "constitutive attitudes" (section 2.2.5, above). They represent in words how things are in the world (word-to-world) and by virtue of this linguistic operation, they cause how things are in the world to match the words (world-to-word). A classic example is, "I now pronounce you husband and wife." We shall see in chapters 5, 8, and 9 that Roman religious practice bristles with Declarations.

Speech acts involve norms, but unlike private mental states such as beliefs, desires, and intentions, these norms are *public*, placing speakers under various sorts of obligations to others.[62] An Assertive publicly commits the speaker to the truth of his or her assertion, a Commissive publicly commits the speaker to doing what the speaker says he or she will do, and so on. I follow Searle in ranging these obligations, along with all other duties and responsibilities, rights, prerogatives, powers, and all social norms, under the rubric of "deontology."[63] The term "deontology" covers all *normative social* (rather than physical, biological, or chemical) empowerments to and restrictions on action. A deontology may be thought of as a package of norms—a set of *oughts, musts, mays*, and their negatives. Language is the logically prior deontology, the basic set of norms—oughts, oughtn'ts, musts, mustn'ts, mays, and may nots—on which all other human social powers, permissions, and restrictions depend. We leave these provocative notions for now and explore them further in sections 3.3.2–3 and especially 5.3.2, as well as in chapter 8.

2.4. Belief-in

Before we move on to discuss our two psychological features of belief, that is, degree of intensity and the distinction between nonreflective and reflective beliefs, we must briefly address the question of *belief-in*.[64] We have been discussing, and this book is about, *belief-that*, which is sometimes also called "factual,"[65] "propositional,"[66] or "existential"[67] belief, among other descriptors. *Belief-that* amounts to, as we have seen, a representation that some state of affairs is the case.

---

62. See Seuren 2009: 139–59; Brandom 2014: 351–53.
63. See Searle 2008a; Searle 2009; Searle 2010: 61–89.
64. Famously introduced into the study of religion by H. Price 1965 (= 1969: 426–54).
65. H. Price 1965 (= 1969: 426–54).
66. Audi 2015: 48–51.
67. Audi 2008: 88–90.

Existential *belief-that* is often contrasted (and, by Pouillon and his followers, mistakenly conflated) with a class of attitudes expressed by the locution *belief-in*, to wit, "evaluative belief,"[68] "attitudinal belief,"[69] or "axiological belief in."[70] These sorts of *beliefs-in* amount to attitudes of trust, faith, or some other positive evaluative state. Indeed, "belief," in the sense of *belief-in*, is often used as a synonym for "faith," in both religious and nonreligious contexts.[71] The Romans, too, had ways of speaking of and expressing faith, *fides*, but we have no space here to investigate this. Readers interested in *belief-in* as "faith" should start with Teresa Morgan's recent, comprehensive book on Roman *fides*.[72]

Note that *belief-in* is not limited to axiological or evaluative attitudes, such as faith, trust, and so on. Sometimes its import is instead existential, in which case one may speak of "intellectual belief in."[73] As Robert Audi points out, "belief in, say wood nymphs may simply come to believing that there *are* such beings."[74] In this connection, note that a *belief-in* locution expressing an existential belief may represent its content not as a proposition but simply as an object,[75] as in "I believe in wood nymphs."

Existential *belief-that* and axiological *belief-in* may relate to one another in various ways, though they need not. If, for example, I *believe in* my friend, that is, if I have a positive attitude toward her, trust her, or have faith in her, I surely must also entertain all sorts of relevant *beliefs-that* about her. Conversely, of course, I can have various *beliefs-that* about her without necessarily *believing in* her.

Consider, in this connection, the Latin creed, which from its earliest attestations commences with the novel locution *credo in*. This locution would appear to express attitudes both existential and axiological, that is, both *belief that* there exists one God (a controversial thesis in a polytheistic society)[76] and one Lord, Jesus Christ, and an attitude of *belief in*, in the sense of hope or trust, with respect to God and Christ. In a sermon touching on these topics, Augustine contrasts *credo in* with *belief-that*. It is worth quoting him at modest length (*Serm.* 144.2.2):

---

68. H. Price 1965 (= 1969: 426–54).

69. Audi 2008: 88.

70. Mulligan 2013: 123–26.

71. Audi 2008: 90. See Audi 2011: 52–88 for philosophical analysis of seven different "faith-locutions," the attitudes they name, and their various relationships to existential belief.

72. T. Morgan 2015.

73. Mulligan 2013: 124–25 illuminatingly discusses such nonaxiological "intellectual belief in."

74. Audi 2008: 90, emphasis in the original.

75. Szabó 2003: 600–606, discussed less technically in Mulligan 2013: 123–26. Cf. the related discussion of "predicative" (or "objectual") vs. propositional belief in Audi 2015: 48–51.

76. But see the essays collected in Athanassiadi and Frede 1999; Mitchell and Van Nuffelen 2010a and 2010b.

Sed multum interest utrum quisque credat ipsum Christum et utrum credat in Christum. Nam ipsum esse Christum et daemones crediderunt, nec tamen in Christum daemones crediderunt. Ille enim credit in Christum, qui et sperat in Christum et diligit Christum. Nam si fidem habet sine spe ac sine dilectione, Christum esse credit, non in Christum credit.

It makes a big difference whether someone believes *that* the man himself is Christ and whether he believes *in* Christ. For even the demons believed that the man himself was Christ, but the demons did not believe in Christ. Truly, that person believes in Christ who both hopes in Christ and loves Christ. For if he has credence [*fides*] without hope and without love, he believes that Christ exists, but does not believe in Christ.

As this passage makes clear, Augustine interprets *credo in* to express an attitude of *belief-in* that is quite distinct from and hence quite distinguishable from *belief-that*. *Credo in*, for Augustine, is a locution that denotes two attitudes held simultaneously: hope and love. To *believe in* Christ in this sense also entails, as Augustine's account implies, *belief-that*. However, the converse clearly does not hold. For Augustine admonishes his congregation that one may, like the demons, have *beliefs-that* with respect to Christ while not *believing in* Christ. The novel locution *credo in*, then, does not name a novel mental attitude, but refers to two well-known attitudes occurring together, and presupposing or entailing (as so very many attitudes do) *belief-that*.

The evidence of Augustine shows that Pouillon and others (see section 1.3.3) are mistaken to suppose that all belief locutions must express simultaneously existential and axiological attitudes. "Belief" and its lexemes in Latin, not to mention in other languages, can have existential import *simpliciter*. Of course, this does not entail that traditional Romans could not take other attitudes beyond *belief-that* toward their gods. For as a character in Plautus affirms, "I both love and fear the gods," *deos ... et amo et metuo* (*Poen.* 282). Love and fear entail that he also entertains various *beliefs-that* about them.

While this book deals primarily with existential belief, that is, *belief-that*, we shall nonetheless see the occasional pagan example of *belief-in*, as in the next section, where we shall see some worshippers of Isis exhibiting not only existential *belief-that* but also an attitude of *belief-in* with respect to their goddess.

2.5. Belief Intensity

Now that we have laid out the logical aspects of belief and illustrated its relationship to belief-in, we turn, as promised, to two psychological aspects of belief. The first, with which we deal in this section, is the fact that belief admits of degrees of intensity.[77] Scholars of Greek religion have recognized this.[78] Intensity refers to the felt strength of a given psychological state. It is a matter of metacognition.[79] I might hold one belief with such intensity that I feel that I overwhelmingly *know* it to be true. It might be so central to my psychology and behavior that I would submit to pain or death in order to attest or defend it.[80] (Recalling our discussion of definitions at section 2.2, we may call this belief a *conviction*, to mark its felt strength.) But I might be scarcely confident enough about another belief to admit to it without a great deal of hedging. Latin lexicalizes doxastic states of various degrees of intensity with verbs such as *opinor*, "be of opinion"; *arbitror*, "suppose"; *aestimo*, "reckon"; *credo*, "believe" (also, "trust"); *puto*, "judge, regard"; *confido*, "be assured of"; and *scio*, "know."

Now, there is a risk that this genuinely useful distinction between "high-intensity" and "low-intensity" belief may be misconstrued to imply an essential contrast between Christian belief (high) and pagan belief (low). Henk Versnel, for example, in an illuminating discussion of belief in Greek religion, advises that scholars should "use the term 'believe' in its broad 'low intensity' meaning and not in its Christian 'high intensity' application."[81] We should not, however, shrink from ascribing high-intensity belief, properly understood, to the ancients, when appropriate. We should judge each case on its own merits rather than presume the ancients to be low on psychological energy where their cult and their gods are concerned. Two quite different examples of high-intensity belief in the Roman world should serve to demonstrate this point.

First, a recurring motif in Livy is that outlandish occurrences, military setbacks, and the like result in high-intensity beliefs and fears,[82] and that these in turn lead to cult action. For example, in 218 BCE many *prodigia* occurred, or rather, as Livy says, "what typically happens once minds have been moved to

---

77. Bentham 1825: 40: "Nobody can be ignorant, that belief is susceptible of different degrees of strength, or intensity." Audi 2008: 89: "Intensity is roughly a matter of the felt conviction—the sense of truth—that accompanies a belief when it is occurrent."

78. E.g., Versnel 2011: 548; Harrison 2015a: 23–26; Petrovic and Petrovic 2016: 3.

79. See Mercier and Sperber 2017: 65–66.

80. For "centrality," see Audi 2008: 89: "Centrality is a matter of how influential the belief is in the person's psychology, especially the belief system but also behavioral tendencies."

81. Versnel 2011: 548. Cf. Harrison 2015a: 24, in an otherwise enlightening discussion of belief intensity: "If we look only for 'high-intensity' belief in the Greek world, it is no surprise if we find it to be scarce."

82. Such events were believed to signal a need to secure the *pax deum*, on which see now Satterfield 2015.

religio, many prodigies were announced and rashly believed [*credita sunt*]."[83] Only the public performance of expiatory rites "relieved people's minds, in large part, of religious care."[84] Five years later, the ravages of Hannibal occasioned yet more high-intensity episodes of religious psychology and action. Many people had been driven from the countryside to the city by want and fear (*egestate et metu*; 25.1.8). Under these conditions, strange observances (*tanta religio*; 25.1.6) displaced traditional public cult in the forum as "sacrificers and soothsayers took hold of the minds of men."[85] When magistrates attempted to empty the forum and remove the novel implements of cult that had been placed there, they narrowly escaped violence at the hands of an incensed crowd (25.1.10). We would be remiss not to interpret Livy's presentation of such episodes—and there are many—as cases of high-intensity belief and high-intensity fear motivating high-intensity cult action.

Consider, second, a tale from Apuleius's *Metamorphoses*. Obviously, this imperial-era fiction scarcely counts as documentary evidence, but neither does it reflect a *Lebenswelt* utterly alien to the late republic. Apuleius's hapless protagonist Lucius, who has spent most of the book transformed by magic into an ass, reverts back to his original human form amid a throng of worshippers of Isis (*Met.* 11.13):

> *populi mirantur, religiosi venerantur tam evidentem maximi numinis potentiam . . . claraque et consona voce, caelo manus adtendentes, testantur tam inlustre deae beneficium.*

> The people wonder at and the pious reverence the power, so evident, of so great a deity . . . and with a clear and harmonious voice, stretching their hands to heaven, they bear witness to the favor, so manifest, of the goddess.

The obvious interpretation of this passage is that Isis's worshippers are in the grip of high-intensity beliefs about Isis: they believe that the goddess has restored Lucius to human form, and thus that she is powerful, that she dispenses

---

83. Liv. 21.62.1: *Romae aut circa urbem multa ea hieme prodigia facta aut, quod evenire solet motis semel in religionem animis, multa nuntiata et temere **credita sunt***. Cf. 24.10.6: *prodigia eo anno multa nuntiata sunt, quae quo magis **credebant** simplices ac religiosi homines, eo plura nuntiabantur*; 29.14.2: *impleverat ea res superstitionum animos, pronique et ad nuntianda et **ad credenda** prodigia erant* (emphasis added). Linderski 1993: 66n2 points out that in such passages Livy expresses not blanket skepticism but rather a concern to distinguish genuine from false *prodigia*.

84. Liv. 21.62.11: *haec procurata votaque ex libris Sibyllinis magna ex parte levaverant religione animos.* Cf. 7.3.1, 25.1.11, 27.37.5.

85. Liv. 25.1.8: *sacrificuli ac uates ceperant hominum mentes.*

favors, and so on. These beliefs—empirically grounded in Lucius's public cure cum epiphany of the goddess[86]—occasion feelings of awe and reverence. The manifest signs of the goddess's power and favor (*tam evidens potentia, tam inlustre beneficium*) move her worshippers not merely to believe and to feel awe but also to *avow* their beliefs. That is, like Innocentius and his household on the occasion of the cure recounted by Augustine (section 1.3.4, above), the Isiac cultists engage in religious action directly expressive of their belief (the verb is *testantur*, "bear witness") as to the beneficence of the goddess.[87]

Not all ancient religious cognition and action can match the high intensity of the Livian and Apuleian examples presented here.[88] Yet we must recognize that both low- and high-intensity religious belief existed among pagans and that both low- and high-intensity episodes of religious cognition involved *causal connections* among belief, desire, intention, emotion, and action. We shall return to this latter assertion, and to these passages from Apuleius and Livy, at section 3.2.2.

2.6. Intuition and Inference Produce Nonreflective and Reflective Beliefs

Now we introduce our second psychological aspect of belief, namely, that it comes in two broad types, nonreflective and reflective.[89] We shall also look at two processes from which such beliefs derive, to wit, intuition and inference (both explored more fully below, at sections 2.6.2 and 2.6.3). Roman examples of "social cognition," that is, intuitions, inferences, and beliefs about *agents*, will illustrate our discussion. These examples will allow us to show the relevance to Roman religious cognition of agential intuitions, inferences, and beliefs. The theory that beliefs about gods and ritual are grounded in cognitively natural intuitions and inferences about agency and action, that is, in social cognition, has been developed extensively in the cognitive science of religion (CSR), on which I draw in this subsection.[90]

---

86. On the many manifestations, so to speak, of ancient epiphany, see Versnel 1987.

87. Cf. Apul. *Met.* 11.23 (Lucius speaking): *igitur audi, sed crede, quae vera sunt.*

88. A final example: in Acts 19:23–41 Paul denies the divinity of idols, οὐκ εἰcὶν θεοὶ οἱ διὰ χειρῶν γινόμενοι (19:26), thus moving the Ephesians vehemently to assert their beliefs as to Artemis's greatness: Μεγάλη ἡ Ἄρτεμιc Ἐφεcίων (19:28).

89. In terminology and in much of substance I follow Barrett 2004a: 1–19. Sperber 1997 speaks of reflective vs. intuitive beliefs. Cf. more broadly Pyysiäinen 2004.

90. Central publications include E. T. Lawson and McCauley 1990; Guthrie 1993; McCauley and Lawson 2002; Boyer 2001; Barrett 2004a; Barrett 2011a; McCauley 2011. See now Larson 2016 for a CSR approach to Greek religion and an expert overview of the CSR field.

2.6.1. The Two Systems and "Theological Incorrectness"

Worth noting right away is that the distinction between two types of belief, one *nonreflective* or spontaneous, the other *reflective* or deliberate, follows from "dual process" or "dual system" accounts of cognition.[91] The *reflective/nonreflective* distinction (which should not be conflated with the *occurrent/dispositional* distinction) captures the fact that some cognitive processes are fast, automatic, and inaccessible to consciousness while others are slow, controlled, and inherently conscious. These processes produce nonreflective and reflective beliefs, respectively, as their products. Various names for these two basic types of cognition have been proposed. I adopt those of Daniel Kahneman, who calls fast cognition "System 1" and slow cognition "System 2."[92] We shall see that both systems contribute to social and hence religious cognition.[93]

This is a lot to unpack. Let us start with the point about not conflating *nonreflective/reflective* with *occurrent/dispositional*, and then move on to the more important concept, the two systems. The occurrent/dispositional distinction reflects the presence to consciousness or not of a given belief (a cognitive *product*) at a given time (see section 2.2.1). In contrast, the nonreflective/reflective distinction refers to the cognitive process that gave rise to a given belief. These four categories vary independently. Thus, a nonreflective belief produced by fast, unconscious processes may be dispositional (if not currently in consciousness) or occurrent. For example, a spontaneously arising nonreflective belief, produced by fast social-cognitive processes, with the content *she's angry at me*, may be uncomfortably occurrent. Equally, reflective beliefs produced by slow, deliberate cognitive processes may at any given time be either occurrent or dispositional. For example, your hard-won belief that natural selection is a nonteleological process was likely dispositional until I brought it into occurrence by mentioning it just now.

We now turn to the two systems. System 1 cognition is irresistible. Examples of System 1 cognition include detecting the source of a sound and reading a word written in your native language when you see it. System 1 does these and innumerable other things for you automatically. You have no choice but to detect the source of a sound you hear or to read a word you see. As these

---

91. See J. Evans and Stanovich 2013 for an overview of dual process accounts of cognition and response to some criticisms of them. Mercier and Sperber 2017: 43–48 suggest that the dual process model no longer accommodates the psychological findings. I appeal to dual process here only as a useful heuristic.

92. Kahneman 2011: esp. 19–30. Cf. Barrett 2011a: 44–53 for an overview from a CSR perspective.

93. For a dual process account of social cognition, see Fiske and Taylor 2013: 31–58.

two examples suggest, fast, automatic cognition ranges from a matter of biological endowment to a matter of cultural learning. In this connection, Robert McCauley usefully distinguishes between "maturational naturalness" and "practiced naturalness."[94] Most animals undergoing a typical ontogeny will, among many other things, come to orient automatically toward sounds.[95] This is maturational naturalness. In contrast, acquiring practiced naturalness in reading, among many other skills, requires learning and effort, which are functions of System 2.

Like Eratosthenes discovering that the earth is round, we employ System 2 in careful observation and reasoning in order to arrive at some of our beliefs. But this is not how we arrive at most of our beliefs. As Kahneman writes, "When we think of ourselves, we identify with System 2, the conscious, reasoning self that has beliefs, makes choices, and decides what to think about and what to do."[96] In fact, however, System 1 is always humming along unnoticed, "effortlessly originating impressions and feelings that are the main sources of the explicit beliefs and deliberate choices of System 2."[97] System 1 constantly offers suggestions to System 2 and System 2 generally accepts them. In this way, "impressions and intuitions turn into beliefs, and impulses turn into voluntary actions."[98] System 2 acquires nonreflective beliefs by taking on board the intuitions that arise in System 1, and it acquires reflective beliefs, in part, by scrutinizing intuitions and nonreflective beliefs. As a result, "most of what you . . . think and do originates in your System 1, but System 2 takes over when things get difficult, and it normally has the last word."[99]

Let us pause over this assertion that System 2 has the last word. Kahneman illustrates this with the example of the Müller-Lyer illusion (see figure 2.1).[100] When you look at the two figures, System 1 tells you that one of the two parallel horizontal lines is longer than the other. It is just obvious. Yet when you measure the two lines, you see that they are the same length. System 2 now *knows* that the two lines are the same length, but it is powerless to stop System 1 from delivering the impression that one line is longer than the other. Still, in

---

94. McCauley 2011: 4–7.

95. Human infants do this from birth (Mills and Melhuish 1974) or before (Moon et al. 2013).

96. Kahneman 2011: 21.

97. Kahneman 2011: 21.

98. Kahneman 2011: 24.

99. Kahneman 2011: 25.

100. Kahneman 2011: 27. Deregowski 1989 discusses cross-cultural variation in susceptibility to this illusion.

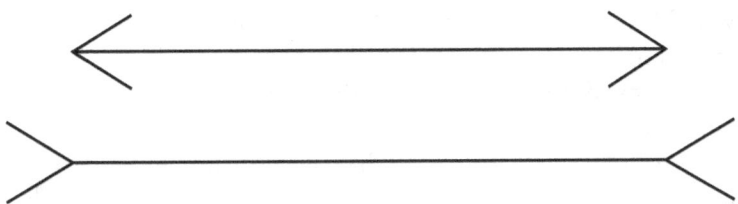

FIGURE 2.1. The Müller-Lyer illusion. (Created by Kate Stanchak after Kahneman 2011: 27, fig. 3.)

this case, you trust your measurements, not your eyes, so System 2 gets to dictate what you reflectively believe.

Typically, the two systems do not come into conflict as starkly as in the Müller-Lyer illusion. And yet they do often contradict one another in ways that may escape our notice. A signal example of this comes from experiments on religious cognition. Justin Barrett's work on "theological correctness" (1999) with subjects in the United States and India shows that regardless of their explicit, reflective theological commitments—the abstruse creeds or doctrines typically considered definitive of religious beliefs—people often reason, without reflecting on doing so, about gods as anthropomorphic agents, in terms of the mundane social-cognitive categories that we examined in the introduction (section 0.2 and especially section 0.3) and alluded to at section 1.3.4.[101]

Christians and Hindus can provide a "theologically correct" description of their god when prompted. However, when asked to reason on the spot, in real time, about their god's activities, people's implicit concept of god becomes "theologically incorrect." Gods turn out to think and to act much as we do, within the limits to which we are subject. It is cognitively easier to "humanize" gods, to conceive supposedly incorporeal, omnipresent, and omnipotent beings as, in fact, localized in space and time and as having to finish one task before going elsewhere to attend to another. Contradicting our reflective theological beliefs, we nonreflectively attribute to gods the "limited focus of attention," "fallible perceptual systems," and incomplete knowledge that characterize mundane agents.[102] This would, at first blush, appear to explain why in petitionary prayer, the ancients *invoked* the gods to get their attention, *reminded* them of their previous interactions, and made so carefully *explicit* what

---

101. Some of the initial work in this area is to be found in Barrett and Keil 1996; Barrett and van Orman 1996; Barrett 1998 and 1999. For discussion and further references, see Slone 2004; McCauley 2011: 207–21; Mercier 2020: 222–30.

102. Barrett 1999: 329.

they wanted (see section 8.4). For gods are not only physically anthropomorphic, as Xenophanes noted, but also *psychologically* anthropomorphic. (We explore prayer and the psychological anthropomorphism of the gods in detail in chapter 8.)

The upshot of Barrett's work is not that people do not "really" believe in the creeds or doctrines they profess. Nonreflective religious cognition does not replace one's explicit theology or reveal one's "true" theology. Rather, cognition about gods moves fluidly along a continuum, depending on context. System 2 cognition permits the memorizing, scrutinizing, accepting, and professing of cognitively demanding theological doctrines. However, when people reason about gods in "real-life" situations, such as during prayer, they often revert to System 1's cognitively less demanding intuitions about how mundane agents perceive, think, and behave. As in the Müller-Lyer illusion, our reflective cognitions tell us one thing about gods while our nonreflective cognitions tell us another. As Barrett points out, intuitions and nonreflective beliefs do not clash with reflective theology but rather "do a tremendous amount of work in filling out religious beliefs, motivating behaviors, and making the fancier theological notions possible." Indeed, "all folk theology and religious practices gain structure and support from nonreflective beliefs,"[103] especially nonreflective beliefs about agents and action.

The broad lesson is that while theological doctrine may tend, like scientific thinking, toward the cognitively "unnatural" and effortful, much religious thinking "in the wild" tends toward the nonreflective naturalness and effortlessness of social cognition.[104] Despite the reflective theological efforts of writers like Varro, Cicero, and Lucretius, explicit, philosophical theology did not play a central part in Roman religion. Varro's cognitively demanding "natural theology" (*theologia naturalis*), which strove to provide a philosophical account of the gods as they truly were, did not serve as a counterpart to the sort of explicit theologizing found in Christian works such as Augustine's *De libero arbitrio voluntatis*. Roman religion was instead primarily a matter of Varro's "civic theology"—*theologia civilis*, the religion of cult acts—and "mythical theology"—*theologia fabulosa*, the religion of mythical narratives transmitted in drama and poetry.[105] That is to say, it amounted to what we saw Barrett characterize, in the previous paragraph, as an implicit "folk theology." Folk

---

103. Barrett 2004a: 10.
104. See McCauley 2011: 230–37.
105. For Varro's tripartition of theology, see Varr. *Ant. Div.* fr. 6 Cardauns = Aug. *Civ.* 6.5 and 6.12. See at section 3.3.2–3 for more on Varro's theology.

theology (or "implicit theology")[106] consisted of reflective cultural representations about divine agents as transmitted in cult and through testimonies, stories, prayers, and so on, along with System 1's spontaneously produced social-cognitive intuitions, inferences, and nonreflective beliefs about them. This Roman folk theology was cognitively quite natural. Cognitively demanding *theologia naturalis* was left to the philosophical schools. We examine Roman folk theology further in chapter 8.

2.6.2. Intuition and Roman Religious Culture

Let us now move on to distinguish *intuition* (a word we defined at section 0.2 of the introduction) from *inference*.[107] The intuitions that occur to us and the inferences at which we arrive tend to become our more or less reflective beliefs. As processes, intuition belongs to System 1, while Systems 1 and 2 may both engage in inferential processes.[108] Intuition and inference both yield beliefs, but they differ in the directness with which they do so.

Inference is, as we shall soon see in more detail, a process of deriving "new information from information already available."[109] In contrast, intuition is a process whereby new information carrying a degree of self-evidence simply appears in consciousness, just as in perception certain features of the world simply become present. When we perceive something, it just *seems*, in an immediate way, to be there. When we intuit something, it just *seems*, in an immediate way, to be the case. Intuition may thus be called "intellectual perception."[110]

Intuition as a cognitive product, that is, an intuition *that* a state of affairs obtains, has much in common with the belief to which it gives rise. Both are doxastic states that have an *Intentional content*; that is, both represent an Intentional object under a particular aspect (see section 2.2.3, above). Some hold that intuition is really just belief, others that it is nonreflective belief, and still others that it is a sui generis psychological mode or attitude, on par with belief

---

106. Thus Larson 2016: 13 and 66–126.

107. On intuition in CSR, see Horst 2013. For an assessment of intuition, inference, and agency in CSR, see Audi 2016: 25–28.

108. See Mercier and Sperber 2009.

109. Mercier and Sperber 2017: 53.

110. Chudnoff 2013: 1. Mercier and Sperber 2017 hold that intuition, like perception, is the output of inferences of which we are unaware, below the level of conscious accessibility: see esp. 63–67. In contrast, Audi 2013: 83–96 offers an account of intuition as a noninferential process.

and desire.[111] Whatever the case, it is clear that unlike beliefs, intuitions are always occurrent, not dispositional (see section 2.2.1, above). It makes no sense to say, "I have an intuition, but I am unaware of what it is about."[112] Rather, in intuition, it consciously *seems* to you, in the moment, that some state of affairs obtains.[113] So, a defining metacognitive property of intuitions is their presence to mind.[114]

We can illustrate these considerations with some social-cognitive examples. One may intuit, say, that one person is happy and another is lying. Neither of these is strictly a perceptual property of the persons in question, like shape, size, color, and distance, yet these are properties that one quite directly perceives or intuits.[115] Such social intuitions tend to pass into more or less reflective beliefs. These beliefs may then serve as premises for inference: *She must be happy because she just won* or *he must be lying in order to conceal from me what she did*.

A telling example of such social intuition, which aptly illustrates its connection to religious cognition, is provided by a passage that we touched on in the introduction and now examine more fully: some verses by the republican satirist Lucilius and their interpretation by the Christian Lactantius, who quotes them in his *Divinae Institutiones*. Lactantius faults mythical Roman figures such as Numa for bequeathing false rites to their descendants. Yet, he assures us, only the foolish are deceived: all *prudentes* see through the error of pagan cult. Lactantius supports this claim by quoting Lucilius, prefacing his citation with the words, "in the following verses, Lucilius scoffs at the stupidity of those who suppose that cult images are gods."[116] Among the verses he quotes are these (Lucil. 15.526–28 = Lact. *Inst.* 1.22.13):

> *ut pueri infantes credunt signa omnia aena*
> *vivere et esse homines, sic isti somnia ficta*
> *vera putant, credunt signis cor inesse in aenis.*

---

111. For "psychological mode," see section 2.2.4, above. For the debate over the status of intuition, see Pust 2019.

112. Mercier and Sperber 2017: 66.

113. Chudnoff 2013: 41–44.

114. Mercier and Sperber 2017: 66.

115. On intuition or "direct perception" in social cognition, see Gallagher 2008a and 2008b; Scholl and Gao 2013; and the articles in a 2015 special issue of *Consciousness and Cognition* (vol. 36).

116. Lact. *Inst.* 1.22.13: *nam Lucilius eorum stultitiam, qui simulacra deos putant esse, deridet his versibus.*

Just as infant children believe all bronze statues live and are human
    beings,
so those [i.e., the superstitious] suppose that imagined dreams
are true, they believe that a heart lies within bronze statues.

For Lactantius, the superstitious adults—that is, of course, pagans—come off worse than Lucilius's children. "For," he says, "the children suppose images are people, but the adults suppose they are gods."[117] Moreover, the children's error owes to age (*aetas*), whereas the pagan adults' error owes to stupidity (*stultitia*). The children will cease to be deceived when they mature, whereas the foolishness of the adults will not diminish.[118] Whatever one's assessment of Lactantius's argument, he does prove himself sensitive here to children's cognitive development. Let us analyze the cognitive implications of this passage and its interpretation, beginning with Lucilius's *infantes pueri* and ending with Lactantius's credulous adults.

When Lucilius's *infantes* encounter statues, they come to believe (*credunt*), quite nonreflectively, that the molded bronze possesses the qualities of animacy (*vivere*) and humanity (*esse homines*). No one *teaches* the infants this, nor presumably do they *infer* it from a set of premises. Rather, they simply *intuit* it upon being confronted with a statue. Neurotypical human beings begin to have intuitions of animacy and agency very early in ontogeny.[119] Such System 1 cognition is "smart": it parses the reflected light that reaches the retina into discrete objects and delivers the intuition that some of these objects are agents. Nonetheless, even smart cognition is not infallible, as Lucilius's infant shows. Happily, as Lactantius points out, the infant's condition is a temporary one. As children mature, they cease to believe that statues are animate.

I would submit that Lactantius here takes note of a maturing System 2's interference with the intuitions offered up by System 1. It is not that, in adults, System 2 shuts down System 1's intuitions of animacy. The intuitions continue to come, but System 2 does not allow them to become beliefs. That System 1 continues to give such intuitions you may have experienced for yourself if you have ever had an uncanny sensation of "presence" while looking at what you "know" to be a mere statue, perhaps of Roman make, in a museum. Indeed, Romans themselves could experience such dueling cognitions in their encounters with naturalistic depictions of living things, as suggested by the

---

117. Lact. *Inst.* 1.22.14: *illi enim simulacra homines putant esse, hi deos.*

118. Lact. *Inst.* 1.22.14: *illos aetas facit putare quod non est, hos stultitia. illi utique breui desinunt falli, horum uanitas et durat semper et crescit.*

119. See, e.g., Opfer and Gelman 2011; Gergely 2011.

common observation that well-made statues seem to breathe, *spirantia signa*.[120] Intuitions of animacy fight against the reflective belief that one is looking at mere bronze. Adults have to learn *not* to see statues as living things.

However, Lucilius's superstitious people never learn. Like children, they continue to believe (*credunt*) the statue contains a living heart (*signis cor inesse in aenis*). Lactantius applies this to non-Christians, "who suppose that cult images are gods" (*qui simulacra deos putant esse*). His interpretation is not reducible to antipagan calumny. He knew that traditional Romans could see in *simulacra* more than artifacts or representations: they *encountered* their gods materially and perceptually in cult images.[121] In such cases, cultural learning shapes cognition,[122] causing System 2 to *endorse* rather than reject intuitions of animacy and agency. The result is nonreflective or even reflective belief that the represented god is actually *present*. Note that the cultural learning that prompts System 2 to endorse rather than reject intuitions of animacy and agency works *with* not *against* System 1's spontaneous intuitions, making such cultural learning cognitively quite "natural."[123]

In this way, Roman religiocultural cognition builds on and reinforces rather than cuts against or undermines the intuitions of agency delivered by natural social cognition. We should take the resulting beliefs, nonreflective and reflective, seriously as cognitions that guided Roman religious action. Consider, for example, the historiographic tradition, elaborated by Livy, of the removal of Juno's statue from her temple at Veii, following Camillus's *evocatio*, a ritual by means of which attackers "call out" a deity from the city they have besieged. As victorious Romans remove gifts to the gods and the very gods themselves (*ipsos deos*) from the fallen city's temples, a young Roman asks Juno if she wishes to go with them. She nods or in some versions even voices her consent.[124] We should surely see here cultural learning about *simulacra* endorsing and even enhancing the intuitions of animacy delivered by System 1 in the

---

120. Verg. *G.* 3.34. Cf. Verg. *Aen.* 6.847–48: *spirantia . . . aera; vivos . . . de marmore vultus*; Apul. *Met.* 11.17: *simulacra spirantia*; Plin. *Ep.* 3.6.2: *etiam ut spirantis*; Petr. *Sat.* 52.1 hilariously sends up the trope: *pueri mortui iacent sic ut vivere putes*; Plin. *H.N.* 35.95 notes that even animals can be fooled, as by a picture of Apelles: *picturas inductis equis ostendit: Apellis tantum equo adhinnivere, idque et postea semper evenit*.

121. Rüpke 2010; Ando 2010b, 2011b, 2015b; Bremmer 2013; from a cognitive perspective, Pongratz-Leisten and Sonik 2015.

122. On cultural learning, see chapters 7 and 8.

123. For more along these lines, see the dual process account of how religious beliefs arise from intuitions in Baumard and Boyer 2013a.

124. Liv. 5.22.3–8. See Ogilvie 1965: 669–71 for the "threads" drawn together by Livy. See Bremmer 2013: 13 for references to further ancient accounts of this event and brief discussion.

presence of Juno's statue, and making those endorsed, enhanced intuitions acceptable as reflective beliefs to System 2.

Take another example: Seneca's observations about the behavior of his contemporaries at the temples on the Capitol. Some wait on Jupiter, announcing callers, telling him the time, washing and oiling him. Others, standing outside the temples of Juno and Minerva, at a remove from the *simulacra,* imitate the motions of dressing hair. People pray over and discuss legal affairs before the gods. An aged mime performs for them.[125] The gods of Rome intuitively *seemed* present *in* or even *as* their *simulacra,* which were treated accordingly. Such "intuitive seeming" supported the transmission of the cultural practices Seneca describes. No doubt the practices in turn enhanced the "seeming." Intuitions guided cult action, while cult action lent credence to intuitions.

2.6.3. Inference and Agency

Let us turn now to inference. Inference is not as direct as intuition. It is a mental process through which we derive new information from information we already have. It takes givens and extracts from them more or less reflective beliefs. Let's distinguish three inferential processes here: *deductive, inductive,* and *abductive.* (We look at a fourth type, *analogical inference,* which was important in ancient theorizing about religious belief, at sections 6.4 and 6.6.1.) One could say that "inference," as the *product* of one of these three inferential *processes,* is nothing more than a word for *belief* that emphasizes its origin.

In deduction, a conclusion follows directly from premises. Here is the classic example. Major premise: All men are mortal. Minor premise: Socrates is a man. Conclusion: Socrates is mortal. Induction is the less tidy process of generalizing from particulars.[126] The classic example is this: All swans thus far observed are white. Therefore, all swans are white. Here, the conclusion goes beyond the information in the premises and may be wrong. Finally, there is abduction, an explanatory process related to induction and also error prone. Abduction explains a situation, taken as an *effect,* by reasoning to the most plausible hypothesis as to its *cause.*[127]

Cicero provides an example of abduction in a story about Plato. When the philosopher and his companions had been shipwrecked on an island, he rejoiced to notice geometric figures drawn in the sand. He abductively inferred

---

125. Sen. *Superst.* fr. 36 Haase = fr. 69 Vottero = Aug. *Civ.* 6.10. On this passage see especially Corbeill 2004: 27–28.

126. On induction, see Johnson-Laird 2006: 174–84.

127. On abduction, see Johnson-Laird 2006: 185–96.

from these "traces of people," *hominum vestigia*, that he and his friends had landed in a place populated not just by human beings, but by cultured human beings.[128] Cicero takes care to spell out Plato's inference from *hominum vestigia* to civilized inhabitants: the verb is *interpretabatur*, "he concluded." Yet he takes for granted the foundation on which Plato's inference rests, that is, his intuitive recognition—the verb is *videre*—of the geometric figures as artifacts, that is, as *hominum vestigia* rather than spontaneously occurring patterns. Cicero does not linger over Plato's intuition of artifactuality. Instead, he focuses on Plato's abductive inference from this intuition and the resulting reflective belief.

Abductive inference played a large role in Roman religious cognition.[129] We have seen that for Romans, some objects intuitively *seemed* to be animate agents. In addition, like Plato in Cicero's story, Romans could intuit some objects to be *reflections* of agency, that is, "the physical manifestations of an (absent) historical creator's intentional goals."[130] To intuit artifactuality in this way is to "recognize" that an object, a situation, or an event embodies the *purposes* and *purposive action* of an agent. Such intuitive recognition potentiates a chain of powerful inferences. What is the artifact's *function*? What were the designing agent's *intentions*? What *kind of mind* designed such an artifact? What *causal powers* might such a designer possess? As Robert Audi points out, the greater the *causal potential* attributed to a designer, the greater the *explanatory potential* of inferences about design.[131] Thus, artifact cognition has religious implications, because it allows us to see features of the natural world in terms of the intentions and actions of causally powerful gods. Though obviously not biblical creationists, Romans did see divine agency at work, however obscurely, in the natural world.[132]

Take, for example, the case of strange sounds (*strepitus cum fremitu*) heard in the *ager Latiniensis*, a district northeast of Rome.[133] We owe our knowledge of this episode to Cicero's De haruspicum responsis, a speech delivered before

---

128. Cic. *Rep.* 1.29. The story is usually told of Aristippus, not Plato (see the comment of Zetzel 1995 on Cic. *Rep.* 1.29).

129. Boyer 1992a offers arguments for appealing to abduction in the anthropological study of causal reasoning. See Boyer 1994b: 215–19 and 236–42 for abduction in religious cognition.

130. Kelemen et al. 2012: 440. For artifact cognition, i.e., "the design stance," see Dennett 1987: 16–17; Casler and Kelemen 2005; Kelemen and Carey 2007; Kelemen et al. 2012. For the design stance applied to CSR, see Boyer 1998, 2000, 2001.

131. Audi 2016: 21.

132. Consider the functions of *indigitamenta* or "Sondergötter" (Usener 1896): Scheid 2003c and Perfigli 2004.

133. Cic. *Har. Resp.* 20.

the college of pontiffs in which he makes a target of his enemy Clodius.[134] The *haruspices*, or Etruscan diviners, inferred that this *prodigium*—an omen officially accepted for expiation by the state[135]—was caused by profanation of sacred places, sacrifices owed but not given to the gods, and other religious offenses.[136] That is, they assumed that a natural event, the *strepitus*, "noise," was in some sense artifactual and explained it abductively, by appeal to what struck them as its most likely agentive causes, divine responses to human offenses against the gods. Cicero endorses this explanation and further advises seeing an earthquake at Potentia, not yet declared a *prodigium*, as equally portentous.[137]

Agentive explanations foster inferences about the agents implicated. Thus, Cicero's enemy Clodius abductively explained the haruspices' explanation of the *prodigium*. He offered that the offences identified by the haruspices were best explained as religious faults of Cicero. *That* is what the *prodigium* responds to. In his turn, Cicero pointed to the religious crimes of his enemy as the likely causal factor. To explain the haruspical explanation, the profanation of sacred places and so on, one must refer to the behavior of Clodius.[138] *That* is why the gods sent a *prodigium*. Regardless of which man's account best explains the haruspical explanation, note that both agree at a deep level. For both accept that the strepitus is an artifact and thus somehow connected to agents human and divine and to their purposeful activities.

Roman religious cognition thus permits *intuitions* that natural events are artifactual as well as *inferences* positing causal links between natural events and the activities of agents. That the precise causal linkages between agents and events might remain murky only added further inferential potential to the original inferences. For example, recall that the haruspices had cast their explanations of the *prodigium* in terms of *human* offenses against and *human* debts to the gods. Clodius and Cicero follow them in this but add further inferences. Cicero fills out the gods' side of the explanation, asserting that the events also represent *divine* agency and *divine* intentions. For the *strepitus* and the earthquake are clearly epiphanic warnings from the gods, the "voice of

---

134. See Beard 2012 for background and reflections on this speech's participation in religious, political, and other discourses.

135. See MacBain 1982; Rasmussen 2003: 35–116.

136. Cic. *Har. Resp.* 9–10 and 20. See North 2000b: 94 for a reconstruction of the full response of the haruspices.

137. Cic. *Har. Resp.* 62–63.

138. On this episode, see Lenaghan 1969; Tatum 1999; Corbeill 2010; Santangelo 2013: 98–107.

Jupiter," *vox Iovis Optimi Maximi*.[139] If we accept this, he asks, "will the very voice of the immortal gods *not* persuade the minds of all?"[140]

Every one of these is an agential inference about the causes of the strepitus and the earthquake, whose artifactuality was intuited. Other explanations, naturalistic ones for instance, were of course available to the Romans in such cases.[141] We have no record of recourse to a naturalistic explanation in the present case, but we should not ignore the fact that Romans could overdetermine such events as *both* natural *and* agential.[142] Regardless, inferences to agency are uniquely appealing. Agency is the causal mechanism with which we are most intimately familiar, not only third-personally, as a result of seeing others make things happen, but also first-personally, as a result of experiencing ourselves make things happen.[143] Agentive inferences appeal to the social-cognitive mind even as they appeal to the cultural mind practiced in *prodigia*.[144] Intuiting and inferring divine agency in strange events and accepting *prodigia* were thus not effortful cognitive accomplishments for a Roman, in the way of some other cultural feats, such as mastering Stoic theology or learning to read.

As with cult images, here, again, we see that the appeal of a cultural conceptual scheme involving divine agency is predicated on the appeal and naturalness of cognition about agents.[145] The fact that sometimes intuitions and inferences about divine agency were institutionalized in such forms as *prodigia* and their public expiation does not detract from the effortlessness of these cognitions; rather the cognitive ease partly accounts for the institution's success. Indeed, even the groping, murky quality of some such agentive intuitions and inferences could be codified. Writing on the question "to which god sacrifice ought to be made when the earth moves,"[146] Gellius quotes Varro: the pontifices had decreed that for earthquakes, there should be sacrificed "a victim 'to god or goddess' [*si deo, si deae*], since it was uncertain both by what force and

---

139. Cic. *Har. Resp.* 10.

140. Cic. *Har. Resp.* 62: *vox ipsa deorum immortalium non mentis omnium permovebit?* Cf. 63: *etenim haec deorum immortalium vox, haec paene oratio iudicanda est, cum ipse mundus, cum maria atque terrae motu quodam novo contremiscunt et inusitato aliquid sono incredibilique praedicunt.*

141. E.g., Lucr. 6.535–607; Sen. *Q.N.* 6.

142. As suggested at Gell. *N.A.* 2.28.3 (quoted more fully just below): earthquakes occur *et qua vi et per quem deorum dearumve.*

143. Audi 2016: 27–28.

144. See Lisdorf 2004 and Lisdorf 2011 for the role of natural cognition in *prodigia*.

145. Cf. Boyer and Walker 2000: 152: "religious concepts are parasitic on intuitive ontology."

146. Gell. 2.28: *non esse compertum cui deo rem divinam fieri oporteat, cum terra movet.*

through which of the gods or goddesses the earth trembled."[147] The formula *si* (or *sive*) *deus, si* (or *sive*) *dea*, "whether god or goddess," was employed in Roman religious language in cases of certainty as to a god's involvement but uncertainty as to that god's identity.[148]

The fundamental point of this section has been to suggest that from a psychological point of view, intuitions and inferences tend to produce and support reflective as well as nonreflective beliefs, which may undergird more reflective, discursive thinking. These cognitive processes and their products were all deeply relevant to Roman cult. We saw that beliefs arrived at through intuitions of agency or inferences that explain events in terms of agent-causation had a particular appeal, given the proclivities of the social-cognitive mind. These considerations have allowed us to present an argument to the effect that the cognitive appeal of those Roman practices and conceptual schemes that built on, promoted, or institutionalized intuitions and inferences of agency enjoyed cognitive advantages that promoted their cultural longevity and success.[149]

2.7. Conclusion

This chapter introduced the theory of Intentionality, that is, of the mind's capacity to represent its objects. There is one manifestation of Intentionality whose job it is to represent states of affairs as obtaining. "Belief" is the most unmarked English word for this Intentional state. Belief depends for its existence on minded subjects, though it is not something created by such subjects through conceptualization or naming. It exists whether we conceptualize it and name it or not. The name "belief" is thus not a matter of deep ideological significance, but a matter of convention and convenience. It allows us to pick out a basic Intentional state that any subject, Roman or modern, may entertain.

We discussed six logical features and two psychological features of belief. We saw that beliefs may be dispositional or occurrent as well as reflective or nonreflective. We examined the roles of intuition and inference in generating beliefs. All these are features of belief regardless of whether belief turns out to be a spiritual power granted to immaterial souls or a state caused by and

---

147. Gell. 2.28.3: *hostiam "si deo, si deae" immolabant, idque ita ex decreto pontificum observatum esse M. Varro dicit, quoniam et qua vi et per quem deorum dearumve terra tremeret incertum esset.*

148. See Alvar 1985.

149. This is a core argument of CSR. See, e.g., Boyer 1994a, 1996, 1998, 2000, 2001; Boyer and Walker 2000; Boyer and Ramble 2001; Barrett and Nyhof 2001; Barrett 2004a, 2011a, 2011b; McCauley 2011.

realized in a physical brain. Scholars will continue to discover truths such as that, in some usages, "'I believe' encapsulates (and permits) both *my* certainty but also *your* doubt,"[150] as well as any number of other possibilities (e.g., "Oh, believe me!," "I believe in you," "atheists do not believe in God," and "I believe I'll have another beer," just for starters). These pragmatic and semantic potentials of the English lexeme are not logical features of belief qua belief but rather contingent facts about using words. I have tried to clarify the logical properties of that mental state that we call belief in the conviction that only once we have done so can we at last identify and discuss this cognitive phenomenon in Roman religious life.

In the next chapter, we address the place of belief in religious emotion and in cult action. I continue to proceed on the assumption that it is instructive to see the systematic relationships that obtain among belief, other Intentional states, such as desire, and other Intentional episodes, such as emotion and action.

I summarize, and thus oversimplify, this chapter's main lessons about belief:

1. Mental episodes (events, states, acts) require a *subject* to bear them: they are *ontologically subjective* or subject dependent for their existence.
2. *Intentionality* is the *aboutness* or *directedness on objects* of certain mental episodes, which may thus be called "Intentional."
3. Belief is an *Intentional state*. That is, belief is *about* or directed *on* an object or state of affairs, which may be called the belief's (*Intentional*) *object*.
4. A belief's (*Intentional*) *content* is the *perspective* from which, the *way* in which, or the *aspect* under which it represents its Intentional object.
5. The *content* of belief has a propositional structure, but beliefs are not *about* propositions; that is, they do not take propositions as their *objects*.
6. "Belief" names an *attitude toward* or a way of *relating to* an Intentional content. To *believe* is to take an Intentional content *to be the case*.
7. Belief therefore has a *mind-to-world* direction of fit. Belief relates subjects to the world by "fitting" their minds to the way the world *is*. In contrast, Intentional states like desire have a *world-to-mind* direction of fit. Desire relates us to the world by "fitting" the world to how we *want* it to be.

---

150. J. Davies 2011: 406. Cf. Pouillon 1982: 1, endorsed by Giordano-Zecharya 2005: 330n20: to believe "paradoxically expresses both doubt and certainty."

8. Beliefs and desires spell out their own *conditions of satisfaction*. With its mind-to-world direction of fit, a belief is "satisfied" or not when it represents accurately or inaccurately. In contrast, desire's world-to-mind direction of fit entails that it is satisfied or not depending on whether it is fulfilled or not.
9. Belief is *normative*. Intentional states have in their conditions of satisfaction a normative dimension. Belief is constituted *as* belief by the fact that it "aims" at satisfaction, defined as accurate fit between mind and world. Accuracy is belief's natural, internal *norm*. This norm explains why ancient philosophers could debate, criticize, or attempt to salvage religious beliefs.
10. Belief admits of *degrees of intensity*, ranging from low to high. One may hold a belief tentatively, more or less neutrally, or with great conviction.
11. Beliefs range from *nonreflective* to *reflective*. The former arise automatically and effortlessly from System 1's intuitions and inferences. The latter arise when System 2 attends to nonreflective beliefs and from conscious or effortful processes such as instructed learning and deliberation. Reflective beliefs tend to rest on a foundation of intuitive, nonreflective beliefs.
12. Intuitions, inferences, and nonreflective beliefs about agency served to guide Roman thinking and contributed to reflective beliefs about agentive gods as well as about religiously salient events and actions, which could be ascribed to or related to such gods, and to their knowledge, wishes, intentions, and actions.

3

Belief and Emotion, Belief and Action

3.1. Introduction

The previous chapter illustrated the Intentionality of belief. As minded subjects, we are "open to the world,"[1] in a way that mindless beings are not, and thus are able to represent the world and how things stand in it. The mind-to-world Intentionality of perception and of doxastic states such as belief allows us to accommodate ourselves to the world. Conversely, the world-to-mind Intentionality of practical states such as desire and intention allows us to accommodate the world to ourselves.

This chapter builds on the findings of chapter 2 by addressing the way belief informs Roman religious emotion and Roman religious action. We shall see that if we discard belief, then we shall also have to discard emotion and action, for both depend on belief. We must grasp this point if we hope to understand Roman, or indeed any, religion. Section 3.2 examines emotion and the Intentionality of emotion. Emotions were constitutive components of Roman religious psychology and religious action, and they typically owed their very existence to religious beliefs. For one cannot feel anger, joy, or fear *about* a state of affairs unless one *represents* that state of affairs, that is to say, entertains a belief about how things stand in the world.

Section 3.3 addresses action. We shall see that cult action, by all accounts a central feature of Roman religion, depended causally on belief, among other Intentional states. Purposive action results from a conjunction of the two broad types of Intentional state examined at section 2.2.5, the doxastic and the practical. Mind-to-world doxastic states such as belief picture how the world *is*.

---

1. Crane 2006: 134.

World-to-mind practical states picture the world as one *wants* it to *be*, that is, one's *desiderata* and *goals*, or they picture one's *interventions* in the world, one's plans of action, to effect one's goals.

Beyond individual wants and desires, however, *social norms* also served as pervasive and potent motivators to action in the world of Roman cult. The motivational power of any "desire-independent" social norm or of any package of such norms—I call a package of social norms a *deontology* (see section 2.3, above, and section 3.3.2, below)—flows from agents' *beliefs* about the content of the norms and the legitimacy of the obligations the norms impose. Thus, the belief-action dichotomy anatomized in chapter 1 dissolves when we see that no human action, not even action under obligation or other deontic/normative pressure, is causally possible or explanatorily intelligible without reference to belief.

3.2. Belief and Emotion

In the previous chapter, we encountered not only belief, but also fear, reverence, and evaluative attitudes such as trust (one possible kind of "belief-in"). This anticipates and brings us to the considerations I now offer regarding emotions[2] in Roman religion.[3] Since belief is the focus of this book, I emphasize of emotions that they are Intentional episodes that inherit their Intentionality from mind-to-world episodes such as perception, belief, and memory.[4] Where perception is presentational and belief is representational, emotions are *evaluative* of presentations and representations. Emotions, as the ancients

---

2. The emotional turn in classical scholarship is in full flower. Among so many other worthy contributions on emotions in ancient literature and culture, see Braund 1988; Cairns 1993; Braund and Gill 1997; Braund and Most 2003; Kaster 2005; Konstan 2006; Cairns 2008; Fitzgerald 2008; Fögen 2009b; Konstan 2009; R. Caston 2012; Chaniotis 2012; Chaniotis and Ducrey 2013; Fulkerson 2013; Cairns and Fulkerson 2015a; R. Caston and Kaster 2016.

3. For various takes on emotions in Roman religion, see, e.g., Stevenson 1996; Mueller 2002: 17–20; Scheid 2011; Scheid 2016: 113–24. In Greek religion, Chaniotis 2006; Chaniotis 2010; Chaniotis 2011. For reflections on the fate of emotion in scholarship on Roman religion, see Bendlin 2006.

4. Cf. Kaster 2005: 8–9 on the significance of cognition's return to the study of emotion. See further, Nussbaum 2001: 100–125. For an excellent assessment of modern theories of emotion and their relevance to classical scholarship (and vice versa), see Cairns and Fulkerson 2015b.

knew, often *depend on* beliefs (so-called cognitivism about emotion).[5] Beliefs are typically neither incidental nor dispensable to emotion.[6]

The nexus between belief and emotion works both ways: emotions contribute to the formation and fixation of beliefs by disposing us to attend preferentially to and draw inferences from information that is more rather than less emotionally salient. Thus, beliefs and other doxastic states may themselves have affective origins and supports.[7] Some Romans recognized this. Tacitus notes that fear, *metus*, will cause people lost at sea to believe that they have seen all sorts of horrors when in fact they have merely imagined them. Similarly, Livy writes that when people's minds are already moved by religious emotion, they are more apt to lend credence to reports of *prodigia*.[8]

We shall explore these twin contentions regarding belief and emotion in more detail in the next two subsections. As we do, bear in mind that if we open the door to *emotion* in Roman religious life, we must recognize that we are letting *belief* in with it. Conversely, if we insist on closing the door to belief, we must accept that we thereby shut out emotion as well. The overarching question is how much cognitive and affective content we are willing to evacuate from Roman religious life, how willing we are to see Roman cult as, in Mommsen's words, "a painstaking and mindless liturgy."[9]

---

5. For ancient thought on the Intentionality and cognitivism of the emotions, from the Pre-Socratics to Plotinus, see Sorabji 2000: 17–28, and, more expansively, Knuuttila 2004: 5–110. On the cognitivism of the emotions in ancient thought, see Konstan 2006: 3–40. From Aristotle to Seneca, Nussbaum 1994 is seminal; Nussbaum 2001 is "neo-Stoic." Aristotle's emotions: examples, Rhet. 2; in brief, Curran 2016: 184–86; in detail, Fortenbaugh 2002. Stoic emotions: Annas 1992: 103–20; T. Brennan 2005: 49ff.; Graver 2007: 35ff. Epicurean emotions: Annas 1989; Annas 1992: 189–99; Tsouna 2007; Armstrong 2008; Gill 2009; Tsouna 2009; Warren 2009. Cicero on the emotions: Graver 2002.

6. I present here what is essentially a cognitivist appraisal theory of emotion as opposed to a feeling or embodiment theory. Jesse Prinz summarizes the difference thus: "Embodiment theorists think that appraisal judgments often trigger emotions, but aren't essential, and appraisal theorists say that bodily feelings are often triggered by emotions, but aren't essential. One view emphasizes thought, and the other feelings" (2012: 244). This book you are reading emphasizes thought but does not wish to discount feelings.

7. See Harmon-Jones 2000. Frijda et al. 2000: 5: "emotions can awaken, intrude into, and shape beliefs, by creating them, by amplifying or altering them, and by making them resistant to change."

8. Tac. *Ann.* 2.24: *ex metu credita*. Liv. 21.62.1: *quod evenire solet motis semel in religionem animis, multa nuntiata et temere credita sunt*. Cf. Luc. 7.172–73: *dubium, monstrisne deum, nimione pavore crediderint*.

9. Mommsen 1856: 160: "ein peinlicher und geistloser Ceremonialdienst."

3.2.1. What Is Emotion?

Emotions are symptoms of the fact that we are conscious creatures, susceptible to feelings of pain and well-being and also motivated by these feelings. The states of affairs and objects that we perceive and represent appear to us as more or less *relevant* to ourselves, to the people and things we care about, and to our well-being and theirs. Insofar as things appear to us to relate to our well-being, they *matter* to us. Indeed, if things did not matter at all, if they did not have differential value to us, we could scarcely direct our perceptual attention toward one object in preference to another or move our bodies purposely here rather than there.

The point is that we intrinsically *care* about things.[10] From this caring, emotions spring. As Hans Bernard Schmid puts it, "To care about something is to be *afraid* when it is in danger, to *hope* for its escape from danger, to be *relieved* when it is saved, to be *content* when it is well, to be *angry* when it is subject to wrong, and to be *joyful* at its thriving and success."[11] The care or concern at the heart of emotion stretches from the basic bedrock of valuing a sense of well-being to the social heights of caring about, and caring about being *seen* to care about,[12] a cultural convention. Note in passing that here we encounter again the normativity of Intentionality: from the natural norms of basic, organism-preserving emotions all the way up to the purely cultural norms involved in such cases as anxiety over being seen to wear one's toga properly.[13]

To see that *care* or *concern* is at the heart of emotion puts us in a position to see that *emotion* is at the heart of Roman religion, at least in the young Cicero's definition: "*Religio* is that which occasions care [*cura*] for and worship [*caerimonia*] of a certain higher nature, which men call 'divine'"[14] As a matter

---

10. Frijda 1986: 333ff.; and Frijda 2007: 123–52 writes of "concerns" rather than care. Nothing hinges on the difference. I have found the following treatments of emotion especially useful: Frijda 1986; Goldie 2000; Ben-Ze'ev 2000; Nussbaum 2001. For crisp accounts, from both psychological and philosophical perspectives, see Frijda and Mesquita 1998; Goldie 2002; Mulligan and Scherer 2012.

11. Schmid 2017: 154. Cf. Mulligan and Scherer 2012: 349: "it is not controversial to claim that emotions and emotional attitudes have an especially intimate link to values and goods."

12. Cf. Kaster 2005: 28–29 on *pudor*: "All experiences of pudor depend upon notions of personal worthiness (*dignitas*) and value (*existimatio*), which in turn derive from seeing my self being seen in creditable terms."

13. A social anxiety Juvenal attempts to make Creticus feel at Sat. 2.65ff.

14. Cic. *Inv.* 2.161: *religio est, quae superioris cuiusdam naturae, quam divinam vocant, curam caerimoniamque affert.* Cf. 2.66, where Cicero uses *metus* instead of *cura*.

of *cura* and *caerimonia*—that is, attitudes and acts (both are implied) of concern and worship—Roman cult was constituted and motivated by god-directed human emotion. We shall return to Cicero's definition in the following section as well as to the motivational role of emotions in action, including cult action.

In what follows, I want to draw attention to five features of emotion. Emotion is (1) an affective episode that is experienced by a subject, involving (2a) mind-to-world Intentionality, that is, presentations or representations of states of affairs, as well as (2b) world-to-mind—that is, practical or motivational—Intentionality. Emotion is caused by (3) an appraisal of (re)presentations. Emotion results in (4) action or tendencies to act as well as (5) bodily feeling.

We can thus understand emotion in terms familiar from our analysis of the Intentionality of belief in section 2.2. An emotion is characterized by at least one affective episode, experienced by a subject, which has a determinate duration, ranging from moments to years.[15] Emotion features mind-to-world Intentionality.[16] This means emotion has an *Intentional object*, or is *about* something, beyond its own raw feel. One does not typically experience undirected reverence or free-floating fear, but rather reverence or fear *about, at, for*, or *of* some object, person, state of affairs, event, or the like. This is not to say that we do not have *moods*, such as generalized anxiety, with rather less specific objects than *emotions* like acute fear. It is merely to say that even our moods have Intentionality. They are *about* something, "even if the best available description . . . is 'everything,' or 'nothing in particular.'"[17]

The *Intentional content* of emotion, that is, the perspective from which or the aspect under which its object is presented, is "inherited" from the Intentional content of sensory perception, anticipation, memory, belief, and other doxastic states.[18] This is to say, the Intentional content of emotion embodies the perspectival presentations or representations of mind-to-world cognitions, including, most importantly for our purposes, beliefs.[19] As Martha Nussbaum puts it: "beliefs are essential to the identity of the emotion."[20]

---

15. See Goldie 2000: 12–16.
16. Cf. Goldie 2000: 16–28; Ben-Ze'ev 2000: 49–52; Nussbaum 2001: 27; Mulligan and Scherer 2012: 346–48.
17. Goldie 2000: 143, and cf. 17–18 and 141ff.
18. Mulligan and Scherer 2012: 348.
19. Mulligan and Scherer 2012: 346–48; Nussbaum 2001: 27–30; Ben-Ze'ev 2000: 52–56; Goldie 2000: 20–28, with acute remarks about "over-intellectualization" of the emotions; cf. Salmela 2014a: 15–43 on conceptual and nonconceptual content of emotions.
20. Nussbaum 2001: 29.

In this, Nussbaum echoes the ancient Stoics. Cicero, for example, presents a Stoic theory of emotion in *Tusculan Disputations* thus (3.24): "The entire cause, not only of distress but also of all the remaining emotions, is in belief" (*est igitur causa omnis in opinione, nec vero aegritudinis solum, sed etiam reliquarum omnium perturbationum*). The belief in question is that a thing is either good or bad, *aut boni aut mali*. When we believe that a thing is bad for us and for what we care about, this belief gives rise to negative emotions, like sorrow and fear. When we believe that it is good for us and for the objects of our concern, it gives rise to emotions like longing and exhilaration. (Neither of these two sets of emotions is, on Stoic theory, conducive to peace of mind.)[21] Thus, on both ancient Stoic and modern cognitivist theories, one's fear may be caused by the belief that one is in danger, one's anger by the belief that one has been wronged, and so on. If the content of the belief changes (e.g., *I am not in danger*), the emotion changes.

As the foregoing already suggests, an emotional episode is *triggered* or *caused* by our appraising or evaluating the significance, for ourselves and for people and things we care about, of the Intentional contents of our perceptions, beliefs, and other cognitions.[22] "Emotions ... are *value-suffused*."[23] If Julia cares about her life, her "valuing"[24] of her perception that her ship is sinking will likely result in or amount to *fear*. The cognitive content of her perception together with her appraisal or valuing of that content constitute her fear. No part of this process need be any more intellectual than her "gut reaction"[25] or "embodied appraisal,"[26] based on her intuitive sense of what matters. Appraisal is sometimes misconstrued as a slow, deliberative process, but, in fact, it ranges "from completely automatic unconscious processing to

---

21. There is much more to the theory Cicero presents: see further Cic. *Tusc.* 3.52–62 with the commentary of Graver 2002. See also the theory of emotion presented in Sen. *Ira* 2.1.3–2.2 and Sen. *Ep.* 113.18.

22. Nussbaum 2001: 30–33; Mulligan and Scherer 2012: 348–52, esp. 351; Ben-Ze'ev 2000: 56–59. See Salmela 2014a: 45–74 for more detailed discussion.

23. Nussbaum 2001: 130.

24. An alternative to "appraisal" suggested by Mulligan and Scherer 2012: 349.

25. Prinz 2004b.

26. For "embodied appraisal" theory, see Prinz 2004b: 52–78 and 2004a: 57: "Let us define an appraisal ... as any representation of an organism-environment relation that bears on well-being. Evaluative judgments can serve as appraisals, but they are not alone. If a nonjudgmental state represents an organism-environment relation that bears on well-being, it too will count as an appraisal on this definition.... Certain bodily perceptions ... represent roughly the same thing that explicit evaluative judgments represent, but they do it by figuring into the right causal relations, not by deploying concepts or providing descriptions."

highly effortful representational or propositional inferences."[27] That is, emotion can arise out of the autonomous System 1 or deliberative System 2 cognitions that we examined at section 2.6.1.

Although this book seeks to emphasize the role of belief in emotion, it is nonetheless important to understand the point that emotions *can* arise as gut reactions, from an automatic, unconscious processing of stimuli that one hesitates to call belief. Take the example of skin-conductance responses in subjects conditioned to fear certain images. Their fear-response persists even when the image is masked beyond conscious recognition.[28] The point is not that there is no Intentionality at play here or that this is "pure," physiological emotion, untethered from cognitive content and its appraisal. Rather, there is still mind-to-world perceptual Intentionality, even when subjects are not consciously aware of the image. Their minds are appraising a perceptual content that is registering below the level of conscious awareness and that may be in principle inaccessible to consciousness. In other words, it is possible that these subjects could not "see" the image if they wanted to, yet it is still registering with unconscious cognitive processes and triggering an appraisal. This account may be extended to emotions that have dispositional beliefs, beliefs not occurrently present to consciousness, at their base. That is, some emotions may arise not from perceptions of which we are not consciously aware, but from beliefs of which we are not consciously aware.

We must note that the same Intentional *object*—whether the object of a perception or of a (reflective or nonreflective) belief—may be viewed under different aspects (as Intentional *content*) and thus inspire quite different appraisals. Take a simple perceptual example. A glimpse of the dog in a *cave canem* mosaic, as in the vestibule of the House of the Tragic Poet at Pompeii, might elicit *reassurance* in the residents (that represents our protective dog), *hesitation* in a thief (that is a warning about a guard dog), or *terror* in the impressionable, such as Encolpius in the *Satyricon*, the content of whose perception was: *a dog!*[29] Thus, a single Intentional object (the same depiction of a dog), presented or represented under differing aspects (a depiction of our dog, a guard dog, or a dog!), may elicit quite differing emotions.

Encolpius's response to the mosaic—he falls over backward—exemplifies comically the "action readiness" or "action tendencies" that emotions arouse, that is, their world-to-mind motivational element.[30] Encolpius's fear readied

---

27. Mulligan and Scherer 2012: 352. Cf. Frijda and Mesquita 1998: 281–83.

28. Öhman 2000.

29. Petr. *Sat.* 29, and cf. 72: *ego . . . qui etiam pictum timueram canem.*

30. Frijda 1986: 69–93; Frijda 2007: 26–46; Ben-Ze'ev 2000: 60–64. Cf. Nussbaum 2001: 129–37; Goldie 2000: 28–49. For a neuroscientific view of emotion's role in behavior holistically, see Damasio 1994.

him to act in order to avoid danger, and he acted, or reacted, immediately and spontaneously. The terminology of action "readiness" or action "tendency" signifies not only that emotions may be motivational and practical—they may involve *ends*, such as avoiding danger—but also that a given emotion need not mechanically produce a given action. Fear need not result in falling over or in any action at all, but fear does *prepare* us to act or to form intentions to act in ways appropriate to our concerns. Not all emotion-driven action need rise to the level of acting on an intention toward a goal. One may feel relief and joy, like Innocentius, whose tribulations we witnessed at section 1.4, and the corresponding action may be nothing more than bodily *expression* of the emotion. Innocentius cried tears of joy (*lacrimantia gaudia*), an uncontrollable outward manifestation of feeling.

Note that Innocentius expressed his joy not only through the involuntary bodily response of weeping, but also purposely and discursively, through prayer. This suggests that while some of the actions for which emotions provide tendencies might be biological primitives such as weeping, fight, and flight, others may be culturally learned. For presumably Innocentius had to *learn* to offer prayer to God as a response to the joy of relief. And yet even basic responses like weeping will have cultural elaborations, as we shall now see. Indeed, learned, cultural elaborations are certainly part and parcel of the Stoic theory of emotions that Cicero presents. We saw that on his theory, emotion results from the evaluative belief that a thing is *good* or *bad* for us. He goes on, using the example of distress for purposes of illustration (*Tusc.* 3.61–63):

> sed ad hanc opinionem magni mali cum illa etiam opinio accessit oportere, rectum esse, ad offĭcium pertinere, ferre illud aegre quod acciderit, tum denique efficitur illa gravis aegritudinis perturbatio. [62] ex hac opinione sunt illa varia et detestabilia genera lugendi: paedores, muliebres lacerationes genarum, pectoris feminum capitis percussiones.... [63] sed haec omnia faciunt opinantes ita fieri oportere.

> But when to this first belief (*opinio*) in a great evil a second belief (*opinio*) is added that it is proper, that it is right, that it is a suitable thing to do, to be aggrieved by what has happened, then and only then does the oppressive emotion of distress come into being. [62] Out of this latter belief arise various revolting forms of mourning: covering oneself with filth, womanly lacerations of the cheeks, beating the chest, thighs, and head.... [63] But people do all these things believing that it is proper that they behave thus.

On Cicero's theory, emotions and their concomitant behaviors require the conjunction of two beliefs: an evaluative belief that a given thing is good or bad coupled with a normative belief that one ought to respond to this value judgment in a certain prescribed way. This response, in turn, has two components: first, one ought to *feel* the relevant emotion ("to be aggrieved") and second, one ought to *act out* ("various revolting forms of mourning").

Cicero's Stoic theory holds that these second, normative beliefs are learned and so can be unlearned. That is, we can learn not only to give up the cultural practice of lacerating our cheeks in grief, but also to stop *grieving*. Here, I would not seek to draw a sharp line between purely "natural" and universal responses, such as weeping, and purely "learned" or "culturally specific" responses, such as praying. It seems clear that covering oneself in filth and tearing at one's own cheeks are "cultural" responses to grief, though they probably rest on and are supported by biological predispositions. This is not a question we need to answer to see the important point: the modern doctrine of emotion's "action tendencies" has a rough counterpart in the ancient theory that full-blown emotion requires beliefs about the appropriate behavioral *response* to our evaluative beliefs.

The final, but scarcely least important, feature of emotion is that it is embodied or somatically *felt*: it has a phenomenology.[31] Innocentius felt his joy, and Encolpius his fear, bodily. The latter was still catching his breath (*collecto spiritu*) even after he'd revised his initial impression of the dog and settled on the belief that it was mere depiction, thus allowing his fear to pass. But, crucially, emotion is not *mere* phenomenology. Subtract appraisal of a content, and subtract the content itself (whether it is delivered by perception, belief, or some other cognition), and we are left with a raw *feel* that tells us nothing about what matters to us, that has no object and no perspective on the world, and that fails to dispose us to act in any particular way, "a mere seizure of mind and body that is *about* nothing at all."[32]

In summary, an emotion may be defined as an affective episode borne and experienced by a subject, characterized by both mind-to-world and world-to-mind Intentionality, arising upon appraisal of a state of affairs, and resulting in a tendency to act as well as a distinctive bodily feeling.

3.2.2. Belief and Emotion in Apuleius and Livy

We may render the foregoing abstract considerations more concrete by briefly recurring to our examples from Apuleius and Livy from section 2.5. In Apuleius's *Metamorphoses*, 11.13, a throng of Isiac worshippers *perceived* Lucius transformed from ass to man. They *believed* that this transformation was accomplished by Isis. And they *appraised* this transformation and Isis's power as

---

31. Explored in Goldie 2000: 50–83; Nussbaum 2001: 56–67. Cf. Ben-Ze'ev 2000: 64–67; Mulligan and Scherer 2012: 346–48, 353–55.

32. Kaster 2005: 8, emphasis in the original.

good. Emotions of awe and reverence resulted. In turn, the *inreligiosi*, "nonbelievers," were expected to feel both awe and admonishment and to confess Isis's power on the basis of the perceptual evidence of Lucius's metamorphosis. As a priest of Isis declares, "Let the nonbelievers behold, let them behold and recognize their error!"[33] In this episode, religious beliefs cause religious emotions, and the emotions, in turn, contribute to the formation and fixation of religious beliefs.

Recall Livy's presentation of the psychological effects of *prodigia* and other distressing events. Early in the Second Punic War, things are not going well for Rome. Livy describes the situation in the city (21.62.1):

> *Romae aut circa urbem multa ea hieme prodigia facta aut, quod evenire solet motis semel in religionem animis, multa nuntiata et temere credita sunt.*
>
> During this winter, at Rome or in the vicinity many *prodigia* occurred or, what typically happens once minds have been stirred with religious concern, many *prodigia* were announced and rashly believed.

The *prodigia* included an infant shouting "Triumphe!" in a public place, a rain of stones, and several other bizarre occurrences (21.62.2–5). In such circumstances, the people's belief that *prodigia* have occurred and their appraisal of that situation elicit an emotion that Livy captures with the term *religio* (21.62.1).[34] Recalling Cicero's definition from section 3.2.1, above, we may gloss *religio* as a religious emotion of care or concern (*cura*) that carries an "action tendency" to perform cult (*caerimonia*). Alternatively, we might speak of the "second belief" from Cicero's theory of the emotions, that is, the learned, normative belief that has us respond to emotion in prescribed ways. Here, the prescribed behavior in response to the religious *cura*, "concern," is cult action, *caerimonia*. Thus, Livy's Romans are gripped by religious *cura* as a result of their appraisal of certain events (Intentional objects), which they represent under the aspect of *prodigia* (Intentional content). (Indeed, merely to represent an event as a *prodigium* amounts to appraising it, for a *prodigium* is by definition concerning.)[35] This emotion of religious *cura*, triggered by appraisal,

---

33. Apul. *Met.* 11.15 (priest of Isis speaking): *videant inreligiosi, videant et errorem suum recognoscant.*

34. For the role of culture-specific beliefs, such as beliefs about *prodigia*, in generating culture-specific emotions, such as *religio*, see the principles laid out in Mesquita and Ellsworth 2001. Cf. De Leersnyder et al. 2015.

35. For the senate's process for accepting certain reported events as *prodigia*, thereby in effect publicly appraising them with a negative religious valence, see Linderski 1993: 58. See Satterfield 2012 for an important reassessment of the timing and relative chronology of the stages of the process.

motivates them to cult action. Thus, the content of the people's belief, as well as their evaluation of that content's significance, produce and together constitute the emotion that Livy calls *religio*. This *religio* then motivates religious action.

The interplay of belief and emotion in this and many similar Livian episodes is subtle. The Roman people come to *believe* that certain events count as *prodigia*, a religious category that they antecedently *believed* to signal a need to secure the *pax deum*.[36] The role of the people's beliefs about *prodigia* in eliciting from them the emotion of *religio* and the reciprocal role of *religio* in promoting their belief in *prodigia* are both on display here. For it was because their minds were already disposed by *religio* to form beliefs about *prodigia* (their minds were already "moved *in religionem*") that they "rashly" (*temere*) came to believe in these particular prodigies in the first place (21.62.1). Note the emotion-belief / belief-emotion feedback loop Livy describes here. The emotion of *religio* produces a disposition to form certain sorts of beliefs, here, beliefs about *prodigia*; these beliefs about *prodigia* then play a part in eliciting more *religio*.

Religio motivates *caerimonia* in this episode, and it is through *caerimonia* that the Romans achieve relief from *religio*. Livy's formula to describe successful cult's psychological effect is *animos* (or *mentes*) *religione levare* (or *liberare*), "relieve minds of religious care" (21.62.11).[37] This relief depends, like *religio* itself, on preexisting beliefs about the efficacy of cult as well as on the Romans' appraisal of the relevance to their current religious concerns of the cult that they actually perform. In other words, what the Romans believe about the cult that they perform causes cult's psychological effects; here, relief. This passage, then, presents a kind of "script"[38] for the unfolding of an entire collective cognitive-affective-behavioral episode composed of causally interconnected beliefs, emotions, and actions.

Thus, we see that the Romans' religious emotions, whether of religious awe and veneration, as in Apuleius, or of religious anxiety and religious relief, as in Livy, depended on their religious beliefs—what they took to be the case—and their evaluations—how they valued what they took to be the case. Note, incidentally, that ancient philosophical therapy operated on precisely the foregoing assumptions: remove vain or empty religious beliefs, and vain or empty religious emotions, such as fear, vanish, too.[39] Conversely, Roman emotions

---

36. Prodigies did not, as often supposed, signal "breaches" in the *pax deum*: see Satterfield 2015.

37. See, e.g., Liv. 7.3.1, 25.1.11, 27.37.5.

38. In the sense of Kaster 2005: 7–9 passim with references at 151n17.

39. For ancient *therapeia* generally, see Nussbaum 1994; Sorabji 2000. For Epicurean therapy generally, see Tsouna 2007: 74ff.; Tsouna 2009; religious fear in particular: Warren 2009;

could help generate and fix religious beliefs in place by giving a "numinous" valence to circumstances that might otherwise either go relatively unremarked or be susceptible to nonreligious, naturalistic explanations.

"Emotions are not *just* features of language and culture; but among all the other things they are or may be, they are features of language and culture *as well*."[40] The emotions we saw on display in Apuleius, while generically of the awe family, possessed irreducibly *cultural* and distinctively *religious* features. The awe was culturally conditioned by the ancient belief in "miracles" as epiphanic, that is, as manifestations of the divine. In chapter 7 we shall ask how, from an ontogenetic perspective, young Romans might have acquired such beliefs and how they might have come to invest them with emotional valence.[41] We shall see that the young of *Homo sapiens* can become socialized and enculturated only if they enter the world with some primitive capacities that are not themselves owed to socialization and enculturation. Such capacities include sensitivity to the beliefs, normative attitudes, and emotional responses of others, as well as a disposition to learn from others and adopt their attitudes and emotional responses.

As we close this section, we point the way forward. We have seen that emotions are *Intentional* (they are *about* something), *evaluative* (they include *appraisals* of what they are about), and *motivational* (they ready us for or inspire action). In the following section, we explore further the etiology of action, focusing primarily on the causal roles of belief, desire, and especially intention. Finally, our examples from Apuleius and Livy illustrated that beliefs and emotions may have a *collective* dimension. Chapter 4 will offer an account of such collective forms of Intentionality.

3.3. Belief and Action

We turn now to the theory of action. We shall see that modern action theory, like modern theories of Intentionality and of emotion, is built on ancient foundations.[42] We surveyed, in chapter 1, a dichotomy between belief and action that for centuries has informed scholarship on the religions of antiquity. Here,

---

Hankinson 2013; Mackey 2021. For the rather different Stoic approach to traditional religion, see Algra 2009. For Stoics and Epicureans compared vis-à-vis traditional religion, see Algra 2007.

40. Cairns and Fulkerson 2015b: 6, emphasis in the original.

41. See the highly relevant discussion of the "education of the emotions," i.e., the way we can learn or be taught evaluative attitudes toward things, in Goldie 2000: 28–37 and 106ff.

42. Anscombe 1957 and Davidson 1963, both taking Aristotle as a point of reference, are seminal. Cf. Davidson 2005.

I propose to dissolve that dichotomy by offering reasons to suppose that human action is causally impossible and explanatorily unintelligible without reference to belief.

We shall see that when Romans engaged in religious action, they were guided by their *beliefs* and motivated by their emotions and desires. The right beliefs coupled with the right emotions or desires contribute to the formation of *intentions*, the central action-causing practical state (see section 2.2.4). However, even more than emotion and desire, I emphasize here, in section 3.3.2, the motivating role in Roman cult of *norms*. Norms, from codified legal norms to unwritten social norms, provided reasons for action and contributed to the formation of intentions in ways that could be (but needed not be) independent of desire and emotion. I call these "desire-independent reasons for action" *normative* or more often *deontic* reasons.[43] (If a deontology is, for our purposes, a package of norms or a set of *musts, mays, must nots*, and *may nots*, "deontic" is the corresponding adjective, meaning "pertaining to such norms, musts, must nots, etc.")

My central contention is this: for a Roman to have deontic reasons to engage in cult, he or she must have beliefs. For in order to have deontic reasons to act, agents must *believe*, reflectively or not, that they are subject to certain restrictions on, entitlements to, or obligations to action. I call agents' beliefs about the normative claims on them—about, that is, what *may, ought*, or *ought not* be done—"deontic beliefs." The upshot, we shall see, is that purposeful cult action in ancient Rome is always attributable to the conjunction of an agent's beliefs and practical states. An appreciation of the relationships among beliefs, norms, the deontic reasons for action that norms provide, and practical states such as desire and intention will allow us to assess more accurately belief's place in the cognitive ecology of Roman cult.

Now, in speaking of purposive action we are dealing with *agency*. Agency remains undertheorized among historians of Greco-Roman religions.[44] A recent account of agency in Roman religion attempts to remedy this by drawing on sociological theory.[45] On the proposed account, *agency* amounts to "subjectively significant action, which has to be comprehended in the light of socially produced meaning," while *action* "means, above all, acting in order to solve problems." People act and exercise agency when confronted with

---

43. I borrow the term "desire-independent reasons for action" from Searle 2001: 167–213 and Searle 2010: 9.

44. Exceptions include Katajala-Peltomaa and Vuolanto 2011; and Vuolanto 2016. The latter provides an account of agency consonant with and complementary to what I offer here.

45. All quotations from Rüpke 2015: 351, which draws in part on Emirbayer and Mische 1998.

"situations which simply cannot be treated in preconceived ways and be addressed by employing and referencing established strategies and meanings." Under such conditions, an "agent can develop new solutions and can be creative." Moreover, agency is "something created through communication."[46]

On the proposed account, agency is a matter of subjective significance, social meaning, problem solving, creativity, and communication. These are all excellent suggestions. And yet the account is incomplete, for it presupposes the very phenomenon it purports to define or explain. For example, to begin with a notion of agency as "subjectively significant action" in the context of "socially produced meaning" is to start on the top floor, as it were, of the structure of agency, rather than at the foundation. That is, a subject must first of all be able to act purposely, and groups of subjects must somehow be able to act purposely together, before we ascend to a level where we encounter the subjective significance let alone wider social meaning of action. Likewise, "solving problems" already assumes agency, because "problems" arise only for agents with goals, plans, projects, and concerns. Finally, to see agency as created through communication is to put the cart before the horse.[47] For even the simplest modes of communication beyond reflexive signaling (such as blushing) require complex agential capacities for initiating one's own and comprehending others' purposive action.[48]

A second difficulty in this account is that it restricts the scope of agency and action so narrowly as to impede our understanding of ancient materials. Why should action be primarily a matter of "solving problems"? Surely, a great deal of what the Romans did as religious agents had nothing to do with problem solving, for example, celebrating the Caristia.[49] Moreover, why should developing "new solutions" and being "creative" count as exercising agency, but not acting in accord with "preconceived ways" and "established strategies"? Is religious action that is "preconceived" and "established," that is to say, traditional, not also purposive and hence agential? We risk denying the agency in a lot of Roman religious action on this theory, because after all, for the Romans, the supposedly traditional, unchanging nature of cult was itself a part

---

46. The account only becomes more perplexing, e.g., "It is not the individual who 'has' agency, but in dealing with the structural context in a given situation the individual acts agentically."

47. Agency may of course be, e.g., conferred on one person by another through communication and indeed new forms of agency, new social functions, such as that of pontifex, may be created through performative rituals and speech acts (see chapters 5 and 9): this is likely what Rüpke 2015: 355 refers to.

48. Signaling vs. communication: Tomasello 2008: 13–55.

49. For the sources describing this festival, see Scullard 1981: 75–76.

of cult's subjective significance and social meaning. Indeed, in some circumstances, traditional action along "established" and "preconceived" lines might amount to a veritable *assertion* of agency, as when C. Fabius Dorsuo defied the Gauls besieging the Capitol in order to perform his family's annual cult on the Quirinal.[50]

As with belief, if we are to understand agency we must start not with the phenomenon's most complex expressions—filigreed theological doctrines in the case of belief, subjectively significant action in contexts of communication and social meaning production in the case of agency—but with the biologically basic foundations on which these cultural expressions rest.[51] Subjective significance, social meaning, problem solving, creativity, communication: all of these are indeed crucial issues for historians to contend with. But before we can begin to do so, we require the rudiments of a theory as to what agency is, most basically. We need to know how and why agents act at all.

Cicero offers just such a starting point.[52] An agent is anything that moves "by an internal impulse of its own," *motu interno et suo* (*Rep.* 6.28). On this view, entry-level agency amounts to an entity's capacity to initiate its own motion. Entities without such capacity have no agency. However, here a concern immediately arises, to wit, "If everything done by any person is categorized by 'agency,' the category becomes vacuous and devoid of analytical importance."[53] True enough, and yet not everything "done" by a person falls under the category of agency. One may digest food or sweat but these are not agential doings.[54] Neither is Encolpius's terrified backward tumble, seen in section 3.2.1, above; nor, perhaps more surprisingly, is having intuitions or acquiring automatic, nonreflective beliefs, as examined at section 2.6. We have seen Innocentius weep, first for sorrow, then for joy (section 1.4). He "did" these things, but neither doing reflects any agency on his part. In contrast, his desperate praying in the pit of sorrow and his thanksgiving at the height of joy *do* attest his agency, his purposeful responses to his changing circumstances.

Thus, much Roman religious experience would have been nonagential: sensing a *numen* in a grove,[55] being overcome by *religio* because of the *res publica*'s misfortune, as in Livy, or feeling awe at the manifest power of a goddess, as in Apuleius. All these things are "done," accomplished, or caused by

---

50. Liv. 5.46.1–4.

51. See Burge 2010: 326–41 for an account of biologically more and less primitive modes of agency.

52. As we saw in the introduction, at section 0.3.

53. Vuolanto 2016: 15.

54. The reflections on agency here follow Burge 2010: 326–41.

55. Sen. *Ep.* 41.3, discussed in the introduction, at section 0.2; cf., e.g., Quint. *Inst.* 10.1.88.

autonomous subsystems in a subject's body and mind, not by his or her exercise of agency. They are psychological *events*, not purposive *actions*. So, not everything done, and certainly not everything undergone, by any person is to be categorized as an exercise of agency, but only those things the person does purposely, however reflective or unreflective his or her intentions. Here we explore this agential class of "things done," that is, purposive, *intentional action*. Only when we become clear about the nature of purposive action, and especially belief's role in it, will we be equipped to analyze historical episodes of agency involving social meaning and the rest.

3.3.1. A Simple Belief-Desire Model of Action

Let us turn, then, to one of Cicero's more detailed reflections on agency as an avenue into our argument. Presenting a Stoic theory of *oikeiōsis*,[56] Cicero begins from the intuition that nature grants to all animate beings self-concern and the agential capacity to avoid what harms and to seek what promotes their well-being. This agency is graded by cognitive complexity. Beasts have only immediate sensory perceptions, while humans are capable of past- and future-oriented cognitions. This difference in beast and *homo* cognition entails a consequential difference between bestial and human action (*Off.* 1.11):

> sed inter hominem et beluam hoc maxime interest, quod haec tantum, quantum sensu movetur, ad id solum, quod adest quodque praesens est se accommodat, paulum admodum sentiens praeteritum aut futurum. homo autem, quod rationis est particeps, per quam consequentia cernit, causas rerum videt ... rebusque praesentibus adiungit atque adnectit futuras, facile totius vitae cursum videt ad eamque degendam praeparat res necessarias.

> But between human being and beast this is the main difference: that the beast adapts itself, insofar as it is moved by sense-perception, only to what is present and in front of it, with very little sense of the past or the future. But the human being—because he partakes of reason, through which he recognizes consequences, sees the causes of events ..., and joins and connects future affairs to present ones—easily visualizes the course of his entire life and prepares the necessities for living it out.

I draw attention here to the relationship between cognition and action envisioned by Cicero. Animals act out of self-concern, but only on the basis of their immediate perceptions. They recall and anticipate very little. Human beings,

---

56. As so often, in various versions: cf. Cic. *Fin.* 2.45, 3.16–71, 5.24–74. On Cic. *Off.* 1.11, see Dyck 1996: 83–90.

however, possess *ratio*, a suite of cognitive endowments that permits recollection and reasoning about the past as well as anticipation of the future. We are, so to speak, "autobiographic agents,"[57] able to represent our past in memories, our present in perception and belief, and our future in desires and intentions. These cognitions, coupled with the motivations provided by our self-concern, shape the arc of actions that structures our agentive lives.

Since our focus is on belief, let us begin with belief in fleshing out our broadly Ciceronian picture. Beliefs, as representations of states of affairs that are taken to obtain, "have *actual and potential consequences*"[58] for action. To take a mundane example, if I believe it is about to rain, I may grab my umbrella, or run outside naked, or stay indoors, or inspect my compluvium, or cancel a picnic, or any of an infinite number of actions. A given belief has no particular consequence necessarily associated with it. Rather, a belief's contribution to action depends first of all on our desires,[59] which relate to our concern for our own well-being. Our beliefs and desires give us *reasons* to act. So, given my belief about the rain, I may take my umbrella if I wish to stay dry or I may run outside naked if I wish to get wet. If asked why I have my umbrella, I appeal to my beliefs and desires as reasons: *because it is raining and I want to stay dry.*

A belief-desire picture of action akin to this had already been proposed by Aristotle. The Stagirite allowed beasts greater cognitive power than Cicero would do, but the former's theory surely lies behind the latter's Stoicizing connection of cognition and action.[60] In *De motu animalium*, Aristotle presents his action theory (*M.A.* 700b15–16):

πάντα γὰρ τὰ ζῷα καὶ κινεῖ καὶ κινεῖται ἕνεκά τινος, ὥστε τοῦτ' ἔστιν αὐτοῖς πάσης τῆς κινήσεως πέρας, τὸ οὗ ἕνεκα.

All living beings both move and are moved for the sake of something, so that this is the end of all their movement, that-for-the-sake-of-which.

Living things act toward goals. So, for Aristotle, to explain their behavior is to give a teleological account of their movements. Explanatory as opposed to descriptive accounts attempt to determine the ends toward which action is directed, ends that arise from both practical and doxastic episodes in an agent's psychology (*M.A.* 700b17–19):

---

57. Dautenhahn and Nehaniv 2002: 7.
58. Crane 2001a: 104, emphasis in the original.
59. Crane 2001a: 105, emphasis in the original: "The consequences of a belief are its consequences *given* other states of mind, especially desires."
60. For the influence of Aristotle in Stoic action theory, see, e.g., Inwood 1985: 9–17.

ὁρῶμεν δὲ τὰ κινοῦντα τὸ ζῷον διάνοιαν καὶ φαντασίαν καὶ προαίρεςιν καὶ
βούληςιν καὶ ἐπιθυμίαν. ταῦτα δὲ πάντα ἀνάγεται εἰς νοῦν καὶ ὄρεξιν.

We see that what moves the living being are its thinking and representation
and choice and wish and appetite. And all of these reduce to thought and
desire.

Thought and desire move agents. Thought represents for the agent the space
of possible action, while desire represents his or her destinations within that
space. Another way to say this is that agents act on their volitions in light of
their cognitions. Thus, the causes of action are desires that represent goals and
thoughts that represent states of affairs relevant to those goals. In short, action
is goal directed or teleological.

Aristotle expounds the logic of action syllogistically. In various places, he
offers versions of his "practical syllogism," modeled on the theoretical syllogism.[61] Purposive action (πρᾶξιc) is the conclusion that follows from a major
premise, conceived as a desire (ὄρεξιc), combined with a minor premise, conceived as a sensory perception, or a thought or belief (νοῦc, νόηcιc, ἔννοια).
Thus, the desire to drink may be represented linguistically as the major premise, *I must drink*, and the belief or thought may be represented as the minor
premise, *This thing is a drink*. The action of drinking follows immediately
(εὐθύc).[62] Thus, for Aristotle, the conjunction of appropriate practical and
doxastic states causes and hence explains purposive action. Most significant
for our purposes, *given* an underlying practical attitude such as desire, the
occurrence of relevant information via sensory perception or doxastic representation activates the desire (ἡ τῆc ὀρέξεωc ... ἐνέργεια) and thus triggers
appropriate action.[63]

There are all sorts of details and qualifications to Aristotle's picture of teleological action that we must perforce ignore here.[64] Yet I hope that this backward glance, through Cicero to Aristotle, has shown that the ancients could
posit causal connections, not a dichotomy, between belief and action. For
Aristotle's νοῦc, νόηcιc, and ἔννοια encompass, among other doxastic cognitions, "belief," that is, a mental representation of an existing state of affairs.
Beliefs, when relevant to an agent's concerns and desires, may play a causal role

---

61. Arist. *M.A.* 701a–702a; *de An.* 433a–b, *E.N.* 1147a–b.

62. Arist. *M.A.* 701a32–33.

63. Arist. *M.A.* 701a30–36. Belief-desire conjunctions result in action "unless something
hinders or compels the agent" (ἂν μή τι κωλύῃ ἢ ἀναγκάζῃ, *M.A.* 701a16). Cf. Nussbaum 1978:
184–210, esp. 187 and 205.

64. For Aristotle's theory of action in *De motu animalium*, see Nussbaum 1978. For a holistic
account of action in Aristotle, see Reeve 2012: 130–94.

in generating action. We shall see, in chapter 6, that Lucretius, too, promoted a theory of action based on belief and desire, and he applied it to Roman cult action. But now we must turn to deontology's contribution to action.

3.3.2. Deontology: Desire-Independent Reasons for Action

We have been speaking of desires as motivators of action. We saw that desires, coupled with beliefs, give agents *reasons* to act. When asked why they acted as they did, agents may cite their desires and beliefs as their reasons. But, of course, agents do not or cannot always act on all their desires.[65] We are doomed to see most of our desires go unsatisfied. For the Intentional contents of a desire may picture the irrevocable past or represent non-existent or unattainable states of affairs. But even given a satisfiable desire as well as information—perceptions, beliefs, and so on—relevant to its satisfaction, an agent may decline to act. External constraints may exert pressure. Some such constraints may be quite coercive. Roman slaves, for example, were compelled to act against their own inclinations by implicit and explicit threats of violence or other forms of extreme compulsion. Other constraints are normative. I may have promised and thereby obligated myself, despite my current whims, to stay dry (to recur to our example about the rain). Or, no matter my wishes, it may be a religious infraction, or merely a social faux pas, for me to run naked in the rain.

Given these limits on desire as a motivator, we must introduce the notion of *intention* into our action theory (see section 3.3.4, below). Desires do not of themselves cause a person to act, but intentions do. When one *commits oneself* to act in a certain way on one's desire, one forms an intention to act. One's intentions to act may also derive from one's emotions, as discussed in section 3.2, above.[66] Sometimes, however, an agent's intentions and actions, as in the case of the Roman slave, may derive only minimally from his or her own independent desires and emotions, as when he or she is commanded to act or is subjected to coercion.[67] In such cases, agents *intend* to act, and they act *intentionally,* however much they may not desire, and may fear or hate, to do so.[68]

---

65. For more on the considerations about desire in this paragraph, see Searle 2005a: 56–66.

66. See, too, for action-theoretic, or practical-reasoning, accounts of emotion, Pacherie 2002; Döring 2003; Döring 2007. For a neuroscientific account of emotion's role in action, see Damasio 1994, esp. 165–222.

67. Of course, all sorts of desires, such as that *I do not get hurt or die,* and emotions, such as fear, will come into play for an individual and guide his or her action when he or she is subjected to coercion.

68. See Nozick 1969, a classic treatment of coercion as an input into intention formation.

However, more central to Roman cult than personal desire, emotion, or coercion are cases in which agents form intentions to act because they recognize or accept, and so "internalize" the claims on them of "external" obligations, in the form of normative phenomena ranging from laws, to social norms, conventions, and commitments such as promises.[69] Kindred notions were not alien to the Roman jurists, whose job it was to think about normativity. The classical jurist Salvius Iulianus, for example, held that legal norms, as well as customary and social norms (*consuetudo* and *mores*), bind us just because (*nulla alia ex causa*) we collectively recognize and approve them as binding (*iudicio populi*).[70] Indeed, the jurists report that unwritten social norms could command stronger recognition and approval than written laws.[71]

As I explained at section 2.3, I range all socially normative phenomena— codified laws, rules, social norms, obligations, permissions, prohibitions, rights, responsibilities, powers, duties, social empowerments and disempowerments to action, dos and don'ts—under the rubric "deontology." *Deontology* is my term for a more or less coherent package of such norms. It is worth pausing briefly to distinguish deontology as defined and used here from morality. The norms that make up a deontology need not include, though they may often abut, *moral* norms. That Roman religion might embody anything resembling morality has often been denied, and only occasionally entertained.[72] To deny moral content to Roman religion is to endorse the condemnations of its Christian attackers, such as that of Augustine, at *City of God* 2.4. This is not to say that such denial is necessarily or always wrong, but the terms of that debate do appear outdated in light of evolutionary and cognitive research that sees religion not so much as conferring morality ex nihilo but instead as piggybacking on and helping to train up and extend an evolved moral faculty that includes intuitive System 1 capacities for empathy and sympathy and for detecting fairness and proportionality.[73] A discussion of Roman

---

69. See Miller 2006 for a philosophical treatment of the most general form of this claim.

70. *Dig.* 1.3.32.1 (Iulianus, *Dig.* 84): *nam cum ipsae leges nulla alia ex causa nos teneant, quam quod iudicio populi receptae sunt, merito et ea* [sc. *consuetudo* and *mores*], *quae sine ullo scripto populus probavit, tenebunt omnes.*

71. E.g., *Dig.* 1.3.36 (Paulus *ad Sab.* 7): *immo magnae auctoritatis hoc ius habetur, quod in tantum probatum est, ut non fuerit necesse scripto id comprehendere.* See Harries 1999: 31–35.

72. E.g., Liebeschuetz 1979: 39–54; Tatum 1993; Wiseman 1994: 49–53; Tatum 1999; Mueller 2002; T. Morgan 2007.

73. For evolved morality, see, e.g., De Waal et al. 2006; Tomasello 2016. For morality and religion, see Norenzayan 2013; Purzycki, Henrich, et al. 2018; cf. Baumard and Boyer 2013b; De Waal 2013; and McKay and Whitehouse 2015.

religion in terms of morality is beyond the scope of this book, but I do insist here on the neighboring notion that Roman cult had a strong other-regarding and behavior-regulating deontological component, to wit, *pietas*, discussed as such below, at section 3.3.3.

The deontology of Roman cult, like any deontology, derived its motivating force, in part, from agents' beliefs, even if only reluctant or grudging, as to its contents and legitimacy. Thus, if I believe that the dead should be honored at their tombs on 21 February (the Feralia), then my belief goes some way toward motivating me to honor the dead thus on 21 February, whatever my countervailing desires about how to spend that day.[74] I call these beliefs—beliefs that represent, as their content, what we should or should not do, may or may not do—*deontic beliefs*.[75]

A recent cognitive account of normativity describes the relationship between Intentional states and obligation thus:[76]

> From a cognitive point of view ... obligations cannot stand alone in the mind. They can only be represented within the scope of another mental state. If Bob says that there is an obligation to do something, this obligation is in the scope of a personal belief of his. If Bob [promises[77]] to accomplish it, the obligation is also in the scope of an intended action of his. If, when doing the right thing, Bob gets inflamed by a sense of duty, the obligation is in the scope of his emotions.

On this account, deontic phenomena such as social norms and obligations are not themselves mental states or episodes but are rather represented as the content ("in the scope") of mental states and episodes such as belief, intention, and emotion. The philosopher of normativity Cristina Bicchieri puts it thus:[78]

> a norm is a social construct reducible to the beliefs and desires of those involved in its practice; if individuals for some reason stopped having those beliefs and desires, the norm would cease to exist.

We shall see momentarily that Varro had a not dissimilar insight into norms, in his case, the norms of cult. He wrote his *Antiquitates rerum divinarum* in

---

74. Ov. *F.* 2.533ff.

75. Bicchieri 2016: 11: "Beliefs can be factual or they can be normative." G. Harris 1999: 196 distinguishes "normative" from "deontic" beliefs: "A normative belief is one that can be expressed in the form, A ought to do x. A deontic belief is a normative belief that, in normal circumstances, results in a felt sense of obligation when the agent sincerely believes it."

76. Andrighetto and Conte 2014: 82.

77. The text reads "asks you," which makes no sense in light of the talk of intention in the apodosis.

78. Bicchieri 2006: 22.

order to ensure that the gods and norms of Roman cult would not cease to exist by ceasing to be represented in the Intentional state of *memoria*, "memory."[79] (See also at section 7.3 for Varro's theory of *mos*, "custom" or "practice," and its transmission.)

So, to reiterate, norms, obligations, and other deontic phenomena are not distinct cognitive states but are rather represented as the content of familiar cognitive states. Thus, a newly acquired obligation "will form the content of a new belief,"[80] that is, a new deontic belief. This deontic belief will then inform our intentions to act as well as lend its Intentionality to our emotions (as discussed above, at section 3.2.1). An important point follows: If this account of deontology/normativity is correct, then insofar as we suppose Roman religion to have been characterized by norms and rules, whether formal or informal, we must perforce confess that it was characterized by beliefs.

There is more to say about beliefs and their relationship to deontology, and we shall return to the topic in the next chapter (section 4.4). For now, merely note that agents' deontic beliefs about what is obligatory, prohibited, and permitted provide them with *deontic reasons* to act. Just as agents may in some cases cite their desires as reasons for action, so in other cases they may cite their deontic beliefs as deontic reasons for action. These deontic reasons provide agents with what are, in principle, *desire-independent* motivations for their actions.[81] This desire independence holds even if, in any given case, an agent also happens intrinsically to desire to act in that way. Yet even when an agent lacks a desire to act in a given way, he or she may still recognize norms and other deontological phenomena as providing reasons, independent of desire, for him or her to act that way.

Let us now take a moment to distinguish *social norms* both from more formal deontological phenomena, such as laws, and from other informal deontological phenomena, such as conventions. For I shall argue below that *pietas*—for all that many of its components were embodied with some degree of formality in the *ius divinum*—should be seen as, in no small part, a system of social norms and the individual's commitment to that system of social norms (see also section 4.4). A social norm, on one influential account, "is a

---

79. E.g., on forgetting / not forgetting gods: *ut vix inveniatur qui Summani nomen quod audire iam non potest, se iam legisse meminerit* (Varr. *Ant. Div.* fr. 42 Cardauns = Aug. *Civ.* 4.23); *illos* [sc. *deos*] *velut ruina liberari a se dicit, et in memoria bonorum per huiusmodi libros recondi atque servari* (Varro *Ant. Div.* fr. 2A = Aug. *Civ.* 6.2).

80. Andrighetto and Conte 2014: 82.

81. On this point, see Searle 2001: 167–218; Searle 2005a: 66–73; briefly: Searle 2010: 9 and 123–32; cf. Miller 2006.

rule or principle that specifies actions which are required, permissible or forbidden independently of any legal or social institution."[82] While not every society codifies laws (or for that matter has writing), every society has social norms, which are distinct from laws. Social norms vary widely in their content, though they tend to pertain to the same domains across cultures, domains that represent the most pressing human concerns: the fair division of goods, reciprocity, cooperation, violence, sexual activity, food.[83] As Michael Tomasello writes, "Social norms represent another mode of existence. . . . The normative world is not the actual world but rather a possible world, that is, a possible world that there is good reason to bring about."[84]

Social norms are distinct not only from laws but also from conventions. It is in the immediate interest of individuals to conform to conventions, but not to social norms, which typically "prescribe behavior that differs from what people would do in the absence of norms."[85] The informal "rules" of a language provide an example of conventions. If Vibius, a native speaker of Oscan, is visiting Rome from Campania, and wishes to get directions to the forum from Marcus, it is in his interest to address Marcus in Latin. He follows the linguistic conventions of Latin because to do so allows him to communicate with Marcus and get the information he needs. So, he follows the local linguistic conventions because of self-interest, not because he will be punished by Marcus or by a third party for not following them.[86]

Social norms, in contrast, motivate us to do things that are not in our immediate interest, narrowly conceived. That is, they give us, as we saw, desire-independent reasons to act. Social norms have at heart the interests of *everyone*, of the group, not of this or that individual. They promote "prosocial" behavior, that is, behavior that benefits others, such as cooperation, fairness, reciprocity, and so on. As the anthropologist Joseph Henrich points out, in a great many circumstances, "the group does best if everyone cooperates but the individual does best if he or she acts selfishly while everyone else cooperates."[87] Social norms serve to prevent selfish behavior and to promote cooperation: "Internalized social norms help guide us through complex social

---

82. Sripada and Stich 2006: 281.

83. Sripada and Stich 2006: 282–84.

84. Tomasello 2021: 466.

85. Boyd and Richerson 2005b: 84. Cf. Bicchieri 2006: 29: "We conform to social norms because we have reasons to fulfill others' normative expectations. These reasons often conflict with our self-interest, at least narrowly defined."

86. On conventions, see further Bicchieri 2006: 34–42.

87. J. Henrich 2015: 193.

environments, allowing people to automatically do the right thing (i.e., comply with local norms)."[88]

It has been proposed that an evolved "norm psychology" helps us identify, learn, and comply with social norms.[89] There is good evidence that people reliably develop "intrinsic motivations" to follow social norms as "ultimate ends" in themselves rather than as means to other ends, even at the expense of purely individualistic self-interest.[90] That is, the motivational force of a recognized social norm can be just as intrinsic as—and can override—the motivational force of a "personal" desire. Our norm psychology is ostensibly an evolutionary adaptation for living in a social world of cooperative norms. We have "self-domesticated" as a species, becoming "prosocial, docile, rule-followers who expect a world governed by social norms monitored and enforced by communities."[91] As prosocial, docile rule followers, each of us "self-domesticates," eagerly conforming to social norms, monitoring our own and others' norm following, and punishing norm violators.

Although people clearly experience intrinsic motivations to comply with social norms, not all normative phenomena mesh so seamlessly with our motivation systems. More formal deontic claims on our behavior, such as duties and obligations related to laws or one's institutional status, may be experienced as onerous. So, I want again to emphasize here that just because an agent *recognizes* or *believes* that he or she has a deontic reason to act in a certain way does not entail that he or she *desires* to act in that way. This is why any deontology, including the obligations, permissions, and restrictions provided by social norms, may be said to provide "desire-independent" reasons to act.

Instances in which Romans *believed* themselves to have cult obligations without being *delighted* to have these obligations are not hard to find. An illustration is offered by Cicero's extended discussion, in *De legibus*, of the deontic fallout of his proposed law, "Let private rites remain in perpetuity," *sacra privata perpetua manento*.[92] Like many of the other laws proposed in this book, this one is merely the codification of a customary social norm. The pages Cicero spends in deliberation as to whom responsibility for maintaining

---

88. J. Henrich 2015: 193.

89. Chudek and Henrich 2011; Chudek, Zhao, and Henrich 2013; J. Henrich 2015. Cf. Kelly and Davis 2018.

90. Sripada and Stich 2006: 281, 284–87. Cf. J. Henrich and Ensminger 2014: 20–26. The question as to how Roman children *learned* ritual norms will be taken up in chapter 7. On the psychology of norm learning, see M. Schmidt and Rakoczy 2018; and J. Henrich and Ensminger 2014: 20–26.

91. J. Henrich 2015: 5, and see further 185–210.

92. Cic. *Leg.* 22.13.

family cult should devolve on following the death of the head of household (*paterfamilias*) amply indicate that this norm and its obligations were not always welcome even when recognized.[93] Presumably, at least some Romans who complied with this deontology acted against their druthers and formed their intentions to act on the basis of desire-independent reasons to act, that is, obligations, that this norm afforded.

Let us consider another, cognate example of potential motivational conflict. A man's status as pontifex might oblige him to accept certain premises or act in ways he might not otherwise wish to act, independently of holding that status. An intuition of such a conflict appears to inform an exchange between Balbus and Cotta in Cicero's *De natura deorum*. Balbus had chided Cotta that as Cotta, as an academic philosopher, and as a pontifex, he should not hold an *errans et vaga sententia*, "a wandering and wavering judgment," about the gods. Balbus thereby implies that the intersection of Cotta's identities might result in cognitive and motivational collisions (2.2; cf. 2.168). Cotta responds to this challenge and spells out what he takes Balbus to have meant, to wit (3.5):

> *ut opiniones, quas a maioribus accepimus de dis immortalibus, sacra, caerimonias religionesque defenderem. Ego vero eas defendam semper semperque defendi nec me ex ea opinione, quam a maioribus accepi de cultu deorum inmortalium, ullius umquam oratio aut docti aut indocti movebit.*

> that I should support the beliefs that we have received from our ancestors concerning the immortal gods, the rites, the ceremonies, and the religious traditions. But I will always support and always have supported these beliefs, nor will the discourse of any person, erudite or otherwise, ever budge me from the belief that I have received from our ancestors about the cult of the immortal gods.

Cotta claims to accept traditional beliefs, *opiniones*, about gods and rituals. He goes on to say that he respects the practices of traditional religion and acknowledges their rationales, such as the tradition that Romulus and Numa, by establishing *auspicia* and *sacra*, "laid the foundations of our city," a city whose greatness owes to the peaceable relationship with the gods that successive generations built on those foundations. He echoes Balbus's words in closing his reply to him: "Balbus, now you've got what Cotta and a *pontifex* thinks," *habes, Balbe, quid Cotta, quid pontifex sentiat* (3.6).

Cotta's expression of traditionalism "as Cotta and a *pontifex*" rules out any notion that he finds his priestly status to demand that he must accept beliefs

---

93. Cic. *Leg.* 2.47–53. An heir could even free himself, through *detestatio sacrorum*, of the obligation to perform the *sacra* of his *gens*: Gell. *N.A.* 15.27.3.

about the gods or endorse and engage in religious activity that he personally (i.e., as Cotta, not as a priest) would find uncongenial. The dialogue highlights the fact that doxastic and deontic expectations might fall on him qua priest that do not fall on him as "Cotta" or as a philosopher. Different positions, identities, and institutional statuses carry different deontologies. Since individuals are likely to inhabit multiple positions, identities, and statuses, they are likely to participate in multiple intersecting, nonintersecting, and even mutually exclusive "norm circles,"[94] each with its associated doxastic commitments. In affirming his unequivocal commitment to traditional beliefs and practices both as Cotta and as a priest, Cotta affirms the harmony or untroubled overlap of his various statuses and their attendant doxastic and deontic demands.[95]

Balbus and Cotta's exchange (not to mention Cicero's discussion of *sacra privata* in *De legibus*) suggests that some Romans might have found themselves under normative pressure to accept propositions, endorse practices, or perform actions that their reasoning in other contexts or their preferences might militate against.[96] It offers a glimpse of a culturally distinctive concern: the possibility and therefore potential worry that a person's beliefs and practical attitudes concerning his or her institutional obligations might conflict with beliefs and practical attitudes that he or she had arrived at in other, perhaps private or discursive, contexts.[97] We perhaps tend to take for granted the cognitive and motivational unity of the individual.[98] We supposedly value being "true to ourselves." The Romans did not take any such thing for granted. They recognized that deontological and hence motivational conflicts were inherent to communal life in a republic.

A dramatic Roman example of an individual experiencing but overcoming motivational conflict due to the clashing deontologies of his different statuses

---

94. For norm circles, see Elder-Vass 2010: 122–33; and Elder-Vass 2012: 22–34 (and see below, section 4.4); and for the individual as a site of "normative intersectionality," see Elder-Vass 2010: 131–33; and Elder-Vass 2012: 160–63.

95. In effect, as Ando 2010a: 68–69 shows, Cotta asserts that his beliefs, based on the *authority* of tradition, cannot be justified by appeal to any *rational* argumentation. By the same token, rational argumentation cannot controvert them and thereby disabuse him of them.

96. Cf. Cicero's Cotta-like endorsement of tradition at *Har. Resp.* 18 and the careful position on traditional cult staked out by "Marcus" in Cic. *Div.* 2.

97. Kant confronted a similar problem of "private reason" vs. "public reason" in 1784.

98. This "we" does not include cognitive theorists: see Cherniak 1981 for "minimal rationality"; for belief fragmentation, or compartmentalization, and the divided mind, see Egan 2008; M. Davies and Egan 2013. For our "hidden motives" in many domains of our lives, see Simler and Hanson 2018.

is found in Livy's story of Brutus and his sons. Shortly after Brutus led the expulsion of the kings from Rome and won the first consulship, his sons were discovered conspiring to restore the monarchy. As consul, Brutus was under an obligation to execute his sons for treason. It is clear from Livy's narrative that readers were expected to see this obligation as clashing violently with Brutus's motivations as their father. Livy draws the tension tight:

> *poenae capiendae ministerium patri de liberis consulatus imposuit*
>
> consulship imposed on the father the duty of exacting the penalty from the sons

and

> *pater voltusque et os eius spectaculo esset, eminente animo patrio inter publicae poenae ministerium*
>
> the father, his expression, and his countenance, created a spectacle, as his paternal feelings shone forth during his administration of the public penalty.[99]

In these selections, Livy juxtaposes Brutus's private and public statuses, his fatherhood and his consulship, his paternal feelings and his duty to the state. Brutus's statuses and the motivations they bring, one familial and personal, the other official and public, do not harmonize. Typical of a Roman, and indeed establishing the *exemplum* that sets a Roman norm,[100] Brutus's public obligation wins out over his paternal duty and preferences.

Varro makes a useful comparison with Cotta and Brutus. Augustine reports that the Roman polymath wrote his *Antiquitates rerum divinarum* in order to promote traditional norms of worship of the traditional Roman gods, despite the fact that neither traditional cult nor traditional theology accorded precisely with his own judgment (*non iudicio proprio; non . . . iudicio suo*).[101] As to cult practice, Varro would have preferred that the gods be worshipped "more purely," *castius*, "without images," *sine simulacris*, as he supposed they had

---

99. Liv. 2.5.

100. On Roman "norm setting" through *exempla*, see Roller 2018. (The example of Brutus is not discussed.)

101. Varr. *Ant. Div.* fr. 12 Cardauns = Aug. *Civ.* 4.31 (quoted below, n. 95). Cf. Varr. *Ant. Div.* fr. 2A Cardauns = Aug. *Civ.* 6.2. Let us take this opportunity to allay a common suspicion (voiced by, e.g., North 1989: 573): Did Augustine radically misrepresent Varro? Most likely he did not, given the fidelity of his many other classical citations that we can check, which fill Hagendahl 1967. See further, Burns 2001.

originally been worshipped at Rome.¹⁰² As to theology, he would have preferred not only to name but even to posit gods "in accord with nature's rule," *ex naturae formula*.¹⁰³ Yet Varro declines to assert his own considered beliefs over those handed down by tradition. He endorses traditional cult norms and traditional theology.¹⁰⁴ As with Brutus, Varro privileges the cultural group, manifested as a religious tradition, over himself as individual. Unlike Cotta, Varro faced a live choice. Where Cotta's mind was in harmony not only with traditional worship but also with the traditional beliefs (*opiniones*) that underwrote that worship, Varro had to choose between his own considered beliefs and the preservation of tradition—indeed, that preservation was his entire project.

Romans like Cotta would find their intentions and actions in religious contexts deriving more or less straightforwardly from relevant beliefs and desires, with some of these desires following effortlessly from internalized norms. Here we see consonance between individual motivations and social and institutional demands. However, Romans like Varro (and, without reference to religion, Brutus) might experience their intentions and actions in the domain of cult embodying not a *lack* of belief or an *unimportance* of belief, but rather the *very importance* of their beliefs about the binding force, legitimacy, or significance of the norms of cult. They would find themselves acknowledging and endorsing these norms *despite* their personal reservations, desires, and druthers regarding the forms of worship and conceptions of the gods enshrined therein.

These considerations extend beyond individual action to take in "collective acts" of cult as well, which are sometimes asserted to be a matter of "precise obligation ... and constituted in no way by abstract belief."¹⁰⁵ I would submit, in contrast to this dichotomy between obligation and belief, that the motivational power of any collective obligation—its capacity to provide a *collective* reason for action—will correlate directly with collective belief as to the

---

102. Varr. *Ant. Div.* fr. 18 Cardauns = Aug. *Civ.* 4.31: *dicit* [sc. *Varro*] *etiam antiquos Romanos plus annos centum et septuaginta deos sine simulacro coluisse.* "*Quod si adhuc,*" inquit, "*mansisset, castius dii obseruarentur.*" Augustine returns to this again, at *Civ.* 7.5, using the plural *sine simulacris* in place of the singular *sine simulacro*.

103. Varr. *Ant. Div.* fr. 12 Cardauns = Aug. *Civ.* 4.31: *quid ipse Varro, quem dolemus in rebus diuinis ludos scaenicos, quamuis non iudicio proprio, posuisse, cum ad deos colendos multis locis uelut religiosus hortetur, nonne ita confitetur non se illa iudicio suo sequi, quae ciuitatem Romanam instituisse commemorat, ut, si eam ciuitatem nouam constitueret, ex naturae potius formula deos nominaque eorum se fuisse dedicaturum non dubitet confiteri?*

104. Cf., with rather different emphases, Scheid 2016: 50–51.

105. Scheid 2016: 123.

legitimacy or binding force of that obligation. (We shall approach the question of what it might mean to believe or act "collectively" in chapter 4.)

The central idea I am pressing here is simply that one's *belief* that one has an obligation to do something gives one a highly motivating deontic *reason* to do it. Such a deontic reason motivated Brutus to kill his own sons. Similarly, but less poignantly, in cases like that of Varro, one's considered personal preferences may not align with the deontic claims to which one feels oneself subject, but one nonetheless acknowledges and even celebrates those claims and acts accordingly. In such cases, one might not ex ante or independently *want* to do as some norm prescribes, but the belief that one has an obligation, and perhaps even that the obligation represents its own sort of *good*, may still give one a desire-independent reason to act. In contrast to both Varro and Brutus, in cases like that of Cotta, one's recognized normative obligations and one's personal motivations align, so one's desires unproblematically supply one with reasons to act.

3.3.3. Pietas *as a Deontology*

The previous section's discussion has led us to the conclusion that in the norm-governed world of cult, a Roman's intentions to act, whether motivated by desire or not, frequently sprang from his or her deontic beliefs as to the lay of the normative landscape. I want to suggest now that that normative landscape was the province of *pietas*.

Pietas was a deontology. It was a package of informal social and formal legal norms that provided representations and grounded intuitions and inferences as to actions permissible (*fas*), obligatory (*religio*), and forbidden (*nefas*). It was also, as commonly translated, a sense of commitment to that package of norms. *Pietas* could be seen by Romans as the foundation of all other norms, including moral norms.[106] *Pietas* was not only action oriented but also other regarding. It was not individualistic but social. For obligations, permissions, and prohibitions oblige, permit, or prohibit agents in direct or indirect relation to other agents. In the case of *pietas*, those other agents included kin and even the state but also, and most importantly here, gods.[107] *Pietas*, then, was the system of obligations, permissions, and prohibitions—offering agents desire-independent, deontic, and other-regarding reasons for action—that

---

106. E.g., Cic. *N.D.* 1.4: *atque haut scio, an pietate adversus deos sublata fides etiam et societas generis humani et una excellentissuma virtus iustitia tollatur.*

107. Cic. *Off.* 2.11: *deos placatos pietas efficiet et sanctitas*; *N.D.* 2.153: *cognitionem deorum, e qua oritur pietas.*

bound together gods and mortals, governing their intercourse in what Cicero called their "fellowship and partnership among themselves," *communitas et societas inter ipsos*.[108] Deontic reasons appealing to *pietas* and deontic cognition about *pietas* were central to Romans' intention formation with respect to cult action.[109]

It will be instructive here to return to Varro. In his *theologia tripertita*,[110] he had articulated a deontic position toward the cult traditions of his city. *Theologia fabulosa*, primarily the province of poets, expressed itself in narratives about the gods.[111] *Theologia naturalis*, concerned with the divine nature and the sources of our knowledge of it, that is, with ontology and epistemology, expressed itself in philosophical discourse.[112] His *theologia civilis*, however, formalized a deontology, or "theology of practice,"[113] a *pietas*, that expressed itself in norms of cult action. Varro writes (*Ant. Div.* fr. 9 Cardauns = Aug. *Civ.* 6.5) that civic theology is the *genus*

> quod in urbibus cives, maxime sacerdotes, nosse atque administrare debent. in quo, est quos deos publice colere <quae> sacra et sacrificia facere quemque par sit.[114]

> that citizens in cities, most of all priests, ought to know and attend to. In this *genus* are the gods whom everyone must publicly worship, the rites and sacrifices that everyone must perform.

Civic theology provides neither the forum nor the resources for assessing the morality of mythic narratives or the truth claims of natural theology. Instead, it provides a system of norms, a framework for our obligations and duties

---

108. Cic. *Off.* 1.153.

109. See especially Jensen 2010 and 2013 on religion as a fundamental case of "normative cognition." For a brief account of deontic reasoning, see Johnson-Laird 2006: 320–31. For empirical studies of deontic cognition such as inference from social norms, deontic rules, and deontic representations, see Beller 2010.

110. For Varro's tripartition of theology, see Varr. *Ant. Div.* fr. 6 Cardauns = Aug. *Civ.* 6.5 and 6.12. For more holistic accounts of Varro, the *theologia tripertita*, and the *Ant. Div.* than I can offer here, see Pépin 1956; Lieberg 1973; Cardauns 1976; Lieberg 1982; Lehmann 1997; Cardauns 2001; Ando 2008: 53–57 and 83–86; Van Nuffelen 2010; Rüpke 2014. For Augustine's accuracy in presenting Varro's arguments, see Burns 2001. For Augustine's reading of Varro, see Dihle 1996; O'Daly 1996; G. Clark 2010.

111. E.g., Varr. *Ant. Div.* fr. 7 Cardauns = Aug. *Civ.* 6.5.

112. E.g., Varr. *Ant. Div.* frr. 8 (= Aug. *Civ.* 6.5) and 226 (= Aug. *Civ.* 7.6) Cardauns.

113. Ando 2010a: 77.

114. This is the reading of the *editio princeps*, not Cardauns: on the textual history, see Ravenna 2007–8.

vis-à-vis the gods, instituted to govern the intercourse of mortals and immortals. But it would be wrong for this reason to reduce civic theology to mere know-how or savoir-faire. For it manifestly had propositional content concerning, among other things, "what force and skill and power each god has in each domain,"[115] and therefore "which god to invoke and summon" in any given context.[116] The latter, that is, which god to invoke and summon, was presumably not merely a prudential but a normative question for Varro, a question not just of instrumentality but of *pietas* and treating the gods as was their due.

As a deontology embodying practical knowledge relevant to Roman relations with divine agents, Varro's civic theology took for granted that the gods were much as pictured in the *theologia fabulosa*, in poetry and on the stage: that is, they were social agents.[117] The defining difference is that in civic unlike in fabulous theology they are social agents with whom we have bilateral relationships and thus reciprocal obligations.[118] The presupposition of divine availability to both mortal petition and mortal ministration found in Varro's *theologia civilis* derives neither from speculation about the gods' "true nature" nor from mythic narratives, but from the historical record of divine-human interactions and the civic flourishing and institution building that resulted from those interactions.[119]

Indeed, I would tender that Varro's project itself constituted a kind of cult act, motivated by at least two intertwined deontic considerations. The first of these considerations was the obligation, recognized by Varro, to promote and sustain the traditional cult practices of an ancient people (*vetus populus*).[120]

---

115. Aug. *Civ.* 4.22: *eo modo nulli dubium esse adserens ita esse utilem cognitionem deorum, si sciatur quam quisque deus uim et facultatem ac potestatem cuiusque rei habeat.*

116. Varr. *Ant. Div.* fr. 3 Cardauns (= Aug. *Civ.* 4.22): *ex eo enim poterimus ... scire, quem cuiusque causa deum invocare atque advocare debeamus.*

117. Aug. *Civ.* 6.5: *nec alii derideantur in theatris, quam qui adorantur in templis, nec aliis ludos exhibeatis, quam quibus uictimas immolatis.* Varro himself saw civic theology as drawing on both the fabulous and the philosophical (fr. 11 Cardauns = Aug. *Civ.* 6.6): *quae sic abhorrent, inquit, ut tamen ex utroque genere ad ciuiles rationes adsumpta sint non pauca. quare quae erunt communia cum propriis, una cum ciuilibus scribemus.*

118. See the reasoning of Cicero propria voce at *N.D.* 1.3–4.

119. See Cic. *Har. Resp.* 19: *eorum* [sc. *deorum*] *numine hoc tantum imperium esse natum et auctum et retentum.* Cf. *N.D.* 2.8 and the commentary of Pease 1955–58 ad "superiores." On civic institution building, see Varro fr. 5 Cardauns apud Aug. *Civ.* 6.4: *Varronis haec ratio est: sicut prior est, inquit, pictor quam tabula picta, prior faber quam aedificium, ita priores sunt civitates quam ea quae a civitatibus sunt instituta,* thus Augustine finds Varro *apertissime confitens quod etiam istae res divinae, sicut pictura, sicut structura, ab hominibus institutae sint.*

120. Varr. *Ant. Div.* fr. 12 Cardauns = Aug. *Civ.* 4.31: *sed iam quoniam in vetere populo esset, acceptam ab antiquis nominum et cognominum historiam tenere, ut tradita est, debere sedivit, et ad eum finem illa scribere et perscrutari ut potius eos magis colere quam despicere vulgus velit.*

The second consideration was thereby to discharge an obligation to ensure that the gods of that ancient people did not die social deaths (*ne pereant*) through "the citizens' neglect" (*civium neglegentia*) of their cult practices.[121] I use "social death" in a way adjacent to but not identical with Orlando Patterson' famous usage. Here, it signifies what happens when a community ceases to recognize the mutual and reciprocal deontic ties that bind one agent to his fellows and his fellows to him. In that case, the agent ceases to exist as a social being and member of the community. Such, at any rate, was the fate of Summanus, whose cult the Romans forgot, and with it, all obligations to the god, and with those obligations, the god himself.[122] So, Varro's project is itself an act of civic *pietas*, on a par, as Varro himself styled it, with Aeneas's rescue of the *penates*, the gods of Troy.[123]

With Varro's *theologia civilis*, we are dealing, of course, with *cultural* normativity, though from a Roman perspective the deontology of *pietas* might have appeared at least as much a matter of *nature* as of culture.[124] At section 4.4 we shall see how norms natural and internal to cognition support cultural norms, such as those that guided Roman cult. For now, I merely wish to emphasize again two points. First, that for an agent to have a deontic reason to act, he or she must have a deontic belief or beliefs as to relevant and applicable norms and, second, that deontic motivators of action need not, despite their desire independence, be felt as coercive or as undermining of one's own agency, as Varro's case attests. Rather, Varro's example shows that beliefs regarding the propriety of traditional norms of cult—and, indeed, beliefs regarding the value to a community of its traditional theological beliefs, that is, a "belief in

---

121. Varro *Ant. Div.* fr. 2A = Aug. *Civ.* 6.2: *cum Varro deos ita coluerit colendosque censuerit, ut in eo ipso opere litterarum suarum dicat, se timere, ne pereant, non incursu hostili, sed civium neglegentia*. Varro's term *neglegentia* is loaded, referring to ritual error that necessitates *instauratio*: see Cic. *Har. Resp.* 23 and Liv. 5.52.9 with Cohee 1994.

122. Varr. *Ant. Div.* fr. 42 Cardauns = Aug. *Civ.* 4.23: *Romani veteres nescio quem Summanum cui nocturna fulmina tribuebant, coluerunt magis quem Iovem, sed postquam Iovi templum insigne ac sublime constructum est, propter aedis dignitatem sic ad eum multitudo confluxit, ut vix inveniatur qui Summani nomen quod audire iam non potest, se iam legisse meminerit.*

123. Varro *Ant. Div.* fr. 2A = Aug. *Civ.* 6.2: *de qua* [sc. *neglegentia*] *illos* [sc. *deos*] *velut ruina liberari a se dicit, et in memoria bonorum per huiusmodi libros recondi atque servari utiliore cura, quam Metellus de incendio sacra Vestalia et Aeneas de Troiano excidio Penates liberasse praedicatur.* For this line of thinking about Varro's project, cf. Ando 2010a and 2015a: 80–81.

124. For the origins of *religio* in *natura*, see Cic. *Inv.* 2.65–66 and 2.160–61. More generally, belief in gods was a matter of *natura* not of convention: Cic. *N.D.* 1.2; *Tusc.* 1.30; *Leg.* 1.24 and 2.27. But see Ando 2010a: 75–79 and Ando 2015a: 53–86 for emphasis on Roman recognition of the conventionality or relativity of religious institutions.

belief"[125]—could coexist with rather different private reasoning about cult and the gods, perhaps because, as Fontenelle glimpsed long ago, Roman religious culture made no effort to enforce cognitive conformity on the individual.[126] For Varro himself would have configured the gods and their worship differently, more in accord with the *theologia naturalis*, if he were founding a city from scratch.[127] Yet he respected the way his countrymen had historically worshipped and believed, and he thought it fitting to preserve these historical cult norms and concomitant theological notions.

The foregoing considerations not only undermine the belief-action dichotomy but also cast in a new light another dichotomy pervasive to the study of ancient religions, that is, the one between "individual choices" and "social expectations," the latter of which of course derive from social norms. Here is an example: "Religious involvement of women and men . . . generally resulted not from individual choices but from social expectations."[128] I would not belabor the point, but by now it should be clear that this dichotomy is false. For even if we grant that some ancients may sometimes have acted solely on "social expectations," we must concede that in so doing they necessarily held deontic beliefs as to what those expectations were, they still found in those social expectations desire-independent reasons to act, and they still chose, unlike Diogenes the Cynic, to form intentions and to act in accord with, and thereby to accede to and to endorse, however tacitly, those expectations. It was exactly such beliefs about social expectations and exactly such endorsement of those expectations by way of appropriate action that sustained religious norms in Roman society, as Varro of all Romans knew well.

3.3.4. An Enriched Model of Action

With this, we return to intentions, which I mentioned but set to one side when we transitioned from desire to deontology as a source of reasons to act in section 3.3.2.[129] Whether intentions derive from desires or from deontic beliefs

---

125. Dennett 2006: 200ff. Cicero evinces similar "belief in belief" at *Leg.* 2.16 (see at section 8.6). For "belief in belief," see the introduction at section 0.1, and section 1.2.

126. See at section 1.2. Marcus, in Cic. *Div.* 2, represents a similar case of deontic belief in the propriety of cult norms in the absence of any belief that the gods were agents who intervened in mundane affairs, as traditionally figured in cult.

127. See, e.g., Varr. *Ant. Civ.* fr. 18 Cardauns = Aug. *Civ.* 4.31 (and cf. 7.5).

128. S. Price 1999: 108, writing about Greek *polis* religion. Cf. Beard et al. 1998: 1.42–43.

129. This section owes a lot to Bratman 1987. Bratman's BDI (belief-desire-intention) model of action is widely accepted both as theory and in practical AI applications. For a review of the history of philosophical theory and psychological research on *intention* that is uniquely relevant

and deontic reasoning, two types may be distinguished: prior intentions and motor intentions.[130] When in the introduction (section 0.4) and chapter 2 (section 2.2.4) we defined "intention" as a *plan* of action, we were speaking of prior intentions. We are, as Cicero would agree, "planning agents."[131] As such, we represent our goals and the means-actions necessary to achieve them as the content of our prior intentions (see section 2.2.4). Motor intentions, in contrast, cause our immediate, purposeful *acting*.

I point out in passing that intentions, both prior *commitments* to act and motoric *endeavorings* to act, reflect again the natural normativity of cognition. First, practical reasoning involves internal, natural norms of consistency among beliefs and intentions as well as means-ends coherence.[132] I cannot both believe that it will rain and intend to keep dry by intending to run naked outside. Second, intentions involve internal, natural norms of satisfaction. If I intend to run in the rain but do not leave the house, my intention fails of satisfaction. Third, these norms *internal* to our intentions remain constant even when *external* norms, such as obligations that we accept, or "social expectations" (i.e., social norms) that we recognize, influence the intentions that we do form.

To understand (without broaching neurology) how intentions actually *cause* action, it may help to recur to the symmetry between perception and action: both are examples of *Intentional causation* (see section 2.2.5). As John Searle summarizes it, "cases of Intentional causation occur when the Intentional content of an Intentional state functions as either cause or effect in a causal relation."[133] Let us spell this out.

Perceptions have a mind-to-world *direction of fit*, which is to say that they take on, or come to "fit," the shape of the world. As such, they have the converse *direction of causation*, that is, world-to-mind. The shape of some feature of the world causes the Intentional content of our perception. We experience the content of that perception as caused by that very feature of the world. If we see that it is raining, we experience that perceptual content as caused by the fact that it is raining.

---

to this book's focus on shared Intentionality (to be introduced in chapter 4), see Seebaß et al. 2013.

130. For "prior intentions" vs. "motor intentions" (or "intentions-in-action"), see Searle 2001: 44–45; and Jacob and Jeannerod 2003: 34–41, 179–80, and 202–8 (and for the perception of intentions in others, see Jacob and Jeannerod 2003: 211–46).

131. Bratman 1987; and Bratman 2014: 15–25.

132. Bratman 1987: 109.

133. Searle 2015: 43. See more fully, Searle 2001: 40–49.

Symmetrically, actions have a world-to-mind direction of fit and thus a mind-to-world direction of causation. The Intentional content of our intention causes our action, and we experience our action as caused by the Intentional content of our intention. Based on Gaius's belief that a festival is being celebrated in the forum and his desire to participate, he forms an intention whose Intentional content may be represented linguistically as *I walk to the forum*, and he experiences his walking to the forum as caused by that very intention. That is, he does not wonder what he is doing when he finds himself walking to the forum. His intention *causes* the state of affairs in the world that it represents, to wit, that he *walk to the forum*, and his subjective experience of his own action includes experience of this Intentional causation.[134] Indeed, a subjective sense of our own agential causation pervades our conscious lives. Have you ever had the sense that, say, you were not the one raising your arm or that your leg was doing something independently of you? Such a sensation would be uncanny.[135] I hope it is obvious that these points about Intentional causation held as much for the Romans as they do for us.

In this theory of action, as always, I want to emphasize the role of belief. If we consider belief in terms of Intentional causation, we see that it may be both effect and cause. The Intentional content of a belief may be an *effect* of sensory perception, of memory, of intuition and inference, as we saw in chapter 2, or of forms of social learning to be examined in detail in chapters 6, 7, and 8. Conversely, the Intentional content of a belief may be *causally implicated* in inferences, reflections, further beliefs, and, as we saw in section 3.2, above, emotions. Most importantly for present purposes, not only emotions and desires but also *beliefs* about states of affairs in the world and *deontic beliefs* about our obligations may enter into our practical reasoning and guide our formation of intentions to act, both prior intentions, or "plans," and motor intentions, the actual endeavorings to act that move us. This, then, is Intentionality in action.

We saw that Cicero had already verged on a view of human beings as "autobiographic agents," whose "experiences in the past" and "predictions about the future" enable them "to represent, access, and to some extent control [their] behavior and relationship" to an environment that includes other

---

134. An alternate formulation, using terminology introduced at section 2.2.6, is this: the state of affairs Gaius's intention represents (*I walk to the forum*) is its *conditions of satisfaction*, and his intention is satisfied if it *causes* its conditions of satisfaction, i.e., if he does, in fact, intentionally walk to the forum.

135. Such sensations accompany depersonalization syndrome: see Stone et al. 2012 on the experience described in Sacks 1984.

agents,[136] including divine agents. An autobiographic agent's Intentional episodes—emotions, desires, beliefs, deontic beliefs, and intentions—work together to guide his action. We have seen that these Intentional episodes are classified by direction of fit.[137] Some, such as perceptions, memories, and doxastic states like belief, exhibit *mind-to-world* direction of fit. They picture things as they *are*. Others feature *world-to-mind* direction of fit. These include desires and intentions, that is, plans to act and endeavorings to act. To borrow a cartographical metaphor from Robert Audi, our perceptions and beliefs[138]

> serve as our maps of reality. *Given* motivation, and intentions in particular, they determine our itineraries. A map alone pictures destinations, but does not incline us to go to them. And if we had motivation without a cognitive map, we would be at a loss to find our way.

Agents require a sense of a world and its affordances for action. Sometimes this sense comes through direct sensory coupling of the agent with his or her environment. However, social, other-regarding, norm-following, past-respecting, future-oriented planning agents such as us require a cognitive map composed not only of immediate perceptions, but also of memories and imaginings, and most importantly here, of doxastic states, including beliefs and deontic beliefs. The latter define the space of possible, permissible, impermissible, and obligatory action. Moreover, we need emotions and practical attitudes such as desire, desire-independent motivations, and most importantly intentions to get us moving within the space so defined. Finally, we must recall that when we explain our own actions to others and others' actions to ourselves, we adduce our own or their perceptions, beliefs, desires, normative commitments, and intentions as *reasons* for our or their actions.

3.4. Action Theory and Folk Psychology

I have presented in the second part of this chapter what I take to be the theory of action that should inform our interpretation of ancient cult.[139] In closing, let me ask why, beyond the arguments offered here, a hardheaded skeptic should discard the belief-action dichotomy and embrace my enriched, neo-Aristotelian action theory. The answer is that anyone who joins Aristotle in

---

136. Dautenhahn and Nehaniv 2002: 7.
137. See just above and at section 2.2.5.
138. Audi 2008: 89, emphasis in the original.
139. For a guide to the many topics in action theory perforce neglected here, see O'Connor and Sandis 2010.

supposing that people sometimes drink because they are thirsty already possesses *implicitly* in his or her stance toward agents the elements of the theoretical apparatus detailed *explicitly* above. That is, even the skeptic possesses a *folk psychology*, that is, a suite of intuitions about minded creatures that makes it as obvious to him or her as it was to Aristotle that sometimes people drink because they desire water. Of course, sometimes Romans drank not out of thirst, but because they wanted to get drunk (a desire-based reason), or because Galen prescribed it, or to celebrate the Vinalia (both deontic reasons), but none of these reasons alters the underlying logical structure of their action or its Intentional causation.

A teleological, Intentionalist, folk-psychological stance is not just one way among others that we may choose, learn, or become socialized to see agents. Rather, it is the condition of the possibility of seeing *anything* as an agent in the first place. As such, Aristotle did not invent the teleological explanation of action so much as he made a biologically inherited cognitive disposition of *Homo sapiens* explicit and attempted to spell out its implications.[140] The Intentionality of others is invisible yet transparently obvious. None of us has ever seen another's belief or intention. Yet we cannot choose *not* to see the physical gestures of others as doings, tryings, choosings, and rejectings, as embodying intentions, wants, emotions, and beliefs. A neurotypical human being cannot "un-see" the Intentionality of other agents any more than he or she can un-see the edges of objects.[141] All of this was, as we saw in the introduction, taken for granted by Romans.

In any event, a theoretical account of action, such as Aristotle's, Cicero's, or the one offered here, is a rather different matter from this automatic and intuitive disposition to see the emotions and *mores* of others on their faces, to read their motions as doings, actings, reactings, tryings, choosings, avoidings, reachings, rejectings, and so forth. As mooted at section 1.4, it is an appreciation, even if only implicit, of such Intentionality in action that makes disciplines such as classics, history, and religious studies possible at all. Yet we gain theoretical purchase on ancient religious phenomena when we refine our intuitions and make explicit the logical structure and Intentional causation of human action. If nothing else, we limit the space of plausible theories and approach asymptotically the truth of the matter about agency's cognitive foundations.

---

140. Cf. Matthews 2003.

141. See, e.g., Gallese and Metzinger 2003; Blake and Shiffrar 2007; Gallagher 2008a and 2008b; Gallese 2009.

We shall return to social cognition in the next chapter because we need to see how developmentally natural intuitions about other minds make possible the sorts of collective cult cognition and action described by Apuleius and Livy. And we shall return to social cognition in later chapters, too, when we probe further the contributions of social cognition to Roman intuitions and beliefs about gods and the divine mind. In this chapter, I have proceeded on the assumption that it is instructive to see belief's integral, constitutive role in emotion and to see the causal role of belief in purposive action. Emotion and action *causally depend on* and cannot be *explained* without belief. If we banish belief from Roman religion, we banish emotion and action as well as agency with it.

4

Shared Belief, Shared Agency, Social Norms

4.1. Introduction

This chapter takes us from individual cognition to the *sharing of Intentionality*[1] in collective cognition as well as from individual agency in solo action to the *sharing of agency* in collective action. In the previous chapter, section 3.2.2, we examined an account of collective cult in Livy. Nearly the whole city of Rome (*prope tota civitas*) cooperated in expiating a series of terrible *prodigia*. What skills of collective cognition and action allowed so many people to believe *together* that the prodigies Livy records had taken place? To experience *together* the religious anxiety that Livy describes? To intend *together* to perform cult? To act *together* on those intentions? And, finally, to feel *together* a sense of relief upon successfully completing the prescribed rituals?

Such questions become especially pressing when we reflect on a trenchant question posed by Arnaldo Momigliano. He famously asked himself what he knew about the religious beliefs of Athenians, Romans, and Jerusalemites in the first century before Christ.[2] In the case of Rome, he noted "a strange absence of information about religious education."[3] Lacking any pagan parallel

---

1. "Shared Intentionality" is often found in the psychological literature, "collective Intentionality" often but not exclusively in the philosophical literature. The two terms typically denote roughly the same phenomenon, and the two fields exert mutual influence. See, e.g., Tomasello 2019, a book of developmental psychology: "For precision, the account borrows theoretical tools from philosophical accounts of shared Intentionality. . . . Individuals are able to create with one another a shared agent 'we,' operating with shared intentions, shared knowledge, and shared sociomoral values" (7).
2. Momigliano 1987: 74.
3. Momigliano 1987: 85.

to Christian catechism, which might ensure a degree of doctrinal uniformity,[4] how could Romans "get on the same page," cognitively and practically, with respect to cult? How, that is, could they share Intentionality?

Momigliano posited that Roman religious education came through observation: "the way to find out about religious practices was to be taken around or, if grown up, to go around the city."[5] In support of this thesis, he adduced a passage from Ovid's *Fasti*, set during the Robigalia festival, on 25 April (4.905–9):[6]

> hac mihi Nomento Romam cum luce redirem,
>   obstitit in media candida turba via:
> flamen in antiquae lucum Robiginis ibat,
>   exta canis flammis, exta daturus ovis.
> protinus accessi, ritus ne nescius essem.

> As I returned on this day from Nomentum to Rome,
>   a white-clad crowd blocked my way:
> a *flamen* was going into the grove of ancient Robigo,
>   to offer entrails of a puppy and a sheep to the flames.
> I went straight up in order not to remain ignorant of the rite.

Ovid presents himself here as an interloper on a collective cult action. Indeed, the uniformity of the crowd's white garb underscores the collective nature of its project. Perhaps, as the *Fasti Praenestini* records, they seek to perform "a sacrifice and games with older and younger runners,"[7] in honor of the festival's eponymous agricultural deity, Robigo (or sometimes masculine Robigus), with the goal "that mildew not harm the grain," *ne robigo frumentis noceat*.[8] If so, the worshippers' collective purpose and intentions suggest that they share knowledge and beliefs, for example, about the nature of these rites and the deity to whom they are addressed. In sharing doxastic attitudes with respect to their collective undertaking, the worshippers stand in contrast to

---

4. See Horn and Martens 2009: 161–63 for catechism of children in early Christianity. See Schwartz 2013: 1–6 and 17–25 for late antique catechism. For a convenient outline of ancient Christian catechetical practices, see M. E. Johnson 2007: 111.

5. Momigliano 1987: 86.

6. For the festival, see Fowler 1899: 88–91; Scullard 1981: 108–10.

7. *Fast. Praen.*, quoted in Fowler 1899: 88: *sacrificium et ludi cursoribus maioribus minoribusque*.

8. *Fast. Praen.*, quoted in Fowler 1899: 88. Cf. Ov. F. 4.921–22: *parce, precor, scabrasque manus a messibus aufer, / neve noce cultis*. Varr. L.L. 6.16: *ne robigo occupet segetes*; Colum. 10.342: *mala robigo virides ne torreat herbas*.

Ovid, in his individual ignorance. He draws closer to hear the flamen's prayer, which occupies the next twenty-one lines.[9]

By listening in, he learns of Robigo, how the god blights crops with mildew and causes iron to rust, and he learns the prayer through which the priest seeks to ward off her action. He then asks the flamen about the puppy he sacrifices, for it is an unusual offering, *nova victima* (4.937). The flamen responds with an idiosyncratic aetiology for the rite. He connects the puppy to the rising of the constellation Canis, with its "Dog Star," Sirius, despite the fact that Canis is at this time of year *setting*.[10] Whatever we think about this case of pontifical, or perhaps poetic, fallibility, and whatever our judgment as to the sincerity of Ovid's autobiographical intentions, the fact remains that cognitive diversity of just this sort—from the shared beliefs and purpose of the worshippers, to the ignorance of the interloping Ovid, to the idiosyncratic "knowledge" of the flamen—is just what we should expect in a tradition that does not enforce cognitive conformity but permits to individuals a large degree of what I have called cognitive autonomy.[11]

Yet Ovid's depiction of a throng of worshippers in matching garb—never mind Livy's account of a city swept by collective belief and anxiety, united in expiatory cult action[12]—suggests that Roman religious culture was also characterized by significant *consensus*, literally, "a feeling together." So, let us begin this chapter by surveying, in section 4.2, the Roman emic discourse of *consensus*. For *consensus* is how the Romans conceptualized the twin topics of this chapter, that is, the *shared Intentionality* that enables *shared agency*. In section 4.3, we shall explore an etic theory of shared Intentionality and shared agency. Section 4.4 returns to the discussion of social norms whose role in individual cognition and action we explored at section 3.3.2. Shared norms, which, as we shall see, exemplify a kind of shared Intentionality, give rise to the large-scale cooperation and behavioral regularities that characterize communities such as Rome. The theory of shared Intentionality developed here and summarized in section 4.5 will allow us, in the coda of section 4.6, to warn against an implausible account of the collective, inherited from Durkheim, whose echoes are still heard in scholarship.

---

9. Ov. *F.* 4.911–32. Cf. learning about the gods from listening to prayer at Ov. *F.* 1.631–33: *siquis amas veteres ritus, adsiste precanti; / nomina percipies non tibi nota prius. / Porrima placatur Postvertaque*. In chapter 8, we examine cultural learning as a result of hearing and intoning prayers.

10. Ov. *F.* 4.937–42. See Fantham 1998 ad 4.902, 4.904, and 4.939.

11. See at sections 1.2 and 3.3.3.

12. At sections 2.5 and 3.2.2.

4.2. Roman Consensus

Cicero provides a convenient point of departure. Drawing on Stoic theory,[13] he maintained that a fundamental social motivation underlies all the cognitive and practical skills that human beings manifest. Our skills of cognition and action, that is to say, are inherently social. Consider this passage from Cicero's *De officiis* (1.157):

> *atque ut apium examina non fingendorum favorum causa congregantur, sed, cum congregabilia natura sint, fingunt favos, sic homines, ac multo etiam magis, natura congregati adhibent agendi cogitandique sollertiam.*

> As swarms of bees do not gather for the sake of making honeycombs, but rather make honeycombs because they are naturally sociable, so human beings, and indeed much more so, when their nature has gathered them together, exercise their resourcefulness in acting and thinking.

Like bees, we do not congregate *in order* to act and to think; rather we act and think in our distinctive ways *as a result* of our natural gregariousness. Our social disposition and our social life together are the wellsprings of all our other properties and capacities.

Cicero expanded on this idea elsewhere, seeking "the natural foundations of human fellowship and partnership (*communitas et societas*)."[14] What he found is "a certain natural partnership (*naturalis quaedam societas*)" of the human *genus*. This "natural partnership" is not itself a product of *consensus*, but rather its source. It consists in *ratio et oratio*, "capacities for reason and speech."[15] The latter—speech—allows us to share the former—reason—with one another through communicative acts of "teaching, learning, sharing, debating, and deciding,"[16] and thus to arrive at common beliefs, intentions, and other forms of shared Intentionality. *Ratio et oratio* stand, therefore, as the conditions of the possibility of *consensus*.

---

13. See Dyck 1996: 339–40 for evaluation of Panaetius or Posidonius as a possible source for Cicero here.

14. Cic. *Off.* 1.50: *sed quae natura principia sint communitatis et societatis humanae, repetendum videtur altius.*

15. The pun is significant. Later sources attest a Roman etymology according to which *oratio* derives from or at least amounts to *oris ratio*, "reason of the mouth": *oratio quasi oris ratio* (see Maltby 1991 s.v. *oratio*).

16. Cic. *Off.* 1.50: *est enim primum quod cernitur in universi generis humani societate. eius autem vinculum est ratio et oratio, quae docendo, discendo, communicando, disceptando, iudicando conciliat inter se homines coniungitque naturali quadam societate.*

Cicero sometimes offers friendship as the strongest expression of *consensus*. For him, the "entire meaning of friendship" resides in the fact that it is based on "a perfect consensus [*summa consensio*] regarding preferences, interests, and opinions."[17] In friendship, minds with "the same interests and inclinations"[18] mingle such that a single mind is made from two, *unus animus ex duobus*,[19] a very strong psychological sharing indeed.[20] Descending from friendship's heights, one finds, outside of Cicero, in colloquial contexts, talk of the communion of mind with mind, as when Plautus's *miles gloriosus* says to his flatterer, "adeptly do you direct your own mind to my mind."[21]

Consensus was also a matter of professional interest to Roman jurists, who theorized that it entailed mutual obligations and potentiated shared agency.[22] Ulpian could illustrate the *consensus* on which contracts, joint ventures, and their obligations were founded with an embodied metaphor. Just as those who share a physical location come together bodily "from different places into a single place," so those who share intentions to act jointly (*consentiunt qui inter se agunt*) come together cognitively *ex diversis animi motibus in unum*, "from diverse mental episodes into a single one," that is, *in unam sententiam*, "to a single purpose."[23] For Ulpian, when we agree on a shared practical pursuit, we figuratively *come together* to stand on common cognitive ground.

Some forms of cognitive coming together in pursuit of practical goals could be viewed with suspicion by the state, as shown by the *Senatus consultum de Bacchanalibus* (186 BCE), a senatorial decree that attempted to curtail the cult

---

17. Cic. *Am*. 15: *id in quo est omnis vis amicitiae, voluntatum, studiorum, sententiarum summa consensio*.

18. Cic. *Off*. 56: *eadem studia . . . eaedem voluntates*.

19. Cic. *Am*. 81: *qui et se ipse diligit et alterum anquirit, cuius animum ita cum suo misceat ut efficiat paene unum ex duobus*; cf. Cic. *Off*. 156: *ut unus fiat ex pluribus*. At *Am*. 80, Cicero presents the true friend as a second self: *tamquam alter idem*.

20. For a cognitive perspective on this Aristotelian idea, see Konstan 2019.

21. Plaut. *Mil*. 1.1.39: *Facete advortis tuom animum ad animum meum*.

22. Extensive treatment of *consensus* in Cascione 2003. Q. Mucius (d. 88 BCE), whose father founded the study of Roman law, already regarded contracts as formed *consensu*: see Fiori 2012: 42–45 on *Dig*. 46.3.80 (Pomp. 4 *ad Q. Mucium*).

23. *Dig*. 2.14.1.3 (Ulp. 4 *ad ed*.): *"conventionis" verbum generale est ad omnia pertinens, de quibus negotii contrahendi transigendique causa consentiunt qui inter se agunt: nam sicuti convenire dicuntur qui ex diversis locis in unum locum colliguntur et veniunt, ita et qui ex diversis animi motibus in unum consentiunt, id est in unam sententiam decurrunt*. Here *conventio* seems to refer to the content of *consensus* (*omnia de quibus consentiunt*) but it could also be a synonym of *consensus*: see *Dig*. 50.12.3; Zimmerman 1990: 563; Fiori 2012: 56–60.

of Bacchus. The senate specifically proscribed shared religious Intentionality with a redundancy of verbs: worshippers will not *coniurare*, "swear common oaths," *convovere*, "vow together," *conspondere*, "pledge in common," *compromittere*, "promise jointly," or *fidem inter se dare*, "give mutual assurances of loyalty."[24] Pledging, promising, vowing: these verbs are significant. For they denote the speech acts, the distinctive uses of *oratio*, through which we express, affirm, and thus generate common knowledge of our *consensus*.[25] That is, in promising and pledging, the parties to *consensus* affirm their first-order beliefs as to the *contents* of their mutual commitments, while they simultaneously engender second-order mutual beliefs, or common knowledge, as to the *fact* that they are jointly committed. People's second-order mutual beliefs to the effect that they are jointly committed to an ideal or a course of action, that is, their belief that they have *consensus*, enables their coordination and cooperation. We shall see in the next chapter (at section 5.3.4) that for Cicero a *populus*, a "people," as opposed to a mere crowd or mob, amounted to a group of individuals united by their *consensus*. Thus, Livy can describe the cult of Bacchus as a menacing "second people," *alter populus*,[26] within, yet apart from, the Roman people.

Licit applications of *consensus* included Roman "partnerships," *societates*, which were formed for the purpose of coordinating joint action toward a shared goal.[27] We have already seen that Cicero could invoke the language of *societas* to characterize figuratively our "natural partnership" of *ratio et oratio*. Partnership, as a legal concept, was considered natural to rational beings and seen to be part of the "law of nations," the *ius gentium*.[28] In Roman law, a *societas* was the collective creation of *socii*, "partners," but it was not an independent "corporate person" in its own right.[29] It existed so long as the *consensus* of the *socii* obtained[30] and ceased to exist when *consensus* ceased to unite the

---

24. CIL I² 581, lines 13–14: *neve post hac inter sed conioura[se nev]e comvovise neve conspondise (14) neve conpromesise velet, neve quisquam fidem inter sed dedise velet.* Lines 19ff. limit the size of cult gatherings. On the Bacchanalian affair, see Pagán 2004: 50–67.

25. On speech acts, see at section 2.3 and chapter 8.

26. Liv. 39.13.14.

27. For the four basic types of *societas*, see *Dig.* 17.2.5pr. (Ulp. 31 *ad ed.*), and see Crook 1967: 229–36; Randazzo 2005; Mousourakis 2012: 234–37; Fleckner 2015.

28. E.g., Gai. *Inst.* 3.154: *sed ea quidem societas, de qua loquimur, id est, quae nudo consensu contrahitur, iuris gentium est; itaque inter omnes homines naturali ratione consistit.*

29. Duff 1938; Abatino et al. 2011; Fleckner 2015.

30. Gai. *Inst.* 3.154, and see the references in the following note. In addition to *consensus*, we sometimes hear of *affectio societatis*, as at *Dig.* 17.2.31 (Ulp. 30 *ad Sab.*).

socii, that is, in cases of *dissensus*, "disagreement," or *contrarius consensus*, that is, agreement to reverse a prior agreement.³¹

Societas generated a deontology, specifically, a set of mutual obligations. Insofar as *socii* endorsed and thereby sustained their *societas* through *consensus*, they thereby also endorsed and sustained their mutual obligations.³² As suggested by Ulpian's metaphor of psychologically "coming together" *in unam sententiam*, "to a single purpose," the point of forming a *societas* was to undertake joint action toward a shared goal. This commitment came with corresponding obligations to act jointly toward the shared goal. Should a partner begin to act on his or her own (*separatim*), for him- or herself (*sibi*), this partner thereby tacitly abandons the joint venture and destroys the *societas*.³³

Let us end this section as we began, with Cicero on "fellowship and partnership," *communitas et societas*.³⁴ He had found that all human beings partake of a "natural" partnership based on shared capacities for reason and speech. These capacities permit us to join in cognitive communion, *consensus*. On our *consensus* are founded our partnerships, *societates*, with their mutual obligations. Seen in this light, Cicero's identification of a "fellowship and partnership [*communitas et societas*] of gods and humans among themselves"³⁵ takes on a new cast. Presumably, he intended by this locution to suggest that a *sharing of Intentionality*, a *consensus*, obtained among gods and mortals, for after all it is from *consensus* that *societas* is formed. The obligations entailed by this particular *societas* are those of *pietas*. As we saw at section 3.3.3, *pietas* offered representations and grounded intuitions and inferences as to religiously obligatory (*religio*), permissible (*fas*), and forbidden (*nefas*) conduct with regard to the gods.³⁶ As such, *pietas* amounted to the deontology, or package of shared norms, that governed the intercourse of gods and mortals in their age-old

---

31. Gai. *Inst.* 3.151; Gai. *Ep.* 2.9.17; *Dig.* 17.2.4.1 (Mod. 3 *reg.*); *Dig.* 17.2.63.10 (Ulp. 31 *ad ed.*); *Dig.* 17.2.65.3 (Paul. 32 *ad ed.*). For *dissensus* and *contrarius consensus*, see *Dig.* 46.3.80 (Pomp. 4 *ad Q. Mucium*); Gai. *Ep.* 2.9.17; *Dig.* 50.17.35 (Ulp. 48 *ad Sab.*); De Ciutiis 2007. See also Daube 1938.

32. Gai. *Inst.* 3.135: *consensu fiunt obligationes in . . . societatibus*. Cf. Gai. *Inst.* 3.136; *Dig.* 50.17.35 (Ulp. 48 *ad Sab.*).

33. *Dig.* 17.2.64 (Call. 1 *quaest.*): *itaque cum separatim socii agere coeperint et unusquisque eorum sibi negotietur, sine dubio ius societatis dissolvitur*.

34. Cic. *Off.* 1.50.

35. Cic. *Off.* 1.153: *deorum et hominum communitas et societas inter ipsos*.

36. *Pietas* underlies all other deontologies: Cic. *N.D.* 1.4: *atque haut scio, an pietate adversus deos sublata fides etiam et societas generis humani et una excellentissuma virtus iustitia tollatur*. Cf. Cic. *Off.* 2.11: *deos placatos pietas efficiet et sanctitas*.

communitas et societas. We pick up *societas* again at section 5.3.4, that is, in the penultimate section of the next chapter, which stands in ring composition with this, the second section of the present chapter. There we shall find that the notion of *societas* pervades and informs Cicero's conception of social reality, especially as a metaphor for that distinctively Roman political arrangement, the republic, whose basic institutional structure depended on the sharing among citizens of certain normative beliefs and political commitments.

4.3. Shared Intentionality and Shared Agency

I have described Roman *consensus*—a cognitive capacity for "coming together," which, as we saw, enabled partnerships, mutual obligations, and collective action—as a form of *shared Intentionality*. Let us now spell out the elements of shared Intentionality more explicitly. As we saw in the introduction and chapter 2, "Intentionality" refers to the mind's directedness on the world. "Shared Intentionality," then, refers to the capacity of individuals to direct their minds on the world *together* and thus to *share* Intentional episodes such as perceptual attention, beliefs, desires, emotions, and intentions. It is, in a sense, a kind of empathic capacity, not just a "tuning in to" but rather a "joining in with" the psychology of others. So, shared Intentionality is cognition *with* other agents, not just cognition *about* other agents. The latter is what usually goes under the rubric "folk psychology."[37] And yet it is cognition *with* others that truly *socializes* our cognition.

Shared Intentionality is not taught or socially learned, for it is the precondition of teaching and social learning. As John Searle puts it, each of us has a "biologically primitive sense of the other person as a candidate for shared Intentionality," and it is this sense of the other that "is a necessary condition of all collective behavior."[38] Cicero might agree: social interaction presupposes not that we meet in the state of nature and strike a deal to be social, as in Lucretius,[39] but that we come to our encounters always already social, always already aware of the other as a potential partner in cognition and action. So, let us now "socialize" the theories of cognition and action that we established in chapters 2 and 3 in order to see how these individual capacities can be shared intersubjectively.[40]

---

37. I draw this distinction between cognition *about* and cognition *with* from Carpenter 2011.
38. Searle 2002: 105.
39. Lucr. 5.1019–27.
40. In what follows I drastically oversimplify a complex field of research. For an overview of the issues, see Schweikard and Schmid 2013. I have found the following to be the most illuminating individual treatments of both of these topics: Gilbert 1990; Searle 1990, 1995, 2002,

4.3.1. Shared Intentionality

We saw, just above, that shared Intentionality is the capacity of individuals to share Intentional episodes such as perceptual attention, beliefs, desires, emotions, and intentions. We can refine this by adding that they must share in the mutual *awareness* that they are sharing. It is not enough if Gaius and Julia both believe that the eagle is the shield bearer of Jupiter but neither has any idea that the other believes this. Instead, in terms of the theory of Intentionality developed in chapter 2, they must share a first-order Intentional content in some psychological mode (in this example, belief) along with a second-order *mutual awareness* or *mutual belief* to the effect that they share the first-order Intentional state.

Recall that *Intentional content* amounts to the perspective from which or the way in which an *Intentional object* or state of affairs is presented or represented, while *psychological mode* distinguishes how the content is held, that is, as perception, belief, desire, fear, intention, and so on.[41] The parties to shared Intentionality share a first-order perception, belief, desire, emotion, or intention (*psychological mode*) regarding, say, a sheep (*object*), which they represent under the aspect of *victima* (*content*). They also share a second-order mutual attitude—some sort of awareness—as to the "sharedness" of the first-order Intentional episode. This second-order awareness may range from a mutual, intuitive sense that "we are on the same page" that this sheep is a *victima*, to a mutual knowledge based in explicit verbal agreement that this sheep is a *victima*. I call this second-order mutual attitude *mutual belief*, because "belief" is our least marked doxastic term. Note that neither first- nor second-order shared Intentional contents need be (and given our cognitive limitations, cannot be) shared as a digital file is shared, as identical copies.[42] Still, our

---

and 2010; Bratman 1992 and 1993; Tomasello, Carpenter et al. 2005; Knoblich and Sebanz 2008; Tomasello 2009; Fiebich and Gallagher 2013; Schmid 2014; Guala 2016: 102–14. My use of the term "shared Intentionality" follows Searle 2002: 105; and Tomasello 2014: 1–6. Fundamental philosophical treatments include Searle 1990; Searle 1995: 23–26 and 37–43; Searle 2010: 8 and 42–60; Gilbert 1990; Bratman 1993; see further, e.g., Tuomela 2007; Schmid 2009; Chant et al. 2014. Syntheses of empirical data for shared Intentionality are Tomasello, Carpenter et al. 2005; and Tomasello and Carpenter 2007. "Shared agency" I borrow from Bratman 2014. Important texts on shared (joint, collective) agency and actions: Searle 1990; Gilbert 1990; Bratman 1992 and 2014; Fiebich and Gallagher 2013. See further Schmid 2009; Gilbert 2013; Tuomela 2013: 97–122. For psychological research and perspectives, see Sebanz et al. 2006; Knoblich and Sebanz 2008; Knoblich et al. 2011.

41. For Intentional content and psychological mode, see at sections 2.2.3 and 2.2.4.

42. Contra Tarde's conception of imitation as an "empreinte de photographie interspirituelle" (1895: viii). At the other end of the theoretical spectrum, Durkheim, Bourdieu, and

social-cognitive capacities—empathy, taking another's perspective, inferring and reasoning about another's beliefs and desires, not to mention linguistic and pragmatic competence as well as conversational feedback and repair[43]—ensure a rough-and-ready sharing of Intentional contents adequate to successful communication and to the practical purposes of sharing agency in joint action. To shared agency we now turn.

4.3.2. Shared Agency and Joint Action

How do individuals transcend parallel action[44] and mutually responsive action[45] to *share* agency in truly cooperative action, where *you* and *I* do something together, as a *we*? To begin with, shared agency requires shared Intentionality. You and I share agency when we act together because we share a common goal and an intention to act together toward that goal, along with mutual belief that we share the goal and the intention. Sharing an intention to act together, that is, a "we-intention,"[46] amounts to you and I each intending to act, not each of us by our own self toward our own goal, and not even each by our own self toward a common goal, but rather jointly, as a "we," each of us contributing our own part to *our* joint action with *our* common goal in view. Each of us acts only as part of *our* acting *together*, in the mutual belief that each of us *intends together* with the other. Note that our common goal may be to bring about some state of affairs in the world, but it need be no more than the joint action itself, for example, dancing together.[47] Action resulting from we-intentions may be called, let us stipulate, *joint action*.

In figure 4.1, I have attempted to illustrate the cognitive structure of sharing agency in joint action. In joint action, two (or more) individuals share a common or joint goal. They also have "we-intentions," that is, as we saw, a joint plan of action, which represents each doing his or her own part in their joint action to realize their joint goal. Thus, the agents fill complementary roles (ROLE X and ROLE Y in figure 4.1). That is, each acts according to an individual subplan that meshes efficaciously with the other agent's or agents' subplan(s).

---

like-minded theorists face a "downloading problem," to wit, "the idea that people can in effect download frameworks or practices from some collective server" (Turner 2002: 17, summing up Turner 1994). See section 4.6, below.

43. For conversational repair, see Hayashi et al. 2013.
44. You do what you do, while I do what I do.
45. You and I each adjust our own doings in light of the doings of the other.
46. On "we-intentions," see Searle 1990; Tuomela 2007: 83–105; Tuomela 2013: 62–96. For an interactionist approach to "we-mode" social cognition, see Gallotti and Frith 2013.
47. Fiebich and Gallagher 2013.

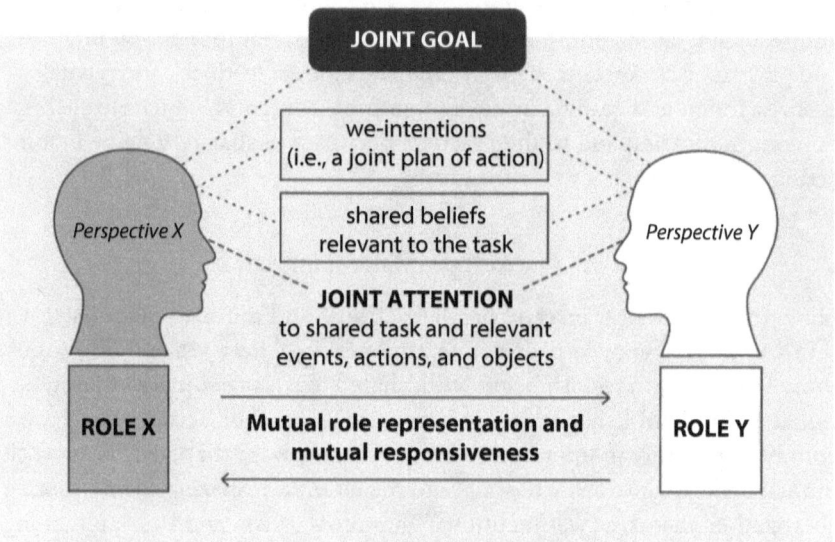

FIGURE 4.1. The cognitive structure of joint action.
(Created by Kate Stanchak, after Tomasello 2014, fig. 3.1.)

Note that this entails that each agent's we-intention represents the joint goal, and the overall action plan, and his or her own and his or her partner's (or partners') action subplan(s). Each agent brings his or her own perspective (Perspective X and Perspective Y), both perceptual and cognitive, to the shared task. Yet the agents share (and mutually believe that they share) beliefs relevant to the joint goal and to the task that they plan jointly to undertake. In the course of performing the shared task, they jointly attend, each from his or her own unique perspective, to the task itself as it unfolds, and thus to the events that occur during its unfolding, to the objects that are relevant to the task, and to their own and their partner's (or partners') actions. This joint attention to one another's actions permits each agent to be mutually responsive to the other and to adjust his or her own actions and subplan to those of his or her partner(s).

What we see, then, is that shared agency, like the joint action that it enables, and like the shared Intentionality on which it depends, "has a dual-level structure which combines social sharedness with individual differentiation."[48] In joint action, agents take into account—through observation; empathy; perspective taking; inferring beliefs, desires and intentions; and explicit

---

48. B. Gordon and Theiner 2015: 160.

communication—the individual Intentionality and roles of their collaborators. Jointly acting agents implicitly recognize that no one agent shares with any other precisely identical Intentional contents or action roles, yet each tries to take the perspective of collaborators and imagine how things look through their eyes. Of course, the parties' "perspectives never fuse with one another."[49] Rather, the joint Intentionality of joint action requires constantly taking others' perspectives and roles into account in order to repair breaches of sharing relevant to the interaction and thus to sustain the jointness of Intentionality and the meshing of action roles in real time.

This is the skeletal structure of shared agency and joint action.[50] Note that the "bones" that compose the skeleton include shared perceptual episodes, shared doxastic states, and shared practical states. In this, joint action amounts, in a sense, to a "cooperativization" of the individual action we examined at section 3.3. In section 4.3.5, we shall put some flesh on the bones of this skeleton by way of a consideration of the cognitive structure of a simple collective sacrifice.

4.3.3. Mutual Belief

For now, let us note that the conditions for both shared Intentionality and shared agency that we have just put forward specify a role for mutual belief. This is a condition for the genuine sharing of Intentionality and agency.[51] It again highlights the importance of belief. For when two or more subjects share an Intentional episode, as I have outlined it, they share both a first-order Intentional content in a psychological mode (that is, a determinate belief, desire, intention, etc.) and a second-order Intentional content in the form of a mutual belief that the first-order state or episode is shared. In other words, each subject has a perception, a belief, a desire, an intention, or some other Intentional episode, and each is *aware* of sharing that Intentional episode with the other.[52]

Mutual belief has excited controversy,[53] in part because it seems to require that *you* believe that *I* believe, and *I* believe that *you* believe, and you believe

---

49. Zahavi and Rochat 2015: 547; the entire article is highly relevant to the present discussion.

50. My discussion of joint action here depends on Bratman 1992 and Tomasello 2014: 32–79, which also owes a great deal to Bratman 1992.

51. See Schweikard and Schmid 2013.

52. See H. Clark 1996: 93–94 and 120.

53. Compare Lewis 1969: 52–60 on "common knowledge"; Sperber and Wilson 1995: 38–46 on a "mutual cognitive environment"; H. Clark 1996: 92–121 on "common ground"; List 2014: 1609–11 on "common attitudes"; and the "mindreading"-based solution of Guala 2016: 89–101.

that *I* believe that you believe, and I believe that *you* believe that I believe, and so forth, ad infinitum. We should obviously not suppose that anyone represents this infinite regress in their head. Rather, mutual belief may amount merely to a nonreflective sense that we share attitudes—beliefs, intentions, and so on—in common.[54] Note that this latter scenario depends on nothing more than empathy and basic folk psychological capacities for inferring others' beliefs and Intentional states. And, of course, mutual belief may top out, at a reflective level, with explicit verbal confirmation as to the attitudes shared.

It is easy to see why we need mutual belief for shared ageny. The *flamen Quirinalis* and Ovid may walk into the grove of Robigo side by side, but they are engaged in *joint* action only if they *both* intend to do so *together* and if this shared intention is a matter of mutual belief between them. Without shared Intentionality, they are merely two men chancing to show up in the grove of Robigo at the same moment. Alternatively, if Ovid intends to walk into the grove with the flamen but the flamen does not share this intention, then Ovid is perhaps following or even stalking the flamen.

Note that in neither of these latter two cases could or would the flamen reproach Ovid if he abruptly peeled away just before reaching the grove and headed on to Rome. However, in the case of genuine joint action, the flamen could complain, and his complaint would depend on the fact that in abandoning him, Ovid would be defecting on their *consensus*, that is, their we-intention to walk to the grove together. This shows that truly joint action is constituted of internal norms, especially obligations, that derive from mutual commitments.[55] If we "we-intend" to act together, and one of us fails to act, a kind of "social rationality of interdependence"[56] has been violated. Joint actions, and their mutual obligations and norms, arise only in conditions of true shared Intentionality, which requires mutual belief. That is, each party intends to *act*, but only as part of *acting together*, and each believes that the other so intends, and each believes that the other believes that he or she so intends.

A further scenario brings out our essential point about the necessity of mutual belief. Imagine, for example, that thousands of Romans bear roughly similar Intentional states, say, *desire* for debt relief, but with no mutual

---

54. Moll et al. 2010 shows that young children *overestimate* the extent of mutual knowledge shared with partners. Apparently, we start out in life *assuming* that information is shared in common and have to *learn* to think or *mature* into thinking otherwise.

55. My example is adapted from Gilbert 1990; on joint commitment as the basic building block of social reality, see Gilbert 2013.

56. Tomasello 2009: 41.

awareness that they share such a desire. They have a classic "coordination problem," with obvious implications for shared agency and joint action.[57] Their lack of mutual belief will make cooperation and coordination—deliberating, bargaining, and acting—to address their shared desire impossible. The desire that each has individually is not out in the open among them and so cannot ground coordinated action. These Romans "share" the desire in only the weakest sense of sharing. Each has the desire, unbeknownst to the others.

However, if *collective* belief as to the shared desire should arise among them, perhaps at one of the public occasions enumerated by Cicero as conducive to the expression of the popular will, the *contiones*, voting *comitiae*, or the games,[58] then everyone's desire for debt relief comes out in the open and becomes mutually manifest. This shared Intentionality sets the stage for shared agency. The like-minded communicate and jointly commit themselves to acting on their shared desire. They try to force a meeting of the senate in order to address their shared desire.[59] Each individual commits to acting with the others and coordinates his or her own actions with the actions of the others because of sharing with them we-intentions to act together, as a group, toward their common goal.

In this light, a remark of Seneca about the lack of distinctive dress for slaves reveals its full import: without any identity marker, the extent to which slaves outnumbered their masters could not become mutually apparent to them. Mutual ignorance precluded any joint action on the part of the slaves against their masters.[60]

4.3.4. Aggregate versus Collective versus Joint Intentionality

We are now in a position to distinguish truly *shared* from merely *aggregate* Intentionality.[61] Aggregate Intentionality is but a summing up of individual attitudes. It is the most weakly "collective" form of Intentionality. As in the

---

57. The classic treatment of "coordination problems" is Lewis 1969: 5–51. Chwe 2001 treats ritual as a "rational" source of common knowledge and hence as a coordination facilitator. See below, chapter 8, for my development of Chwe's theory of rational ritual: I call rituals that include gods in the circle of common knowledge "superrational rituals." See Ober 2008 and Teegarden 2013 for coordination problems and their solutions in ancient Greece.

58. Cic. *Sest.* 106, on which, see Kaster 2006: 330ff. Such public occasions could also, of course, reveal dissension rather than accord, as at Plu. *Cic.* 13.3.

59. As at Liv. 2.2.23.

60. Sen. *Clem.* 1.24.1.

61. *Aggregate* (or *summative*) Intentionality: List 2014: 1602–9; Tollefsen 2015: 1–15. *Shared* Intentionality admits of further distinctions: see below. For further discussion, see Searle 2010:

example of debt relief, Seius desires such a policy, and Titius desires such a policy, but they lack mutual awareness. One could say that they "collectively" hold this desire and thus form a collective or group defined by this desire, but their "sharing" is very weak because they do not mutually recognize that they share this desire. Similarly, there were surely all sorts of things that Romans believed in this weak, aggregate sense. And there would also have been various forms of only weakly collective aggregate agency, such as that exercised by all Romans who drank Falernian wine and who thereby constituted an aggregate collective of Falernian wine drinkers, acting "together" to drive up demand for the wine.

Compare aggregate collectives such as the following: Romans under four feet tall; Romans privately against Cicero's exile; Romans whose *lararium* contains a statuette of Fortuna. These aggregate collectives "share" in only the weakest sense. They have little emic value because individuals do not identify as part of a collective of, for example, short Romans or Fortuna worshippers. However, such groups do have etic value:[62] they are analytically and descriptively useful for scholars interested in discovering, say, median heights in Roman Italy, distributions of Fortuna in *lararia*, or why some wines were more expensive than others. Aggregate collectives *do* affect the social world.

In contrast, *shared Intentionality* amounts, as we have seen, to individuals having a belief, a desire, an intention, or another Intentional episode, with mutual belief that the Intentional episode is shared. Individuals who share Intentionality may form a weaker or stronger "we." At the weaker end of the spectrum, individuals need not interact or cooperate directly, as they did in our idealized joint action in section 4.3.2 (with figure 4.1), but instead merely pursue their individual activities on the basis of their (fallible) belief that certain knowledge, beliefs, values, or normative attitudes are "common ground"[63] between themselves and others around them. This weak shared Intentionality is what makes everything from spontaneous and uncoordinated crowds, such as, perhaps, Apuleius's throng of Isiac worshippers (examined at sections 2.5 and 3.2.2), to large-scale communities, such as Rome, possible. Let us distinguish this weak sharing from stronger instances by calling it *collective Intentionality*.

42–58; List 2014: 1609–21; Tomasello 2014: 32–79 and 80–123; B. Gordon and Theiner 2015: 159–64 and 164–68.

62. List 2014: 1606.

63. H. Clark 1996: 92–121.

Collective Intentionality is everywhere in evidence. Ovid, for example, took for granted, as matters of shared belief and knowledge between himself and the flamen, that the grove of Robigo was a cult site, that the white-clad crowd was there to worship, that they were engaged in an act of cult, that the flamen was the presiding religious authority, and indeed that he could understand and respond to Ovid's questions in Latin. Ovid simply assumed that these and countless other things were matters of *cultural* or *communal common ground* among himself, the troupe, and its leader.[64] Had he not made such an assumption, he would have approached the worshippers and their priest rather differently, perhaps seeking to determine what language they spoke or to discover what sort of activity—cultic, culinary, political, dramaturgic, and so on—they were engaged in.

Cicero deploys much this notion of communal common ground in describing the *communia*, "shared things," that bind together citizens (*cives*) in a city-state (*civitas*). These *communia* include "a forum, temples, piazzas, roads, laws, rights, courts of law, and elections."[65] This enumeration of *communia* maps the literal and figurative topography of the communal common ground on which *cives* stand together. Communal common ground makes even strangers, such as Ovid and the flamen, intelligible to one another and able to cooperate, because they can simply assume that they share the same language, local knowledge, norms, practices, institutions, and so on.

We may now distinguish the more intimate or stronger form of shared Intentionality, on which we have primarily focused in this chapter (see section 4.3.2), as *joint Intentionality*. It goes beyond unreflectively assuming that one shares—as a matter of weaker collective Intentionality—beliefs, knowledge, and norms with those around oneself. Indeed, joint Intentionality may arise from collective Intentionality, as it did when Ovid and the flamen initiated conversation. Joint Intentionality is, as we have seen, interactive and cooperative. It is the level of shared Intentionality at which we-intentions are formed.[66] It thus enables the sharing of agency in joint action. In cases of joint Intentionality, agents may experience their togetherness as a "plural pre-reflective self-awareness,"[67] a sense of themselves as a plural subject, a strong "we." The mutually manifest fact of their strong sharing, their sense of being a

---

64. On "communal common ground," see H. Clark 1996: 100–112.

65. Cic. *Off*. 1.53: *multa enim sunt civibus inter se communia: forum, fana, porticus, viae, leges, iura, iudicia, suffragia.*

66. We return to joint Intentionality at section 7.4.

67. Schmid 2014: 7.

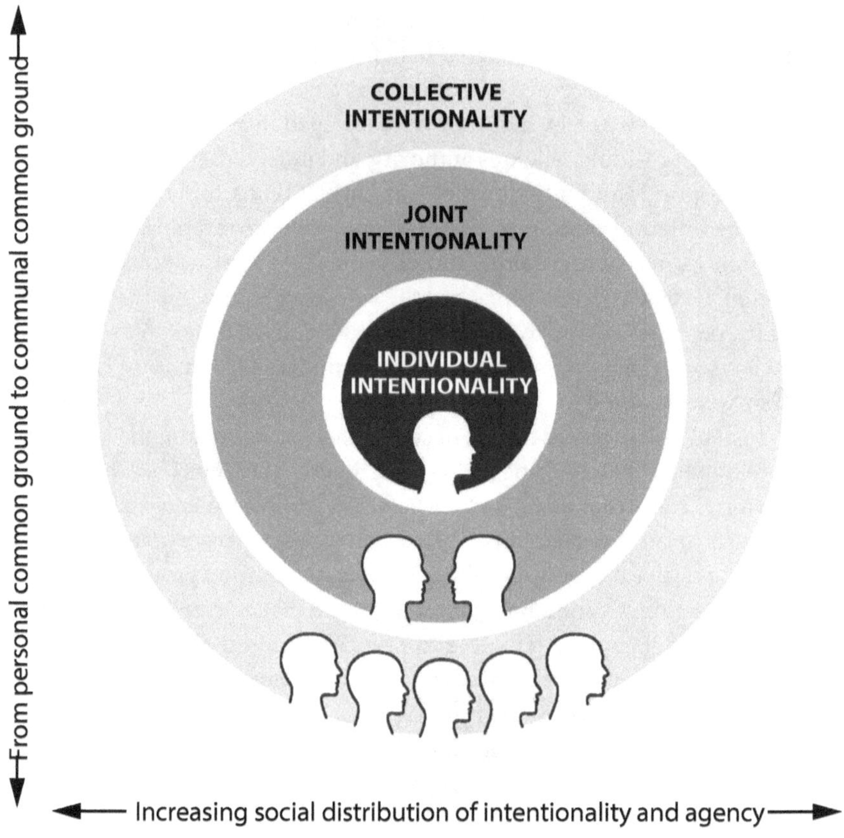

FIGURE 4.2. Relationship of *individual* Intentionality to *shared* Intentionality, differentiating the levels of individual Intentionality, the stronger *joint* form of Intentionality (see fig. 4.1), and the weaker *collective* form of Intentionality. (Created by Kate Stanchak, after Gordon and Theiner 2015, fig. 1.)

"we," along with the content of their shared sensory perceptions, perspectives, beliefs, memories, desires, norms, and intentions makes up the agents' constantly updating *personal common ground*.[68] Thus, joint Intentionality not only enables but also arises from shared agency, in the form of the intersubjectively shared experience that makes up personal common ground. Figure 4.2 depicts schematically the expanding circles of individual, joint, and collective Intentionality.[69]

---

68. On "personal common ground," see H. Clark 1996: 112–20.

69. It will perhaps be noticed that my distinction between joint and collective Intentionality parallels a distinction proposed by Jan Assmann between "communicative" and "cultural"

4.3.5. Jointly Sharing Beliefs and Agency in Sacrifice

Let us now imagine, as a concrete example of joint Intentionality, with shared agency, shared belief, and other shared attitudes, a two-person sacrifice, such as that depicted in the fresco that stood outside the kitchen in the House of C. Julius Polybius at Pompeii (figure 4.3).[70] Here we see the "guardian spirits" of the wife and husband, her *juno* and his *genius*, sacrificing at an altar, framed by the much larger twin household gods, the *Lares*. We should almost certainly take the *juno* and *genius* to represent, in an idealized scene of domestic cult, the wife and husband themselves, as they make an offering to their *Lares*.[71] Usually, in literary and graphic representations, the *genius* of the *paterfamilias* is depicted, whether alone or with the *juno*, as the leader of sacrifice.[72] Here, however, as Harriet Flower notes, the figures' "precisely choreographed identical gestures suggest harmony and parity over any sense of precedence between *juno* and *genius*."[73] They are depicted as being on a par with one another as officiants of sacrifice.

Now, it must be conceded that there may be some modes of action that require only that organisms interact dynamically and "enactively" with their environments and one another through immediate perception and action. However, it seems likely that a norm-governed joint action such as this sacrifice to the *Lares* requires the participants to entertain and share a variety of practical and doxastic representations. Cultural joint actions that reflect cultural beliefs and norms, such as this one, are, I would submit, "representation-hungry" tasks.[74] Figure 4.4 attempts to capture some of these representations. It updates figure 4.1, which depicted a hypothetical

---

memory (Assmann 2011). I see the theory proposed here as complementary to but broader than Assmann's, which limits itself to but one form of mind-to-world Intentionality, i.e., memory.

70. For discussion of this fresco, see Flower 2017: 59–61, with further references. In practice, as in this fresco, most sacrifices would have featured more than two participants, including such attendants as *victimarius*, *popa*, *tibicen*, *camillus*, and others: see Fröhlich 1991: 114–19. For two participants in domestic sacrifice, see, e.g., Tib. 1.10.19–24, and for more than two, see Ov. *F.* 2.645–58 (both discussed at section 7.4, below) and Hor. *Ep.* 2.1.139–44.

71. Flower 2017: 60. On the *juno*, see Rives 1992.

72. E.g., Cato *Agr.* 143.1: *dominum pro tota familia rem divinam facere*.

73. Flower 2017: 60.

74. See Andy Clark 1997: 166–70. Cognitively "leaner" theories of joint action have been proposed (e.g., Vesper et al. 2010; Pacherie 2013; Knoblich et al. 2011: 62–64), but I submit that complex conventional joint actions like sacrifice require a cognitively rich account. An ideal account of joint ritual action, well beyond the scope of this book, would integrate a cognitively

FIGURE 4.3. Fresco from the House of C. Julius Polybius at Pompeii, showing the *juno* and *genius* ("spirits" of the family's matron and patron) sacrificing at an altar to the twin household gods, the Lares, who frame the composition. Note, too, the diminutive flute player (*tibicen*, left), and altar boy (*camillus*, right). (Wikimedia Commons.)

generic joint action, by depicting the cognitive structure of a normative cultural joint action.

As figure 4.4 shows schematically, the husband and wife share immediate joint perceptual attention to cult objects such as the altar and the offerings, as well as to other relevant aspects of the environment. And, indeed, this is how they are depicted in the fresco (figure 4.3). They also share practical attitudes, such as the shared goal of making sacrifice and we-intentions (a joint action plan) to attain their goal. They share doxastic attitudes, not only beliefs about the *Lares*, the sacrificial act, and the significance of these things, but also

---

rich account with accounts of lower-level entrainment and alignment mechanisms, as in Knoblich and Sebanz 2008; and Tollefsen and Dale 2012.

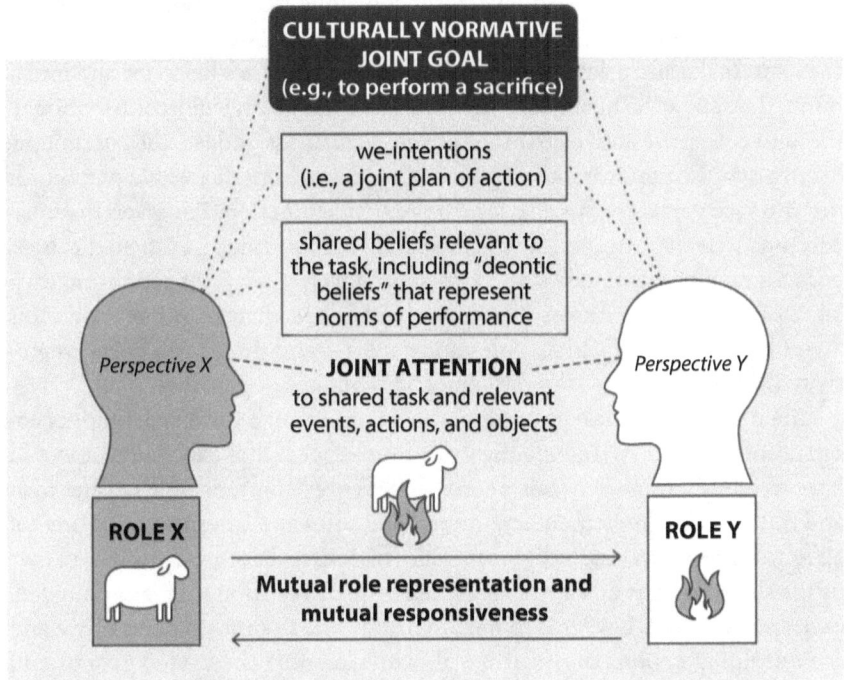

FIGURE 4.4. The cognitive structure of joint cultural action as exampled by sacrifice. From top to bottom: shared representations of the *goal* to sacrifice, *we-intentions* to act jointly toward the goal; and shared *beliefs* about the nature, purpose, and gods of the practice, and shared deontic beliefs about ritual *norms*. Participants *jointly attend* to the task and its objects. Each participant has his or her own *perspective* on the scene and represents his or her own *role* in the joint action but also remains *responsive* to the perspectives and actions of others and *represents* how their roles mesh with his or her own. (Created by Kate Stanchak, after Tomasello 2014, fig. 3.1.)

deontic beliefs about when and why they should sacrifice as well as about the "constitutive rules"[75] that govern sacrificial performance.

It is worth lingering briefly over the deontic beliefs shared by the husband and wife in the context of this sacrifice. Some of these shared deontic beliefs represent norms of sacrificial practice. These norms of practice have action-guiding, action-evaluative, and action-predictive functions. The guiding function is perhaps most obvious: norms spell out permissions, prescriptions, and

---

75. For constitutive rules of ritual, see Humphrey and Laidlaw 1994: 117–21 (drawing on Searle 1969: 33–42) and section 5.3.2, below.

prohibitions on action. The evaluative function follows from these shared beliefs about permissions, prescriptions, and prohibitions. For shared norms allow agents to make and acknowledge claims on one another's behavior and intentions. They allow the husband to monitor and evaluate his wife's contribution to the joint enterprise and her to monitor and evaluate his. Indeed, they permit the "normative self-monitoring,"[76] by which he makes himself a viable partner for her and vice versa. Norms also have a predictive function. For given that husband and wife share norms, she can predict his behavior, and he can predict hers, because each of them knows the norms that govern their joint action and each knows that the other knows the norms (and knows that the other knows this about him- or herself). Shared deontic beliefs—and the shared norms represented as their content—thus smooth and facilitate cooperation.

The couple's identical gestures in the fresco, though idealized, put this cooperation on display. The identical gestures suggest that each partner would have to entertain more or less determinate representations of his or her own and the other's complementary, interrelated roles and "meshing subplans" of action.[77] These meshing subplans would, of course, have been guided in part by the shared norms of the ritual. As their respective action subplans unfolded, each spouse would have had to remain responsive to shifts in perspective and the unfolding actions of the other, all while keeping the shared goal or end point in view. Thus, the collaborators would share perceptual attention, beliefs, and we-intentions against a background of their own individual perspectives, roles, and subplans relevant to the joint action.

Let us switch from the *lararium* sacrifice back to Ovid's Robigalia in order to take note of just how deep the cognitive sharing in such joint actions can go. We must suppose that the white-clad worshippers shared, as Ovid did not, a certain *savoir rituel*,[78] including deontic beliefs about liturgical norms, about the proper use of implements—*patera*, "libation bowl"; *acerra*, "incense box"; and *focus*, "portable altar"[79]—and about the hierarchically organized, interlocking roles of at least some participants. It is also likely that the worshippers shared (and mutually believed that they shared) a reflective belief that they were celebrating the Robigalia, as required by the festival calendar on that day, VII Kal. Mai., in honor of the divinity whom they (also reflectively) believed to avert *robigo*.[80]

---

76. Tomasello 2014: 87–90 and 118–20.
77. I owe "meshing subplans" to Bratman 2014: 53–56.
78. Scheid 1990: 673.
79. All mentioned at Ov. *F.* 4.934–35.
80. Robigo, *quem putabant robiginem avertere* (Fest. 325 Lindsay).

These reflective beliefs would have been founded on shared nonreflective beliefs and intuitions, such as that the deity was an agent and could thus be *pleased* or *displeased* by states of affairs that he or she could perceive, represent, and so appraise.[81] Thus, the worshippers presumably attributed, quite nonreflectively, to the deity all the representational and motivational faculties of agents in general, to wit, perceptions, beliefs, and preferences (see section 2.6.2). This intuitive sort of reasoning about agents in general supported the reflective belief that Robigo was capable of being pleased, that is, was *placable*, in culturally specific ways. Indeed, the worshippers—but not Ovid, who had to learn this detail from them—shared the reflective belief that the god preferred sacrifices "with the blood and entrails of a suckling puppy."[82] Finally, to engage together in the cult act was to presuppose collectively that the god had a social mind receptive to and reciprocal of such communications. (Note that all these nonreflective beliefs and intuitions are perfectly consistent with confusion, uncertainty, disagreement, or lack of interest as to the divine gender.)[83] All these observations could be repeated, mutatis mutandis, for the joint sacrifice to the *Lares* depicted in figure 4.3.

These considerations suggest that collective ritual, whether on the scale of Ovid's public sacrifice or the domestic scale of the *lararium* painting, is cognitively much richer than mere savoir faire or "know how." Figure 4.4 attempts to represent but some of this richness, by putting the flesh of a collective cultural practice on the skeleton of joint action that was depicted in figure 4.1.[84] I say, "but some of this richness," for in this chapter I have not even broached the fact that joint ritual action might flow from or result in shared emotions, as suggested by our earlier discussions of Livy's *prodigia* and Apuleius's Isiac throng. I refer readers to those earlier discussions (sections 2.5 and 3.2.2) and limit myself here to just a few words about shared emotion in Roman cult.[85]

---

81. The god is thus subject to the "appraisal" theory of emotions explicated at section 3.2.

82. Colum. 10.342–43: *hinc mala robigo virides ne torreat herbas, / sanguine lactentis catuli placatur et extis*. Divine placability in general: Cic. *Off.* 2.11: *deos placatos pietas efficiet et sanctitas*.

83. *Robigus* in Varro R.R. 1.6.0 and the *Fasti Praenestini* but *Robigo* in Ov. *F.* 4.907 and 911. Perhaps it was simple metonymy that allowed Ovid to call the god Robigus by the term more appropriate to his domain, *robigo*: see Fantham 1998 ad 4.907–8 and Fest. 325 Lindsay.

84. I have not here even attempted to capture the cognitive richness of *individual* skilled, habitual action, for which see Sutton et al. 2011; and Christensen et al. 2016.

85. For theoretical reflections on shared emotions, see J. Michael 2011; Von Scheve 2012; Von Scheve and Ismer 2013; Schmid 2017. For some Roman reflections on collective emotions, see Sen. *Ira* 3.2.2ff., 3.16.2.

We are in a position to make an important theoretical point about the relevance of all this shared Intentionality, especially shared beliefs, to shared emotion in Roman cult. Research in the cognitive sciences continues to substantiate the Durkheimian hypothesis that participating together in ritual binds people socially and fosters in-group cohesion.[86] However, a sense of bonding, or in-group cohesion, or even the shared emotion of relief, as in our example from Livy (at section 3.2.2)—in short, any affective *effect* of group ritual—can occur only insofar as people already share at least *some* Intentionality.[87] That is, without shared perceptions and doxastic representations—for example, beliefs about the nature and valence of the ritual act, its gods, its occasion, its purpose, and its other concomitants—individuals are unlikely to share emotional responses to group ritual.

To illustrate this point, consider the following hypothetical scenarios. The husband and wife depicted in the fresco in figure 4.3 are substantially divided on the question as to whether sacrifice *placates* or *enrages* the *Lares*. The Roman *populus* described by Livy does not collectively believe that cult expiates *prodigia*—that is, individual cognitive diversity within the *populus* is so great that various individuals variously suppose sacrifice to be a matter of religious indifference,[88] a travesty of piety,[89] or a cult of demons.[90] In these scenarios of belief diversity, husband and wife are highly unlikely to sacrifice to the *Lares* together, and Livy's *populus* is hardly going to experience the shared emotional response of relief upon the performance of expiatory rites. Differing beliefs would sponsor not only differing practical attitudes with respect to cult action but also differing emotional responses to it.

I want to emphasize that only when certain beliefs are already collectively shared in common ground can collective ritual take place, let alone contribute to strengthening social bonds or to a shared emotional response such as relief. This latter point is central to the argument of this book, so it deserves reiteration. We saw at section 3.2 that emotions depend on beliefs and other representations, such as memories and perceptions, of how things stand in the world. Given this dependence of emotion on belief, we need *shared* beliefs to account for *shared* emotions in response to cult. Thus, if we suppose the Romans ever experienced collective emotions in religious contexts, we must accept that they could share beliefs (and other forms of Intentionality), as well.

---

86. For reviews, see Legare and Wen 2014; and Whitehouse and Lanman 2014.
87. A point well made by Von Scheve 2012.
88. E.g., Sen. *Ben.* 1.6.3. Cf. Plin. *Pan.* 3.
89. E.g., Lucr. 5.1198–203.
90. 1 Cor. 10:20, on which, see Ullucci 2012: 73–74. Cf. Aug. *Civ.* 8–10 passim.

Let us now close this section by reflecting on how cultural, conventional, and social normativity depends on natural normativity. All sharing of agency, from spontaneous joint action to deliberate, culturally scripted, group ritual, such as a family's sacrifice to the *Lares*, or a troupe's sacrifice to Robigo, involves natural, internal norms. At sections 2.2.6 and 3.3.4, we discussed norms natural and internal to individual forms of Intentionality such as belief, intentions, and action. Similarly, there are norms natural and internal to the sharing of Intentionality and agency, norms, that is, that must obtain among agents in any cooperative enterprise if it is to succeed qua cooperative enterprise.

Call these "norms of cooperation" or "cooperative norms."[91] Cooperative norms, unlike social norms, are not cultural products, though they render cultural norms, such as social norms and conventions, possible. They amount simply to those standards that make joint action *joint*. To flout them is to decline to act jointly. As we saw in our imaginary case of the flamen protesting Ovid's abandonment of their joint walk (section 4.3.3), cooperative norms allow agents to make and acknowledge claims on one another's conduct. In our imaginary scenario, the flamen implicitly appealed to a constitutive norm of cooperation in protesting when Ovid veered off in another direction. In this event, cooperation failed, and the flamen's expectations of Ovid as a cooperative partner were frustrated. Cooperating individuals expect certain conduct from one another and know that others expect certain conduct from them, given the content of the we-intentions in their personal common ground. Culturally distinct social norms, to which we turn in the next section, will of course also come to bear, even on activities as seemingly "natural" and "universal" as walking together.[92] However, any joint action where social norms apply, such as a joint sacrifice to the *Lares*, can occur only if participating agents observe natural norms of cooperation. Culturally specific social normativity depends on the normativity natural and internal to cooperation as such.

4.4. Norms, Collective Intentionality, Communal Common Ground, and Large-Scale Cooperation

We now turn to a consideration of social norms and packages of social norms, such as *pietas*, which serve to coordinate collective behavior on both small and large scales, thus giving rise to group-level regularities. We shall focus on the central role of shared belief in sustaining these social norms. At sections 2.3 and especially 3.3.2, I placed all normative phenomena under the rubric

---

91. Here I follow closely Tomasello 2009: 34–44 and 88–98.
92. For walking in Roman culture, see O'Sullivan 2011.

deontology. We saw that social norms and other deontic phenomena exist and motivate individual action, in part, because individuals *believe* they exist and make legitimate claims on their conduct. Agents represent mays, may nots, oughts, and ought nots, musts and must nots, as the contents of deontic beliefs. If they did not do so, the relevant permissions (mays), obligations (oughts and musts), and prohibitions (may nots, ought nots, and must nots) would not exist. Because agents take mays, may nots, and the rest to make legitimate claims on them, the packages of social norms that constitute deontologies supply them with desire-independent, normative reasons to act in one way rather than another.

We began to "socialize" this picture of norms with our discussion of shared deontic beliefs and shared norms in the previous section. Let us now continue exploring the role of shared Intentionality in underlying and supporting norms and packages of norms, such as *pietas*. Here I draw on the work of Cristina Bicchieri, a philosopher of normativity. She suggests that social norms exist when a substantial number of agents in a group not only believe (1) that there is a given rule that applies in a given situation, but also follow that rule because they believe (2) that many group members believe that there is such a rule and conform to it (she calls this an "empirical expectation"), and (3) that many group members believe that there is such a rule and expect and prefer *them* to conform to it, too, and may punish them for failure to conform (a "normative expectation").[93]

The first belief, about the existence of a given rule applicable to a given situation, is just the sort of deontic belief we examined in the previous chapter, at section 3.3.2. It is a matter of a subject representing, in the Intentional content of a belief, a determinate permission, prescription, or prohibition. People will follow this rule conditionally, that is, on the condition that they have two further beliefs, both of which depend critically on our capacities for social cognition. The first of these additional beliefs (number 2, above) is an empirical expectation based on what we have seen or heard about what others usually do. For example, a Roman man might have observed among his neighbors that upon the birth of a baby, the parents set up, in the atrium of the home, a *lectisternium* as an offering to the gods. This amounts to a couch (*lectus*) with an image of a god or gods, and a table (*mensa*) bearing food offerings, all of which

---

93. This paragraph reflects my adaptation of "Conditions for a Social Norm to Exist" of Bicchieri 2006: 11, and see further 8–28. See also Bicchieri 2016: viii, xiii–xiv, and 11–15. For an illuminating comparison of Bicchieri's account of norms with the important cognitive evolutionary account of, e.g., Chudek and Henrich 2011 and Chudek, Zhao, and Henrich 2013, see Kelly and Davis 2018.

might remain in place for a week.[94] He may come to believe as a result of observing this behavior that new parents believe they should, and usually will, set up a *lectisternium* upon the birth of a baby.[95]

The second additional belief (number 3, above) amounts to our second-order normative expectation concerning *other people's* deontic beliefs about what *we* should do. This belief does not track what others typically will do themselves (that is the job of belief number 2), but rather what others expect *us* to do, that is, what norms they expect us to follow. This belief may go hand in hand with a highly motivating belief, which supplies a further desire-independent reason to act, to the effect that others will punish our failure to follow the norms in question. This punishment can be as mild as an expression of disapproval.

Thus, in addition to the deontic belief that one should set up a lectisternium upon the birth of a baby, and the empirical expectation that parents usually will set up a lectisternium upon the birth of a baby, our Roman might believe that *others* believe that *he* (and his wife, and all other relevant group members) *should* set up a *lectisternium* upon the birth of a baby. Using this example, we may schematize as follows the beliefs that are required for the social norm of setting up a *lectisternium* to obtain:

Belief 1 (deontic belief):
one should set up a lectisternium upon the birth of a baby.

Belief 2 (empirical expectation):
new parents hold Belief 1 and usually set up a lectisternium upon the birth of a baby.

Belief 3 (normative expectation):
other people hold Belief 1, expect me to set up a lectisternium upon the birth of my baby, and may punish me if I do not.

Note that Belief 1, the deontic belief, exhibits the universality that is characteristic of social norms. That is, its obligation applies not to you alone or to me alone, but to all group members (here, Romans) in a given situation (here, the

---

94. Lectisternia could be set up for Juno (Tert. *An.* 39: *per totam hebdomadam Junoni mensa*), for Juno and Hercules (Serv. *ad Ecl.* 4.62: *in atrio domus Iunonis lectus, Herculi mensa*), or for Pilumnus and Picumnus (Varr. *Vit.* apud Non. 848L): *dis coniugalibus Pilumno et Picumno in aedibus lectus sternebatur*; cf. Varro apud Serv. *ad Aen.* 10.76: . . . *eisque* [sc. *Pilumno et Picumno*] *pro puerpera lectum in atrio sterni.*

95. Observation is crucial to norm acquisition, as we shall see. Evidence suggests that we adopt a "ritual" or "normative stance," which powerfully disposes us to infer a rule from behavior. See at section 7.4.1.

birth of a baby).[96] The universality of the deontic belief explains not only what we observe, that is, that others tend to follow the norm (the content of our Belief 2). It also explains our normative expectation (Belief 3) regarding the deontic beliefs of others. That is, because the norm is of universal applicability, others not only should conform to it themselves but also should expect and prefer that we conform to it, too, and may punish us for nonconformity.

The fact that norms require agents to have beliefs about others' beliefs, as in Beliefs 2 and 3, shows that norms are collective phenomena involving a degree of shared Intentionality, specifically, what I have called collective Intentionality (4.3.4, above). This is to say that to count as a social norm, a given permission, prohibition, or obligation must be a matter of communal common ground (see again figure 4.2). To see the role of collective Intentionality in sustaining norms in communal common ground, imagine that every Roman held a deontic belief (Belief 1) whose content amounted to *one should set up a lectisternium upon the birth of a baby*. Imagine, too, that no Roman had any inkling that any other Roman held this belief. In this case, the deontic belief would be a matter of merely *aggregate* Intentionality (as described at section 4.3.4).

In this hypothetical scenario, we would hesitate to say that the setting up of *lectisternia* was a social norm existing in Roman communal common ground.[97] For no Roman would expect any other to set up a *lectisternium*, and no Roman would believe that any other expected him or her to set up a *lectisternium*, and no Roman would expect to face any sort of punishment, not even mild disapproval, for not setting up a *lectisternium*. There would be, that is, no question of the social expectations about behavior that characterize social norms. As Cristina Bicchieri writes, "collective awareness is constitutive of" a norm's "very existence."[98] Or as another recent account of norms has it: "In order for there to be a norm, it seems that the way people think and feel about certain behaviour must be known by others."[99]

An upshot of all these beliefs, of the individual norms they sustain, and of the resulting deontological packages of permissions, prescriptions, and prohibitions such as *pietas* is that agents' actions are rendered "interdependent." That is, each agent's actions are determined by what he or she takes to be the beliefs and actions (or likely actions) of others.[100] Thus, *my* choice to set up a

---

96. See Tomasello 2014: 87–90 on the generality, or "agent-neutral, transpersonal, generic" quality (88), of social norms.

97. Cf. G. Brennan et al. 2013: 30–31.

98. Bicchieri 2006: 13.

99. G. Brennan et al. 2013: 31.

100. Here I draw on Bicchieri 2016, chapter 2.

lectisternium is predicated not only on my belief about what I *should* do (deontic belief) but also on my belief about what my neighbors *do* or *will do* (empirical expectation), as well as on my belief about what my neighbors believe I *should* do, and how they might treat me if I do not (normative expectation). *Your* choice is similarly determined by your corresponding beliefs about me and others. My action is not independent of your beliefs and behaviors, nor yours of mine. Rather, our actions are interdependent in that what I do depends on what I take to be your beliefs and actions, and vice versa.

Note that the interdependence of action that I have described here is distinct from the interdependence of intimate joint action, involving joint Intentionality and personal common ground (see section 4.3.5). When a husband and wife (and perhaps other family members) work together to set up a *lectisternium*, this is a case of two (or more) people sharing agency in joint action, each doing his or her part, as a "we," in pursuit of a common goal. In contrast, I have described here a broad *collective* rather than intimate *joint* interdependence of agents' actions in a social group. Neighbors in Rome collectively (but not jointly) observed the norm of setting up natal *lectisternia*. Neighbor did not cooperate directly with neighbor in performing this cult act, as they did when they came together in a white-robed group to sacrifice jointly to Robigo. Rather, at the level here described, each neighbor acted as he or she did because of what he or she took to be the beliefs and behaviors of his or her neighbors. This is the broad, groupwide interdependence of action to which social norms and systems of social norms such as *pietas* gives rise. This interdependence results in observable group-level behavioral patterns and regularities (often termed simply "culture"), which we may characterize as large-scale cooperation.

It remains to say a word about norms and the groups that share them. Those for whom a deontology, such as *pietas*, is part of communal common ground, whose conduct the constituent norms tend to guide, and who are inclined to endorse and enforce the constituent norms form what the sociologist Dave Elder-Vass calls a "norm circle."[101] In abiding by, endorsing, and enforcing the norms, individuals in the norm circle exert a causal influence on one another and on others, whom they induce to adopt and abide by the norms, thereby perpetuating the norms horizontally across a population and vertically from generation to generation.[102]

---

101. Elder-Vass 2010: 122–33 and 2012: 22–34. Cf. section 3.3.2, above, on norms.

102. This interindividual causal influence is often attributed to "structure" or some other supra-individual entity: see section 4.4, below. Section 7.4.1 considers the transmission and acquisition of norms at greater length.

Often without consciously intending to do so, people display signals of norm-circle membership and hence of communal common ground that may be called "identity markers." As anthropologist Joseph Henrich writes, "the cultural transmission pathways of social norms are often the same as those for other more observable markers, like language, dialect, or tattooing practices."[103] Thus, the norms that a stranger endorses, which of course are invisible, but which you urgently need to know whether you share with him or her, can often be inferred from the visible, outward cultural markers he or she exhibits. On these cultural markers depend our "folk-sociological" cognitive abilities, that is, our facility in assigning those we meet to our own or some "other" norm circle.[104]

Ovid's folk-sociological faculties effortlessly and automatically identified the white-clad crowd as Roman worshippers and the flamen as a Roman priest. Though he did not know precisely what they were up to, he recognized that he and they stood together in the broad norm circle of cultic *pietas*. The folk-sociological information he gleaned from the crowd's dress, and perhaps speech, allowed Ovid to predict the norms the worshippers were likely to endorse, abide by, and enforce, and thus the likely behavioral repertoire of crowd members, and thus the odds that they would make good partners for cooperation and joint action.[105] This is why Ovid could feel confident approaching the flamen and could assume they shared enough ritual common ground that, for example, he would be understood when he referred to the puppy as an "unusual victim," *nova victima*.[106]

Think of such visible identity markers as dress and speech, and the folk-sociological, norm-circle categorization they permit, as social-cognition aids for potential partners in shared Intentionality and agency. They provide rich starting points for interlocutors to use in generating inferences about one another's beliefs, preferences, normative commitments, and hence cooperative potential.

The point of these reflections on norms is to demonstrate again the centrality of belief to Roman cult. The analysis I have provided in this section should suggest that neither social expectations about religious behavior, nor social norms, nor the cultic obligations to which they give rise, nor indeed the deontological system of *pietas* itself could exist without the interrelated deontic

---

103. J. Henrich 2015: 201. Variations in usage and dialect of Latin would have told Romans a great deal about speakers. See Adams 2007 for geographic variation and Adams 2013 for social registers of Latin.

104. See J. Henrich 2015: 199–205.

105. See H. Clark 1996: 100–106; McElreath et al. 2003; Tomasello 2014: 82–93.

106. As implied at Ov. *F.* 4.936–37.

beliefs concerning oughts, mays, and ought nots, and the beliefs concerning the deontic beliefs of others concerning those oughts, mays, and ought nots, that I have enumerated in this section. If we suppose that Roman religious culture was marked by group-level regularities, large-scale cooperation, and widely subscribed-to norms of conduct and practice—in other words, that it was constituted by the *religio*, the *fas*, and the *nefas*, the obligatory, the permitted, and the prohibited—then we must suppose that Roman religious culture was sustained by shared beliefs.

4.5. Conclusion

Individuals have Intentional episodes such as perceptions, attention, beliefs, memories, desires, emotions, and intentions. All these forms of Intentionality may be shared, and at least some must be shared if individuals are to engage in joint action. When two or more people mutually believe that they share one or more of these forms of Intentionality, say, a perceptual episode, a belief, a desire, or an intention, then the sharing itself becomes a bit of common ground for them.

Shared Intentionality and hence common ground come in degrees of intimacy. I distinguished joint Intentionality from collective Intentionality. Joint Intentionality both potentiates and arises from interactions among individuals, such as shared attention, interlocution, collective ritual, and other joint actions. The perceptions, experiences, beliefs, memories, and so on that are shared in such contexts become the personal common ground of interacting agents. Collective Intentionality, by contrast, includes the beliefs, norms, and so forth that we believe, often quite nonreflectively, that we share with others in communal common ground, not by virtue of our history of direct interaction but by virtue of their visible identity markers and other cues.

Indeed, more basic than communal common ground is the *human* common ground we share even with cultural "others" by virtue of recognizing them as "like us" in the most elementary of respects—being alive; breathing; possessed of beliefs, desires, and the capacity for sharing Intentionality—and thus as candidate partners for joint action. Shared Intentionality thus permeates our common ground at every level, enabling us to engage others in all sorts of cooperative ventures, from Ovid's curious questioning, to a Pompeian couple's joint domestic offering, to Livy's citywide collective cult action.

As always, I wish to emphasize the importance of *belief* to my account of shared Intentionality. That the deity who presides over *robigo* is pleased to receive a sheep and a puppy may become a shared belief and hence a bit of personal common ground between the flamen and Ovid, and Ovid may go on to assume that he shares this datum in communal common ground with other

Romans. However, his second-order belief concerning his common ground with the priest, that is, concerning the *sharedness* of their first-order belief about the god's sacrificial preferences, is critical to their genuine sharing of that first-order belief in personal common ground.

The same analysis applies to shared agency. When the flamen and Ovid act jointly by engaging in conversation, they are "acting on [their] individual beliefs or assumptions about what is in [their] common ground."[107] Each comes to the conversation believing that some beliefs can and some beliefs cannot be taken for granted as features of the other's mind. So, in joint as in individual action, belief turns out to hold a central position. For people act jointly based on what they (fallibly) *believe* to be cognitively common or psychologically shared among them, for instance, as in Ovid's conversation, the belief that certain kinds of *victimae* are or are not the norm.

The lesson is that there can be no sharing of Intentionality or of agency in contexts of cult—but only individual Intentionality and agency and, at most, aggregates thereof—unless individuals hold second-order beliefs about the extent to which "we" share first-order beliefs concerning rites, their conduct, their purposes, and so on. If we are to suppose that the Romans engaged in group religious activity, as we surely must, then we need to recognize that this group activity was enabled by individuals holding beliefs at two levels: first-order beliefs about the ritual itself and second-order mutual belief that the first-order beliefs were shared among self and others. If two or more Romans did *not* mutually believe that they shared certain beliefs about the activity in which they were engaged, if they did *not* mutually assume that they saw the activity under roughly the same description, then it is hard to see how they could have engaged, in any sense, in *that* particular activity *together*. Moreover, as we saw in our discussion of social norms, in some cult contexts, Romans acted as they did because of what they took to be the normative behaviors and beliefs of other Romans. Thus, sharing beliefs—whether in the weaker collective or the stronger joint sense—was vital to Roman religion, insofar as Roman religion had a genuinely "group" or "collective" dimension.

4.6. Coda: Durkheim among the Ruins

Let us close with a cautionary tale of Durkheim's reception among classicists. The tale illustrates a conception of shared or collective Intentionality and agency to be avoided. Durkheim had famously hoped to find laws of society that would make sociology an autonomous science, not reducible to

---

107. H. Clark 1996: 96. Cf. Searle 2010: 53–54.

psychology, on par with physics, chemistry, and biology.[108] Every science needs its own distinct object, so Durkheim reified society as a distinct, "collective consciousness" that exerted a causal influence on individual minds, and thereby generated social facts, such as rates of suicide.[109] See, for example, in *The Rules of Sociological Method* ([1895] 1901):[110]

> Now, once the individual is ruled out, only society remains. It is therefore in the nature of society itself that we must seek the explanation of social life.

For Durkheim, society represented a "psychic individuality of a new kind,"[111] distinct from and greater than the sum of the psychologies of the individuals that constituted it. He supposed this "psychic individuality" to consist in a fabric of "collective representations," which "to a certain extent ... are exterior to individual minds."[112] In a letter of 1895 he emphasized this distinction: "one has no right to treat collective psychology as an extension, an enlargement or a new illustration of individual psychology."[113] This dualism, in which society is not only susceptible to *methodological* analysis at its own discrete level but is also a separate *ontological* entity,[114] an organism in itself that transcends individuals and their interactions, has sponsored untenable assumptions that have left their mark on classical scholarship.

Durkheim's dualism informed Simon Price's *Rituals and Power*, whose denial of belief we discussed in chapter 1. Price invoked Durkheim in faulting what he characterized as "the conventional approach in ancient history."[115] This involved "an improper emphasis on the individual," in which the scholar "attempts to locate meaning at the level of individuals and their mental

---

108. See section 2 of "Preface to the Second Edition" in Durkheim (1895) 1901 (= Durkheim 1982: 38–43).

109. For collective consciousness (French "conscience collective"), see, e.g., Durkheim 1982: 40. For a charitable reading of Durkheim in recognition of the difficulties he himself created for his interpreters, see A. King 2004: 140–61. For a brisk assessment of Durkheim's failure in "discovering the laws of the collective mind, thus establishing it as a causal order," see Turner 1994: 24–27 (quotation at 25). For *imitation* as a cause of suicide, see J. Henrich 2015: 49–50.

110. Durkheim 1982: 128.

111. Durkheim 1982: 129.

112. Durkheim 1974 (originally Durkheim 1898): 25–26.

113. Durkheim 1982: 250.

114. See in contrast the elegant arguments for *methodological collectivism* within a framework of *ontological individualism* in Tollefsen 2015. Cf. Tuomela 2013.

115. S. Price 1984: 11.

states."[116] Price proposed instead to study the "collective constructs" or "collective representations"[117] that shape but do not depend on individuals.

Here, however, we encounter a methodological problem.[118] Price followed Clifford Geertz and especially Dan Sperber[119] in viewing "ritual as a cognitive system."[120] However, this conception of ritual sits uneasily with Price's theoretical commitment to a mésalliance of Durkheim and Needham. For what sort of mind was supposed to bear the cognitive content of the ritual system? Following Durkheim, Price supposed individual minds and their "mental states" to be verboten. Instead, we must imagine society itself as a minded being. But in what psychological mode would society hold the cognitive content or "collective representations" of ritual? Following Needham, Price supposed that belief was out of the question. It is not clear what alternative sorts of psychological attitudes Price envisioned, or who exactly was supposed to bear them.

Not only in the literature, but in conversation, too, one frequently encounters a sub-Durkheimian insistence that the ancients should be characterized in "collective" rather than "personal" or "individual" terms.[121] Allow me to present but one recent published example of this contrast, cast as a dichotomy between "collective" and "individual belief," along with rejection of the latter. In the introduction to his erudite book *Ancestral Fault in Ancient Greece*, Renaud Gagné considers and rejects, for some of the reasons familiar from chapter 1, a cognitivist definition of belief as of limited "analytical value."[122] He goes on to contrast collective and individual belief as follows:[123]

> The synchronic and diachronic complexity of culture in movement, moreover, the dynamic rhythms of transformation constantly at work at the seams of social life, make the study of *collective belief* a rather different proposition from the study of *individual belief* on which the cognitive definition of the term is so often based.

---

116. S. Price 1984: 9.
117. S. Price 1984: 11 and 102.
118. Already alluded to in Fishwick 1986: 229–30.
119. Geertz 1973: 87–125; Sperber 1975.
120. S. Price 1984: 8. As noted in chapter 1, this is an underappreciated merit of Price's book.
121. Cf. Rüpke and Spickermann 2012: 2: "Must we question the common assumption of the collective character of pre-modern religions?"
122. Gagné 2013: 6–7 (quotation at 7), considering the definition of Barrett and Lanman 2008: 110, discussed in chapter 1, above. Gagné is of course under no obligation to write in terms of belief, and he does not. But he still cannot avoid attributing *representations of what is the case*, i.e., beliefs, to the Greeks.
123. Gagné 2013: 7–8, emphasis added.

These evocative words about the "complexity of culture in movement" and "the dynamic rhythms of transformation constantly at work at the seams of social life" appear to be intended to motivate the contrast drawn between collective and individual belief. Specifically, "the study of collective belief" is supposed to be a unique undertaking, incommensurable with what we are apparently to understand is an overly reductive "study of individual belief."

Now, I do not mean to imply that Price, Gagné, or any classicist is committed to an ontology of society as a "psychic individuality." And yet there is a Durkheimian hangover to be felt in this and other scholarship, even if it often manifests as rhetorical flourish rather than substantive commitment. Yet even the rhetorical flourish reflects a troubled conception of the relationship between individual and collective belief. We need to clear this up if we are to make progress. I have argued in this chapter that we should imagine Roman cult as a product of individuals capable of the full range of practical and doxastic Intentionality, intentions as well as beliefs, who could share such mental episodes jointly, in contexts of shared agency and joint action, and collectively, as communal common ground.

This focus on individuals and their more or less intimate interactions should preempt any need to appeal to a hypostasized group mind, or to a disembodied realm of collective beliefs or representations, or to any reification of culture, practice, or tradition, that is, to borrow a page from the philosopher Stephen Turner, to any "collective mental element that is out there, in some sense" to be "assimilated or acquired by"[124] individual Romans. All we need to appeal to are empirical facts about individual human cognition, the forms of social interaction that same cognition enables, and the social learning and cultural transmission that results from such interaction.[125] Without any reference to a shadowy collective entity external to individuals, human cognition and human social interaction can account for observed behavioral regularities, for cultural transmission, and thus for the vertical longevity of traditions and the horizontal distribution of cultural practices and representations. Indeed, cognitive theory allows us to take a non-essentialist view of culture itself as, in Dan Sperber's words, "the precipitate of cognition and communication in a human population."[126]

In appealing solely to individual cognition and interindividual interaction, my project here bears a certain affinity to that of Durkheim's bête noire,

---

124. Turner 2014: 191.

125. See the provocative arguments of Turner 1994 (esp. 97–100) and Turner 2014 (esp. 101–19 and 189–209). Cf. Bloch 1989: 106–36.

126. Sperber 1996: 97.

Gabriel Tarde, who formulated a sociology based on causal interactions among individual agents, notably through imitation, rather than on the causal powers of a collective mind over individuals.[127] As Tarde put it, "where there is any social connection between two living beings, there is imitation" ("où il y a un rapport social quelconque entre deux êtres vivants, il y a imitation"). Imitation amounted to "a remote action of one mind on another" ("une action à distance d'un esprit sur un autre"), which could be "intended or not, passive or active" ("voulue ou non, passive ou active"). In this, Tarde sounds not unlike Seneca, who could moralize, "*mores* (habits) are picked up from those we spend time with and ... the mind passes its own faults to those who are closest" (*sumuntur a conuersantibus mores et ... animus mala sua proximis tradit*; Sen. *Ira* 3.8). Tarde envisions a similar process, an "inter-spirituelle" relation among agents that transmits from one to another not only external forms of behavior but also "a certain amount of *belief* and of *desire*" ("une certaine dose de *croyance* et de *désir*").[128]

Tarde's excellent insight was that imitation alone was powerful enough to account for observable patterns of thought and behavior in a given community. Unfortunately, he could not adduce the empirical and theoretical resources that are now available to us in support of his thesis. Durkheim, in contrast, dismissed imitation a priori as no more than mimicry: "mechanical monkey business that makes us reproduce the movements that we witness" ("la singerie machinale qui nous fait reproduire les mouvements dont nous sommes les témoins"), and thus as insufficient to account for anything as collective and social as *moeurs*, "customs."[129] Romans like Seneca, who emphasized *imitatio* and exemplarity as mechanisms of social learning, the inculcation of *mores*, and cultural transmission (see at section 7.3), might have found Tarde's project amenable. Roman thought on *imitatio*, Tarde's theory of imitation, and recent empirical research shows that the *quality* of our conception of imitation determines the *quantity* of work imitation can do for us in explaining observable facts about collective practices and the transmission of culture.

---

127. On the recent revival of interest in Tarde, and for the debate between Durkheim and Tarde, see Candea 2010. I closely follow the interpretation of Tarde offered by Schmid 2009: 197–214.

128. Tarde 1895: viii and 157.

129. Durkheim 1897: 113, and cf. 110: "C'est la singerie pour elle-même." This book, *Le suicide*, features an entire chapter ("L'imitation," 107–38) devoted to discrediting imitation. We now know that Durkheim dramatically underestimated imitation's power to sustain the cultural traditions of both humans and other primates: see, e.g., Whiten, McGuigan, et al. 2009; and see chapter 7, below.

Before we turn, in chapter 7, to imitation and its contribution to cultural learning and cultural transmission we must take up, in chapter 5, the question of how the shared Intentionality that we examined here permitted the creation and maintenance of Roman social reality, including Roman religious reality, along with its deontology, which I have called *pietas*, that is, the package of norms, rights, duties, permissions, prescriptions, and prohibitions that socially empower and disempower individual and collective action.

5

Shared Belief, Social Ontology, Power

5.1. Introduction

This chapter offers a *social ontology* for the Roman religious world,[1] a theory of the nature of social reality in general that explains Roman socioreligious reality in particular.[2] It explores the creation and maintenance of institutions, such as the augurate and augural college; practices, such as *inauguratio*; statuses, such as the position of augur; and most consequentially, the deontologies, that is, the strictly *social* powers, obligations, permissions, and restrictions that attend these things, such as the augur's right of *obnuntiatio*.

I argue that *shared Intentionality*, the previous chapter's topic, sustains the ontology of the social world, with its institutions, practices, positions, statuses, and deontic powers. Sharing Intentionality allowed Romans *collectively* to create institutions and practices, to impose statuses and positions on objects, actions, and persons, and to bestow and recognize the deontic powers of these institutions, practices, objects, actions, and persons. They did all of this by collectively *representing*—in their beliefs, practical attitudes, and speech acts—these institutions, practices, statuses, positions, and deontic

---

1. I see my account of social ontology as complementary to the project of Ando 2015a: 53, where the phrase "ontology of the social" appears for the first time known to me in classical scholarship.

2. There is no space here to contrast social ontology against the bundle of theories that go under the name "social constructionism." For an assessment of several social constructionisms vis-à-vis a "realist" social ontology, see Elder-Vass 2012; for an assessment of social constructionism and its critics, see Hacking 1999; for arguments against some social-constructivist claims, methods, and presuppositions, see Turner 1998; Boghossian 2001; Boghossian 2006.

powers as existing, and by reflecting these representations in their consequent behavior.[3]

We shall see that "there are things that exist only because we believe them to exist."[4] The point of these belief-dependent things—institutions, statuses, and so on—is to serve practical purposes. They give socially positioned agents *reasons for action* based on the deontology associated with their status; they warrant *beliefs* about how other socially positioned agents will act based on their statuses; and they ground one socially positioned agent's *judgments* about the behaviors of another, given his status. Thus, the representational, motivational, and normative aspects of social reality *interrelate* the agents that compose the social world and *interlock* their activities in coherent ways.

The theory proposed here is, as in the previous chapter, etic. However, it will permit us to appreciate emic Roman conceptions of the "consensual" ontology of the social. We shall see most importantly that Roman socioreligious reality and socioreligious power depended existentially on belief, especially shared belief. The thesis, stated baldly, is that all Roman religious reality—not only puppy sacrifice, *flamines*, and festivals but also the obligations, permissions, prohibitions, and norms attendant upon such things—existed only insofar as it was collectively believed to exist.

5.2. Objective and Exterior or Subjective and Interior?

One result of fleshing out this chapter's thesis will be, to repurpose the words of Andreas Bendlin somewhat, "to surmount the traditional subject-object dichotomy" ("jene traditionelle Subjekt-Objekt-Dichotomie zu überwinden") and thus, in a sense, "to reintegrate the two realms ... of institutionalized religion and the psychological-emotional dimension of religious action and sensibility" ("die beiden Bereiche ... von institutionalisierter Religion und der psychisch-emotionalen Dimension religiösen Handelns und Empfindens, zu reintegrieren").[5]

This chapter effects this reintegration by showing that Roman socioreligious reality was at once *ontologically subjective* and *epistemically objective*. That is, the sorts of institutions, practices, social facts, and social powers that this chapter deals with *existed* only insofar as *subjects* represented them and therefore treated them as existing. They were mind dependent, which is to say,

---

3. This chapter fleshes out a thesis adumbrated in sections 1.3.2 and 2.2.3 and, with special reference to deontology, sections 3.3.2 and 4.4.
4. Searle 1995: 1.
5. Bendlin 2006: 230–31.

ontologically subjective. (In contrast, *ontologically objective* things, such as molecules, trees, and animals, exist independently of any mind, independently of whether any subject cognizes them.) Yet *claims* about ontologically subjective social realities could be *objectively* true or false: they were epistemically objective.[6] For example, Julia's promise to Gaius existed only because she made it, he accepted it, and they both represented it and therefore treated it as obtaining. And yet because it obtained and was a social fact, anyone could have knowledge and make claims about it that could be evaluated for accuracy. (In contrast, an *epistemically subjective* claim, such as "Vergil's poems are more beautiful than Horace's poems," is not objectively true or false but, as we say, "subjective," a matter of taste.) To grasp at a deep theoretical level the simultaneous subjectivity and objectivity of social phenomena is, as we shall see, the key to resolving long-standing confusions regarding belief and ritual practice, belief and religious institutions, "interiorized" and "exteriorized" religion.

So, one intervention of this chapter is to reassess the long-standing subject-object dichotomy referred to by Bendlin, which has pitted subjective, "interiorized" religious psychology against objective, "exteriorized" religious institutions, while preferring the former for Christians and the latter for non-Christians.[7] W. Robertson Smith provides an early example. In his *Lectures on the Religion of the Semites*, he proposed to leave belief to one side and to study instead "the religious institutions which governed the lives of men of the Semitic race."[8] Smith's methodology was grounded in his ontology of ancient religions: they "consisted entirely of institutions and practices."[9] Almost a hundred years later, S.R.F. Price echoed Smith, presumably unintentionally, by denying belief to the Romans and asserting, instead, "Ritual is what there was."[10]

Cognate oppositions of the institutional to the psychological are not hard to find, as witnessed by John Scheid's recent defense of the *polis*-religion model.[11] Praising Georg Wissowa for adopting, like Smith, an institutional

---

6. For more on this distinction, see at section 1.3.4 and section 2.2.3.

7. This is but one more reflex of the belief-action dichotomy that I disassembled in chapter 1.

8. W. R. Smith 1889: 23.

9. W. R. Smith 1889: 18.

10. S. Price 1984: 11. On this assertion, see at section 1.2.

11. For *polis* religion, see, e.g., Sourvinou-Inwood 1990. Scheid 2016 takes issue with, among others, Woolf 1997; Krauter 2004; Bendlin 2009.

methodology,[12] Scheid activates a host of oppositions, not only "experience," "emotions," and "feelings" as opposed to "institutions," but also "interiorization" versus "exteriorization," all of which are grounded in a dualism of the "subjective" over against the "objective."[13] Scheid faults *polis* religion's critics for what he sees as their undue attention to the first, "subjective" terms in these oppositions. According to Scheid, only the second, "objective" terms are relevant to Roman religion: "All is in the institution."[14]

In some of these dichotomizations, institutions do not *preclude* but do *precede* belief, logically and chronologically. For W. R. Smith, "sacred institutions . . . are primary," while "ideas as to the specific divine nature" are "secondary formations," arising organically out of "the orderly relations and stated activities that connected [gods] with their worshippers."[15] In this view, institutions are a seedbed of theology. Similarly, Talal Asad, seeking to soften Needham's denial of belief, held that "belief is a mental state, a grounded disposition, but it is confined to people who have certain social institutions and practices."[16] So belief does exist, but only in societies with institutions designed to create and propagate it. Now, the idea that institutions can generate, spontaneously or by design, theological speculation or particular beliefs, obviously has merit. The troubled common denominator in these quotations, however, the assumption on which I wish to cast doubt, is that institutions and practices—or more broadly, religious reality and its associated deontologies—*can* exist and *do* exist prior to and independently of belief.

These considerations suggest that more than a century after Smith and Wissowa, little progress has been made in theorizing the relationship between institutions and cognition, that is, between the epistemically objective social world, with its practices and institutions about which historians may make true or false claims, and the attitudes of the human subjects who not only make up but also *make* that ontologically subjective, mind-dependent socioreligious world. I submit that progress is possible only when we recognize that where socioreligious reality is concerned, a simple dichotomy between objective and subjective, exterior and interior, cannot help but lead us astray.

12. Scheid 2016: 7–21 on Wissowa 1912 (comparison of Wissowa to W. R. Smith is my own, not Scheid's).

13. Scheid 2016: 16–21 passim.

14. Scheid 2016: 52.

15. W. R. Smith 1889: 88. This is not to deny that Smith could also acknowledge "unspoken ideas embodied in the traditional forms of ritual praxis" (27).

16. Asad 1993: 48, seconding the criticism of Needham 1972 of Harré 1981: 82. For my own criticisms of Needham 1972, see chapter 1.

Now, I would scarcely propose, as an alternative to the troubled dichotomy that I have identified, that Roman institutions were founded on a "creed" that holds "the key to ritual and practice,"[17] much less on some universal sentiment of "Religiosität."[18] Nor would I dream of faulting the methodological choice of Smith, Wissowa, or Scheid to make institutions their focus. Instead, what I propose here is that if we aspire to the study of religious institutions, then we must comprehend their logical and ontological dependence on the Intentionality, including the beliefs, of human subjects. When I say that religious institutions depend logically and ontologically on human subjects, I mean that religious realities—including institutions; practices; the religious statuses of actions, objects, and persons; as well as the deontic powers associated with these institutions, practices, and statuses—depend for their sheer existence on the shared conceptual schemes of interacting individuals, that is, on their collective recognition, acceptance, and belief as well as on the speech acts in which they explicitly express or pragmatically presuppose such recognition, acceptance, and belief.

A thought experiment illustrates the point I am trying to make. In a world without human subjects, there obviously could be no institutions, practices, statuses, obligations, and so on. This entails that institutions and the rest are subject-dependent entities, that subjects are logically and ontologically prior to institutions. So, institutions and the other features of the social world depend on subjects for their existence. How, precisely? On what property, faculty, or activity of Roman subjects depended an institution such as the flaminate, a practice such as puppy sacrifice, or a cult obligation to Robigo such as that exerted by the calendrical recurrence of VII Kal. Mai.? These social realities and deontologies depended on subjects *treating* them as existing (at a practical, "objective" level) as a result of *representing* them as existing (at a psychological, "subjective" level) in speech acts and in doxastic cognitions such as recognition, acceptance, and belief.

At this juncture I must point out that I am not denying that individuals are "thrown" into a world of institutions, practices, and deontologies, that is, into a preexisting social reality to which they must accommodate themselves.[19] Of course this is so. Yet, it is so not because culture, society, or social reality are discrete entities over and above individuals, from which the latter "download" their culture, their forms of social relations, or their institutions and practices. Rather, it is so because individuals arrive in a world of preexisting

---

17. W. R. Smith 1889: 18.
18. See Wissowa 1912: viii.
19. Chapter 7 explores the process of this accommodation in human ontogeny.

human subjects, who are actively maintaining social reality in its existence by virtue of the representations they entertain and communicate as well as the actions and interactions they undertake in light of these representations. So, subjects create, adopt, and sustain (but also transform and reject) sacerdotal institutions, puppy sacrifice, and cult obligations by recognizing, accepting, and believing (or by refusing to recognize or disbelieving), as well as by declaring, stating, and pragmatically presupposing in speech acts (or by denying) that such things exist, and of course by acting accordingly.

Thus, the beliefs and representations of subjects are logically and ontologically prior to institutions even when a given institution chronologically preexists any given subject's representations about it. Moreover, and most importantly, the dichotomy that opposes religions of "exterior" or "objective" practices to religions of "interior" or "subjective" mental episodes is a misbegotten one. For "exterior" religious practices, about which we may make *objective* claims, are themselves ontologically *subjective*, created and maintained by the "interior" states of subjects.

5.3. A Social Ontology

So let us flesh out this social ontology to see exactly how it works. The theory I propose here builds on my account of Intentionality and belief in chapter 2 and on my account of shared Intentionality from section 4.3. My account draws primarily on the social ontology of John Searle,[20] while incorporating insights from the social ontologies of the economist Tony Lawson and the sociologist Dave Elder-Vass.[21] While there are, as one might expect, areas of disagreement among theorists of social ontology, there is nonetheless broad agreement on the central point I wish to emphasize, that is, that institutions, practices, social statuses, and their deontological powers depend on uniquely human faculties of shared Intentionality. This book's focus on belief and the sharing of belief constrains me to offer not an exhaustive account of the

---

20. Searle 1995 and 2010; more briefly, Searle 2008a; and more briefly still, Searle 2016.

21. T. Lawson 2012 and 2016, especially valuable for an account of emergent social objects. Elder-Vass 2010 and 2012, especially useful for the theory of norm circles and for situating current social ontology research in the context of the sociological classics. Gilbert 2013 offers a joint commitment account of the social ontology, while Tuomela 2007: 182–214 and 2013: 214–41 spell out a very fine-grained collective acceptance theory. The social ontology research program has exploded. I point the interested reader to just a few recent publications to indicate its breadth: Schmid 2009; Ikäheimo and Laitinen 2011; List and Pettit 2011; Schmitz et al. 2013; Gallotti and Michael 2014; Tollefsen 2015; Ziv and Schmid 2014; Guala 2016.

ontology of the social but a minimalist account that is maximally skewed toward my principal preoccupation of belief.

The basic framework for analyzing the ontology of the social will consist of three components: the imposition of function (5.3.1), constitutive rules (5.3.2), and, once again, shared Intentionality (5.3.3). To this trio now we turn.

5.3.1. Imposition of Function

The first thing to note is that human beings, like some other animals, have an ability to impose functions on features of the world around them, often to solve practical problems.[22] Chimpanzees turn twigs into ant-dipping tools, early humans turned flint into hand axes, and Romans turned wood and metal ore into grappling hooks (*corvi* or *harpagones*).[23] The functions of such artifacts derive from the intentions of the makers. Ant-dipping tools are for catching ants, hand axes are for butchering and digging, and the *corvus* is for immobilizing and boarding Carthaginian ships.

Each of these artifacts or tools succeeds or fails in performing its function by virtue of its materials' properties and the arrangement imposed on its materials by its creator(s). The ant-dipping tool functions insofar as its physical constitution conduces to catching ants, the hand axe insofar as it permits butchering and digging, and the corvus insofar as it facilitates defeating enemies at sea. Such objects can be repurposed. But the imposition of any new function is constrained by the object's natural "affordances,"[24] its physical potentials for sensorimotor manipulation. Thus, a hand axe can be turned into a borer[25] but not into, say, a belt, while a *gladius*, "sword," to take another Roman example, can be converted into a *vomer*, "ploughshare," but not into a *stola*, "robe."

Unlike other animals, however, human beings also impose statuses on things or persons where the status brings with it functional capacities that go beyond or are not causally limited by the physical properties and affordances of the thing or person in question. These status-dependent functional capacities are deontic; that is, they are powers, responsibilities, rights, and so on that do not reduce to the physics, chemistry, or biology of the thing or person on which they are imposed. Consider, for example, a boundary marker, a *terminus*, that demarcates Seius's field from that of his neighbor Titius.[26] The *terminus* is not a physically impregnable barrier. Perhaps it is just a line of stones. However,

---

22. This discussion draws directly on Searle 1995: 13–23; Searle 2010: 58–60.

23. Poly. 1.22–23 with Wallinga 1956, and, for the numismatic iconography, Morello 2008.

24. Gibson 1986: 127, emphasis in the original: "The *affordances* of the environment are what if *offers* the animal, what it *provides* or *furnishes*, either for good or ill."

25. Vaquero et al. 2012.

26. Example adapted from Searle 1995: 39–40; and Searle 2010: 94–96.

it keeps Seius and his crops on one side and Titius and his crops on the other side. To the extent that the *terminus* succeeds in fulfilling this function, this success is due not to some causal power intrinsic to lines of stones in general or to this line of stones in particular but to Seius's and Titius's cognitions: their representation of the line of stones as a *terminus* with the power or function of demarcating property.

Something like the *terminus*'s power of demarcation is implicated in the myth of Rome's foundation. In Livy's telling, Romulus killed his twin brother for jumping over the rising walls of his new city and declared, "so from now on for anyone who leaps over my walls."[27] Romulus's admonitory pronouncement was an attempt to impose a deontology on his walls, over and above their physical affordances. He was not saying, "May my walls become physically impregnable," but rather, in effect, "Let these walls constitute a boundary that no one is *permitted* [a social, deontic concept] to transgress."

The historical *moenia* of Rome might have served as a reasonably effective, purely physical, barrier. However, as inaugurated structures, *loca inaugurata*, the walls were also "holy things," *res sanctae*. This additionally fortified them with a deontology of sanctions and prohibitions.[28] This deontology determined the *Intentional affordances* of the walls. Intentional affordances are "the intentions of other persons as embodied in the artifact,"[29] intentions that determine what the object is socially *for*, its normative sociocultural action potential. Intentional affordances go beyond the sensorimotor possibilities for and constraints on action proper to natural affordances. For they provide *social*, *normative*, and *cultural* possibilities for, and constraints on, action.

It is important to see that none of this is merely "symbolic."[30] Rather, the walls' deontic powers were quite as real as their physical properties, their Intentional affordances quite as consequential as their natural affordances. Romulus could impose or build up the walls' physical properties and affordances just by moving earth and stones. Yet he could impose deontic powers and Intentional affordances on his walls only by getting others, through the persuasive appeal of fratricide and admonition, to represent and believe these powers and affordances obtained and so to treat the walls accordingly.

---

27. Liv. 1.7.2: *sic deinde quicumque alius transiliet moenia mea*. For discussion of the variants of this myth, see Wiseman 1995: 9–11. For more on the normative dimensions of the myth, see De Sanctis 2009.

28. Gai. *Inst.* 2.8: *sanctae quoque res, uelut muri et portae, quodam modo diuini iuris sunt*. Cf. *Dig.* 1.8.9.3 (Ulp. 68 *ad ed.*); Ov. *F.* 4.837–48; Plu. *Rom.* 11.3. On the inauguration of *loca sancta*, see Valeton 1892: 338–54. For religious law governing *res sacrae, religiosae*, and *sanctae*, see Rives 2012.

29. Tomasello 1999b: 157. See further Tomasello 1999a: 84–87; and especially Fiebich 2014.

30. As argued by, among others, Fichtl 2005. On Rome's wall, see De Sanctis 2007.

Here it is instructive to return to our contrast between such things as the *terminus* and Romulus's walls over against artifacts such as the *corvus* and *gladius*. Like the *terminus* and the walls, the *corvus* and *gladius* were social objects constructed by human beings for social purposes. But there is a crucial difference, which is evident in the fact that the *corvus* and *gladius* performed their functions not by virtue of collective representations and beliefs as to their functions but by virtue of the sheer physical affordances of their materials and design. Anyone could use a *gladius* to kill or a *corvus* to board a ship, regardless of anyone else's beliefs or attitudes about these artifacts. In contrast, the *terminus* and the *moenia* functioned as they did solely because of their Intentional affordances, that is, because their status and attendant deontic powers were part of communal common ground and thus collectively believed to exist and collectively accepted as obtaining, functioning, and in effect.

This very real power of the *terminus* and the *moenia* to demarcate boundaries—among a host of other functions, and so to regulate social interactions, a power that goes beyond the strictly physical properties of these objects—is in technical terms a "Status Function."[31] A Status Function is a *function* that an entity possesses by virtue of the *status* imposed on it. The Status Function and its social use are precisely the point of this section. To bear a certain status is typically to have certain social powers or functions, that is, to have a deontology, a package of rights, obligations, prerogatives, duties, permissions, prohibitions, and so on. "*Moenia*" and "*terminus*" denoted Status Functions in the Roman world. Further examples could be multiplied indefinitely. "*Augur*" and "*pater patratus*," for instance, name Status Functions. Cicero functioned as an *augur*, and Spurius Fusius as *pater patratus*, with all the deontic powers thereby conferred,[32] not because of any special physical or biological properties of their persons, but because they bore the relevant statuses and with those statuses the relevant deontologies.

5.3.2. Constitutive Rules

All such examples—a line of stones counting as a boundary or a city wall, Cicero counting as augur—reflect one of two simple but powerful forms of *constitutive rules*.[33] A constitutive rule is a species of norm (for norms, see at

---

31. Searle 1995: 40–43 and 94–103; Searle 2010, esp. 7, 11–15, 58–60, 105–6.

32. For the augur's powers, see Cic. *Leg.* 2.20–21, 2.31, 3.43; and Linderski 1986a. For the *pater patratus* of the college of *fetiales*, and the *fetiales* generally, see Rüpke 1990: 97–124. On Spurius Fusius, see at section 8.5.

33. Searle 1995: 43–51; and Searle 2010: 9–10 and 96–104.

sections 3.3.2 and 4.4). The two constitutive rules discussed here arguably represent the two basic, abstract, logical forms of all social reality. These constitutive rules can be deployed to create and sustain social reality by means of "communicative interactions that alter the way we think about the world" and, in so doing, alter those "features of the world that depend on how we think."[34]

The first constitutive rule I shall discuss has the abstract logical form *X counts as Y in context C*. This constitutive rule makes it the case that a preexisting entity, X, counts as having a Status Function, Y, in a given context, C. So, the line of stones (X) counts as *terminus* (Y) in the context (C) of Seius's and Titius's properties. Likewise, Cicero counts as an augur in the context of augural rituals. The operation of this constitutive rule allowed Romans to populate their social world with all sorts of Status Functions, such as *moenia*, *termini*, and augurs, and their corresponding deontologies.

Before we proceed, note that the *X counts as Y in C* rule presupposes a category of mind-independent objects, properties, and relations.[35] Early humans crafted independently existing flints into hand axes, and Romans crafted independently existing wood and ores into *corvi* and *gladii*. Analogously, there are some independently existing entities, Xs, on which human cognition imposes Status Functions, Ys. These X terms are mind independent, that is to say, they exist and have properties, including causal properties, that do not depend on human attitudes or beliefs in the way that the Y terms do. Conversely, just as flints cannot function as hand axes and ores cannot function as *gladii* unless human beings *physically* impose certain causal properties on them, so these Xs cannot exercise any of the powers conferred with the Y term unless human beings *cognitively* impose these Y-term properties on them.

Now, there are cases in which an X term may already count as a Y, that is, it may already be a mind-dependent Status Function–bearing entity. In such cases, new Status Functions may be recursively imposed on preexisting Status Functions, without upward limit.[36] Constitutive rules always allow us, in principle, to put Y_n in the role of X_n and count it as Y_{n+1}. So a *homo* (X_1) counts as a Roman (Y_1), but then the Roman (here Y_1 becomes X_2) comes to count as a *cooptatus*, that is, a candidate for the augurate (Y_2). Then the *cooptatus* (here $Y_2 \rightarrow X_3$) becomes augur (Y_3). Finally, the augur ($Y_3 \rightarrow X_4$) may come to count as "chief augur," *augur maximus* (Y_4).[37] In each of these cases, the X term can count as the Y term only because of its preexisting nature or status.

---

34. Elder-Vass 2012: 55.
35. So-called brute facts: Searle 1995: 2, 27, 34–35, and 55–56; and Searle 2010: 10.
36. Searle 1995: 80; Searle 2010: 201.
37. See further, below, at section 9.4.

Only *homines* could be Romans, only a Roman could be *cooptatus*, only a *cooptatus* could become an augur, and so forth. Thus, constitutive rules permitted Romans to order, interrelate, and hierarchize social roles and statuses and therefore powers of social action and practice.

The second constitutive rule to discuss takes the logical form *Y exists in context C*. This "freestanding Y term"[38] rule accounts for cases where there is no preexisting X to which to assign a Status Function, Y, but instead the Status Function is created by fiat. The *Y exists in C* form is the underlying logical form of institutions such as the augurate, slavery,[39] and dice games of *alea*,[40] where there are no preexisting X terms out there in the world on which to impose Y-term Status Functions, but instead the Status Functions, and hence the institutions, are in effect conjured out of thin air. The resulting institutions amount to *systematic arrangements of constitutive rules*, while "institutional facts" are the facts that arise within and because of the institutions.[41] So, once the institutions of the augurate, slavery, and *alea* were created, the *X counts as Y in C* rule could operate in appropriate contexts to create "institutional facts" such as that Cicero was an augur, Tiro was a slave, and this or that was a winning throw.

Here I wish to pause in order to distinguish the subclass of institutions and institutional facts within the broader class of social facts.[42] Social facts are roughly any facts resulting from human interaction. The fact that Clodius and Cicero hated each other, the fact of a new fashion in Roman wall painting,[43] the fact that collective emotion mastered a crowd at the *munera*,[44] and the fact of steep inflation in the late third century:[45] these sorts of things and many more besides are facts of the Roman social world and therefore of historical interest. However, what concerns us here is the subcategory of *institutions* and *institutional facts*, which—unlike Clodius and Cicero's mutual hatred, trends in wall painting, crowd emotions, and inflation—exist only insofar as they are represented and so believed to exist. The mark of this institutionality is a more or less determinate deontology,[46] such as the distinctive powers and

---

38. Searle 2010: 20–21 and 97–100.

39. Slavery was seen both as *contra naturam* and as a universal institution of the *ius gentium*: *Dig.* 1.5.4.1.

40. On *alea*, see Purcell 1995.

41. Searle 1995: 31–57; Searle 2008a: 452–55; and Searle 2010: 10–11 and 90–122.

42. Searle 1995: 26.

43. Plin. *H.N.* 35.116–17.

44. See Coleman 1998; and for an interpretation informed by social psychology, Fagan 2011.

45. See Graser 1940.

46. Searle 1995: 94–97 and 100–101; Searle 2010: 8–9, 84–86, and 105–6.

prohibitions that mark the augurate, slavery, and *alea*, as well as augurs, slaves, and winning throws.

Now, to return to our constitutive rules, it is important to see that these need not be codified or otherwise made explicit, as they might be in *alea*, in order to operate. No one, for example, has to think of him- or herself as performing the operation of counting X as Y.[47] Thus, the imposition of Status Functions via the logic of constitutive rules, and hence the creation of institutions and institutional facts, need not be "a matter of a deliberate act or set of actions." Institutions can of course be created through the deliberate passage of laws and so forth, that is, by way of other institutions, and also, as we shall soon see, through the speech act of Declaration, but nonetheless "the creation of institutional facts is typically a matter of natural evolution, and there need be no explicit conscious imposition of function."[48]

A likely example of the natural evolution of institutions and institutional facts is slavery. Even before the legally defined Roman institution of slavery came into existence, one person could presumably come to dominate another, and thus, so to speak, "enslave" him or her. This seems to be what happened to Cabeza de Vaca in the New World, as he recounts in his 1542 *The Relation of Álvar Núñez Cabeza de Vaca*. He spent a period of time in what he describes as highly informal slavery or subjection to native people he encountered. That is, by informal and spontaneous application of a more or less ad hoc constitutive rule, de Vaca had the Status Function of "captive slave" (*vel sim*) imposed on him. Historically, such informal types of domination were presumably the basis from which formal, legally defined institutions of slavery such as the Roman evolved.

As natural and nonreflective as the process of imposing Status Functions via constitutive rules may be, it presupposes capacities for representation and communication. Consider another example. Seius and Titius might, after living in proximity for a time, come to treat a line of stones as a boundary separating what they have come to regard as their respective fields, each in growing mutual recognition that the other does so, too. The line of stones became a boundary by natural evolution rather than by some deliberate moment of formal agreement. Thus, each eventually comes to represent the line of stones as a boundary in mutual awareness that the other does, too.[49] However, they do require *some* communicative means by which to bring this representation into

---

47. Searle 1995: 47–48, and cf. 145.
48. Searle 1995: 125.
49. An example of a so-called ad hoc imposition of Status Function: Searle 2010: 19–20 and 94–96.

mutual awareness. Perhaps this amounts to nothing more than grunts and gestures toward the line of stones, much like the *voces et gestus* through which, Lucretius theorized, prelinguistic early humans struck history's first pact.[50]

In any case, a genuine deontology with respect to the boundary must amount to more than the neighbors' having fortuitously matching *dispositions* not to cross the line of stones.[51] They must, instead, share a way of *representing* the line of stones: it (X) counts as boundary (Y) of their properties (C). The deontology results not from the two men chancing to have matching individual aversions to crossing the line. Rather, it is a result of the two sharing the representation, in mutual awareness of so sharing, that the line counts for them as a boundary to their properties. Note that without mutual belief as to their shared representations, they would have no personal common ground on which to stand in making and acknowledging deontic claims on one another's conduct with respect to the boundary and their properties.[52]

In more complex cases such as that of Cicero's augurate, one can only imagine Cicero counting as an augur by virtue of speech acts that represent and communicate his augural status and its deontology. (Presumably, here again, augural Status Function was conferred less formally on early augurs, like Attus Navius. Perhaps it was conferred, as in Cicero's telling, through mere *recognition*.)[53] Many statuses and their powers are complex, and that complexity requires linguistic resources. There can be no Status Function "augur," nor any right of *obnuntiatio* and all the rest, without semantic representations, that is, propositional contents expressed symbolically. So, both the creation by fiat of a freestanding Y-term Status Function, such as the augurate (Y), and the imposition of a Y-term Status Function on a preexisting X term, as in making Cicero (X) an augur (Y), require not only cognitive but also semantic and linguistic representations that embody the logic of one of our two constitutive rules.

Be this as it may, we must recognize—in line with my earlier remarks about the *moenia* as more-than-symbolic—that the deontic powers of, for example, an augur, go beyond the semantic or symbolic power of the speech acts that represent those deontic powers. For the augur's deontic powers relate him and his possibilities for action to other agents and their possibilities for action, not just semantically or symbolically but practically, materially, and causally. So,

---

50. Lucr. 5.1019–23. On the communicative power of gesture, see Kendon 2004. Sterelny 2012b defends the "gestural origins" (2141) of language. Kendon 2017 offers a trenchant critique of the gesture-first hypothesis.

51. Searle 2010: 95–96.

52. Cf. at section 4.4.

53. Cic. *Div.* 1.17.30–33.

you need *language* to bestow almost any social powers over and above sheer physical dominance, or prestige,[54] or Weberian charisma, but the *social* powers thus bestowed exceed the *symbolic* or *semantic* powers of the speech acts that bestow them.[55]

These remarks about language and representation bring us to the speech act of Declaration and to the forms of Intentionality that correspond to it.[56] We have just seen that the representational powers of language are indispensable to the creation and maintenance of much of social reality. The refinement I offer now is that social reality is created and maintained by the *logic* if not always by the explicit *performance* of the speech act of Declaration. Declaration is familiar from speech act theory: "In declarations the state of affairs represented by the propositional content of the speech act is brought into existence by the successful performance of that very speech act."[57] In other words, Declarations "get the world to match the propositional content by saying that the propositional content matches the world."[58] Classic examples of Declarations are "I hereby pronounce you husband and wife" and "I declare the meeting adjourned." The propositional contents *you are husband and wife* and *the meeting is adjourned* come to obtain in the world by virtue of being represented as and accepted as obtaining. Declarations *create* the states of affairs represented in their propositional contents by publicly enunciating that content *as created*.

As Malinowski noted long ago, "Words in their primary and essential sense *do, act, produce,* and *achieve*."[59] So, anyone who has words can create social realities through a subclass of Declarations called "performatives."[60] If one says, "I promise," one thereby makes a Declaration that one is promising, and in making that Declaration, one thereby makes it the case that one does in fact promise.[61] In promising, one creates a public deontology that *commits* one to

---

54. For prestige as a human-specific status system, over and above the dominance system we share with apes, see J. Henrich 2015: 117–39. Unlike dominance, which compels deference, prestige garners "freely conferred" deference (347n12), predicated on the prestigious individual's perceived success and skill.

55. See further, Searle 2010: 14, 93, and 109–15.

56. On speech acts, see at section 2.3 and chapter 8.

57. Searle 1995: 34.

58. Vanderveken 1990: 106.

59. Malinowski 1935: 52.

60. Searle 2002: 156–79.

61. Of course, one may make false promises, but to the extent that promising falsely has any point or efficacy, it is because promising characteristically involves the public creation of a commitment.

fulfilling the promise.[62] A promise creates a "socially binding relation" or "accountability relation" between speaker and hearer.[63] This simple example presupposes and instantiates joint Intentionality between at least two individuals, a promisor and a promisee. It creates a local bit of social reality with a local deontology, sustained by joint Intentionality. We can extend the logic of this example to the *terminus* recognized by our two farmers. The Status Function they impose on the line of stones is, like a promise, a local social reality with deontic powers, which are brought into existence by their shared representations and mutual recognition.

These points put us in a position to extend the logic of the promise and the *terminus* beyond joint Intentionality and personal common ground to collective Intentionality and communal common ground. The very strong claim Searle makes for his social ontology is that not only promises and boundary markers but "all of human institutional reality, and nearly all of human civilization, is created in its initial existence and maintained in its continued existence by a single logico-linguistic operation," to wit, Declaration and, as we shall see soon enough, linguistic and cognitive representations that manifest the same logic, if not the same surface structure, as Declaration.[64]

Roman examples of explicit, reality-creating Declarations abound. Livy relates that Numa was declared king (*declaratus rex*) upon his inauguration.[65] He also tells of P. Decius and M. Valerius, "whom the people with great consensus declared [*declaravit*] consul and praetor, respectively."[66] We shall examine in some detail several Roman cultic Declarations presently, but for now it is important to note that the point of such speech acts is not just to go around declaring things. Rather, the point is to use the speech act to change people's representations of reality and in so doing to change reality to match their representations. Declaration does this by deploying the logic of constitutive rules. That is, it enunciates that *X counts as Y*, and, insofar as others come therefore to see X as Y, it thereby *causes* X to count as Y. Or it enunciates that *Y exists*, and, insofar as others therefore come to see Y as existing, it thereby *causes* Y to exist.

Declaration is merely the most direct speech act through which to effect this operation, but constitutive rules are deployed all the time, even by speakers not intending to "declare" per se, as in these examples: Assertive: "It

---

62. As Roman law recognized: Gai. *Inst.* 3.92–93.
63. Seuren 2009: 140, and cf. 133–55. Cf. Searle 2010: 80–84.
64. Searle 2010: 201, and cf. 12–13.
65. Liv. 1.18.10. This episode is explored in detail at section 9.4.
66. Liv. 9.40.21: *quos populus . . . ingenti consensu consulem alterum, alterum praetorem declaravit*.

appears that Numa is now king"; Directive: "Please tell the people that Numa is king"; Commissive: "I shall do as the new king, Numa, asks"; Expressive: "I thank the gods that Numa is king!" In these speech acts, *that Numa counts as king* is either explicitly represented or implicitly presupposed and thereby reinforced as fact. As Searle puts it, "Recognition in the form of speech acts functions like Declarations, even when the speech acts are not in the form of a Declaration. By continuing to use the vocabulary of the status functions we reinforce the status functions."[67] Talk of Numa being king reinforced Numa actually *being* king.

Let us follow speech acts all the way through to cognition. Corresponding to and underlying both explicit Declarations and those speech acts that function like Declarations by representing or presupposing the existence of Status Functions, there are what I call *constitutive attitudes*, including beliefs.[68] Some attitudes play no role in constituting their objects as the objects they are. If Seius believes that his ox is tired after a day at the plough, he is more or less correct, but he does not in any sense *constitute* his ox as tired. His ox is independently either tired or not, and his belief either "fits" this state of affairs or does not. However, if Titius and Seius each believe that their line of stones is a boundary (and if they believe this in mutual awareness that the other does too, and if each intends to treat the line of stones as a boundary as part of *their* treating it as such), then between them they *do* thereby constitute the line of stones as a boundary.

Such shared constitutive attitudes, including intentions and beliefs, *represent a state of affairs as existing* (mind-to-world) and by means of so representing, they *cause that very state of affairs to exist* (world-to-mind). So, the representational content of Seius and Titius's shared constitutive belief—paralleling that of a Declaration such as "Let this line of stones count as a *terminus*"— *makes* the line of stones a *terminus* by *representing* it as a *terminus*. The logical form of all such representations, whether embodied in Declarations, in other speech acts, or in constitutive beliefs and other attitudes, is that of one of our two constitutive rules: *Y exists in C* or *X counts as Y in C*.

I have used the *terminus* as an example. But let us take another, say, a temple (*aedes sacra, templum, fanum*) consecrated to a god. Insofar as the *aedes* is the *aedes* that it is, it is a piece of institutional reality created and sustained in

---

67. Searle 2010: 104.

68. See at section 2.2.5. Searle 1995 speaks of "beliefs" (e.g., 1). Searle 2010 largely speaks of "representations" (e.g., 27–30) in order to capture all the sorts of *thinking about* and *speaking about* that have the same logical form as Declarations. M. Flynn 2012: 47 introduces the term "Declarative belief."

existence by Declarational linguistic and cognitive representations. In the "normal science" of scholarship, the question, "what makes a given structure an *aedes*?" might be answered in any number of ways that would all beg a deeper question about the *aedes*'s ontology. At a certain level of superficiality, one might suppose that it is just *obvious* that the *aedes* is an *aedes*, for it is marked as such by the way it instantiates the relevant canons of architectural design in wood, terra-cotta, and stone.[69] However, if we ask the further questions, "What caused structures exhibiting such design features to differ from non-*aedes* structures? What made them *sacred* space?" we might get an answer that appeals, with Servius, to rituals of *inauguratio* and *consecratio*, by which temples were constituted as such.[70] And if we then ask, "what granted inaugurated, consecrated space its special functions or significance?" our inquiry might bottom out in the *ius divinum*, the "divine law," which specified the legal and hence deontic distinctions among *res sacrae*, *res sanctae*, and *res religiosae*.[71]

Of course, all these factors were critical to the creation and hence to our understanding of Roman *aedes sacrae*, and yet the ontology of our *aedes* depended, at rock bottom, on none of them. For each of these answers only pushes the question back a step: What determined certain architectural forms as sacral? What made a set of gestures a sacralizing ritual? What allowed some sentences in Latin to be part of *ius divinum*, with the power to distinguish *res sacrae* from other *res* and to determine their status?

The answer to *these* questions is that the *ius divinum* was sustained as law, that is, as an instrument with the power to determine *res* as *sacrae*, only by the collective acceptance of the people to whom it legislated, a fact the Romans quite appreciated.[72] *Inauguratio* and *consecratio* were the rituals that they were, and possessed the power to inaugurate or consecrate, only because they were collectively represented as such. Without shared beliefs regarding their nature, purpose, effects, and normative forms, these action sequences would not confer sanctity and sacrality but would be nothing more than empty vocalizations and gestures. Finally, regarding the physical structure of the temple, nothing inherent in its materials or their disposition in space makes them an

69. As described, for example, in Vitr. 3.
70. Serv. *ad Aen.* 1.446: *antiqui enim aedes sacras ita templa faciebant, ut prius per augures locus liberaretur effareturque, tum demum a pontificibus consecraretur, ac post ibidem sacra edicerentur.* ("The ancients used to turn *templa* into *aedes sacrae* as follows: first, a place was freed and defined by augurs, then consecrated by the *pontifices*, and after that the *templa* were declared '*sacra*.'")
71. Gai. *Inst.* 2.2–2.9.
72. See *Dig.* 1.3.32.1 (Iulianus 84 *Dig.*), discussed at section 5.3.3.

aedes with the deontology that this status carries. Roman law, Roman ritual, and Roman architectural canons possessed their respective powers to define, confer, and mark sacrality only by virtue of the shared Intentionality of human subjects.

This is because, as we saw, the *function* of any material artifact is imposed on it by the intentions and representations of the people who made or used it. When an archaeologist identifies physical remains as an *aedes* he or she makes a social-ontological identification that carries "paleopsychological" implications about ancient minds, ancient intentions, and ancient beliefs. The archaeologist's identification may be objectively true: the stones found either are or are not the foundations of a temple of Diana. While the archaeologist's claim is thus *epistemically objective*, the temple's mode of existence, its *ontology*, was *subjective*, because its existence *as* temple depended entirely on the collective intentions and beliefs of the Romans who built, appropriated, or used the structure, inaugurated and consecrated it, marked it off by religious law from other sorts of space, and recognized and respected in their practices and behaviors its unique deontology.

In all of this, we see the workings of *constitutive* cognitions and other representations, which get the world to match a given propositional content by representing that propositional content as matching the world. Again, some representations succeed or fail to match a world that exists independently of them. However, Roman representations to the effect of "that is an *aedes*" contributed to causing the world to match their contents just by claiming that their contents matched the world. It is today *historically* (etically) accurate because it was in antiquity *then* (emically) accurate to represent the structure as an *aedes*, but this claim is and was accurate only because ancient people represented the structure as an *aedes* and, in the last analysis, thereby made it an *aedes*. So, some *objectively cognizable* aspects of Roman socioreligious reality depended, odd as it may seem, on the *subjective cognitions* of subjects. The Roman religious world was, therefore, at once *epistemically objective* and *ontologically subjective*.

Let us close this subsection by considering some cases in which Roman practice exposes the logic of the process by which a Declaration authoritatively "defines the situation"[73] and so creates or alters religious reality. Take the votive formula for the *ver sacrum*, "sacred spring," of 217 BCE, by means of which all the livestock born in that season were vowed as an offering (*donum dare*) to Jupiter, provided Rome be preserved through her wars.[74] The vow

---

73. Nock 1939: 93.
74. Liv. 22.10.2.

provides a number of stipulations concerning this offering, of which the first two run as follows (Liv. 22.10.4):[75]

> *qui faciet, quando volet quaque lege volet facito; quo modo faxit probe factum esto.*

> Let him who performs it, perform it whenever he wants, and in whatever manner he wants; however he performs it, let it be well performed.

The first imperative, *facito*, regulates the *how* of the officiant's action. It regulates the *how* by stipulating that the officiant is to offer the *donum* at a time and in a manner of his own choosing (*quando volet quaque lege volet*). In so stipulating, it also implicitly constitutes the *what* of the officiant's action, that is, his action's content. For the formula declares, albeit indirectly and implicitly, that *whatever actions* the officiant performs (X), those actions will count as *donum dare* (Y) in the context of the vow (C). So, this stipulation defines and constitutes the *what*, that is, the actions that will count as the offering.

The second stipulation, *probe factum esto*, is a direct Declaration that reinforces the first stipulation by further stipulating, in the form of a constitutive rule, that whatever offering is made (X), it will count as a *successful* offering (Y), devoid of ritual flaw, in the context of the vow (C).[76] The parts of the formula I have not quoted continue in this vein, proposing, through Declaration, constitutive rules for the creation of religious facts. What we see here, then, is a quite explicit case of what Caroline Humphrey and James Laidlaw have called the "ontological stipulation" of ritual, that is, the stipulation that certain actions (X) *count as* a performance of the ritual (Y).[77]

This votive formula makes explicit the underlying logic of its own construction of religious reality, the logic by which Declaration and the constitutive rules it embodies impose status and function. The formula is unusual in rendering so transparent the "constructedness" not only of the imposed Y Status Function, but more strikingly of the X term on which the Y term is imposed. That is, the vow does not take the X term as "given," that is, as some determinate set of actions, which will then, by Declaration, count as sacrificing the animal, Y_a, rather than as a profane activity, say, butchering the animal for food, Y_b, or killing it for sport, Y_c. Instead, the formula states that the officiant's actions, whatever yet-to-be-determined form they may take (X_1), will count as

---

75. Liv. 22.10.4. On this vow, see Nock 1939; and Ando 2015a: 70–71.

76. See Ando 2015c: 305–8 for more examples, from law and religion, of this use of *esto* to create facts.

77. Humphrey and Laidlaw 1994: 96–97 and 103, explicitly connecting ontological stipulation to constitutive rules on 117–21 (with reference to Searle 1969: 33–42).

an offering (Y_1), and that this offering ($Y_1 \rightarrow X_2$) will count as a successful offering (Y_2). In this, we have an example of the constitutive rule iterating upward, creating one institutional fact on top of another, imposing Status Function upon Status Function.

Presumably the self-consciousness exhibited here was not entirely the norm.[78] One imagines that the Romans were typically no less blind than we to the logic of the constitutive rule and its role in imposing function and thereby creating socioreligious reality. Surely Romans believed that certain structures were temples because they *just were* temples, certain gestures were sacrifice because they clearly *just were* sacrifice, certain arrangements of stones were *termini* and certain persons, such as Cicero, were augurs because that is *just what they were*. One suspects that for Romans, most such things and their deontologies were naturalized, just part of the furniture of the world. Yet sometimes, as we have just seen, Romans could utilize the constitutive "counts as" rule with a degree of self-consciousness, recognizing that they were stipulating an ontology, that they were imposing status and function on entities that would not have had any such status or function without human imposition.

Indeed, the Romans could perform this operation with varying degrees of what we might call "ontological commitment." For example, constitutive rules underlie the Roman religious practice of substitution, in which bread or wax may *stand in for*, without quite *counting as*, a sacrificial animal, that is, without any pretense that the substitute actually *is* or *becomes* the thing substituted.[79] Indeed, this is precisely the point of those substitutions whereby, in narratives of ritual progress, one sort of object or another comes to stand in for human heads, and thus animal or vegetal sacrifice comes to stand in for human sacrifice.[80] There is no "commitment" to the new object being "ontologically" identical to the old, even if, by stipulation, the new can fill the functional role of the old.

Finally, consider a case not of substitution but of deontic equivalence, created by a legal fiction, in Gaius's *Institutes*.[81] There it is stipulated that what has been consecrated in the provinces, without the authority of the Roman people, while not properly *sacrum*, is still to be counted *pro sacro*, "as if" truly sacred, with all the attendant permissions and prohibitions regarding its

---

78. Although Nock 1939 (and cf. Ando 2015c) does adduce numerous other such examples.

79. Serv. *ad Aen.* 2.116: *in sacris simulata pro veris accipi*. On substitution in Roman cult, see Ando 2011b.

80. E.g., Plut. *Num.* 15.6; Macr. *Sat.* 1.7.34–36.

81. See Ando 2015a: 70 and 2015c: 310–12.

treatment.[82] That is, the entity in question, X, is to be treated as *sacrum*, Y, and so is to be deontically equivalent to a genuine *sacrum*, while not in fact being genuinely *sacrum*.[83] Unlike the vow of the *ver sacrum*, examined above, but much as we just saw in cases of sacrificial substitution, here the constitutive rule is employed with a measure of *ontological diffidence*. That is, the entity, X, does not assume a new status, a new ontology, Y, but is nonetheless treated *as if* it had that status, Y.[84]

5.3.3. Shared Intentionality and Social Ontology

So how do constitutive rules, the Declarational speech acts that implement them, and the cognitions that reflect them create social reality? How did a line of stones come to count as a *terminus*, a material structure as an *aedes*, certain gestures as sacrifice, or certain persons as augurs? How did these things acquire their Status Functions and thus come to bear their deontic powers? How did these X terms come to count as the specified Y term? And how did Romans conjure Y terms such as the augurate or slavery out of thin air?

We have been alluding to the answer throughout our discussion and can now state it explicitly: the answer is the shared Intentionality, including of course the shared beliefs, to which the previous chapter was devoted. Searle puts it thus: "The intuitive idea is that the point of creating and maintaining institutional facts is power, but the whole apparatus—creation, maintenance, and resulting power—works only because of collective acceptance or recognition."[85] Constitutive rules derive their force from collective acceptance of the logical operation they perform, and a Declaration succeeds if the propositional content that it enunciates is recognized as obtaining by the relevant audience. Recognition and acceptance are forms of doxastic uptake. When we recognize and accept, we add to our beliefs, and if these beliefs are widely shared among us, they change those features of the world that depend on our collective belief. So, the stones count as a *terminus* and exercise their boundary-marking deontic power if they are collectively recognized as a *terminus* and thus collectively believed to mark a boundary. Certain gestures count as *donum dare*, and thus do their deontic duty in fulfilling the terms of

---

82. Gai. *Inst.* 2.7: *quod in provinciis non ex auctoritate populi Romani consecratum est, proprie sacrum non est, tamen pro sacro habetur.* I follow Ando 2015c: 309 in translating *pro* with "as if."

83. Cf. Gaius's discussion of the power of legal fiction at *Inst.* 3.194 with Ando 2015c: 314.

84. For further, complementary observations on this text of Gaius, see Ando 2015c: 310–12.

85. Searle 2010: 103.

the *ver sacrum*, only if those gestures are collectively accepted and believed to serve the requisite donative function.

The Romans could, in some contexts, recognize this dependency of institutions on collective acceptance. The second-century jurist Julian theorized in the following way the sources in shared Intentionality and shared practice of the deontic power of laws written and unwritten (*Dig.* 1.3.32.1 [Iulianus 84 *Dig.*], Watson trans., modified):

> nam cum ipsae leges nulla alia ex causa nos teneant, quam quod iudicio populi receptae sunt, merito et ea, quae sine ullo scripto populus probavit, tenebunt omnes: nam quid interest suffragio populus voluntatem suam declaret an rebus ipsis et factis? Quare rectissime etiam illud receptum est, ut leges non solum suffragio legis latoris, sed etiam tacito consensu omnium per desuetudinem abrogentur.

> Given that statutes themselves are binding on us for no other reason than that they have been accepted by the judgment of the populace, certainly it is fitting that what the populace has approved without any writing shall be binding on everyone. What does it matter whether the people declares its will by voting or by the very substance of its actions? Accordingly, it is absolutely right to accept the point that statutes may be repealed not only by vote of the legislature but also by the silent *consensus*[86] of everyone expressed through desuetude.

Julian's point goes not only for written and unwritten law but for all institutions and institutional facts. They exist and exercise their deontic powers to the extent that they are part of a group's communal common ground, and so recognized, accepted, believed to be—and treated as being—legitimately in force. This can also be demonstrated *ex negativo*. Without shared Intentionality, we cannot impose laws or any Status Function, for that matter. Without shared belief that the line of stones is a *terminus*, people will cross over it indifferently because "it" will be of no deontic significance. Without shared belief that certain gestures amount to sacrifice, we have a slaughtering of animals but not the fulfillment of a vow.

In this way, shared beliefs about social reality not only constitute that reality but also guide agents' practical reasoning within the spaces for action distinctive to and embodied in that reality. This is because Status Functions always come with a deontology, and deontologies always give social agents *reasons* to act. So, recognizing a *terminus* as a *terminus* amounts to recognizing its

---

86. Cf. *Dig.* 1.3.35 on the *tacita civium conventio*.

deontology, and this recognition serves as a deontic input into an agent's practical reasoning, causing him or her to represent constraints on and enablements to his or her action.[87]

As Tony Lawson has it, shared recognition or acceptance of an institution or institutional fact amounts to "a shared belief that such and such a situation is so, and a willingness of each ('accepting') individual (for the time being) thereby to go along with that situation."[88] As I emphasized in the previous chapter, such sharing of beliefs is no mere aggregation of individual attitudes, but rather a social and other-regarding mode of shared Intentionality. For a subject's second-order belief as to the sharedness of his or her first-order beliefs is crucial to motivating his or her individual action. That is, an individual's beliefs about the beliefs of others condition that individual's actions. It is because *we* do things a certain way, and I know it, that *I* do things that way.

The role of shared Intentionality in creating Roman social reality is exposed by the Livian example, cited above, in which the *populus* declared P. Decius and M. Valerius consul and praetor *ingenti consensu*, "with great consensus." The important thing here, from a Roman point of view, is the *consensus* (as we saw at section 4.2). Shared Intentionality was likewise implicated in the creation of the vow of the *ver sacrum*, for its wording was put to a vote to ensure collective endorsement of its proposed interventions in the religious order.[89] In this way, the vow became a collective speech act, regardless of which individual eventually spoke its terms.[90] Note that even the gods join the vow's circle of shared Intentionality, for when Jupiter satisfies the vow's request, he thereby accedes to its provisions and commits himself to regard as *probe factum* whatever is offered to him.[91]

5.3.4. Societas *versus "Emergent Social Entity"*

In Jupiter's acceptance of the stipulations of the *ver sacrum* vow, we see a manifestation of the *communitas et societas* of gods and mortals identified by Cicero, with which we opened the previous chapter (4.2). Jupiter's acceptance of the vow's terms marks his entry into *consensus* with his mortal *socii*.

---

87. As discussed at section 3.3.2.
88. T. Lawson 2016: 361–62.
89. Liv. 22.10.1: *iniussu populi voveri non posse*.
90. See Meijers 2007 for a theory, highly relevant to ancient modes of public discourse, of (otherwise often ignored) *collective* speech acts.
91. Cf. at section 8.6 on "superrational rituals."

We also saw, at section 4.2, that consensus among *socii* constituted Roman *societates*, partnerships dedicated to cooperative or joint, rather than individual, action in service to a goal. We noted that Cicero could extend the notion of *societas* as a metaphor for the natural relations of the members of the whole *genus humanum*. Humankind amounts, on this view, to "a sort of natural *societas*," *naturalis quaedam societas*, created not by *consensus*, but by our common faculties of reason and language, *ratio et oratio*, which condition the very possibility of sharing any Intentionality and agency at all.

Now let us see how, in the same passage, *societas* serves Cicero as a tool for thinking about ontological and deontological aspects of the social world. Here is *De officiis* 1.53:

> *gradus autem plures sunt societatis hominum. ut enim ab illa infinita discedatur, proprior est eiusdem gentis, nationis, linguae, qua maxime homines coniunguntur. interius etiam est eiusdem esse civitatis. multa enim sunt civibus inter se communia: forum, fana, porticus, viae, leges, iura, iudicia, suffragia, consuetudines praeterea et familiaritates multisque cum multis res rationesque contractae.*

> There are many levels of *societas* among men. Descending from that unlimited *societas* [sc. of the *genus humanum*], more exclusive is the *societas* of the same ethnic group, nation, or language, by which human beings are united most strongly. An even more intimate *societas* consists in being of the same *civitas*; for many things are shared by *cives* among each other: a forum, temples, piazzas, roads, laws, rights, courts of law, elections and, moreover, familiarity and intercourse, and the affairs and transactions that many have contracted with many others.

Cicero goes on to include families and friendships, as ever more closely and affectively bonded *societates*.[92] The only literal, legal *societas* to be found in this nested set of metaphorical *societates* is the final one above, implicit in the words *res rationesque contractae*, "affairs and transactions contracted."[93] Cicero's ultimate goal in this exercise is to define the deontologies of each level of *societas*, our *officia*, "duties," as regards our various *socii* and our various *societates*.[94] For example, our duty to other humans in the *societas* of all humans is to render such aid as does not harm us as givers, while our duty to friends is to share our lives, advice, and even our rebukes.

---

92. E.g., *Off.* 1.54: *sanguinis autem coniunctio et benivolentia devincit homines <et> caritate.*

93. Gai. *Ep.* 2.9.17: *societas ... consensu contrahitur*; Gai. *Inst.* 3.154: *societas ... quae nudo consensu contrahitur*; *Dig.* 17.2.5pr. (Ulp. 31 ad ed.): *societates contrahuntur*; etc.

94. See esp. *Off.* 1.51–52, 57–58, 160.

Most relevant to our aims here is Cicero's characterization in this passage of *civitas*, the "city-state," as a *societas*. This characterization echoes an equation that Cicero had made only a few years earlier, when he figured the *res publica* in similar terms.[95] In *De re publica*, Scipio states the following (1.39):[96]

> *est igitur... res publica res populi, populus autem non omnis hominum coetus quoquo modo congregatus, sed coetus multitudinis iuris consensu et utilitatis communione sociatus.*

> A *res publica*, therefore, is the thing [*res*] of a people [*populus*], but a people [*populus*] is not every coming-together of human beings gathered in just any way, but rather a coming-together of a large group partnered (*sociatus*) by a consensus about norms (*iuris consensu*) and by a sharing of benefits (*utilitatis communione*).

Cicero imagines a *populus* not as a random aggregation but as an association of individuals who have come together and partnered (*coetus... sociatus*) as *socii*. The basis of their association is a sharing of both a "consensual commitment to a particular normative order"[97] and the benefits that accrue from adherence to that normative order.[98] So, the *res* of the *populus*—the *res publica*—amounts to a shared project or joint venture, aiming at the common good. It is the *societas* of an entire *populus* of *cives*.

Note the ontological and deontological implications of this metaphor. For *societates*, and thus, in Cicero's metaphor, the *populus* itself, had no legal personality, no Durkheimian independent existence as a collective entity, a reified "society" bearing a sui generis "group mind." Instead, the *populus* was just its members, unified by a consensus with respect to their mutually agreed norms and goals, in accord with which and toward which they jointly acted. So, for Cicero, the *populus*, and even the *civitas* itself, was best conceived by

---

95. If Cicero and his contemporaries could conceive the *res publica* on the model of a *societas*, under the empire the reverse will hold: partnerships come to be conceived as *res publicae*: see the expressions *ad exemplum rei publicae* and *tamquam in re publica* at Dig. 3.4.1.1 (Gai. 3 ad ed. provinc.). I thank Clifford Ando for pointing this out to me *per litteras*.

96. On Cicero's conception of the *res publica* as a *societas* and its distinctively Roman flavor, see Asmis 2004; Arena 2012: 119–20 and 154–68; Hammer 2014: 46–69.

97. So Ando 2011a: 3 and 116. On *ius* as the entire normative order, see Quint. Inst. 12.3.6. On *ius* as a body of higher-order norms dependent on *mores*, standing above and authorizing enacted *leges*, see Straumann 2016: 54–62 and 168ff. The phrase *consensu iuris* occurs again at Cic. Rep. 3.45: *populus non est*, without it; cf. Cic. Rep. 6.13: *concilia coetusque hominum iure sociati, quae "civitates" appellantur*.

98. On "*utilitatis communione*," see the commentary of Zetzel 1995 on Cic. Rep. 1.39, aptly citing in comparison Cic. Sest. 91: *res ad communem utilitatem quas publicas appellamus*.

analogy with a *societas*, that is, "an association of individuals each of whom conditions his actions to accord with the terms of a joint agreement," and no more.

In contrast to *societas*, Roman law *did* recognize a type of collective entity that could be denoted by the term *universitas*, that is, "an association of individuals considered collectively to form a single entity itself capable of action."[99] *Collegia*, such as those of tradesmen, of merchants, and of priests,[100] for example, the *collegium pontificum*, were *universitates*. *Universitas* differed from *societas* not only ontologically but deontologically. For example, in a *societas*, "the partners were liable for the debts of the *societas*" while "the claims of the *societas* against its debtors were claims of the partners."[101] In contrast, in a *universitas*, according to Ulpian, "whatever is owed to the *universitas*, is not owed to the individual members; nor do individual members owe what the *universitas* owes."[102] The *universitas* thus amounts to an entity distinct from its members. Let us call such organizations "emergent social entities."[103]

It is worth taking a brief excursus to explore this concept, because such "emergent social entities," including *collegia* and, in certain respects, the senate, featured in the ontology of the Roman social world.[104] Indeed, the relationship between emergent social entities and individuals bears, if obliquely, on recent scholarship concerned with the status of the ancient individual vis-à-vis the collective.[105] Let us define "emergent social entities" by contrasting them with composite material objects. The former differ from the latter in that:

99. This and the previous quotation come from Runciman 1997: 13–14.

100. See J. Liu 2009 for *collegia* of textile dealers, and see 105 for a list of attested *collegia*.

101. A. Berger 1953 s.v. *societas*. In *societas*, agency was exercised by, and all liabilities and obligations devolved on, the individuals involved: See Duff 1938; Abatino et al. 2011; Fleckner 2015.

102. *Dig.* 3.4.7.1 (Ulpianus, 10 *ad ed.*): *si quid universitati debetur, singulis non debetur: nec quod debet universitas singuli debent.*

103. On this concept, see Elder-Vass 2010: 13–39 and 144–68; Elder-Vass 2012: 15–22; T. Lawson 2012; T. Lawson 2016, esp. 362–63.

104. On Roman groups generally, see Waltzing 1895: 195ff.; Waltzing 1900: 431ff.; and the relevant essays in, e.g., Kloppenborg and Wilson 1996; Rüpke 2007b; Rebillard and Rüpke 2015. Despite the tendency to see Roman culture as collectivist, I would hazard (and hope to argue at length elsewhere) that it was in fact quite individualistic in important respects. For example, properly *collective* functions of sacerdotal *collegia* appear to be few compared to functions of individual members (see n. 110, below). Moreover, Roman law tended to be parsimonious about recognizing discrete collective entities such as *universitates*.

105. For recent framings of the issues, see Rüpke and Spickermann 2012; Rüpke 2013 and 2015; Fuchs 2015; Fuchs and Rüpke 2015; Rebillard and Rüpke 2015.

the relations that bind them together and generate their causal powers are not *spatial* relations but rather *Intentional* relations: They depend on the beliefs and dispositions that individuals hold, and in particular on the commitments to each other that these entail.[106]

Emergent social entities, such as a *collegium* or the senate, can *act*, but the agency they possess is not the intrinsic agency of a minded creature but, as Christine Korsgaard puts it, "normatively constituted" agency. That is to say, the senate's "*capacity* for agency consists in or depends on the existence of certain normative relations" among individual senators and other Romans. In turn, "the *realization* of that capacity," that is, the senate's "success in action," "depends on conformity" on the part of individual senators "to the norms in question."[107]

The material analogy is illustrative. A clock, for example, functions as it does because of spatial, mechanical, and hence *physically causal* relations among its parts. If the parts were arranged in any other configuration, the clock function would not emerge. Analogously, an emergent social entity like the senate functioned as it did because of determinate *Intentional relations* among the relevant individuals, that is, the practical, doxastic, and normative attitudes shared by senators, which permitted them to function together *as a group* in ways that the sharing individuals could not function singly.[108]

In this way, the senate, acting qua group, issued *senatus consulta* and declared *prodigia*,[109] just as the *collegium pontificum*, acting qua group, issued pontifical *decreta* and prescribed expiations.[110] The senate and the priestly *collegia* were, of course, composed of individuals without whom the groups could neither exist nor function. Yet neither could individual senators or *pontifices* function singly as could their respective groups. Each of these groups was a social actor qua group, empowered by its parts (the relevant individuals)

---

106. Elder-Vass 2012: 20, emphasis in the original.

107. Korsgaard 2014: 191, emphasis in the original.

108. Note that emergent social entities are not the same as aggregate groups, such as, for example, the set of all Romans under four feet tall (see further, section 4.3.4, above). Nor are they Durkheimian, hypostasized, collective entities, ontologically floating free of the individuals that constitute them (see further, section 4.6, above).

109. On *senatus consulta*, see esp. Schiller 1978: 442–62; Lintott 1999: 75–93. On *prodigia*, see at section 3.2.2.

110. On *decreta* and other group functions of the *collegium pontificum*, see M. J. Johnson 2007: 123–50. Cf. Linderski 1986a: 2151–89 for the group functions of the *collegium augurum*.

and by the normative relationships among them to act in ways in which the individuals could not act in isolation.[111]

In this light, when the senate qua senate considered a reported *prodigium*, when it issued orders to the *quindecemviri*, and when it prescribed cult (as in the example from Livy at section 3.2.2), the senate's agency and actions were possible and successful only insofar as the individual senators that constituted the group endorsed and acceded to certain norms, that is, to a deontology, which guided their interactions among themselves as well as their transactions with the priestly *collegia* and the *populus* at large. So, Roman collectives could possess agentive causal powers qua group, but only by virtue of the *shared attitudes* of group members who did not *as individuals* possess those agentive causal powers.

Our faculties of social cognition, and indeed our bias to cognize the world in social terms, allow and even incline us to *personify* some social phenomena, such as groups, and so to see them as agents.[112] However, we *see* groups as agents only because our social-cognitive faculties permit us to cooperate collectively to *make* certain social phenomena *agentive*, bestowing on groups, such as the senate and priestly *collegia*, powers of action and causation that we might deny to individuals or that are beyond individual capacities. In the bottom-up view that I advocate here: "People ... interact in groups to form social entities that have causal powers, and it is these entities ... whose powers produce the effects commonly attributed to *social structure*"[113] and to other Durkheimian top-down collective notions, such as a *group mind* (see section 4.6).[114]

Let us return now from our excursus on emergent social entities to Cicero's metaphor that casts *civitas* and *populus* as *societates* (*De officiis* 1.53 and *De republica* 1.39, quoted above). The metaphor has ideological implications. Scholars have stressed the extent to which Romans, not only in the republic, but especially during the transition to the principate, and still under the empire, subscribed to an ideal of political legitimacy through consensus, Weberians *avant la lettre*, as it were.[115] So, Cicero's core message, the central ideological

---

111. Thus, it is not quite right to affirm, with Woolf 2013: 136, "Ritual action has always been about individuals: there are, after all, no other conceivable social actors." Emergent social entities are also social actors.

112. See, e.g., J. A. Michael and Szigeti 2018.

113. Elder-Vass 2012: 22, emphasis in the original.

114. For further theorizing along related lines, see List and Pettit 2011; Tuomela 2013: 9–13; Tollefsen 2015; B. Gordon and Theiner 2015.

115. See, e.g., Instinsky 1940; Hölkeskamp 1993; Jehne 1995 (esp. Flaig's chapter); Ando 2000, esp. 6–7 and 30–31; Flaig 2003; Lobur 2008; Arena 2012: 113–20; Rich 2015.

implication of casting *civitas* and *populus* as *societates*, is that absent a constitutive *consensus*, a sharing of Intentionality as to a common *res* and as to a deontic order to govern that *res*, there is no *populus*, but only a *multitudo*, a chance aggregation of individuals. And without a *populus*, that it, without individuals united by their consensual sharing of Intentionality, there is no *civitas*, no joint political venture.[116]

One final point now remains to be made in order to bring the gods into our *societas*, as Cicero would insist that we should. We have touched on and will recur to Roman "folk theology," informal and often nonreflective beliefs, shared and unshared, about the gods.[117] For present purposes, it suffices to recall that the previous chapter opened with an allusion to Cicero's notion of "a fellowship and *societas* of gods and men among each other," *deorum et hominum communitas et societas inter ipsos*.[118] In the *De legibus*, Marcus offers, as a preface to his proposed legal code, a theology, inflected with Stoic theory, clarifying the relations among gods and mortals in their shared *societas* (*Leg.* 2.15):

> sit igitur hoc iam a principio persuasum ciuibus, dominos esse omnium rerum ac moderatores deos, eaque quae gerantur eorum geri iudicio ac numine, eosdemque optime de genere hominum mereri, et qualis quisque sit, quid agat, quid in se admittat, qua mente, qua pietate colat religiones, intueri, piorumque et impiorum habere rationem.

> Let the citizens first of all be persuaded of this: that the gods are masters and moderators of all things, and the things that take place do so by their judgment and power, and they are the greatest patrons of the human race, and they observe what each person's character is, what he does, what license he permits himself, in what frame of mind and with what *pietas* he performs cult, and they take an accounting of the pious and the impious.

This theology, to which Marcus proposes that every Roman subscribe, holds that the gods attend carefully to the purity of human minds and human conduct, above all in religious matters. He goes on to express the view, more specifically Ciceronian than generically Stoic,[119] that such beliefs about the gods are *good* for human community (*Leg.* 2.16):

---

116. Cf. Cicero's postexile political program based on *consensio omnium bonorum* in *Sest.* and elsewhere. For discussion, see Zarecki 2014: 45–76.

117. See at section 2.6.1. We return to folk theology especially in chapter 8.

118. Cic. *Off.* 1.153. Cf. Cic. *Fin.* 3.64: the *mundus* is *quasi communis urbs et civitas hominum et deorum*.

119. So Dyck 2004 ad 15b–16.

utilis esse autem has opiniones quis neget, quom intellegat quam multa firmentur iure iurando, quantae saluti sint foederum religiones, quam multos divini supplicii metus a scelere revocarit, quamque sancta sit societas civium inter ipsos, diis inmortalibus interpositis tum iudicibus <tum> testibus?

Who could deny that these beliefs [sc. about gods] are useful, when he perceives how much is shored up by oaths, how important are religious obligations for the preservation of treaties, how many people a fear of divine punishment has restrained from wickedness, and how *sancta* is the *societas* of citizens among one another, when the immortal gods have been brought in at once as judges and as witnesses?

A shared theology of the sort Marcus recommends confirms the socially binding force of oaths, guarantees compliance with treaties, deters immoral acts, and generally preserves our *societas*, our partnership as citizens. For the gods are immanent, not transcendent, arbiters of our adherence to our own *iuris consensus*, the "consensus about norms" that informs our oaths, our treaties, and most of all, our civic relations with one another.[120] The gods stand as our *iudices* and *testes*, passing judgment not only on our conduct but also on the character, frame of mind, and intentions that inform it. A shared belief in such gods reinforces our *consensus* and sanctifies our *coetus*, our "coming together," rendering it not a chance aggregation but a "sacred partnership" (*sancta societas*).[121]

5.4. Concluding Caveats and Possible Objections

In allowing us to create institutions, institutional facts, and deontologies, our capacity for shared Intentionality, including shared belief, allows us to build a social world of limitless practical possibilities. This social world is "structured by interlocking, internally related, often spontaneously emergent collective practices, carrying, in the sense of manifesting, (often contested) rights and obligations interrelating the human beings who undertake these practices as positioned components of communities."[122] Moreover, these "rights and obligations," that is, these deontologies, "rest on a shared belief that every member, or at least a relevant subset, of the community has implicitly 'agreed' or

---

120. Divine immanence is the subject of Cic. *Leg.* 2.26: *delubra ... in urbibus* increase piety (*ut augerent pietatem in deos*) by inculcating the belief that the gods live among us; "this belief imparts a *religio* that is useful to states" (*adfert ... haec opinio religionem utilem ciuitatibus*).

121. Cf. Enn. *apud* Cic. *Off.* 1.26 (and cf. *Rep.* 1.49): *nulla sancta societas, nulla fides regni est.*

122. T. Lawson 2016: 367.

'accepted' to abide by, or go along with, them."[123] These recognized deontologies, in turn, give status-bearing social actors desire-independent *reasons* to act in ways that go beyond their momentary urges and druthers. These deontologies also sponsor *beliefs* about how other status-bearing social actors with their own desire-independent reasons for action can be expected to behave. In addition, the mutuality of such beliefs, the fact that all of this is common ground for most people, gives everyone grounds for making and acknowledging deontic claims on one another's behavior. In other words, deontologies have action-guiding, action-predictive, and action-evaluative functions (see at section 4.3.5).

This social reality in all its practicality—all these interlocking, internally related practices, manifesting deontic powers that interrelate status-holding social actors—is cognition dependent. It exists and enables all the practical possibilities for action that it does only as a result of *shared* attitudes and beliefs. So, to bring together all three components of our social ontology, to wit, imposition of function, constitutive rules, and shared Intentionality: we create by fiat a Status Function, Y, or alternatively we impose a Status Function, Y, on an entity, X, insofar as we collectively adopt shared beliefs and practical attitudes, where the Intentional content of those shared beliefs and practical attitudes represents *Y as existing* or *X as Y*. And to recognize Y as existing or to recognize X as Y is, simultaneously, to recognize a deontology, a field of practical constraints, possibilities, and empowerments to action.

We saw in chapter 1 that belief has often been denied a place in Roman religious life. In particular, we saw that "beliefs . . . had no particularly privileged role in defining an individual's actions, behaviour or sense of identity."[124] I have offered reasons to suppose the contrary. That is, without a sharing of beliefs among Romans, there were no socioreligious statuses or positions (sources of identity), no deontic powers associated with them, and no actions or behaviors whose motivating reasons derived from recognition of such deontic powers. True, in Rome there was power beyond that conferred and sustained by shared belief, but this power was not the deontic power of a *votum* or an *ex voto* offering, of augural priestly status, or of a *locus sacer*, but rather the power of charisma, noninstitutionally conferred prestige, or superior physical force.

So, to state this chapter's thesis about shared belief and social ontology starkly: *all Roman socioreligious reality and socioreligious power was produced and sustained by the shared beliefs and other attitudes of Romans. These shared*

---

123. T. Lawson 2016: 366.
124. Beard et al. 1998: 1.42.

attitudes and beliefs were "constitutive." They produced and sustained institutions, institutional facts, practices, statuses, and their associated deontic powers just by representing these things as existing in representations embodying one of two constitutive rules, Y exists in C *or* X counts as Y in C.

In closing, let us consider some caveats and anticipate some objections. First the caveats. It is important to recognize precisely what religious realities Romans could and could not create through their sharing of Intentionality. They could create a temple, an *aedes*, and they could create, through the ritual of *consecratio*,[125] the sacrality attached to the *aedes*, rendering it an *aedes sacra*. The sacrality conferred by *consecratio* and denoted by the adjective *sacer* amounted not to that mysterious numinous property of the Capitoline Hill that King Evander called *dira religio*, "forbidding sanctity," at *Aeneid* 8.349 (discussed at section 0.2, above); rather this sacrality amounted to the social permissions, prohibitions, and obligations that follow upon the conferral of sacral status and that serve to surround the *aedes* with a "deontic aura."[126] It was this deontic aura, not a numinous aura, that shared Intentionality created.

Nonetheless, any *dira religio* antecedently possessed by a place (or a person or object) could presumably contribute to the felt force of any deontic aura subsequently conferred on it. Conversely, a place with a strong deontic aura might as a consequence come to exude a sense of numinous awe for those sensitive to its normative power. These two things, separable in analysis, must have come inextricably bundled in Roman experience. The deontic aura bestowed by collective recognition on an *aedes* might, in its palpable power, mystify the very people whose recognition had created that aura, thereby giving rise to intuitions of the *aedes*' numinousness. And some things and places, such as the *terminus*, could be so enveloped in an aura of deontic power that it became Terminus, not merely numinous but a *numen*.

This is not to say that the Romans could create, through shared Intentionality, *actual gods*, no matter how many beliefs and other representations they shared about them, with whatever intensity. *Nonconstitutive beliefs* about gods—a folk theology—underlay much cult practice and many religious institutions, as we have seen and shall see in more detail. Similarly, shared but *nonconstitutive* beliefs about divine authorization might underlie religious institutions, such as the augurate, and institutional statuses, such as that of augur, that were themselves created and maintained by *constitutive* beliefs and

---

125. Gai., *Inst.* 2.4: *sacrae sunt, quae diis superis consecratae sunt*; cf. Serv. *Ad Aen.* 1.446. See M. J. Johnson 2007 (a dissertation) and forthcoming.

126. I borrow "deontic aura" from Buekens 2014: 33.

attitudes.[127] We return to these shared but nonconstitutive beliefs, which may form part of the theology of an institution even if they are not strictly *constitutive* of that institution, in chapter 9. These beliefs were properly theological. Because Roman religious culture exerted no pressure toward cognitive conformity in matters of cult, they were also debatable and even dispensable in ways that constitutive beliefs and attitudes were not.

The second point to make is this: We should not suppose that sharing the constitutive beliefs that created and sustained Roman socioreligious reality (or sharing the nonconstitutive but still central beliefs about that socioreligious reality) entailed downloading identical Intentional contents from a central server into Roman minds or digitally copying Intentional contents from one Roman mind to another. Instead, we should think of this sharing of Intentionality on the model of Ovid and the flamen, from chapter 4. The latter possessed specialized and, as we saw, idiosyncratic knowledge about the Robigalia, while the former knew only enough to recognize what he saw as a *ritus*. The point is that *even this* modest sharing, this narrow patch of common ground, was enough to enable a broadening of the Intentionality they shared, enough to facilitate their cooperation, and, ultimately, enough to sustain Roman socioreligious reality in existence.

Third and finally, we should not suppose that the shared attitudes of recognition, acceptance, and belief that sustain social reality need to be valenced positively by the individuals who hold them.[128] A Roman might believe with enthusiasm, with boredom, or with resentful rage that Numa is king, but believe it he does, because after Numa's inauguration he recognizes and accepts it. This recognition, acceptance, and belief contribute to *making* Numa king but do not imply that the subject who believes *approves* of Numa's kingship. We recognize and thereby sustain all sorts of institutional facts, some of which we approve, some of which we disapprove, and some of which we are indifferent toward.

Let us now turn to two possible objections. The first is this. I have argued that Roman religious institutions and other features of Roman social reality existed only because Romans represented them and therefore treated them as existing. They were *ontologically subjective*. Yet it might appear that the direction of causation goes the other way, that is, that we entertain representations of institutions and so forth simply because there *are* such things "out there." For example, in the previous chapter, Ovid learned about the practice of puppy sacrifice from the flamen Quirinalis in the grove of Robigo on the god's

---

127. See Buekens 2014; Searle 2010: 107 and 118–19.
128. Searle 2010: 103–4.

festival day. He came to entertain representations of these institutions and practices only because these institutions and practices were there for him to learn about. We could say that the representations he acquired amounted to *knowledge* of independently (pre)existing institutions and practices.

Here we have simply stumbled into the *epistemic objectivity* associated with institutions. That is, we can form beliefs and make claims about institutions that are objectively accurate or inaccurate. In this sense, Ovid can gain knowledge and false beliefs, information and misinformation, about the Robigalia. However, there are three things about such knowledge that we should not forget. First, as we saw at section 0.4 of the introduction and at section 2.2.5, knowledge is a form of belief with the same mind-to-world direction of fit as any doxastic state. Second, when we create social reality—institutions, institutional facts, practices, statuses, and so on—we create new entities in the world about which to have beliefs and knowledge, new possibilities for the acquisition of (accurate or inaccurate) information.

Third, and perhaps most important, Ovid's knowledge about institutions—quite unlike his knowledge or lack thereof about the rising and setting of Sirius—also has a world-to-mind dimension, because, as Varro could have told him, his very knowledge of the institutions helps to preserve the institutions in existence and use. So, for all their epistemic objectivity, institutions are *ontologically subjective*. They exist and function only because of how they are represented in the cognitions, and hence treated in the actions, of minded subjects. If Ovid and his contemporaries ceased to make or have any representations—linguistic, doxastic, or otherwise—about the Robigalia, they would cease to act as if it existed, and it would perish. Again, this is because institutions depend ontologically on being in the common ground of a community of subjects. That is, they depend on collective representations, beliefs, knowledge, and speech acts as well as on the collective second-order presumption that such Intentionality is shared, and finally on the behavior that all this shared Intentionality supports and inspires.

A final objection to consider is one that I have occasionally encountered in conversation, to wit, that many people and perhaps especially the Romans "just do stuff," and that a great deal of action, Roman ritual action in particular, reflects only procedural knowledge, savoir faire, or know-how. My response is that where the cult phenomena dealt with in this book are concerned, the Romans did not "just do stuff." Instead, they did stuff *under a description*. As I have been arguing, they represented what they were doing in their beliefs, intentions, and speech acts. As we have seen, it was these representations that made their doings the doings that they were.

PART II
Case Studies

6

Belief and Cult: Lucretius's Roman Theory

6.1. Introduction

Chapter 1 was critical and polemical. It sought to contextualize and rebut two positions that have been influential in the study of ancient religion. The first position posits a dichotomy between belief and behavior according to which there is no particular connection between them. Religions divide into those that are matters of cognition and those that are matters of action. The second position more or less denies the existence of belief before the Christian era. Neither of these positions turned out to be tenable.

Chapter 2 was constructive. It examined logical and psychological properties of the mental state that we call belief. In chapter 3, we saw that belief underlies emotions and that beliefs, along with practical attitudes such as desire and intention, are implicated in the etiology of action. In chapters 4 and 5 we saw how beliefs and other attitudes may be collectively shared and how such sharing potentiates shared agency and joint action, gives social norms their force, and underlies social reality and social power. Along the way, we tried to illustrate the value of looking at belief in this way for scholars of religion.

The arguments offered in the previous chapters are, despite their sometimes ancient roots, modern arguments. What happens if we ask a Roman how he or she imagines the relationship between belief and cult action? Are our etic theories alien to this Roman's emic perspective? To explore these questions, we turn to the Epicurean poet Lucretius (section 6.2) and his Roman theory about the origin of theological belief, the origin of cult, and the causal relation of religious believing to cultic doing. Most scholarship on Epicurean religious thought has addressed issues metaphysical, that is, concerning the nature of the gods;[1] epistemological, that is, concerning knowledge of the gods;[2] or ethical, that is, concerning piety.[3]

Here, I draw out the implications of Epicurean philosophy of action (section 6.3) for Lucretius's view of the religious motivations and commitment to cult of his fellow Romans (section 6.9). Lucretius offered an aetiology of cult in intuitions and beliefs about the gods (sections 6.4 and 6.7). He saw some of these intuitions and beliefs as deriving from epiphanic experience: we shall investigate the Roman phenomenon of epiphany and the discourse of belief around it in section 6.5. His views about the human propensity to see agency in mindless natural processes will afford us the opportunity (section 6.6) to delve into a kindred hypothesis from the modern cognitive science of religion (CSR). The upshot is that Lucretius's theory is in important respects a *cognitive* rather than functionalist or hermeneutics-of-suspicion "social manipulation" theory (section 6.8).

Lucretius gives us one of the most sustained surviving Roman reflections on the question of belief. He endorsed a cognitivist theory of action, according to which the religious behavior of his contemporaries was *caused* by their beliefs and affective episodes. And he theorized that cult behavior in turn influenced religious belief. Historically, cult sprang from naturally arising theological beliefs. Then cult had cognitive effects, both transmitting and altering beliefs, typically for the worse. Fortunately, with the help of Epicurean theory, one may nurture more accurate beliefs about the gods, and thus foster a healthier religiosity (section 6.10).

6.2. Why Lucretius?

I focus on Lucretius for three reasons. First, Lucretius shows that already in antiquity, approaches to Roman cult consonant with the one offered here, which posit an essential role for religious belief in religious action, could be proposed and accepted.[4] At least some Romans were perfectly capable of conceiving religious belief and action not as terms in a dichotomy but as causally related. Second, bringing out the *cognitive* in Lucretius's approach will afford us an opportunity to explore some closely related theories from the

---

1. See Konstan 2011; Essler 2011; and, with further bibliography, Mackey 2021, which treats of many of the texts discussed here.

2. See Sedley 2011; and, e.g., Kleve 1963.

3. See Summers 1995; Obbink 1996; and Algra 2007, comparing Stoic and Epicurean attitudes toward cult.

4. Theories of religion that were not especially cognitive were, as now, available in antiquity, e.g., that of Theophrastus, on which see Obbink 1988.

modern cognitive science of religion (CSR).[5] Particularly significant is the Lucretian insight that our minds are predisposed to intuit divine agency and purposeful activity where there is in fact nothing to be found but blind astronomical, meteorological, or physical processes.[6] Third, Lucretius's theoretical approach to religious phenomena offers an occasion to delve into some of those phenomena, especially the phenomenon of epiphany and the Roman discourse around it (section 6.4).

It is, alas, all too common to find the relevance of ancient philosophical discourse to ancient religious life impugned, as if Academics, Skeptics, Stoics, and Epicureans ceased to live in their own societies as soon as they grew out their beards, as if their "speculations and meditations were located to one side of religion," and as if "religion was something other than or, perhaps, something apart from these more or less erudite reflections."[7] In this spirit, we are offered the following admonition:[8]

> It would be a serious mistake to believe that we could take the thoughts and debates of philosophical observers concerning religion and translate them directly into thoughts, feelings, and "beliefs" of adherents of religious activities. Life is not so simple.

Neither is life so simple that we can afford to discount an entire class of Roman materials that *explicitly claim* not only to speak about but also to participate and intervene in Roman religious life. So perhaps we may take a page from Denis Feeney and suggest that there was no more essential a distinction between religion in philosophy and religion in real life than there was between "religion in literature" and "religion in real life." Or perhaps we may prefer to say, with Mary Beard, that "there is no reason necessarily to regard the illiterate... peasant as a truer representative of the Romanness of Roman religion than Hellenized Roman intellectuals or Roman Greeks."[9]

---

5. We first encountered CSR at introduction, section 0.2, and again at section 2.6.

6. Cf., similarly, Cicero's account of Plato's shipwreck, recounted at section 2.6.3.

7. Propositions endorsed in Scheid 2016: 49.

8. My trans. of North 2003: 344: "Ce serait une erreur majeure que de croire que nous pourrions prendre les pensées et les débats des observateurs philosophiques de la religion et les traduire directement en des pensées, sentiments et 'croyances' des adherents des activités religieuses. La vie n'est pas si simple."

9. Quotations attributed to Feeney from Feeney 1998: 1, which takes a page from G. B. Conte. Quotations attributed to Beard from Beard 1987: 3. See now the holistic "lived ancient religion" model of Raja and Rüpke 2015: 4: "The specific forms of religion-as-lived are barely comprehensible in the absence of specific modes of individual appropriation..., cultural techniques such as the reading and interpretation of mythical or philosophical texts, rituals, pilgrimages

Whatever approach we choose, when we turn to Lucretius's poem and other Roman Epicurean materials we find a great deal of data and analysis that purports to be relevant to religion as lived in antiquity. For Epicureans were observers of and participants in cult and in fact constituted, in a sense, a voluntary religious society, with its own cults and feast days.[10] These were people attempting to negotiate the religious world in which they lived, to interrogate their own religious traditions, and to construct their own ways of *being religious*, their own *pietas*, from materials both found and invented.[11]

Lucretius participated in this trend. He was one among countless Romans of various backgrounds thinking and talking about religion from Epicurean perspectives.[12] *De rerum natura* emerged within a tradition of Latin Epicureanism. Cicero speaks of a previous generation of Epicureans like Amafinius and his *aemuli* who "took over all Italy" with their Latin books of Epicurean doctrine.[13] These early works in Latin may have responded to a demand among the Greekless "well-to-do citizens of the *municipia*."[14] Many elite Romans, in contrast, such as Cicero's friend Atticus, would have come by their Epicureanism in Greek, whether at Athens or in Italy, under the tutelage of men like Philodemus.[15] For these Romans, it was a point of pride to take their philosophy in Greek.[16] Lucretius's poem was thus only one among many

---

and prayer, and the various media of representation of deities in and out of sanctuaries." See further Gasparini et al. 2020. See also MacRae 2016: 4–6.

10. Clay 1998: 75–102 (= Clay 1986) collects and discusses the evidence. Cf. Picavet 1888 and Koch 2005. See also Sedley 1989 on the quasi-religious allegiance of ancient philosophers to their sects and Sedley 2009 on Epicureanism in the republic.

11. The classic study is Festugière 1955. On the Roman side, see Summers 1995, and for a defense of Lucretius's approach to contemporary religious realities, Gale 1994: 85–95.

12. The history of Epicureanism and its diffusion in Italy has been much studied: see Erler 1994: 363–80, with extensive bibliography.

13. *Tusc.* 4.3.6–7: *Italiam totam occupaverunt*. For Amafinius, see Castner 1988: 7–11. Epicurean proselytizing: Epic. *Sent. Vat.* 41; Diog. Laert. 10.9.

14. Howe 1951: 60. But it does seem that Lucretius's addressee Memmius read Greek (Cic. *Brut.* 247).

15. For a portrait of Romans and their Epicurean teachers at Athens, see Raubitschek 1949. For Philodemus's Italian itinerary and influence, see Gigante 1995; and Armstrong et al. 2004, esp. 1–24. For a prosopography of Roman Epicureans, see Castner 1988. Momigliano 1941 addresses the political activities of prominent Epicureans at the end of the republic.

16. See Murphy 1998. Roman Epicureans with Greek could denigrate their Latin-writing fellows: Cassius refers to Amafinius and Catius Insuber as *mali verborum interpretes* (Cic. *Fam.* 15.19.2). We know only that Catius Insuber translated εἴδωλα as *spectra* (Cic. *Fam.* 15.16) and that Amafinius's Latin word for atoms was *corpuscula* (Cic. *Acad. post.* 1.2.6).

works, in Greek and in Latin, that made the doctrines of the Atomists widely available to Romans.

Given the prominence of theology in the Epicurean therapeutic program,[17] the outlines of Lucretius's account of cognition and cult would have been familiar to many late republican readers, quite independently of his poem. To what extent did prayer, ritual, or any aspect of cult practice depend, for Epicureans, on religious belief? Put the other way around, to what extent, if at all, was belief a motivating factor in the performance of cult acts? In answering these questions, Lucretius attempted to account for how individuals acquired religious beliefs and for the causal relations among religious beliefs and religious actions. In this sense, his theory was a cognitivist one.

6.3. Epicurean Action

Epicurus's theory of action resembled that of Aristotle, which we examined at section 3.3.1.[18] In Aristotle's "practical syllogism," purposeful action (πρᾶξις) is the conclusion that follows from a major premise, conceived as a desire (ὄρεξις), combined with a minor premise, conceived as a sensory perception or a doxastic representation (νοῦς, νόησις, ἔννοια). For example, given the practical representation, "I must drink," the occurrence of a doxastic representation such as "This particular thing is a drink" will yield *drinking* as conclusion.[19] Given a desire, the addition of relevant information in the form of sensory perception or belief triggers appropriate action.[20]

On this model, the conjunction of appropriate practical and doxastic states causes and hence explains Intentional action. Note that this picture takes no account of deontic motivators of and reasons for action (as offered starting at section 3.3.2). And it makes no effort to explain shared agency (as at section 4.3). The emphasis is on action as an individual rather than collective phenomenon.[21]

Epicurus's theory of action was similar to that of Aristotle. However, he was a psychological hedonist. For him, pleasure, ἡδονή, was a kind of master desire or ultimate value, the innate motive and goal, ἀρχὴ καὶ τέλος, of all our

---

17. Epicurus dispatches divine passibility in *KD* 1; Lucr.'s first remarks on *religio* come at 1.62ff.; and Diog. Oen. places fear of the gods first on his list of disturbing emotions at fr. 34.VII (Smith).

18. See O'Keefe 1997 and 2005.

19. Arist. *M.A.* 701a32–33.

20. See Arist. *M.A.* 701a30–36.

21. Lucretius is explicit in his individualism at 2.919–22.

actions.[22] "From pleasure," he writes, "we begin every act of choice and avoidance."[23] Our desire for pleasure, coupled with the right beliefs as to its attainment, leads to actions conducive to the happy life. The trouble is that socioculturally acquired "empty beliefs" (κεναὶ δόξαι)[24] confuse us, leading us away from natural desires that subserve the end of pleasure, and filling us with unnecessary, unnatural desires in their place, which inspire us to actions injurious to our well-being.

Epicurus's descriptive, *psychological* hedonism would not have required a prescriptive, *ethical* hedonism were it not for this tendency of our beliefs to become corrupted and to corrupt our desires in turn. The Epicurean program was devoted to "driving out" such noxious beliefs and desires and replacing them with "sober reasoning that searches out the motives for every act of choice and avoidance."[25] Epicurean therapy instilled, in a word, practical wisdom, φρόνηϲιϲ.[26] Once we reform our beliefs and desires, we naturally act in ways conducive to our well-being.

In what follows I hope to show that Lucretius's thinking about religion assumes, and makes sense only in light of, this theory of action. The poet thought that cult action resulted from doxastic forms of Intentionality, such as belief; and practical forms of Intentionality, such as desire; as well as affective episodes, such as, especially, fear. He emphatically did not see religious action as a matter "of doing not of believing,"[27] but rather as the inevitable result of our usually mistaken beliefs and desires.

6.4. A Lucretian Archaeology of Religious Belief

Lucretius's account in the fifth book of *De rerum natura* is our fullest exposition of the Epicurean archaeology of religion.[28] In a discussion of the development of civilization, Lucretius theorizes about the cause, *causa* (5.1161), of theological belief and of cult. He proposes the following (5.1169–71):

quippe etenim iam tum divom mortalia saecla
egregias animo facies vigilante videbant
et magis in somnis mirando corporis auctu.

---

22. Epicur. *Ep. Men.* 128.
23. Epicur. *Ep. Men.* 129.
24. Epicur. *K.D.* 15, 29 30.
25. Epicur. *Ep. Men.* 132.
26. Epicur. *Ep. Men.* 132–35.
27. Cartledge 1985: 98; cf. Beard 2015: 103: "a religion of doing, not believing."
28. The poet closely followed Epicurus's *De natura*, here relying on book 12. See Sedley 1998: 134–65.

> Already, long ago, mortal generations used to see / with waking minds, and even more in sleep, / the appearances of the gods, dazzling in the marvelous size of their bodies.

The earliest people, awake or asleep, perceived apparitions of anthropomorphic beings. They could not yet, of course, interpret the appearances as epiphanies, not until they had arrived at the belief that they were appearances of gods. Epicurus explained these appearances by positing that anthropomorphic "images," εἴδωλα—films of atoms that flow from objects, retain their sensible properties, and cause perception[29]—had befallen earliest man's *sensoria*.[30] The resulting sensory experience of marvelous anthropomorphic forms gave rise to the notion of gods and the belief that they existed.

These apparitions revealed marvelous beings, who seemed to suffer no aging or deterioration and showed no sign of fearing death. On this empirical basis, the earliest people inferred their way to the additional belief that these gods were imperishable and blessed. Consider these two passages:

5.1175–76:

> *aeternamque dabant vitam, quia semper eorum*
> *subpeditabatur facies et forma manebat.*

> They granted them eternal life, since the appearance [*facies*] / of them was in constant supply and their forms endured.

5.1179–80:

> *fortunisque ideo longe praestare putabant,*
> *quod mortis timor haut quemquam vexaret eorum.*

> And they supposed them to be far superior in their fortunes, / because fear of death [*mortis timor*] never bothered any of them.

On this theory, our earliest ancestors' inferences about the gods remained closely linked to the sensory evidence of the *facies* and were thus correct. Note that we have thus far outlined a two-stage theory. First, the earliest people simply *saw* (*videbant*) certain forms that led them to conceptualize gods and believe they existed. Second, on the basis of the details of what they saw, they further *inferred* (*dabant, putabant*) that the gods were immortal and perfectly untroubled.

---

29. Epicur. *Ep. Hdt.* 46–50.
30. See Sedley 2011; and Mackey 2021.

Sextus Empiricus confirms the orthodoxy of Lucretius's account and supplements it. He reports that Epicurus explained belief in gods by positing that images of superhuman aspect had appeared to the sleeping mind and were taken to indicate the divine existence (*M.* 9.45):

οἱ δὲ καὶ ... φαcιν, ὅτι ἡ μὲν ἀρχὴ τῆc νοήcεωc τοῦ εἶναι θεὸν γέγονεν ἀπὸ τῶν κατὰ τοὺc ὕπνουc ἰνδαλλομένων.

And they [sc. the Epicureans] ... say that the origin of the idea that there is a god arose from images in sleep.

Like Lucretius, Sextus attributes to Epicurus a theory in which people first came to believe that gods existed as a result of perceiving certain images.

Sextus also adds a second stage in which people came to believe through inference that the gods existed immortally and blessedly. But where Lucretius says that it was the perceptible qualities of the images that inspired early humans' inferences about divine immortality and happiness, Sextus reports that early conceptions of the gods' nature arose through analogical inference from human beings (*M.* 9.45):

τὸ δὲ ἀίδιον εἶναι τὸν θεὸν καὶ ἄφθαρτον καὶ τέλειον ἐν εὐδαιμονίᾳ παρῆλθε κατὰ τὴν ἀπὸ τῶν ἀνθρώπων μετάβαcιν.

But that god is eternal and imperishable and perfect in happiness came about by analogical inference [μετάβαcιc] from human beings.

So, according to Sextus, belief in the existence of gods came from epiphanic perceptions, but beliefs as to the divine attributes resulted from a process of inference for humans.

Here we must pause briefly to address Sextus's term μετάβαcιc (inference). The word and its cognates are good late Epicurean terms for inference by analogy, used regularly, along with Epicurus's own term ἀναλογία (analogy),[31] in for example Philodemus's *De signis*.[32] As for Sextus's usage of the term, at *M.* 11.250 he employs the term ἀναλογιcτικὴ μετάβαcιc, "analogical inference," as a catchall for any reasoning from sensory experience. At *M.* 11.250–51 he proceeds, in a passage resembling Epicurus's own account of concept-formation,[33] to subdivide ἀναλογιcτικὴ μετάβαcιc into ὁμοιωτική ("by resemblance," as when we identify Socrates from his representation), cυνθετική ("by

---

31. D.L. 10.32. See below, section 4.6.

32. See, e.g., Phld. *Sign.* XXXVII. See further in the index of De Lacy and De Lacy 1978; cf. De Lacy and De Lacy's remarks about the use of μετάβαcιc in Epicurean theology (204–5). For more on inference by analogy in Philodemus, see Allen 2001: 208–41.

33. At D.L. 10.32. See Bett 1997: 252–53, who also notes Stoic parallels.

composition," as when we compose a centaur out of a man and a horse), and ἀναλογία, "analogy," that is, the process by which we mentally transform an ordinary man into a Cyclops "by amplification" (παραυξητικῶc) or into a pygmy "by diminution" (μειωτικῶc). The latter, that is, analogy, obviously involving amplification, must be the sort of μετάβαcιc Sextus has in mind in his characterization of the Epicurean theory of theological μετάβαcιc "from human beings," and so I have translated it, above.

Sextus thus attests an Epicurean theory to the effect that by analogy with their own experience of limited happiness and longevity, human beings inferred that the gods enjoyed happiness and longevity in the superlative degree. They attributed to the gods, in the mode of eminence, those imperfect goods that they themselves enjoyed. These two inferential processes—Lucretius's inference from the sheer appearance of the divine images and Sextus's inference "by amplification" from human beings—complement each other to provide a fuller picture of the Epicurean aetiology of theology. We shall see both inferential processes reflected again in Lucretius's account of *false* belief formation (6.6).

Taking a step back, we see that the Epicurean archaeology of theological belief is itself a product of inference, a reasoned reconstruction of an empirically inaccessible past. As Lucretius put it in another context, *ratio vestigia monstrat*, "reason points out the traces" of the long-lost past.[34] Such reasoning from the observable to the unobservable was good Epicurean epistemological practice.[35] So we can hardly accuse the Epicureans of having dropped the epiphanic "images," εἴδωλα, into their argument as *dei ex machina*, in order to solve ad hoc the problem of the origins of theological belief. Rather, they spoke of epiphany as the *historical* origin of theological belief only because, as we shall see, they were also convinced that epiphany was one of the *ongoing* causes of theological belief.

Thus does Lucretius speak of the *simulacra* (likenesses; images) that flow "from the holy body into the minds of men, messengers of the divine form."[36] Thus does Velleius, Cicero's Epicurean spokesman in *De natura deorum*, similarly refer to the *simulacra* (calling them *imagines*) when he declares (1.49):

> *cum maximis voluptatibus in eas imagines mentem intentam infixamque nostram intellegentiam capere quae sit et beata natura et aeterna.*
>
> our minds, attending and fixed to these images [sc. of gods] with the greatest delight, grasp an understanding of what a nature both blessed and immortal is.

---

34. Lucr. 5.1446–47. Cf. Cole 1967: 44.
35. E.g., Epicur. *Ep. Hdt.* 38–39.
36. Lucr. 6.76–77: *de corpore ... sancto ... / in mentis hominum, divinae nuntia formae.*

Thus, epiphany helps even now to establish what Epicurus terms ἡ κοινὴ τοῦ θεοῦ νόηcιc, "the common notion of god," to wit, "an indestructible and happy living being," ζῷον ἄφθαρτον καὶ μακάριον.[37] This "common notion" comprises, as we have seen, the *chronologically* earliest complex of theological beliefs. Perhaps it also makes up the *ontogenetically* earliest theological cognitions of each of us. At any rate, the "common notion" is *logically* prior to any further theological belief, for whatever else we attribute to a god, he or she must exist and be immortally happy, or else he or she can hardly be reckoned a god.[38]

"Gods exist, for our knowledge of them is clear."[39] Our knowledge that the gods exist and are immortally blessed is true, and we know it to be true because it is ἐναργής, "clear," a term that in the Epicurean idiolect indicates a secure foundation in sensory experience.[40] A further corollary of the ἐνάργεια, "clarity," of this "common notion" is its universality, indicated by Lucretius when he speaks of "the divine presence of the gods," *deum numina*, that has spread "throughout great nations," *per magnas gentis*.[41] The universality of the common notion is made most explicit by Velleius in his argument for the gods' existence in Cicero's *De natura deorum* (1.43–45, with text abridged):

[43] *quae est enim gens aut quod genus hominum quod non habeat sine doctrina anticipationem quandam deorum, quam appellat* πρόληψιν *Epicurus id est anteceptam animo rei quandam informationem . . . ?* [44] *cum enim non instituto aliquo aut more aut lege sit opinio constituta maneatque ad unum omnium firma consensio, intellegi necesse est esse deos, quoniam insitas eorum vel potius innatas cognitiones habemus.* [45] *quae enim nobis natura informationem ipsorum deorum dedit, eadem insculpsit in mentibus ut eos aeternos et beatos haberemus.*

[43] What people or race of men is there that does not have, without being taught, a certain "preconception" of the gods, which Epicurus called πρόληψιc [*prolēpsis*], that is, a certain delineation of a thing preconceived by the mind . . . ? [44] Since belief has been established without any institutional act or custom or law and remains to a man the firm consensus of all, it must be understood that there are gods, because we possess implanted or rather innate cognitions of them. [45] The same nature, which gave us a

---

37. Epicur. *Ep. Men.* 123–24. The "common notion" is termed, more technically, πρόλήψιc (*Ep. Men.* 124).

38. See below, n. 67.

39. Epicur. *Ep. Men.* 124: θεοὶ μὲν γὰρ εἰcίν· ἐναργὴc γὰρ αὐτῶν ἐcτιν ἡ γνῶcιc.

40. See D.L. 10.33: ἐναργεῖc οὖν εἰcιν αἱ προλήψειc. Cf. Epicur. *Ep. Hdt.* 82; S.E. *M.* 7.216; Phld. *De signis* XV.21 (De Lacy and De Lacy 1978).

41. Lucr. 5.1161.

delineation of the gods themselves, engraved them in our minds in such a way that we hold them to be eternal and blessed.

Velleius's reference here to "implanted or rather innate cognitions" of the gods brings us to an aspect, not explicitly discussed by Lucretius but perhaps implicit in Sextus's doctine of "amplification," of the Epicurean theory of theological belief formation: what David Sedley calls "dispositional innatism" (2011: 41).

On this account, epiphanies depend not only on the physics of perception, that is, the impingement of films of atoms, but also on a feature internal to our minds. As Sedley interprets Velleius's argument, "human beings are born with an innate *predisposition* to form, as they mature, that conception of gods,"[42] that is, the notion of gods as "eternal and blessed." This predisposition flows from our innate psychological hedonism, discussed above. In Sedley's telling:[43]

> Each of us has an innate propensity to imagine—and in particular to dream of—the being we would ideally like to become. By doing so, we are *ipso facto* giving a concrete realization to the *prolēpsis* of god. Hence our innate predisposition to form this *prolēpsis* is likely to amount to our natural tendency to form a graphic picture of our own equally innate moral agenda.

So, our inherent valuing of life and happiness leads us to conceive of ourselves in a superlative state, the state of being forever imperturbably happy. We come to see this very state graphically instantiated in gods when we perceive their apparitions.

As Sedley puts it, "in this one special case it is not the nature of the object that determines the *prolēpsis*, but the innate predisposition of the human subject."[44] We project our own hedonistic moral agenda onto the epiphanic images that we perceive. Thus, our innate predisposition to form the "common notion" of immortally blessed gods amounts, for Sedley as for Sextus, to our natural tendency to imagine in the mode of eminence, "by amplification," those goods we enjoy in limited supply: life and happiness.

What we have here, then, is in important respects a *cognitive* explanation of the origin of religious ideas. This account stipulates an interaction between *psychological* and *environmental* factors in the generation of religious beliefs. That is, an innate disposition to imagine beings such as immortally blessed gods and the adventitious εἴδωλα, which supply us with images on which to work our inferences and project our imaginings. These two factors combine

---

42. Sedley 2011: 38, emphasis in the original.
43. Sedley 2011: 49.
44. Sedley 2011: 48.

in a way that is universal and entirely natural, not culturally, socially, or historically contingent.

Its cognitive naturalism distinguishes the Epicurean theory from other rationalizing ancient theories such as, for example, the "functionalist" theory exemplified in a fragment of the *Sisyphus*,[45] which asserts that religion was a human invention designed to enforce morality through fear of retribution. Human invention is not required, in the Epicurean analysis, for the generation of religious beliefs. Rather, all one needs is a typical human mind. Indeed, typical human minds cannot help but generate these beliefs. We have seen that these cognitive mechanisms operated in human history and continue to operate to compel theological belief formation.

6.5. Excursus: Roman Epiphanies

Here we pause to ask how the Lucretian theory of epiphany might have struck a Roman audience. Would it have been received as abstract philosophical theorizing? No. As Clifford Ando writes, "private individuals saw gods on a regular basis."[46] We shall survey some inscriptions that attest to this fact, and we shall sample the Roman discourse on epiphany and the question of credence. Presumably, there was no question as to whether or not the gods existed. Yet the Romans were not therefore simply credulous. It will emerge that even if the gods' existence was never in doubt, a Roman might question what beliefs were licensed with respect to any given epiphany and even whether a given experience should count as "epiphanic." For it was not properly an epiphany unless it was accepted as and believed to be a god's apparition. The point of this excursus, then, is to show that *belief* was essential to the Roman experience of epiphany.

A story of an epiphanic encounter related by Valerius Maximus illustrates the centrality of belief. In the early third century BCE, the consul C. Fabricius Luscinus won a battle against the Bruttii and Lucani. At a crucial moment in the struggle, when the Romans were wavering in their resolve, an unusually large young man (*eximiae magnitudinis iuvenis*) appeared, exhorted them to fight, and then assisted them in securing victory. Valerius reports that on the

---

45. DK 88 B 25 = S. E. *M.* 9.54. Polybius 6.4 likewise offers a functionalist interpretation of Roman religion. On these theories, religion was explicable in terms of the functions it fulfilled: social control, social cohesion, maintenance of elite dominance. But even these ancient functionalisms necessarily assume that religion relied on the distinctive psychological states it inspired in most people for its power to promote control, cohesion, or dominance. For a concise critique of modern functionalist explanations of religion, see C. King 1998: 326–35.

46. Ando 2010b: 45. On ancient epiphany Pfister 1924, Pax 1955, and Pax 1962 are fundamental. I've found Versnel 1987 the most useful concise study, Platt 2011 the most sophisticated longer study. On epiphany in Atomist theology, see Mackey 2021.

day following the battle, Fabricius announced that he had reserved a special crown of honor for the young man who had played such a decisive role in the Roman victory. However (1.8.6):

> cum ... nec inueniretur qui id praemium peteret, cognitum pariter atque creditum est Martem patrem tunc populo suo adfuisse.

> when ... nobody could be found to claim the prize, it was recognized as well as believed that Father Mars had been present to aid his people at that time.

When the heroic young soldier was nowhere to be found, it was immediately recognized (*cognitum est*) that the only explanation was an epiphany of Mars. What is more, this explanation was accepted and believed (*creditum est*).

Valerius's two verbs point to two distinct cognitive operations: the moment when an intuition, a "recognizing," nonreflectively presents itself, and the moment when this intuition is reflectively accepted as true. The remainder of Valerius's tale attests the value of empirical evidence in conducing to acceptance and belief (1.8.6):

> inter cetera huiusce rei manifesta indicia galea quoque duabus distincta pinnis, qua caeleste caput tectum fuerat, argumentum praebuit.

> Among the other clear signs of this fact, a helmet, too, adorned by two wings, with which the heavenly head had been covered, furnished evidence.

There would have been no question as to whether or not Mars existed. Yet one could always doubt whether an apparent manifestation of his divinity was genuine and warranted credence. Here the mystery of the young warrior intuitively suggested an epiphany of Mars, and the empirical supports, *manifesta indicia*, in favor of this interpretation were overwhelming. Fabricius ordered a *supplicatio* be made to the god, and the soldiers complied with joy. (Note the connections of belief, emotion, and action: see chapter 3.)

The episode in Valerius is hardly unique. The appearance of gods in military contexts formed a well-populated class of epiphanies. Balbus, the Stoic in Cicero's *De natura deorum*, recounts several. For example, Castor and Pollux were said to have appeared, fighting on the Roman side at the battle of Lake Regillus. And they were supposed to have appeared again to advise the Romans of the defeat of Perseus. Balbus's account emphasizes that the Romans were not a credulous people (*Cic. N.D.* 2.6):

> P. enim Vatinius ... cum e praefectura Reatina Romam venienti noctu duo iuvenes cum equis albis dixissent regem Persem illo die captum, <cum> senatui nuntiavisset, primo quasi temere de re publica locutus in carcerem coniectus est, post a Paulo litteris allatis, cum idem dies constitisset, et agro a senatu et vacatione donatus est.

For two youths with white horses told P. Vatinius, as he came to Rome by night from his prefecture at Reate, that king Perseus had that day been taken captive. At first when he announced this to the senate he was tossed in jail as if he had spoken recklessly about a public matter. Later, when letters were sent from Paulus establishing that same day for Perseus's defeat, he was rewarded with land and exemption from military service by the senate.

The senate rejected Vatinius's report, not because announcing an epiphany was per se absurd, but because the matter on which the epiphany purported to bear was as existential for the *res publica* as it was lacking in independent corroboration. However, upon receipt of that corroboration the senate promptly accepted the truth of Vatinius's story—how but for divine visitation could he have known of Perseus's defeat?—and rewarded him.

This concern with credence frames Balbus's digression on manifestations of the divine in Cicero's *De natura deorum*. For the Stoic, as for Lucretius, the experience of seeing gods is probative of both the divine existence and presence (*N.D.* 2.5–6):

> *itaque et in nostro populo et in ceteris deorum cultus religionumque sanctitates existunt in dies maiores atque meliores;* [6] *idque evenit non temere nec casu, sed quod et praesentiam*[47] *saepe divi*[48] *suam declarant.... saepe faunorum voces exauditae, saepe visae formae deorum quemvis aut non hebetem aut impium deos praesentes esse confiteri coegerunt.*

> Thus, among both our people and others the worship of the gods and the sacredness of religious practices emerges greater and better every day. [6] And this is happening neither at random nor by chance, but because deities often manifest their presence.... Often fauns' voices are heard, often the forms of gods are seen, and these events compel anyone who is neither a fool nor impious to confess that there are gods present.

The gods reveal themselves to us, aurally and visually, and although it is *possible* to deny these revelations their veracity, it is not *wise* to do so. Note that where Valerius Maximus had spoken of *inferring* divine action based on various pieces of evidence, Balbus speaks of the *direct experience* of a god's presence. Yet even he acknowledges that what *feels* like epiphanic experience *need* not be taken as transparent proof of a god's visitation. There is always a choice, to believe or disbelieve, even if to disbelieve would be a mark either of foolishness

---

47. Pease 1955–58 prints *praesentes*, which is the reading of *A*: *praesentiam HNOB* (*in ras.*) *FM*.

48. Pease 1955–58 prints *dii vim*, again, the reading of *A* (*in ras.*): *divi HNOBFM*.

or of the intellectual perversity called impiety. However, when we *do*, wisely, accept visual or auditory phenomena as genuine epiphany, when we *do* believe that the gods have shown themselves, then, Balbus says, our commitment to religious action increases, and our acts of worship grow "greater and better," *maiores atque meliores*. (Note the implication of *intensity*: see section 2.5.)

We see traces of the worship Balbus references in votive inscriptions testifying to epiphanic encounters. Numerous inscriptions bearing formulas such as *ex visu* ("on account of a vision"), *ex iussu* ("on account of a command"), and *somno monitus* ("advised in sleep") record the dedications of individuals claiming to have encountered gods,[49] some of them the very gods we just met in Valerius and Cicero's literary epiphanies. Here, for example, is testimony to an epiphany of Mars, in an inscription from Numantia, in modern Spain:[50]

EX VI(SU) / MAR/TI
On account of a vision, to Mars.

And here we see attested the appearance of one of the divine twins in an inscription on an altar unearthed at Brescia (ancient Brixia):[51]

CASTORI / DEO / EX VISU /
S[E]X(TUS) SEXT(IUS) / EPAGATHUS

To the god Castor, on account of a vision,
Sextus Sextius Epagathus [sc. dedicates this].

The formula *ex visu* indicates, simply and without elaboration, the worshipper's reason for dedicating the altar or stele: a vision of the god.

The formula could be varied or expanded, as in this inscription recording a dedication to Jupiter Optimus Maximus from Mediolanum (modern Milan):[52]

I(OVI) O(PTIMO) M(AXIMO) /
L(UCIUS) V[ICTULL]I/[E]NUS / [VICTO]RI/[NUS] VI[SU] / MONITUS

To Jupiter Optimus Maximus
Lucius Victullienus Victorinus, advised by a vision
[sc. dedicates this].

---

49. See especially Renberg 2003; Renberg 2017; and Ando 2010b. Given this wealth of epigraphic evidence, one can hardly say that "theophanies" are "ill-attested" (Pease 1955–58 ad Cic. N.D. 2.4).

50. *AE* 1999: 0926.

51. *ILS* 3392 (2).

52. *CIL* V 05597 (B).

The dedicator set up this inscription as a result of having received an admonition in a vision, *visu monitus*. Another votive to Jupiter Optimus Maximus from Köngen, Germany, varies the wording to indicate precisely what the worshipper saw: *visu dei monitus*, "advised by a vision *of the god*."[53]

At other times the epiphany comes not in a vision but in a command, as is attested by the class of *ex iussu* inscriptions, such as this one from Puteoli (modern Pozzuoli):[54]

[EX] IUSSU I(OVIS) O(PTIMI) M(AXIMI) HELIOPOLITAN[I] /
[AEDE]M DILAPSAM M(ARCUS) ULPIUS SABINUS AEDITUS
I[NSTAURAVIT]

On account of a command, Marcus Ulpius Sabinus, the temple-keeper, restored the crumbled temple of Jupiter Optimus Maximus of Heliopolis.

Here we learn of the god's command, *ex iussu*, to restore his crumbling *aedes*. The restorer commemorates his fulfillment of the god's *iussus* with this inscription.

The examples we have surveyed so far harmonize with Lucretius's claim that epiphanies can appear to the waking mind, *animo vigilante*. However, as we saw, Sextus and Lucretius both proposed that images of the gods filter into our dreaming minds as well. So it is that we find inscriptions reporting communications of the gods neither to the ears nor to the eyes, but in dreams while asleep, *somno monitus*, as here:[55]

NUMINI C[AE]LESTI	To the celestial power,
P(UBLIUS) CLODIUS [FL]AVIUS	Publius Clodius Flavius
VENERA[N]DUS	Venerandus,
VIVIR [A]UG(USTALIS)	*sevir Augustalis*,
SOMNO MONITUS FECIT	advised in his sleep, placed this.

The deity of this inscription, from the so-called Sabazeum in Ostia, marking a dedication by a *sevir Augustalis*,[56] has been identified as the Carthaginian Dea Caelestis.[57] If so, she is called simply *numen caeleste* here. More important for us is that the dedicator, P. Clodius Flavius Venerandus, was "advised in his sleep," *somno monitus*, by the deity.

It is unclear whether this last inscription attests a spontaneous dream-epiphany or a vision sought through *incubatio*, ritual sleep for the purpose of

---

53. *AE* 1996: 1147. *CIL* XIII 11729 (B). Dated AD 151–250.
54. *ILS* 4289 (5). First published, Dennison 1898: 374. Dated AD 101–200.
55. *AE* 1909: 0110.
56. A municipal honorific office usually held by freedmen.
57. L. Taylor 1913: 93.

receiving a dream-vision, often to secure health. The following inscription from Sibiu, Romania, appears to have resulted from *incubatio* on account of its reference to Aesculapius:[58]

I(OVI) O(PTIMO) M(AXIMO) D(OLICHENO) /
EX PRAECEPTO / NUM(INIS) AESCULAPI(I) / SOMNO MONIT(US) /
VETURIUS MARCI / AN(US) VE(TERANUS) L(EGIONIS) XIII G(EMINAE)
P(RO) S(ALUTE) S(UA) SUOR(UM)Q(UE)

To Jupiter Optimus Maximus Dolichenus,
advised in his sleep by instruction of the *numen* of Aesculapius,
Veturius Marcianus, veteran of the 13th twin legion [sc. dedicates this],
for his own health and that of his family.

Aesculapius visits the soldier, Veturius Marcianus, in a dream and instructs that he make a dedication to Jupiter Dolichenus, "for his own health and that of his family." *Incubatio* was open to men and women, as an inscription of (Af)rania Afra, bearing the words "advised by a vision, [*ex*] *visu monita*, for her own and her family's heath," indicates.[59]

Now, let us grant that these inscriptions betray a certain formulaic quality, and let us grant that some of them might have been pro forma, "merely" responding to some contextual demand, social norm, or sense of obligation. Still, it is hard to believe that none of this religious behavior was a response to the subjective experience of having heard or seen a god, while awake or asleep. Balbus certainly insisted, as we saw, that epiphany could drive Romans both to confess (*confiteri coegerunt*) the presence of a deity, and to engage in cult action. These inscriptions amount to a small sampling of precisely such confessions and actions.

Balbus wished to insist on the probative value of epiphanic experience and the cult commitment it could engender. Yet, as we saw, Romans like Valerius Maximus could acknowledge the gap between an intuition of divine manifestation and sober acceptance, as when Fabricius both perceived and then with the help of tangible evidence came to believe (*cognitum atque creditum est*) that Mars had assisted him in battle.

Indeed, the Roman discourse on epiphany could be subtler still. Take Cicero's denial, in a speech to the senate on a matter of *religio*,[60] that the gods appear to us *ex visu*, that the sort of epiphanic manifestations narrated in *fabulae* should be lent any credence (*Har. Resp.* 62):

---

58. *CIL* III 01614 (= *CIL* III 08044). Dated between AD 151 and 270.

59. *CIL* XIII 06415 [*ex*] *visu monita / ob salute sua et / suorum*. Found in Mannheim, Germany, and dated AD 101–250.

60. We touched on this episode and its context at section 2.6.3.

Nolite enim id putare accidere posse quod in fabulis saepe videtis fieri, ut deus aliqui delapsus de caelo coetus hominum adeat, versetur in terris, cum hominibus conloquatur.

Do not suppose that what you often see take place in plays can happen: that some god, slipping down from heaven, may approach the gatherings of men, may haunt the earth, may speak with men.

Cicero's next move is significant. He denies neither the existence of gods, nor that they manifest themselves and their will to us. Instead, he suggests that the epiphanies of the gods come to us indirectly, mediated through mundane phenomena (*Har. Resp.* 62–63):

Cogitate genus sonitus eius quem Latinienses nuntiarunt, recordamini illud etiam quod nondum est relatum, quod eodem fere tempore factus in agro Piceno Potentiae nuntiatur terrae motus horribilis. . . . [63] *Etenim haec deorum immortalium vox, haec paene oratio iudicanda est, cum ipse mundus, cum maria atque terrae motu quodam novo contremiscunt et inusitato aliquid sono incredibilique praedicunt.*

Consider the sort of sound that the Latins have announced and remember also that event that has not yet been referred to the senate, that at about the same time a terrible earthquake is said to have taken place in the Picene district, at Potentiae. . . . [63] In fact, *this* should be judged the voice of the immortal gods, *this* their way of speaking, as it were, when the world itself, when the seas and lands tremble with an unusual quaking and prophesy something in unaccustomed and incredible sounds.

Cogitate genus sonitus eius: Cicero closes his speech by admonishing the senate to reflect on the nature of a sound that has been heard. This sound, which he urges the senate to regard as the "voice of the gods," *vox deorum*, was not human speech, but rather the more ambiguous medium of extraordinary, if nonetheless terrestrial, phenomena.

If Cicero's argument and the other examples we have examined tell us anything, it is that epiphany represented both a possible experience and a topic of doxastic contestation in the Roman world. Thus, Lucretius's theory as to its historical and continuing role in religious life did not reside at some philosophical distance from his readers' own concerns and experience. The gods' *existence* does not emerge as a matter of debate from these texts on epiphany, but the question of what should count, and on what evidence or arguments, as a genuine manifestation of their presence, power, or voice often does. What counted or did not count as epiphany was a matter of belief.

6.6. False Beliefs

We saw at section 6.4 that Lucretius had a story to tell about the origin of belief in gods. In this story, theological belief results from our propensity to imagine, through inference, in the mode of eminence the limited goods that we already enjoy, as well as from our tendency to project those eminent goods onto the beings that we see in epiphanic visions. In this way, the earliest people arrived (as we may still arrive) at the theologically correct "common notion" of god as immortally blessed.

However, our ancestors strayed from this common notion, erring when they attributed to the gods a mundane agency inconsistent with their perfect tranquility. In the Intentionalist terms introduced in chapter 2, the *object* of our ancestors' beliefs remained constant but the *content* changed. The gods came to be represented inaccurately. The Lucretian passage describing how this came to pass is worth quoting (5.1183–95):

> *praeterea caeli rationes ordine certo / et varia annorum cernebant tempora verti / nec poterant quibus id fieret cognoscere causis. / ergo perfugium sibi habebant omnia divis / tradere et illorum nutu facere omnia flecti. / in caeloque deum sedes et templa locarunt, / per caelum volvi quia nox et luna videtur, / luna dies et nox et noctis signa severa / noctivagaeque faces caeli flammaeque volantes, / nubila sol imbres nix venti fulmina grando / et rapidi fremitus et murmura magna minarum. / O genus infelix humanum, talia divis / cum tribuit facta atque iras adiunxit acerbas!*

> They [i.e., early humans] observed the patterns of the heavens and the / various seasons of the years turning in their sure order, / and they were not able to understand by what causes this happened. / Therefore their refuge was to entrust everything to the gods / and to make all things directed by their nod. / And they located the seat and abode of the gods in the sky, / since night and the moon are seen revolving through the sky, / moon, day, and night, and the austere constellations of night / and the night-wandering torches of the sky and flying flames, / clouds, sun, rains, snow, winds, lightning, hail, / and the rapid roarings and great rumblings of threatening thunder. / Oh unhappy human race, to attribute such doings / to the gods and to attach to them bitter wrath!

These mistaken theological beliefs arose from erroneous inferences about the *causae* of natural phenomena. Not grasping the obscure but strictly physical principles involved, early humans took celestial occurrences to reflect the causal agency of the gods. That is, they mistakenly inferred that effects explicable with reference to merely *physical* causal processes instead reflected *agential* causal processes.[61] Worse still, they read into events such as thunder and lightning expressions not only of divine agency but of divine wrath.[62]

In this passage, we see two kinds of inference gone wrong: abductive inference from sensory experience and analogical inference.[63] When our ancestors "attributed such doings" as lightning and thunder "to the gods," they abductively inferred agential causes for what they saw in the sky, thus stacking false and inconsistent beliefs about divine agency on the foundation of the preexisting "common notion." And when they "added bitter angers to the gods," they inferred by analogy with human beings—recall Sextus's μετάβασις—that the gods could experience negative emotions (see further, section 6.7, below). Thus, they joined false and inconsistent beliefs—the "false suppositions" to which "the many" subscribe[64]—to the true beliefs of the "common notion."

It is important to stress that for Epicureans, these false beliefs about the gods' agency and passions hurt us not only because of their alarming content but even more because they are inconsistent with the core precepts of immortality and blessedness that make up the "common notion." It is not logically consistent with the gods' blessedness and immortality to believe that they experience "labors and cares and anger and favor,"[65] or that they undertake the *leitourgia*, "public service," of managing the cosmos and directing the weather.[66] Such cognitive dissonance is its own punishment, because logical "inconsistency creates the greatest upset in men's souls."[67]

Note that the pattern of argument outlined here hews closely to Epicurus's general, descriptive theory of cultural development. First, earliest man learns his first lessons directly, from "things themselves," αὐτὰ τὰ πράγματα. Later, he employs his faculty of reason, λογισμός, to form inferences based on

---

61. Cf., e.g., Epicurus K.D. 11, Ep. Pyth. 97, 113, and 115–16, and Ep. Hdt. 76–77 and 81.

62. For Epicurus against astral gods, see Festugière 1955: 73–93; for Epicurean arguments about illicit recourse to divine explanations of celestial phenomena, see Hankinson 2013.

63. We explored abductive inference and its role in religious belief formation at section 2.6.

64. Epicur. Ep. Men. 124: ὑπολήψεις ψευδεῖς.

65. Epicur. Ep. Hdt. 77.

66. Epicur. Ep. Pyth. 97, 113, 115–16.

67. Epicur. Ep. Hdt. 77: τὸν μέγιστον τάραχον ἐν ταῖς ψυχαῖς αὐτὴ ἡ ὑπεναντιότης παρασκευάσει. Cf. Ep. Hdt. 81. In therapeutic mode, Epicureans argue that both basic false beliefs—divine agency and divine anger—logically contradict the "common notion" and thus can be reduced to absurdity. For given the "common notion" that gods are immortal and blessed, we cannot without contradiction further suppose that they trouble themselves with managing the heavens, much less partake of unpleasant emotions such as anger. See Epicurus K.D. 1 and Ep. Hdt. 77; and see further Warren 2009.

perceptions and experience.[68] The argument reflects, too, the shape of Epicurus's prescriptive epistemology.[69] Sense evidence is "true" (the gods seen in epiphany exist), as is licensed inference from it (these gods are immortally blessed), while error results from inferences neither entailed by nor consistent with the deliverances of the senses (angry gods control the weather).[70] Our tendency to form beliefs from bad inferences underlies the Epicurean aetiology of erroneous theological beliefs and fears. These false beliefs and illegitimate fears, as we shall soon see, could be adduced to explain cult.

First, however, I would submit, without wishing to risk anachronism, that Epicureans had noticed some features of human cognition that underwrite the research program of the cognitive science of religion (CSR). We see this both in Lucretius's emphasis on epiphanic experience and in his diagnosis of faulty inferences of agent-causation. The poet saw that we are prone to intuit the presence of agents and to overattribute agential processes even where no agents or agential processes really exist.

In this, Lucretius recognized an even profounder anthropomorphic bias in our cognition than what we find in his theory of divine epiphany. For he saw not only that we are prone to encounter human-like apparitions in our dreams but also that we tend to project human-like *intentions* and *agency* onto an environment and events that are susceptible to explanation in strictly physical terms. This anthropomorphic impulse is particularly relevant to religious ideation in the case of astronomical and other causally opaque phenomena.[71] For it requires sophisticated observation and reasoning to discover, for example, that an eclipse is the result of predictable celestial events rather than the result of the purposive activity of superhuman beings. It requires minimal cognitive effort for us to ascribe almost any sort of event to the activity of agents like ourselves, exercising the kind of Intentional causality with which we are first-personally familiar.

Even more basic than inferences to agential causation is our predisposition simply to *sense*, in "epiphanic" intuitions, the presence of human-like or superhuman beings. This experience of divine presence, as described by Lucretius, and also by Balbus, and as witnessed in numerous inscriptions, may be credited to a social-cognitive "tool" called the Hypersensitive Agency Detection Device (HADD). This tool's job, as explored in the introduction (section 0.3), is to sense or intuit animacy and agency. If the cultural discourse tells us that

---

68. Epicur. *Ep. Hdt.* 75–76.
69. Epicur. *Ep. Hdt.* 49–52; D.L. 31–34.
70. On Epicurean epistemology, see, e.g., C. Taylor 1980; Everson 1990; Asmis 2009.
71. See esp. Guthrie 1993; Boyer 1996; Barrett 2004a: 31–44.

gods lurk all about, HADD may easily come to detect *divine* agents.[72] As Marc Andersen hypothesizes, "religious systems communicate estimates of the distribution of supernatural agents in certain environments." Expectations about the likely presence of such "supernatural" agents (*superhuman* might be preferable: for nymphs and satyrs, even ghosts and gods, were not "unnatural" for the Romans) "are often induced through exposure to higher-order verbal or written information," such as *ex visu* inscriptions. Epiphanies and testimony about epiphanies combine to create, according to Andersen:[73]

> a cyclical feedback loop where the transmission of religious ideas facilitates culturally endorsed supernatural agent experiences, further strengthening expectations that such agents exist and may be encountered, which in turn strengthens the religious system itself.

The Roman cultural environment—saturated with rites such as prayer, which presupposes the existence of superhuman agents, and testimonies such as those offered by Cicero before the senate, by Balbus, by Valerius Maximus, and by inscriptions that record epiphanic experiences—vouches for the authenticity of divine visitation and action. Religious culture may thus convert our natural disposition to detect agents into a cultural disposition to detect divine agents in appropriate contexts.

Not every culture need recruit HADD in the service of epiphanic visions, yet there presumably could have been no Roman culture of epiphany without HADD. This is the larger lesson: cultural beliefs are not radically relative. Neither are they simply inscribed onto the tabula rasa of the mind by culture. Rather, cultural representations get purchase on human minds insofar as, in the process of being communicated from person to person, they succeed in exciting cognitive systems, such as HADD, that make up the developmentally natural architecture of the human mind. Narratives such as those in Valerius Maximus and Cicero, as well as inscriptions such as those we sampled, did just this, leading to epiphanic encounters, which in turn led to ever more testimonies of such encounters. In the profusion of such testimonies, Romans likely encountered the world culturally prepared to accept the intuitions generated by HADD, and thus to believe that their agential intuitions and experiences reflected genuine epiphanies.

These observations gain support from another Lucretian episode that evinces his shrewd recognition of our hypersensitivity to agency, his

---

72. For our cognitive predisposition to trust in such testimony, see P. Harris et al. 2006; P. Harris and Koenig 2006; Bergstrom et al. 2006; P. Harris 2012.

73. All quotations from Andersen 2019: 77–78.

discussion of echoes at *De rerum natura* 4.563–94. Having explained the physics of sound in the preceding lines (4.524–62), Lucretius shows that echoes are merely a feature of natural acoustics.[74] Yet people who do not understand the physical principles of echoes frequently infer the activity of superhuman agents. Wherever echoes are commonly heard (5.580–83):

> *haec loca capripedes satyros nymphasque tenere / finitimi fingunt, et faunos esse loquuntur / quorum noctivago strepitu ludoque iocanti / adfirmant volgo taciturna silentia rumpi.*

> the neighboring people imagine that goat-footed satyrs and nymphs / haunt these places, and they say that there are fauns, / by whose night-roaming noise and joking play / they commonly affirm the deep silence to be broken.

This passage, like the one about celestial phenomena with which this section opened, shows that Epicureans recognized the human propensity to find agents and agency where none exists, especially when the phenomena to be explained are causally opaque, not transparently explicable in nonagential terms. This cognitive tendency authorizes the historical picture Epicureans paint of the origin of mistaken theological beliefs and fears. We shall soon see that these mistaken beliefs and fears can be adduced to explain cult action intended to influence the behavior of the divine agents so imagined.

6.6.1. Philodemus on Religious Inference

Before we turn to cult, let us cast a glance at Philodemus's *De pietate* in order to see what this Syrian Greek tutor to the Roman elite[75] can add to our investigation of Epicurean theological inference and the origins of false belief. In his fragmentary treatise, we find in columns 8 to 11, lines 225–318, a characteristically Epicurean theory about religious origins in a fragmentary digression on the "first people," which forms a digression to a defense of Epicurean piety. Philodemus cites Epicurus's *De natura*, book 12, on the origin of belief in gods among early human beings.[76] All we learn before the column disintegrates is that the earliest people began to conceive of "imperishable entities."[77] These

---

74. For a discussion of these passages, see Koenen 1999 and 2004.

75. On Philodemus's activities in Italy, see Gigante 1995, and Armstrong's contribution to Armstrong et al. 2004: 1–24.

76. Phld. *Piet.* col. 8, 225–31.

77. Phld. *Piet.* col. 8, 230–31: ἀφθάρτων | φύcεων. Trans. Obbink.

words are followed by a lacuna of one column,[78] in which, perhaps, Philodemus set out the theory of epiphanic belief formation we have seen in Lucretius and Sextus.

When the text resumes (column 9), we find Philodemus describing the first degradation of theological belief. Early people "initiated no dispute"[79] about the fact that the gods are "unbitten in respect of harm,"[80] that is, not *troubled* by any prospect of injury. Thus, at this stage, god was still conceived, in good Epicurean terms, as a ζῷον ἄφθαρτον, "an incorruptible living thing." Nonetheless, early people *did* wrongly attribute to god "psychological disturbance" by *analogy* with the psychological disturbance[81] to which other living beings (τἆλλα ζῶια; col. 9, 236) were subject, though presumably any such disturbance was not related to the possibility of receiving injury.[82] Similarly, at a later stage, toward the end of Philodemus's digression on cultural history (column 11), our ancestors began telling stories about the gods that had them suffering emotions and passions similar to our own (ὁμ]οίοις πάθ[εςι; col. 11, 307).

The key to column 9 is analogy, ἀναλογία (col. 9, 236–37).[83] The preserved text of these columns strongly suggests that the perversion of theological beliefs early in cultural history resulted from faulty inference by analogy. This Philodemean passage must be read in light of the account Sextus gives (section 6.4, above) of the Epicurean theory that early humans reasoned about the gods by μετάβαςις, that is, by analogical inference from human beings. As we have seen, Lucretius attests that μετάβαςις from human beings can go wrong when he complains that early people overanthropomorphized and "added

---

78. Obbink 1996: 309 ad 231–32. Note that this lacuna between columns 8 and 9 is not reflected in Obbink's continuous numbering of his columns.

79. Phld. *Piet.* col. 9, 233–34: οὐ] καθίσταν|τ[ο] διαλογισμόν. Trans. Obbink.

80. Phld. *Piet.* col. 9, 232–33: ἄδηκ]τον εἰς τὴν | [βλά]βη[ν. My translation. Obbink translates ἄδηκτον as "insusceptibility." But δηγμός and its cognates have a technical meaning in Philodemus, i.e., the "bite" of a natural and acceptable emotion: see Tsouna 2007: 7 and 44–51; Armstrong 2008; and Sanders 2011: 229.

81. Phld. *Piet.* col. 9, 236–38: τῆς ἀ|[ν]αλογίας ... | ... τοῦ ταράγματος.

82. It seems we reason by *analogy* only about the psychological states of gods, not about those of other animals. In Lucretius, for example, we simply *intuit* in the behavior of subhuman animals their psychological states (e.g., the mother cow anxious for her calf at Lucr. 2.352–66 and animals' vocalizations as expressions of their feelings at Lucr. 5.1059–86). Cf. Atherton 2005: 110–12.

83. Epicurus held that we form conceptions by (among other things) ἀναλογία from sensory data (D.L. 10.32): see Allen 2001: 195–205. On analogy in *Piet.*, see Obbink 1996: 306–7 ad 225–31, 310–11 ad 234–35, and 311 ad 235–38 (cf. 571 ad 2084). D.L. 10.32 and Sextus on μετάβαςις, discussed above at section 4.2, are omitted.

bitter angers to the gods" (*divis... iras adiunxit acerbas*; 5.1194–95). I submit that Philodemus's ἀναλογία, through which the "psychological disturbance" (τάραγμα) proper to "other living things" (τἄλλα ζῷια) was attributed to the gods, correlates precisely with Lucretius's account of early people's attribution of "angers" to the gods.

These results suggest that Philodemus's views on the origins and development of theological belief map neatly onto and also supplement what we know independently. In Philodemus, early humans came to believe in deathless gods. I would conjecture that in a column now lost he described the same process of epiphanic belief formation found in Lucretius and Sextus. At a later stage, early people arrived at false theological beliefs. What Philodemus does uniquely is to fill out this picture by making explicit the role of analogical inference in producing *false* beliefs. Sextus refers to μετάβαcιc only in discussing licit inferences (immortality and happiness). Lucretius explicitly mentions that early people attributed anger to the gods but leaves the reasoning that led them to do so implicit. Philodemus makes that process of reasoning explicit: ἀναλογία.

6.7. A Lucretian Aetiology of Cult

We turn now to cult. Lucretius's account of the origin of belief in gods and belief in their causal agency is framed by references to religious practice. He introduces his archaeology of religion in book 5 by ascribing to religious beliefs a *generative* role in the origins of cult. False beliefs about interventionist gods "has filled the cities with altars / and has caused customary rites, *sollemnia sacra*, to be undertaken."[84] Lucretius closes this section by decrying as misguided and impious the beliefs that motivate traditional *pietas* and religious action, beliefs about the gods' anger, favor, and receptivity to persuasion (5.1198–202):[85]

> *nec pietas ullast velatum saepe videri / vertier ad lapidem atque omnis accedere ad aras, / nec procumbere humi prostratum et pandere palmas / ante deum delubra, nec aras sanguine multo / spargere quadrupedum, nec votis nectere vota.*

> It is no piety to be seen often to turn, / with head covered, toward a stone and to approach every altar, / nor to lie prostrate on the ground and to extend your hands / before the shrines of the gods, nor to sprinkle altars with much blood of animals, nor to join vow to vow.

---

84. Lucr. 5.1162–63: *ararum compleverit urbis / suscipiendaque curarit sollemnia sacra*.
85. And see to 5.1240. Cf. Epicur. *K.D.* 1 and *Ep. Men.* 123–24.

On the Epicurean view of cultural history, then, cult practices are both chronologically and logically secondary to religious beliefs, which cause them. Chronologically, cult is secondary to theological belief because early humans could hardly institute worship of gods until they entertained at least some beliefs about gods, their existence, and their nature. Logically and action-theoretically, cult is secondary to religious beliefs because the performance of cult acts follows on the entertaining of certain theological beliefs.

So, in human history, belief gave rise to cult. Once established, cult and belief reciprocally reinforce and perpetuate one another. Cult may be secondary to belief, but once established, cult propagates noxious theological attitudes and emotions. Specifically, cult engenders *horror*, and *horror* in turn engenders further cult acts. Lucretius writes of this reciprocal relationship when he describes (5.1164–67):

> *quae nunc in magnis florent sacra rebu' locisque, / unde etiam nunc est mortalibus insitus horror / qui delubra deum nova toto suscitat orbi / terrarum et festis cogit celebrare diebus.*

> the sacred rites that now flourish in great states and places, / as a result of which even now is implanted in mortals the awe [*horror*] / that raises new shrines of the gods all over the world / and drives men to gather together on feast days.

Cult inspires *horror*—an emotion of religious awe predicated on belief in the gods' superhuman causal agency and human-like susceptibility to passions—in its participants, and *horror* in turn motivates further acts of cult. No doubt we should see the *horror* that is inspired by cult as itself engendering theological beliefs, in turn (cf. section 3.2 for emotion's role in promoting belief). Lucretius is explicit that emotions such as fear can have this effect, as when he writes that our fear in the face of natural catastrophes readies us to believe in gods.[86]

Earlier in book 5, Lucretius had alluded to *divom metus*, "fear of the gods," a synonym for *horror*, when he had advertised his intention to explain (5.73–75):

> *et quibus ille modis divom metus insinuarit / pectora, terrarum qui in orbi sancta tuetur / fana lacus lucos aras simulacraque divom.*

> by what means that fear of the gods has penetrated / our hearts, which all over the world keeps sanctified the temples, lakes, groves, altars, and images of the gods.

86. Lucr. 5.1233–40.

So, *horror* and *metus* motivate acts of cult. It is *horror* that "raises new shrines of the gods," and it is *metus* that "keeps sanctified the temples, lakes, groves, altars, and images of the gods." Cult, then, in its turn, perpetuates in its participants these attitudes of *horror* or *metus*, that is, awe of the gods predicated on belief in their passional nature coupled with belief in their superhuman causal agency. As a result of cult, "even now *horror* is implanted in mortals."[87] Examples of cult's effects are everywhere, for instance, in Lucretius's portrayal of the cult of Magna Mater, whose worship is able, through the perceived power of the goddess, *numine divae*, "to terrify with fear [*metu*] the thankless minds and impious hearts of common folk."[88]

To summarize, Lucretius says he will offer an aetiology of cult, an account of its *causa* (5.1161). Then, at 5.1170–202, he lays out the empirical, intuitive, and inferential origins of theological belief, followed by early people's mistaken inferences about the gods' celestial agency and powers of mundane intervention. This is followed by an injunction against traditional piety as manifested in cult action. The implication is that early people's inferences about the gods motivated them to cult action. He calls this motivation to cult action *horror* and asserts that cult in turn perpetuates *horror*.

But how, precisely, does such cult cause *horror* to become "implanted in mortals"? Our discussion of inference suggests an answer. Cult offers a wealth of inputs for inference, from the pageantry of festivals, to the anthropomorphism of idols, to the donative pragmatics of sacrifice, to the propositional content of petitionary prayers.[89] These and other features of cult almost compel *horror* by licensing false inferences, and from those inferences, false beliefs, that the gods are passional beings, receptive to address and persuasion, possessed of agency and causal power in our world. The Intentional content of such beliefs is then appraised in such a way as to give rise to the emotion of *horror*, a mingling of what we call awe and perturbation (on this "appraisal theory" of emotion, see at section 3.2).

6.8. A Cognitive Theory?

In Lucretius's archaeology of religious error and in his aetiology of cult, we find once again a theory that is notably cognitive. If we could ask him Dan Sperber's question—"how do beliefs become cultural?"[90]—he could provide

---

87. Lucr. 5.1165, quoted just above.
88. Lucr. 2.622–23: *ingratos animos atque impia pectora volgi / conterrere metu*.
89. On prayer, see chapter 8, below.
90. Sperber 1996: 77.

answers that appeal to our uniquely human cognitive endowments. First, as we have seen, *everyone* acquires the true, "common notion" of god, because of the interactions among innate characteristics of the human mind, perceptual stimuli, and legitimate inference from that stimuli. Then some people, just as naturally, read divine agency into the workings of the natural world and in so doing carry their inferences about the gods too far, attributing to them the full panoply of human emotions and intentions, including anger and other "disturbances." Indeed, because, according to Lucretius, early people saw the gods "do many amazing things"[91] in dreams, it was an easy next step to conceive the gods as exercising control over celestial phenomena. In any event, Lucretius held that we are predisposed to see agent causation where only the blind workings of physics are to be found.

These erroneous inferential beliefs—as opposed to the natural and ubiquitous "common notion"—then "become cultural" as a result of, to employ Sperber's epidemiological metaphor, vertical and horizontal transmission.[92] Vertical transmission, that is, from generation to generation, is signaled explicitly by the trigenerational exclamation with which Lucretius concludes his aetiology of false belief (5.1196–97):

> *quantos tum gemitus ipsi sibi, quantaque nobis / volnera, quas lacrimas peperere minoribu' nostris!*

> How many groans they created for themselves, and how many / wounds for us, what tears for our children!

And horizontal transmission is exemplified by, for example, Lucretius's *vates*, whose terrifying utterances lead their contemporaries astray in their thinking about the gods.[93] Both of these modes of transmission are at work in the diachronic and synchronic effects of cult, its capacity to produce *horror*.

6.9. Action Theory and Cult in Lucretius

These Lucretian theses about belief and cult raise questions. For instance, are *false* beliefs necessary or merely *sufficient* causes of cult activity? Is it of the essence of cult to communicate theological beliefs and other attitudes, and, if so, must these beliefs and attitudes invariably be harmful? We return to these issues in section 6.10. For now, let us see, in light of the Epicurean theory of

---

91. Lucr. 5.1181–82: *multa et mira . . . / efficere*.
92. Sperber 1996: 56–76 and 77–97.
93. Lucr. 1.102–3: *vatum / terriloquis . . . dictis*.

action, what role the cultural beliefs, whose generation we have just described, play in contemporary cult practice.

Thus far, I have presented Lucretius's general theory on the acquisition of theological beliefs and the role of those beliefs in the diachronic development of religious practices. Other passages in *De rerum natura* provide vivid synchronic illustrations of the Epicurean theory of religious action, a theory that is essentially an application of their general action theory to cult. The most famous such illustration emerges from the description in book 1, at lines 80–101, of the sacrifice of Iphigeneia. Lucretius chooses this mythical sacrifice for its exemplarity; it illustrates the sorts of toxic beliefs, at their most extreme, that typically motivate sacrifice.[94]

He opens the episode by stating that "religious belief has engendered criminal and impious deeds."[95] Assuming his readers know the outlines of the Aeschylean version of the myth, Lucretius details how Agamemnon sacrificed Iphigenia "so that a fortunate and auspicious departure might be granted to his fleet."[96] He closes by reiterating how "religious belief was such a powerful persuasion to evil deeds."[97]

What is pertinent for us in these lines is not so much Lucretius's criticism of religion or his engagement with myth and literature, but rather the fact that he analyzes Agamemnon's deed in teleological terms, as a goal-directed action that was motivated by desire and religious beliefs relevant to the realization of that desire. The clause of purpose introduced by *ut*—that is, *exitus ut classi felix faustusque daretur*, "so that a fortunate and auspicious departure might be granted to his fleet"—indicates what Agamemnon wanted to achieve. He believed that cult interaction with the gods would help him get it. As in his archaeology of religion, Lucretius here implicitly posits causal connections between sacrifice and religious beliefs, beliefs about the gods' existence, their agency, and their susceptibility to the blandishments of ritual.

A related example, also with a maritime theme, comes not from myth but from a situation that would have been a genuine source of fear in antiquity.[98] Lucretius presents the captain of a fleet praying in vain for deliverance from a storm: "does he not apply for the gods' peace [*divom pacem*] with vows and seek in prayer, / trembling, the pacification of the winds, and favoring

---

94. For the relevance of this passage to a Roman audience, see Minyard 1985: 37–40.
95. Lucr. 1.83: *religio peperit scelerosa atque impia facta*.
96. Lucr. 1.100: *exitus ut classi felix faustusque daretur*.
97. Lucr. 1.101: *tantum religio potuit suadere malorum*.
98. Lucr. 5.1226–35.

breezes?"[99] Lucretius's point here is that in situations such as this, in which any Roman could imagine him- or herself, one's beliefs about the gods and the scope of their agency (especially when one believes they and their agency are directly relevant to one's fears and concerns) *motivate* and *cause* one's religious actions, such as prayer.

A final example, also from Roman daily life, analyzes sacrifice in order to show that at times we may not be consciously aware that we entertain the beliefs that do in fact inform our action. Lucretius appeals to the cult of the *manes* (roughly, deified ancestors) in order to distinguish between beliefs actually held and those merely professed.[100] The causal connection between underlying beliefs and ritual action is brought out especially well here. While the Iphigenia passage laid stress on the way beliefs motivate religious action, this passage approaches the belief-action nexus from the opposite direction, showing that actions can sometimes be a more reliable index of a person's true beliefs than that person's words.

Lucretius speaks of those who profess physicalist theories of the soul and claim that they fear present ills—disease or bad reputation—more than any putative afterlife.[101] However, when they experience misfortunes (3.51–58):

> *parentant*
> *et nigras mactant pecudes et manibus divis*
> *inferias mittunt multoque in rebus acerbis*
> *acrius advertunt animos ad religionem.*
> *quo magis in dubiis hominem spectare periclis*
> *convenit adversisque in rebus noscere qui sit;*
> *nam verae voces tum demum pectore ab imo*
> *eliciuntur et eripitur persona manet res.*

they sacrifice to their ancestors / and slaughter black sheep, and to the *dii manes* / they send offerings, and in their bitter affairs much / more eagerly they turn their minds to religion. / Therefore, it is more expedient to observe a man in the fluctuations of danger / and to learn, in his adverse fortunes, what sort of man he is. / For true words [*verae voces*] are then at last forced from / his breast and his mask is torn away, the reality remains.

This passage has been subject to debate. Martha Nussbaum, for example, reads it as exemplary of a "moment of acknowledgement," in which the patient

---

99. Lucr. 5.1229–30: *non divom pacem votis adit ac prece quaesit / ventorum pavidus paces animasque secundas?*

100. On ancestral cult, or the worship of the manes, see especially C. King 1998: 336–80; C. King 2009; C. King 2020.

101. Lucr. 3.41–44.

undergoing Epicurean therapy at last recognizes that it is fear of death that motivates his or her behavior.[102] By contrast, for Gladman and Mitsis, Lucretius "is merely, in the tradition of diatribe generally, pointing to inconsistencies in beliefs—or between beliefs and actions—which make one vulnerable to ridicule or censure."[103]

From an action-theoretical point of view, however, the "inconsistency" is not so much "between beliefs and actions" as between *professed* and *actual* beliefs, where only the latter actually inform action. Of course, the fear of death that Nussbaum identifies is clearly operative in this passage.[104] However, Lucretius primarily wants to point out the disjunction between a person's *claim* not to believe in the afterlife and his or her *actual* beliefs, implicit in that person's cult action, about the agency of dead ancestors. This person may be honestly confused as to his or her true beliefs about the afterlife, or the person may be a hypocrite. He or she may have harbored an unconscious (i.e., dispositional) belief about the existence and agency of the ancestors that he or she did not recognize until the experience of a crisis, or the person may have been all insincere talk. In any event, and most generally, Lucretius's point is that no matter one's public assertions, one's actions under duress will flow from one's desires and fears and one's actual, not merely professed, religious beliefs.

For Aristotle, as we saw at section 3.3.1 and in section 6.3, above, actions follow directly from the conjunction of our desires and our beliefs relevant to those desires. Similarly, for Epicureans, our practical or motivational states, such as desires and fears, conjoined with doxastic states such as beliefs, compel our actions. Thus, the cryptoreligious believer is overwhelmingly motivated to act as he or she does. The person's behavior in a crisis infallibly indicates his or her real beliefs and reflects his or her *verae voces*. As Nussbaum notes, this recognition has implications for therapy. If our beliefs and desires *determine* our actions, then we can correct our behavior and undertake appropriate actions, that is, make choices and avoidances conducive to the happy life, only if we first recognize our mistaken beliefs and noxious desires for what they are and purge ourselves of them.

6.10. A Prescription for Cult Practice

Epicureans saw traditional cult as motivated and underwritten by false beliefs. Our examples suggest that these false beliefs amount, at a minimum, to these: there are psychologically anthropomorphic gods, susceptible to anger and favor, and possessed of superhuman agential powers; these gods are tractable

---

102. Nussbaum 1994: 195–201.
103. Gladman and Mitsis 1997: 215–17.
104. Cf. Konstan 1973: 20–22.

through cult action.[105] Surely in this these philosophers cannot be accused of constructing a theoretical edifice remote from the concerns and cognitive world of their fellows.

The diachronic archaeology of theological belief, sketched above, was no disinterested intellectual exercise. To understand the origin and transmission of false belief in cultural history is to be freed from false belief now. Likewise, to understand the sources of true belief for earliest mankind is to grasp the ongoing grounds of true belief. On the Epicurean view, belief in the gods' existence, immortality, and blessedness is both temporally and logically prior to all other theological beliefs. Early man's, and our own, false theological beliefs clash with these more primal true beliefs. The cognitive dissonance that results from accepting mutually exclusive propositions—for example, that the gods are eternally happy *and* that they are apt to be consumed with rage—creates, on the Epicurean theory, "the greatest upset in men's souls."[106] Indeed, "the greatest harms and benefits are brought upon us from the gods,"[107] not as a result of cult per se, but as a result of the false beliefs that that lead us to and that we take away from cult.

Likewise, the Epicureans' synchronic explanation of cult action does not stem from mere scientific curiosity. To understand, in causal terms, the beliefs, fears, and desires that underlie cult is the first step in the project of our own cognitive housecleaning. But if cult is the natural result of mistaken theology, and if cult action serves to keep the horror of the gods alive in men's hearts, how can its practice be reconciled with a true theology?

Certainly the opponents of the Epicureans resorted to this argument.[108] Epicureans denied such charges, devoting sections of works such as Philodemus's *De pietate* to proving the founder's assiduous participation in traditional cult.[109] Let me suggest an approach to this issue of Epicurean religious observance and to two related questions, which I raised early in the previous section, first, whether Lucretius thought it was specifically *erroneous* beliefs that gave rise to and must continue to motivate cult and, second, whether traditional cult *necessarily* expresses or communicates erroneous beliefs.

---

105. Lucretius had thus already reached the conclusion of Linder and Scheid 1993: 55: "il existait une foi dans la religion romaine. . . . Elle . . . se réduisait à un ou deux 'articles' fondamentaux. Elle donnait pour acquise l'existence des dieux et posait la nécessité et l'efficacité du commerce rituelle avec eux."

106. Epicur. *Ep. Hdt.* 77, quoted above, n. 67.

107. Epicur. *Ep. Men.* 124: αἱ μέγισται βλάβαι ἐκ θεῶν ἐπάγονται καὶ ὠφέλειαι.

108. See Phld. *Piet.* col. 49 Obbink, with accompanying commentary.

109. See Obbink 1996: 10, with nn. 1–7, for a catalog of attested Epicurean religious activities. Cf. the discussion of *POxy.* 215 in Obbink 1984.

I submit that Lucretius might have seen in traditional cult practice the same core of soundness that he saw in traditional religious beliefs. Just as the common denominator and sine qua non of the cognitive side of religion was the "common notion" of blessedly immortal gods, so the basic underlying foundation of the practical side was a sense that gods of this description are beings whom it is worthwhile to venerate.[110]

This thesis can perhaps be brought out through closer study of a Lucretian passage we examined earlier. Lucretius speaks of (5.1164–67):

quae nunc in magnis florent sacra rebu' locisque, / unde etiam nunc est mortalibus insitus horror / qui delubra deum nova toto suscitat orbi / terrarum et festis cogit celebrare diebus.

the sacred rites that now flourish in great states and places, / as a result of which even now is implanted in mortals the awe [*horror*] / that raises new shrines of the gods all over the world / and drives men to gather together on feast days.

Cult action produces religious *horror* and, conversely, *horror* produces cult action. Lucretius chose the word *horror* carefully. On the one hand, it is redolent of the fear of the gods, *metus*, that we saw him decry as a motive in religious action. On the other hand, *horror* recalls *divina voluptas atque horror* (3.28–29), the almost religious joy and awe that Lucretius claims to feel when contemplating Epicurus's teachings and the nature of reality those teachings disclose.

Lucretius equivocates purposely with *horror*, using the term to point in two directions at once. For *horror* directs us toward the mistaken beliefs at the root of *divom metus*, which motivate most cult and stand in need of correction. Yet *horror* also points us toward the awe and reverence that correct beliefs about the gods inspire and that might constitute a cognitively healthy motive for engaging in cult. Lucretius's wording makes both readings available. Thus, for Lucretius, cult action does not *require* that we entertain disturbing beliefs about the gods and court the bad kind of *horror*. As in other areas of Epicurean therapy, so too here, we must free ourselves of the false beliefs and empty desires that hurt us.[111]

So, Epicureans could recommend the continuation of cult because they held that if properly understood, what was *really* expressed by these rites was

---

110. Cf. the Stoic idea that although myth and cult contain some inkling of true theology, "the purity of the original preconception is almost inevitably compromised in the transmission through myth and cult" (Algra 2009: 246; cf. Algra 2007).

111. Epicur. *Ep. Men.* 127; K.D. 29. See Algra 2007 for a comparison of Stoic and Epicurean attitudes to traditional cult, with special attention to Phld. *Piet.*

reverence for beings of surpassing perfection, beings whose tranquility, if meditated on in worship, could serve as exemplary for us. Epicurus himself, according to whom "every wise man holds pure and holy beliefs about the divine,"[112] practiced cult under this description. He held that "praying is naturally suited to us."[113] As to his own prayer practice, "at festivals he proceeded to an understanding of the divine nature, through having its name the whole time on his lips."[114] So, cult logically *entails* very little by way of belief beyond the "common notion" and very little by way of affective episode beyond the awe, the "good" horror, which meditation on the divine nature, rightly understood, inspires. The "common notion" was, on the Epicurean view, *sufficient* to motivate cult.

In this light, we should read Lucretius's words about approaching the *delubra deum* in peace. Once false beliefs and the "bad" *horror* they cause are excised from the mind, what remains is "good" *horror*, which allows us both to attend to epiphany and to practice cult in peace.[115] It is only if you fail to reject false conceptions that (6.75–78):

> nec delubra deum placido cum pectore adibis, / nec de corpore quae sancto simulacra feruntur / in mentes hominum divinae nuntia formae / suscipere haec animi tranquilla pace valebis.

> you will not approach the shrines of the gods with a placid heart, / nor will you be able to receive in tranquil peace of mind / the images of the gods that flow from the divine body / into the minds of men, announcing the divine form.

Only if we accept the terrifying words of Lucretius's *vates* does the good sort of awe we should feel during cult become the fearful awe that marks and is propagated by traditional practice.

6.11. Conclusion

Now to close. We have been warned that any "question about the 'real beliefs'" of the ancients is illegitimate, because it is "implicitly Christianizing."[116] However, in Lucretius we find an ancient Roman concerned explicitly with the "real

---

112. Phld. *Piet.* col. 27, 758–61 trans. Obbink.
113. Phld. *Piet.* col. 26, 737–40 trans. Obbink.
114. Phld. *Piet.* col. 27, 765–70 Obbink.
115. Pace Summers 1995, who argues that Lucretius, alone among known Epicureans, recommended rejection of all cult activity.
116. S. Price 1984: 10–11.

beliefs" of his contemporaries, both the "true" and the "false" ones. I have rehearsed the Lucretian theory at such length to show that the ancients could conceive cult in cognitive terms, seeing doxastic states, such as belief; practical states, such as desire; and emotional episodes, such as fear, as causally implicated in cult action.

I have not meant to imply that Lucretius's answers are the last word or necessarily "correct." However, Lucretius's *questions* are very much to the point, for he asked what it was about the inherent workings of the human mind that made religious beliefs and practices what they are. A cognitive theory must also ask, as did Lucretius, how religious beliefs were acquired and communicated. These are questions we address at greater length in chapters 7 and 8. Chapter 7 considers Roman children as social agents who participated actively, as apprentices, as it were, in their own religious learning. Chapter 8 considers the role of the contents and contexts of Roman prayer in belief transmission.

The book's final chapter, chapter 9, addresses the causal role of cognition in the conceptualization and performance of religious ritual via a treatment of that distinctively Roman institution, *inauguratio*. The choice of this ritual, by means of which augurs and other priests were created, allows us to close the book with a concrete examination of belief's place in the construction of social reality and social power.

7

Ad incunabula

CHILDREN'S CULT AS COGNITIVE
APPRENTICESHIP

7.1. Introduction

The theoretical resources we have assembled in the previous chapters have prepared us now to explore the *cognitive agency* exercised by Roman children, both individually and jointly, in their own religious learning. Roman children can best be described not as *students*, for they typically did not receive formal instruction (though we shall examine the case of choral song, in which they did), but as *apprentices* in cult.

The "apprentice model" of learning, developed by Kim Sterelny, fairly describes the approach I have assembled, mostly from research in developmental psychology, in this chapter. The apprentice model is a form of "learning by doing" that "is often social and collaborative." In apprentice learning, the "reliable transmission of skill can begin as a side effect of adult activity, without adult teaching." Moreover, "apprentice learning is known to support high-fidelity, high-bandwidth knowledge flow."[1] There is much more to Sterelny's model than this, but these features of the model neatly characterize this chapter's approach to Roman children's religious learning.

The account offered here is an alternative to those in which Roman children figure as passively molded by socializing agents or external forces.[2] I contend that as apprentices, these young religious learners were *agents* of their own learning in their own right and were recognized as such by Roman adults. In turn, children recognized adults as agents *from* and *with* whom they could

---

1. See Sterelny 2012a: 35–36. A version of this chapter originally appeared as Mackey 2016.
2. Such as T. Morgan 1998. For agency-centered approaches consistent with my own, see Laes and Vuolanto 2016; and Vuolanto 2016.

learn. Thus, Roman children's religious learning was not only active but also social.

It is true that Romans sometimes did describe children as passively shaped by adults. Plautus attests this in the architectonic metaphor he uses to capture child rearing. Ideally, he writes, "parents are the builders of their children."[3] However, Plautus recognized children's agency, too, noting that even the best-built child eventually comes into his or her own *ingenium*, or unconstructed nature, and destroys "the work" of his or her "builders," *opera fabrorum*.[4] Two further examples, far more optimistic about children's powers of self-edification, attest the chronological sweep of the sources on which this chapter draws. Cicero could aver that children learn without instruction, *sine doctrina*, motivated by examples of virtuous behavior, while Augustine could insist centuries later that he learned of his own accord, by paying attention, *advertendo*, rather than under coercion.[5]

I focus here on children's acquisition of traditional Roman cult because, as noted, this domain of culture was not primarily an object of formal pedagogy, and certainly not of catechesis, but of apprenticeship, of informal "social learning," which unfolds through children's observation of and interaction with others.[6] Even when religious knowledge was taught formally—as in the case of choral hymns, examined below—the pedagogy was, so far as the evidence permits analysis, such as to yield to children significant cognitive autonomy (cf. at sections 1.2; 3.3.3; 4.1; 5.4). That is, the culture of Roman polytheism did not exert significant pressure toward cognitive and especially doxastic conformity.

Roman children's religious learning and its role in the transmission of religious culture is receiving renewed interest.[7] We saw in chapter 1 that we can no longer follow S.R.F. Price in supposing that the capacity for belief

---

3. Plaut. *Most*. 84–156; *Most*. 120: *primumdum parentes fabri liberum sunt*.

4. Plaut. *Most*. 135–36: *postea quom immigravi ingenium in meum, / perdidi operam fabrorum ilico oppido*.

5. Cic. *Fin*. 5.42 and Aug. *Conf*. 1.14.23.

6. See Scheid 2006: 18: "There was no religious teaching other than practice and assistance to the divine services. By the day of his majority, every young male had to be capable of sacrificing or performing a consultation of the gods. He learned these procedures, like all the other features of social life, during the preceding years at the side of his father or of a friend of his family." For "social learning," see Hoppitt and Laland 2013: 3–5.

7. Recent contributions include Bremmer 1995: 36–38; Mantle 2002; Rawson 2003: 311–35; Prescendi 2010; Vuolanto 2010. See Tulloch 2012 for graphic depictions of children in cult. Previous work includes Fowler 1896; Spaulding 1911; van der Leeuw 1939; Néraudau 1979: 183–241; Néraudau 1984: 223–50.

originated with Christianity. However, we should not fail to recognize the value of his suggestion that we view Greco-Roman "ritual as a public cognitive system." I take this formulation to mean that ritual was a matter of representations arranged in a fairly standardized way (a "cognitive system") and *publicly* conveyed, in the form of speech acts, iconography, and gestures. That is to say, the public cognitive system is the subject of this and the next two chapters. Nor should we neglect Price's question about "the sort of knowledge . . . contained in ritual."[8] A parsimonious answer to this question is "performative knowledge" or "savoir rituel."[9] To study Roman children's religious learning is to explore one avenue for the transmission of such performative knowledge. Yet the ontogenetic perspective we take here will also reveal just how complex the cognitive structure of this "savoir" was.[10]

Roman children's social learning of their religious culture involved cognitive *processes*: perceiving the Intentional episodes of others, sharing Intentional episodes with others, and imitating others. These processes resulted in distinctively cultural cognitive *products*: shared practical representations, such as goals and intentions with respect to cult action; shared doxastic representations, such as theological beliefs; and shared deontic representations, such as deontic beliefs; all of which had practical consequences for cult performance.[11] When process yields product, religious transmission has occurred.[12]

Before outlining what is to come, it will be useful to recapitulate some findings from previous chapters. Since our focus here is children's agency, we

---

8. S. Price 1984: 8–9.

9. Performative knowledge: Feeney 1998: 138–39. Savoir rituel: Scheid 1990: 673. Performative knowledge did not, of course, foreclose the possibility of "systematising expositions of religious knowledge," as in "philosophical, literary or antiquarian" works (Feeney 1998: 139–40).

10. Prescendi 2010: 74 follows Borgeaud 1988 in dividing Roman children's religious learning into "mechanical memorization" and "deliberate memorization." (For a scientifically informed discussion of types of memory and their relationship to ritual, see Larson 2016: 192–96.) I would submit that Prescendi's characterization of informal learning as "mechanical" elides Roman children's agency and the complexity of the cognitive processes they brought to bear in the course of such learning. Moreover, Prescendi neglects some important evidence for Roman children's learning of the "deliberate" sort that I present here: choral training.

11. For the distinction between practical (or motivational) and doxastic (or theoretical) cognitions, see at sections 2.2.4–2.2.5. For deontic beliefs, see section 3.3.2.

12. For a complementary but quite different account of religious transmission from a cognitive perspective, see Larson 2016: 301–72.

should recall, from section 3.3, that *agency* denotes a subject's capacity to act purposely or to cause things to happen within a space of possibilities for and constraints on action. The capacity to act purposely presupposes the cognitive faculty of *Intentionality*, which as we saw at sections 0.4 and 2.2 amounts to having *contentful* mental episodes, that is, cognitions *about* objects, states of affairs, situations, one's own actions and goals, and so on. Such episodes include perceptual attention, beliefs, desires, fears, and intentions (i.e., plans). Beliefs are Intentional states in that they are contentful. That is, they are *about* or are mental representations *of* states of affairs that a subject takes to obtain. Compare desires, which are about states of affairs that a subject wishes *did* obtain.

In chapter 4, we saw that Intentionality and agency may be shared. Two or more people share Intentionality when they are *engaged* with one another in such a way that they share attention, a belief, a desire, a plan, a goal, or another Intentional episode in mutual awareness that they are so sharing. Sharing agency, in turn, requires sharing Intentionality. Two or more people share agency when they act together as a result of intending to act together, in mutual awareness of sharing such intentions. That is, *you* and *I* each intend to act *only* as part of *our* acting *together*: we share "we-intentions." The resulting action is, as we saw, joint action. This is important in the present context because it was the ability to share Intentionality and agency that allowed Roman children to become socialized, that is, to acquire cultural knowledge both by observing and understanding the actions of others and by cooperating with others in joint actions of calculated or fortuitous pedagogical value. Successful socialization of Roman children, in its turn, preserved in existence the socio-religious institutions, realities, and associated deontologies and social powers examined in chapter 5.

The underlying assumption of this chapter is worth making explicit: the young of *Homo sapiens* can become socialized only if they enter the world with some primitive capacities that do not themselves result from socialization. Our biological line of inheritance grants us our characteristic human physiology as well as some core cognitive competencies that enable our sociability. These biologically inherited social-cognitive capacities allow us to acquire the cultural lines of inheritance prevailing in our particular communities.[13] Our early developing social-cognitive skills include the predisposition to treat others as agents like ourselves and the motivation to share Intentionality with them. The biologically primitive capacity to see others *as* agents and the biologically

---

13. Cf. Tomasello 1999a: 13–55.

primitive motivation to *share* Intentionality with them potentiate social life and social learning, thereby opening cultural lines of inheritance, in all their local specificity, to children.[14]

In what follows, I discuss the contributions that these core cognitive competencies made to Roman children's active social learning—their religious apprenticeship—in three different modes: (1) imitative learning, (2) participatory learning, and (3) instructed learning.[15] The first section, 7.2, sketches very briefly the ontogeny, that is, the development and maturation, of some aspects of social cognition relevant to our account of Roman children's religious learning. The following section, 7.3, explores imitation as an individualistic mode of social learning in which Roman children learned to pray by observing others in prayer. Section 7.4 turns to the Roman child's participatory learning through sharing Intentionality and agency in collaborative ritual actions. Section, 7.5 takes up the question of formal religious pedagogy by examining some evidence for children's choral training. We shall see that this religious pedagogy was orthoprax, a matter of training children *how* to sing hymns correctly. And yet hymns, *carmina*, express propositional contents that make reference to divine agents. In doing so, they were rich sources of both theological information and theological inference. In the absence of doctrinal coaching, children were left to receive that theological information and to make those theological inferences as relatively autonomous cognitive agents.

7.2. Ontogeny of Social Cognition

Let us now trace the ontogeny of some of the social-cognitive skills that contribute to the sharing with others of Intentionality and agency.[16] The basic developmental trajectory is as follows. Neonates emerge from the womb with a sense of "self-world differentiation" and an "innate ability to discriminate and empathize with people as distinct sentient and animated entities in the world."[17] By about six weeks of age, infants begin entering into *dyadic relations* with others. These one-on-one engagements may amount to "protoconversations" in which infant and adult share reciprocal eye contact, smiling,

---

14. E. Herrmann and Tomasello 2012: 709: "human beings biologically inherit the cognitive skills necessary for developing in a cultural environment." See Searle 2002: 104–5; Tomasello 1999a; Moll and Tomasello 2007; Behne et al. 2008; Tomasello and Moll 2010.

15. I follow the tripartition of Tomasello, Kruger, and Ratner 1993. For an update, see Tomasello 2016.

16. For what follows, I rely primarily on the treatments of Rochat 2001; Tomasello, Carpenter, et al. 2005; Tomasello and Carpenter 2007; Moll and Meltzoff 2011; Zahavi and Rochat 2015.

17. Zahavi and Rochat 2015: 547.

vocalizations, and affective states.[18] Around their first birthday, infants begin to engage with others in *triadic relations,* in which they share attention with others toward third objects or situations. In these triadic relations, children begin to appreciate that others may have unique perspectives on a mutually apprehended object or situation. When a child can appreciate and eventually adopt others' perspectives, the child's *cultural* ontogeny begins in earnest.

This is the narrative in outline. Let us develop it a bit. Neonates both identify others and identify *with* them, seeing other people as beings that are in some sense "like" themselves.[19] The self-other correspondence appreciated even by babies enables them to imitate or learn to imitate others.[20] Romans could regard newborns as, in a sense, *precognitive,*[21] but perhaps for that very reason they took note of what they saw as the emergence of the infant's first social-cognitive capacities, that is, the infant's awareness of other people not merely as external objects but as animate beings, and not just as animate beings but as agents and candidates for interaction.[22] Indeed, Romans could see that young children might also *overattribute* animacy and agency, as in Lucilius's observation that infants take naturalistic images, such as bronze statues, to be alive.[23] This developmentally early awakening to agency includes a motivation, from about six weeks of age,[24] to *share* with others through the exchange of smiles, gestures, and vocalizations, in that ontogenetically primal social space, the infant-caregiver dyad.[25]

---

18. A term coined by Bateson 1971. See Trevarthen 2012.

19. See Meltzoff and Brooks 2007a; Meltzoff 2007a and 2007b; cf. Opfer and Gelman 2011.

20. For imitation by neonates, see Meltzoff and Moore 1977; Meltzoff and Moore 1983; and for some theoretical implications, Meltzoff 2011a. Neonate imitation has been challenged: Oostenbroek et al. 2016; cf. Heyes 2016.

21. E.g., Cic. *Fin.* 5.42: *parvi enim primo ortu sic iacent, tamquam omnino sine animo sint.* Lucr. 5.222–25: *puer . . . / . . . nudus humi iacet, infans, indigus omni / vitali auxilio.* Aug. *Conf.* 1.6.7: *nam tunc sugere noram et adquiescere delectationibus, flere autem offensiones carnis meae, nihil amplius.* Utilizing many of the texts referenced here, I have argued for a relatively coherent Roman "developmental psychology" in Mackey 2019.

22. E.g., Cic. *Fin.* 5.42: *cum autem paulum firmitatis accessit, et animo utuntur et sensibus conitunturque, ut sese erigant, et manibus utuntur et eos agnoscunt a quibus educantur.* Aug. *Conf.* 1.6.8: *et ecce paulatim sentiebam ubi essem, et voluntates meas volebam ostendere eis per quos implerentur, et non poteram, quia illae intus erant, foris autem illi.*

23. Discussed at section 2.6.2.

24. The "two-month revolution" in infant cognition: Rochat 2001: 182–84.

25. For the Roman infant's smile, see, e.g., Cat. 61.212–16: *Torquatus volo parvulus / matris e gremio suae / porrigens teneras manus / dulce rideat ad patrem / semihiante labello.* Verg. *Ecl.* 4.60: *incipe, parve puer, risu cognoscere matrem.* Ov. *Met.* 4.516–17: *deque sinu matris ridentem et parva . . . bracchia tendentem.* Plin. *N.H.* 7 pr. 2: *risus praecox ille et celerrimus ante XL diem nulli datur.*

Very young infants are especially interested in eyes. Going beyond dyadic, face-to-face social interactions, they begin to note the direction of other people's gaze, which they follow.²⁶ Gaze following soon grows into a comprehension that others direct their perceptual *attention* to objects and situations. With this development, infants begin not only to *follow* another's attention to a third entity, but also to *direct* the attention of others, especially by pointing.²⁷ Lucretius notes this phenomenon in his account of the origin of language.²⁸ He digresses to remark on the ontogeny of communication in infants: "the very speechlessness [*infantia*] of the tongue appears to lead children to gesture, when it makes them point out with a finger objects that are present."²⁹

Lucretian pointing of this sort attends and attests the emergence of triadic social cognition, or *joint attention*, at the "nine-month revolution."³⁰ Now the infant transcends both the infant-caregiver dyad and the gaze following to enter with adults into triadic relations, in which *you* and *I* attend to a third object or situation *together*, in mutual recognition that we are so attending.³¹ This is precisely the scenario that Lucretius presents. His pointing infant directs the attention of another person to some third object in their common environment, perhaps simply to share attention to it or to serve some other goal that itself presupposes joint attention, such as making a request.

The larger point illustrated by the emergence of joint attention is that *social* cognition, as embodied in the Lucretian infant's prelinguistic communicative gestures, precedes *cultural* cognition, as exemplified by fluency with the conventions of a language.³² It is in the joint-attentional space of triadic engagement that cultural learning begins, because it is here that the young encounter the attitudes that their elders take toward the world, and it is here that they learn the names of things. Thus, a *natural* capacity and motivation for

---

26. See Meltzoff and Brooks 2007b.

27. Moll and Meltzoff 2011: 288–90. On infant pointing cross-culturally, see Liszkowski et al. 2012.

28. For the Epicurean theory of the origin of language and some new papyrological evidence for it, see Mackey 2015.

29. Lucr. 5.1030–32: *ipsa videtur / protrahere ad gestum pueros infantia linguae, / cum facit ut digito quae sint praesentia monstrent*. For such deictic pointing, cf. Hor. C. 4.3.22: *monstror digito*; Pers. 1.26: *digito monstrari*; Mart. 9.97.4: *monstramur digito*; Tac. Dial. 7.4: *digito demonstrat*.

30. Tomasello 1999a: 61ff.; Rochat 2001: 185ff.

31. Joint attention is explored in the essays in Eilan et al. 2005; Seemann 2012; Metcalfe and Terrace 2013.

32. A formally similar point about social-cognitive competence preceding and enabling cultural cognition is often made by Roman authors discussing the infancy not of individuals but of the human race: see, e.g., Lucr. 5.1019–23; Vitr. Arch. 2.1.1; Lact. Div. Inst. 6.10.13–14.

contentful communication with others through the production and interpretation of gestures in the space of joint attention is the foundation for learning *cultural* technologies of communication, such as language.[33]

As children's social-cognitive powers for joint-attentional engagement mature, they gradually come to recognize that others have their own perspectives, whether those perspectives are perceptual (e.g., a unique vantage point) or epistemic (e.g., unique beliefs), and that these perspectives may differ from their own.[34] In the Intentionalist terms of chapter 2, children come to see that two or more people may entertain different *attitudes* with different *Intentional contents* with respect to the same *Intentional object*. That is to say, people may represent the same *entity* or *situation* under differing *aspects* (as being *this* way versus *that* way) and have differing *attitudes* (e.g., belief, fear, desire) toward it. When this cognitive development is well established, by about four years of age, children can "confront"[35] the perspectives of others, that is, compare others' perspectives to their own perspectives, consciously adopt others' perspectives, and modify their own perspectives in light of the perspectives of others. Taking others' perspectives in this way allows children to exploit their powers of *social* cognition to bootstrap their way into *cultural* cognition. As we shall see, Augustine illustrates precisely this process in his account of his own language acquisition in *Confessions*. He suggests that seeing things the way others see them is central to cultural learning through imitation.

7.3. Learning to Pray: Imitation and Individual Agency

Let us approach the target of this section—Prudentius's depiction of the Roman child learning to pray—by exploring Romans' recognition that children's imitation was not passive but rather active, or "agent-based,"[36] and that their imitative agency was crucial to their cultural learning.[37] Surveying

---

33. This and the preceding sentence amount to a rather brutal summary of chapter 3 of Tomasello 2008.

34. Moll and Meltzoff 2011: 296–300. Cf. Hobson and Hobson 2012.

35. Moll and Meltzoff 2011: 287.

36. Dautenhahn and Nehaniv 2002: 1: "imitation is best considered as the behavior of an *autonomous agent* in relation to its environment, including other autonomous agents" (emphasis in the original). The "autonomous agent" here is simply a being (7) "able to represent, access, and to some extent control its behavior and relationship to the (social) environment, based on experiences in the past and predictions about the future."

37. More on Roman theories of children's imitation: Harders 2010; Bloomer 2011: 94–108. My thesis contrasts with that of T. Morgan 1998: 240–70 (esp. 252), where Roman children's imitation is seen as passive.

Quintilian and Augustine on language acquisition, we shall see that Romans could connect imitation to the child's perception of others' Intentional episodes, to the child's ethical and social development, and more broadly to cultural transmission.[38]

That a child must perceive others' minds in order to imitate, and that a Roman could recognize this, emerges from Augustine's account of his own acquisition of language. His account dramatizes the way children's *social* cognitive abilities underlie their acquisition of *cultural* cognitive abilities. Augustine builds his narrative from what he has been told of his own infancy, from his observation of other infants, and (he claims) from memory.[39] As an infant, Augustine had tried to communicate his needs to his caregivers: "I wanted to express my desires to those who could fulfill them."[40] Frustration over his inability to share his desires had led him "to seek out signs through which" he could make his "feelings known to others."[41]

Yet how to acquire such communicative signs? Augustine noted that language is not learned through formal instruction.[42] Rather, his linguistic learning depended not only on his experience of his own feelings but also on a social-cognitive capacity to attune himself to the psychological states of those around him. He began to grasp that adult's *attended* to objects and that they had *attitudes* and *intentions* toward the objects of their attention. The relevant passage is worth quoting at modest length (*Conf.* 1.8.13):

> cum ipsi appellabant rem aliquam et cum secundum eam vocem corpus ad aliquid movebant, videbam et tenebam hoc ab eis vocari rem illam, quod sonabant, cum eam vellent ostendere. hoc autem eos velle ex motu corporis aperiebatur tamquam verbis naturalibus omnium gentium, quae fiunt vultu et nutu oculorum ceterorumque membrorum actu et sonitu vocis indicante affectionem animi in petendis, habendis, reiciendis fugiendisve rebus.

> When my elders uttered a word for some thing and when they moved their body toward the thing upon uttering the word, I saw and I grasped thereby that that thing was referred to by them because they made the sounds when they wished to point it out. Moreover, what they wanted was made clear by

---

38. I treat of these texts and several others, but with different ends in view, in Mackey, 2019.
39. Aug. *Conf.* 1.6.8, 1.7.11, 1.7.12, and 1.8.13.
40. Aug. *Conf.* 1.6.8: *et voluntates meas volebam ostendere eis per quos implerentur.*
41. Aug. *Conf.* 1.6.10: *signa quibus sensa mea nota aliis facerem iam in fine infantiae quaerebam.*
42. Aug. *Conf.* 1.8.13: *non enim docebant me maiores homines, praebentes mihi verba certo aliquo ordine doctrinae sicut paulo post litteras.*

the motion of the body, a kind of natural language of all peoples [*verba naturalia omnium gentium*], which by means of facial expression [*vultus*], and by the glance of the eyes, and by the movement of the other limbs, and by inflections of the voice, indicates the mind's intention [*affectio animi*] to seek, acquire, reject, or avoid things.

Augustine's discovery *of* other minds allowed him to learn the linguistic signs through which he could share his mind *with* other minds. As in the case of Lucretius's pointing infant, Augustine's engagement with others' Intentionality preceded and grounded his learning of language as a conventional code.[43] In moving beyond his own self-centered perspective and attuning himself to the perspectives of others, Augustine perceived that adults had *perspectives* on the objects to which they attended. Where Lucretius's pointing infant sought to *elicit* another's attention to an object, the Augustinian infant *followed into* the attentional and Intentional states of others, as manifested in their *vultus*, their glances, and their gestures, the *verba naturalia omnium gentium*.[44] He saw that the Intentionality of adults, their *affectio animi*, not only was directed at objects but also embodied perspectives on those objects, for example, their desirability or the converse. By intuiting an adult's attention to, perspective on, and intentions toward an object, he associated that object with the adult's concomitant utterances and thereby learned the names of things, thus bringing his infancy, in the etymological sense, to an end.

In this way, Augustine's social-cognitive ontogeny preceded and enabled his *cultural* ontogeny. In the process, his social cognition was *transformed* into cultural cognition. For the Latin that he learned was of course the product and embodiment of a specific culture. But what does this cultural-specificity entail? A first pass at an answer is that Latin allowed Augustine to represent states of affairs under a variety of culture-specific *aspects* or from a variety of cultural *perspectives* that were unavailable to him without Latin. This aspectual, perspectival quality of language is continuous with, builds on, and enriches what we have already seen in Augustine's *verba naturalia*. For in the language of gesture, which is at a certain level universally intelligible via social cognition, Augustine could perceive people's primitive perspectives toward states of affairs, the fact that they viewed objects under elementary aspects such as *desirable, not desirable, to be sought, to be avoided*, and so forth. Language extends

---

43. For more on the prelinguistic foundations of coded linguistic communication, see Tomasello 2008: 57–71; Searle 2007. The "Augustinian Infant" returns to the study of language-learning: Bloom 2000: 55–87.

44. Similarly, for Cicero, *imago animi vultus* (*De Or.* 3.221), on which see my discussion in the introduction.

and transforms these potentialities of social cognition. To learn a language is to *acquire* new cognitive capacities for entertaining Intentional contents in propositional form and for adopting the perspectives and representing the world under the aspects encoded in that language. There is a representational difference that is also a cultural and cognitive difference in referring to one and the same entity as, for example, *animal* (living being), *sus* (pig), *caro* (meat), *porcina* (pork), or as *victima* or *hostia* (sacrificial victim). The differences are *linguistically* cultural—one needs Latin to represent in these ways—and *cognitively* cultural—each term determines under what cultural aspect or from what cultural perspective one mentally represents the selfsame entity.

Language thus constitutes a form of shared *cultural cognition*. Augustine signals that language initiated him into a new category of shared cognition when he writes that with linguistic mastery, "I shared with those about me signs for expressing our wills, and I entered more deeply the stormy *societas* of human life."[45] This notion that to share a language is to join a *societas*—a distinctively Roman metaphor, as we have seen[46]—is already found in Cicero, who speaks of being "connected by the *societas* of the same language." Unlike the *vultus*, which for Cicero and Augustine is open to anyone with basic social-cognitive competence, language for these authors is like a *societas*, an exclusive partnership. It is cognitively exclusive because culturally exclusive, moving the minds only of those among whom it is a matter of common ground.[47] As cultural cognition, fluency in a given language is not biologically inherited like the communicative capacities manifested in Lucretian pointing, but rather is entered into as one enters a *societas*, through social-cognitive understanding of others, imitation of them in interaction, and the consequent sharing of Intentionality.[48]

Augustine's language learning was precisely such an *imitative* and *interactive* enterprise.[49] He claims that he learned Latin by attending to, *advertendo*, and interacting with adults, "amid the coaxing [*blandimenta*] of nurses, and the

---

45. Aug. *Conf.* 1.8.13: *sic cum his inter quos eram voluntatum enuntiandarum signa communicavi et vitae humanae procellosam societatem altius ingressus sum.*

46. Sections 4.2 and especially 5.3.4.

47. Cic. *De Or.* 3.223: *verba enim neminem movent nisi eum qui eiusdem linguae societate coniunctus est.* Cf. *Off.* 1.50: *oratio ... homines coniungit ... naturali quadam societate.*

48. Further on "cultural cognition": Tomasello 1999a: 8–9, 118–29, 153–56, 166–73, and 201–17.

49. Augustine does not use *imitatio* or its cognates in *Conf.*, though he does imply that the language learning of *infantes* occurs *imitando* at *Doct. Chr.* 4.3.5. *Imitatio* typically carries a

jokes of those laughing with me, and the delights of those playing with me."[50] His account reflects a tradition of Roman thought about language learning through imitation and interaction. Lucretius, for example, supposed that infants required "the coaxing and broken speech [*blanda atque infracta loquella*] of a doting nurse," that is to say, "motherese," a cross-culturally well-attested mode of child-directed speech.[51] And nurses expected infants to imitate them in return: "when coaxing infants [*blandientes*] people tend to break up their own speech so that the infants may imitate them [*ut ... imitentur*]."[52] Finally, Quintilian, whose theory of early imitation we shall peruse presently, observed that infants did in fact try to imitate what they heard: "A child's nurses are the first people he will hear, and he will try [*conabitur*: note the emphasis on agency] to form their words by imitating them [*imitando*]."[53] For this theorist of rhetoric, imitation was an innate and profoundly *social* cognitive capacity with implications far beyond language learning. Let us survey Quintilian's theory.

Quintilian held that a robust faculty of *imitatio* was the surest sign, after a quick and exact memory, that a child possessed a "teachable nature."[54] Even beyond the domain of rhetoric, *imitatio* served Quintilian as a general theory of cultural transmission.[55] There can be no doubt, he wrote, "but that a great part of *ars* consists in imitation," given that "it is useful to follow what has been well invented."[56] Not only do aspiring orators, musicians, and painters imitate

---

negative valence in *Conf.*, e.g., at 1.16.25, 1.18.28, and 1.19.30. Explicit discussion of *imitatio* as a learning modality in Aug. *Mus.* 1.4.6ff.

50. Aug. *Conf.* 1.14.23: *nam et Latina aliquando infans utique nulla noveram, et tamen advertendo didici ... inter etiam blandimenta nutricum et ioca adridentium et laetitias adludentium.*

51. Lucr. 5.229–30: *nec cuiquam adhibendast / almae nutricis blanda atque infracta loquella*. On the universality of the inaptly named motherese, see Falk 2009.

52. Ps.-Acr. ad Hor. *Sat.* 1.3.48: *blandientes infantibus infringere linguam suam solent ut eos imitentur* (cited by Merrill 1907 ad Lucr. 5.230). I adopt the text of Keller's Teubner edition of Ps.-Acr.

53. Quint. *Inst.* 1.1.5: *has* [sc. *nutrices*] *primum audiet puer, harum verba effingere imitando conabitur.* On Roman children's speech, see Heraeus 1904.

54. Quint. *Inst.* 1.3.1: *ingenii signum in parvis praecipuum memoria est. ... proximum imitatio: nam id quoque est docilis naturae.*

55. Cf. Fantham 1995: 131 on Quintilian's "recognition of imitation as the method by which writing and all physical crafts are developed—the method which also shapes the first steps in every intellectual discipline."

56. Quint. *Inst.* 10.2.1: *neque enim dubitari potest quin artis pars magna contineatur imitatione. nam ut invenire primum fuit estque praecipuum, sic ea quae bene inventa sunt utile sequi.*

in order to learn, but even peasants follow the *exempla* of experience-tested agricultural practices.⁵⁷ So cultural inheritance per se—the acquisition not only of language but also of the *artes*—depended on an inborn capacity to imitate as well as the discrimination and agency to choose *what* and *how* to imitate. Of course, in the case of children, who possessed imitative agency but lacked discrimination, the "what" and "how" had to be carefully mediated by adults.

More than a means to transmit language and other cultural achievements, children's imitation had for Quintilian all sorts of cognitive, ethical, and social dimensions. *Frequens imitatio transit in mores*, "regular imitation turns into character/habit."⁵⁸ Therefore children should not imitate the behaviors of drunks or slaves, of lovers, of the avaricious, or of the fearful, as these behaviors may "infect" (*inficiunt*) their receptive minds (*mens*), implanting in them corresponding attitudes and dispositions.⁵⁹ Moreover, children should learn socially, in groups of their age mates, rather than alone at home. For the *schola* affords children not only direct but also indirect instruction⁶⁰ and allows them to learn by imitating and even trying to rival more accomplished peers.⁶¹ This last observation shows that Quintilian's imitation does not reduce to slavish conformity.⁶² Imitation may be *conservative* in that it enables the inheritance of cultural achievements, but this conservatism positions heirs to "ratchet up" their cultural patrimony in "cumulative" fashion,⁶³ expanding and building on (rather than reinventing) past achievements with their own *inventiones*.⁶⁴ Quintilian's prohibitions and prescriptions all represent attempts to foster such an ideal of imitation in the child so that he might not only

---

57. Quint. *Inst.* 10.2.2: *rustici probatam experimento culturam in exemplum intuentur*. On the centrality of *exempla* to Roman culture, see Roller 2018.

58. Quint. *Inst.* 1.11.3.

59. Quint. *Inst.* 1.11.2: *nec vitia ebrietatis effingat neque servili vernilitate imbuatur nec amoris, avaritiae, metus discat adfectum; quae ... mentem, praecipue in aetate prima teneram adhuc et rudem, inficiunt*.

60. Quint. *Inst.* 1.2.21: *domi ea sola discere potest quae ipsi praecipientur, in schola etiam quae aliis*.

61. Quint. *Inst.* 1.2.29: *utile igitur habere, quos* [sc. *condiscipulos*] *imitari primum, mox vincere velit*. Cf. 1.2.26.

62. Cf. T. Morgan 1998: 240–70 (esp. 250–54), where Roman children's imitation is inherently conservative.

63. Tennie, Call, and Tomasello 2009.

64. Quint. *Inst.* 10.2.4: *quid enim futurum erat temporibus illis quae sine exemplo fuerunt si homines nihil nisi quod iam cognovissent faciendum sibi aut cogitandum putassent? Nempe nihil fuisset inventum*. Cf. 10.2.8.

become "a good man skilled at speaking,"[65] but also perhaps one day outdo his predecessors, the touchstones of his own *ars*.

Our discussion to this point suggests that the ancients could appreciate what developmental psychologists have discovered, to wit, that children imitate not only the overt behaviors but also the perspectives, beliefs, desires, goals, and other psychological characteristics that they attribute to their models.[66] Indeed, as Augustine showed so eloquently, imitation *depends on* a social-cognitive capacity to intuit others' mental states. Similarly, we saw Quintilian draw causal connections between imitation and the youthful *mens*, between imitation and *mores*. In this, he was surely looking back to Cicero, who wrote that we imitate, *imitamur*, others' inclinations and habits, *studia* and *instituta*, as well as their practice, *consuetudo*, and way, *mos*.[67] Taken together, these authors testify to a Roman tradition of seeing imitation not as mere behavioral mimicry but rather as a source of our *mores*, that is, our character, ways, and habits.

Now, I wish to linger briefly over two of the words that we have just seen paired by Cicero, *consuetudo*, something like "practice" or "custom," and *mos*, which I have translated as "way." A late republican discourse around these terms has recently been reconstructed.[68] Romans could recognize both individual and collective dimensions of *mos*. As Terence put it, "there are as many *sententiae* as there are people, everyone has his own *mos*."[69] Varro confirms the cognitivism implicit in Terence's juxtaposition of *sententiae* and *mos* by writing that *mos* depends on one's *iudicium animi*, "act of mental judgment." Mental judgment and the resulting *mos*, in turn, have implications for one's settled practice, *consuetudo*.[70] In Macrobius's paraphrase of Varro, "*mos* came first, and the cultivation of *mos*, that is, habitual practice [*consuetudo*], followed."[71] This is the individual dimension of *mos*, but Varro could also

---

65. Quint. *Inst.* 12.1.1: *vir bonus dicendi peritus*.

66. See, e.g., Tomasello, Kruger, and Ratner 1993: 497–99; Meltzoff 1995; Jacob and Jeannerod 2003: 230–34; Goldman 2005; Tomasello and Carpenter 2005; Carpenter, Call, and Tomasello 2005; Carpenter 2006; Trevarthen 2012; Hobson and Hobson 2012; Oostenbroek and Over 2016.

67. Cic. *Off.* 1.118. Imitation runs through *Off.*: cf. esp. 1.78, 116, 121, 133, 140, 146. See also, e.g., Sen. *Ira* 3.8 for the transmission of *mores* and *vitia* from mind (*animus*) to mind.

68. Bettini 2011; Arena 2015.

69. Ter. *Phorm.* 454: *quot homines tot sententiae, suos cuique mos*.

70. Varr. *Logist.* fr. 74 Bolisani (*apud* Macr. *Sat.* 3.8.9) *morem esse in iudicio animi, quem sequi debeat consuetudo*.

71. Macr. *Sat.* 3.8.12: *mos ergo praecessit et cultus moris secutus est, quod est consuetudo*. Cf. 3.8.10: *ille* [sc. *Varro*] *dixerat morem praecedere, sequi consuetudinem*. For the whole Macrobian context: 3.8.8–14.

identify a collective dimension, according to which "*mos* amounts to the shared *consensus* of all who live together." *Consensus*, or shared attitude, may result in collective *mos*, which eventually results in a common custom or shared practice, *consuetudo*.[72]

The question arises: Whence this shared *mos* with its implications for collective practice, *consuetudo*? The answer suggested by our passages from Augustine, Quintilian, Cicero, and Varro is that it emerges gradually from one person's imitation of another in social contexts. A given *mos* spreads from individual to individual via imitation until it becomes a matter of communal common ground.[73] It is significant in the present context that a collective *mos* was thought to "pertain to religious obligations and the modes of worship of the *maiores*."[74]

Precisely this social-cognitive account of religious socialization through imitation, rather than through deliberate indoctrination, is implicit in Prudentius's description of a child learning to pray, as we are about to see. Most broadly, in his *Contra Symmachum* the Christian polemicist is exercised by children's inadvertent but inevitable acquisition via observation and imitation of the traditional religious *mos*, which he marks both as "hereditary," *mos patrius*, and more ominously as "dark," *mos tenebrosus*.[75] Prayer is but one aspect of this *mos*.

Learning to pray in antiquity no doubt sometimes involved explicit pedagogy, even if this is not where Prudentius will lay emphasis.[76] We have, for example, a depiction of a mother trying to instruct her daughter, Sulpicia, in her prayer to Iuno Natalis. The girl resists, silently petitioning the goddess for love.[77] Most often, however, children must have learned to pray much as Augustine described learning Latin, that is, indirectly, through observing others and grasping the intentions guiding their behaviors. Indeed, this is how the saint characterizes his own social learning of prayer: "O Lord, we came upon

---

72. Serv. ad Aen. 7.601: *Varro vult morem esse communem consensum omnium simul habitantium, qui inveteratus consuetudinem facit.* Cf. Ulp. Reg. 1.4: *mores sunt tacitus consensus populi, longa consuetudine inveteratus*, and see further Dig. 1.3.32 (= Salvius Iulianus 84 *Dig.*) and Inst. 1.2.9.

73. Cf. Bettini 2011: 100–101; Arena 2015: 224. For "communal common ground," see at section 4.3.4.

74. Macr. Sat. 3.8.9: *Iulius* [sic] *Festus de verborum significationibus libro tertio decimo: mos est, inquit, institutum patrium, pertinens ad religiones cerimoniasque maiorum.*

75. Prud. c. Symm. 1.154 and 1.244.

76. For example, Roman magistrates "learned" prayers by having them dictated to them: see, e.g., Klinghardt 1999. More on Roman prayer in chapter 8, below.

77. Tib. 3.12.15–16: *praecipit et natae mater studiosa, quod optat: / illa aliud tacita iam sua mente rogat.* On the authorship of these poems, see Keith 2006.

people petitioning you in prayer, and we learned from them."[78] A sensitivity to the Intentionality and psychology of others is implicit in this account of how Augustine learned to pray to God, just as the same sensitivity had conditioned the very possibility of his imitative learning of language. We shall see something similar in Prudentius's account of the Roman child learning to pray to pagan gods.

Prudentius's *Contra Symmachum* 1.197–244 surely contains our most extensive ancient meditation on the religious socialization of Roman children and their imitative induction into traditional cult. Prudentius begins by locating the earliest religious learning right where we might expect to find it, in the home, with women playing a central role (*c. Symm.* 1.205–11):[79]

formatum Fortunae habitum cum divite cornu
sacratumque domi lapidem consistere parvus
spectarat matremque illic pallere precantem.
mox umeris positus nutricis trivit et ipse
inpressis silicem labris, puerilia vota
fudit opesque sibi caeca de rupe poposcit,
persuasumque habuit, quod quis velit, inde petendum.

The child had observed a stone, shaped in the appearance
of and consecrated to Fortuna with her rich horn,
standing in the home, and his mother going pale as she prayed to it.
Then he himself, placed on his nurse's shoulders,
pressing the stone with his lips, poured forth childish vows [*puerilia vota / fudit*], and begged good things for himself [*opes . . . sibi*] from the blind rock,
convinced [*persuasum . . . habuit*] that what he wanted should be sought there.

Note that what Prudentius describes here is not mindless mimicry of behavior; indeed, the scene could scarcely irk his ire if behavior alone were at

---

78. Aug. *Conf.* 1.9.14: *invenimus autem, domine, homines rogantes te et didicimus ab eis.*

79. This is the place to recommend Bodel 2008 as the single best short account of Roman domestic religion I have read. For the family as locus of early education: Marrou 1956: 313–15; Wiedemann 1989: 143–75; Corbeill 2001, esp. 269. For religious learning and the family, see Bremmer 1995; Prescendi 2010: 76–79. Role of mothers generally: Cic. *Brut.* 211: *filios non tam in gremio educatos quam in sermone matris*; cf. Tac. *Dia.* 28.4; Dixon 1988: 104–40. Role of nurses: Bradley 1986, 1991, and 1994. Hrdy 2009 offers an account of the evolutionary role of such "allomothers" (22n) that is uniquely germane to shared intentionality and this book.

stake.[80] No, he is primarily worried about the beliefs, *vana superstitio*, "empty superstition,"[81] that the child internalizes through imitation.

On Prudentius's account, the child overhears the prayer that his mother directs to her statuette of Fortuna and grasps the Intentional states that motivate her action. Social-cognitive competence, of the sort the infant Augustine began with, as well as linguistic competence, of the sort Augustine gained, grants the child access to his mother's beliefs about the statuette and her desires and goals in praying to it. Her pallor, a signal of emotional arousal—marked but not interpreted for us by Prudentius—may plausibly be read as testifying to the child the authenticity of her beliefs and desires.[82] Like Augustine's *verba naturalia omnium gentium*, the gestures and expressions that disclose others' inner attitudes, the mother's pallid face communicates the solemnity of her entreaty. Motivated by the maternal example,[83] the child imitates his mother's beliefs (*persuasum habuit*), her desires and goals (*opes sibi*) and, with his nurse's help, her prayerful actions (*puerilia vota fudit*).

Strikingly, these *vota* offered to the "blind stone" (*caeca de rupe*) reveal that from the child's perspective—a perspective descried and decried by the poet—his mother and nurse are not the only agents in the scene. The statuette is also an agent. Recall our discussion of Lucilius at section 2.6.2.[84] There we saw that Roman children could suffer faulty intuitions about anthropomorphic but inanimate objects. Lucilius presented us with a child who mistakenly attributed animacy to a bronze statue. Yet whereas Lucilius's child will come to recognize the error of his intuition, Prudentius's child is imitatively inheriting a practice that will support, confirm, and enhance any intuitions he may have as to the image's animacy and agency, which he is learning to identify more specifically with Fortuna. The statue's *physical* anthropomorphism

---

80. Jacob and Jeannerod 2003: 231: "mimicry does not require the retrieval of the intention involved in the mimicked behavior, since there is none."

81. Prud. *c. Symm.* 1.198. On superstition, see R. Gordon 2008: 75: "In the Roman case, ... it makes most sense to view the notion of superstition as a strategy for delimiting an imagined community by claiming the existence of consensual frontiers between traditional/sanctioned/proper and non-traditional/unsanctioned/improper/religious action."

82. The mother's pallor is a "hard-to-fake emotional or physiological cue," and as such a "credibility enhancing display" (on such "CREDs," see further, below, at section 8.7): Norenzayan, Shariff, et al. 2016: 19n4. Cf. Alcorta and Sosis 2005: 333; Bulbulia and Sosis 2011: 365–66.

83. We see here classic *social referencing*, in which children modulate their behavior toward a third entity based on the perceived attitude toward that entity of a trusted adult: see Feinman et al. 1992.

84. Lucil. 15.526–27 (= Lact. *Div. Inst.* 1.22.13).

combined with the petitionary practice of prayer will bolster the child's intuitions and inferences as to the goddess's *psychological* anthropomorphism, including (but not only) her susceptibility to entreaty.[85]

Thus, the Christian poet describes the contributions that the child's faculties of social cognition make to his acquisition of religious beliefs. What the child learns in the company of his mother and nurse are, most immediately, the *Intentional affordances* of the statue for them and, most broadly, the *cultural affordances* of the statue for his larger social group.[86] Let us approach these Intentional and cultural affordances by way of some contrasts. Consider: There are things the child can learn on his own, nonsocially, about the *physical* affordances, that is, the possibilities for motoric action, of the statue qua object.[87] He might learn just by manipulating the statue that its solidity and weight suits it to the task of smashing nuts, holding papyrus in place on windy days, or supporting the weight of other objects. Assuming that the child is developing neurotypically, he would also note the statue's anthropomorphism and perhaps take it to be a living being, as Lucilius would have it, or perhaps treat it as a doll, that is, as a likeness of a living being.

Such individual-learning scenarios contrast sharply with what the child learns socially, as described by Prudentius. As Shaun Gallagher points out: "we start to learn about the world by seeing how others relate to objects in that world. Objects take on meaning in the pragmatic contexts within which we see and imitate the actions of others."[88] Not individual learning (even granting the child full-blown Lucilian intuitions of agency) but social learning, that is, learning by observing and interacting with others, teaches the child that the statue has a *function* or teleology, that it serves human *purposes*, to wit, as an object of cult to be addressed in Directive speech acts. Through social learning, not individual learning, does the child discover the cultural fact that the object is a *simulacrum deae*, a representation of the goddess Fortuna.

These aspects of the *lapis* are not among its physical but rather its Intentional and cultural affordances. That is, the child's mother and nurse have not only physical but also *Intentional* relations with the lapis: they have *perspectives* on it, *expectations* and *beliefs* about it, and *desires, goals*, and other *practical attitudes* with respect to it.[89] They see the *lapis* as surrounded by a deontic aura,

---

85. See Barrett and van Orman 1996.

86. Tomasello 1999a: 84–87; and Tomasello 1999b. See further, on "cultural affordances," Fiebich 2014 as well as Ramstead et al. 2016.

87. Gibson 1986: 127: "The *affordances* of the environment are what if *offers* the animal, what it *provides* or *furnishes*, either for good or ill."

88. Gallagher 2008c: 171.

89. See Barresi and Moore 1996.

a penumbra of norms regarding its treatment—the permitted, the forbidden, and the obligatory. These aspects of the lapis are irreducible to its physical properties: they are cultural properties, part of its social ontology. So, the statue of Fortuna—what it *is*, what it is *for*, how it must be *treated*—are matters of Intentionality, most broadly, and of belief, more narrowly. The Intentional affordances that the child discovers by observing and imitating his elders transform a world of *physical* and even *social* entities, which offer opportunities for *instrumental* action and social *interaction*, into a *cultural* world of divine *simulacra*, bearing deontic statuses, such as *sacer* and *sanctus*, which open spaces for culturally specific *ritual* action. The child's discovery of the statue's Intentional affordances for his family's practices inducts him, most broadly, into his society's cultural possibilities for thought and action. His family's practices and beliefs initiate him into a world of cultural affordances, which augment and constrain the physical and social possibilities for action afforded by his material and human environment.

Only when the child possesses the requisite social-cognitive equipment can he grasp the intentions and beliefs of others, including their Intentional relations with the statue. With this developmental milestone, the child is equipped to perceive and learn the *Intentional* affordances of the *lapis*, that is, the beliefs and attitudes that individuals collectively share toward it, which make it the *cultural* object that it is, with all its specifically cultural possibilities for thought and action. What we see here is the ontogeny of culture, where "culture" amounts to not a Durkheimian hypostasis floating above and somehow participated in by individuals but rather the cumulative result of the interactions of individuals. On this view, culture is the fallout or "precipitate of cognition and communication in a human population"[90] or, from the individual's perspective, "those things the organism knows and learns that are derived from acts in which it attempts to see the world through the perspective of other persons (including perspectives embodied in artifacts)."[91]

As these considerations have already made manifest, Prudentius has in his sights much more than merely learning to pray. Indeed, he echoes, from a Christian perspective, Quintilian's big-picture concern about the effect of *imitatio* on *mores*. Imitation passes into character as "the credulous boy" learns to pray, learns his rites, and so goes on to become a traditional Roman man,

---

90. Sperber 1996: 97.
91. Tomasello 1999a: 51, and cf. 52: this "narrower definition of cultural inheritance—and therefore cultural learning and the cultural line of development—is focused on intentional phenomena in which one organism adopts another's behavior or perspective on some third entity."

"maintaining the absurd practice" of his family's cult.[92] This implies that Prudentius, like Quintilian before him, saw imitation as a mode of cultural transmission: Roman religion "has run uninterrupted through a thousand generations" in this imitative fashion.[93]

Even if Prudentius's polemic scarcely counts as documentary evidence, he was surely on to a fundamental fact about the nature of traditional religious socialization. The Roman child was a kind of apprentice, observing, imitating, and thus adopting beliefs and practices of domestic cult.[94] In this way, he or she could acquire much of "la culture rituelle commune des Romains."[95] Such learning was, as we have noted, manifestly social, insofar as it involved the observation of others. Nonetheless, it was individualistic in the important sense that it was driven by the child's own initiative and agency, not by cooperation between adult and child, much less by the pressure of an external, inculcating force.[96] Like Augustine learning language, Prudentius's Roman child exploits his models by retrieving their intentions from their actions and then imitating both their intentions and their actions for his own benefit.

Yet ultimately, of course, the benefit to the child was a social and cooperative one. Learning to pray enabled Prudentius's child to share his wishes with the gods, just as learning to speak allowed Augustine to "share"[97] his desires with adults, in the expectation in each case that the addressees would respond cooperatively. Beyond this, the acquisition of religious knowledge aligned Prudentius's child horizontally with his family and vertically with his ancestors, just as the acquisition of language aligned Augustine with fellow users of Latin, dead and alive, in the "stormy partnership [*societas*] of human life."[98] Indeed, it is precisely this vertical and horizontal alignment of beliefs—this sharing of Intentionality—that so troubles Prudentius.

The examples we have surveyed here suggest that Romans could conceive of children as agents of their own enculturation. Children could learn *sine doctrina*, without instruction, by paying attention, *advertendo*, in the manner of apprentices. Infants' natural social-cognitive competence empowers them

---

92. Prud. *c. Symm.* 1.213–14: *insulsum tenuit . . . credulus usum, / privatos celebrans agnorum sanguine divos*.

93. Prud. *c. Symm.* 1.198–99: *non interrupta cucurrit / aetatum per mille gradus*.

94. Wiedemann 1989: 158: Roman children learn by "watching and copying the behaviour of someone who already possesses the *ars*."

95. Scheid 1990: 673: "le citoyen apportait un savoir rituel, oralement transmis dans le cadre familial."

96. Cf. Tomasello 1996: 320–25.

97. O'Donnell 1992 *ad Conf.* 1.8.13 recommends "shared" for Augustine's *communicavi*.

98. *Conf.* 1.8.13.

to inherit the cultural modes of cognition unique to their communities. We have seen that in ontogenesis, social cognition progresses from awakening to others as agents, to reading in the *vultus* and *motus* of those agents their attitudes, perspectives, and Intentional states. It culminates in taking those other agents and their perspectives as models of thought and action for imitation. Through imitation, Roman children transformed their powers of social cognition into powers of cultural cognition. They were imitative agents of their own cultural ontogeny. Thus, imitation is or can be a relatively individualistic social-learning *process* even if the resulting *product*, that is, culture as transmitted beliefs and practices, ensures cognitive and behavioral conformity with others. But let us turn now from this relatively individualistic mode of social learning, in which children see others as agents whose intentions and actions they may borrow and exploit, to a fully cooperative mode of apprenticeship and social learning, in which children approach others as agents *with* whom they may *share* Intentionality and agency.

7.4. Religious Participation: From Joint Attention to Cultural Cognition

What cognitive endowments are required to collaborate, that is, to participate cooperatively, in joint activity? As we saw at section 4.3.2, to engage in joint action, agents must be able to share Intentionality. Minimally, two or more people share agency in joint action when they act together as a result of sharing intentions to act together, with these shared "we-intentions" mutually manifest. So, for example, Gaius and Quintus may walk into the forum side by side, but they are engaged in joint action only if they both intend to go *together* and if this shared intention is manifest between them. Without shared Intentionality, Gaius and Quintus are merely two people chancing to show up in the forum at the same time. Here we discuss the cognitively more complex case of collective cult with an eye to how children learned about cult by participating in it.

Just as Romans could theorize about imitation, so too, as we saw at section 4.2, they could theorize about sharing Intentionality and agency. Ulpian illustrated the shared Intentionality underlying joint action with an embodied metaphor in which those who share intentions (*consentiunt*) to act jointly (*qui inter se agunt*) come together "from different affections of the mind" to a single purpose (*una sententia*), just as those who share a physical location come together bodily from different places.[99] I submit that contexts of shared

---

99. *Dig.* 2.14.1.3 = Ulp. 4 *ad ed.*

Intentionality and joint action formally similar to what Ulpian describes constituted potent spaces of social learning for Roman children. In traditional societies, without formal institutions of instruction,[100] children tend to learn through "intent participation" with adults.[101] In such contexts, they undertake more or less formal apprenticeships with culturally fluent elders from whom they acquire specifically *cultural* forms of Intentionality as well as specifically *collective* forms of culture.

Indeed, joint attention alone—an elementary joint action[102] in which two people purposefully attend to a third entity together—opened the cultural line of inheritance for Roman children in ways that went beyond the imitative learning sketched in the previous section. We saw that Romans like Lucretius knew that even prelinguistic children could jointly attend with another person to a third object. As the poet notes, the "speechlessness of the tongue" (*infantia linguae*) makes children point in order to share attention.[103] This Lucretian sharing creates an ontogenetically primitive "we." In the context of this "we" the first properly *social* facts emerge for children, facts, that is, that are jointly recognized and even jointly created. These social facts soon scale up to an entire social ontology, created and maintained by collective Intentionality.[104]

There was of course more to Roman children's religious learning than Lucretian joint attention. We shall see that by acting jointly in cult, Roman children could learn "our" collective liturgical *norms*. By forming joint goals to perform acts of cult, they could ultimately develop a shared *commitment* to "our" ritual institutions and their associated social norms, or deontology: to wit, a sense of *pietas*. And by perceiving the intentions and perspectives of others toward the cult act within a shared space of joint attention, they could acquire "our" beliefs about a given ritual's nature, purpose, and theology. All the latter, cultural forms of cognition are built on the former, elementary abilities to perceive and share Intentionality and agency.

Tibullus—to take a simple example of joint ritual action—depicts a father and daughter sacrificing together. Father offers cakes, *liba*, to his household *Lar*, while his little daughter, *filia parva*, offers honeycomb, *purus favus*

---

100. Scipio Aemilianus praises Rome for her lack of such institutions at Cic. *Rep.* 4.3. See Corbeill 2001.

101. Rogoff et al. 2003.

102. So Fiebich and Gallagher 2013.

103. Lucr. 5.1030–32, quoted at n. 29, above.

104. For social ontology, see chapter 5, above. For the ontogeny of social ontology, see Tomasello and Rakoczy 2003; Rakoczy 2007; Rakoczy and Tomasello 2007; Wyman and Rakoczy 2011.

FIGURE 7.1. *Lararium* from the House of the Arches (Casa degli Archi), Pompeii, picturing the *genius* of the *paterfamilias* making an offering with a *patera* (libation bowl). A *camillus*, or young assistant, perhaps his son, holding a jug, participates. (Photo credit: Lydia Herring-Harrington.)

(compare figure 7.1).[105] Ovid alludes to this tableau in his depiction of the Terminalia festival of 23 February. On this day, the state religious authorities arranged for the sacrifice of a sheep to Terminus, god of boundaries, at the sixth milestone outside the city on the Via Laurentia (*F.* 2.679–82). Meanwhile,

---

105. Tib. 1.10.19–24.

in the countryside children joined their parents and neighbors joined neighbors in order to honor the god's *numen* in the stone or stump that marked the common border of their fields (*F.* 2.645–58):

> ara fit: huc ignem curto fert rustica testu
>   sumptum de tepidis ipsa colona focis.
> ligna senex minuit concisaque construit arte,
>   et solida ramos figere pugnat humo;
> tum sicco primas inritat cortice flammas;
>   stat puer et manibus lata canistra tenet.
> inde ubi ter fruges medios immisit in ignes,
>   porrigit incisos filia parva favos.
> vina tenent alii: libantur singula flammis;
>   spectant, et linguis candida turba favet.
> spargitur et caeso communis Terminus agno,
>   nec queritur lactans cum sibi porca datur.
> conveniunt celebrantque dapes vicinia simplex
>   et cantant laudes, Termine sancte, tuas.

> An altar is made. Here the country wife herself brings
>   in a potsherd fire taken from the warm hearth.
> The old man chops wood and arranges the pieces with skill
>   and struggles to fix branches in the hard ground.
> Then he encourages the first flames with dry bark.
>   His son stands and holds a wide basket in his hands.
> Then, when he has tossed grain thrice into the flames,
>   his little daughter offers sliced honeycombs.
> Others hold wine. Each pours a libation to the flames.
>   Dressed in white, the group watches, and maintains silence.
> Terminus, common to all, is sprinkled by the slaughtered lamb,
>   and he doesn't complain when offered a suckling pig.
> Neighbors gather and throng the sacrificial feast in sincerity,
>   and they sing your praises, holy Terminus.

Ovid's recounting of this rite, set in the Augustan present, alludes to Tibullus's apostrophe to his ancestral *Lar,* in the course of which he had asserted the superiority of the *maiores'* worship: "in those days, they kept faith better."[106] Where Tibullus imagines a little daughter, *filia parva,* offering *purus favus,* honeycomb as wholesome as the antique rite of which it is a part, Ovid's *filia parva* offers sliced honeycomb, *incisi favi,* perhaps more appropriate to a god of

---

106. Tib. 1.10.19: *tum melius tenuere fidem.*

divisions. The change undergone by the girl's honeycomb in its transition from Tibullus to Ovid, from nostalgic past to idealized present, alerts the reader to the poets' divergent purposes in their ritual depictions. For the effect of Ovid's allusion is to suggest, in quiet dissent from his Tibullan model, the integrity and diachronic continuity of Roman religious practice.[107]

So, poetry mingles with ideology in the portrayal of collective ritual practices. Ovid's ritual expands on that of Tibullus, amplifying the number, roles, and types of agents involved. Ovid's farmer enjoys the companionship of not only his daughter, but also his wife and son, close kin united in the shared goal of worship.[108] Each family member, beginning with mother and ending with *filia parva*, with father and son in between, in that order, has his or her own age- and gender-appropriate task to do in the coordinated action of the ritual. Fittingly, for example, it is the matron who brings the fire from the household *focus*. Each participant must act appropriately, in careful coordination with every other participant, or else the ritual falls apart. Parents and children successfully coordinate their worship, while as a family they coordinate their worship with that of their neighbors, and finally the neighborhood coordinates its worship with the rites of the state. The inescapable suggestion is of concentric circles of harmony: within the family, among neighbors, between citizens and civic institutions, between realms human and divine. Hierarchies among humans, and among gods and humans, are enacted and affirmed in the complex choreography of ritual roles (as in figure 7.2).[109]

That the ritual actors experience a sharing of doxastic and practical attitudes with respect to the ritual is important to Ovid's harmonious portrait and implicit in it. For example, everyone had to know and believe that everyone else knew certain liturgical norms, such as when to maintain ritual silence (*favere linguis*). Indeed, participants had to share a sense that everyone was committed to observing such norms *now*. Most generally, participants had to share a mutually manifest commitment to the ritual's enactment, that is, a joint goal to perform the cult act together. If not, cooperative action could scarcely get started. Moreover, Ovid suggests, the worshippers shared an informal folk theology, including the culturally transmitted belief that the god was immanent in the stone or stump at the center of their worship.[110] Such a belief motivated their shared conception of the ritual's purpose. For they jointly

---

107. Cf. Robinson 2011: 418–19.

108. Recalling Hor. *Ep.* 2.1.139–44: *agricolae prisci . . . cum sociis operum pueris et coniuge fida*, etc.

109. See Scheid 2005 and 2012.

110. Ov. *F.* 2.641–42: *Termine, sive lapis sive es defossus in agro / stipes.*

FIGURE 7.2. Wall painting in the kitchen *lararium* of the House of Sutoria Primigenia at Pompeii. Twin *Lares* frame their worshippers. Left to right: a *tibicen* plays while *juno*, *genius*, and *camillus* make an offering at an altar. The rest of the *familia*, presumably household slaves, participate with right hands raised to their chests. This may represent a celebration of the Caristia (so, e.g., Bernstein 2007: 534). See also Fröhlich 1991: 178–79; Giacobello 2008: 156–58. (Photo credit: Lydia Herring-Harrington.)

intended to honor Terminus in performing the rite, or so Ovid frames the episode. The passage opens with the exhortation, "let the god be worshipped with customary honors."[111] And it closes with neighbors feasting and singing the god's praises after the sacrifice: *cantant laudes, Termine sancte, tuas*. This act of rural *pietas* thus depends on exquisite cognitive attunement among worshippers: joint-attentional engagement, the sharing of beliefs and norms, the coordination of agency in pursuit of collective goals. (For more, see section 4.3.5.)

We may contrast the joint cognition and joint action implicit in Ovid's Terminalia against the collective cognition and action of a crowd, such as we saw in our brief discussion of Apuleius's Isiac worshippers (section 2.5). He presents a gathering of people who share at least some doxastic and practical attitudes regarding Isis praising the goddess in synchrony as they witness what they take to be a manifestation of her power. We must not suppose that we are

111. Ov. F. 2.639: *solito celebretur honore*.

carving nature at any putative joints here, but it is analytically useful to note that these worshippers are not sharing agency quite as Ovid's do. In Apuleius, each worshipper has his or her own emotional and behavioral response, as a result of his or her beliefs and other attitudes, to the scene he or she witnesses. The worshippers' responses happen to converge, because their doxastic and practical attitudes happen to converge. They share the sort of common ground that we have termed "collective Intentionality" (section 4.3.4). The crowd's collective action does not require that any individual *intend* to act *together* with any other, but merely that their individual actions add up to the scene Apuleius describes. Of course, such behavioral synchrony will typically lead to affective attunement, emotional contagion,[112] and some sense of cohesion or solidarity among the worshippers. This is broadly *collective* Intentionality but not intimately Ovidian *joint* Intentionality.

Ovid's ritual is exemplary of intimately shared cult's unique cognitive and actional jointness, and thus of the richness of such contexts for enculturation, for the acquisition of the shared intentions, beliefs, norms, and goals that constituted Roman religious culture. An adult might have learned about a rite just by *asking*, as did Ovid at the Robigalia (section 4.1). Children, however, would typically have learned by *engaging*. They would not, in their earliest ritual engagements, have shared with other participants properly *cultural* forms of Intentionality: ritual norms, cult commitments, folk-theological beliefs. But by three years of age, they would have been set to *acquire* such cultural Intentionality through techniques of cognitive communion, such as inferring others' beliefs, desires, and intentions; taking their perspectives; and especially joining with them in joint attention and joint action. Romans seem to have intuited this, for Tibullus and Ovid both witness the important fact that Roman children participated in cult as *camilli* or *camillae*, "assistants" with apprentice-like roles complementary to those of adults.[113] In such roles they were active acquirers, rather than passive recipients, of ritual norms, of joint commitments to put those norms into action, and of shared religious beliefs. Let us explore these contentions.

---

112. Such crowd emotions were first investigated by Le Bon 1895. See now the distinctions made by Von Scheve 2012; Salmela 2012; Von Scheve and Ismer 2013; Salmela 2014b. Fagan 2011 applies, with splendid results, a social-psychological framework to crowd responses to blood sport in the Roman arena.

113. Serv. *ad Aen.* 11.558: *ministros enim et ministras inpuberes camillos et camillas in sacris vocabant*. Romans could even imagine a child *taking over* domestic worship in the face of parental neglect, as in Plaut. *Aul.* 23–25, where the *Lar familiaris* says of the daughter of the house: *ea mihi cottidie / aut ture aut vino aut aliqui semper supplicat, / dat mihi coronas*.

7.4.1. Ritual Norms, Overimitation, and Orthopraxy

By the age of three, children have been engaging in joint action for some time. This implies that they are sensitive to natural norms internal to cooperation as such (on which, see section 4.3.5). This sensitivity to the natural norms of cooperation underwrites children's acquisition of conventional norms.[114] For it is through adhering to cooperative norms in episodes of joint action that children learn the conventional norms of cultural activities. That is, they learn norms just by cooperatively participating in rule-governed activities. Here again we see that norms natural and internal to cognition and action underlie conventional norms.[115] Let us look briefly at some details.

Children (and adults, too) infer the existence of rules from the behavior they observe. Indeed, they may only need to see an action performed once to infer that it is governed by norms.[116] Children appear to adopt a "normative stance"[117] or "ritual stance"[118] toward the actions of adult partners, inferring from an adult's performance of an action sequence that the sequence is a ritual, that is, that it must be executed precisely *thus* and not otherwise. This stance amounts to more than the mere adoption of external performances or behavioral mimicry. For children not only faithfully imitate performances (showing the guiding function of the perceived norms) but also expect others to behave "correctly" in their own performances (the norms' predictive function). And, indeed, children enforce norms on third parties by protesting what they see as breaches of those norms (the norms' evaluative function).[119] Thus, we see in cult scenes such as Ovid's "the birth of a social practice and its normative dimension"[120] in individual ontogeny, as a causal result of interindividual interaction among children and adults.

Cooperative joint action affords children new opportunities for social learning, including new forms of imitation. For example, they take complementary roles with partners in collaborative actions[121] and in so doing learn their partners' roles. Such learning enables "role-reversal imitation,"[122] in

---

114. See Tomasello 2009: 86–98; DuBreuil 2010: 63–67.
115. See at sections 2.2.6, 3.3.2–3, 4.3.5, and 4.4.
116. M. Schmidt et al. 2016.
117. Rakoczy and Schmidt 2013: 17.
118. P. Herrmann, Legare, et al. 2013: 537.
119. Rakoczy et al. 2008; Rakoczy and Schmidt 2013.
120. Tomasello 2009: 92–93.
121. Warneken et al. 2006.
122. By eighteen months: Carpenter, Tomasello, and Striano 2005; Fletcher et al. 2012; cf. Hobson and Hobson 2012.

which a child switches roles with partners and assumes one of their roles in a joint action. Unlike the individualistic imitation exhibited by Prudentius's child, role-reversal imitation is inherently collaborative, or "we"-based, for it involves representing oneself and one's partner(s) acting together in interdependent, complementary ways. This form of imitation surely contributed to children's cultural learning when they served their parents as *camilli* or *camillae* in cult and thereby learned not only their own roles but also those of their parents.

Such role-reversal imitation appears to be connected to young children's motivation to discover how "we" do things, that is, the group's accumulated practical wisdom as well as its values and conventions. I have already mentioned that children adopt a "normative stance" or "ritual stance," that is, a perspective from which they interpret actions as performed *this* way, not *that* way, that is, as governed by norms or conventions that must be internalized and endorsed. Children's internalization or "ownership" of these norms is revealed by the fact that three-year-olds not only spontaneously *act* in accord with norms in contexts such as rule-based game playing, but also *protest* breaches of norms and *enforce* norms on others in such contexts.[123]

Possible triggers for the adoption of the ritual stance are the "teleological opacity" and the "causal opacity" of many ritualized or conventional actions.[124] Let us distinguish these two terms.[125] We inexorably interpret the behavior of agents as goal-directed. But ritual actions are often *teleologically opaque* in that there is no obvious goal, no clear end to which they are a means. To what end, for example, does Ovid's *camillus* throw grain into the fire during the Terminalia festival? And why three times?[126] These actions have no transparent teleology, no clear end or goal. *Causal opacity* differs in that the *goal* of the action is relatively clear but its *instrumental rationale* is not. The goal of, say, petitionary prayer is clearly to entreat a god, but why raise one's right hand to one's lip and spin oneself around?[127] The causal contribution of these gestures to the end of entreating the god is obscure.[128] Both teleological and causal opacity may trigger the ritual stance in culture learners, which leads behaviorally

---

123. Rakoczy et al. 2008; Rakoczy and Schmidt 2013. See Tomasello 2009: 28–44.

124. See, with the discussion of Gergely and Csibra 2006, Boyer 2001: 232–33; Whitehouse 2012; P. Herrmann, Legare et al. 2013; Legare et al. 2015.

125. Following Csibra and Gergely 2011: 1149.

126. Cf. Rüpke 2007d: 87–90 on Roman ritual's frequent lack of a "pragmatic basis."

127. Plin. *H.N.* 28.5.25: *in adorando dextram ad osculum referimus totumque corpus circumagimus*. See further, Corbeill 2004: 28–29.

128. See further at section 8.2.

to what has been dubbed "overimitation,"[129] that is, high-fidelity copying of actions that have obscure ends or unclear causal relevance. I submit that the teleological and causal opacity of Roman ritual action, together with children's and indeed adults' propensity to overimitate such action, contributed to the orthopraxy of Roman religion.[130]

Let us indulge a brief excursus on the implications for Roman ritual orthopraxy of the ritual stance and overimitation. First, a note on overimitation, for which various explanations have been offered.[131] On one theory, the "causal account," learners encode opaque actions as non-obvious but crucial *causal* components in an overall action sequence, so they imitate such actions with precision.[132] A competing theory, the "normative account," holds that learners encode causally opaque actions as *normatively* indispensable, as part of "our" conventional cultural repertoire, and thus imitate them with high fidelity.[133] At first blush, it might appear that the causal account of overimitation best explains Roman orthopraxy. After all, as Clifford Ando explains it: "in light of the terrifying superiority of the gods, and knowing what had worked before, one had an overwhelming obligation scrupulously to recreate precisely that earlier performance."[134] The critical phrase here is "what had worked." The Romans' was an *efficacious* system of cult. Pliny, for example, could connect orthoprax prayer with desired ritual outcomes and defective prayer with ritual failure.[135] Indeed, he held that even *mutae religiones*, rituals without prayer, could be effective.[136]

Ritual efficacy and ritual orthopraxy are easily seen in the case of magic, where we find highly scripted words and gestures that are undoubtedly

---

129. The literature on overimitation is now extensive. See, e.g., Kenward 2012; Keupp et al. 2013. Overimitation among Bushmen: Nielsen and Tomaselli 2010.

130. I have developed this argument in Mackey 2018a. The excursus that follows summarizes those results. It is important to note that orthoprax ritual is driven by more than just overimitation. For example, the so-called hazard-precaution system is a suite of cognitive tools that directs behavior in response to perceived threats and may support ritualized behavior and adherence to ritual norms (Boyer and Liénard 2006; for the hazard-precaution system and Greek ritual, see Larson 2016: 189–91). I have not had the space here to pursue the connections between overimitation and the hazard-precaution system (on which see Kapitány and Nielsen 2017).

131. See Over and Carpenter 2012a for a review and assessment.

132. Lyons et al. 2007; Lyons and Keil 2013.

133. E.g., Keupp et al. 2013. I have borrowed the terminology of "causal" and "normative accounts," with minor modifications, from this publication (393).

134. Ando 2008: 14.

135. Plin. *N.H.* 28.3.11, a text we examine in chapter 8.

136. Plin. *N.H.* 28.5.25: *etiam mutas religiones pollere manifestum est.*

efficacious no matter how causally opaque. Take an example from Cato. To heal a dislocated hip, perform a series of gestures with a reed that has been split down the middle and pressed to your hips, while chanting "motas vaeta daries dardares astataries dissunapiter."[137] The causal opacity of these vocalizations and gestures is high. Though the gestures with the reed appear "sympathetically" to mimic the healing of the hip, the precise mechanisms by which that mimicry (or sympathy) contribute to the physical effect of healing remain vague at best. And the incantation is, at least in its preserved state, entirely opaque of reference, though *dissunapiter* is suggestive of a god, looking as it does like "Diespiter" (a version of "Jupiter") or "Dis Pater."[138] Because the causal relationship among the gestures, the incantation, and the healing of the dislocation is so difficult to infer, beyond intuitions about "sympathy," the entire sequence must be overimitated in the causal account's sense of overimitation. That is, learners must encode actions and vocalizations as *instrumentally necessary*, in some not-perfectly-transparent way, to obtaining their putative effect in the physical world.

A second—and at first glance similar—example comes from Pliny. He relates a story from L. Calpurnius Piso Frugi to the effect that Numa used to call down lightning "by means of certain rites and prayers."[139] Numa's successor, Tullus Hostilius, attempted the same ritual but failed *to imitate* the ritual accurately (*imitatum parum rite*) and so was struck by lightning.[140] Pliny seems to imply that causally opaque actions capable of producing effects in the physical world had failed as a result of Tullus's lack of imitative fidelity. If, however, we consult Livy, who also relates Frugi's story, we see that he explicitly preserves the reason for the rite's failure. The "improper ritual," excited Jupiter's anger—*ira Iovis sollicitati prava religione*—and he communicated his wrath by striking Tullus with lightning.[141]

Livy's version of the story removes the failed ritual from the domain of strictly physical causality and supports the *normative* account of overimitation. For, in effect, Jupiter *protests* a breach of orthoprax ritual norms by smiting the king. Yet even if it is correct to say that Tullus's botched ritual does not reduce to the causation of an unintended physical effect, we need not therefore

---

137. Cato *Agr.* 160.

138. Guittard 2007: 181–83.

139. Plin. *N.H.* 2.140: *sacris quibusdam et precationibus vel cogi fulmina vel impetrari.*

140. Plin. *N.H.* 2.140: *tradit L. Piso ... quod imitatum parum rite Tullum Hostilium ictum fulmine.*

141. Liv. 1.31.8: *sed non rite initum aut curatum id sacrum esse ... ira Iovis sollicitati prava religione fulmine ictum cum domo conflagrasse.*

discard the causal account of overimitation. Instead, Livy shows that we may unite the normative and causal accounts.

For it is precisely by adhering to certain norms, in this case norms of ritual practice, that one *causes* certain effects. However, these effects are not in the first place *physical* but rather *psychological*, affecting the god's mind. A *normatively* proper ritual would not have produced lightning through some obscure causal mechanism within the physical domain, in the way that Cato's sympathetic magic produced healing. Rather, a normatively proper ritual would have affected Jupiter's *mind* in the right way, eliciting his intervention in the physical world. So, the normative is causal, but the effects of proper norm following are in the first place psychological. Any physical effects follow from the psychological, when the ritual prompts the god to act. Normative actions, even when teleologically opaque, have real effects, but these effects are realized in the minds of others, in this case, gods, who share or recognize the same norms.

We may adduce the distinctively Roman institution of *instauratio* in support of this hypothesis.[142] As Camillus summarizes it, *instauratio* is the repetition from scratch of a ritual or ceremony "because something from the ancestral rite [*ex patrio ritu*] has been omitted [*praetermissum*] owing to negligence [*neglegentia*] or chance."[143] Cicero dilates on *instauratio* at length in *De haruspicum responsis*. The haruspices had interpreted certain portents as evidence that "games [*ludi*] have been performed without due attention and have been desecrated." It was then up to the *septemviri epulonum* to determine if anything had been "omitted [*praetermissum*] or done wrong," and to the *pontifices* to decide whether "those same *sacra* are to be celebrated anew and from the beginning [*instaurata*]."[144] Cicero goes on to list in detail some of the seemingly minor infractions that could cause games or ceremonies to require *instauratio*: "if a dancer has stopped, or if a flute player suddenly falls silent, or if a boy ... has let go of the rein of a chariot." In such cases the games have not been correctly performed (*non rite facti*).[145]

Cicero presents the rationale behind *instauratio* as follows: repetition from scratch "expiates ritual errors and the minds of the gods are appeased."[146] Surely *instauratio* represents a very extreme cultural deployment of overimitation. It is not enough just to get the rites *right*. One must *start all over again* in

---

142. See Cohee 1994.

143. Liv. 5.52.9: *recordamini ... quotiens sacra instaurentur, quia aliquid ex patrio ritu neglegentia casuve praetermissum est.*

144. Cic. *Har. Resp.* 21. See section 2.6.3 for discussion of this episode.

145. Cic. *Har. Resp.* 23.

146. Cic. *Har. Resp.* 23: *errata expiantur et mentes deorum immortalium ludorum instauratione placantur.*

the event of the least error. Here we see the practical antidote to Piso Frugi's cautionary tale about Tullus Hostilius. Incorrect ritual, *prava religio*, excites divine anger. Fortunately, *instauratio*, correct reperformance from scratch, can turn aside that anger and appease the "god's minds," *mentes deorum*.

Now, we must pause to consider the nature of the divine minds that are appeased in this way. If the rituals through which we affect these minds are causally opaque, and hence must be imitated with high fidelity, it is also true that the divine minds to which the rituals are addressed are relatively *psychologically opaque*. We explored in the introduction (section 0.3) and have seen in this chapter (section 7.3) that the transparency of the human mind was a commonplace. The human expression, the *vultus*, speaks the "silent speech of the mind," the *sermo tacitus mentis*,[147] disclosing the contents of one mind to another with direct clarity. But the divine mind is comparatively psychologically opaque. We have no unmediated access to a divine *vultus* on which to glimpse the divine mind.

What we have instead is ritual, which is like language in being governed by norms. And, as Cicero points out, language is opaque to the minds of those not united in the *societas* of common linguistic norms. Unless we share a set of linguistic norms, neither of us can move or affect the mind of the other through speech.[148] Where the gods are concerned, all the Romans had was the language of ritual, a system of norms for producing effects in, and reading the state of, the divine mind. So, humans indicate their will in prayer and cult action, while the gods indicate their will through the entrails of victims or by means of prodigies and *auspicia*. This language of entrails, prodigies, and *auspicia* is itself a language to be mastered through high-fidelity imitation. Yet even given a mastery of this language, human beings must ensure that their communications are free of ambiguities and errors in order to guarantee that they cause the desired effect in minds so opaque. Hence the Roman insistence on orthopraxy in ritual action. Hence the cautionary tale of Tullus Hostilius, inadvertently inciting the divine mind to anger through a breach of ritual norms. Hence, finally, *instauratio*, which permitted Romans to repair their breaches of ritual norms and begin anew their communications with the gods, in order to produce in their minds propitious effects.

To summarize the argument thus far baldly: in order reliably to exert *causality* in the domain of divine *psychology*, Romans had to overimitate in ritual performance. Only meticulous adherence to *normatively* determined action sequences could ensure achievement of the desired *effects* in the divine mind.

---

147. Cic. *Pis.* 1.1.
148. Cic. *De Or.* 3.223.

Only overimitation of causally opaque actions could ensure the desired psychological effect, because the psychology to be affected, the divine mind, was only mediately available, through ritual.

So, we should view overimitation as at once normative and causal. In the social world, especially in a social world that embraces gods along with mortals, the culturally *normative* aspects of our actions are often instrumental to their *causality*. And that causality is not *physical* but *psychological*, insofar as it was divine minds that were affected. Adhering to ritual norms causes divine pleasure, while breaching those norms causes divine displeasure. This causality, psychological and social though it be, is every bit as real and consequential as the physical causality involved in push-pull, object-to-object contact.

This understanding of overimitation as driven by motivations both normative and causal positions us to explain Roman orthopraxy itself. If Roman ritual was a system of causally opaque, normative actions, then its very *opacity* will have triggered an overimitation response in Roman culture learners, not only children but also adults.[149] Overimitation in response to the causal opacity of Roman ritual will have ensured high-fidelity copying of the ritual and hence high-fidelity cultural transmission. Roman ritual—with its concomitant cautionary tales about imperfect imitation, and its remedy, *instauratio*, for underimitation—is a paradigm and indeed extreme case of causally opaque cultural knowledge transmitted by overimitation. Thus, the causal opacity of Roman ritual triggered overimitation in learners, resulting in high-fidelity ritual copying, that is to say, the very orthopraxy that characterized Roman religion.

There are two fallouts from my overimitation account of orthopraxy, at which we can barely glance here. First, we know that Romans declined to insist on authoritative explanations of their cult practices. Indeed, the famous story of the discovery and subsequent burning of Numa's seven books on the pontifical law, *de iure pontificum*,[150] itself amounts to an aetiology for this lack of authoritative explanations. Had the books survived, the authoritative explanations for the cult tradition that Numa instituted would have become known. The resulting explanatory vacuum meant that Roman inference about ritual causality could remain open-ended, and this resulted in the proliferation of multiple aetiologies for opaque rituals, of the sort found in Plutarch's *Roman*

---

149. Particularly relevant here is Gergely and Csibra 2006. For adult overimitation, see McGuigan et al. 2011; E. Flynn and Smith 2012; Whiten, Allan, et al. 2016.

150. Liv. 40.29.7; Varr. *Curio de cultu deorum* fr. 3 Cardauns (= Aug. *Civ.* 7.34–35); Val. Max. 1.1.12; Plin. *N.H.* 13.84–87; Plu. *Num.* 22; Lact. *Div. Inst.* 1.22; Aur. Vict. *Vir. ill.* 3.2.

Questions and Ovid's *Fasti*.[151] These aetiologies took the form of origin stories, physical explanations, and functional explanations.[152]

Here we see a chief difference between orthoprax and orthodox religions. It is not that orthodox religions lack causally opaque rituals, composed of purposive actions with no clear instrumental rationale, but rather that orthodox religions tend to assert authoritative explanations for them. Orthoprax traditions, in contrast, may decline to do so, as the Roman tradition did. Orthopraxy permits polydoxy, and one of the ways that polydoxy could express itself at Rome was through multiple aetiologies.

A second fallout from my account of orthopraxy is that as paradoxical as it may sound, overimitation accounts for ritual change. For overimitation preserved instrumentally opaque ritual technologies for context-sensitive innovation and refinement. Orthopraxy notwithstanding, Roman religion was constantly evolving.[153] In older accounts, Roman religious change was mostly a matter of decline due to decadence, Greek rationalism, ritualism's failure to meet spiritual needs, and so forth. I prefer a less value-laden perspective from overimitation. In an orthoprax system, the relatively stable norms of practice create a zone of latent ritual solutions, that is, a zone of possible modifications to ritual technology to meet new needs, which are just within reach, given the very norms of the ritual system. Overimitation and the orthopraxy it enables, by dint of their very conservativeness, *preserve* ritual technologies to be built on in this way. Transmitted ritual technologies, however much they are supposed or assumed to remain eternally unchanged, inexorably suggest possibilities for repurposing and refinement, albeit still in accord with norms internal to the orthoprax system, in order to address new religious problems. The result is a "ratcheting effect" in which new ritual technologies are made possible by and built on older ones, resulting in a "cumulative," evolving, ever more elaborate ritual culture.[154]

Romans, with their tolerance for multiple understandings of opaque ritual, were relatively free to explore within the zone of latent ritual possibilities. Take, for example, Macrobius and what he terms *permutatio sacrificii* or *emendatio sacrificiorum*.[155] We learn that Apollo had originally specified that the Compitalia was to be celebrated with "heads on behalf of heads," *pro capitibus capita*. Like all Apolline oracles, this recommendation is hermeneutically opaque. The god's precise intentions hide behind his inscrutable words. King

---

151. See Feeney 2020 and Mackey 2018a.
152. See, e.g., Plu. Q.R. 93 for all these types of aitia in response to a single ritual question.
153. For a recent, thorough account of this process, see Rüpke 2012.
154. For the ratchet effect and cumulative culture, see Tennie, Call, and Tomasello 2009.
155. Macr. *Sat.* 1.7.34–36.

Tarquin took Apollo to mean that human heads should be offered on behalf of human heads, that is, behead some to preserve the heads of many. Brutus offered another interpretation. He proposed that "heads" of garlic and poppy be offered in place of (*pro*) human heads. This interpretation follows to the letter the ritual prescription. Orthopraxy is maintained, but "head" is seen in a new perspective; this perspective comes to guide practical attitudes; and these attitudes guide cult practice. In an orthodox tradition, such a reinterpretation might well have occasioned a schism. However, an orthoprax tradition of open speculation about the rationale for causally opaque ritual action allowed Romans to explore freely the zone of latent cognitive and practical possibilities afforded by the prescribed cult regulations and thus to modify the ritual.

To summarize our excursus on overimitation, Roman ritual orthopraxy was *causal*, but it was primarily *psychologically* causal and only secondarily *physically* causal, insofar as ritual instigated gods to act in the world. Additionally, cult was psychologically causal because it was *normative*. Producing effects in the divine mind required opaque actions stipulated by convention to be imitated with high fidelity. As a system of causally opaque behaviors, Roman ritual engendered and was sustained by the cross-culturally well-documented tendency of human beings to overimitate. In Rome, these overimitated ritual behaviors—orthopraxy itself—could sponsor open-ended inference about causes, that is, multiple aetiologies. Finally, orthopraxy allowed for ritual change both because it preserved ritual technology faithfully for modification and innovation and because it afforded the ritual system a flexibility to respond substantively to the inference and speculation that it itself engendered and refused to curtail.

7.4.2. Joint Commitments

Joint action, in which people act together cooperatively toward a shared goal, whether the goal is just the action itself or some outcome, necessarily creates commitments and obligations. If Gaius could not count on Quintus to do his part in their plan to take a walk, and vice versa, it is hard to see how they could ever reach the forum together. Children's proclivity to cooperate in joint action was not lost on the Romans. Cicero, for example, channeling Antiochus, remarks that soon after children begin to walk, "they delight in the company of their peers, gather happily with them, and devote themselves (*dant se*) to playing games."[156] Once a Roman child has learned the conventional norms

---

156. Cic. *Fin.* 5.42: *deinde aequalibus delectantur libenterque se cum iis congregant dantque se ad ludendum*. Roman children's games: Väterlein 1976; and Wiedemann 1989: 148–53.

of behavior that govern a game or cult act, he or she and other participants must still "devote themselves" to performing it together, that is, form a joint commitment to enact the joint action. Such commitments, involving norms of cooperation, may arise explicitly or tacitly. The normative nature of joint commitments and the obligations they generate is best seen in the breach. For example, if on the way to the forum Quintus abruptly peels away from Gaius and wanders into a *taberna,* Gaius has good cause to protest.[157]

Even infants are sensitive to others' commitments to cooperative enterprises, for they expect adults to share their attention toward objects to which they point, and they remain unsatisfied until they achieve truly cooperative, joint attention.[158] By three years of age, children's understanding of the joint commitments entailed by joint activities have deepened. Sensing that joint commitments carry obligations, they will reliably attempt to reengage derelict partners, and they will exhibit leave-taking behavior when they themselves disengage from the activity. In other words, joint action entails, even for young children, a sense that they and their partners have entered into a mutual obligation, or that they are subject to a norm of cooperation, to act together toward their joint goal.[159]

For a very young Roman, joint commitments might at first have been limited to spontaneous, isolated moments of joint action, such as the game playing mentioned by Cicero. However, recent empirical studies offer reasons to accept the Durkheimian thesis that repeatedly cooperating in collective cult actions, such as those depicted by Tibullus and Ovid, contributed to children's sense of identity and group cohesion.[160] Indeed, Cicero had already voiced a similar notion. He held that kinship alone, *sanguinis coniunctio,* entailed cognitive and affective bonds of *benevolentia* and *caritas;*[161] but he also held that sharing *sacra* and other forms of cult was significant for familial bonding.[162]

The upshot is that it is easy to suppose that regularly committing to specific cult actions with one's family might contribute to the development of a larger sense of commitment to "our" cult tradition and its norms. This sense of *pietas* was surely in Cicero's sights when he wrote of the importance of preserving

---

157. See further, Gilbert 1990. Note that Roman law formalized one person's legal *obligationes* to another because of their joint commitment (*consensus*) in certain contexts: *consensu fiunt obligationes* (Gai. *Inst.* 3.135). See Mousourakis 2012: 183–87; Birks 2014: 2–5.

158. Tomasello, Carpenter et al. 2005: 682–83; Tomasello, Carpenter, and Liszkowski 2007.

159. Gräfenhain et al. 2009; Tomasello 2009: 60–67; Tomasello and Hamann 2012.

160. Von Scheve 2012; Legare and Wen 2014; Whitehouse and Lanman 2014.

161. Cic. *Off.* 1.54.

162. Cic. *Off.* 1.55: *magnum est enim eadem habere monumenta maiorum, eisdem uti sacris, sepulchra habere communia.*

family traditions, the *ritus familiae patrumque*.[163] And such a sense of *pietas* is surely at the heart of stories such as that of C. Fabius Dorsuo, who braved the Gauls besieging the Capitol in order to perform his family's annual cult on the Quirinal.[164] Here, then, we see the *ontogeny of community* in the joint commitments that are the precondition for acting together at all. That is, we see how Roman children might have constructed a sense of their community, and of commitment to their community's traditions, through sharing Intentionality and agency in joint ritual actions of the sort Ovid describes.

7.4.3. Shared Beliefs

Prudentius's child acquired his beliefs about Fortuna by perceiving and adopting his mother's attitudes toward the goddess's *effigies*. In Ovidian joint action, this sort of intention-perception and intention-adoption deepens into *intention sharing*. The children's joint attention with culturally experienced elders to the ritual act—its implements, gestures, prayers, and hymns—allows them to enter and share with adults a space of cognitive common ground, where the attitudes and perspectives of all participants are mutually manifest. In this joint-attentional space, the children not only perceive but also share with adults their doxastic and practical states regarding the ritual (e.g., its nature and purpose), and its gods (e.g., who they are and how "we" feel toward them). As these beliefs, perspectives, goals, and feelings become part of the common ground that the children share with others, they come to hold them, not as "mother's," "father's," or "mine," but as "ours."[165] Needless to say, this might have been a largely tacit process. It need not, and for Romans did not, involve explicit declarations of theological creeds, but rather the sort of social-cognitive competence for attuning oneself to the psychological states of others that we saw Augustine describe in section 7.3.

Thus, we should not imagine a Roman child entering into his or her first act of domestic cult with a fully formed cultural-cognitive architecture in place: certainly not shared *beliefs* about the nature or purpose of the ritual or the gods invoked in it, nor any clear sense of the *norms* of ritual practice. We should, however, expect the child to *attend* actively and jointly with others to the cult act, however innocent she may yet be as to its cultural and cultic nature. As she learns the ritual's performative norms in the course of practice—for example, what to do with her honeycombs and when—and as she learns the nature of

---

163. Cic. *Leg.* 2.19.
164. Liv. 5.46.1–4.
165. Cf. Tomasello 1999a: 56–93. See also Tomasello and Moll 2010: 339–45.

her family's worship and the "theology" of Terminus in the joint-attentional space she shares with her elders, including listening to and eventually joining in the singing of the hymn—her *commitment* to the ritual as what "we" do will deepen. This is cultural transmission.

I have suggested simply this. Within a space of "precultural" joint attention and joint action, Ovid's Roman children would have come to share both a primitive sense of collective commitment and the cultural forms of Intentionality and agency distinctive of their community. In this "precultural" joint-attentional space, the children not only got their own perspective on the object of shared attention but also intuited and inferred others' perspectives. In this way, through sharing attention to and agency in ritual performance, Roman children grasped and gradually came to share with experienced elders more properly cultural forms of Intentionality, such as informal folk-theological beliefs, a sense of a ritual's purpose, and commitment to the practical norms and deontology of ritual, its *pietas*. The Roman child who started out with a capacity to share attention and to act jointly (cognitive processes) would soon have found him- or herself launched into a cultural reality of norm-governed practices and gods (cultural cognitive products).

Ovid's simple act of domestic *pietas* was thus structured by, and supported the acquisition of, a complex matrix of shared Intentionality. Though Ovid does not use overtly psychological language, if we are to recover the agency of Roman children, we must allow ourselves reasonable inferences about their cognitive processes of cultural learning in the episode as he describes it. I have tried to show that from the perspective of ontogeny, what Scheid has called "savoir rituel" and what Feeney has called "performative knowledge" possessed a cognitive structure that included, first, joint attentional engagement and the joint goal to act together, and then, eventually, shared folk-theological beliefs, shared norms of performance, in sum, a shared sense of *pietas*. Ovid's ritual thus promoted group cohesion as well as the sharing of cultural Intentionality—that is, distinctively Roman beliefs and norms—even as it was reproduced with reasonable accuracy across generations. Cicero wrote that "it is consequential to practice the same *sacra*." I have tried to show how and why, from a cognitive perspective, this was so.

7.5. Religious Instruction: Beyond Apprenticeship

Thus far, I have argued that Roman children were religious apprentices, agents of their own enculturation, in two ways. First, they apprehended the Intentionality of their elders and imitated their beliefs, purposes, and actions. Second, they shared Intentionality with adults in joint actions, such as collective ritual. Through such sharing of Intentionality and agency, Roman children joined adults in an intimate space of *cognitive* common ground, where they could grasp adults' perspectives and so gradually come to share with them a larger *cultural* common ground: "our" commitments, "our" performative norms, and "our" beliefs.

Now we turn to a rarer phenomenon: deliberate religious instruction in the singing of choral hymns. Songs and singing permeated Roman culture, often as a means of pedagogy.[166] And yet the choral training of children qua religious pedagogy has been overlooked in recent discussions of religious transmission at Rome.[167] Note that the two contexts of religious learning that we have so far examined featured verbal productions. Prudentius's child learned to pray from hearing his mother pray. And Ovid's children heard and presumably took part in the singing of hymns. In chapter 8 we shall ask what these ubiquitous linguistic aspects of Roman cult might portend for Roman belief. Here, in the final section of this chapter, we merely try to sort out the cognitive effects of this one, distinctive, Roman mode of religious pedagogy: choral training. Here, our apprentices become students.

For Cicero, our social nature predisposes us to learn from as well as teach one another.[168] Instructed learning represents a cooperative, albeit hierarchical, joint activity, underwritten by recursive layers of shared Intentionality. For instruction is a species of cooperative communication. As in communication a speaker has intentions toward the Intentional states of auditors (e.g., "I *intend* to get you to *know*"), so in instruction a teacher has intentions toward the Intentional states of students ("I *intend* to get you to *learn*"). And just as auditors recognize that speakers have intentions toward their Intentional states (e.g., "this person *intends* to get me to *know*"), so students recognize that teachers have pedagogical intentions toward their Intentional states ("this person *intends* to get me to *learn*"). Teachers and students thus *know together* that they are sharing intentions to teach and to learn.[169] Thus, to conclude on a Quintilianic note, instruction depends on children's natural sociability, *congressus naturalis*, a faculty we share with some animals, but it transforms it into the

---

166. See esp. Horsfall 2003: 11–19 and 31–47. Music in Roman religion: Wille 1967: 26–74 (for "*sakraler Chorgesang*," see 47–52); and Quasten 1983 (75–77 on choirs of women or girls, and 87–88 on boys' choirs). Singing (including choral) in early Christianity: J. A. Smith 2011: 174ff.

167. E.g., by Prescendi 2010. However, see the study of "Rhythmisch-musikalische Heilpädagogik" in Wille 1962.

168. Cic. *Fin.* 3.66: *ita non solum ad discendum propensi sumus, verum etiam ad docendum*. Cf. *Off.* 1.50.

169. On cooperative communication, see Grice 1989: 86–116 and 213–23, esp. 220; Sperber and Wilson 1995: 21–31 (esp. 29) and 54–64; Tomasello 2008: 72–99.

civilized virtue of a *sensus communis*, a "shared sensibility" that unites us culturally with our fellows.[170]

When we point to the training of Roman choruses for civic cult, we must admit that formal instruction in sacred hymn singing was scarcely the rule for all Roman children at all times. We know, rather, that it would have occurred on special occasions, such as times of crisis or the secular games.[171] It would have been reserved for select children, especially girls, as we shall see, who had both parents living (*patrimi matrimique* or *patrimae matrimaeque*) and were typically from the elite classes.[172]

Figure 7.3, however, in which a *schola cantorum* (a sacred choir of Diana and its singing master) appears to be depicted, suggests that choral training of children was perhaps more widespread than literary sources would lead us to believe.[173] It must be the case that hymn-singing in "private" contexts was common, as witnessed by the chorus in Ovid's Terminalia, even if not necessarily a matter of formal pedagogy. Whatever its incidence, choral training represented, in a sense, a formal, collective analogue of the prayer learning that we have already seen Roman children do informally and individually.[174]

With this preamble and these caveats in mind, let us turn to our evidence for what appears to be the first introduction of choral hymn singing at Rome, in order to expiate prodigies in 207 BCE, during the Second Punic War (Liv. 27.37.7):

---

170. *Inst.* 1.2.20. For *sensus communis* cf. Cic. *De orat.* 2.16.68; Sen. *Ep.* 5.4.

171. Attested public singing of hymns by children's choruses: Macr. *Sat.* 1.6.14 (217 BCE?), *obsecratio*; Liv. 27.37.7 (207 BCE); Liv. 31.12.9 (200 BCE); Liv. 37.3.6 (190 BCE?); Jul. Obs. 27a (133 BCE); Jul. Obs. 34 (119 BCE); Jul. Obs. 36 (117 BCE); Jul. Obs. 43 (104 BCE); Jul. Obs. 46 (99 BCE); Jul. Obs. 48 (97 BCE); Jul. Obs. 53 (92 BCE), all to expiate prodigies; Hor. *C.S.* (17 BCE), for secular games; Cass. Dio 59.7.1 (37 CE) for dedication of a shrine to Augustus; sestertius of Domitian (88 CE) for secular games (so Mantle 2002: 88); Cass. Dio 75.4.5 (193 CE), for the funeral of Pertinax; Vop./*Hist. Aug.* 19.6 and 20.3 (reign of Aurelian) for a threat to Rome. See Mantle 2002: 86–91.

172. *Patrimi matrimique* and upper class: Mantle 2002: 105–6. Vestals also received and gave religious pedagogy for periods of ten years (learning) and ten years (teaching): D.H. 2.67.2; Sen. *Ot.* 2.2; Plu. *Num.* 10.1.

173. On this mosaic, see Fogagnolo 2012: 235ff. For children singing hymns to the gods, see, e.g., Hor. *C.* 1.21 and Cat. 34. See Green 2007: 138–40; Wille 1967: 47–52; Mantle 2002: 86–91.

174. This is not to elide the distinction proposed in Scheid 2007a between prayer (*precatio*: a verbal formula that "performs" the cult act) and hymn (*carmen*: a verbal "œuvre d'art" to delight the gods). The distinction is valuable but should not obscure the fact, discussed below and in chapter 8, that our evidence suggests that prayers and hymns alike had at their core Directive speech acts requesting divine intervention.

FIGURE 7.3. Mosaic (third century CE) depicting a chorus of children with their singing master from the temple of Diana Tifatina on Monte Tifata near Capua. Now in the Museo Provinciale Campano di Capua. (Photo courtesy of museum.)

decrevere item pontifices ut virgines ter novenae per urbem euntes carmen canerent. id cum in Iovis Statoris aede discerent conditum ab Livio poeta carmen, tacta de caelo aedis in Aventino Iunonis Reginae.

The priests decreed that twenty-seven young girls should sing a hymn [*carmen canerent*] while walking through the city. When they were learning [*discerent*] this hymn, composed by the poet Livius, in the temple of Jupiter Stator, the temple of Juno Regina on the Aventine was struck by lightning.

Rather than inquire into either the nature of Livius Andronicus's hymn, which Livy professed to find less than sophisticated, or the historical context—political, religious, and literary—of its composition,[175] let us ask what we can recover of the children's cognitive agency from this evidence.

The active verbs *discere* and *canere*, to which we shall return below, immediately jump out.[176] The *virgines* had convened in a *locus sacer*, the temple of Jupiter Stator in the forum,[177] in order to learn (*discere*) a *carmen* uniquely composed for the occasion of their novel expiatory ritual. We have to infer that the girls devoted considerable mental energy to memorization of this new material over a brief period of time (they surely had a deadline). The fact that they undertook this learning together in a special place suggests, moreover, that they were taught or trained, perhaps by priests or by Livius himself.

What can we say about the young girls' experience of memorizing the *carmen*? We might look, though with all due caution, to Catullus 62, a wedding poem structured as if to be sung antiphonally in a contest between a chorus of boys and a chorus of girls. In the following lines the boys bemoan the girls' superior preparation (Cat. 62: 12–14):

> *adspicite, innuptae secum ut meditata requirunt.*
> *non frustra meditantur; habent memorabile quod sit.*
> *nec mirum, penitus quae tota mente laborant.*

> Behold how the unwed girls recollect what they have studied [*meditata*].
> Not in vain do they study [*meditantur*]; they have something worth remembering.
> No wonder they have immersed their entire mind [*tota mente*] deep in their work.

The thing to note here is Catullus's emphasis on the strenuousness of the girls' cognitive effort, their commitment to memorizing the song, eminently memorable though it was, and their devotion of all their mental energy, *tota mente*, to the task. Indeed, it was imperative to memorize songs in antiquity, especially

---

175. See G. Boyce 1937; Forsythe 2012: 64–67; Santangelo 2013: 165–68; Feeney 2016: 225–32.

176. The lightning strike on the temple of Juno, for whom the hymn was composed (Liv. 27.37.12: *carmen in Iunonem Reginam canentes*), also jumps out. We might imagine that it caused cognitive *distress* for the *virgines*: on emotions in Roman religion, see section 3.2.

177. Coarelli 2007: 89–91.

their music, which might not be written down or, if written, might not be legible to the singers.[178] We need believe neither that Catullus's song describes a particular "real life" situation nor that it was itself ever sung in a ritual context to suppose that the poet does in fact depict a facet of the world of Roman children's experience that would have been recognizable to his audience.

Thus far, our *virgines* have received instruction in the singing of their hymn, and they have labored to practice and learn it. The reward would have been successful performance, which Livy marks, as we saw, with the verb *canere*. Indeed, they did not merely sing the hymn together but marched through the city as they sang and, linked together by a rope, danced in the forum, "matching the sound of their voice with the rhythm of their feet."[179] Servius tells us that the *maiores* made a place for both dance (*saltatio*) and song (*cantus*) in cult because they wanted both body (*corpus*) and mind (*animus*) "to experience *religio*."[180] What Livy offers goes beyond Servius's holistic but individualistic picture, for his *virgines* experience *religio* collectively, jointly acting as a kind of plural subject, in apparently perfect cognitive and motoric attunement.[181]

While we can recover the experience of these young women only through educated inference and imagination, we do have some Roman evidence (slippery, because self-interested) regarding the experience of the *memory* of having sung a sacred hymn. In a poem published in 13 BCE, Horace imagines a young woman, now married, looking back with satisfaction on having learned and sung his *Carmen saeculare* four years earlier (C. 4.6.41–44):

nupta iam dices, "ego dis amicum,
saeculo festas referente luces,
reddidi carmen docilis modorum
vatis Horati."

Married now, you will say,
"When the age brought round the festal days again,
I recited a hymn [*reddidi carmen*] that pleased the gods,
trained [*docilis*] in the meters of the poet Horace."

Our Livian and Catullan texts emphasized children's agency with verbs such as *discere*, *meditari*, and *laborare*. Here we find rather more explicit reference

---

178. Isid. *Orig.* 3.15: *nisi enim ab homine memoria teneantur soni pereunt quia scribi non possunt.*
179. Liv. 27.37.14: *sonum vocis pulsu pedum modulantes incesserunt.*
180. Serv. *ad Ecl.* 5.73: *sane ut in religionibus saltaretur, haec ratio est, quod nullam maiores nostri partem corporis esse voluerunt, quae non sentiret religionem: nam cantus ad animum, saltatio ad mobilitatem pertinet corporis.*
181. See Von Scheve 2012; Legare and Wen 2014; Whitehouse and Lanman 2014.

to the teacher's role in the word *docilis*, which echoes the *Carmen saeculare*'s *docilis iuventa*, "teachable youth" (*C.S.* 45) and *doctus chorus*, "trained chorus" (*C.S.* 75). The effect is to remind us that the children learned through the instruction of an expert, perhaps Horace himself.

Horace coordinates the verbs *discere* and *docere*, reflecting the cooperative nature of teaching and learning, the active roles of both student and teacher, in another recollection of the *Carmen saeculare* (*Ep.* 2.1.132–37):

> *castis cum pueris ignara puella mariti*
> *disceret unde preces, vatem ni Musa dedisset?*
> *poscit opem chorus et praesentia numina sentit,*
> *caelestis implorat aquas, docta prece blandus,*
> *avertit morbos, metuenda pericula pellit,*
> *impetrat et pacem et locupletem frugibus annum.*

> How would innocent boys and unmarried girls
> learn [*disceret*] prayers, if the Muse had not granted them a poet?
> The chorus begs for aid and feels the divine presence,
> pleads for heavenly rain—persuasive with the prayer that has been
> taught [*docta prece*]—averts disease, dispels dangers feared,
> requests peace and a bounteous year for crops.

This passage opens up a new aspect of children's religious agency for us. All our passages thus far, with their emphasis on learning, teaching, and cognitive effort, describe a mode of pedagogy that is, in a sense, orthoprax rather than orthodox. The important thing was that the children learned to sing their hymns, and perhaps as in the Livian example, to march and dance, correctly and in unison. The instruction and learning that we must imagine in these cases is instruction and learning *how*. Correspondingly, we have until now largely been discussing a first domain of cognitive agency exercised by Roman children during religious instruction: the domain of active learning and memorizing in response to the pedagogical intentions of adults.

However, we may now identify a second domain in which Roman children exercised cognitive agency. Recall that we have no evidence for catechistic pedagogy, for creedal instruction, for authoritative explanations of ritual of the sort found in late antique Christian homilies.[182] The absence of catechesis in the training of Roman choruses left open to Roman children the exercise of *inferential agency* as to the existence and nature of the gods whose *carmina* they

---

182. See Schwartz 2013: 1–6 and 17–25 for late antique catechism. See the outline of catechetical practices at M. E. Johnson 2007: 111. Catechism of children in early Christianity: Horn and Martens 2009: 161–63.

were learning. Creeds and catechisms present their propositional contents in Assertive speech acts.[183] That is, speakers expressly assert the propositional contents of creeds and doctrines as truths that they accept and intend auditors to accept. However, Roman hymns and prayers alike often conveyed their propositional contents not as truths to be believed, but as desiderata, under the Directive illocutionary force of wish, plea, or request.

In Horace's *Epistle*, the children's *preces* do not assert as an article of faith that Apollo *does* bring aid, that he *does* send rain, that he *does* avert disease, and so forth. Rather, the chorus begs and pleads (*poscere, implorare, impetrare*) that Apollo bring aid, send rain, and the rest. The psychological state expressed toward the propositional content of a petitionary prayer or hymn is thus often one of hope or desire rather than belief per se. To plead that Apollo bring aid, rain, or peace, is tacitly to *presuppose* rather than explicitly assert that he has the power to fulfill such requests.[184] Thus, the texts of choral *carmina* did have a theological content, but they communicated that content nondogmatically and indirectly, permitting children an inferential agency or cognitive autonomy that doctrinal, creed-based religions at least attempt to foreclose. Belief and other psychological attitudes were left up to the Roman child, who was thus in important respects cognitively autonomous, relatively free to exercise his or her own inferential agency without doctrinal pressures.

The children's inferential agency, their availing themselves of their own cognitive autonomy, will have begun from the pragmatics of the prayer or hymn qua speech act. Absent any theological instruction, the sheer pragmatics of singing a *carmen* for the gods would have sponsored children's theological inferences, and even their theological experiences, as Horace suggests when he writes of his choristers' epiphany: *praesentia numina sentit*, the chorus "feels the divine presence."[185] That is, to sing a hymn *for* Apollo, in which they begged for help and rain *from* Apollo, permitted children to *infer* and so implicitly to *presuppose* and even explicitly to *believe* that Apollo did in fact exist and had the power to offer help, send rain, ward off disease, and so forth. Moreover, insofar as the children made such theological inferences and presuppositions and arrived at such beliefs, they implicitly joined their fellow choristers and their elders—their approving parents, the poet who composed the hymn, the civic authorities sponsoring its production—in a space of *theological*

---

183. For propositions and speech acts, see section 2.3 and chapter 8.

184. On such presuppositions, part of the "preparatory conditions" of speech acts, see Searle and Vanderveken 1985: 16–18; Vanderveken 1990: 113–17.

185. Ovid recounts a similar prayerful epiphany at *F.* 6.251: *in prece totus eram: caelestia numina sensi.*

common ground, where certain beliefs about the gods were shared and presumed to be shared.[186] Given their cognitive autonomy, it was, of course, always possible for children to have opted not to believe anything about the gods, not even that they exist, without fear of social sanction. Yet the materially and temporally costly ritual *contexts* of hymn singing and praying, with their associated religious pageantry, will have strongly implied that adults had committed to the propositional contents of these verbal productions and to the inferences about gods that they sponsored. Such contextual cues would have channeled the young toward belief.

Thus, we have seen that choral hymn singing afforded Roman children a rich context in which to make theological inferences, arrive at more or less reflective theological beliefs, and so join their community in shared, cultural cognition. In the following chapter, we expand on the theory limned in this section. We turn to prayer and the pragmatics of prayer in order to explore the consequences for Roman belief of encountering the *content* of prayers in cult *contexts* of praying. That is, we delve more deeply into the sources and nature of Roman belief, or folk theology.

7.6. Conclusion

I have aimed in this chapter both to account for Roman children's religious learning *sine doctrina*—for traditional Roman religion knew no catechism—and to supplement the accounts of religious socialization found in the scholarship, where we read of contexts of socialization, such as the *domus*, and adult agents of socialization, such as nurses, mothers, and fathers, with a fine-grained, cognitive account of religious socialization. I attempted to maintain a focus on Roman children's agency in their own socialization and on the cognitive endowments that underlay that agency. I have argued that Roman children's capacities for social cognition—not only *understanding* but also *sharing* the Intentionality of others—potentiated their apprenticeship in cult. Roman children's religious imitation, ritual participation, and choral hymn learning constituted powerful, nondogmatic, inferential modes and contexts of social learning. Such nondogmatic, inferential social learning sustained Rome's religious traditions and contributed to the flexibility and informality of Rome's noncompulsory theology, over which not a single religious war was ever fought.

---

186. On such pragmatic presupposition and common ground, see Stalnaker 2014: 2–4 and 54ff.

8

The "Folk Theology" of Roman Prayer

CONTENT, CONTEXT, AND COMMITMENT

8.1. Introduction

We ended the previous chapter with the thought that prayers were contentful verbal productions by means of which Romans communicated with their gods.[1] I have noted that many religious beliefs derive from contexts of discourse or testimony, that is, from *social* sources, rather than from individual experience.[2] It is time now to examine this claim in some detail. This chapter's fundamental task is to show how *public* representations in the form of spoken prayers, with their requests, expressions of gratitude, and so on, not only arise from but also produce *private* representations in the form of beliefs.

Prayer was central to Roman religious culture and ubiquitous in cult.[3] In a sense, every act of cult communicated, through its accompanying prayer, a public linguistic representation *of itself*, that is, of its presuppositions, purposes, and significances (which is not to say that prayers exhausted the

---

[1]. The classic study of communication between man and god in Rome, covering all sorts of topics that I cannot touch on here, is Scheid 1987–89. Among cognitive accounts of prayer, I have found the following helpful: Goody 1995; Barrett 2001; Barrett 2002; Martin 2004; Boudry and De Smedt 2011; Sharp 2012.

[2]. See at section 2.2 passim, especially 2.2.5.

[3]. The fundamental collection of evidence for Roman prayer is Appel 1909; crisp discussion of the basic issues: Hickson 1993, esp. 1–15; comparative study of prayer among Greeks, Romans, Jews, and Christians: Klinghardt 1999; review of scholarship to 1998: Freyburger and Pernot 2000; useful selection of Roman prayers with introduction and commentary: Chapot and Laurot 2001; compelling study of Roman prayer and gesture: Corbeill 2004: 26–33; Roman prayer in its Italic context: Fisher 2014.

"meaning" of the rituals to which they were integral). This chapter proposes that we take quite seriously these public linguistic representations in three of their features. First, prayers are speech acts; second, as such, they express or make public their speakers' psychological states; third, hearing speakers make public their psychological states by means of precatory speech acts in cult contexts has cognitive consequences for the private psychological states of hearers. I address two such cognitive consequences, one doxastic, namely, religious belief, and the other practical, to wit, commitment to cult and its deontology, or *pietas*. That is, put simply, why did Romans have the religious beliefs they had? And why did they bother with and persist in time- and resource-consuming god-focused practices such as animal sacrifice, votive offering, temple construction, and of course prayer?

These two questions appear especially urgent when we reflect that Roman life did not feature practices designed to inculcate religious beliefs and promote commitment to their behavioral fallout. The Romans had no creed, no catechism, no evangelists advocating the salvific virtue of faith or warning of the perils of unbelief. Instead, Roman religion was marked by "a ritual savoir-faire, orally transmitted from father to son, from public officer to public officer, relying on written formulas of prayer and an orally-enacted calendar."[4] Such considerations inspire a third question: What was the *nature* of Roman religious belief, given the nondogmatic way that it was transmitted? I merely pose this third question here. We shall return to it in this chapter's conclusion.

I propose to seek answers to our two questions of belief and commitment in the *content* and the *context* of Roman prayer.[5] In preference to any other religious behavior, I focus on prayer—under which heading for present purposes I include hymns, vows, oaths, and all other god-focused linguistic productions—because as a form of discursive Intentionality (see section 2.3), prayers, like all speech acts, possess *content*. Speech acts derive their discursive Intentionality—their *aboutness* or *contentfulness*—from the psychological Intentionality of their speakers, that is, from speakers' beliefs, desires, intentions, and other mental episodes, which are (as we saw at section 2.2.3) *about* states of affairs and objects in the world. Put otherwise, speakers' mental episodes represent states of affairs and objects in the world as their *content*. Prayer expresses these mental episodes, including beliefs, and in so doing may transmit them to hearers as well. Since prayer was integral to all cult activity, all cult

---

4. Scheid 2006: 19.

5. For this content-cum-context approach to cultural learning, see N. Henrich and Henrich 2007: 10–11, and for its application to religious belief and commitment, see Norenzayan 2013: 112–13; and especially Norenzayan, Shariff, et al. 2016.

"FOLK THEOLOGY" OF ROMAN PRAYER   293

activity therefore featured discursive Intentionality, that is to say, communicative content. The communicative content of prayer initiated in hearers processes of "doxastic uptake" or belief formation. From the content of prayers, Romans could derive a great deal of information about their religious world and a great deal of what I have called their folk theology, an informal suite of reflective and nonreflective beliefs about the gods.

Beyond discursive content, I also address in a coda the fact that Romans produced and attended to prayers in ritual *contexts*. These contexts possessed properties, quite apart from discursive content, that served to promote among participants not only belief in but also practical and deontological commitments to the gods and their cult, in a word, *pietas*, a virtue in which the Romans judged themselves peerless.[6] The contextual cues of prayer performance could induce the adoption of or reinforce in culture learners corresponding attitudes of belief and commitment, precisely the attitudes required to motivate further time- and resource-consuming cult action and thus transmit the tradition.

What I am arguing, then, is that an appeal to *content* situated in appropriate *contexts* partly explains Roman belief and practice. My approach here is, broadly speaking, Lucretian. As we saw in chapter 6, the poet described content-based mechanisms of transmission, whereby the mind is naturally disposed to form and entertain representations of immortally blessed gods. He complements this approach with a context-based mechanism, whereby the spectacle of cult activity induces a *horror* that promotes transmission of theological beliefs and cult commitments horizontally, from person to person, and vertically, from generation to generation.

In this chapter, we explore content, context, and commitment, with an eye to what it all means for Roman belief. The status of Roman prayer as speech act is not news to scholars.[7] However, my two questions have largely gone unexplored. The first concerns the relevance of belief to the pragmatics of prayer. What must one believe simply in order to lodge a request with a divine agent? The second question has to do with the relevance of prayer to the beliefs of third-party hearers. For when one (over)hears a prayer, one encounters a discursive content, explicitly expressed semantically. However, especially in light of the prayer's ritual context of utterance, this expressed content also

---

6. Cic. *Har. Resp.* 9.19: *pietate ac religione . . . omnes gentes nationesque superavimus*. Cf. Cic. *ND* 2.8: We Romans are *religione, id est cultu deorum, multo superiores*. Cf. Val. Max. 1.1.1: *studium antiquis non solum servandae sed etiam amplificandae religionis fuit*; 1.1.9: *omnia namque post religionem ponenda semper nostra civitas duxit*. For *pietas* as a deontology, see at section 3.3.3.

7. See, e.g., Meyer 2004: 73ff.; Hickson-Hahn 2007; Kropp 2010; Rüpke 2015: 355. See also Versnel 2002 and the references collected at 146n105.

carries considerable pragmatic inferential potential, that is, a variety of implications and entailments. Let us explore these contentions systematically.

8.2. Some Guiding Theoretical Principles

We have already ventured into the theoretical weeds. Let us pause in order to make some distinctions that we shall take for granted in what follows. In praying, Roman agents *uttered*, that is, *spoke aloud* (less often *silently*) or *wrote out* speech acts.[8] We shall limit ourselves to spoken speech acts.[9] We may distinguish *addressees* from *hearers* (including *overhearers*). Speakers typically directed prayers to divine addressees. But prayers could also be heard and overheard by third parties, who might learn from them.

As speech acts, prayers are *contentful* uses of language. That is, prayers are *about* states of affairs past, current, desired, feared, imagined, and so forth. In addition to having content, prayers also have, like all speech acts, pragmatic *force*. Pragmatic force has *illocutionary* and *perlocutionary* dimensions.

We saw at section 2.3 that as an *illocutionary* act, every speech act applies a force F to a propositional content p, giving all speech acts the logical form $F(p)$. The five basic illocutionary forces are Assertive, Directive, Commissive, Expressive, and Declaratory. These forces have different illocutionary *points*. The point of Assertives is to *describe* the world; of Directives, to *request* that someone change something about the world; of Commissives, to *commit* speakers to changing something about the world; of Expressives, to *express* feelings about the way the world is; of Declarations, to *change* something about the world by linguistically representing the world as changed.[10] (For illustrative examples, see ahead to figure 8.1.) One may apply any illocutionary force F to one and the same propositional content p, such as, for example, the Assertive, Directive, or Expressive force to the proposition *Apollo averts disease*. The respective speech acts might run, "Apollo averts disease," "Apollo, avert disease!," and "I thank Apollo for averting disease." Directive force is the signal

---

8. On silent prayer, see Van der Horst 1994; and Freyburger 2001. Roman priests and magistrates often had prayers dictated to them or read them from written scripts (see Benveniste and Lallot 1973: 389ff.; Valette-Cagnac 1997: 247ff.; Meyer 2004: 73ff.), but the writing of spells on, e.g., lead tablets as in some sense *itself* a performance was characteristic of magic: see Gager 1992; Graf 1997: 205ff.

9. On speech acts, Austin 1962 is the seminal anglophone theorist. Further development in Searle 1969 and 1979a; Searle and Vanderveken 1985; Vanderveken 1990 and 1991. More information at section 2.3.

10. Searle 1979a: 12–20; Searle and Vanderveken 1985: 52; Vanderveken 1990: 22–23.

illocutionary force of petitionary prayer, but we shall certainly encounter the other forces in Roman prayer.[11]

We need to take a moment here to discuss the *sincerity conditions* of speech acts.[12] This is important because I shall use "sincere" and "sincerity" in their technical sense throughout this chapter. I do not want my usage of the term to be mistaken as denoting "doe-eyed earnestness" or anything of the sort. Each type of speech act has a *sincerity condition*. Assertives, for example, express beliefs; the sincerity condition of Assertives is therefore that the speaker *believes* the propositional content of his or her Assertive speech act. Directives express desires; the sincerity condition of Directives is that the speaker actually *wants* what he or she represents in the Directive speech act. Commissives express intentions; the sincerity condition of Commissives is that the speaker actually *intends* to do what he or she represents in the Commissive speech act. These sincerity conditions may have differing *degrees of strength*, ranging, for example, from mild wish to burning desire for Directives, and from high-intensity conviction to low-intensity belief with little felt sense of certitude for Assertives.

Not every speech act is sincere. A lie is an Assertive that expresses a belief that the speaker does not actually hold. It is also possible to request something without wanting it and to promise something without intending to do it, and so on. Such speech acts, whose sincerity conditions are not fulfilled, are *insincere*. Thus, it is always possible, in any tradition, for people to utter insincere prayers. Importantly, an insincere speech act may still be *successful*. For example, one may *succeed* in asserting something one does not believe, promising something one does not intend to do, or praying for something one does not really want. The insincerity of these speech acts renders them *defective* but not unsuccessful qua speech act.

For a speech act to be *unsuccessful*, or to *fail*, there must be a problem with the status of its speaker or the institutional context of its utterance.[13] Thus, if anyone but the appropriate magistrate should intone the formula to dedicate a temple, no matter with what sincerity, that dedication (a Declaration) would *fail*. This was the essence of the argument of the pontifex maximus Cornelius Barbatus in 304 BCE, when he was compelled by the people, asserting themselves against the nobles, to dictate (*praeire verba*: see section 8.3) the words

---

11. See also at section 1.3.3 for further reflections on Assertives and chapter 5 (especially at section 5.3.2) for much more on Declarations.

12. The following discussion of sincerity conditions and their degrees of strength relies on Searle and Vanderveken 1985: 12–20; Vanderveken 1990: 103–24.

13. For the relationships among "successful," "defective," "non-defective," and "failed/unsuccessful" speech acts, see Searle and Vanderveken 1985: 12–23; Vanderveken 1990: 129–30; and Vanderveken 2004.

of the prayer of dedication to a mere curule aedile, Gnaius Flavius, who wished to dedicate a temple of Concordia. Barbatus argued, in effect, that only a consul or imperator could *successfully* perform that particular speech act.[14] Since such questions of appropriate status and institutional context are matters of social ontology, they are almost always up for renegotiation, which is part of the point of Livy's story.

There is one final technical term to grapple with: the *conditions of satisfaction* for speech acts (compare the discussion at section 2.2.6 of the conditions of satisfaction for Intentional states). It is one thing *successfully* to utter an Assertive (as in a statement), a Directive (as in a prayer), a Commissive (as in a promise), and so on. However, the successful Assertion is not *satisfied* unless it is true, nor the Directive unless it is granted, nor the Commissive unless the action it represents is carried out by the speaker as promised.[15]

Aristotle did not develop a full-fledged theory of speech acts, but he did recognize a distinction between assertion and other speech acts. He made the point that only assertive sentences can be true or false and noted that nonassertive sentences—he takes εὐχή, "prayer," "vow," or even just "wish," as his example—have no truth value one way or the other (*Int.* 17a1–5):

ἔστι δὲ λόγος ἅπας μὲν cημαντικόc . . . κατὰ cυνθήκην· ἀποφαντικὸc δὲ οὐ πᾶc, ἀλλ' ἐν ᾧ τὸ ἀληθεύειν ἢ ψεύδεcθαι ὑπάρχει· οὐκ ἐν ἅπαcι δὲ ὑπάρχει, οἷον ἡ εὐχὴ λόγοc μέν, ἀλλ' οὔτ' ἀληθὴc οὔτε ψευδήc.

Every sentence signifies . . . by convention. Yet not every sentence is assertive, but only those in which truth or falsity subsists. These values do not subsist in all sentences, *for example, a prayer is a sentence, but is neither true nor false.* (My emphasis.)

Assertives may represent either truly or falsely. However, while prayers do represent, on Aristotle's account, they do so neither truly nor falsely. Aristotle goes on to discuss Assertives (usually translated as "propositions"), dismissing Directives such as those of prayer as the province of the study of rhetoric and poetry.

Aristotle did not have the broader concept of satisfaction. Directives, such as petitionary prayers, do not state, either truly or falsely, how things stand in the world. Instead, they are *satisfied* when they get the addressee to change how things stand in the world. Similarly, the propositional content of Commissive and Declaratory speech acts represents not *reality*, but rather how the speaker him- or herself *intends* to or actually *does* alter reality. Unlike the

---

14. Liv. 9.46.4–7.
15. Vanderveken 2004: 712.

Assertive, which is satisfied when it is *true*, these other types of speech acts are satisfied when they *change states of affairs in the world*. This can be done directly, as in the case of a Declaration, which changes the world by representing it as changed, or indirectly, as in the case of a Directive, when it gets an addressee to do something.

Our discussion of satisfaction has taken us to the *perlocutionary* aspect of speech acts. Recall that as an *illocutionary* act, a speech act applies Assertive, Directive, Commissive, Expressive, or Declaratory force (F) to a proposition (p) with the illocutionary point of describing, requesting, committing, expressing, or changing the world. In contrast, as a *perlocutionary* act, a speech act's point is to produce an *effect* in an addressee, that is, in his or her psychological state or behavior. Thus, for example, a speaker might use an Assertive in order not only to describe the world but also to get an addressee to believe something, or a Directive, such as a prayer, not only in order to express a desire but also to get an addressee to do something. When, in its capacity as a perlocutionary act, a speech act gets an addressee to believe something or to do something, it has had a *perlocutionary effect*.[16] In the case of Directives, this effect may be related to the *satisfaction* of the speech act.

Any speech act may additionally have an *informative* illocutionary point and perlocutionary effect, that is, it may be intended to inform and succeed in informing its (over)hearers that a speech act of a given sort has been directed to a given addressee.[17] Thus, a prayer might have the informative effect of apprising third-party hearers that a given speaker has made a certain request of Apollo. In this way, hearers not only derive the information in the content of the speech act; they also derive information about who has asked what of whom and how. As we shall see when we look at the oath of the fetial priest, public prayers in the Roman world exhibited "audience design."[18] That is, prayers took into account and indeed constructed the different roles—addressee, participant, (over)hearer—of different hearers. Prayers relied for their intelligibility on, while informatively adding to, the beliefs of their addressees and hearers.

Now, in any speech act, a speaker *presupposes* propositional content that he or she does not *state* or encode semantically in the content of the utterance.[19]

---

16. The original discussion of perlocution is Austin 1962: 101–31.
17. See H. Clark and Carlson 1982.
18. On "audience design," see H. Clark and Carlson 1982: 342–47.
19. On *presupposition*, see Levinson 1983: 167–225; Yule 1996: 25–34. "Presupposition" does not name a mental state distinct from belief. Rather, the term distinguishes one pragmatic *role* among many that doxastic representations with mind-to-world direction of fit, i.e., beliefs, may play in discourse.

As Dan Sperber and Dierdre Wilson argue, "verbal communication involves both coding and inferential processes."[20] Thus, hearers not only *decode* the semantics of a speech act but also pragmatically *infer* and *accommodate* its speaker's presuppositions. Accommodation is the process through which we adopt a speaker's presuppositions and add them to the "common ground" of beliefs we share with the speaker.[21] That is, in the give and take of conversation, speakers and hearers dynamically alter their beliefs to match those of their interlocutors (barring reason for doubt or disagreement). In any speech-act scene, "certain information might be given ... 'common ground status' by a certain speech act even though it was not common ground before the speech act occurred."[22] Consider this example:

Hegio is grateful to Jupiter that Philopolemus has been returned to his father.[23]

The hypothetical speaker of this sentence *asserts* that Hegio is grateful. However, he or she *presupposes*—and this speaker may well be wrong—that Hegio, Jupiter, and Philopolemus exist ("existential presuppositions"), that the latter was separated from and then returned to his father, and that Jupiter was causally implicated in this event ("factive presuppositions"). Hearers infer and accommodate these presuppositions of the speaker, incorporating them as new information into their own database of beliefs, and tagging them as common ground between the speaker and themselves. Thus, in what is a form of the perspective-taking ability that we explored at section 7.3, the parties to a speech-act scene update the information in their common ground—their shared beliefs—in the course of interaction. This inferential process yields strongly shared *joint* Intentionality and *personal* common ground among interlocutors in conversation, but weaker *collective* Intentionality and *communal* common ground in cases of mere (over)hearing.[24]

Although I do not mechanically spell it out in every paragraph, the emphasis throughout this chapter should be felt to fall on the *effects* that hearing prayers has for third-party hearers, especially with respect to their doxastic uptake. I call these third-party hearers "culture learners," not because every Roman (over)hearing a prayer was necessarily encountering this aspect of Roman culture for the first time but rather to draw attention to the fact that because prayers were ubiquitous, integral, and content-rich components of all

---

20. Sperber and Wilson 1995: 3.
21. On *accommodation*, see Beaver and Zeevat 2007.
22. Stalnaker 2014: 56, citing Grice 1989: 274.
23. From Plaut. *Capt.* 922–23, quoted and discussed below.
24. For the joint/personal vs. collective/communal distinction, see above at section 4.3.4.

ritual activity, hearing prayers, not to mention learning and reciting them, constituted a critical part of any Roman's ongoing, lifelong social learning of his or her religious culture.[25]

I emphasize here prayers that embody *communicative intentions* and ignore cases where the intention in praying was arguably just to produce a locution or to make certain nonsemantic sounds and not thereby to communicate a discursive content, as perhaps was the case with the *Carmen Saliare*.[26] Of such cases, I would note only that even here speakers will have acted on beliefs: beliefs as to the appropriate sounds to utter, beliefs as to when and how to utter them, possibly even beliefs as to the sounds' ritual purpose.[27] In contrast to such cases, most Roman prayers embodied communicative intentions, that is, a speaker's intentions, by means of an utterance (1) to produce an effect in a hearer, and (2) to have the hearer recognize the speaker's intention to produce that effect.[28] Romans typically intended, by praying, to produce an effect in a god (for example, to get the god to respond in some way), and they intended that the god recognize that by praying they intended to

---

25. Prayer was not, of course, the only way a Roman learned his or her religious culture: see chapter 7, above, for some other contexts of cultural learning, and consider the roles of storytelling, the theater, and the artifactual environment, especially graphic representations of the gods, this latter remarked on by authors as widely separated in time and context as Cicero and Augustine: Cic. *N.D.* 1.29.81 and Aug. *Ep.* 91.4–5. I focus on prayer because Intentionalism is the theoretical center of this book and prayer possesses discursive Intentionality. I largely ignore philosophical approaches to prayer (e.g., Sen. *Ep.* 41.1; and see H. Schmidt 1907) though of course philosophical approaches to prayer would equally admit of an Intentionalist analysis. Of course, inscriptions, which were also ubiquitous, possess discursive Intentionality, too, and were an important source of religious information for the literate especially: see section 6.5 and Haensch 2007. Storytelling, the famous *aniles fabulae*, were another such source and did not presume literacy: see Massaro 1977; Heath 2011; and especially Johnston 2016.

26. As Quintilian remarks of this hymn, of which *cozeulodorieso* (FPL^4 3 *apud* Varro L.L. 7.26) is a notable fragment: *et saliorum carmina vix sacerdotibus suis satis intellecta* (*Inst.* 1.6.40).

27. Consider the *sounds* of Cato's spell (*Agr.* 160), which though devoid of semantic content were uttered with the *purpose* of effecting healing: *motas vaeta daries dardares astataries dissunapiter*. See further Versnel 2002: 106–8; and Mackey 2018a.

28. Grice 1989: 213–23. Let me be clear about the rationale for this characterization of communicative intentions. First, it is possible for a speaker's utterance to produce an effect in a hearer entirely *inadvertently*. For example, in response to pain I involuntarily yell, "ouch!" and upon hearing this you rush over to assist me. Second, it is possible for a speaker to *intend* to produce an effect in a hearer but to intend to produce this effect *without the hearer recognizing his or her intention for what it is*, as when, at Plaut. *Mil.* 1219ff., Milphidippa and Acroteleutium intend their words to produce an effect in the eavesdroppers Pyrgopolynices and Palaestrio, but also intend that this intention not be recognized by the eavesdroppers.

produce this effect. Roman prayer was thus, ideally, a matter neither of contentless, nonsemantic vocalization nor of merely going through the motions. Instead, at least ideally, Romans prayed with purpose and assumed that a speaker's prayers expressed his or her Intentional states.

Various sorts of evidence support this latter thesis. It is worth dwelling on this briefly because I have often encountered the notion, when publicly or privately sharing my theory about belief and cult, that the Romans "just did" such things as sacrifice and auspication without thinking too much about these activities and without having any beliefs one way or the other about them. One might rejoin that merely going through the motions, as well as merely "doing what's expected," is logically possible for anyone, for an Evangelical as much as for a Roman. Yet I would submit that what the Romans tell us about their praying renders any thesis as to its perfunctory nature less than compelling.

Consider an exemplary story. Valerius Maximus reports that when Scipio Aemilianus was performing his duties as censor (142/1 BCE), a scribe dictated to him the censor's prayer, which asked the gods to make Roman affairs, *populi Romani res*, "better and more extensive," *meliores amplioresque*. This formula gave Scipio pause. Roman affairs, in his estimation, were already "good and great enough," *satis bonae et magnae*. So, he altered the prayer to ask instead that the gods preserve the extant Roman *res* "unharmed," *incolumes*, and he had the prayer formula changed in the record books.[29] Presumably, if praying was a matter of mindlessly going through the motions, Scipio would not have worried about the content of the censor's prayer.

We hear, too, of people absorbed in meditative prayer, hardly something that happens to someone performing an "empty" routine. Thus, Ovid states: "I was entirely in my prayer: I sensed the divine presence" (*in prece totus eram: caelestia numina sensi*; Ov. *F.* 6.251). We also hear of petitioners making silent requests that reflect their true intention while masking these intentions with an insincere prayer spoken aloud. For example, the young Sulpicia prays silently for love even as she speaks aloud the prayer her mother dictates to her.[30] And Horace writes tellingly of the "good man," *vir bonus*, who prays loudly, *clare*, to Janus and Apollo, while secretly, afraid to be heard, *metuens audiri*, he prays to Laverna, goddess of thieves, that he might *appear* to be good, *da iusto sanctoque videri*, so that he can get away with all sorts of

---

29. Val. Max. 4.1.10: *qui censor* [sc. Scipio], *cum lustrum conderet inque solitaurilium sacrificio scriba ex publicis tabulis sollemne ei precationis carmen praeiret, quo di immortales ut populi Romani res meliores amplioresque facerent rogabantur, "satis" inquit "bonae et magnae sunt: itaque precor ut eas perpetuo incolumes seruent," ac protinus in publicis tabulis ad hunc modum carmen emendari iussit.*

30. Tib. 3.12.15–16, cited at chapter 7, n. 77.

wickedness.³¹ Moreover, it would make no cultural sense to advise a man, as the Sibyl advises Palinurus, that praying will not induce the gods to change his fate, unless it were commonly assumed that people do in fact express their sincere desires in prayer and pray because they hope to get the gods to fulfill those desires.³²

Finally, we must suppose that Romans would not have bothered to fulfill vows if their vowing had been devoid of content and sincerity.³³ Romans could theorize the sincerity proper to the related speech acts of oaths and promises³⁴ as *bona fides*, "good faith," and mark the sincerity of an oath with the phrase *ex animi sententia*.³⁵ Cicero, for example, writes (*Off*. 3.108):

> *Non enim falsum iurare periurare est, sed, quod "EX ANIMI TUI SENTENTIA" iuraris, sicut verbis concipitur more nostro, id non facere periurium est. Scite enim Euripides:*
> *Iuravi lingua, mentem iniuratam gero.*

> It is not perjury to swear an oath falsely [sc. as when you swear to pirates an oath that you do not intend to fulfill and that there is no requirement to fulfill], but it is perjury not to carry out that which you swore "in accord with your own mind's will," as we phrase it according to our custom. See Euripides [*Hipp*. 612]:
> I have sworn with my tongue, I bear a mind unsworn.

Here, Cicero looks behind the speech act of oath taking to the psychological state that the speech act expresses or deceptively appears to express, distinguishing the former as sincere and the latter as insincere. Sincerity, in this case, amounts to a commitment to the force (Commissive) and propositional content (p), insincerity a lack of such commitment. There is another form lack of commitment can take, beyond sincerity and purposeful insincerity, and that is the purely perfunctory. It is always possible that some Romans, maybe even

---

31. Hor. *Ep*. 1.16.57–62. Cf. Tib. 2.1.83–84.

32. Verg. *Aen*. 6.376: *desine fata deum flecti sperare precando*.

33. A monumental and very public index of Roman sincerity in this domain is the roughly fifty temples vowed and then duly dedicated between the years 396 and 219 (listed in Ziółkowski 1992: 187–88). See also Italian figurines and anatomical votives recorded in, e.g., the twenty-one volumes so far of *Archaeologica*'s *Corpus delle stipi votivi in Italia* (published by Giorgio Bretschneider Editore under the direction of Lucio Fiorini). For other means of publicizing one's fulfillment of a vow, such as displaying a notice in a procession, see Veyne 1983.

34. For promises in Roman law, see Gai. *Inst*. 3.92–93.

35. See Cic. *Off*. 3.43ff., esp. 58ff.; 3.102–10. For *bona fides* in Roman law, see Schermaier 2000. Fides also of course had a temple on the Capitoline from the middle of the third century: Ziółkowski 1992: 28–31. See, too, the complaint of Livy at 3.20.5.

most of them most of the time, prayed perfunctorily or "went through the motions." However, the texts I have surveyed here suggests that Romans, both in praying and in hearing prayers, took the *discursive* Intentionality of prayer, its Assertives, Directives, Commissives, and so on, as (ideally at least) a sincere expression of speakers' *psychological* Intentionality—their beliefs, desires, and intentions.

Thus, we may say that in Roman religion, what a culture learner is *given* is the words of a speaker's prayer, for example, to Apollo, asking him to send rain. The hearer might *infer* certain things about the speaker: for example, that the speaker entertains certain beliefs about Apollo and recognizes certain commitments to him. The hearer might also infer and *accommodate*, that is, come to believe, the speaker's presuppositions that Apollo exists and is capable of fulfilling his or her request by intervening causally in the physical domain to send rain. Building on these new beliefs, the hearer might infer additional things and form additional beliefs about Apollo. Finally, the hearer might as a result of all of this adopt a cult commitment toward the god similar to the speaker's commitment. In sum, prayers communicated theological representations as content. Cognition enriched that content through accommodation and other inferential processes. If culture is, as Dan Sperber has it, "the precipitate of cognition and communication in a human population,"[36] then a precipitate of prayer was Roman religious culture, with all its beliefs and practices.

Unlike a creedal religion such as Christianity, whose central speech act is that of asserting truths believed and to be believed, traditional Roman religion left hearers *cognitively autonomous*, free to infer speakers' beliefs from their prayers, to accommodate those beliefs or not, and to reflect on and form inferences from them, that is, to decide what they themselves believed about the gods, their causal powers, their dispositions toward worshippers, and so forth. As we shall see, various features of the human mind respond to *context* in ways that would have caused hearers' to appropriate quite seamlessly as their own (often nonreflective) beliefs (what they took to be) speakers' beliefs. These context-based cognitive biases include an overall bias to trust in testimony, reinforced by a bias to trust preferentially speakers of prestige and authority, and a bias to conform. In section 8.7 we discuss one such contextual factor, so-called credibility enhancing displays (CREDs), that is, actions that are consistent with or reflect, and so lend credence to, the content of what a speaker says. However, to get there we must first take an overview of Roman prayer.

---

36. Sperber 1996: 97.

8.3. Roman Prayer

Let us start with a passage central to the study of Roman prayer. Pliny the Elder asks whether the words of prayers, hymns, and incantations have any power: *polleantne aliquid verba et incantamenta carminum*. He notes that the wisest, *sapientissimi*, reject this belief, *respuit fides*, but that everyone else believes it quite nonreflectively: *credit ... nec sentit*: "they believe it and don't even realize it."[37] Thus, he points out, prayer is an indispensable component of all Roman religious action: "without prayer [*sine precatione*], it appears to do no good for victims to be sacrificed or for the gods to be ritually consulted."[38]

Pliny presents a taxonomy of prayer types, according to the purposes for which they are employed. Impetrative prayers elicit signs from the gods, as in auspice taking; others avert evil, as in expiation; and a third category, the *commendatio*, allows petitioners to entrust a person or thing to the gods.[39] Valerius Maximus presents an alternative taxonomy, which overlaps with *commendatio* and impetration, including in addition vows and prayers of thanksgiving.[40] We may add that there are also distinctions among prayer proper (*precatio*), which invokes the god(s) and accompanies ritual, enunciating its purpose, and hymn (*carmen*), which is typically conceived as an offering to the god(s).[41]

These remarks on the variable functions of prayer present an opportunity to follow up, in passing, on our discussion of the opacity of ritual from section 7.4.1. I would merely propose now, following an observation of John Scheid, that prayer tends to expose the *goal* of cult, thereby rendering it *teleologically* transparent. That is, the formulas of prayer, which "pronounce and realize through speech that which is accomplished by the ritual gesture,"[42] manifest the *end* to which the sequence of cult gestures is a *means*. Typically, as we shall see, Roman prayer asks the god(s) to do something, and it is enough

---

37. Plin. *Nat. Hist.* 28.3.10: *sed viritim sapientissimi cuiusque respuit fides, in universum vero omnibus horis credit vita nec sentit*.

38. Plin. *Nat. Hist.* 28.3.10: *quippe victimas caedi sine precatione non videtur referre aut deos rite consuli*.

39. Plin. *Nat. Hist.* 28.3.11: *praeterea alia sunt verba inpetritis, alia depulsoriis, alia commendationis*.

40. Val. Max. 1.1.1: *prisco etiam instituto rebus diuinis opera datur, cum aliquid conmendandum est, precatione, cum exposcendum, uoto, cum soluendum, gratulatione, cum inquirendum uel extis uel sortibus, inpetrito*. On these classificatory schemes, see Guittard 1987.

41. See Scheid 2007a and 2008, which carefully distinguish between prayer (*precatio*) and hymn (*carmen*).

42. Scheid 2007a: 445: "l'officiant prononce toujours une formule consacrée qui énonce et réalise par la parole ce qu'il accomplit par le geste cultuel." Cf. Scheid 2003a: 98–99.

to know that divine agents are doing that thing. Their (unseen) agency is the means. What remains opaque are the causal contributions of the ritual gestures. These actions remain causally opaque, for participants and observers alike, even when their teleology or purpose is disclosed in the content of the prayer.

Returning to Pliny, we find that he goes on to note the care that magistrates took in articulating the formulas of prayers with perfect precision. The result of fumbling a prayer could be a failed ritual (*H.N.* 28.3.11):

> *videmusque certis precationibus obsecrasse summos magistratus et, ne quod verborum praetereatur aut praeposterum dicatur, de scripto praeire aliquem rursusque alium custodem dari qui adtendat, alium vero praeponi qui favere linguis iubeat, tibicinem canere ne quid aliud exaudiatur, utraque memoria insigni, quotiens ipsae dirae obstrepentes nocuerint quotiensve precatio erraverit; sic repente extis adimi capita vel corda aut geminari victima stante.*

> we see that our highest magistrates supplicate with fixed prayers [*certae precationes*] and, so that no word is passed over or spoken out of place, that someone recites in advance from a script [*de scripto*] and, again, another attendant is provided to keep an eye on the recitation, another is appointed to order people to hold their tongues, and a flutist plays so that no other sound is heard. And there are in memory two kinds of remarkable instances, where bad omens have ruined the ritual with their noise, or where the prayer went wrong. Thus suddenly the lobe of the liver or the heart has disappeared from the entrails or been doubled while the victim was still standing.

This passage shows that Romans prayed with fixed, unchanging formulas: *certae precationes* written down and read *de scripto* for accuracy. Moreover, Romans declaimed prayers aloud. And finally, prayers accompanied all ritual activity. Thus, prayer formed a relatively invariable, pervasive, and unavoidable part of the religious environment and thus a relatively invariable, pervasive, and unavoidable source of cultural knowledge.

The fixity of prayer formulas reflects a need for precision. Servius writes: "In prayers nothing should be ambiguous."[43] It was not enough to mean well. One had to speak well too. If a speaker botched the wording of a prayer (*precatio erraverit*), however earnest his intentions, his verbal mistake might cause the god to reject his sacrifice, as indicated by cases where the victim was found to have extra or missing entrails.[44] To ensure accuracy, Roman magistrates could have as many as four attendants on hand, one to dictate, *praeire*, the

---

43. Serv. *ad Aen.* 7.120: *in precibus nihil esse ambiguum debet.*

44. Cf. Cicero's argument that the novice pontifex L. Pinarius Natta failed to dedicate his house to Libertas because in speaking the formula, "his mind and tongue wavered," *mente ac lingua titubante* (*Dom.* 139).

formulas of the prayer to the magistrate *de scripto*,[45] a second to guarantee the fidelity of the first, a third to maintain ritual silence among participants while the prayer was recited, and a fourth to play the flute, in order to mask any sound other than the words of the prayer.[46] In light of these and various other prayer-related practices and beliefs that he mentions, Pliny allows that we might well suppose that "the gods hear certain prayers and are moved by certain words,"[47] and we might, thus, have to answer Pliny's question about the power of words, with which this section opened, in the affirmative.

We happen to possess a prayer preserved in a priestly inscription. Between the eras of Augustus and Diocletian, the Fratres Arvales recorded their proceedings on marble in their sanctuary just outside Rome, where their prayer to the Lares, Marmar, and the Semones survives to us in an inscription dated to 218. Indeed, the priestly inscription describes the context of the prayer's utterance, stating that the Arval priests, after sequestering themselves in the *aedes* of Dea Dia, read the prayer from booklets, *libelli*.[48] The prayer, the *Carmen Arvale*, and its introductory words run as follows:[49]

> *Ibi sacerdotes |*
> *clusi, succincti, libellis acceptis, carmen descindentes tripodaverunt in verba haec*
> *Enos Lases iuvate, |*
> *[e]nos Lases iuvate, enos Lases iuvate! Neve luae rue Marma sins incurrere in pleores, neve lue rue Marmar |*
> *[si]ns incurrere in pleoris, neve lue rue Marmar sers incurrere in pleores!*
> *Satur fu, fere Mars, limen |*
> *[sal]i, sta berber, satur fu, fere Mars, limen sali sta berber, satur fu, fere Mars, limen s(al)i sta berber! |*

---

45. For the written prayers kept by the pontifices, see Aul. Gell. 13.23.1: *conprecationes deum immortalium, quae ritu Romano fiunt, expositae sunt in libris sacerdotum populi Romani et in plerisque antiquis orationibus*. For the *libri* of the priests, see Norden 1939; and North 1998.

46. Such care was taken with prayers but not with ritual gestures: Scheid 1990: 674–75: "Seules les prières étaient enregistrées intégralement et lues, éventuellement, *de scripto*, au cours du culte."; "Seules les paroles étaient notées avec précision, sans doute parce que, d'après une vieille tradition... elles étaient réputées plus trompeuses que les gestes simples composant les unités rituelles."

47. Plin. H.N. 28.3.13: *si semel recipiatur ea ratio, et deos preces aliquas exaudire aut ullis moveri verbis, confitendum sit de tota coniectatione*. Cf. 28.3.12: *cuius sacri* [sc. the live burial of Greeks in the *Forum Boarium*] *precationem qua solet praeire XVvirum collegii magister si quis legat, profecto vim carminum fateatur, ea omnia adprobantibus DCCCXXX annorum eventibus*.

48. On the Arvales' *libelli*, see Scheid 1990: 616ff.

49. CIL VI, 2104a, lines 31–38. The text I provide is that of Scheid 1990: 619n103 (cf. Courtney 1995: 34–35). My translation is deeply indebted to Scheid's French translation.

[Sem]unis alternei advocapit conctos, Semunis alternei advocapit conctos,
  Simunis alternie advocapit |
[conct]os! Enos Mamor iuvato, enos Mamor iuvato, enos Mamor iuvato!
  Triumpe, triumpe, triumpe, trium | [pe, tri]umpe!

  Enclosed there,
toga clad, having received their books, the priests tapped out a
  triple-time beat while scanning the song in the following words:
"Help us, Lares,
help us, Lares, help us, Lares! Mars, do not let plague and ruin fall
  upon your
people, Mars, do not let plague and ruin
fall upon your people, Mars, do not let plague and ruin fall upon your
  people!
  Be sated, savage Mars, jump
to the border, stand firm, be sated, savage Mars, jump to the border,
  stand firm, be
sated, savage Mars, jump to the border, stand firm!
Invoke, by turns, the Semones, all together, invoke, by turns, all the
  Semones,
  invoke, by turns, all the Semones!
Help us, Mars, help us, Mars, help us, Mars!
  Triumph, triumph, triumph, triumph, triumph!"

The *Carmen Arvale* was recited as just one part of a larger ritual for Dea Dia, an agricultural goddess. According to Varro, the task of the Fratres Arvales was to perform rituals to ensure that the fields bore fruit (*L.L.* 5.85). In John Scheid's interpretation, the *carmen* invoked Mars in order to secure the war god as guardian of the productive activity of the goddess Dea Dia. The Lares, gods of the earth, and the Semones, gods of seed, also invoked, attend to specialized tasks within the agricultural goddess's larger field of activity.[50]

The words of the *Carmen Arvale* date to the fourth century BCE. Writing preserved it for recitation long after its language had ceased to resemble ordinary usage. It is worth noting immediately that the "orthopraxy" of Roman prayer, as exampled especially graphically here, owes at least in part to the fact that Roman religion is rooted in a post-oral era. Unlike Vedic or Greek culture, Roman culture always already had writing, and this literacy impacted the fixity, exactness of transmission, and prescriptiveness that we have observed to be

---

50. Scheid 1990: 621–23.

characteristic of Roman prayer.[51] In their communications with their gods, it was not enough for the Romans simply to express their intentions or requests. Instead, communicating their intentions to the gods and obtaining their objectives required first and foremost that they pronounce exactly the right formulas, whose power was guaranteed by their observed efficacy over the course of hundreds of years.[52] All linguistic communication is of course conventional and norm governed, but none more strictly so than Roman prayers.

The point of these meditations on the fixity and prescriptiveness of prayer formulas is this: The very stability that was thereby conferred on Roman prayer will have guaranteed the communication of highly similar propositional contents and hence of similar conceptions of the gods over the generations. Although Roman prayers do not typically spell out an explicit theology, we shall see that, nonetheless, these prayer formulas, even those as difficult as the *Carmen Arvale*, contain in their propositional contents their own implicit folk theology, whose grasp and acquisition would not have required explicit theological instruction. Importantly, this folk theology represents a *practical* theology, ideal as a basis for religious action.

8.4. Prayer Form

In order to approach this implicit folk theology, let us take on board another prayer, and examine the highly typical tripartite formal structure it evinces. Cato prescribes an unostentatious little petition for the *porca praecidanea*, a preharvest sacrifice. He recommends that before the farmer harvest his fields he do as follows (*Agr.* 134):

> *fertum Iovi ommoveto et mactato sic: "Iupiter, te hoc ferto obmovendo, bonas preces precor uti sis volens propitius mihi liberisque meis, domo familiaeque meae, mactus hoc ferto."*

> Offer a cake to Jupiter and honor him thus: "Jupiter, in offering you this cake I pray to you good prayers (*bonas preces precor*) that you be willingly well disposed (*volens propitius*) toward me and my children, toward my house and my family, since you have been honored by this cake."

---

51. See further, Mackey 2018b: 624–25.

52. For Pliny, strange language was central to the effect of prayer: *H.N.* 28.4.20–21: *neque est facile dictu externa verba atque ineffabilia abrogent fidem validius an Latina inopinata et quae inridicula videri cogit animus semper aliquid inmensum exspectans ac dignum deo movendo, immo vero quod numini imperet.*

We see here a prayer of Pliny's *commendatio* type. The farmer is entrusting or commending himself and his family to Jupiter and his goodwill.

Cato's prayer neatly illustrates the formal analysis of Greek prayer, easily extended to Roman prayer, proposed over a century ago by Carl Ausfeld.[53] He noted that prayers tend to fall into three distinct parts: *invocatio*, *pars epica*, and *preces*. The point of the *invocatio* is to specify and get the attention of the divine addressee, here, Jupiter. The overall purpose of a prayer is contained in its *preces*, or petition, which makes a request of the god that has been invoked. Here, the farmer simply asks Jupiter to be "willingly well disposed." Ausfeld's *pars epica*, renamed the "argument" by Jan Bremer,[54] is an optional component. It is absent, for example, from the *Carmen Arvale*. It typically explains *why* the god should grant the petitioner's request. In our prayer, the "argument" consists of the fact that the farmer has offered a cake to Jupiter and thereby "honored" or "magnified," *mactare*, the god.

This typical structure contains its own implied theology, what I have called a folk theology. Let us take only the *invocatio* for now and note that in order to invoke a god at all, one must possess at least elementary theological knowledge.[55] As Varro admonished, we need to know "what force and ability and power" a god has in a given domain, and so "which god we ought to call upon and invoke" for a given purpose.[56]

The *invocatio*, flowing directly from this rudimentary, practical theological knowledge, contains not a complete speech act but a pragmatic feature of discourse known as deixis.[57] The vocative "Iupiter," like "Marmar" and "Lases" in the *Carmen Arvale*, is a "person deixis," singling out a god as addressee, including him in the context of the prayer's utterance, and thereby rendering the god as, in a sense, present.[58] The vocative would likely have been accompanied by a deictic gesture, which would have introduced the deity into the group of participants and linked him even more closely to the utterance and its context.

---

53. Ausfeld 1903.

54. Bremer 1981.

55. See Guittard 1998 for an analysis of the distinctively Roman features of the *invocatio*.

56. The fact that Varro felt he had to point this out suggests that he thought some of his contemporaries were confused: Aug. *Civ.* 4.22 = Var. *Ant. Div.* fr. 3 Cardauns: *eo modo nulli dubium esse asserens* [sc. Varro] *ita esse utilem cognitionem deorum, si sciatur quam quisque deus uim et facultatem ac potestatem cuiusque rei habeat. ex eo enim poterimus, inquit, scire quem cuiusque causa deum aduocare atque inuocare debeamus, ne faciamus, ut mimi solent, et optemus a Libero aquam, a Lymphis uinum.*

57. For deixis, I draw on Levinson 1983: 54–96; Yule 1996: 9–16; and Senft 2014: 42–75.

58. Sometimes quite literally present: e.g., Hor. *Ep.* 2.1.134: *poscit opem chorus et praesentia numina sentit*; Ov. *F.* 6.251: *in prece totus eram: caelestia numina sensi.*

The gesture in question in Jupiter's case would likely have consisted of raising hands to the sky,[59] a "spatial deixis" that localizes the god absolutely as well as in relation to the speaker and his context.[60] Etymologically, the name "Jupiter," and perhaps the gesture toward the sky, too, reflect a "social deixis" that distinguishes the god as "father" (*dyeu-pəter) and as the speaker's superior. Even if the etymology was obscure to Cato, the implication of a social hierarchy would have been crystal clear.[61]

So, in the act of invocation alone, the petitioner presupposes the existence, relative location, and status of the god he or she invokes. Any hearer would tend to *infer* that the speaker is acting on such presuppositions. Some contextual cue, such as the utterance of the prayer by an actor in a drama, would be required for an observer to infer otherwise. The point I wish to insist on is that the *mere act* of invoking a god put a speaker's beliefs, however nonreflective, into practice. That practice, the practice of praying, could inform a hearer / culture learner's folk theology by supplying him or her with material for inferences about the agency of the gods invoked.

As this analysis already suggests, Romans' prayers imply that their gods are rather human-like, especially in their psychology. It is not merely that the *invocatio* solicits the attention of a being who is therefore presupposed to be at least sentient and the *preces* addresses a discursive content to a being who is therefore presupposed to be sapient. It is also that the gods have affect and can make evaluative judgments. Jupiter, for instance, can be "honored," *mactus*, by his worshipper's offering. Presumably, he would not appraise every act or offering as "honoring." The god can, in response to the act, come to feel "well disposed" toward his worshipper, and do so willingly, *volens*. Merely to ask that Jupiter be "willingly well disposed" is to imply that the god can display the opposing attitudes: that he can be unwilling, or badly disposed, that he can refuse the *fertum* or fail to appraise it as an honor.

Thus, the gods were as *psychologically* anthropomorphic when invoked in prayer as they were *physically* anthropomorphic when represented graphically, in frescoes and *simulacra*. Indeed, this symmetry did not escape the notice of Roman philosophers.[62] However, the folk theology of prayer attributed to

---

59. Macr. *Sat.* 3.9.12: *cum Iovem dicit, manus ad caelum tollit.* Cf. Liv. 10.19.17, quoted below.

60. Cf. Lipka 2009: 11: the gods "had a place in this world, in which they moved freely"; "This conclusion is unavoidable, if we consider that all Roman gods could be invoked, and that invocation implied spatial proximity to the invocator."

61. See Dickey 2007: 121–22. Romans who considered the question saw the "*pater*" in *Iuppiter* but tended to suppose that *Iu-* derived from *iuvare*: see Maltby 1991 s.v. Iuppiter.

62. See the Epicurean Velleius's apology for physical anthropomorphism at Cic. *N.D.* 1.48. Quite different is Varro's allegorization of *simulacra*, whose similarity to human form, though

the gods not the abstract perfections of the philosopher's theology but the concrete *limitations* of human beings. For, generically, the *invocatio* of a prayer presumes that gods, like mortals, have limited focuses of awareness or attention. In Ovid's *Fasti*, at Romulus's founding of the city, he calls on all the gods to pay attention (4.829): *advertite cuncti!* The divine attention must be called away from wherever it may be if one hopes to have one's prayers heard. Similarly, the *pars epica* or argument, which establishes the "credentials" or "solvency" of the petitioner,[63] reminding the god of the parties' past interactions and calling the god's attention to present interactions, like Cato's cake offering, implicitly assumes a less than all-knowing and all-seeing deity. The god's memory of his petitioner's good works must be jogged.

The psychological anthropomorphism of Jupiter presupposed by Cato in this prayer, and of Mars and the Lares in the *Carmen Arvale*, appears so natural as to be unremarkable, because it taps our social-cognitive expectations so effortlessly. Representations of divine beings, such as those communicated by the Arval brethren and by the speaker of Cato's prayer, infiltrate human minds less because of their otherworldliness than because of their *this*-worldliness. As Henk Versnel once put it:[64]

> the believer of Antiquity approached his god, in word and deed, as though he was a great and powerful human being. Indeed, he had few other alternatives, either psychological or linguistic.

To represent the god in this way is to make him highly cogitable, for such representations recruit our folk-psychological resources for reasoning about mundane agents. As Justin Barrett writes, "people implicitly understand humans and gods by elaborating tacit assumptions about ... [human] agents."[65] Or as McCauley and Lawson put it, people's "intuitive assumptions about the psychology of agents purchase them vast amounts of knowledge about [gods] for free."[66] So, the *Carmen Arvale*, even if otherwise quite obscure, and certainly Cato's prayer would have conveyed, to speakers and hearers, through their vocatives and appeals, the gods' strange familiarity. These prayers presupposed gods with human-like, if inhuman, minds. Herein lies the foundation of Roman folk theology.

---

false, mystically reveals a truth: the similarity of divine and human minds: Var. *Ant. div.* fr. 225 Cardauns = Aug. *Civ.* 7.5.

63. Graf 1991, esp. 189.
64. Versnel 1981: 37–38.
65. Barrett 2002: 95.
66. McCauley and Lawson 2007: 227.

8.5. The Force of Prayer

Ausfeld's formal analysis, combined with an appreciation of pragmatics and social cognition, gave us one avenue by which to approach Roman folk theology. We can, however, probe the form and content of Roman prayers more deeply still, by analyzing a further aspect of their pragmatics, that is, the patterns of their speech acts. Speech act theory has been invoked to point out that Roman prayers are "performative." That is, prayers do things with words, such as submit requests, make promises, and so forth. We examined the five basic kinds of speech act, constituted by and named for the five basic illocutionary forces, above, at section 8.2 (and cf. at section 2.3). These five basic kinds of speech act may be described and exampled as laid out in figure 8.1:

Assertive: Expresses a speaker's belief that a state of affairs obtains.
Example: "This building is a *taberna*."

Directive: Expresses a speaker's desire that a hearer alter a state of affairs.
Example: "Pour me some *vinum*."

Commissive: Expresses a speaker's intention to alter a state of affairs.
Example: "I'll pay for it tomorrow."

Expressive: Expresses a speaker's attitude about a state of affairs.
Example: "Thanks for the *vinum*!"

Declaration: A speaker's creation of a state of affairs by declaring it created.
Example: "I ban you from my *taberna*."

Put otherwise:

Force	Psychological Mode	Propositional Content	
Assertive	Belief	that	this building is a *taberna*
Directive	Desire	that	you pour me some *vinum*
Commissive	Intention	that	I pay for it tomorrow
Expressive	Gratitude	that	you gave me some *vinum*
Declaration	Belief, desire, and intention[67]	that	I ban you from my *taberna*

FIGURE 8.1. Speech acts and psychological states.

---

67. Vanderveken 1990: 126; and cf. Vanderveken 1991: 73: "a speaker who makes . . . a successful declaration is . . . necessarily sincere. Indeed, he cannot mean to make the propositional content true in virtue of his utterance without *eo ipso* believing, desiring, and intending this utterance to bring out success of fit between language and the world."

We shall see in this section that any Roman prayer may contain and even be dominated by any of these five types of speech acts. However, perhaps the largest category of Roman prayer is the *petitionary*. Petitionary prayers express propositional contents not with the force of Assertion, that is, to state how the world *is* (word-to-world), but rather with the Directive force, as entreaties to addressees to *make* the world match speakers' verbal representations (world-to-word).[68] In petitionary prayer, a speaker tries to get his or her addressee, a divine being, to do something, where this "something" is contained in a propositional content, which the Directive expresses as the *substance* of its request.

The Directive speech act portion of a petitionary prayer falls naturally into Ausfeld's *preces*, Bremer's "petition." Looking back to Cato's prayer from the previous section, we may note that it explicitly signals its own petitionary pragmatics and employs redundancy to avoid ambiguity. For example, the farmer uses three different terms to capture his domestic scene—"children," "house," and "family"—and he refers twice to the cake he offers the god. In addition, he overspecifies Jupiter's desired psychological state, begging him to be "willingly well disposed" (*volens propitius*). Moreover, he does not merely pray, asking, "Please be well disposed." Rather, he uses a performative verb and internal accusative, constituting a *figura etymologica*, to mark metapragmatically that he "prays good prayers," *bonas preces precor*.

The speech acts of Cato's prayer map onto Ausfeld's scheme as follows.

invocatio: "Jupiter" Speech Act: (deixis)
pars epica: "in offering you this cake" Speech Act: Declaration
           "you have been honored by this cake" Speech Act: Assertive
preces: "I pray . . . you be . . . well disposed" Speech Act: Directive

We have already seen that the *invocatio* contains not a complete speech act but a deixis. In the *pars epica*, or argument, we find Declaratory and Assertive speech acts. First, Cato's farmer *performs* his offering by indirectly *declaring* that he is offering a cake to Jupiter.[69] That is, he offers the cake not only with a physical gesture but also by signifying the import of the gesture with the words, "in offering you this cake," *te hoc ferto obmovendo*. This clause verbally performs and thus *creates* the offering.[70] It also makes the fact of the offering public, creating common knowledge among mortal, god, and any third parties

---

68. For mind-to-world and world-to-mind direction of fit and speech acts, see at section 2.2.5.

69. See Searle 1979b on indirect speech acts, where the speech act's surface structure does not reflect its illocutionary function. Cato's Declaration, stated directly, would run, "I hereby offer you this cake."

70. Cf. Scheid 2003a: 32: prayer "was performative in that it realized" the ritual "gesture."

present. At the end of the prayer, the farmer asserts, as a fait accompli, that he has made an offering and notes the honor that has thereby accrued to Jupiter. Finally, as expected, the *preces* contains a Directive, a request that Jupiter adopt a positive disposition toward the farmer and his family. In order to ask this, the speaker must presuppose not only that the divine addressee *exists*, but also that he has the *causal capacity* to act in the way the request represents him as acting. Those hearing this prayer would pragmatically accommodate these presuppositions, barring any reasons that they might have (such as a considered atheism) not to do so.

If petitionary prayer is thus characterized by Directive speech acts, Expressives mark *supplicationes* of thanksgiving, as in Hegio's prayer in Plautus, *Captivi* (922–27):

> *Iovi disque ago gratias merito magnas,*
> *quom te redducem tuo patri reddiderunt*
> *quomque ex miseriis plurumis me exemerunt,*
> *quae adhuc te carens dum hic fui sustentabam,*   925
> *quomque hunc conspicor in potestate nostra,*
> *quomque haec reperta est fides firma nobis.*

> To Jupiter and the gods I give much well-deserved thanks,
> since they returned you, brought back to your father
> and since they released me from so many miseries,
> which I was enduring 'til now, while I was here without you,   925
> and since I see that *this* guy is under our control,
> and since *this* guy's promise has been shown firm to us.

This prayer is one long Expressive, in which the propositional contents, expressed in the five *cum* clauses, represent states of affairs that the speaker presupposes to obtain. The illocutionary force is one of expressing thanks for these states of affairs to the gods.[71] Obviously, in addition to beliefs about how things stand in the world, beliefs about the gods are also typically presupposed in such acts of thanking.

Commissive speech acts characterize *vota*. Livy attributes the following *votum* to the consul Appius Claudius Caecus. During the Third Samnite War, he turned for aid to the Italic goddess of war (10.19.17–18):

> *Dicitur Appius ... ita ut inter prima signa manibus ad caelum sublatis conspiceretur, ita precatus esse: "Bellona, si hodie nobis victoriam duis, ast ego tibi*

---

71. For some reflections on the state of our evidence regarding such prayers of thanksgiving, which we know were quite common, see Hickson-Hahn 2004.

templum voveo." [18] *Haec precatus, velut instigante dea, et ipse collegae et exercitus virtutem aequavit ducis.*

Appius ... in such a way as to be seen among the first standards, with hands lifted to heaven, is said to have prayed as follows: "Bellona, if today you grant us victory, then I vow you a temple." [18] Having prayed thus, as though the goddess were rousing them, Appius matched the courage of his colleague and his army to that of its leader.

invocatio: "Bellona"	Speech Act: (deixis)
pars epica: "I vow you a temple"	Speech Act: Commissive
preces: "today you grant us victory"	Speech Act: Directive

The conditional structure of this *votum* is straightforward.[72] The *preces* lies in the protasis (or antecedent): it is an indirect Directive, a request that the goddess grant the Romans victory. The *pars epica* indicates Appius's "solvency," that is, his capacity to offer the goddess something in return. It is found in the apodosis (or consequent), which expresses a Commissive, publicly committing Appius to a future action: the dedication of a temple to Bellona. Yet he commits himself to this action only on the condition that the goddess satisfy the Directive of his *preces*. For this prayer to be sincere, Appius must presuppose both that Bellona would *want* a temple and that she *can* grant the Romans victory. (Note, too, the way Appius plays to his human overhearers, by choosing a prominent place to pray.)

Our final prayer, an oath or *iusiurandum*, also comes from Livy. Many Roman prayers, such as those offered to Fortuna by a mother and her young child (as described by Prudentius at section 7.3), are individualistic. Such prayers feature a single petitioner addressing the deity as a *privata* or *privatus*, with a personal objective. In contrast, Ovid's hymn to Terminus from the previous chapter was collective. It was offered by a *group*, a family and neighbors, who sing together with the *shared* objective of praising the god. Less well-organized groups can also make collective speech acts. In Apuleius's *Metamorphoses*, for example, the aggregated crowd of Isiac worshippers testify *consona voce*.[73]

Livy's oath is collective in a different sense than is Ovid's group hymn or the testimony of Apuleius's crowd. It features a *collective agent*, that is, an individual who represents, and so can vow, on behalf of a group.[74] Here, the group

---

72. On conditional speech acts, see Searle and Vanderveken 1985: 157.

73. Apul. *Met.* 11.13, quoted and discussed at sections 3.4 and 4.1.

74. For such collective speech acts, see Meijers 2007. For Roman thinking about collective representation, see, e.g., Cic. *Off.* 1.124: *est igitur proprium munus magistratus intellegere se gerere personam civitatis debereque eius dignitatem et decus sustinere, servare leges, iura discribere, ea fidei*

is the Roman people, and the collective agents are nested: Marcus Valerius, a fetial priest, secures the right for himself and his colleagues (*comites*) to speak for the Roman people, whereupon he appoints a colleague, Spurius Fusius, as *pater patratus* to represent the fetial college in pronouncing the oath.[75] Fusius does not swear the oath as a *privatus*; he can swear only as a group member, as a Roman *fetialis*, and then only from the institutional position of *pater patratus*, with a collective, not personal, objective in view.[76] He does not swear on his own behalf alone, and, as we shall see, the oath is not binding on him alone, as was Appius's vow, but on the whole *populus* on whose behalf he swears.

According to Livy, Fusius seals with an oath Rome's first recorded treaty (*foedus*) between Rome and Alba Longa, dating to the reign of Tullus Hostilius.[77] The two parties agree to abide by certain conditions, and then (Liv. 1.24.7–8):

> *legibus deinde recitatis, "audi," inquit, "Iuppiter, audi, pater patrate populi Albani, audi tu, populus Albanus. ut illa palam prima postrema ex illis tabulis cerave recitata sunt sine dolo malo, utique ea hic hodie rectissime intellecta sunt, illis legibus populus Romanus prior non deficiet. [8] si prior defexit publico consilio dolo malo, tum ille Diespiter populum Romanum sic ferito ut ego hunc porcum hic hodie feriam; tantoque magis ferito quanto magis potes pollesque."*

> After reciting the conditions of the treaty, [Spurius Fusius, *pater patratus*] said: "Hear, Jupiter! Hear, *pater patratus* of the Alban people! Hear, Alban people! As these conditions have been openly rehearsed from first to last from these tablets or wax without malicious intent, and as they have been most exactly understood here today, from these conditions the Roman people will not be the first to defect. [8] If they will be the first to defect as a matter of the people's resolution, with malicious intent, then you, Jupiter, strike the Roman people just as I here today shall strike this hog, and strike them the more as you are greater in ability and power."

---

suae commissa meminisse. On the model of the *res publica*, Roman law comes to recognize that other groups such as *societates* and *collegia* may have representatives: e.g., *Dig.* 3.4.1.1 (Gaius 3 *ad ed. provinc.*): *actorem sive syndicum, per quem tamquam in re publica, quod communiter agi fierique oporteat, agatur fiat*.

75. Liv. 1.24.5–6.

76. The treaty and its attendant oath could not be made *inussu populi* (Liv. 9.5.1). For Status Functions, i.e., functions that can be performed only by persons of a certain status or position, see above, at section 5.3.1.

77. Liv. 1.24.4. On this *foedus*, see Gladhill 2016: 25ff., with full references to the scholarship on this episode. Rich 2011: 193–95 discusses the historical continuity of fetal treaty making.

invocatio: "Jupiter"	Speech Act: (deixis)
pars epica: "populus Romanus prior non deficiet"	Speech Act: Commissive
preces: "Audi"	Speech Act: Directive
"si prior defexit . . . populum Romanum . . . ferito"	Speech Act: Directive

The *fetiales* on the Alban side will have sworn a complementary oath (Liv. 1.24.9).

The prayer of the *pater patratus* features a complex configuration of interrelated speech acts, which I have mapped onto Ausfeld's tripartite structure (above). In this prayer the Commissive speech act consists not in a promise to do something for the god, as in the case of Appius's prayer, but rather in a promise not to violate a treaty among mortals. The main Directive speech act asks Jupiter to punish the group, the *populus Romanus*, but only provided the Romans fail to fulfill the conditions of their Commissive. That is, the god is directed to act, but only in case the Romans defect. This is the converse of Appius's prayer, where he commits himself to act, but only in case Bellona responds positively to his Directive.

Thus, the oath creates the practical commitments and obligations among speakers and hearers that it expresses in its propositional content. The prayer commits the Romans to *doing* and to *not doing*: to not defecting on their agreement with the Albans, to accepting divine punishment in the case of their defection, and so on. In this way, the oath creates a "socially binding force,"[78] that is, a deontology, a regime of rights and responsibilities among parties. Yet even as it does so, it also *informs* its hearers of the creation of this deontology and so alters or adds to their beliefs, which in itself carries potential practical outcomes. Herein lies its "audience design" (see section 8.2). The oath *addresses* only Jupiter. It performs a Commissive and a Directive with respect to the god, publicly making a request of and a promise to him. But the oath also explicitly *informs* the Alban people—*audi tu, populus Albanus*—of the commitments that it has created and of their content. The Romans' stated commitment to certain actions and inactions thus becomes itself a matter of Alban belief. Presumably, the belief that the Romans recognize certain commitments vis-à-vis both Jupiter and themselves will guide future Alban action with respect to the Romans. Note that all of this is intelligible, and certainly most effective, only given a shared background of theological beliefs among the human parties, such as that Jupiter is apprised of and cares about the

---

78. Seuren 2009: 133ff.

commitments entered into by mortals. We return to the theology of Jupiter presupposed by this prayer in section 8.6.

For now, let us consider one last prayer, employed by augurs in the ritual of *inauguratio* for creating priests. We may reconstruct its relevant features with the help of Varro and Livy. (We return to this ritual in the following chapter in order to explore it further and trace some of its other cognitive implications.) The augur stands with the candidate for priesthood on the Capitoline *arx*, or "citadel," and creates a *templum in aëre*,[79] that is, an augurally significant space within his visual field. He does this, Livy tells us, by mentally dividing his visual field into sections—*animo finivit*—and by reciting a prayer to the gods.[80] The words that the augur spoke were, Varro tells us, as follows (*L.L.* 7.8):[81]

*templa tescaque m(eae) (fines) ita sunto
quoad ego easte lingua nuncupavero.
ollaber arbos quirquir est quam me sentio dixisse
templum tescumque m(ea) f(inis) esto in sinistrum.
ollaner arbos quiquir est quod me sentio dixisse
templum tescumque m(ea) f(inis) esto dextrum.
inter ea conregione conspicione cortumione
utique ea f(ini) rectissime sensi.*

Let temples and wild lands, my boundaries, be thus,
as I shall have named them with my tongue.
That tree, whatever it is, which I deem myself to have named,
let it be temple and wild land, my boundary, to the left.
This tree, whatever it is, insofar as I deem myself to have named it,
let it be temple and wild land, my boundary, to the right.
Between these points, by delimiting, viewing, internally seeing,
as far as I have most correctly deemed, this being the boundary.

Much is obscure in this prayer.[82] Yet it seems certain that the augur is demarcating his *templum in aëre*, the space within which he will look for divine signs. He chooses a tree to his left and a tree to his right to form the boundaries of his *templum*, and hence of his field of augural vision. After establishing the boundaries of the *templum*, the augur bisects it into left and right halves in his

---

79. For the *arx*, see Varro, *L.L.* 7.6; for the *templum in aëre*, see Serv. *ad Aen.* 1.92.

80. Liv. 1.18.7: *deos precatus*.

81. Linderski 1986a: 2273. I cite the text of the prayer from Linderski 1986a: 2269, which reproduces the text of Norden 1939. I have modified the translation of Beard et al. 1998: 2.86.

82. See esp. Varro's own interpretation at *L.L.* 7.9ff. and see Linderski 1986a: 2267ff.

mind, *animo finivit*, by reference to a landmark, a *signum*, on the horizon opposite him.[83] Varro's prayer marks all these operations with the words *conregio*, "delimiting"; *conspicio*, "viewing; and *cortumio*, a word that Varro, claiming to follow the augurs' own interpretation, glosses as "from the vision of the heart," *a cordis visu*.[84] According to Livy, the augur then asks Jupiter to send "clear signs," *signa certa*, and he requests that the signs appear "within the boundaries that I have established," *inter eos fines quod feci*.[85] Jupiter will send auspices into the left half or the right half of the *templum* to mark his approval or disapproval of the inauguration of the candidate, the *inaugurandus*.

Note that Varro gives us a prayer composed largely of Declarations.[86] It does not conform easily to Ausfeld's tripartition, having no *invocatio* or *pars epica*. If we assume that the prayer as transmitted by Varro is incomplete and should be filled out by the request for *signa certa* recorded by Livy, then it does have a Directive *preces*. It serves solely to construct a piece of religious reality through its Declaratory speech acts, which consist grammatically of imperatives: *meae fines ita sunto, mea finis esto* (twice). Moreover, the augur metapragmatically marks these Declaratory speech acts as such: "as I shall have named them with my tongue," *quoad ego easte lingua nuncupavero*, and "which I deem myself to have named," *quiquir est quam* (also *quod*) *me sentio dixisse*. The augur builds his *templum* through acts of visual attention, mental division, and Declaratory prayer. Words, then, have the power not only to entreat the gods, promise the gods, and thank the gods, but also to construct institutional religious realities recognized and respected by the gods.

This small sample of Roman prayers permits us to draw some preliminary conclusions about their speech-act components. The primary *point* of a great many Roman prayers is to prompt a divine addressee to do something, so prayers tend to feature a Directive speech act in the *preces* or petition. The Directive unites a variety of cultic uses of language, such as the magical incantation and the hymn (both can be denoted by *carmen*, though they are distinct genres), and the prayer proper (*precatio*), all of which otherwise belong to different contexts.[87] Meanwhile, in the *pars epica* or argument we have seen

---

83. Liv. 1.18.8: *signum contra quod longissime conspectum oculi ferebant animo finivit*. See further, Magdelain 1969: 261; and Linderski 1986a: 2287–89.

84. *L.L.* 7.9. See Linderski 1986a: 2289n570.

85. Liv. 1.18.9.

86. See at section 5.3.2 for more on the role of Declarations in the construction of Roman religious reality.

87. For magical incantations, see the examples collected from Plin. *Nat. Hist.* and discussed in Gaillard-Seux 2014. For the distinction between prayer (*precatio*) and hymn (*carmen*), see Scheid 2007a and 2008.

Commissives, Declarations, and Assertives. With a Commissive, the petitioner attempts to motivate the addressee to fulfill a Directive by committing to perform some action in return. This is the *votum* type of prayer. Other prayers, for example, those intended to thank the gods, may employ Expressives. Finally, prayers may use Declarations. In some, the petitioner tries to motivate the addressee by performing a service on the spot, such as making an offering. Here, the worshipper creates through Declaration some new state of affairs he or she presupposes the divine addressee will value. (The worshipper may then refer to the state of affairs his or her Declaration has created with an Assertive.) This is the *do ut des* type of prayer. Yet other prayers, such as that of Varro's augur, use Declaratory speech acts to create religious realities or institutions within the context of which humans and gods may act cooperatively.

8.6. Counterintuitive Content

Now that we have surveyed, all too hastily, the illocutionary forces characteristically applied in Roman prayer, we may turn to the question of prayer's larger *cognitive implications*. What does it imply about a speaker's beliefs and other Intentional states that he or she makes requests of the gods? What does it imply for a hearer to hear such requests made? What of promising the gods and of hearing such promises made? Of thanking the gods and of hearing such thanks? Of creating and using such institutional realities as the *templum in aëre* as a space for cooperative religious action with the gods? We may approach our answer by considering not only the expressed *propositional content* of prayer but also what is *presupposed* but not explicitly expressed in praying.

We have already seen that the sheer pragmatics of Roman prayer implies that the gods are psychologically anthropomorphic, like other social agents, with at least mundane mental capacities and proclivities. Thus, to focus on Directives for a moment, we note that requests made of divine agents will sometimes be correspondingly mundane. For example, the prayer of Cato's farmer requests only that Jupiter be well disposed toward him and his family. That an agent might come to be psychologically well disposed is entirely intuitive, in line with our normal expectations about agents. In such cases, where Romans interact with gods in practical contexts rather than theorize about them in the abstract, one would not expect cognitively unnatural, highly abstruse, theologically sophisticated representations of gods to arise.[88] Instead,

---

88. For "theological correctness," see at section 2.6.1, above.

one expects and sees quite intuitive folk-theological representations of the gods such as this.

We have seen, thus far, that Roman prayer implicitly represents the gods as rather *similar* to human beings. However, research into the transmission of religious representations isolates some precise ways in which representations of gods *differ* from our intuitive understanding of human agents and are, thus, in a technical sense that we shall explore, *counterintuitive*. Often in petitionary prayer, the substance of the request or the divine agent addressed, or both, are counterintuitive in this way. That is, the prayer's propositional content represents the god, his mind, or his requested action in ways that go beyond our intuitive folk-psychological expectations about ordinary agents, their minds, and their potentialities for action. Such counterintuitive properties appear to be the hallmark of religious representations. In a sense, the cognitive research we are about to explore spells out in psychological terms what careful historians have noted about ancient gods. Albert Henrichs, for example, identified the defining properties of the Greek gods as anthropomorphism (intuitively like human agents), but also immortality and extraordinary power (counterintuitively unlike human agents).[89] Here, we focus especially on the counterintuitive powers of the Roman gods, as disclosed in prayer.

Pascal Boyer hypothesized that the appeal, memorability, and cultural salience of representations of gods in different times and places owes to the fact that these representations systematically tend to violate the intuitive expectations of such cognitive faculties as folk psychology, folk physics, and folk biology.[90] Boyer calls the intuitive expectations about the properties of objects, agents, and their interactions that are brought to bear by folk psychology and these other faculties "intuitive ontologies." That is, a typically developing human being with a typical neurology will tend intuitively and nonreflectively to divide up the world of existing things into certain categories and to expect that the entities in these categories just *are* a certain way. He provides evidence for five basic intuitive ontological categories: NATURAL OBJECT, ARTIFACT, PLANT, ANIMAL, and HUMAN.

Throughout this book we have dwelt at some length on the intuitive expectations that our faculties of social cognition bring to bear to define our intuitive ontological category HUMAN. Humans, for example, have minds with (often hard to infer) beliefs, desires, and intentions, and their behavior is both explicable and predictable with reference to the contents of these minds. All our

---

89. Henrichs 2010.

90. Boyer's work in this area begins with Boyer 1992b and develops through, e.g., Boyer 1994a, 1994b, 1996, 2000, and 2001.

intuitive ontologies—such as the folk-psychological expectations in the HUMAN category—may be violated in one of two ways: *breach* or *transfer*. The notion of an invisible stone *breaches* our expectation that midsized natural OBJECTS are visible. The notion of a talking bush involves a *transfer* of at least some intuitive expectations from the category HUMAN to the category PLANT. Invisible stones and talking bushes are "counterintuitive," in Boyer's terms, in that they violate the tacit expectations about the nature and properties of such objects embodied in our developmentally natural cognitive faculties. Counterintuitive representations can be memorable and appealing, making them highly transmissible and likely to find their way into a repertoire of cultural representations. These representations rub our intuitions the wrong way, which makes them jump out and spurs inferences: for example, what might the talking bush have to say to me?

Many successful representations of gods tend to be counterintuitive in precisely these ways. Gods characteristically make heavy use of the category HUMAN, while at the same time *breaching* select intuitive expectations about humans, such as our physical expectations (with, for example, invisibility or the ability to be present anywhere), our biological expectations (with, say, immortality), and our psychological expectations (with, for example, super-knowledge). Many gods will tend to be "minimally counterintuitive agents" or "MCI agents,"[91] breaching (or transferring) very few of our intuitive expectations,[92] so as to be attention grabbing and memorable, without requiring a great deal of conscious deliberation and reflection to recall, reason about, and communicate to others. Note that such theological beliefs are culture specific and will tend to be *reflective*, because they are not straightforwardly *intuitive*.

None of this is to say that massively counterintuitive gods, such as the deity of the monotheistic traditions, have not been dramatically successful. Yet even the G-d of Moses Maimonides, about whom nothing predicable of human beings could be positively predicated, is still fundamentally an *agent* who depends on our social cognitive intuitions to be conceptualized at all (even if only to insist that we cannot conceptualize Him). Such massively counterintuitive gods require constant, deliberate, reflective cognitive effort to be "thought" in theologically correct ways, and believers always risk defaulting to cognitively more natural, and "theologically incorrect," thinking.[93]

---

91. See Barrett 2004a: 22ff. The term "minimally counterintuitive," or MCI, was coined by Justin Barrett in Barrett 2000: 30.

92. How many violations of intuitions are "minimal" has been debated: see Barrett 2008.

93. Cf. McCauley 2011: 242.

The full range of categories and their possible breaches and transfers, adapted from Boyer 2000, is schematized below:

1) NATURAL OBJECT + *breach* of physical expectations
2) NATURAL OBJECT + *transfer* of biological expectations
3) NATURAL OBJECT + *transfer* of psychological expectations
4) ARTIFACT + *breach* of physical expectations
5) ARTIFACT + *transfer* of biological expectations
6) ARTIFACT + *transfer* of psychological expectations
7) PLANT + *breach* of physical expectations
8) PLANT + *breach* of biological expectations
9) PLANT + *transfer* of psychological expectations
10) ANIMAL + *breach* of physical expectations
11) ANIMAL + *breach* of biological expectations
12) ANIMAL + *breach/transfer* of psychological expectations
13) HUMAN + *breach* of physical expectations
14) HUMAN + *breach* of biological expectations
15) HUMAN + *breach* of psychological expectations

The hypothesis is that a representation of a god can be only so counterintuitive if it is to find secure purchase in people's minds and become widespread in a population, without the benefit of the extensive theological training that has often been characteristic of the Abrahamic religions. Experiments suggest that counterintuitive representations have a circumscribed "cognitive optimum" in terms of the number and kinds of violations of intuitive expectations they may manifest.[94] In memory experiments, for example, subjects tend not to recall representations that are entirely intuitive, such as, for example, a normal old man. Conversely, subjects recall only slightly better representations that are just bizarre, *too* counterintuitive. These tend to baffle domains of intuitive knowledge such as folk psychology. Consider the following representation: an invisible old man who knows what will happen to you next week but ceases to exist whenever you think about him. This violates a host of our default assumptions about agents and in so doing places excessive strain on our cognitive processing or reasoning systems. However, minimally

---

94. Empirical testing of Boyer's theories with subjects from a variety of religious traditions and countries is documented in Boyer and Ramble 2001; and Barrett and Nyhof 2001. Such testing has become a cottage industry: see, e.g., Norenzayan, Atran, et al. 2006; Barrett et al. 2009; Gregory and Barrett 2009; C. Johnson et al. 2010; and Banerjee et al. 2013. See Lisdorf 2004 for an analysis of the prodigies reported by Livy that finds that 99 percent of them are strictly minimally counterintuitive, featuring only a single violation. See Purzycki and Willard 2016 for a critical reassessment of MCI theory.

counterintuitive (MCI) representations may attain a "cognitive optimum"[95] for memorability, transmissibility, and inference-generating potential. These mostly conform to our developmentally natural expectations, which makes them cognitively manageable, while still violating a few expectations, which makes them attention grabbing and salient. Examples would include an invisible old man and an old man who knows your future.

So, how does Boyer's theory help us understand the representation of Roman gods in prayer? The folk theology implicit in Cato's little prayer to Jupiter (section 8.4) draws primarily from the category HUMAN, as we saw, and imputes few if any counterintuitive properties to the god. Yet one regularly encounters the gods represented otherwise, as significantly more than human, with counterintuitive properties, as Boyer defines these, attributed to or implied of them. To take a single example, consider Cicero's description of *Iuppiter Optimus Maximus, cuius nutu et arbitrio caelum, terra, mariaque reguntur,* "Jupiter Best and Greatest, by whose nod and will heaven, earth, and sea are governed."[96] Representations such as this suggest gods with counterintuitive properties of causation, properties that breach our ordinary physical expectations. For the default, observed already in infants, is to assume that an agent can have effects on or enter into causal relations only with those physical objects with which the agent can come into contact.[97] This expectation would make Jupiter's governance of *caelum, terra,* and *maria* by means of *nutus* or *arbitrium* counterintuitive indeed. As we shall see, in prayer the Roman gods were often represented in equally counterintuitive ways, and the requests made of them frequently presupposed that they had similarly counterintuitive powers.

Let us ease into this field of contentions by noting that at times the Roman *manner* of praying could of itself imply that the gods possessed counterintuitive properties. Cicero tells us, for instance, that people implicitly assume that the gods can "hear" their wishes even in silent prayer.[98] Of course, it must be acknowledged that the vast majority of praying was done out loud. But the cases of silent (or at least quiet) prayer that we have are compelling. For example, a Roman might explicitly appeal to the gods' extraordinary perceptual powers in the context of silent prayer, as Sulpicia does with the verb *sentio*: "since, as a god, you perceive all things (*omnia sentis*), grant it: what does it

---

95. Boyer 1994b: 121.

96. Cic. *Rosc. Am.* 131.

97. For research on these intuitive expectations in infants, see Spelke, Phillips, and Woodward 1995.

98. Cic. *Div.* 1.129: *homines, etiam cum taciti optent quid aut voveant, non dubitent quin di illud exaudiant.* On silent prayer generally, see Van der Horst 1994.

matter if he asks in secret or openly?"[99] The mere act of praying silently thus suggests that Romans might represent divine addressee(s) as superperceptive, as *breaching* ordinary expectations about the psychology of agents, in whose consciousness, we normally assume, anything not communicated aloud or appearing sensibly goes unregistered. In silent prayer, the gods are presupposed as capable of "hearing" petitions stated only in the mind (or perhaps under the breath, or behind closed doors).

Other prayers we looked at in the previous section (8.5) reinforce the thesis that the gods could, at least in some contexts, perceive private thoughts. Even if not consistently represented as omniscient per se, Roman gods were nonetheless presupposed to be "full-access strategic agents," that is, sapient beings with access to information of existential importance or pressing social relevance to *us*.[100] The gods know, even if we do not, who among us is plotting, cheating, lying, or hiding something. Thus, the prayer of Livy's *pater patratus* presupposes or at least invites the inference that Jupiter can know whether or not the treaty truly has been entered into *sine dolo malo*, "without malicious intent," as the *pater patratus* states.[101] This flirts with, even if it does not outright amount to, an implicit folk theology in which Jupiter can access individuals' private mental states. For how else could he know the Romans' inmost intentions? The prayer also presupposes that Jupiter can know if the Romans defect from the treaty "as a matter of the people's resolution, with malicious intent," *publico consilio dolo malo*. If it is a matter of "the people's resolution," it is hardly a matter of private mental states. Nonetheless, we see here the notion that the god has privileged access to social information relevant to our terrestrial cooperation and conflicts. You may be able to fool your human treaty partners about your public deliberations back home, and you may be able to disguise your malicious intent, but the prayer's implication is that these things do not escape the god.

Even if we leave the god out of consideration, the public prayer of Livy's *fetialis* functions as what Michael Chwe has called a "rational ritual," because it advertises the shared beliefs, intentions, and commitments of the human

---

99. Tib. 3.11.19–20: *at tu, Natalis, quoniam deus omnia sentis, / adnue: quid refert, clamne palamne roget?*

100. Boyer 2001: 150–60; Purzycki, Finkel, et al. 2012; Norenzayan 2013, esp. 13–32 and 118–39.

101. *Dolus malus* is the opposite of *bona fides*, discussed above (see at n. 35). On *dolus malus*, see Cic. *Off.* 3.60, reporting the definition of the jurist C. Aquilius: *cum esset aliud simulatum, aliud actum*. Cf. Labeo's definition at *Dig.* 4.3.1.2: *dolum malum esse omnem calliditatem fallaciam machinationem ad circumveniendum fallendum decipiendum alterum adhibitam. Dolus malus* versus *bona fides*: *Dig.* 17.2.3.

actors, Roman and Alban alike, thereby generating common knowledge among them and thus fostering their cooperation.[102] Note in this connection that Varro etymologically associates the words for the priest (*fetialis*) and treaty (*foedus*) with *fides publica*, the public "trust" or "trustworthiness" that allows for cooperation between peoples.[103]

Factoring the gods back in, Roman folk theology allows us to extend Chwe's formulation of rational ritual. Given an implicit attribution of extraordinary perceptual powers to Jupiter and other gods, I would posit that what we have in Livy's *fetial* oath is a *superrational ritual*. The prayer promotes cooperation and coordination even more effectively by including the god (*"audi, Iuppiter!"*) as a transaction partner, along with the human partners, within its circle of common knowledge. The god knows not only what the mortals know but critical additional information besides. Jupiter has unique insight into the good faith (*fides*) or deceptiveness (*dolus malus*) of the swearers of the oath, and he is in a unique position to monitor the decisions later taken by the peoples on either side. His inclusion guarantees that the parties are not mistaken in their beliefs about one another's intentions, and this increased certainty promotes mutual trust. With his access to the intentions, malicious or otherwise, of all parties, Jupiter acts as referee and hence as guarantor of nondefection.

Cicero makes precisely such a point about the nexus of folk theology and cooperation when he alludes to the *utility* of such beliefs about the gods (*Leg.* 2.16):

> *utilis esse autem has opiniones quis neget, quom intellegat... quam... sancta sit societas civium inter ipsos, diis immortalibus interpositis tum iudicibus tum testibus?*

> Who could deny that these beliefs [sc. about gods] are useful, when he perceives how holy is the partnership [*societas*] of citizens among themselves, when the immortal gods have been brought in at once as judges [*iudices*] and as witnesses [*testes*]?

Gods such as Jupiter render social bonds inviolable by keeping a superseeing eye on all parties to contracts and agreements. Note especially the term

---

102. Chwe 2001. For similar arguments applied to Greek oaths, see Williamson 2013. I thank Christina Williamson for discussion *per litteras* of this topic.

103. Var. *L.L.* 5.15.86 *Fetiales, quod fidei publicae inter populos praeerant: nam per hos fiebat ut iustum conciperetur bellum, et inde desitum, ut foedere fides pacis constitueretur. Ex his mittebantur, ante quam conciperetur, qui res repeterent, et per hos etiam nunc fit foedus, quod fidus Ennius scribit dictum.*

denoting privileged sensory knowledge: *testes,* "witnesses." Such gods possess, if perhaps not omniscience, then counterintuitive powers of superperception and so, as "full access strategic agents," serve as reliable *testes* and *iudices*,[104] attending with moral concern to (at least some domains of) human interactions.

My suggestions about Cicero and the fetial ritual are broadly congruent with two partially overlapping theories: the "supernatural punishment hypothesis" of Dominic Johnson and the "big gods" theory of Ara Norenzayan.[105] On these theories, the cultural evolution of moralizing gods who were disposed to punish or reward human behavior deepened and broadened human cooperation by providing superhuman incentives to adhere to social norms and other obligations. I ignore all sorts of controversial aspects of these theories, but the basic idea is that when we all know that we are being watched (and we all know that we all know it) by concerned full-access strategic agents, as represented in Livy's fetial prayer and in Cicero's *iudices* and *testes*,[106] we are less likely to defect on norms and obligations and more likely to behave in prosocial and cooperative ways. This facilitates large-scale cooperation beyond the small band or tribe.

On the account I have just offered, Roman folk theology did not need to attribute to the gods (however implicitly) full omniscience or unambiguous powers of seeing the secrets in the hearts of mortals in the manner of the God of the Psalms.[107] It merely presupposed more-than-human powers of observation. We shall note how Roman prayer presupposes divine powers to intervene in the world in *physically* and *biologically* counterintuitive ways momentarily, but for now please note how skewed toward the *psychologically* counterintuitive Roman gods tend to be on the evidence just reviewed. The gods perceive everything relevant to human beings, far more than any human could intuitively be thought capable of perceiving.

The augural procedure discussed at section 8.5 implies not only that Jupiter has superpowers of perception but that he can, in addition, exert counterintuitive psychological causation, not over his own body, but over the body of other living things, birds in this case, who make up the *auspicia ex avibus* that he sends to signal his will. Livy tells us that the augur specified in words the

---

104. The gods are *iudices* in other authors, too, e.g., Liv. 9.1.7: *quid dis arbitris foederis debeo?*

105. D. Johnson 2015, updated in D. Johnson 2018; Norenzayan 2013, updated in Norenzayan, Shariff, et al. 2016. For some criticisms, see Whitehouse et al. 2019.

106. For a sense of Roman beliefs about divine interest in human treaties and divine punishment for their rupture, see the speech of Gaius Pontius at Liv. 9.1.

107. E.g., Psalm 44:21 (KJV): "Shall not God search this out? for he knoweth the secrets of the heart."

precise *auspicia* that he wanted Jupiter to send.[108] We do not possess the wording of this request.[109] Yet it seems to presuppose that Jupiter can causally usurp the agency of birds, in order to direct their flight and cries. It is one thing for Jupiter to receive the epithet *omnipotens*, as he sometimes does in our literary sources,[110] but it is quite another for counterintuitive causal power over the volition of birds to be made available for inference in the verbal formulas of a prayer and thus made a part of cult practice. (We return to this feature of augural ritual in chapter 9.) We need not suppose that *omnipotens* meant for the Romans anything like what it would later mean in Christian theology. As with the attribution of "all-perceiving," the "all" here (*omni-*) merely means "all that is relevant to us in our present context."

This skewing toward the psychologically counterintuitive can be seen in other ways as well. Sometimes, for example, the wording of a prayer leaves a "theological vacuum"[111] regarding the precise mechanisms of divine action. Given the cognitive autonomy of Roman religion, speakers and hearers may fill this vacuum by inference or not, leaving the causal details hazy. Generally, it appears that people tend in their causal inferences to attempt to *minimize* the counterintuitive properties of the gods. So, they will fill the theological vacuum with natural intuitions about agents, defaulting to assumptions of psychological causation rather than physical or biological causation as the most plausible mode of divine agency.

We saw this in Appius's prayer requesting that Bellona grant victory to the Romans. By what causal mechanism could an agent who is not a soldier on the ground grant victory or decide a battle? Livy represents Bellona's causal agency as psychological or *as if* psychological: the courage of Appius and his men mounts "as if the goddess were rousing them," *velut instigante dea*.[112] It is more consonant with our ordinary expectations that a distant agent—recall that Appius had raised his hands up to heaven—might rouse an army *psychologically* than that she might *physically* hinder or harm the enemy. After all, young children already grasp that one person can affect another psychologically at a distance, through language and gesture.[113] Thus, *instilling* thoughts and emotions in others is more intuitive (less counterintuitive) than *perceiving* the secret Intentional states of others. That an MCI agent might instill thoughts and

---

108. Liv. 1.18.10: *tum peregit verbis auspicia quae mitti vellet*.

109. See Linderski 1986a: 2293–94.

110. E.g., Cat. 64.171; Ov. *M.* 1.154; Val. Max. 1.6.12.

111. Barrett 2001: 260 and 268.

112. Cf. Liv. 10.19.21: *Appius Bellonam victricem identidem celebrans accenderet militum animos*.

113. Shwe and Markman 1997.

emotions as Bellona does is an even more natural inference than that such an agent might exert physical causality from a distance, which in our intuitive understanding requires contact.

With all of that said, we must note that Roman prayers could also represent divine agents as breaching normal expectations in the physical and biological domains. We can see this in a prayer to Mars recorded by Cato. The farmer is to offer the god, in his archaic guise of agricultural deity, a *suovetaurilia*, that is, a sacrifice of a pig, a sheep, and a bull. Then the farmer is to pray to the god (*Agr.* 141):

> *uti tu morbos visos invisosque, viduertatem vastitudinemque, calamitates intemperiasque, prohibessis, defendas, averruncesque; utique tu fruges, frumenta, vineta, virgultaque grandire beneque evenire siris, pastores pecuaque salva servassis duisque bonam salutem valetudinemque mihi, domo, familiaeque nostrae.*

so that you might keep away, ward off, and remove diseases, seen and unseen, barrenness and destruction, ruin and inclement weather; and so that you might permit my produce, my grain, my vineyards, and my plantations to flourish and to turn out well, preserve in health my shepherds and my flocks, and give good health and strength to me, my house, and my family.

The speech act of note here is the single, complex Directive, running from "keep away . . . diseases," through "permit my produce . . . to turn out well," to "preserve in health . . . my family." The farmer presupposes that Mars can intervene in the *biological* domain, that is, the domain of living bodies, in a number of counterintuitive ways. He can ward off disease from the farmer's fields and foster their fertility. He can also protect and promote the health of the farmer and his household. Moreover, Mars can intervene causally in the *physical* domain, the domain of objects and force, in order to protect the fields from inclement weather. Finally, Mars breaches normal expectations about mundane agents' *psychological* powers in that he is represented as able to detect the undetectable: *morbi invisi*, the invisible blights that may afflict the farmer's field. Mars's superknowledge and superhuman causal powers in the biological and physical domains would have made him a compelling agent for an agriculturalist to reflect on. He would have been irresistible to turn to in connection with existential concerns such as food production and bodily health. This relevance to everyday concerns presumably contributed to the successful transmission in communication and retention in memory of representations of the god.

In both Cato's prayer to Mars and Livy's fetial prayer, the prayer represents physical modes of divine causation as the content of its Directive. Recall that the *pater patratus* asks Jupiter to strike the *populus Romanus* with superhuman force should they purposely defect from their treaty with the Albans. The obvious implication is that Jupiter can (somehow) strike the entire Roman people *physically*, as the *fetialis* strikes the hog. The god thus possesses, as part of his folk theology, nonnatural properties of physical causation, even if those properties remain less than fully specified.[114]

The takeaway is this: Roman prayer implied in its mode of performance, encoded propositionally, and made inferentially available an informal, nondogmatic, but reasonably consistent folk theology. This folk theology pictured gods who largely conformed to ordinary expectations about agents and who were thus easy for the mind's developmentally natural cognitive systems to process, reason about, and generate inferences about. However, Roman prayer also represented these same gods as possessing, or implied that they possessed, counterintuitive powers that cut against normal cognitive expectations. As Jennifer Larson writes of the Greek gods:[115]

> According to cognitive scientists of religion, widely distributed "god concepts" combine a preponderance of the naturalistic and intuitive properties that we expect other agents to possess (e.g., occupying physical space; feeling emotions) with one or more non-naturalistic and counterintuitive properties (ability to read minds; invisibility). These counterintuitive properties produce a sense of the gods' "otherness" and their incommensurability with humans.

As we've seen, possessing a small number of these counterintuitive properties also confers mnemonic advantages. These properties grab attention, inspire inferences, and so are easily remembered and transmitted. Successful counterintuitive representations, the ones most likely to get transmitted and thus to join the cultural repertoire, are those most relevant to human concerns, for example, those that represent deities who appeal directly to Roman concerns about divine goodwill, military victory, bodily health, crop success, treaty defection, and so forth.

No Roman will have required explicit theological teaching on the nature and characteristics of the gods. He or she will instead have learned in a cognitively autonomous rather than catechistic way, that is, through normal social interaction, absorbing and inferring a great deal about the gods from the

---

114. In fact, upon violating a treaty, as did the Samnites during the Second Samnite War, the divine wrath could be felt to have been suffered less as a physical blow from a superhuman agent and more as suffering of a strictly mundane sort: *satis scio, quibuscumque dis cordi fuit subigi nos ad necessitatem dedendi res quae ab nobis ex foedere repetitae fuerant* (Liv. 9.1.4).

115. Larson 2016: 67–68.

religious activity, such as prayer, that he or she observed and participated in. It follows that we need not suppose that any two Romans ever had precisely the same concept of the gods. Nonetheless, their folk theologies will have converged enough to facilitate their sharing of Intentionality in joint cult action and thus the perpetuation of the tradition.

The points that I would stress about Roman religious belief are as follows. When they prayed, Romans typically presupposed, however nonreflectively (and therefore believed, however nonreflectively), that their gods were social agents of a sort that neurotypical human beings handle with intuitive facility. However, they also represented, in these episodes of discursive Intentionality, the divine social agents as counterintuitively superhuman in their unique access to information relevant to Roman concerns and in their powers and motivations to intervene in the world of mortals through psychological, biological, or physical causation.

Those attending to these prayers, whether for the first time or for the thousandth, not only *encountered* a folk-theological content but also *accommodated* the unspoken presuppositions of the prayers' speakers. That is, culture learners inferred and adopted worshippers' unstated beliefs about the existence, agency, dispositions, proclivities, and causal capacities of the divine agents addressed. They also encountered, in the content of prayer, propositions about the nature of the gods and their interventions in the human realm. This propositional content was available to hearers for doxastic uptake. Both the presuppositions accommodated by hearers and the propositional content incorporated into hearers' beliefs represented the gods as salient, compelling, and cooperative MCI agents.

8.7. Context and Commitment

Now let us finish with the interrelated questions of context and commitment. Why should any Roman have *believed* the folk-theological content expressed in prayer or *acted on* such beliefs in cult? For it is one thing to *represent* something and quite another to *represent it as the case*. Only the latter is belief. As discussed in chapter 3, belief played a unique role in the etiology of Roman cult action, by picturing a world replete with gods in which to act.

In in our discussion of MCI theory in this chapter, we have focused on the contribution of *content* to belief. We have seen that the counterintuitive content of Roman prayer contributed to its cultural success. This content harmonized with normal cognitive expectations enough to make it fairly intuitive: the gods were rather anthropomorphic. Yet in certain respects, prayer content also violated or exceeded anthropomorphizing expectations. Gods are represented as possessing uncanny access to all sorts of socially and existentially relevant information as well as extraordinary, if opaque, causal powers. In this, the gods were memorably counterintuitive.

Indeed, one could easily suppose that this very counterintuitiveness might itself have *detracted* from the prima facie plausibility of Roman folk theology.[116] How could anyone actually *believe* in entities that can inscrutably turn the tide of battle, strike the *populus Romanus* as a man strikes a hog, ward off invisible disease, or discern secret intentions? Intuitive representations are obviously more inherently *believable* than are counterintuitive representations such as these. Part of the answer is that we believe these counterintuitive representations because they are quite memorable and inferentially rich, and they are supported by HADD and Theory of Mind (introduction section 0.3).

Another important part of the answer, the part that we focus on now, is this: *context* promotes commitment to *content*.[117] The social environment in which religious representations are produced and encountered determines the psychological mode, from intense belief (gods) to mere imagination (cartoon characters), in which we hold those representations. The mind possesses context-sensitive cognitive biases that predispose us to adopt the beliefs of others. These include a general bias to trust in testimony, reinforced by a bias to trust preferentially speakers of prestige, and a bias to conform to the behaviors and beliefs of the majority or at least of a plurality.[118]

Let us return to Prudentius, from the previous chapter, in order to see an example of the prestige bias at work. Prestige, as Henrich and Gil-White have argued, is a uniquely human form of social capital based neither on institutional status (though prestigious individuals may have that, too; on institutional status, see chapter 5), nor on physical dominance (as among chimps), but rather on "freely conferred deference." Prestigious individuals are those

---

116. Cf. Gervais and Henrich 2010: 386: "concepts that systematically deviate from intuitive expectations may actually be less believable than are more intuitive concepts." Cf. Mercier 2020: 221, 222–30.

117. For an early skirmish in the content vs. context wars, compare Barrett 2008, which discusses the contribution of content biases to our belief or disbelief in God and Santa Claus, with Gervais and Henrich 2010, which insists on the primacy of context for our belief or disbelief in God and Zeus.

118. See, briefly, Barrett 2011a: 41–44. For testimony, see P. Harris 2012 (and see at section 6.5, above) and Audi 2015: 217–57. For prestige, see J. Henrich and Gil-White 2001; Chudek, Birch, and Henrich 2012. For conformity, see T.J.H. Morgan and Laland 2012; and Muthukrishna et al. 2016. For much more on social and cultural learning mechanisms, see N. Henrich and Henrich 2007: 11–30; and Hoppitt and Laland 2013.

whom we see *others* watch, defer to, and imitate, and whom we therefore take to be worthy of *our* attention, deference, and imitation. Our imitation of the prestigious is both cognitive and behavioral: we copy what we take to be their attitudes and we commit ourselves to their practices.[119]

Prestige-based belief adoption appears in Prudentius's account of the pagan child's learning. We examined in detail his account of child learning traditional Roman religion in the home, by observing and imitating his caregivers. In the section that follows, which we did not explore, the poet turns to what must be a later stage of childhood, when the child leaves the house (*iamque domo egrediens, c. Symm.* 215). In the public places of the city, he attends festivals, observes priests at work in the temples, and sees processions of sacrificial animals. Prudentius lavishes fifteen lines on descriptions of the various gods whose statues the child sees (226–40). Taking it all in, the child comes to believe in the traditional deities. Note that his cognitive response is not dictated so much by the *content* of the representations, rich as they are, as by *contextual* features of the content's presentation (*c. Symm.* 223–25):

> *vera ratus quaecumque fiant auctore senatu,*
> *contulit ad simulacra fidem dominosque putavit*
> *aetheris, horrifico qui stant ex ordine vultu.*

> Supposing whatever happens with the support of the senate to be genuine,
> he gave credence to the statues and believed them to be the lords
> of heaven, standing in a row with their dreadful expressions.

The key to the child's belief is the *prestige* associated with the senate. The senators support the creation or even *create* the statues (*auctor* can mean both). Had he inferred that the religious pageantry on display lacked the endorsement of the senate or some other prestigious individual(s), his cognitive response might well have been different.

Prestige is not the only or even the most important contextual factor. Social cognition disposes culture learners to infer people's commitment to their beliefs (or lack thereof) from their actions. As Justin Barrett points out (2004a: 62):

> It is one thing to say that one believes in a god, but it is quite another to *act* as if one believes in a god. Such evidence of others' commitment becomes part of the corpus of inputs that support reflective belief.

---

119. See J. Henrich and Gil-White 2001; and J. Henrich 2015: 34–53.

We tend to come to believe in counterintuitive, empirically hard-to-verify entities to the extent that we see others acting as if they believe in them. This goes for everything from Roman gods to modern germs, which every child in a developed country simply *knows*—on the basis of parental representations backed up by actions like hand washing—cause colds.[120]

The theory I am adumbrating is that of "credibility enhancing displays" (CREDs). People's actions serve as CREDs, that is, as indexes of their commitment to the content of their speech acts and the other representations they make.[121] These CREDs have been defined as follows by Joseph Henrich (2009: 258):

> CREDs are actions that (a) are consistent with a model's professed beliefs, and (b) a model would be unlikely to perform if he believed something different from what he expressed symbolically.

Credibility enhancing displays bolster the perceived sincerity of social actors and thereby function as *belief triggers* for culture learners, who weight these CREDs heavily when determining whom to trust and what representations to believe. As Henrich writes in another context (J. Henrich 2015: 258):

> Using CREDs provides learners with a kind of partial immune system, or filter, against manipulators who would exploit the cheap cultural-transmission channel provided by language.

The extension to Roman prayer should, I hope, be obvious. As language-using creatures, we exercise "epistemic vigilance" in contexts where we are exposed to linguistic representations.[122] That is, we are always on the lookout for insincere communicative signals from others. If an epistemically vigilant Roman culture learner exclusively encountered models, such as Cato's farmer, who prayed to Jupiter but failed to offer the cake mentioned in the prayer, or who intoned the oath of the fetial priest but then immediately defected on its terms, or who made vows like Appius Claudius Caecus but then omitted to dedicate a votive upon getting what they requested, then this culture learner would doubt whether the models were committed, practically or epistemically, to their own representations. The culture learner might opt not to imitate the

---

120. For germs, see P. Harris et al. 2006. Cf. Veyne 1988: 28: "Westerners, at least those among us who are not bacteriologists, believe in germs and increase the sanitary precautions we take for the same reason that the Azande believe in witches and multiply their magical precautions against them: their belief is based on trust."
121. J. Henrich 2009. Cf. Norenzayan 2013: 98–100; and J. Henrich 2015: 258.
122. Sperber et al. 2010.

prayer practice of such models or at least to stop short of believing in the gods represented in their prayers.

In contrast, and in fact, as we have seen, the speakers of Roman prayers tended to act in ways not only consistent with but demonstrative of commitment to the content of their prayers. Such CREDs could be extraordinarily "costly" and "hard-to-fake."[123] Think, for example, of the material cost of the *ver sacrum*, which might be vowed during an existential crisis of the community, such as war. By the terms of the vow, an entire season's produce of livestock was dedicated to Jupiter.[124] Just in case that is not already costly enough, if there is the slightest ritual error, the *ver sacrum* would be subject to repetition from scratch, *instauratio*.[125] It is next to impossible to imagine Romans promising or engaging in such costly sacrifice without holding beliefs about the gods and their efficacious action on Rome's behalf in response to the vow. On the CREDs theory, such behavior would have signaled the belief of the religious actors and triggered belief in culture learners. The learner would, in turn, go on to act on his or her new belief(s), providing CREDs for others, thus spreading the belief(s) exponentially. Note that even if the cult actors were entirely insincere in their heart of hearts, as long as they performed the requisite costly cult acts, the doxastic uptake in the learners should be the same.

All that said, I would add one shade of nuance to the CREDs theory, to wit, that from the point of view of pragmatics, speech acts are themselves performances. Thus, we are not dealing with a strict dichotomy between *logos* and *ergon*, speech and action, talk and walk. Instead, a first CRED, for our purposes, will just be performance of a prayer. This is not to say that the words of the prayer will not have to pass through the filter of their hearers' epistemic vigilance. However, the right words could themselves serve as "commitment signals." Recall Cato's farmer (section 8.5) who "prays good prayers," *bonas preces precor*. The performative verb *precor* advertises to hearers his sincerity, As Hugo Mercier notes, "We are more influenced . . . by more committed speakers."[126]

Moreover, as we saw, prayer was a practical, highly formal, and highly formulaic affair, in which words could be thought to have a power of their own. When Romans prayed, they did not ask hearers to consider a series of propositions for acceptance or rejection. Instead, in praying, they entered

---

123. I allude to a constellation of religious signaling theories: for "hard-to-fake," see Irons 2001. For "costly," see Sosis 2003; Ruffle and Sosis 2007; Bulbulia 2013; Norenzayan 2013: 100–105. Norenzayan, Shariff, et al. 2016: 17 brings together signaling theory and CREDs.

124. E.g., Liv. 22.9–10.

125. E.g., Liv. 34.44.

126. Mercier 2020: 92; "commitment signals": 89.

into transactions with their gods in acts of requesting, promising, thanking, and Declaration. The words of these speech acts had power, as Pliny supposed. Their utterance created socially binding forces among speakers, (divine) addressees, and hearers, by publicly committing speakers to the beliefs, desires, and intentions that they expressed as prayer content, and thus made them publicly accountable for, say, the desires they expressed in petitionary prayer and the intentions they expressed in oaths and vows. Finally, prayers were typically accompanied by cult action. They were not words in a vacuum.

Therefore, to perform the cult act of prayer by, for example, making a vow, was itself to perform a CRED manifesting to culture learners one's belief in gods, especially if it was accompanied by a cult. When a vower demonstrated his or her sincerity, or *fides*, by fulfilling this vow, the vower enacted a further, even more powerful CRED that evidenced commitment to the practical intention the Commissive speech act had expressed. This is because, as we have seen, "religious ideas backed up by credible displays of commitment . . . are more persuasive and more likely to spread."[127] The vast number of temples, votive objects, and inscriptions found throughout the Roman world advertising the fulfillment of vows form an archaeology of just such credible displays of commitment or CREDs.[128] In summary: the performance of prayer, especially if it was accompanied by appropriate actions, such as *ex voto* offering or sacrifice, was a behavioral feature of ritual *context* that promoted belief in and commitment to the religious ideas appearing in the prayer's presuppositions and representational *content*.

8.8. Conclusion

If we are asked Denis Feeney's question—"What . . . did a Roman know of his religion, and how did he come to know it?"—we are now in a better position to provide an admittedly partial yet nontrivial answer.[129] I have argued that the representational *content* of prayer, situated in practical *contexts* that demonstrated commitment, transmitted not only Roman folk-theological beliefs but also Roman commitment to cult and its system of norms, or *pietas*. In a cult system with no institutions for promulgating creeds, the conservative formulas in which prayers petitioned superhuman agents transmitted relatively stable representations and fostered the generation of relatively consistent

---

127. Norenzayan, Shariff, et al. 2016: 5.
128. For Roman temples and votive objects, see above, n. 33.
129. Feeney 1998: 138.

theological inferences about the gods, that is, a folk theology. Insofar as Roman gods were prayed to for benefactions both mundane and marvelous, they were represented as agents possessing highly intuitive, anthropomorphic psychologies as well as counterintuitive, nonnatural properties and powers. Finally, the ritual contexts of praying, which often involved costly material and temporal investment, indicated to culture learners that petitioners believed in and had committed to the representational content of prayer. Contextual cues of prayer performance could thus induce culture learners to adopt corresponding attitudes of belief and commitment, which were precisely the attitudes required to motivate cult action and transmit belief and the cult commitment to successive generations.

9

Inauguratio

BELIEF, RITUAL, AND RELIGIOUS POWER

9.1. Introduction

Ritual is action. Yet it is not merely action. It is standardized, recurrent action, or "practice." One might therefore suppose ritual to be largely a matter of practical cognition, a matter of intentions to act. However, in human action, any intention to act can arise only in the context of a background of beliefs—reflective and nonreflective—and other Intentional states.[1] In order to form an intention to perform a given ritual action, one typically needs antecedently to believe that, for example, words, gestures, and actions A enact ritual B, that ritual B creates religious effect C, and sometimes, as in augural ritual, that religious effect C amounts to bestowal of status D along with deontic powers E. Consider the negative: if one does not have such beliefs about one's words, gestures, and actions, then one is likely not performing ritual B but instead acting under some other description.

Finally, of course, those engaged in ritual will also typically have beliefs about gods or other superhuman agents and their place in the ritual's structure. This is a controversial statement, and "ritual" is a contested term. I follow McCauley and Lawson in distinguishing *religious* rituals from other actions and practices, including other "ritualized" actions and practices, on the basis of their associated theological (and other MCI agent) representations.[2] Religious rituals are, in rather unambiguous ways that we shall explore, god involving. But of course, there will always be edge cases. As Aristotle noted long ago, different sciences admit of differing levels of exactness.

In this chapter, I make three related proposals about practice and belief in the Roman ritual of *inauguratio*. These proposals admit of extension to other

---

1. See Searle 1983a: 141; and chapter 3, above.
2. McCauley and Lawson 2002: 8–9.

religious cultures. First, ritual participants' *cognition-in-practice*, including both practical and doxastic representations, guides their ritual actions. Second, participants' (and observers') *cognition-about-practice* guides their intuitions about and evaluations of the ritual actions that they see performed. In keeping with the overall target of this book, I attend primarily to the relevant beliefs, including deontic beliefs, that are mobilized in both cognition-in-practice and cognition-about-practice. My third proposal will emerge from my treatment of the first two. It amounts to the claim that some practical and doxastic representations, including beliefs and deontic beliefs, are *constitutive* of religious practices and their effects. That is, rituals cannot *be* the rituals that they are, let alone be performed, evaluated, or have any effects, in the absence of certain cognitive representations.[3]

The latter point about ritual effects bears emphasizing. I attempt to show that the effects of Roman rituals, effects that frequently involved the creation of very real social statuses and social powers, were not "empirical" effects, residing out there in the world, waiting to be noticed and connected to ritual practice, but instead existed only insofar as they were represented and believed to exist. In this way, the discussion here reiterates and illustrates a central point of chapter 5, to wit, that social practices, institutions, and institutional statuses do not exist independently of the shared practical and doxastic representations of human subjects. Social practices, institutions, and institutional statuses are ontologically subjective, that is, constituted by and hence dependent for their existence on cognition of human subjects.

A few words of review are in order before we move forward. Our discussion here of the beliefs involved in cognition-in-practice and cognition-about-practice follows on our earlier treatments of constitutive belief and deontic belief. A *belief* is, of course, just a subject's representation of a state of affairs that he or she takes to obtain. Any belief that represents a norm—that is, what may, must, or must not be done—may be called a *deontic belief* (section 3.3.2). Norms contribute both to cognition-in-practice, by helping to guide action, and to cognition-about-practice, by helping us to predict and evaluate action (section 4.4). Finally, any belief that represents some X as a Y in context C (for example, Cicero, X, as an augur, Y, in augural ceremonies, C) or that represents a Y as existing in context C (for example, the augurate, Y, exists in Roman civic life, C) may be called a *constitutive belief*. Such beliefs play a role in sustaining the existence and deontology of the Y term, which always names a Status

---

3. I have called such mental representations *constitutive attitudes* (at sections 2.2.5 and 5.3.2, above). From among these constitutive attitudes, I focus here on *constitutive belief*. See just below.

Function such as "augur" (sections 2.2.5 and 5.3.1–2). Note that these distinctions do not define mutually exclusive categories. Any belief, including any deontic belief, may be constitutive if it happens to represent X as Y in C, or Y in C, and, in so doing, helps to maintain the Y Status Function.

In what follows, I draw on two theoretical models. One is the theory of social ontology presented in chapter 5.[4] The other is a cognitive theory of ritual proposed by E. T. Lawson and R. N. McCauley.[5] Relying on these theoretical resources, I argue for my three proposals by way of an examination of the ritual of *inauguratio*. Mark Antony's claim to a novel priesthood, the flaminate of the deified Julius Caesar, will provide our point of departure. The chapter's next section, 9.2, lays the foundation by presenting some relevant features of the cognitive theory of ritual. The following section, 9.3, offers a brief orientation to the Roman auspices (or *auspicia*). In section 9.4, we turn to Cicero's complaint against Mark Antony for his failure to undergo inauguration as a flamen. Here, under the rubric of "cognition-about-practice," we attempt to come to grips with Roman cognitive representations of the ritual of *inauguratio*. Section 9.5 shifts to a brief discussion of "cognition-in-practice," the counterpart to "cognition-about-practice." Finally, section 9.6 discusses the distinction between constitutive and nonconstitutive, or merely "religious," beliefs, as this distinction pertains to *inauguratio* and to ritual more broadly.

9.2. Cognition and Ritual Form

The study of ritual has generated a plethora of theories.[6] Ritual theorists have universally acknowledged—even insisted, when seeking to insulate practice from belief—that ritual is *action*.[7] However, from the cognitive perspective developed by E. T. Lawson and R. N. McCauley, insofar as ritual is action, then we should expect normal human cognition about action to permit as well as constrain our understanding of rituals.[8] Our social-cognitive systems for

---

4. Searle 1995 and Searle 2010. Brief overview in Searle 2008a.

5. E. T. Lawson and McCauley 1990; and McCauley and Lawson 2002. Brief overview in McCauley and Lawson 2007.

6. See Bell 1997 for a convenient historical survey of theories of ritual. For a more recent and more comprehensive survey of theories and an annotated bibliography, see Kreinath et al. 2007.

7. Cf. Bell 1992: 6.

8. E. T. Lawson and McCauley 1990; McCauley and Lawson 2002. For concise statements of their theory, see E. T. Lawson 2007; and McCauley and Lawson 2007. Elements of Lawson and McCauley's theory have been tested empirically: Barrett and Lawson 2001; Malley and Barrett 2003; Barrett 2004b. Lisdorf 2005 applies the theory to Clodius's attempt to have Cicero's house ritually consecrated to Libertas.

identifying, representing, and interpreting action—what E. T. Lawson and R. N. McCauley (1990: 87–95) call our "action representation system"—guides our developmentally natural intuitions and judgments about the agents, components, qualities, and effects of mundane actions. The same system underlies and potentiates our *cultural* intuitions and judgments about the agents, components, qualities, and effects of ritual actions. Thus, as we have seen elsewhere, at section 2.6.2, for instance, universal cognitive processes ground specific cultural forms.

The cognitive theory of ritual does not seek to answer the anthropologist's question about its "meaning" for participants. As McCauley and Lawson write (2002: 36):

> a great deal of ritual participants' (intuitive) knowledge of their religious ritual system does not depend upon their ability to provide interpretations or meanings for the rituals in which they participate.

Indeed, "sometimes all the ethnographer gets is 'we do it because our ancestors did it.'" Similarly, much is made, and with good reason, of the great latitude Roman ritual allowed participants for exegesis and interpretation. Beard, North, and Price, for example, write (1998: 1.48):

> it is characteristic of rituals not only that their meanings change over time, but also that they are always liable to be interpreted in different ways by different people, or, for that matter, by the same people on different occasions.

In this, they echo Catherine Bell, who voiced a similar thesis (1992: 186):

> ritualized activities specifically do *not* promote belief or conviction. On the contrary, ritualized practices afford a great diversity of interpretation in exchange for little more than consent to the form of the activities.

Like Bell, Denis Feeney has contrasted interpretive fluidity with the relative stability of performance. The Romans possessed "performative knowledge"—the knowledge required to perform a sequence of ritual actions. Feeney (1998: 138–39; cf. 127–31) cautions that it is hard for us moderns

> to grasp how easily a religion may maintain itself in an environment where most of its practitioners are genuinely ignorant about practically everything outside the realm of performative knowledge.

Practitioners' performative knowledge does not (or need not) encompass theoretical knowledge about the "meaning" of sacrifice and other ritual actions. The bare frame of ritual action and the naked script of performative knowledge leave interpretation, the domain of meaning, open. For Feeney, as for Bell and Beard, North, and S.R.F. Price, ritual practitioners are more or less free to dress their cult actions in whatever exegetical glosses respond to the needs and purposes of the moment.

These perspectives, whatever their virtues, are organized around a basic opposition of action to cognition, ritual (or performative knowledge) to interpretation. Following Lawson and McCauley, we shall see that uncertainty or diversity regarding "meaning" does not preclude participants' generating and entertaining all sorts of intuitions, inferences, and beliefs about the structure, nature, and consequences of ritual performances. They do, and they do so as a result, in part, of their developmentally natural ability to understand action. In other words, however unconstrained exegesis may be by performance, we should not therefore posit a gulf between action and cognition.

For, after all, ritual is action, and we cognize action as accomplishing things. Thus, qua action, ritual will often be judged as *efficacious*, even when its causal mechanisms remain "opaque."[9] We shall see that in the case of the ritual of *inauguratio*, obtaining certain effects—accomplishing things—was a primary motive. Indeed, that Roman ritual in particular had pragmatic bent, scholars have long supposed. As John North has put it, to Roman eyes (1976: 1, my emphasis):

> the real validation of their religion lay in the fact that *it had worked*: that their ancestors had won battles, survived crises, eaten dinners, begotten children and expanded their power by the practice of the self-same rites and ceremonies as they practised themselves.

Others have cast the same insight in terms of "observation" or "empiricism."[10] Recently, for example, Clifford Ando has described Roman religion as a *scientia* "grounded upon observation," that is to say (2008: 13):

> upon an empiricist epistemology: cult addressed problems in the real world, and the effectiveness of rituals—their tangible results—determined whether they were repeated, modified, or abandoned.

This empirical sensitivity to "the effectiveness of rituals" may even be found in Roman views about the auspices, a central component of *inauguratio* that we shall explore below. In book 1 of Cicero's *De divinatione*, for example, Quintus presents an empiricist argument in favor of divination in general and of auspication in particular. Cicero represents Quintus's empiricism as embodying the view of the ancients, the *veteres*, who discovered and established the

---

9. On the causal opacity of ritual, see at section 7.4.1; and see further, Mackey 2018a.
10. See, e.g., Regell 1878: 3–7; Dumézil 1970: 1.125; Linderski 1986a: 2231–36; Hickson 1993: 9.

practices of divination, "more because they were swayed by outcomes than because they were instructed by reason," *magis eventis moniti quam ratione docti* (*Div.* 1.5). For Quintus, the augural art was based on *observatio diuturna*, "long observation" of, and the discovery of connections between, signs and *eventa*.[11]

None of this should be taken to imply that Romans were protoscientists who attempted to "falsify" their rituals empirically and abandon the ones that did not "work." Rather, ritual cognition is replete with confirmation bias and the explaining away of failures.[12] Any successful result was dispositive, while failures could easily be ignored. Thus, battles won and crises survived were empirical facts that could be attributed to proper ritual performance.

As we shall see, however, in many cases the effectiveness of rituals was not judged by any empirical results that could plausibly be attributed to them. It will transpire that at times a participant's belief that a ritual has been effective turned solely on his or her judgment *that the ritual itself was properly performed* (section 9.4). Obviously, what counts as proper ritual form will vary from ritual to ritual, and from culture to culture. However, the forms that rituals can take are not, as one might suppose, entirely unconstrained or arbitrary. Rather, ritual form and participants' judgments about ritual performance are shaped by developmentally natural cognitive resources for representing action.

So, let us describe some of these features of natural cognition about action and then discuss their relevance for Roman ritual. In previous chapters we have seen that social cognition allows us to represent some entities as agents and to reason about them accordingly, in terms of the perceptions, beliefs, desires, intentions, and goals that drive their behavior. And, of course, we interpret behavior as action, that is, as an event caused by an agent. Our cognitive systems for parsing action include three functional "action roles": AGENT, ACT (including, optionally, INSTRUMENT), and PATIENT or object.[13] The roles of AGENT and ACT together are enough to constitute the representation of an action (e.g., intransitive representations, like "the man runs"), but actions may also include the roles of PATIENT and INSTRUMENT (e.g., transitive

---

11. *Observatio*: *Div.* 1.2, 1.109, 2.26, 2.28, 2.42, 2.146; *Eventa*: *Div.* 1.12, 1.72, 1.84, 1.128, 2.27, 2.79.

12. See Larson 2016: 100–102.

13. For "action roles," see E. T. Lawson and McCauley 1990: 87–95, summarized in McCauley and Lawson 2002: 10–13 (cf. 23–24), with references to literature in developmental psychology. For more on the psychology of action representation, with further references, see E. T. Lawson 2001. Please note that in describing AGENT and PATIENT action roles, I do not mean to imply that all actions involve transitive relations between two distinct entities. Obviously, there are also intransitive actions and reflexive actions.

representations like "the woman cuts the apple with a knife").[14] These roles potentiate but also constrain our action cognition. We cannot, for example, represent actions consisting of acts and objects, but no agents.

All of this is not only logically necessary (it is analytically true that an *act* is performed by an *agent*), but also cognitively indispensable. For whatever the facts about the world may be independently of our representations, if our minds did not possess systems for automatically intuiting these functional action roles, we would be able neither to distinguish some events as actions nor to comprehend the roles of and relationships among the various entities involved.

These developmentally natural cognitive resources that guide and constrain our intuitions about action in general also underpin, guide, and constrain our intuitions about ritual. Religious ritual may now be defined more specifically: it differs from mundane actions, even "ritualized" mundane actions, in that in religious ritual, superhuman agents are represented as connected to one or more of the three action roles described above.[15] Mundane actions feature mundane entities. Religious actions feature nonmundane entities, to wit, the "minimally counterintuitive" (MCI) agents introduced in chapter 8—gods, ancestor spirits, and the like. More precisely, in Lawson and McCauley's technical definition, a religious ritual is a repeated (i.e., standardized) religious action (1) in which at least one MCI agent is represented by participants in direct or indirect connection to an action role, and (2) that is efficacious, serving to "bring about changes in the religious world."[16] Several additional points must be made about points (1) and (2).

Let us begin with (1), the representation of MCI agents in direct or indirect connection to an action role. An MCI agent can be represented either as occupying or as indirectly connected to the PATIENT role of a ritual (e.g., sacrifice in which the god receives the offering); the ACT role, via the INSTRUMENT role (as in rituals that include an implement blessed or given by a god); or the AGENT role, as we are about to see in detail.

Consider, first, mundane actions. Any mundane action will depend causally on a variety of prior actions, in a series that extends back (as good as) infinitely. We grasp this intuitively and generate representations of these prior actions as needed, insofar as they are relevant to the action under consideration. Thus, if a friend hands me an offprint of her latest article, I will, without being so

---

14. The same entity may, of course, fill the AGENT and PATIENT roles, as in the case of reflexive actions.
15. McCauley and Lawson 2002: 8–9, 13–16.
16. McCauley and Lawson 2002: 13–16.

informed, infer that she conducted research for it, wrote it, and submitted it to a journal, whose editors read it, solicited peer review, accepted it, and so on. These inferences arise unbidden as needed: "Is this the one you researched at the Bodleian?"; "Was the second reader a nitpicker?"; and so on.

Likewise, any religious ritual action will depend causally on prior actions, some of which may themselves be rituals. Just as we may infer the prior actions on which a mundane action depends, so participants may represent the requisite "enabling rituals" on which a given ritual depends as "embedded" in its structure.[17] The hypothesis is that a series of religious rituals differs from a series of mundane actions in that the action of an MCI agent will provide the ritual series with "principled closure," a closure that conditions the efficacy of every "downstream," dependent ritual in the series.[18] Lawson and McCauley call this closure-providing action of an MCI agent a "hypothetical ritual," for it "need not occur in the world of space and time, and it need only be done once."[19]

Minimally counterintuitive agents, then, may occupy the AGENT role of a ritual *directly*, as when a god is conceived by participants as acting in the role of AGENT. Or MCI agents may occupy the AGENT role *indirectly*, as for example when a human agent is licensed to carry out his or her ritual duties because of having been so authorized by the action, or "hypothetical ritual," of a god. And this brings us at last to point (2), that is, that rituals are efficacious of change in the religious world. From the participants' point of view, ultimate agency in rituals, that is, the ultimate *source* of the change that they effect, stems from MCI agents participating in the rituals either directly, by occupying an action role in a present ritual, or indirectly, through enabling rituals that bear on an action role in a present ritual.[20] Ultimately, that is to say, rituals effect their change through the direct or indirect agency of a god.

9.3. *Auspicia*

We shall evaluate the import of these theoretical considerations for Roman religion in due course, in section 9.4. But first, a brief orientation to the *auspicia* is in order.[21] *Auspicatio*, or "auspication," was a formal ritual through

---

17. E. T. Lawson and McCauley 1990: 95ff.; McCauley and Lawson 2002: 18–23.
18. E. T. Lawson and McCauley 1990: 95.
19. E. T. Lawson and McCauley 1990: 113 (cf. 127–28). Cf. McCauley and Lawson 2002: 23.
20. E. T. Lawson and McCauley 1990: 95; McCauley and Lawson 2002: 22–23.
21. My notes will show that the following discussion is much indebted to Linderski 1986a; and Vaahtera 2001. Other classic studies of *auspicia* include Valeton 1889, 1890, 1891a, and 1891b; and Catalano 1960.

which an auspicant requested that Jupiter indicate his will on a given matter by means of specified signs, *auspicia*. The signs came *ex caelo*, that is, "from the heavens," in the form of thunder or lightning; *ex avibus*, that is, "from birds," in the form of avian behavior; or *ex tripudiis*, that is, from the manner in which sacred chickens did or did not eat. A great many Roman practices required eligible participants to auspicate, or "take the auspices" (*auspicari*). To "have the *auspicia*" (*habere auspicia*) designated the right to take the auspices. In public life, augurs took the auspices in the course of *inaugurationes* (also called *auguria*), and magistrates did so in the course of carrying out their official duties.[22]

The *collegium augurum*, or "college of augurs," was one of Rome's four most important priestly *collegia*.[23] It consisted, in the late republic, of fifteen members, drawn from both patrician and plebeian families.[24] Cicero, in self-consciously archaic language, legislates what had long been the augurs' primary functions (*Leg.* 2.20–21):

Interpretes autem Iovis optumi maxumi, publici augures, signis et auspiciis operam danto, disciplinam tenento, [21] *sacerdotesque vineta virgetaque et salutem populi auguranto.*

Let the interpreters of *Jupiter Optimus Maximus*, the public augurs, give attention to signs and *auspicia*, let them keep the augural discipline, [21] and let them inaugurate priests, vineyards and brush, and the ritual for the health of the people.

The augurs were experts in all matters that pertained to the *auspicia* and, as such, the custodians of the augural discipline, the precepts and records of which were written up in the college's "augural books," *libri augurales*.[25] Among the augurs' chief ritual functions was the performance of the ritual of *inauguratio*. This ritual permanently altered the status of persons, places, or certain *sacra*, as Cicero's listing of "priests, vineyards and brush, and the ritual

---

22. Here I discuss only the public *auspicia*, though it must not be forgotten that *privati* were entitled to take auspices in conducting their private affairs (cf. Serv. *ad Aen.* 3.20: *auspicari enim cuivis ... licet*). We know very little about these practices.

23. In our period the others are the pontifices, *quindecemviri sacris faciundis*, and *septemviri epulonum*.

24. The *lex Ogulnia* (300 BCE) provided for five plebeians to join the college, bringing total membership to nine (Livy 10.6 and 10.9). Sulla raised the number to fifteen (Livy, *Per.* 89), Caesar to sixteen (Dio 42.51.4).

25. Cic. *N.D.* 2.11; *Div.* 1.72, 2.42–43; Linderski 1986a: 2241–56.

for the health of the people" indicates.²⁶ The ritual turned ordinary people into priests, sanctified man-made and natural places, and inaugurated some other rituals. Thus, the *auguria* concerned substantive matters, altering "the status of an *object* of the ceremony."²⁷ Augurs took the auspices while performing *inaugurationes* in order to seek divine permission for an entity to be inaugurated into a new status.²⁸ Augurs alone were qualified to perform inaugurations.

The augural use of the auspices must be contrasted with the practices of public magistrates. They were required to take the auspices concerning procedural matters in certain circumstances, and when they did so, it was in order to ascertain the divine will concerning "an action to be undertaken by the *subject* (the auspicant) of the ceremony."²⁹ In effect, the auspices established divine approval for the auspicating magistrate's projects. These rituals effected no changes in the status of persons, places, or other entities but rather ensured that Jupiter was willing for a given action to be undertaken by a given individual at a given time. (This approval, it should be noted, did not guarantee a successful outcome.) If a negative answer was received, the auspicating magistrate simply waited until the next day and then took the auspices again.³⁰ Unlike augurs, magistrates could not perform *inaugurationes*; they could auspicate only concerning actions that lay within their legally circumscribed sphere of activity. Magistrates might on certain occasions have an augur present during auspication (*in auspicio esse*) to ensure that the ritual was conducted correctly and to assist in interpreting the signs.³¹ And magistrates could appeal to the expertise of the augural college in cases of uncertainty about the validity of a given taking of the auspices or the nature of signs received.³²

The technical term for the auspices by means of which augurs performed inaugurations and magistrates received divine permission was *auspicia impetrativa*. These *auspicia* were signs explicitly sought, or "impetrated" (*impetrire*), from Jupiter. In impetrative auspication, the auspicant requested that Jupiter signal his will through specified signs, *ex caelo*, *ex avibus*, or *ex tripudiis*, as noted. The augurs sought *auspicia impetrativa* only while performing *auguria*. A magistrate sought *auspicia impetrativa* before he embarked on any public

26. Linderski 1986a: 2218–24.
27. Linderski 1986a: 2296 (emphasis added).
28. Linderski 1986a: 2292; Vaahtera 2001: 103–4.
29. Linderski 1986a: 2296, emphasis added. Cf. Vaahtera 2001: 103–4.
30. Linderski 1986a: 2294–96.
31. Linderski 1986a: 2190–95.
32. Linderski 1986a: 2208–15.

business. Magistrates also had the right to impetrate signs from the sky (*de caelo servare*), and to announce any adverse *auspicia impetrativa* that they observed to the presiding magistrate *before* a public proceeding, thus preventing it from taking place. This right was called *obnuntiatio*.

For clarity, we should distinguish these impetrative auspices from *auspicia oblativa*, which consisted in unsought signs sent by the gods. Jupiter could indicate, unasked, his approval or disapproval of an enterprise that was already in progress by sending appropriate signs. These signs could come *ex caelo* or *ex avibus*, just as in impetrative auspication, as well as *ex quadrupedibus*, that is, from the behavior of four-footed animals, or *ex diris*, that is "from ominous events."[33] Augurs in particular possessed the technical knowledge required to recognize, interpret, and announce *auspicia oblativa*, thereby, in the case of adverse signs, interrupting a public proceeding and declaring it invalid. The right to announce *auspicia oblativa* was called *nuntiatio* (Cic. *Phil.* 2.81). Non-augurs, both private citizens and magistrates, could also report adverse *auspicia oblativa* during a public proceeding, but their *nuntiationes*, unlike the *nuntiationes* of augurs, could be disregarded by the presiding magistrate if he deemed them irrelevant.[34]

With this introduction to the auspices and their uses, let us now turn to the ritual of *inauguratio*, in which the augur used auspices to create a priest. Our avenue into this ritual will be a late republican incident involving a new god, a new priesthood, and a traditionalist's complaint.

9.4. Cognition-about-Practice: Antony's Flaminate

Shortly after Julius Caesar's assassination in March 44 BCE, his longtime supporter and general Mark Antony began to assert his prerogatives as *flamen divi Iulii*, "flamen of Divine Julius," a new priesthood for which Caesar himself, in his capacity as *pontifex maximus*, selected him while he still lived.[35] Cicero responds to this situation in a speech that he circulated, but never delivered, late in 44 BCE. The augur and expert in traditional religion was not pleased at the prospect of a deified Caesar with Antony for a priest. His speech, the Second Philippic, attacks Antony (*Phil.* 2.110):

33. Festus ex Paulo 316–17L: *quinque genera signorum observant augures publici: ex caelo, ex avibus, ex tripudiis, ex quadripedibus, ex diris*. The *auspicia ex tripudiis* were impetrative only.

34. On the *nuntiatio* of augurs and citizens, and the magistrates' *obnuntiatio*, see Vaahtera 2001: 144–45, 151–60; and Linderski 1986a: 2195–208.

35. As pontifex maximus, in anticipation of divine honors, Caesar appears to have exercised his right of *captio* (on which, see the text at n. 47, below) on Antony: so Weinstock 1971: 306. Cf. not only Cic. *Phil.* 2.110 and 13.41, but also Suet. *Iul.* 76.1; Dio 44.6.4; Wardle 2009: 105–7.

est ergo flamen, ut Iovi, ut Marti, ut Quirino, sic divo Iulio M. Antonius. quid igitur cessas? cur non inauguraris? sume diem, vide qui te inauguret; collegae sumus; nemo negabit. o detestabilem hominem, sive quod tyranni sacerdos es sive quod mortui! . . . aut undique religionem tolle aut usquequaque conserva!

So, as Jupiter, Mars, and Quirinus have their *flamines*, so is Marcus Antonius the *flamen* of *divus Iulius*. Why then do you delay? Why are you not inaugurated? Pick a day, see who might inaugurate you; we are your augural colleagues; no one will refuse. O you hateful man, whether priest of a tyrant or of a dead man! . . . Either destroy religious practice altogether or preserve it in its entirety!

It would be easy to see here, in Cicero's biting questions about Antony's failure to have himself inaugurated into his novel flaminate by a member of the augural college, merely one more example of what is often referred to as the Romans' scrupulousness about ritual practice, or orthopraxy.[36] However, Cicero was only proximally concerned here with incorrect ritual practice.[37] For the *practical* scrupulousness on the surface of Cicero's complaint reflects a deeper *cognitive* scrupulousness, a concern about what could legitimately be *believed*, not only about Antony and his novel flaminate, but also about that priesthood's dubious god. For Caesar was after all a dead *man*, and his would-be flamen was a pretender to a priesthood whose legitimacy Cicero could scarcely bring himself to acknowledge, as his tone amply suggests.

"Why are you not inaugurated?" he asks. "Pick a day, see who might inaugurate you." The implication, of course, is that no augur, least of all Cicero, will inaugurate him. To do so would be to legitimize Antony as *flamen divi Iulii* and, in so doing, Caesar's flaminate as an institution. Indeed, it would amount to tacit acceptance of Caesar as god. *Inauguratio*'s legitimizing power owed to the fact that the ritual's proper performance *changed* states of affairs in the Roman religious world. As we saw in section 9.3, above, *inauguratio* altered "the status of an *object* of the ceremony."[38] The conferral of a new status on an inaugurand granted him new deontic powers, which opened up for him new possibilities for socially consequential action. For Cicero, to legitimize the new priesthood of Caesar by conferring the flaminate, with a flamen's deontic powers, on Antony would have been to damage traditional practice. This prompts him to

---

36. See above, chapter 1.

37. Antony was eventually inaugurated in 40 BCE: see Plut. *Ant.* 33.1 with Pelling 1988: 206 (citing Weinstock 1971: 304–8 and 399). For a summary of relevant facts and references, see Rüpke 2008: 537.

38. Linderski 1986a: 2296 (emphasis added).

demand that Antony either *preserve* religious practice (*religio*) or go ahead and *destroy* it entirely.

Let us now take a closer look at the ritual of *inauguratio* in order to see how it could work such significant outcomes in the Roman religious world. Livy preserves our most detailed single description of an inauguration in his account of Numa's mythical regal inauguration, which would have taken place after the death (traditionally dated to 716 BCE) of Rome's first, legendary king, Romulus. (We examined prayer associated with this ritual at section 8.5.) Livy gives us the inauguration of a king, but in the historical republic it was priests who were inaugurated.[39] Indeed, Cicero remembers his own "cooptation" and inauguration into the augural college by his friend, the augur Hortensius.[40] Here is Livy's description of Numa's ceremony (1.18.6–10):

> *Inde ab augure ... deductus in arcem, in lapide ad meridiem versus consedit.* [7] *Augur ad laevam eius capite velato sedem cepit, dextra manu baculum sine nodo aduncum tenens, quem lituum appellarunt. Inde ubi prospectu in urbem agrumque capto deos precatus regiones ab oriente ad occasum determinavit, dextras ad meridiem partes, laevas ad septentrionem esse dixit;* [8] *signum contra quod longissime conspectum oculi ferebant animo finivit; tum lituo in laevam manum translato, dextra in caput Numae imposita, precatus ita est:* [9] *"Iuppiter pater, si est fas hunc Numam Pompilium cuius ego caput teneo regem Romae esse, uti tu signa* [10] *nobis certa adclarassis inter eos fines quod feci." Tum peregit verbis auspicia quae mitti vellet. Quibus missis declaratus rex Numa de templo descendit.*

> When he [sc. Numa] had been led to the citadel by an augur ... , he sat on a stone, facing south. [7] The augur, his head covered, holding in his right hand a hooked staff without knots, which they call a *lituus*, took a seat to the left of him. Then, after he took into his view the city and countryside, prayed to the gods, and marked the regions from east to west, he declared the parts to the south to be "right," those to the north to be "left." [8] He marked with his mind a sign opposite him, as far away as his eyes could see. Then, transferring the staff to his left hand and putting his right hand on Numa's head, he prayed as follows: [9] "Father Jupiter, if it is religiously acceptable that this man, Numa Pompilius, whose head I am touching, be

---

39. For the inauguration of the *rex sacrorum*, see, e.g., Liv. 40.42.8–11. For the inauguration of *augures*, see, e.g., Cic. *Brut.* 1. For the *flamines*, see n. 47, below. Details in Linderski 1986a: 2218–22 and 2224–25.

40. *Brut.* 1: *cooptatum me ab eo* [sc. Hortensio] *in conlegium recordabar, in quo iuratus iudicium dignitatis meae fecerat, et inauguratum ab eodem.*

king of Rome, may you exhibit to us [10] clear signs within the boundaries that I have established." Then he specified in words the *auspicia* that he wanted to be sent. When these *auspicia* were sent, Numa was declared king and he descended from the *templum*.

To accomplish an *inauguratio*, as Livy describes it, the augur demarcates a space in his field of vision, the *templum in aëre*, which he will watch for signs. He recites a prayer, or *precatio*, in which he invokes Jupiter, specifies the purpose of the *inauguratio*, and requests the "clear signs," *signa certa*, that will indicate the god's will. Then he stipulates the precise *signa certa* that Jupiter should send if he wishes to approve the candidate, and thereby effect his inauguration. Livy does not say, but perhaps the augur requested that Jupiter send "a crow singing on the left, a raven on the right" (*cornicem a laeva, corvum ab dextera canere*) in Cicero's formulation (*Div.* 1.12; cf. Plaut. *As.* 259–61).[41]

Now, when an augur performs an inauguration, the actions that make up the ritual may be conceptualized by different observers in different ways. The bare, empirical data in the actions described by Livy, available to the perceptual faculties of any neurotypical, sighted observer, are these: one man produces utterances and gestures while touching the head of another, and then a bird flies or sings. This way of representing the ritual, diagrammed in figure 9.1,[42] shows that the happenings reported by Livy are, at a culturally naive level of description, just two discrete sets of actions, those of a man and those of a bird. Taken individually and taken together, they lack any special significance, religious or otherwise. Nor is there any inherent connection between them for the naive observer.

If, however, we posit an ideal Roman observer, well versed in augury, we find that this observer represents the actions that make up the ritual quite differently, as shown in figure 9.2, where I have represented the historically more realistic inauguration of an augur rather than Livy's inauguration of a king. Insofar as a culturally informed observer judges the actions—of the priest and of the bird(s)—as components in the performance of *inauguratio*, then he or she represents them as causally linked. The observer sees the individual actions as moments in the larger ritual sequence of inauguration (figure 9.2: ACTION 1). For the culturally informed observer, the act of inaugurating (figure 9.2: ACT 1A) involves a subsidiary act (figure 9.2: ACT 1B) in which the augur requests of Jupiter ("impetrates") signs of approval regarding the

---

41. For the augural procedures in Livy's passage, see Linderski 1986a: 2256–96.

42. My diagrams in figures 9.1, 9.2, and 9.3 are inspired by the diagrams in E. T. Lawson and McCauley 1990: 93; and McCauley and Lawson 2002: 14. I am grateful to Kate Stanchak for turning my crude sketches into the crisp illustrations you see here.

BELIEF, RITUAL, AND RELIGIOUS POWER 351

ACTION 1				ACTION 2	
Agent Man 1	Act Touches while uttering, gesturing, etc.	Patient Man 2	THEN	Agent Birds	Act Fly or sing

FIGURE 9.1. Actions of Livy 1.18.6–10 as represented by an augurally naive observer.

candidate. This request engenders the god's response (figure 9.2: ACTION 2): he sends a bird or birds, which appear on the scene flying or singing. Thus, the action of the augur ultimately results in the bird's behavior.

Notice the crucial fact that the action role of the bird differs from observer to observer. In figure 9.1 (ACTION 2), the naive observer represents the bird in the AGENT role, while in figure 9.2 (ACTION 2) the knowledgeable observer represents the bird as PATIENT. The naive observer perceives the bird as the agent responsible for its own flight or song. But the Roman observer in figure 9.2 conceives the bird as the patient of an act performed on it by Jupiter. For the informed observer, the agency of the god has displaced the bird's agency.

Ammianus Marcellinus advocates precisely this way of representing the bird's and Jupiter's respective action roles when he states that in augury, "the god directs the flights of birds" (*volatus avium dirigit deus*; 21.9). This was surely the fundamental idea underlying the use of birds as vessels of divine communications. Indeed, Cicero informs us that the Romans believed (*putamus*) some birds were born for the very purpose of such communication.[43] Philosophical defenses of divine control over augural birds could be mounted, as by Quintus, arguing as a Stoic in Cicero's *De divinatione* (Cic. *Div.* 1.120):

> *Eademque efficit in avibus divina mens, ut tum huc, tum illuc volent alites, tum in hac ... tum a dextra, tum a sinistra parte canant oscines. Nam si animal omne, ut vult, ita utitur motu sui corporis ... eaque ante efficit paene quam cogitat, quanto id deo est facilius, cuius numini parent omnia.*

The divine mind causes the same effects in birds, so that "flying birds" [*alites*] fly here and there ... while "singing birds" [*oscines*] sing now on the

---

43. Cic. N.D. 2.160: *avis quasdam, et alites et oscines, ut nostri augures appellant, rerum augurandarum causa esse natas putamus.*

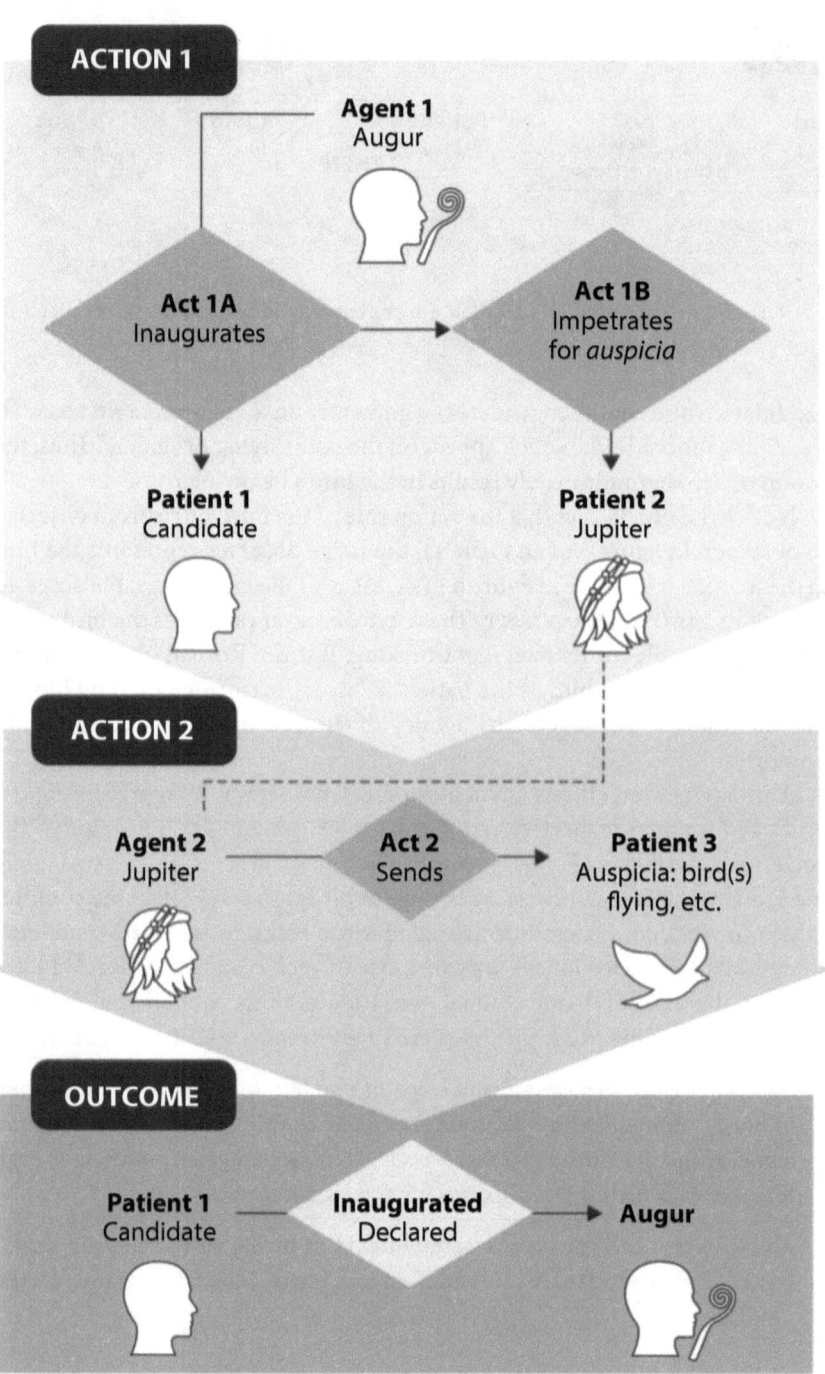

FIGURE 9.2. Actions of Livy 1.18.6–10 as represented by an ideal Roman observer.

right, now on the left. For if every animal moves its body as it wishes ... and causes these effects almost without thinking about it, how much easier is it for the god to cause these effects, whose will all things obey.

Quintus insists on the god's causal control over the doings of *aves*, but he alludes to the mundane intuition that birds might be the agents of their own actions. Indeed, technical augural terminology suggests that Romans could entertain conflicting intuitions on this point. Common formulas for a positive answer in auspication include *aves addicunt*, "the birds assent," and *aves admittunt*, "the birds permit," while a negative answer could be marked by *aves abdicunt*, "the birds refuse."[44] The active verbs, with *aves* as subject, suggest hard-to-shake intuitions about the birds' own agency. The point is simply that mundane intuitions about animal agency could coexist with culturally stipulated, "counterintuitive" beliefs about divine intervention in avian behavior.[45] Perhaps Ovid means to comment wryly on the misfit between augural doctrine and mundane intuition when he writes that it is the *gods*, rather than we mortals, who believe that birds reveal the divine intentions: *dique putant mentes vos* [sc. *aves*] *aperire suas* (F. 1.446).

These statements of Ammianus, Quintus, and Ovid draw our attention to what is surely the most striking feature of the ideal Roman observer's conceptualization of what he sees in Livy's inauguratio: the representation of Jupiter as a participant in the ritual (figure 9.2: ACTION 2). Nothing in the strictly empirical data would suggest the presence of a superhuman agent, as the hypothetical naive observer's representation of the actions in figure 9.1 shows. There is nothing inherent in the behavior of birds, as Quintus concedes, to suggest anything but the most mundane animal agency. And yet figure 9.2 shows that informed observers represent in this tableau an entity that is not directly perceptible, Jupiter, first in the action role of PATIENT, receiving and attending to the augur's petitions, and then in the action role of AGENT, guiding the behavior of birds and thereby either granting or denying the augur's request to translate the candidate to inaugurated status.

The contrast is clear: the two observers' representations of the scene and its constituent actions, agents, and patients are incommensurable. Culturally naive observers see only men and birds. They ascribe no special significance to or causal connections among their respective actions. Culturally informed observers, by contrast, see the actions of men and birds as moments in, and

44. E.g., Liv. 1.55.3 and 27.16.15 (*addicere*); Plaut. As. 259 and Liv. 1.36.6 (*admittere*); Cic. Div. 1.31 (*abdicere*). See further, Linderski 1986a: 2293n589.

45. On the "counterintuitive," and hence attention-grabbing, memorable, and inferentially rich character of many religious representations, see above at section 8.6.

the agents and patients as participants in, a total ritual sequence, in which a divine agent plays a central part.

We have dealt with the god, but what of the human participants, the augur and the candidate? Here, too, the Romans held distinct beliefs about the status and qualifications of both the ritual's agent and its patient. Notice that for the naive observer of figure 9.1, the AGENT and PATIENT roles are filled by two men lacking any salient social qualities beyond gender. However, for the Roman observer of figure 9.2, these roles could properly be filled only by people possessing appropriate social status and ritual qualifications. The PATIENT of the inauguration—in Livy's account, Numa, but in historical practice candidates for certain priesthoods—could occupy this role only if he or she met certain conditions.

In the late republic, candidates for various priesthoods including the flaminate—the major three flamens being those of Jupiter (Dialis), Mars (Martialis), and Quirinus (Quirinalis)[46]—underwent an elaborate procedure. First, the pontifical college nominated (*nominatio*) three candidates. Then one of them was selected (*captio*) by the head priest, the pontifex maximus, as Caesar had selected Antony in anticipation of divine honors. Finally, the selected candidate, the *captus*, had to request that an augur inaugurate (*inauguratio*) him or her.[47] All these prior actions were required before the candidate was eligible to occupy the PATIENT role in the ritual of inauguration where, finally and definitively, Jupiter might grant or deny the candidate's transference to priestly status.

For their part, agents who performed an inauguration had to be augurs. Without such status, any "augural" actions they undertook could not possibly have been judged efficacious; these actions would have been merely a mimicry of augural actions. Augurs were, after all, "the interpreters and mediators (*interpretes internuntiique*) of Jupiter Optimus Maximus," in Cicero's words.[48] They themselves owed their unique status, with its unique deontic powers, to Jupiter and his favorable auspices. To attain augural status, a candidate had, like any other priestly candidate, first to be "coopted" (*cooptatio*), a step that Cicero mentions with respect to his own ritual biography.[49] Then, also like other candidates, the candidate had to be inaugurated. Thus, a man could hold augural status, and could perform *inaugurationes*, only if Romans could

---

46. See Rüpke 2008: 8 and 44–48 for the "major" three and the many "minor" *flamines*.

47. *Nominatio*: Tac. *Ann.* 4.16.2. *Captio*: Liv. 27.8.5; Gell. 1.12.15–16. *Inauguratio*: Liv. 27.8.4; Gai. *Inst.* 1.130 (*flamen Dialis*); Macr. *Sat.* 3.13.11 (*flamen Martialis*). See further Vanggaard 1988: 56.

48. *Phil.* 13.12: *Iovis optimi maximi . . . interpretes internuntiique*; cf. *Leg.* 2.20, quoted above at section 9.3.

49. Cic. *Brut.*, quoted at n. 40, above.

represent him as having himself been an appropriate candidate for the augurate and as having himself successfully undergone the ritual of *inauguratio*. This means that a more complete diagram of the informed observer's conception of the ritual depicted in figure 9.2 would have to include an "embedded" representation of the "enabling ritual" that made the augur a causally effective ritual agent, that is, the augur's own inauguration by an augur.[50] I have provided this in figure 9.3, with abbreviated schemata of the inaugurations themselves.

Before we leave figure 9.2 behind and turn to figure 9.3, however, do note that in the inauguration of a priest, Jupiter is *doubly* active. This double activity is legible in figures 9.2 and 9.3 taken together. First and most obviously, Jupiter is *directly* active in the inauguration that creates an augur. For he is the agent who sends signs of approval by way of auspices. However, the god is also *indirectly* active in every inauguration, in that he is connected to the ritual's primary AGENT role through his authorized terrestrial agent, the officiating augur who performs the inauguration. This is because the augur's own authority to initiate and perform an inauguration derives from his or her augural investiture by Jupiter himself, through his auspices. So, the initial AGENT role of any augural ritual, which is always filled by an augur, mediates the agency of Jupiter in the person of the augur, whose authority derives from Jupiter and who is, as we have seen, the *interpretes internuntiique* of the god.

Turning now to figure 9.3: it shows how an informed Roman might have conceived the immediate ritual basis of the status of any given augur (AGENT x^1). That is, it was necessary for the candidate to have been inaugurated (ACTION X) in order to become an augur (OUTCOME X), just as, Cicero reminds us, it would have been necessary for Antony to have been inaugurated in order for him to be a flamen. This inauguration, which granted an augur or any other priest his or her ritual authority, will ideally have been represented by participants and observers as an embedded enabling ritual. In figure 9.3, ACTION X (leading to OUTCOME X) is the enabling ritual embedded in an observer's representation of AGENT x^1 and of any ritual action he or she undertakes, ACTION x^1 (leading to OUTCOME x^1).

In fact, figure 9.3 oversimplifies for the sake of clarity. For notice that an inauguration is not the only enabling ritual that will be represented as embedded in a given, current ritual, such as ACTION x^1. Recall our constitutive rule, *X counts as Y in context C*, from section 5.3.2. We saw that this constitutive rule could be applied recursively. Entity X_1 may count as Y_1 in context C_1, but then

---

50. For the cognitive "embedding" of requisite, prior "enabling rituals," see above, section 9.2.

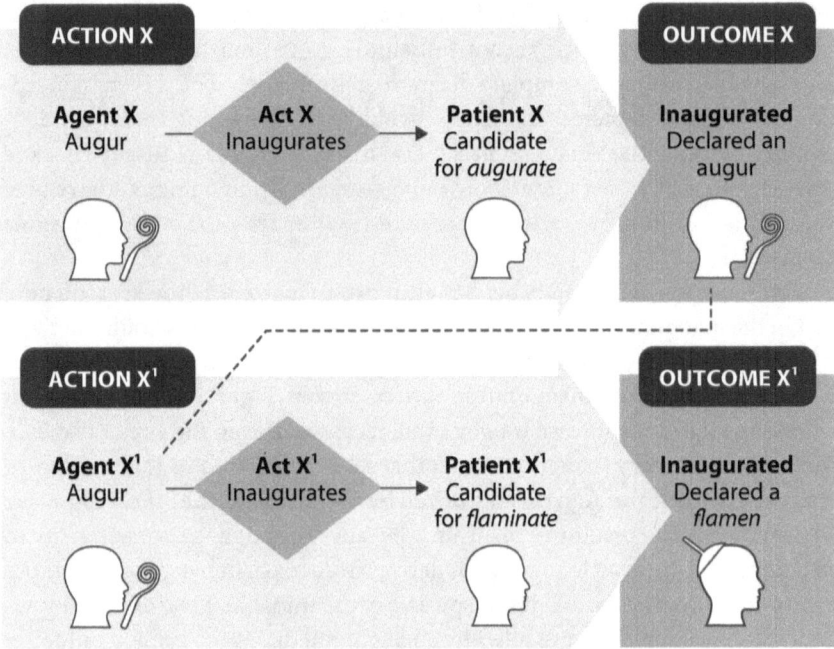

FIGURE 9.3. Ideal representation of enabling ritual bearing on an augur (AGENT X¹).

Y_1 can appear in the role of X_2 and be counted as Y_2 in C_2, and so on recursively, without limit. We have seen an example of this process, just above, in the steps for becoming a flamen. Thus, X_1 (say, *Antonius*) might come to count as Y_1 (*Antonius nominatus*), and then Y_1 (*Antonius nominatus*) might go on, as X_2, to come to count as Y_2 (*Antonius captus*). Finally, Cicero would have had far less ammunition if *Antonius captus* (Y_2) had, as candidate (X_3), been inaugurated and declared to count as flamen (Y_3).

Note the confluence here of the logical, the ontological, the practical, and the cognitive. Recursivity is a *logical possibility* of the underlying form of the constitutive rule, *X counts as Y in C*. This logical possibility inherent in the constitutive rule opens up *ontological possibilities* for human social reality, where social statuses may be stacked recursively one atop the other or where the condition of the possibility of holding one social status, Y_2, may be the prior tenure of some other social status, Y_1. As one might expect, the social practices that bestow new ontological statuses track this recursive pattern, with the ritual of *inauguratio* following on that of *captatio*, which itself follows upon *nominatio*, and so on. Finally, we cognitively represent enabling practices as embedded in current practices, a new social status as overlaying or depending on a prior social status, and so forth, in accord with the recursive logic of the constitutive rule.

Note that this recursivity that we have just described opens up the possibility of an infinite, or at least indefinite, regress. In the case of sacerdotal authority, to represent this recursive process cognitively is to represent the augur who inaugurated the augur who inaugurated the augur, and so on, in a regress of prior enabling rituals bearing on the augur who inaugurated the priest in question. Even leaving all the relevant *nominationes* and *cooptationes* aside, a complete representation of the conditions of a given augur's authority to inaugurate priests would have to embed a series of enabling inauguration rituals stretching back further, and incorporate more inaugurations of more augurs, than any human mind could hope to cope with.

Here aetiology comes to the rescue and does its cognitive work. The myth of Romulus—the founder through augury not only of Rome, but of Rome's *auspicia*, and of the augural college, co-opting one augur from each of the original three tribes[51]—allowed Romans to "theorize" about the origins of augury and its validity, to ground their own augural practice in a foundational agreement between Romulus and the tutelary god of the seven hills, and, most importantly for present purposes, to close the recursive series of augural rituals in the actions of an heroic, even divine, *primus inventor*, or founding figure.[52] Indeed, in the tradition attested by Ennius and Livy, Romulus founded Rome precisely by founding *inauguratio* in his originary consultation of the auspices, *simul auspicio augurioque*, "by auspice and augury at once," in Ennius's words.[53]

So, to Roman eyes, the *proximate* source of any given priest's or augur's status and deontic powers will have stemmed from the auspices sent by Jupiter himself at his inauguration. But the *ultimate* source of that status and those powers—and indeed of the validity and efficacy of every auspicial and augural act, and of the institutionalized practices of *inauguratio* and *auspicatio*—will have traced back to Romulus's establishment of a privileged relationship,

---

51. Cic. *Rep.* 2.16: *ex singulis tribubus singulos cooptavit augures*. Cf. Dion. Hal. 2.22.3. Livy has Numa establish the college (1.18.6): *augure, cui deinde honoris ergo publicum id perpetuumque sacerdotium fuit*.

52. For the divinity of Romulus, his foundation of Rome, and of the auspices, see, e.g., Cic. *Rep.* 2.17; Cic. *N.D.* 3.5; and the references in the following note.

53. Enn. *Ann.* fr. 47 (Skutch). Cf. Enn. *Ann.* fr. 155 (Skutch): *augusto augurio postquam incluta condita Roma est*; Livy 1.6.4: *ut di quorum tutelae ea loca essent auguriis legerent qui nomen novae urbi daret, qui conditam imperio regeret, Palatium Romulus, Remus Aventinum ad inaugurandum templa capiunt*; 1.18.6: *augurato urbe condenda*; 5.52.2: *urbem auspicato inauguratoque conditam*.

mediated by the auspices, with Jupiter on that day when he prayed to local tutelary deities on the Palatine. In the terms established in section 9.2, Romulus's aetiological *inauguratio* represents the "hypothetical ritual" that establishes a ritual bond with Jupiter and guarantees the efficacy and legitimacy of all *inaugurationes* that follow. His founding *inauguratio* originated and legitimated the series of enabling rituals that continued through every *inauguratio* on the *arx*. Denis Feeney has rightly warned against viewing "aetiology as bad history," averring that it was "rather the ancients' way of doing theory."[54] Whatever we think of the historicity of the Romulus story, it clearly did cognitive work for the Romans, allowing them to theorize about the ultimate source of augural authority, posit a (semi)divine charter for augural practice, and close the series of augural rituals in a legendary original.

Now, let us consider the nature of the religious change that has occurred when an augur is inaugurated. We saw in our discussion of cognitive theory (section 9.2) that participants should tend to intuit that ritual action is efficacious, that it causes "changes in the religious world." McCauley and Lawson hypothesize that a predictable cognitive consequence of participants representing a god directly or indirectly connected to an AGENT role in a ritual is that they should have intuitions that the ritual has "permanent" effects and thus never requires repetition.[55] What is done by a god, either directly or indirectly, through an intermediary agent, is done for good and need not be redone. As it happens, Romans conceived inauguration in precisely this manner. Inauguration was a one-time affair. To quote Linderski: "The positive answer at an augury . . . bestowed a kind of permanence upon the object of the ceremony."[56] Augurs were augurs for life once they were inaugurated. Neither imprisonment nor exile affected their special religious status.[57]

McCauley and Lawson hazard the further hypothesis that rituals like this, which feature a god in connection to an AGENT role, will tend to be reversible. That is, as a cognitive corollary of the intuition that their effects are *lasting*, such rituals will under certain circumstances spawn intuitions that they may or must be ritually "undone."[58] In contrast, rituals in which superhuman beings occupy roles other than AGENT will not be intuited to have permanent effects and so will not require special rituals to reverse them. Thus, ritual systems will typically not feature rituals for undoing, say, sacrifice, in which gods

---

54. Feeney 1998: 128.

55. McCauley and Lawson 2002: 30–32. The historical record has not unequivocally confirmed the hypothesis. See Gragg 2011 and Larson 2016: 225–26.

56. Linderski 1986a: 2296.

57. Plin. *Nat. Hist.* 18.2: *honosque is non nisi vita finitur et exules etiam captosque comitatur.*

58. McCauley and Lawson 2002: 31, 132–34.

occupy PATIENT roles, as recipients of offerings. Nonetheless, by virtue of the durability of their effects, rituals such as inauguration may sometimes require undoing.

Here, too, Roman religion lines up with the cognitive hypothesis. We have evidence that some sacerdotal inaugurations could be reversed. For example, a Vestal could be "exaugurated" out of her priesthood at the end of her thirty-year tenure, which freed her to marry.[59] We also know that inaugurated places could be subjected to *exauguratio*. This is well illustrated by the story of the temple of Jupiter on the Capitoline Hill. Our sources explain that when the legendary last king of Rome, Tarquinius Superbus, wished to build a temple to Jupiter on the Capitoline Hill, he had to contend with the fact that shrines to other gods had already been built and inaugurated there. These he had to exaugurate one by one so that he could remove them to clear ground for Jupiter's temple. As Cato writes (*Orig.* 1, fr. 24 [Peter]):

> *fana in eo loco compluria fuere. ea exauguravit, praeterquam quod Termino fanum fuit; id nequitum exaugurari.*
>
> There were a great many shrines in that place. These he exaugurated, except the shrine of Terminus. This could not be exaugurated.

The ritual of *exauguratio* was not successful for Terminus's shrine. The gods refused to allow it. And so his shrine remained, incorporated into the new temple of Jupiter, "visible proof," as Linderski writes, "of that augural rule" that prescribed the ritual of *exauguratio* to reverse an *inauguratio*.[60]

Other accounts add the shrine of Iuventas to that of Terminus.[61] Whatever the diversity in the details of these stories, the underlying intuition that informs their ritual action, and that of the exauguration of Vestals, remains uniform: representations of divine agency in *inaugurationes* occasion intuitions of lasting ritual effects. In accord with the cognitive hypothesis about our ritual intuitions, these lasting effects are reversible only if the original ritual is reversed, thus channeling the agency of the god once again, but now to undo what he had previously done.

The upshot is that Roman intuitions and beliefs about ritual action derive from developmentally natural cognition about mundane action. The Roman

---

59. Gell. 7.7.4: *si quadraginta annos nata sacerdotio abire ac nubere voluisset, ius ei potestasque exaugurandi atque nubendi facta est*. In CIL VI, 1978 we read of *M. Sosius Laelianus Pontius Falco loco L. Anni Ravi exaugurati*, showing that in 170 CE *Salii* could be exaugurated (see Syme 1989: 255; Rüpke 2008: 530).

60. Linderski 1986a: 2296. Livy reports the same story at 1.55.2–4.

61. Livy 5.54.7; Dion. Hal. 3.69; Flor. 1.1.7.8.

ritual system and Roman ritual action were constrained but also fecundated and structured by natural cognition. Given representations of Jupiter as a participating agent in inauguration, a variety of intuitions and beliefs follow, as "cognitive fallout," as it were. These resultant intuitions and beliefs have, as we just saw, implications for the structure of the ritual system, for augural law and norms, and for the religious actions and ritual biographies of individuals.

At this point I want to pause to emphasize that the purpose of the foregoing discussion has *not* been to rehearse the ritual norms that determined how Antony could have been made a flamen or, more broadly, a candidate could have become a priest, in Rome. Nor has my primary point been to provide a comprehensive set of diagrams showing how Romans ideally conceptualized the rituals of inauguration by which priests were made. Nor have I intended to assert that all Romans were "ideal" culturally informed observers of their own rituals, all of them equally well acquainted with the details of ritual form and the niceties of augural doctrine. Nor, finally, have I wished to assert that the details of ritual form and the niceties of augural doctrine remained static or were objects of consensus throughout the republican era. Indeed, the Roman penchant for multiple aetiologies and the welter of traditions surrounding so many Roman institutions attest otherwise.[62]

My point, rather, in presenting and discussing the diagrams in figures 9.1–3, has been to illustrate some features of cognition-about-practice. I have sought to show starkly that insofar as a Roman observer, at any given moment in Roman history, was capable of distinguishing a performance of *inauguratio* from culturally insignificant head touching and bird flight, or indeed from head touching and bird flight under some other cultural description, that observer was necessarily bringing to bear a host of beliefs in forming intuitions and judgments about the actions he or she was observing.

In cognition-about-practice, an observer brought to bear his or her beliefs concerning at least three aspects of the ritual observed. The observer brought, first, his or her beliefs about the actions that constitute the practice as the practice it is, including deontic beliefs that represent its practical norms of performance. For, lest the observer be likened to the naive observer, he or she required beliefs about the normative gestures of *inauguratio* just in order to recognize it as such when he or she saw it, as well as to adjudge *this* performance a well- or ill-formed one. Our observer brought, second, his or her beliefs, including deontic beliefs, about the agents (including the divine

---

62. Compare the foundation stories in Dionysius (*Ant. Rom.* 1.72–75), Plutarch (*Rom.* 1–2), Servius (*ad Aen.* 1.273), and Festus (326–9L), and cf. those in Ennius, Cicero, and Livy (cited in nn. 51–53, above).

agents: more on this at section 9.6) who may or must participate in the ritual. Thus, if Cicero had had no such beliefs about the ritual's normative agents—which human agent must be inaugurated and which human agent must do the inaugurating—he could never have asked Antony, "Why are you not inaugurated?" And he could never have suggested that Antony appeal to an augur. Third, and finally, our observer brought beliefs about the effects or changes in social and religious reality that resulted from such rituals. Without such beliefs, our well-informed observer could no more reckon the candidate in figure 9.2 transformed into an augur than Cicero could reckon Antony *not* transformed into the first *flamen Divi Iulii*. These three categories of beliefs guided observers' and participants' intuitions and judgments about the ritual they were observing or participating in, about the agents and patients of the ritual, and about the ritual's outcomes and effects.

9.5. Cognition-in-Practice

Cognition-in-practice is the flip side of cognition-about-practice. I treat of it only briefly here (see chapter 3; and chapter 4, especially at section 4.3.5). Where cognition-about-practice is, as we saw, evaluative, cognition-in-practice is, as one might guess, practical. Where the former involves observers referring to their beliefs in order to evaluate the actions, gestures, words, and agents associated with a given performance, the latter involves appropriate agents *acting on* their beliefs in order to perform the actions constitutive of a given practice. In both cases, many of these beliefs are *deontic* beliefs: that is, they are *normative* representations, representing not only how things *are* but also how they *should be*. These deontic beliefs, brought to bear in cognition-about-practice for purposes of evaluation and brought to bear in cognition-in-practice for purposes of action production, represent, as their content, the conditions of satisfaction of a well-formed, efficacious *inauguratio*.[63] That is, they picture what it would take to achieve a successful ritual.

When an augur performed the ritual of inauguration in order to make a priest, he believed he was engaging in a distinct practice, that is, *inauguratio*, and he believed that performing it efficaciously consisted in enacting a definite series of gestures, actions, and words, each of which fell under a more or less determinate description. For example, the augur entertained beliefs about the actions required to demarcate the *templum in aëre*, which he would watch for auspices. He entertained beliefs about the verbal formulas and objectives of the *precatio* he uttered in order to specify the purpose of the ritual and to

---

63. On conditions of satisfaction, see at section 2.2.6.

request *signa certa*. He also believed that performing these actions and uttering these formulas would effect a particular outcome, that is, the creation of a *sacerdos*. Ideally, he entertained beliefs about the divine agent to whom he addressed the *precatio* and who would send *auspicia* in response. I say "ideally" because beliefs about the divine agent(s) traditionally associated with *inauguratio* are not deontic but theological; in the polydox Roman context, they admit of a great deal of diversity from one person to another. We explore this further in section 9.6.2, below.

As this enumeration shows, the augur's beliefs were part of the etiology of his actions and behavior. We saw in chapter 3 that the augur also crucially entertained a variety of practical attitudes in order to act, including especially intentions, which represented both his goals and the actions by means of which he would achieve them. Yet these practical Intentional states arose only against the background of his doxastic states. The augur formed the intentions that he formed and did the things that he did, because of what he believed about the augural nature of such doings.

9.6. Constitutive versus Nonconstitutive Beliefs

9.6.1. Constitutive Beliefs

The points made positively in the previous section can be made negatively through the example of Antony's flaminate, as we shall soon see. For the moment, let us linger over the beliefs associated—whether in cognition-about-practice or in cognition-in-practice—with the *effects* of augural ritual. As we saw in section 9.2, above, it has been argued that Roman religion was founded on an "empiricist epistemology," with "tangible results" guiding conservatism and change in cult practice.[64] There is surely something to be said for this with respect to the causal connections a Roman might draw between rituals performed and battles won, crises survived, dinners eaten, children begotten, and imperial power expanded.[65]

However, the creation of a priest is not analogous to battles won, crises survived, dinners eaten, and the rest. The *effect* obtained through augural ritual—the creation of a priest—is not an empirical datum or a "tangible result" on a par with these other events. Battles won, crises survived, and so on are observable, empirical events out there in the world that are available to be construed as effects of proper ritual performance. But no *empirical* effects may

---

64. Ando 2008: 13.
65. I borrow the phrasing of North 1976: 1, which is quoted and discussed in section 9.2, above.

be linked with the transformation of a candidate into a priest in an efficacious *inauguratio*.[66] The change is entirely in the minds of participants and observers, rather than "out there" to be pointed to in the world.

In Livy, Numa descends from the *arx* and is declared king (*declaratus rex*) through the performative utterance of an augur. In the course of the Roman republic, many people must similarly have been declared *sacerdos*, whether flamen, augur, or otherwise. Nothing in the physical, chemical, or biological composition—nothing empirically observable—of those who had undergone inauguration will have changed. And yet something no less real and consequential about them will have changed as a result of the augural ritual. Each of these individuals gained a new status, marked by new deontic powers, that is, by a new set of rights and obligations.

We can only account for this very real change—this genuine effect of ritual action—if we recognize that such effects were predicated on shared beliefs and collective representations *about the mere performance of the ritual*. That is, an individual became a Roman priest, and came to exercise in Roman society the deontic powers associated with his or her specific priesthood, *because* he or she came to be represented, in an augur's declaratory utterance, and thus in collective verbal and mental representations, *as having undergone a well-formed ritual*. The ritual effect, that is to say, turns on cognition-about-practice, especially judgments about the well-formedness of the relevant ritual. The effect is not "out there in the world" waiting to be connected to the ritual but is instead dependent on observers' and participants' beliefs about the ritual itself.[67]

We can sharpen this point by contrasting the approach I am advocating here with the functionalism, ultimately indebted to Durkheim, that is embodied in, for example, Beard and North's edited volume *Pagan Priests*. There, the editors sought the common *functions* that defined priesthood in polytheistic societies. They asked, "What is it that priests *do* within a society that makes them priests?"[68] By my lights, Roman priests were not *made* priests *by* "doing" or performing certain functions, nor by their implication in a nexus of social, political, and religious power. Rather, priests were entitled to

---

66. Of course, the behavior of a bird (or birds) could and no doubt would be seen as an effect of the augur's petition. And the appropriate avian behavior would be seen as connected with the outcome of turning the candidate into a priest. But the point I am making here is that the ultimate practical end of the ritual—to make someone a priest—could not be observed or pointed to as an effect out there in the world.

67. Similarly, in Ovid's *Fasti*, the householder performs a ritual to placate the Manes on the Lemuria. He knows his ritual has been effective insofar as he believes he performed it correctly: "he believes the rites to have been performed without fault," *pure sacra peracta putat* (5.444).

68. Beard and North 1990: 8, emphasis in the original.

perform priestly functions and to wield their special social, political, and religious powers *because* they were collectively represented by their fellow citizens as having ritual histories that authorized them and afforded them special connections to the gods. A Roman priest's capacity to function, to *do* anything qua priest, followed from collective beliefs about and representations of him or her, his or her ritual history, and thus his or her religious and deontological status. Note that on the approach I take here, informed by Lawson and McCauley's ritual theory, not by Durkheim, a priest need not even *do* anything. A successfully inaugurated candidate was a priest regardless of whether he or she ever performed any rituals or not.

"Why are you not inaugurated?"—Cicero's question depends for its power on his audience collectively sharing with him a framework of beliefs about religious institutions, Roman gods, their priests, and the legitimating religious rituals in which both divine and mortal agents play obligatory roles. His attack assumes that his audience conceives *inauguratio* and its role in granting priestly authority more or less as schematized in figures 9.2 and 9.3. In effect, Cicero asserts that even if we accept the dubious flaminate of a dubious god, no Roman could believe that *Antony* was that god's flamen, because no Roman could legitimately represent him as having secured Jupiter's approval in a ceremony of *inauguratio*, which alone could have altered his socioreligious status and granted him the deontic powers of the flaminate.[69]

Cicero's attack thus shows that the Romans' *practical* scrupulousness was also a *cognitive* scrupulousness. Because Antony had not attended properly to practice, Cicero found it impossible to accept, recognize, or believe that Antony was a flamen, and Cicero assumes his audience's intuitions will converge with his own once they have the facts. This shows how misleading is the assertion that "it is a mistake to overemphasize any question of the participants' belief or disbelief in the efficacy of ritual actions."[70] For collective *beliefs* are precisely what cause and sustain the *effects* of rituals like *inauguratio*. If the Romans had not believed in this ritual's efficacy to create Antony as flamen, Cicero's diatribe would have lacked any force.[71]

---

69. I know of no cases in which the god disapproved of a candidate for a priesthood, though we do hear, at Liv. 23.31.13 (on which, see Linderski 1986a: 2168ff.), of C. Claudius Marcellus, who received negative auspices during his *auspicatio* of "investiture" immediately following his election as suffect consul (on these "auspices of investiture," see D.H. *Ant. Rom.* 2.6.1–3).

70. North 2000a: 84.

71. One might object that the bedrock on which the existence of a new flaminate and flamen of Divus Iulius rested was not collective Roman belief but rather the actions of Caesar, or the authority of the senate, the law, or ritual, or even the compulsion of a monopoly on violence. But this objection merely pushes the question of collective belief and acceptance back a level

In the examples of inauguration and Antony's flaminate, then, we see illustrated an important truth about social reality, which happens to be the third thesis I set out to argue in this chapter, namely, that *some beliefs, including some deontic beliefs, are constitutive of social realities as such, including religious practices and the effects of religious practices*. Recall that a belief is a mental representation of a state of affairs as obtaining. Some beliefs have no effect on whether the states of affairs they represent obtain or not. If Cicero believes that Caesar is a dead man, his belief has no causal bearing on whether Caesar is in fact a living or dead human male. Yet in some cases, we *create* states of affairs *by representing them as existing*.[72] Such "constitutive beliefs" constitute or create social realities such as rituals of inauguration, their socioreligious effects such as sacerdotal status, and the deontology consequent upon that status. Constitutive beliefs are *normative* and hence are deontic as well as constitutive, in two senses. First, as components of cognition-in-practice, they *regulate* and guide the performance of rituals by representing the actions, gestures and words that make up well-formed instances of that ritual. In so doing, they additionally provide *the condition of the very possibility* of certain practices. For without beliefs and other representations as to the normative actions, gestures, and words of, for example, *inauguratio*, there would be no possibility of performing *inauguratio*.

It is therefore mistaken to suppose that in Roman religion, "experiences, beliefs and disbeliefs had no particularly privileged role in defining an individual's actions, behaviour, or sense of identity."[73] For the very possibility of *performing* inaugurations, the possibility of *having been inaugurated*, and the possibility of *being* an augur, a flamen, or any priest, depended on the Romans collectively holding certain beliefs about augural practices, about augurs, about flamines, and the rest.

To indulge in some further illustration, look back to Livy's passage on inauguration, quoted in section 9.4. This text, like any text that references Roman religious practice, is strewn with tacit witnesses to the *constitutive* role of

---

or two. Insofar as Romans collectively yielded to Caesar, to the senate, to the law, or to ritual the deontic power to institute new priesthoods, those entities had this power. (Indeed, the sources [e.g., Suet. *Iul.*] are at pains to stress the foundation in popular consensus of Caesar's authority. On the question of consensus about Caesar's divinity, see Pandey 2018: 35–82.) Even monopolies on violence such as late republican armies, which could compel acceptance by force, were products of the collective belief and recognition by soldiers of certain men as leaders and of certain deontologies as compelling in the ranks. Cf. the remarks of Searle 2010: 106–7, 141–42, and 164.

72. For development of this point, see at section 5.3.2 passim.
73. Beard et al. 1998: 1.42.

Roman belief in creating Roman religious reality. In Livy's description, the man is not merely a human organism of the male sex; he is an augur. The staff is a *lituus*, not just a curved length of wood. The actions of the birds count as *auspicia*, as signs sent by a god, not merely as behaviors attributable to avian agency. The *arx* features a built augur's perch, the *auguraculum*, rather than just a random pile of stones. And so forth. Indeed, the whole procedure and all its component actions, agents, and objects constitute moments in or parts of a practice, *inauguratio*. In effect, just as Numa was declared king, or a candidate was declared an augur or flamen, so these otherwise mundane actions, agents, and objects have in effect been *declared* to possess statuses that transcend their physical, chemical, or biological properties, statuses that grant each item its own "deontic aura"[74] of prescriptions, permissions, and prohibitions in the Roman socioreligious world.

These socioreligious realities—*inaugurationes, litui, auspicia, auguracula, augures, flamines*, and so on—existed only because the Romans believed they existed, that is, had accepted the declarations of status, function, and power (Y terms) tacitly or expressly imposed on otherwise unmarked entities (X terms). By contrast, the unmarked entities—human beings, lengths of wood, birds, avian behavior, and piles of stone—can exist independently of anyone's declarations or beliefs. These things possess physical, chemical, or biological features that owe nothing to any speech act or cognitive state of ours. But that *this* man counted as an augur, that *these* actions counted as an *inauguratio*, and so on—expressed in terms of the underlying constitutive rule, that X counts as Y in context C—was due not to inherent features of the entities involved but rather to the Romans' collective acceptance and shared beliefs.

As we saw at some length at section 5.3.1, some entities in the sociocultural world function as they do as a result of their inherent physical properties. The Roman sword, the *gladius*, for example, performed its function just by virtue of the properties of sharpened steel. We illustrated the same point with respect to the defensive function of Rome's Servian Wall. However physically impregnable the wall may have been, it also had a deontic aura, a penumbra of dos and don'ts, which owed not to its physical properties but to its inauguration and its resulting status as *locus inauguratus*.[75]

In just the same way, nothing in the brute physical gestures that went into a performance of augural ritual inherently conduced to the function of *inaugurating*. It was instead because those brute gestures were represented and

---

74. I owe this evocative term to Buekens 2014: 33.

75. Gai. *Inst*. 2.8: *sanctae quoque res, uelut muri et portae, quodam modo diuini iuris sunt*. On the inauguration of *loca sancta*, see Valeton 1892: 338–54.

believed by Romans to be augural and to have certain effects that they *were* augural and *had* those effects. All the religious realities we have been discussing were *constituted as such* not by their inherent features, but by the way they were represented in the Romans' collective beliefs. I have spilled some ink making this point, because its implications are crucial: scholars of Roman religion can oppose practices to beliefs only if they fail to recognize that the fact *that* a practice *is* a practice depends entirely on the beliefs of human beings.

9.6.2. Nonconstitutive Beliefs

It is an objective fact that Cicero was an augur, and as far as we know it is an objective fact that in 44 BCE Antony was not yet a full-fledged flamen.[76] However, these are facts of a peculiar species. They are "institutional facts." Institutional facts are both epistemically *objective*, in that one can have objective knowledge of and make true or false claims about them, and ontologically *subjective*, in that they are created, constituted by, and dependent on subjective states of human beings, such as belief.[77]

Nonetheless, not all the religious beliefs of the Romans were *constitutive* of such institutional facts as ritual practices, auspices, and priestly status. Some religious beliefs were what I call *nonconstitutive* beliefs.[78] Recall the ideal Roman observer's representation of Jupiter's intervention in avian behaviors during *inauguratio* (figure 9.2). A crucial distinction between constitutive and nonconstitutive beliefs may be seen here. For Jupiter's intervention is not an "institutional fact" about the ritual of *inauguratio*, however much it may be a fact about the way Romans ideally represented the ritual. Jupiter's agency neither *simply existed* out there in the world, nor could it be constituted—*made to exist*—by the collective beliefs of the Romans in the same way that a man could be so constituted, or made, a flamen.[79] Nonetheless, Jupiter's agency in inauguration was a genuine Roman belief. Indeed, it is part of the received story about *auguria* assumed by every ancient source on the topic—Ennius,

---

76. See n. 37, above.

77. See further at section 5.2 passim.

78. See Buekens 2014 for more on the distinction between religious beliefs that I call *constitutive* of institutional facts and those that I call *nonconstitutive*.

79. Here my approach differs from that of Revell 2013, which appeals to Giddens 1984. Revell writes, "People made the gods real through the rituals carried out within religious space" (21). I do not deny that the gods were, so to speak, "real to the Romans." They represented the gods as existing and acted accordingly. But they could not "make the gods real" through ritual action in the same way that they could make a person a priest. This is a crucial distinction about the nature of social reality.

Cicero, Dionysius of Halicarnassus, Livy, Plutarch, Servius, and others. So, we must reckon Jupiter's augural agency as a core Roman "religious" belief about the basis of augural authority and indeed about the basis of Roman institutional reality more generally. The same point can be made, mutatis mutandis, about Romulus's aetiological role in founding augural institutions.

It is true that a Roman inclined to take a critical stance might abandon nonconstitutive beliefs about Jupiter or Romulus. Moreover, intellectuals like Polybius could insinuate that such beliefs had been introduced by a cynical elite for social control (6.56.6).[80] A valuable insight implicit in the remarks of incredulous observers like Polybius is that a primary effect of nonconstitutive beliefs, such as the belief that Jupiter indicates his will through augury, is the mystification of the *social* origin of social facts. That is, reference to a divine action, will, or dispensation mystifies or conceals social reality's origin in collective human recognition, acceptance, and belief. If the fact that we are, in the deepest sense, the creators of our own social reality is obscured through theology and other ideologies, we are less likely to attempt to transform that reality.

Polybius and other ancient hermeneuticists of suspicion notwithstanding, the Romans could surely be just as blind to the social origins of their social world as any other historical people. They likely tended not to recognize the ontologically subjectivity of their social reality.[81] Here, we might agree with Durkheim that the Roman social world was, for Romans, objective, external, and coercive.[82] This external, objective social world would presumably have exerted pressure on individual Romans to produce in them that "undisputed, pre-reflexive, naive, native compliance" that Bourdieu calls "doxa."[83] Yet even in this jaundiced sociological mood we must not neglect the fact that

---

80. Even if a given Roman could not entertain the nonconstitutive belief that it was Jupiter who sent auspices, this did not require him to abandon constitutive beliefs about the power of inauguration to create its effects; thus, the ritual and the priests it creates, along with all associated social powers, are preserved. A project of abandoning nonconstitutive beliefs while preserving constitutive beliefs is urged by the Cicero character in *Div.* 2 (see, e.g., 2.148: *nec vero superstitione tollenda religio tollitur*).

81. "Likely": but see Ando 2010a, 2010b, 2015a, and 2015b for discussion of Varro on the human, not divine, origins of religious institutions, and see above at section 5.3.2, toward the end of the section.

82. Durkheim 1982: 50–59.

83. E.g., Bourdieu 1980: "Belief is . . . an inherent part of belonging to a field. . . . Practical faith is the condition of entry that every field tacitly imposes . . . by so arranging things, in practice, that the operations of selecting and shaping new entrants (rites of passage, examinations, etc.) are such as to obtain from them that undisputed, pre-reflexive, naive, native compliance

institutions, however coercive, also open up new possibilities for human action and extend human powers beyond the biological (*you are bigger and stronger than I*) into the deontological (*as an augur, I am entitled to call a halt to your political assembly*).[84] Surely this extension of human powers is the point of institutions and their deontologies. Nor should we lose sight of the fact that Romans could and often did, as in Cicero's *De divinatione*, reflect critically on some if not all of the unspoken "doxic" presuppositions of their own religious culture.

Thus, Romans could hold their *nonconstitutive* beliefs about gods and divine agency quite nonreflectively, as a matter of "pre-reflexive, naive, native" acceptance. And they could also deliberate over, and accept or reject, such beliefs, as when Cicero reminds his audience that Caesar is a mortal man, a very dead one, and not a god. But, whatever the fate of such nonconstitutive beliefs with this or that individual, in this or that era, I hope it is clear that if the Romans had abandoned beliefs *constitutive* of religious practices, effects, statuses, and deontic powers, they would thereby have "destroyed religious practice entirely," as Cicero warned Antony he was about to do (*Phil.* 2.110). (Who can say how many Romans would need to do this in order to reach a tipping point: a majority? All?) To abandon constitutive beliefs is to cease to represent, and so to cease to recognize, the norms of practices, the effects of rituals, the statuses imposed on individuals, and the deontic powers that accompany those statuses. In short, to cease to *recognize* Roman religious institutions amounts to *ending* Roman religious institutions. This was what Cicero accused Antony of doing.[85] It was what Roman Christians eventually succeeded in doing.

9.7. Conclusion: Belief, Religious Reality, and Power at Rome

In this chapter, we have explored the centrality of belief to Roman social ontology, that is, its role in the creation and maintenance of Roman religious reality. Without constitutive beliefs about the normative actions and legitimate participants of augural practices—beliefs that not only inform judgments about but also guide ritual performances—the practices cease to be the practices

---

with the fundamental presuppositions of the field which is the very definition of doxa" (67–68).

84. Cic. *Leg.* 2.31, and cf. 2.21.

85. Surely part of the creative destruction of the late republic was the revision or destruction of accepted institutions and the introduction of new ones, to see which could be made to "stick" in the collective acceptance.

that they are and become instead a series of culturally neutral or insignificant actions carried out by unmarked agents. And without constitutive beliefs about the effects of augury, the social statuses and powers conferred by augural ritual vanish. Finally, beyond these constitutive beliefs about augural practices, priestly status, and power, there existed nonconstitutive, strictly "religious," Roman beliefs about divine agents and their efficacious participation in ritual. I have tried to offer reasons to suppose, contrary to a traditional scholarly tenet, that in Roman religion beliefs *did* play an essential role, not only in cognition-about-practice and cognition-in-practice, but also in constituting and creating the religious practices, effects, statuses, and powers that composed the Roman religious world.

Epilog

COMPARISON, EXPLANATION, AND BELIEF

cetera quoque omnia publica privataque sacra pontificis scitis [sc. *Numa*] *subiecit.*

All other public and private rites Numa subjected to the decrees of the *pontifex*.

LIVY, AB URBE CONDITA, 1.20.6

10.1. Introduction

In this epilog, we briefly recapitulate some central arguments of the book via a look at ancient explanations of sacrifice, that most central of Roman *sacra*. Our epigraph adumbrates two important characteristics of sacrificial ritual. First, in Roman lore, just as Romulus founded the *auspicia* and co-opted the first augurs (section 9.4), so Numa founded the *sacra* and created priesthoods to administer them.[1] Second, just as the augurs supervised the auspices, so the pontifices held authority over the *sacra*, whether public, that is, performed by magistrates, or private, that is, performed by individuals or families.[2]

Here we compare three ancient discussions of sacrifice, two of them treating of Roman *sacra* and one of them treating of barbarian cult—but all three purporting to explain the practices of the "other." We do this in order to see what role in these rituals, if any, either the ancients or we moderns might ascribe to belief. We shall see that ancient polytheists were capable of explaining

---

1. Livy 1.19–21. Cf. Cic. *N.D.* 3.5: *Romulum auspiciis, Numam sacris constitutis fundamenta iecisse nostrae civitatis.* See the note of Pease 1955–58 at Cic. *N.D.* 3.5 for numerous other sources attesting Numa's role in founding the *sacra* and the priesthoods.

2. For the pontifices' role in both public and private *sacra*, see also Cic. *Leg.* 2.30 and *Har. Resp.* 14.

sacrificial action by reference to belief. Moreover, we shall see that even when belief is not part of an emic strategy employed by ancient authors to explain the "other," we are nonetheless licensed to ascribe beliefs in our etic scholarly explanations, in order to peer more deeply into ancient cult practice and render it tractable to our understanding.

Dionysius of Halicarnassus, Arnobius of Sicca, and Julius Caesar produced accounts of the sacrificial practices of the culturally other that were at once explanatory and at least implicitly comparative. They compared the practices of other peoples to their own, more familiar practices and in so doing sought the reasons *why* the peoples under investigation sacrificed as they did. Their accounts are explanatory *because* they are comparative. For the comparative enterprise is a quest for reasons why.

Section 10.3 looks at Dionysius and section 10.4 at Arnobius, both writing about Roman sacrifice, though to very different ends. In section 10.5, we examine Caesar's attempt to explain human sacrifice among the Gauls. In section 10.6, we step back and, by way of reflecting on these three accounts, recapitulate some of the main themes of the book. Before we embark on this project, however, section 10.2 surveys the component actions of Roman sacrifice.

10.2. Prescendi's Model of Roman Sacrifice

Francesca Prescendi has abstracted from the scattered evidence a template of Roman sacrifice.[3] Not every sacrifice will have featured every one of Prescendi's component parts, but the ideal form she extrapolates provides an accurate sense of the lineaments of the procedure. A blood sacrifice proceeded through nine basic steps:

1) Selection of animals,
2) Procession,
3) *Praefatio*,
4) *Immolatio*,
5) Slaughtering of the victims,
6) *Extispicium* and *litatio*,
7) Preparation and cooking of the meat,
8) Offering,
9) Feast.

---

3. Prescendi 2007: 31–51.

A person wishing to sacrifice had first to choose the appropriate animal or animals. These were invariably domesticated animals, usually cows, sheep, or pigs. White animals were selected for celestial deities and black animals for chthonic gods. The sex of the animal typically corresponded to the sex of the god for whom it was destined. Once selected, the animals were led in a procession to the altar by the assistants at sacrifice: *victimarii, popae,* or *cultrarii.* This took place at dawn.[4]

Third came the *praefatio,* a uniquely Roman sacrificial element. Here the sacrificer washed his or her hands, offered a libation of incense and wine on a *foculus,* or portable altar, and invoked the god(s) in prayers. Next, in the *immolatio,* the sacrificer sprinkled the head of the victim(s) with wine and *mola salsa,* a mixture of grain and salt. The slaughter of the victim(s) followed. This was accomplished by the specialized attendants, the *victimarii.*[5]

The sixth step was the *extispicium,* inspection of the carcass to ensure that all the internal organs were in place and normal. If this inspection revealed nothing out of the ordinary, the result was a *litatio,* a successful sacrifice, the gods being thought to have accepted the victim. However, extra, missing, or deformed organs revealed that the gods had not accepted the victim. Another victim had to be offered in its place. This repetition of the slaughtering stage was called *instauratio.*[6] (Recall that the introduction opened with failed sacrifice and *instauratio.*)

The preparation and cooking of the meat, with portions set aside for the gods, followed the establishment of a *litatio.*[7] In the eighth stage, the sacrificer offered the gods their portion of the animal, the blood and *exta,* which were burned on an altar, or *ara.*[8] Finally, the remaining meat was divided up among the human participants and eaten at the feast that closed the sacrifice.[9]

10.3. Roman Sacrifice in Dionysius of Halicarnassus's *Antiquitates Romanae*

We can find most of Prescendi's nine steps in one of the most complete descriptions of Roman sacrifice to have survived from antiquity, written up by Dionysius of Halicarnassus in his *Antiquitates Romanae*. There, Dionysius

---

4. Prescendi 2007: 32–35.
5. Prescendi 2007: 36–39. On the *victimarii,* see Lennon 2015.
6. Prescendi 2007: 39–40.
7. Prescendi 2007: 42–44.
8. Prescendi 2007: 45–48.
9. Prescendi 2007: 48.

describes the celebrations that attended the first-ever Ludi Magni, in 490 BCE.[10] He states, at 7.71.1, that he owes the details of his description of this event to Fabius Pictor, but he also claims to have seen the Romans performing sacrifices exactly like the ones he describes (7.72.18):

> Ταῦτα δὲ Ῥωμαίους ἔτι καὶ εἰς ἐμὲ πράττοντας ἐπὶ ταῖς θυσίαις ἰδὼν ἐπίσταμαι· καὶ μιᾷ πίστει τῇδε ἀρκούμενος οὐ βαρβάρους ἐπείσθην εἶναι τοὺς οἰκιστὰς τῆς Ῥώμης, ἀλλ᾽ ἐκ πολλῶν τόπων συνεληλυθότας Ἕλληνας.

> I know from having myself seen that the Romans do these things at their sacrifices still even in my time. And satisfied with this single proof, I have been convinced that the founders of Rome were not barbarians, but rather Greeks who had come together from many places.

As the final sentence of the quoted text indicates, part of Dionysius's motive in describing Roman sacrifice is to show through structural parallels that it is in fact Greek sacrifice, and thus to prove that the Romans themselves derived originally from Greek stock, a comforting thought, given Roman domination of Greece.[11] Dionysius chooses sacrifice on the theory that it is an inherently conservative practice that will bear accurate witness to its origins. Neither Greek nor Roman would dare innovate or alter sacrificial practice "from fear of divine wrath" (ὑπὸ δείματος ... μηνιμάτων δαιμονίων; 7.70.3).

Dionysius's description of the Ludi Magni begins with the grand procession from the Capitol to the Circus Maximus (7.72.1–4), with its dancers (7.72.5–12) and musicians (7.72.13). As an aside, he indulges briefly in a bit of *interpretatio Graeca*, that is, in showing that the gods worshipped by the Romans are in fact the familiar gods of the Greeks (7.72.13–14):

> τελευταῖα δὲ πάντων αἱ τῶν θεῶν εἰκόνες ἐπόμπευον ὤμοις ὑπ᾽ ἀνδρῶν φερόμεναι, μορφάς θ᾽ ὁμοίας παρέχουσαι ταῖς παρ᾽ Ἕλλησι πλαττομέναις καὶ σκευὰς καὶ σύμβολα καὶ δωρεάς, ὧν εὑρεταὶ καὶ δοτῆρες ἀνθρώποις ἕκαστοι παραδίδονται.

> Last in the procession came the images of the gods, carried on men's shoulders, presenting the same likenesses as those made by the Greeks and having the same dress, symbols, and gifts, of which they are said to be the discoverers and givers to mankind.

---

10. So denominated by Livy, at 2.36.1.
11. See further, *Ant. Rom.* 7.70–71.1; and Gabba 1991: 134–36.

Dionysius then describes the Roman manner of sacrificing (7.72.15):

συντελεσθείσης δὲ τῆς πομπῆς ἐβουθύτουν εὐθὺς οἵ θ' ὕπατοι καὶ τῶν ἱερέων οἷς ὅσιον, καὶ ὁ τῶν θυηπολιῶν τρόπος ὁ αὐτὸς ἦν τῷ παρ᾽ ἡμῖν. χερνιψάμενοί τε γὰρ αὐτοὶ καὶ τὰ ἱερὰ καθαρῷ περιαγνίσαντες ὕδατι καὶ Δημητρίους καρποὺς ἐπιρράναντες αὐτῶν ταῖς κεφαλαῖς, ἔπειτα κατευξάμενοι, θύειν τότε τοῖς ὑπηρέταις αὐτὰ ἐκέλευον. τῶν δ' οἱ μὲν ἑστῶτος ἔτι τοῦ θύματος σκυτάλῃ τοὺς κροτάφους ἔπαιον, οἱ δὲ πίπτοντος ὑπετίθεσαν τὰς σφαγίδας, καὶ μετὰ τοῦτο δείραντές τε καὶ μελίσαντες ἀπαρχὰς ἐλάμβανον ἐξ ἑκάστου σπλάγχνου καὶ παντὸς ἄλλου μέλους, ἃς ἀλφίτοις ζέας ἀναδεύσαντες προσέφερον τοῖς θύουσιν ἐπὶ κανῶν· οἱ δ' ἐπὶ τοὺς βωμοὺς ἐπιθέντες ὑφῆπτον καὶ προσέσπενδον οἶνον κατὰ τῶν ἁγνιζομένων.

When the procession had ended, the consuls and the priests whose duty it was sacrificed oxen. And their manner of performing sacrifices was the same as ours. For after they washed their hands and purified the victims with clean water and sprinkled the fruits of Demeter on their heads, then, having uttering prayers, they ordered their assistants to sacrifice the victims. Some of these assistants struck the temples of the victims with a cudgel while they were still standing, and others held sacrificial knives under them as they fell. And after this, when they had flayed and butchered the victims, they took first fruits from each organ and all the other parts and smearing these with spelt meal they brought them to the officiants in baskets. And the officiants, placing the first fruits on the altars, set fires underneath them and poured a wine offering over them as they burned.

After presenting this tableau to his readers, Dionysius demonstrates at great length that each element of the Roman sacrifice he has described can be paralleled in Greek sacrificial custom, a demonstration that relies on copious quotation of Homer: "That everything took place according to the customs established by the Greeks regarding sacrifice, it is easy to recognize from the poetry of Homer."[12] We shall pass over the details of Dionysius's demonstration and note instead the sacrificial steps identified by Prescendi that may be found here.[13]

The first step, the selection of animals, is referred to obliquely in the verb ἐβουθύτουν, "they sacrificed oxen." The second step, the procession, was Dionysius's object for several chapters before the present one. Dionysius fails to

---

12. D.H. Ant. Rom. 7.72.16–17: ἕκαστον δ' ὅτι κατὰ νόμους ἐγίνετο τοὺς ἀμφὶ θυσίαν ὑφ' Ἑλλήνων καταστᾰθέντας, ἐκ τῆς Ὁμήρου ποιήσεως γνῶναι ῥάδιον.

13. Prescendi, in fact, takes Dionysius's description of Roman sacrifice as one example by which to illustrate her model (2007: 60–70).

mention part of the *praefatio*, the offering of incense and wine on a *foculus*, but he notes the washing of hands and the prayer. Step 4, the *immolatio*, in which the victims are sprinkled with *mola salsa* (here, Δημητρίους καρπούς), is present, as of course is the slaughter of the victim by sacrificial assistants. Dionysius omits mention of step 6, the *extispicium* and *litatio*, but the following step, the preparation and cooking of the meat, is described in some detail, as is step 8, the offering. Dionysius leaves the final feast out of his account.

All in all, Dionysius's description is nearly complete, forming one of the two fullest treatments of Roman sacrifice that survive (I discuss the other one in the following section, 10.4). It is perhaps natural that Dionysius slights the *praefatio* and the *litatio*, two of the most markedly "Roman" elements of Roman sacrifice. For after all, his entire purpose is to establish the Greekness of the Romans, and he can best do this by identifying parallels in their sacrificial procedures and omitting discrepancies.

From the point of view of the aims of this book, there is another, more significant omission than those we have identified thus far. To wit, Dionysius hazards not a single attribution of belief to the Romans, attributing to them solely the psychological state of fear of the gods' wrath. His account is almost pure "behaviorese." He speaks solely of actions, performance, *drōmena*. Beard, North, and Price do not include Dionysius's description of Roman sacrifice in their sourcebook for Roman religion (1998, vol. 2), but at first glance it would seem that the evidence from Dionysius at the very least does not falsify their claim that "experiences, beliefs and disbeliefs had no particularly privileged role in defining an individual's actions, behaviour or sense of identity" (1998: 1.42).

10.4. Roman Sacrifice in Arnobius of Sicca's *Adversus Nationes*

Dionysius's account of sacrifice leaves us faced with some uncomfortable questions: were there *any* beliefs that motivated Romans to undertake the complex sequence of religious actions, the *sacra*, that we have just seen Dionysius describe? Or was it *just* a matter of doing, not of believing, for Roman sacrificers? One ancient author, a convert from traditional Roman polytheism to Christianity, claimed to have answers to these questions. Arnobius of Sicca, in book 7 of his *Adversus nationes*, presents an anatomy of the beliefs that he thought motivated polytheists to sacrifice.[14]

---

14. For Arnobius on sacrifice, see Liebeschuetz 1979: 254–60; Simmons 1995: 304–18; Gilhus 2006: 151–54; and North 2007.

From the start, he signals his intention to *explain* Roman sacrifice rather than merely describe it (7.3.1):

> *primum illud a vobis expetimus noscere, quae sit causa, quae ratio, sacrificia ut faciatis.*

> First, we seek to learn from you [sc. polytheists] what the cause is, what the rationale, that you make sacrifices.

Indeed, in recalling his conversion, in the first book of his work, Arnobius reflects on the days when he was himself a polytheist. *Venerabar, o caecitas, nuper simulacra . . .* : "I recently used to worship (oh the blindness!) images brought forth from the furnace, gods fabricated on anvils and with hammers," and other cult objects, he writes. He is acerbic about the beliefs that had motivated this behavior (1.39):

> *et eos ipsos divos, quos esse mihi persuaseram, adficiebam contumeliis gravibus, cum eos esse credebam ligna lapides atque ossa aut in huius<modi> rerum habitare materia.*

> those very gods, whom I had persuaded myself to exist, I was treating with serious abuse, since I believed them to be wood, stones, and bones, or to inhabit the matter of things of this sort.

Arnobius finds the beliefs (note the psychological language—*mihi persuaseram* and *credebam*) that had motivated his previous religious behavior not only absurd but blasphemous. He singles out the anthropomorphism of the traditional gods for special criticism (e.g., at book 7, chapters 1, 2, 15, 34–35). Of course, he realizes that Christianity, and especially Christ, look equally ridiculous to traditional polytheists, so he spends the remainder of the first book playing defense against the standard attacks of critics: "but he died on the gibbet," *sed patibulo adfixus interiit* (1.40); "you worship one born a man," *natum hominem colitis* (1.42); and so on.

But by book 7, the final book of *Adversus nationes*, Arnobius is ready to devote himself to dissecting the signal institution of Roman state religion. The result is one of the most substantial meditations on Roman sacrifice that we possess from antiquity. Arnobius enumerates a host of beliefs that could serve as *rationes* for performing sacrifice. For example (7.3.3):

> *numquid forte dii caelestes aluntur his sacris?*

> Is it perhaps that the heavenly gods are nourished by these sacrifices?

Or perhaps sacrifice delights and pleases the gods (7.4.1):

> *numquid ... voluptatis alicuius animique ut dicitur causa caeduntur diis hostiae et succensis adiciuntur altaribus?*

> Are victims slaughtered for the gods and piled up on fiery altars for the sake of some pleasure and, as it is said, high spirits?

Or perhaps, as common belief has it, sacrifice placates the gods (7.5.1):

> *sequitur ut illam quoque inspiciamus partem, quam iactari audimus vulgo et populari in persuasione versari: sacrificia superis ea fieri diis causa, ut iras atque animos ponant reddanturque mites et placidi fervidorum pectorum indignatione sedata.*

> It follows for us to examine, too, that opinion that we hear commonly bruited about and circulating in the popular belief: that sacrifices are made to the gods above for this reason: so that they may put down their wraths and bad feelings and be rendered gentle and peaceful, the umbrage of their fevered breasts calmed.

Arnobius goes on in this way for several chapters, stating pagan beliefs about sacrifice and the gods, and then demonstrating their untenability. In the process, he displays a deep knowledge of traditional religion and the discourse around it.

Later in the final book, he returns to the polytheists' rationales for sacrifice, and rehearses some of his criticisms of them (7.36.3):

> *vos pecorum sanguinea vos caedibus et mactationibus hostiarum gaudere, laetari et in gratiam cum hominibus remini offensionibus redire sopitis: nos amorem sanguinis nullum esse in caelitibus ducimus nec esse tam duros, ut miserorum animantium caede saturatas abiciant iras.*

> *You* believe that the gods delight in the blood of cattle, in the slaughter and sacrifice of the victims, that they rejoice and return to favor with men, when their vexations have been soothed. *We* consider that there is no love of blood among the heavenly gods and that they are not so harsh that they give up their wrath when it has been glutted with the slaughter of wretched animals.

Arnobius contrasts *vos*, "you," against *nos*, "we," the beliefs of his prior self against the superior vantage point that his new religion affords him to censure them.

For Arnobius, piety or impiety resides primarily in beliefs and other psychological states, and only secondarily in actions; for action follows upon cognition (7.37.1):

cumque sit opinionum tanta nostrarum vestrarumque diversitas, ubi aut impii aut vos pii, cum ex partium sensibus pietatis debeat atque inpietatis ratio ponderari? Non enim simulacrum qui sibi aliquod conficit quod pro deo veneretur aut qui pecus trucidat innoxium sacrisque incendit altaribus, is habendus est rebus deditus esse divinis.

since there is so great a difference between our beliefs and yours, where are we impious or you pious, when the measure of piety and impiety ought to be weighed on the sentiments of the individual parties? For the man who makes some image to worship as a god or who slays a harmless animal and burns it on consecrated altars is not to be considered to be devoted to divine things.

The dependence of action on belief, and hence the reliability of action as an index of belief, is implied in these words: "the man who makes some image to worship as a god . . . is not to be considered to be devoted to divine things." The cult actions of the polytheist, who worships images and sacrifices animals, indicate his cognitive states, revealing what he is "devoted to." Conversely, right religion, *religio* properly so-called, is constituted by true beliefs: *opinio religionem facit et recta de diis mens*, "belief and correct understanding about the gods constitute religion" (7.37.2).[15]

Opinio religionem facit: with these words, we know unequivocally that we are listening to a Christian. I am scarcely the first to have noticed this. Without explicitly referring to Arnobius, Beard, North, and Simon Price have remarked that by the time we reach the age in which the Christian from Sicca lived and wrote, around the turn of the fourth century (1998: 1.x, emphasis in the original):

we are in a world that is broadly recognisable to us: we can see, for example, issues of religious *belief* being discussed by both pagans and Christians; we can observe religious *communities*, with their own hierarchy and officials, representing a focus of loyalty and commitment quite separate from the political institutions of the state; we can see the range of religious *choices* available (between different communities or different beliefs).

Arnobius perfectly instances the trends that Beard, North, and Price have identified: he is, by choice, a member of a north African Christian community, and he has devoted a book to discussion of issues of religious belief.

---

15. The precise nature of Arnobius's own *positive* beliefs are surprisingly hard to ascertain: see North 2007.

And yet it was not always thus: "So far as we can tell," the same authors write, "the religious world of the earliest periods of Roman history was quite different, and much less recognisable in our own contemporary terms."[16] In fact, this world was so different (1998: 1.x, emphasis in the original):

> that many of our familiar categories for thinking about religion and religious experience simply cannot be usefully applied here; we shall see, for example, how even the idea of "personal *belief*" (to us, a self-evident part of religious experience) provides a strikingly *in*appropriate model for understanding the religious experience of early Rome.

Let us proceed carefully here. Let us grant that the world—not least the religious world—had transformed by the time of Arnobius. And let us note that the Christian's work is qualitatively markedly different from that of Caesar, let alone that of Dionysius. Finally, let us note with due diligence that the authors are speaking of "the earliest periods of Roman history," while our authors date to the late republican and Augustan eras.

Yet even after exercising these cautions, we may question the most radical implications of the historical development proposed by Beard, North, and Price. We may wonder whether it is only because he is part of a new religious world, a Christian (a convert, no less), that Arnobius speaks of belief, attempting to explain religious practices with reference to the psychological states of individuals. In other words, we may wonder whether the causal priority Arnobius grants belief over practice is conditioned by his epoch and a by-product of his new commitments.

It is true that the analysis of sacrifice by Dionysius, a pre-Christian polytheist, differs significantly from that of Arnobius. Unlike Arnobius, Dionysius made no explicit mention of religious belief, attending only to questions of practice. We may well ask whether this was because, in the words of John North, "the whole problem" (i.e., "of participants' belief or disbelief") "derives from later not pagan preoccupations."[17] If belief was not a live issue, perhaps not even conceivable qua issue, for a pre-Christian Roman polytheist like Dionysius, we might expect to find that no treatment of sacrifice from that era will resemble the treatment of Arnobius, and that any account will resemble the treatment of Dionysius. Let us even stipulate that philosophical treatments such as that of Lucretius covered in chapter 6 must be left to one side. For a philosopher's concerns are not those of the average Roman. Fortunately, as it

---

16. Beard et al. 1998: 1.x.
17. North 2000a: 84.

happens, we do have a nonphilosophical treatment of sacrifice that we may use to test this prediction.

10.5. Human Sacrifice in Caesar's *De bello Gallico*

In the sixth book of his *De bello Gallico*, Caesar pauses in his narrative for several chapters in order to deliver himself of an ethnography of the Gauls (6.11–29). No stranger to the technical details of his own religion (he had been a pontifex since 73 BCE and pontifex maximus since 63 BCE), Caesar allots considerable space to the Gallic religion.

Caesar introduces his account by adverting to the Gauls' extreme devotion to their religious practices: *natio est omnis Gallorum admodum dedita religionibus*, "the entire Gallic race is very much given over to religious practices." Their religiosity leads the Gauls to observe some rather un-Roman customs (*B.G.* 6.16):

> *atque ob eam causam, qui sunt adfecti gravioribus morbis quique in proeliis periculisque versantur, aut pro victimis homines immolant aut se immolaturos vovent administrisque ad ea sacrificia druidibus utuntur, quod, pro vita hominis nisi hominis vita reddatur, non posse deorum immortalium numen placari arbitrantur, publiceque eiusdem generis habent instituta sacrificia.*

> on account of this, those who have been affected by very serious illnesses, and those engaged in battles and dangers, either offer or vow to offer human beings as sacrificial victims, and they employ druids as officiants at these sacrifices. They do these things because they believe that unless one human life is paid for another, the will of the immortal gods cannot be appeased. They have sacrifices of the same kind instituted for the sake of the group.

The Gauls practice human sacrifice, some of them burning their victims to death in large wicker enclosures. According to Caesar, they engage in human sacrifice because (6.16, continued):

> *supplicia eorum qui in furto aut in latrocinio aut aliqua noxia sint comprehensi gratiora dis immortalibus esse arbitrantur; sed, cum eius generis copia defecit, etiam ad innocentium supplicia descendunt.*

> they believe that the punishment of those who have been caught in theft or robbery or any other offense is more agreeable to the immortal gods; but, when they lack a supply of criminals, they sink even to the punishment of the innocent.

In attributing human sacrifice to the Gauls, Caesar marks them off as decisively different from his fellow Romans. By the late republic, such rites were not only antithetical to Roman practice, but also expressly prohibited by a *senatus consultum* of 97 BCE.[18] Livy, recalling a rare case of human sacrifice at Rome, avows that these *sacrificia extraordinaria* were not in keeping with Roman practice: *minime Romano sacro*.[19]

In the section that follows immediately on his discussion of the Gaulish penchant for human sacrifice, Caesar turns to the question of the gods of the Gauls. In this early instance of *interpretatio Romana*, Caesar calls the Gallic gods by Roman names and further equates the two pantheons by claiming that the two sets of gods share similar attributes (*B.G.* 6.17):[20]

> *deum maxime Mercurium colunt. huius sunt plurima simulacra: hunc omnium inventorem artium ferunt, hunc viarum atque itinerum ducem, hunc ad quaestus pecuniae mercaturasque habere vim maximam arbitrantur. post hunc Apollinem et Martem et Iovem et Minervam. De his eandem fere, quam reliquae gentes, habent opinionem: Apollinem morbos depellere, Minervam operum atque artificiorum initia tradere, Iovem imperium caelestium tenere, Martem bella regere.*

> The god they worship most is Mercury. There are many images of him. They reckon him the inventor of all arts, the guide of roads and journeys, and they believe him to have the greatest power over money making and trade. After him, they worship Apollo and Mars and Jupiter and Minerva. About these gods they have pretty much the same belief as other peoples: that Apollo dispels diseases, that Minerva transmits the elements of workmanship and of the trades, that Jupiter holds authority over heavenly things, that Mars governs wars.

Surprisingly, the deities who demand human sacrifice of the Gauls turn out to be the familiar gods of Roman religion, identified by their functions.

So, how does Caesar's report on the Gaulish religion, particularly their practice of human sacrifice, compare with Arnobius's critique of Roman religion and its institution of animal sacrifice? Do Caesar and Arnobius diverge sharply in the attention each pays to the issue of belief?

Let us contrast, first, Caesar's procedure in treating of the gods of the Gauls with Arnobius's procedure in dealing with the gods of Roman polytheism. In some respects, the theological evaluations of the two men could not be more different. Arnobius, in section 7.35, for example, criticizes the falseness and

---

18. Recorded by Pliny, *Nat. Hist.* 30.3.12: *senatus consultum factum est, ne homo immolaretur*.

19. Livy 22.57.6. On human sacrifice among the Romans, see Várhelyi 2007, and the works cited there.

20. On *interpretatio Romana* (a Tacitean term: *Ger.* 43.4), see Ando 2008: 43–58.

fatuity of the Romans' beliefs about their gods. Caesar, for his part, asserts the continuity of the Gauls beliefs with Roman beliefs, indeed, with the beliefs of all peoples. But note that the difference between their evaluative judgments is underpinned by a similarity in the terms they are comparing, that is, beliefs. Both polytheist and Christian take belief to be the salient issue, Caesar peppering his account of the Gauls' gods with words like *ferunt, arbitrantur, opinionem*.

Now let us turn to the question of sacrifice, where the rubber of belief, as it were, meets the road of practice. Note that as in Arnobius, Caesar's prefatory remarks signal his intention to explain rather than merely to describe. He tells his readers that the Gauls take their religion very seriously, and for this reason (*atque ob eam causam*) they engage in their religious practices. Indeed, Caesar's account is marked throughout by psychological explanations of the behavior of his informants. These explanations follow the standard form suggested by folk psychology (or Theory of Mind): a person does A because he or she desires B and believes C. Thus, the Gauls *perform* human sacrifices *because* they *desire* to elude death and *believe* the gods will accept the life of another in exchange. And they sacrifice criminals because they believe the gods find the punishment of those who have done wrong agreeable. Caesar uses the verb *arbitrari*, "judge; believe," twice here, emphasizing that the Gauls' beliefs motivate their actions.

Caesar's explanation of the Gauls' sacrificial practices in terms of their beliefs and desires represents much the same sort of analysis as Arnobius produced. For the Christian writer, polytheists sacrifice animals because, for example, they desire to honor the gods or to placate them, and they believe that such actions will conduce to this end. Likewise, for Caesar, the Gauls sacrifice human beings because they wish to placate the gods and believe that such actions will be acceptable to the gods as means to this end. Moreover, both are critical, explicitly or implicitly, of the sacrificial practices they seek to explain, which means, ultimately, that they are critical of beliefs.

These similarities between the accounts of the Christian and the polytheist are, I hope, suggestive. But we can go still further in tracing Caesar's imputation of religious beliefs to the Gauls. Merely counting Caesar's employment of words for "belief" or "believe" hardly represents the horizon of interpretative possibility here and, indeed, fails to give a full account of his explanatory enterprise.

We may note, for example, that if explanatory psychologizing underwrites Caesar's account of the Gauls' behavior, so too does it underwrite his account of their beliefs about other agents, for he represents his informants/subjects as reasoning about the mental states of their psychologically anthropomorphic gods. The Gauls, at least in Caesar's analysis, theorize about the desires of their gods: if the gods are to be placated (*placari*), they require one human life before they will spare another. Moreover, the Gauls infer the gods' preferences: punishment of wrongdoers is desirable, so they prefer sacrifices of criminals (*gratiora*), though they will accept sacrifices of the innocent in a pinch. Implicit in the Gauls' reasoning about the divine will are assumptions about the causes of the gods' own behavior as well. They will act as their worshippers request—whether to cure illness or to benefit the group—if their desires and requirements are met. Thus, even as he himself reasons about the mental states and behavior of the Gauls, Caesar represents them as reasoning, in turn, about the mental states and behavior of highly anthropomorphic divine agents.

Like Arnobius, Caesar explains the Gauls' religious practices by reference to their beliefs. He rationalizes their behavior by recourse to mentalistic, belief/desire explanations. As we have seen, these mentalistic explanations obtain at three levels. Caesar *believes* certain things about the Gauls and their religious behavior. Moreover, Caesar *believes* that the Gauls *believe* certain things (belief about belief is "second-order Intentionality"). He also *believes* that the Gauls *believe* certain things about the mental states (here, the *desires* and *preferences*) of their gods—third-order Intentionality.[21] Without the human mind's ability to nest layers of belief and belief-representation, all this religious behavior could neither be explained by Caesar nor, indeed, exist among the Gauls. Without beliefs about the predilections and susceptibility to persuasion of the gods, the Gauls would have lacked any motivation to engage in religious practices; without beliefs about the Gauls' beliefs, Caesar would have lacked any means by which to rationalize and explain their behavior.

Caesar's report of the Gauls' actions is not merely descriptive of practice; it is also explanatory. And the explanation of human behavior—giving reasons—requires recourse to beliefs, desires, and intentions. The precise details of Caesar's explanations, like his ethnography more generally, may or may not accurately reflect the facts, but assessing Caesar's reliability as an ethnographer has not been our aim here.[22] Rather, Caesar's example has shown that

---

21. Most people can cognitively manage fifth order intentionality. For a philosopher's take on the orders of intentionality, see Dennett 1987: 237–68. For an evolutionary take, see Dunbar 1998, where the orders of intentionality (a necessary component of folk psychology or Theory of Mind) are hypothesized to have evolved as part of the development of "the social brain."

22. For a positive assessment of Caesar's ethnography, see Dunham 1995. It has been pointed out to me that Caesar's explanation of practices by reference to beliefs might have been conditioned by the conventions of ethnography, in which genre he—like Herodotus and others, who also explain practices via beliefs—was working. This strikes me as a case of getting the causal story backward. Psychologizing explanation of customs and practices must have been logically and historically prior to the establishment of ethnography as a determinate genre. The genre of

even a pre-Christian Roman polytheist perceived religious beliefs as structuring and motivating religious practice through and through; moreover, he evidently expected that his Roman audience would find such a belief-based explanation of sacrifice perfectly natural. One might even hazard that Caesar's critical, evaluative model of ethnography, with its emphasis on the way the Gauls' beliefs explained their actions, is the ancestor of Arnobius's still more critical, belief-based explanation of the traditional religion that he had abandoned. In any event, Caesar believed in belief. Religion, whether Roman or Gallic, *was* about belief. For the polytheist no less than for the Christian, *opinio religionem facit*.

10.6. Comparison, Explanation, and Belief in Dionysius, Arnobius, and Caesar

Let us take one step back in order to take in the big picture. All three of our authors more or less explicitly *compare* alien religious practice to their own. Dionysius does so in order to explain how the other, the Roman, is really the familiar, the Greek. For Greeks to understand the Romans thus is to bear more lightly the burden of their rule. Arnobius compares in order to explain the errors of traditional cult in light of Christianity. To understand Roman cult thus is to move toward conversion, as he had done. Caesar compares in order to explain to his fellow citizens why that most un-Roman rite, human sacrifice, is practiced among the Gauls. To understand the Gauls thus is perhaps to feel all the more justified in conquering them. All three of our authors provide theological commentary, Dionysius and Caesar in order to assimilate the essential attributes of foreign gods to familiar ones, Arnobius to expose the Roman deities as theological abominations. Caesar and Arnobius use the same explanatory strategy: appeal to participants' beliefs to explain their actions. Dionysius's aetiological strategy differs: appeal not to belief but to the genealogy of cultural forms.

In all of this, the three authors we have just examined go into some detail about the sacrifices they describe. In this they are unusual. Writing specifically of the Roman historians, John North notes that as a rule they "do not provide us in their narratives with very satisfactory accounts of ritual activities."[23] Typically (2008: 23):

---

ethnography, with its aim to explain why foreign peoples do what they do, merely formalized an intuitive mode of making sense of alien social worlds.

23. North 2008: 23.

They did not produce background information about procedures, laws or social customs unless there was a definite need to do so.

Of course, the three accounts of sacrifice we have examined in this chapter were not written by Roman historians properly so-called. Dionysius was a Greek writing about *res Romanae* for Greeks, Arnobius was a Christian polemicist, and Caesar, however we may wish to categorize his literary productions, was not writing about Roman sacrifice at all.

Still, one might have expected a reasonably detailed description of blood sacrifice somewhere in the many books of Livy, for example. But as North notes (2008: 24):

> Notoriously ... the Roman historians never give us any sustained account of the elaborate ritual of animal sacrifice.

Why are our sources so often silent concerning the details of religious practice, especially sacrifice? North's answer to this question is that it was not the case that religion was unimportant to these authors. Rather, "they simply did not contemplate having readers who would be so ignorant as to need telling how a sacrifice should be conducted."[24]

If North is right, he has offered us an avenue by which we ourselves may explain our three authors and their accounts of sacrifice, which we are comparing. We may perhaps extend his observation from the realm of "conduct" to the realm of belief in order to hazard the thesis that ancient authors typically did not contemplate readers so ignorant as to need telling what beliefs motivated the performance of sacrifice. Let us test this thesis by seeing whether it has any explanatory power. Let us see whether it can help us understand why our three authors present the kinds of accounts they do.

We can make fairly short work of Caesar and Arnobius. First, Caesar. If a Roman writing about his own religion could presuppose knowledge on the part of his readers and thus make relatively few details explicit, as North has noted, we might expect a Roman writing about an unfamiliar religion to adopt a different strategy. As it happens, Caesar discusses an unfamiliar religion, and his discussion takes very little for granted. His account is at once descriptive, describing the Gauls' religious behavior, and explanatory, rationalizing that behavior by reference to their beliefs, desires, and intentions.

Note that Caesar's account is very like that of Dionysius *except* in the emphasis it places on belief. Both authors employ *interpretatio*, the description of a foreign pantheon in terms of their own. And both describe many details of

---

24. North 2008: 24.

sacrifice. However, only Caesar makes explicit reference, and very full reference, to beliefs. If our modification of North's thesis is sound, we may explain this unique feature of Caesar's account as owing to the fact that he knew his readers would be ignorant of and curious about the Gauls' beliefs and would need them spelled out explicitly.

Arnobius, for his part, polemically contrasts a religious tradition he has recently rejected with one he has recently accepted. His interest lies not only in highlighting the divergence in the practices of these two religions—he is, for example, keen to depict the many bizarre niceties of traditional sacrificial practices—but also in explaining *why* people engage in these divergent practices. For it is only in understanding the reasons why people act—reasons that include their beliefs—that Arnobius can argue the folly of their actions. Thus, Arnobius takes very little for granted, whether of practice or belief. He does not presuppose either ignorant or informed readers. Rather, the very nature of his project required him to go into the details, both creedal and practical, of Roman sacrifice, in order to demonstrate the error of the traditional religion.

But what of Dionysius? His account was resolutely descriptive of Roman practice, making no reference of any sort to belief. What could a comparison of Greek and Roman sacrificial practices, in service to an aetiology of the latter as a cultural descendant of the former, possibly have to do with belief? The answer to this question is the argument that this entire book has pressed. It will serve as our concluding statement of the book's themes. Let us approach it methodically.

We begin with Caesar and the emic value of belief. (Let us leave Arnobius to one side. His belief-rich account of Roman polytheism may be suspected of infection with uniquely Christian concerns.) We saw in chapter 1 that attempts by modern scholars to posit a dichotomy between doing religious things and believing religious things, as well as to deny belief to the Romans altogether, were not supportable. Caesar's ethnography drives home the point. The conqueror of Gaul amply demonstrates the emic relevance of belief to his late republican readers. His Latin psychological vocabulary picks out a doxastic mental state that represents states of affairs as obtaining. For example, he claims that the Gauls have the same *opinio* about the gods as other peoples, to wit, the *opinio* "that Apollo dispels diseases," the *opinio* "that Minerva transmits the elements of workmanship and of the trades," and so on. As we saw in chapter 2, to represent states of affairs, expressed here as propositions about the gods, as obtaining is simply the distinguishing feature of the Intentional state that we happen to call "belief," and Caesar calls *opinio*. Other Intentional states represent states of affairs differently. Desire, for example, represents states of affairs not as we take them to *be* but as we would that they *were*.

Caesar's narrative shows that the attitude that we call "belief" was hardly unknown to the Romans or irrelevant to their understanding of religion. It had emic relevance.

Caesar's account of Gaulish sacrifice also evinces an emic theory, whether derived from folk psychology or from his Epicureanism (see the case of Lucretius in chapter 6), to the effect that beliefs play a role in the etiology of religious action. His account is thus intelligible in terms of the etic theory of action put forward in chapter 3. The Gauls, he says, perform human sacrifice "because they believe that unless one human life is paid for another, the will of the immortal gods cannot be appeased." A *desire* on the part of the Gauls to appease the gods is simply presupposed here. We saw in chapter 3 that action's etiology is more complicated than allowed on the Aristotelian and Epicurean theories, in which the conjunction of relevant beliefs and desires results in action. We saw that we must appeal additionally to *intentions* to act, and that such intentions may derive both from desires and, especially in the case of cult action, from desire-independent *deontic* considerations, that is, from deontic beliefs and reasoning about what may, must, or must not be done.

Now we are prepared to turn to Dionysius. Where Caesar demonstrated the emic value of belief, the Greek's account shows the value of the etic scholarly discourse of belief that we have pursued in this book's pages. For everything in his account—prayer, emotion, joint action, norms of sacrificial performance, religious institutions carrying deontologies, and even the gods themselves—begs to be understood in terms of belief, even if he himself uses no Greek terms for such a mental state. Let us take these factors in turn and address beliefs about the gods along the way, for they are central to everything in our list.

Prayer: Dionysius says that the consuls and priests pray (his verb is κατεύχομαι) before ordering the attendants to slaughter the animals. We saw in chapter 8 that Roman prayer is a speech act, carrying a propositional content, and expressing a psychological state with respect to that content. Often, as in the Directive speech acts of petitionary prayer, the psychological state expressed is that of *desire*. But even when a Roman expresses nothing more than desire in praying, he or she does so against a background of beliefs about the gods, their natures, and their powers, that this person simply *presupposes* in praying. Hearers *accommodate*, or infer and adopt, the background beliefs of the person praying in order to make the prayer intelligible. Moreover, the propositional contents of even purely petitionary prayers represent the gods in one way or another, as having capabilities and causal powers that are often "counterintuitive" and hence attractive to human cognition. These attractive theological representations motivate acts of cult and prayer. They are also likely to turn into observers' theological beliefs, especially when they occur, as at Dionysius's sacrifice, in *practical* contexts, where those producing the representations are also acting on them, in dramatic ways that signal to observers belief and commitment.

Emotion: Dionysius appeals to "fear," δεῖμα, in order to explain why neither the Greeks nor the Romans have altered ritual procedure since the era of Homer. We saw in chapter 3 that emotion depends on belief. One must *believe* that a state of affairs obtains in order to *appraise* or evaluate that state of affairs as good or bad for oneself and one's projects. Emotion arises upon that appraising. Here, Dionysius tells us that the emotion is fear and its object is divine wrath (μηνίματα). Embedded in the fear, then, is a belief that carries fear's object, something like the proposition that the gods are prone to anger over solecisms in ritual performance. Appraisal of the state of affairs represented in this belief triggered the fear. Compare this fear to Lucretian *horror*, the awe that results from representing the gods as possessed of superhuman causal agency and all-too-human passions (section 6.7). Neither Dionysius's Romans nor Lucretius's contemporaries could have *felt* as they did about the gods unless they *believed* as they did about the gods. Note, too, that just as Caesar's Gauls reason about their gods' mental states, so too do Dionysius's Romans, at least implicitly. For implicit in their fear of the divine anger is their recognition that the emotion is predicated on divine perception or belief that rites have been altered. Again, emotion arises from appraisal of the Intentional contents of perceptions and doxastic states.

Joint action: Dionysius depicts Romans acting not independently in individual acts of cult but in a complex, choreographed collective act of sacrifice, involving numerous interlocking, hierarchically arranged roles, including consuls, priests, and a variety of specialized attendants. We saw in chapter 4 that sharing agency in cultural joint action, such as Dionysius's sacrificial act, is explicable only in terms of shared representations. Participants must share the *goal* to sacrifice, *we-intentions* to act interdependently toward the goal of sacrificing, *beliefs* about the nature (say, butchering cattle vs. sacrificing cattle), purpose (say, to thank the gods or expiate a fault), and gods of the sacrifice (Jupiter or Minerva, say), as well as *deontic beliefs* about sacrificial *norms*. Dionysius's sacrificers also *jointly attend* to the task and its objects. Each has his own *perspective* on the scene and represents his own *role* in the joint action but remains *responsive* to the perspectives and actions of others and *represents* how their roles mesh with his own. Finally, we saw the importance of mutual belief: participants must mutually believe that they share this Intentionality with the others. Insofar as the sacrifice is not reducible to individuals engaged in their own actions and chancing to converge, that is, insofar as it is a joint action characterized by the sharing of agency, it is explicable only in terms of a richly textured structure of practical and doxastic Intentionality.

Norms of performance: Dionysius is deeply interested in norms of sacrificial performance, although of course he does not use this terminology. For his entire project was to show that the *manner* in which Roman and Homeric sacrifices were carried out (ὁ τῶν θυηπολιῶν τρόπος) was comparable if not identical. But the manner in which rituals are carried out is a matter of ritual norms. We saw in chapters 3 and 4 that norms—their prescriptions, permissions, and prohibitions—are represented as the content of deontic beliefs. That is, the content of a deontic belief represents a religious *may*, *must*, or *must not*, and these beliefs guide the performance as well as the evaluation of cult actions (see chapter 9). Thus, the consuls, priests, and attendants must share (and mutually believe they share) relevant deontic beliefs in order to produce the actions that Dionysius will evaluate as "Greek."

Indeed, for Dionysius himself to notice similarities between Greek and Roman cult, he must also entertain a number of beliefs as to what actions count as Greek and as Roman sacrifice. He does not *argue* that the Greek and Roman activities he describes are both sacrifice and thus comparable. Rather, he comes to the comparative project *presupposing* that the Greek and Roman action sequences are comparable norm-governed activities, that is, that both are *sacrifice*. He must believe that Greek sacrifice normatively runs *thus* and Roman sacrifice *so*, and that the norms governing *thus* and *so* are norms of the same generic type, and thus admit of comparison and, in this case, identification.

More on this latter point in the next section. For now, we have reached a good place to recapitulate what we saw most fully at section 9.6.2, to wit, that in joint cult action, a diversity of theological, nonconstitutive beliefs among participants is acceptable in a way that a diversity of deontic, constitutive beliefs, representing as their content the norms of performance, is not. For the latter make the action the action it is, much as the rules of tennis make it the game that it is. Theological beliefs are central to cult—the gods may be felt to be cult's most important observers or participants, the source of its effect or of its meaning—but they are not constitutive of it as a discrete practice. So, in Dionysius's sacrifice, the magistrate may be an Epicurean who believes the gods do not attend to cult and the priest a Stoic who believes they do, but they may still successfully sacrifice together just as Dionysius describes, provided they share the right rich structure of practical and doxastic, including deontic, Intentionality.

Religious institutions and deontologies: This discussion of constitutive versus nonconstitutive beliefs has already anticipated the recapitulation of our social-ontological thesis of chapters 5 and 9. In order for the actions and behavior of Dionysius's Romans to count as sacrifice—indeed, for his Romans to count as consuls, priests, and sacrificial attendants, rather than as butchers, or as random people wantonly killing animals—a framework of beliefs about what actions count as sacrifice, what people count as licit sacrificers, and so forth must be shared collectively among Romans. These beliefs play an important role in creating and sustaining these social realities.

Look back at Dionysius's description of Roman sacrifice at *Antiquitates* 7.72.15, from section 10.3, above. In order for the sprinkling of water to count as "purification" (the verb is περιαγνίζω), in order for animals to count as "sacrificial victims" (τὰ ἱερά), in order for chunks of organ meat to count as "first fruits" (ἀπαρχαί), indeed, in order for the entire procedure to count as an act of "sacrifice" (θυηπολία; also θυcία at 7.72.16), human beings—Romans—must have imposed the functions of purifying, of being first fruits, and of constituting a sacrifice on these objects and actions. The same analysis goes for the Status Functions borne by the sacrificers of consul (ὕπατοc) and priest (ἱερεύc), along with their associated deontologies, that is, the packages of norms, obligations, permissions, and powers, including the power to offer public prayer and perform public sacrifice, that attend their special statuses.

The fact that these people count as priests, that these objects count as components of sacrifice, and that the sequence of actions Dionysius describes functions as sacrifice for the Romans is due entirely to the collective representations and beliefs of the Romans. There is no reason in principle why, for example, the agents and actions described by Dionysius should count, under their barest possible physical description, as sacrificers and sacrifice, rather than as butchers and butchery, or as sportsmen and sport, or as killers and the unadorned slaughter of animals. In other words, social practices and institutions such as sacrifice, and social statuses such as consul or priest, are constituted *as such* by the beliefs and other Intentional episodes, as well as by the behaviors motivated by those episodes, of the members of the society to which they belong. They are, as we saw, ontologically subjective or mind dependent.

Moreover, Dionysius's entire aetiological project, through which he was trying to rouse his readers to believe that Roman sacrifice is Greek sacrifice in origin, stands as secondary to, takes for granted, and depends on his own elementary belief that certain actions, Greek or Roman, should be counted as sacrifice. The very fact that Dionysius could compare Roman sacrificial actions, one after another, to corresponding Greek sacrificial actions indicates that Dionysius harbored determinate beliefs about the statuses of the actions performed in each case. He did not conceive himself to have been comparing Homeric sacrifice to Roman culinary traditions. He thought the actions he was comparing both had to do with the gods and shared the property of being sacrificial. Thus, Dionysius—but also Arnobius and Caesar—could compare actions and social institutions only because he entertained more generic beliefs about the nature of human phenomena, such as religion and religious activities, that transcended the parochial, more specific bounds of his own culture.[25] He could posit Greek-Other equivalences, in a way that, as we saw in the preface, those who would deny "religion" to the Romans cannot.

Belief is thus deeply implicated in Dionysius's very act of cataloging the actions that constitute Roman sacrifice and comparing them to Greek sacrifice, even if bringing this fact out is an etic, scholarly project. In stating that this or that action or set of actions is part of a Roman sacrifice, Dionysius has gone beyond describing bare behavior. He has tacitly recognized that that behavior bears an additional ontological weight—as religious, as sacrificial, and so on—conferred on it by the beliefs, attitudes, and resulting behaviors of a people. When Dionysius presents his aetiological argument about Roman *actions*, he is at the same time tacitly presenting an argument about the *descriptions* under which those actions should appear, about the *statuses* they bear, and hence by implication about the collective beliefs and representations of the Romans. If we fail to recognize this in our etic discourse, then we unwittingly join Dionysius in naturalizing Roman sacrifice, priesthood, and all the rest. As scholars, we should rather seek to discover these things' underlying social ontology. But that it an etic project.

10.7. Believing in Belief

In closing this epilog, let us see if our extension of North's thesis from behavior to belief has come into its own. Precisely because he believed that Roman sacrifice simply was Greek sacrifice, Dionysius could take the beliefs that motivated it for granted, as understood, as going without saying. In other words, unlike Caesar, writing about the Gauls, or Arnobius, diagnosing the flaws in his previous beliefs, Dionysius felt no need to explain to his readers the reasons for, or the beliefs behind, what he was after all asserting was a single, common, familiar tradition of Greco-Roman sacrifice.

North's thesis allows us to posit, as an explanation for Dionysius's omission of any mention of belief, the possibility that he simply could not contemplate readers so ignorant as to need telling what beliefs motivated the performance of sacrifice, especially sacrifice that he had proved was Greek. Thus, Dionysius's account of sacrifice, which at first encounter had seemed to render talk of belief irrelevant, turns out to show the deep relevance of belief in a properly theorized etic analysis.

In this discussion we have found ourselves inspired by a stimulating observation of John North to refute a problematic position espoused by the very same John North. For I have tried to point out the flaws in North's admonition

---

25. Similarly, Cancik 2008, esp. 408.

that "it is a mistake to overemphasize any question of the participants' belief or disbelief in the efficacy of ritual actions."[26] Instead, we have seen that at least one pre-Christian polytheist could strongly emphasize participants' beliefs about the effects of ritual actions in his discussion of Gaulish religion. For, at least according to Caesar, the Gauls resorted to practices as monstrous as human sacrifice precisely because they believed in its efficacy. As for North's assertion that we have "good reason to suspect that the whole problem [sc. of belief] derives from later not pagan preoccupations,"[27] I have tried to suggest, following a lead from North himself, that when polytheists like Dionysius omit explicit mention of belief from their writing on religion, we may chalk this up to their inability to conceive of readers so ignorant as to need telling.

North has rightly warned that we should not take the Roman historians' reticence to provide abundant descriptions of sacrificial procedure as a sign that they "were taking such matters lightly or without interest."[28] I agree wholeheartedly and would add only that we should extend the same consideration to ancient authors where matters of belief are concerned. If we hope to compare and explain, we must believe in belief.

26. North 2000a: 84.
27. North 2000a: 84.
28. North 2008: 24.

GLOSSARY

agency/agent: An agent is any entity possessing agency, which is the capacity to act, that is, to move on purpose, in order to accomplish a goal, even if that goal is merely the action itself. The term "intentional agent," often found in the psychological and CSR literature, is eschewed in this book. "Intentional agent" not only is often ambiguous, because some (maybe most) authors use "intentional" to mean "purposive" and others use it to mean "possessing representational mental capacities," but it also is redundant, because agents by definition both act intentionally and possess representational mental capacities, even if only perception. See at introduction, section 0.2; and section 3.3.

constitutive belief: Constitutive beliefs and other constitutive attitudes play a role in *constituting* or creating features of social reality by representing those features as existing. They represent a state of affairs as existing, and by means of so representing, they cause that very state of affairs to exist. For example, if Titius and Seius each believe that their line of stones is a *terminus*, and if they believe this in mutual awareness that the other does too, then between them they thereby *constitute* the line of stones as a *terminus*. See at section 5.3.2, and see also entry *nonconstitutive belief*.

deontic belief: Deontic beliefs are beliefs an agent has about the normative claims on him or her—about, that is to say, the permissions, obligations and restrictions to which he or she is subject, that govern what he or she *may, may not, ought,* or *ought not* do. See at section 3.3, especially 3.3.2.

deontology: A deontology is a more or less coherent package of norms and normative phenomena—codified laws, rules, social norms, obligations, permissions, prohibitions, rights, responsibilities, powers, duties, social empowerments and disempowerments to action, dos and don'ts. A deontology specifies powers and disabilities with respect to action, that is, permissions, obligations, and restrictions. See at sections 2.3 and 3.3.2.

direction of fit: Representations with *mind-to-world* direction of fit include perceptions and beliefs, in which the *mind* represents the way the *world* is. Representations with *world-to-mind* direction of fit include desires and intentions, which depict how the *world* should come to match the *mind*. Arguably, some representations have a *double* direction of fit. These representations represent the *world* (mind to world) and just by so doing, bring the world to match the representation in the *mind* (world to mind). The analysis can be extended to speech acts. Assertives have *word-to-world* direction of fit. Commissives and Directives have *world-to-word* direction of fit. Declarations may be said to have *double* direction of fit. See at sections 2.2.5 and 5.3.2.

dispositional versus occurrent: Mental states such as belief are in principle accessible to consciousness but need not at any given moment be consciously accessed. Beliefs that are not currently in consciousness, such as your belief that Cicero was consul in 63 BCE just before you read this, are called "dispositional." Beliefs of which one is at a given moment conscious, such as your belief that Cicero was consul in 63 BCE after reading the previous sentence, are distinguished as "occurrent." Some mental episodes, such as pain, cannot be "dispositional," because pain is its experience. It would make no sense to say, "I'm in pain but I don't feel it." See at section 2.2.1.

episode, mental: See entry *mental episode*.

epistemically objective: A claim or assertion may be epistemically objective or subjective. An epistemically objective claim such as "The temple of Jupiter Optimus Maximus was on the Capitoline Hill" is objectively true or false and thus epistemically objective. Anyone can evaluate the claim for accuracy. (In contrast, an epistemically *subjective* claim such as "The temple of Jupiter Optimus Maximus is more beautiful than the temple of" Juno is not objectively true or false but, as we say, a matter of personal taste.) See at section 5.2, and see entry *ontologically subjective*.

folk theology: Folk theology is a package of beliefs and intuitions about gods that differs from the sorts of theology found in Augustine's *De libero arbitrio voluntatis* or Cicero's *De natura deorum* in that it is mostly implicit rather than explicit, a matter not of formal study and philosophical reflection, but of informal social learning and social-cognitive intuition. Folk theology consisted of the reflective, System 2 cultural representations about divine agents that were transmitted through testimonies, stories, prayers, and so on, coupled with System 1's social-cognitive intuitions, inferences, and nonreflective beliefs about the gods as agents. See the introduction, section 0.3; section 2.6.1; and chapter 8.

inference: The mental process through which we derive new information (i.e., inferences as cognitive products) from information we already have is inference. We distinguished four types of inferential processes: *deduction, induction, abduction,* and *analogy.* In deduction, a conclusion follows from premises. For example: Major premise: All men are mortal. Minor premise: Socrates is a man. Conclusion: Socrates is mortal. Induction generalizes from particulars. For example: All swans thus far observed are white. Therefore, all swans are white. The conclusion goes beyond the information in the premises and may be wrong. Abduction is related to induction and also is error prone. Abduction explains a situation, taken as an *effect*, by reasoning to the most plausible hypothesis as to its *cause*. Example: Situation: There are what appear to be geometric symbols traced in the sand. Conclusion: Human beings must have drawn them. Analogical inference draws conclusions about one thing from its similarities to something else. Example: the gods are similar to human beings; human beings have passions; therefore, the gods have passions. See at sections 2.6.3, 6.4, and 6.6.1.

Intentional affordances: Intentional affordances are the intentions, desires, beliefs and so on of an artifact creator (or of artifact creators) as embodied in the resulting artifact. These intentions determine what the object is *for*, its normative sociocultural action potential. Intentional affordances go beyond the sensorimotor possibilities for and constraints on action proper to *natural* affordances. A knife, for example, may have natural affordances of cutting because of its material composition and sharpness. But a *sacrificial* knife has the added *intentional* affordances of killing victims in sacrificial rituals. The way it is represented by subjects gives it *normative* and *cultural* possibilities for action lacking in mundane knives. See at section 7.3.

Intentionality/Intentionalism/Intentional: "Intentionality" is ambiguous. In an everyday and narrow sense, it means "purposiveness," as when we speak of *intentions* to act (i.e., plans) or actions done *intentionally* (i.e., on purpose). In its technical but also broadest sense, "Intentionality" (spelled in this book with an uppercase *I* to distinguish it from intentionality as purposiveness, spelled with a lowercase *i*) is that property of a mental episode, and also of a speech act, by virtue of which it is *about, of, directed at,* or *represents* some object. Intentional (uppercase *I*) mental episodes include not only intentions but also beliefs, desires, emotions, fears, hopes, and so on. Beliefs, fears, hopes and so on are *about* objects or states of affairs. This "aboutness" is their intentionality. See at the introduction, section 0.4; and section 2.2.

intuition: Intuition is a term for both a cognitive process and its cognitive product. Intuition as process results in new thoughts (i.e., intuitions) that carry a degree of self-evidence simply appearing in consciousness, with no trace of a reasoning process that led to them. Intuition as product is a new thought carrying a degree of self-evidence that simply appears in consciousness with no trace of a reasoning process that led to it. An intuition is experienced as a kind of self-evident *seeming* that thus and such is so. See at the introduction, section 0.2; and at section 2.6.

MCI: See entry *minimally counterintuitive (MCI)*.

mental episode: This is the broadest term for mental "stuff" used in this book. Mental episodes include *emotions*, which are "episodic" in that they typically arise, grow, and then tail off. "Mental episodes" is also used here to refer to mental *events*, such as perceptions or sudden intuitions; mental *acts*, such as calculating a figure in one's head; and mental *states* that perdure indefinitely and that may or may not be present to consciousness at any given moment (see entry *dispositional versus occurrent*), such as memories, beliefs, desires, and intentions. See at section 2.2.

mental state: See entry *mental episode*.

metacognition: Metacognition is our ability to cognize our own cognition, to think (and thus to talk) about our own thinking (and recursively, about our own thinking about our own thinking). Metacognition allows us to monitor, assess, and exert control over our own thought processes. See at section 1.3.2.

mind-to-world direction of fit: See entry *direction of fit*.

minimally counterintuitive (MCI): This is a term of art in the cognitive science of religion. An MCI concept, representation, or agent (hence another term of art, "MCI agent") is one that violates a small number of our intuitive expectations (without verging into the simply bizarre) in ways that make it memorable and a compelling source of inferences. Thus, a talking bush is an MCI agent, because it violates our expectations about plants (they do not talk), it is more memorable than a standard bush, and it has the potential to generate more inferences than a standard bush: "Maybe the bush has something to say to me"; "Perhaps the bush knows what happened to my father"; "What could the bush want?"; and so on. See at section 8.6.

nonconstitutive belief: A belief that does nothing to create the reality that it (purports to) represent is a nonconstitutive belief. If Gaius believes his ox is tired, this belief plays no part in making the ox tired. The ox is either tired or not, independently of Gaius's belief. See entry *constitutive belief*, and see sections 5.4 and 9.5.

ontogeny: Ontogeny is the development and maturation, physical and cognitive, of an organism. See at section 7.2.

ontologically subjective: To be dependent on a minded subject for its very existence makes something ontologically subjective. A pain you feel in your knee is ontologically subjective, because it does not exist apart from your conscious experience of it, and your conscious experience of it depends on your being a subject with a mind. Institutions are also ontologically subjective, because they depend for their existence on the beliefs, intentions, and activities of minded subjects. That is, without minded subjects, no institution could exist. (In contrast, some things are *ontologically objective* in that they do not depend on a minded subject for their existence. Natural objects—molecules, rocks, trees, and animals, for example—are ontologically objective. They exist whether or not anyone knows about them and regardless of what anyone thinks of them.) See at section 5.2, and see entry *epistemically objective*.

religion: Here, *religion* is an etic term that denotes practices that involve doing things to, for, directed toward, with, or significantly implicating gods, spirits, ghosts, and other nonhuman or superhuman (MCI) entities. The emic term *religio* could denote much the same phenomena. See preface.

social cognition: This is the suite of developmentally natural, species-specific human cognitive faculties that give rise to intuitions of *agency*, intuitions about the mental states of *agents*, and intuitions about how agents' mental states inform (and therefore both explain and predict) their *action*.

Status Function: A Status Function is a function that an entity possesses not by virtue of its physical affordances or material makeup but rather by virtue of the status imposed on it and collectively accepted. Thus, "augur" names a Status Function, because it is a status that comes with a function. Status Functions always come with a set of social powers and obligations, that is, a deontology. See at section 5.3.1

world-to-mind direction of fit: See *direction of fit*.

REFERENCES

Abatino, B., G. Dari-Mattiacci, and E. C. Perotti. (2011). "Depersonalization of Business in Ancient Rome." *OxfJLegStud*, 31.2: 365–89.
Adams, J. N. (2007). *The Regional Diversification of Latin: 200 BC–AD 600*. Cambridge: Cambridge University Press.
———. (2013). *Social Variation and the Latin Language*. Cambridge: Cambridge University Press.
Alcorta, C. S., and R. Sosis. (2005). "Ritual, Emotion, and Sacred Symbols: The Evolution of Religion as an Adaptive Complex." *HumNature-IntBios*, 16: 323–59.
Algra, K. (2007). *Conceptions and Images: Hellenistic Philosophical Theology and Traditional Religion*. Amsterdam: Koninklijke Nederlandse Akademie van Wetenschappen.
———. (2009). "Stoic Philosophical Theology and Graeco-Roman Religion." In *God and Cosmos in Stoicism*, ed. R. Salles, 224–51. Oxford: Oxford University Press.
Algra, K. A., M. H. Koenen, and P. H. Schrijvers (eds.). (1997). *Lucretius and His Intellectual Background*. Amsterdam: North-Holland.
Allen, J. (2001). *Inference from Signs: Ancient Debates about the Nature of Evidence*. Oxford: Oxford University Press.
Alvar, J. (1985). "Matériaux pour l'étude de la formule *sive deus, sive dea*." *Numen*, 32.2: 236–73.
Andersen, M. (2019). "Predictive Coding in Agency Detection." *ReligionBrainBehav*, 9.1: 65–84.
Anderson, M., D. Cairns, and M. Sprevak (eds.). (2019). *Distributed Cognition in Classical Antiquity*. Edinburgh: Edinburgh University Press.
Ando, C. (2000). *Imperial Ideology and Provincial Loyalty in the Roman Empire*. Berkeley: University of California Press.
———. (ed.). (2003). *Roman Religion*. Edinburgh: Edinburgh University Press.
———. (2008). *The Matter of the Gods: Religion and the Roman Empire*. Berkeley: University of California Press.
———. (2010a). "The Ontology of Religious Institutions." *History of Religions*, 50.1: 54–79.
———. (2010b). "Praesentia numinis: Part 1. The Visibility of Roman Gods." *Asdiwal*, 5: 45–73.
———. (2011a). *Law, Language, and Empire in the Roman Tradition*. Philadelphia: University of Pennsylvania Press.
———. (2011b). "Praesentia numinis: Part 2. Objects in Roman Cult." *Asdiwal*, 6: 57–69.
———. (2015a). *Roman Social Imaginaries: Language and Thought in Contexts of Empire*. Toronto: University of Toronto Press.
———. (2015b). "Praesentia numinis: Part 3. Idols in Context (of Use)." *Asdiwal*, 10: 61–76.

———. (2015c). "Fact, Fiction, and Social Reality in Roman Law." In *Legal Fictions in Theory and Practice*, ed. M. Del Mar and W. Twining, 295–323. Dordrecht: Springer.

Ando, C., and J. Rüpke (eds.). (2006). *Religion and Law in Classical and Christian Rome*. Stuttgart: Steiner.

Andrighetto, G., and R. Conte. (2014). "Norms' Dynamics as a Complex Loop." In *Minding Norms: Mechanisms and Dynamics of Social Order in Agent Societies*, ed. R. Conte, G. Andrighetto, and M. Campennì, 81–93. Oxford: Oxford University Press.

Annas, J. (1989). "Epicurean Emotions." *GRBS*, 30.2: 145–64.

———. (1992). *Hellenistic Philosophy of Mind*. Berkeley: University of California Press.

Anscombe, G.E.M. (1957). *Intention*. Oxford: Blackwell.

Appel, G. (1909). *De Romanorum precationibus*. Giessen: Impensis A. Toepelmanni.

Arena, V. (2012). *Libertas and the Practice of Politics in the Late Roman Republic*. Cambridge: Cambridge University Press.

———. (2015). "Informal Norms, Values, and Social Control in the Roman Participatory Context." In *Companion to Greek Democracy and the Roman Republic*, ed. D. Hammer, 217–38. Oxford: Blackwell.

Armstrong, D. (2008). "'Be Angry and Sin Not': Philodemus versus the Stoics on Natural Bites and Natural Emotions." In Fitzgerald 2008, 79–121.

Armstrong, D., and J. Fish. (1994). "Emender's Guide to PHerc. 1425 as Read by O and N." *CErc*, 24: 97–107.

Armstrong, D., J. Fish, P. A. Johnston, and M. B. Skinner (eds.). (2004). *Vergil, Philodemus, and the Augustans*. Austin: University of Texas Press.

Arrighetti, G. (1973). *Epicuro: Opere* (2nd ed.). Turin: G. Einaudi.

Asad, T. (1993). *Genealogies of Religion: Discipline and Reasons of Power in Christianity and Islam*. Baltimore: Johns Hopkins University Press.

Asmis, E. (2004). "The State as a Partnership: Cicero's Definition of *res publica* in His Work *On the State*." *HistPolitThought*, 25: 569–98.

———. (2009). "Epicurean Empiricism." In *The Cambridge Companion to Epicureanism*, ed. J. Warren, 84–104. Cambridge: Cambridge University Press.

Assmann, J. (2011). "Communicative and Cultural Memory." In *Cultural Memories: The Geographical Point of View*. ed. P. Meusburger, M. Heffernan, and E. Wunder, 15–27. Knowledge and Space, 4. Dordrecht: Springer.

Athanassiadi, P., and M. Frede (eds.). (1999). *Pagan Monotheism in Late Antiquity*. Oxford: Clarendon.

Atherton, C. (2005). "Lucretius on What Language Is Not." In *Language and Learning: Philosophy of Language in the Hellenistic Age*, ed. D. Frede and B. Inwood, 101–38. Cambridge: Cambridge University Press.

Atran, S. (2002). *In Gods We Trust: The Evolutionary Landscape of Religion*. Oxford: Oxford University Press.

Audi, R. (2008). "Belief, Faith, and Acceptance." *IntJPhilosRelig*, 63: 87–102.

———. (2011). *Rationality and Religious Commitment*. Oxford: Oxford University Press.

———. (2013). *Moral Perception*. Princeton, NJ: Princeton University Press.

———. (2015). *Rational Belief: Structure, Grounds, and Intellectual Virtue*. Oxford: Oxford University Press.

———. (2016). "Intuition, Agency Detection, and Social Coordination as Analytical and Explanatory Constructs in the Cognitive Science of Religion." In *The Roots of Religion: Exploring the Cognitive Science of Religion*, ed. R. Trigg and J. L. Barrett, 17–36. Burlington, VT: Ashgate.
Auffarth, C., and H. Mohr. (2006). "Religion." In *Brill Dictionary of Religion*, ed. K. von Stuckrad (vol. 3), 1607–19. Leiden: Brill.
Ausfeld, C. (1903). *De Graecorum precationibus quaestiones*. Leipzig: Teubner.
Aust, E. (1899). *Die Religion der Römer*. Münster: Aschendorff.
Austin, J. L. (1962). *How to Do Things with Words*. Oxford: Clarendon.
Bailey, C. (1947). *Titi Lucreti Cari De rerum natura libri sex*. Oxford: Clarendon.
Baillargeon, R. (2004). "Infants' Physical World." *CurrDirPsycholSci*, 13: 89–94.
Baillargeon, R., J. Li, Y. Gertner, and D. Wu. (2011). "How Do Infants Reason about Physical Events?" In Goswami 2011, 11–48.
Baillargeon, R., R. M. Scott, and Z. He. (2010). "False-Belief Understanding in Infants." *TrendsCognSci*, 14.3: 110–18.
Baldassarre, I., A. Pontrandolfo Greco, and A. Rouveret. (2002). *Pittura romana: Dall'ellenismo al tardo antico*. Milan: F. Motta.
Baltus, J.-F. (1707). *Réponse à l'histoire des oracles de M. de Fontenelle*. Strasbourg: Jean Renauld Doulssecker.
Banerjee K., O. S. Haque, and E. S. Spelke. (2013). "Melting Lizards and Crying Mailboxes: Children's Preferential Recall of Minimally Counterintuitive Concepts." *CognSci*, 37.7: 1251–89.
Baron-Cohen, S. (1995). *Mindblindness: An Essay on Autism and Theory of Mind*. Cambridge, MA: MIT Press.
Barr, J. (1961). *The Semantics of Biblical Language*. Oxford: Oxford University Press.
Barresi, J., and C. Moore. (1996). "Intentional Relations and Social Understanding." *Behavioral and Brain Sciences*, 19.1: 107–22.
Barrett, J. L. (1998). "Cognitive Constraints on Hindu Concepts of the Divine." *JSciStudRelig*, 37: 608–19.
———. (1999). "Theological Correctness: Cognitive Constraint and the Study of Religion." *MethTheoryStudRel*, 11: 325–39.
———. (2000). "Exploring the Natural Foundations of Religion." *TrendsCognSci*, 4: 29–34.
———. (2001). "How Ordinary Cognition Informs Petitionary Prayer." *JCognCult*, 1: 259–69.
———. (2002). "Dumb Gods, Petitionary Prayer, and the Cognitive Science of Religion." In *Current Approaches in the Cognitive Study of Religion*, ed. I. Pyysiäinen and V. Anttonen, 93–109. London: Bloomsbury Academic.
———. (2004a). *Why Would Anyone Believe in God?* Walnut Creek, CA: AltaMira.
———. (2004b). "Bringing Data to Mind: Empirical Claims of Lawson and McCauley's Theory of Religious Ritual." In *Religion as a Human Capacity: A Festschrift in Honor of E. Thomas Lawson*, ed. B. C. Wilson and T. Light, 265–88. Leiden: Brill.
———. (2007). "Cognitive Science of Religion: What Is It and Why Is It?" *Religion Compass*, 1: 1–19.
———. (2008). "Why Santa Claus Is Not a God." *JCognCult*, 8: 149–61.
———. (2011a). *Cognitive Science, Religion, and Theology*. West Conshohocken, PA: Templeton.

———. (2011b). "Cognitive Science of Religion: Looking Back, Looking Forward." *JSciStud-Relig*, 50: 229–39.
Barrett, J. L., E. R. Burdett, and T. J. Porter. (2009). "Counterintuitiveness in Folktales: Finding the Cognitive Optimum." *JCognCult*, 9: 271–87.
Barrett, J. L., and A. Johnson. (2003). "The Role of Control in Attributing Intentional Agency to Inanimate Objects." *JCognCult*, 3: 208–17.
Barrett, J. L., and F. C. Keil. (1996). "Anthropomorphism and God Concepts: Conceptualizing a Non-natural Entity." *CognitivePsychol*, 31: 219–47.
Barrett, J. L., and J. A. Lanman. (2008). "The Science of Religious Beliefs." *Religion*, 38: 109–24.
Barrett, J. L., and E. T. Lawson. (2001). "Ritual Intuitions: Cognitive Contributions to Judgments of Ritual Efficacy." *Journal of Cognition and Culture*, 1.2: 183–201.
Barrett, J. L., and M. A. Nyhof. (2001). "Spreading Non-natural Concepts: The Role of Intuitive Conceptual Structures in Memory and Transmission of Cultural Materials." *JCognCult*, 1: 69–100.
Barrett, J. L., and B. van Orman. (1996). "The Effects of Image Use in Worship on God Concepts." *Journal of Psychology and Christianity*, 15: 38–45.
Barton, C., and D. Boyarin. (2016). *Imagine No Religion: How Modern Abstractions Hide Ancient Realities*. New York: Fordham University Press.
Bateson, M. C. (1971). "The Interpersonal Context of Infant Vocalization." *Quarterly Progress Report of the Research Laboratory of Electronics*, 100: 170–76.
Baumard, N., and P. Boyer. (2013a). "Religious Beliefs as Reflective Elaborations on Intuitions: A Modified Dual-Process Model." *Current Directions in Psychological Science*, 22.4: 295–300.
———. (2013b). "Explaining Moral Religions." *TrendsCognSci*, 17.6: 272–80.
Beard, M. (1986). "Cicero and Divination: The Formation of a Latin Discourse." *JRS*, 76: 33–46.
———. (1987). "A Complex of Times: No More Sheep on Romulus' Birthday." *PCPhS*, 33: 1–15.
———. (2012). "Cicero's 'Response of the Haruspices' and the Voice of the Gods." *JRS*, 102: 20–39.
———. (2015). *SPQR: A History of Ancient Rome*. New York: W. W. Norton.
Beard, M., and M. Crawford. (1985). *Rome in the Late Republic*. London: Duckworth.
Beard, M., and J. North (eds.). (1990). *Pagan Priests: Religion and Power in the Ancient World*. Ithaca, NY: Cornell University Press.
Beard, M., J. North, and S.R.F. Price. (1998). *Religions of Rome*. Vol. 1, *A History*; vol. 2, *A Sourcebook*. Cambridge: Cambridge University Press.
Beaver, D., and H. Zeevat. (2007). "Accommodation." In *The Oxford Handbook of Linguistic Interfaces*, ed. G. Ramchand and C. Reiss, 503–38. Oxford: Oxford University Press.
Beck, R. (2004). "Four Men, Two Sticks and a Whip: Image and Doctrine in a Mithraic Ritual." In Whitehouse and Martin 2004, 87–104.
———. (2006). *The Religion of the Mithras Cult in the Roman Empire: Mysteries of the Unconquered Sun*. Oxford: Oxford University Press.
Behne, T., M. Carpenter, M. Gräfenhain, K. Liebal, U. Liszkowski, H. Moll, H. Rakoczy, M. Tomasello, F. Warneken, and E. Wyman. (2008). "Cultural Learning and Cultural Creation." In *Social Life and Social Knowledge: Toward a Process Account of Development*, ed. U. Müller, J.I.M. Carpendale, N. Budwig, and B. Sokol, 65–101. New York: Erlbaum.

Bell, C. (1992). *Ritual Theory, Ritual Practice*. Oxford: Oxford University Press.
———. (1997). *Ritual: Perspectives and Dimensions*. Oxford: Oxford University Press.
———. (2002). "'The Chinese Believe in Spirits': Belief and Believing in the Study of Religion." In *Radical Interpretation in Religion*, ed. N. K. Frankenberry, 100–128. Cambridge: Cambridge University Press.
———. (2008). "Belief: A Classificatory Lacuna and Disciplinary 'Problem.'" In *Introducing Religion: Essays in Honor of Jonathan Z. Smith*, ed. W. Braun and R. T. McCutcheon, 85–99. London: Equinox.
Beller, S. (2010). "Deontic reasoning Reviewed: Psychological Questions, Empirical Findings, and Current Theories." *CognProcess*, 11: 123–32.
Bendlin, A. (2000). "Looking beyond the Civic Compromise: Religious Pluralism in Late Republican Rome." In *Religion in Archaic and Republican Rome and Italy: Evidence and Experience*, ed. E. Bispham and C. Smith, 115–35. Edinburgh: Edinburgh University Press.
———. (2001). "Rituals or Beliefs? 'Religion' and the Religious Life of Rome." *ScrClassIsr*, 20: 191–208.
———. (2006). "'Eine wenig Sinn für Religiosität verratende Betrachtungsweise': Emotion und Orient in der römischen Religionsgeschichtsschreibung der Moderne." *ARG*, 8: 227–56. (Translated into French as Bendlin 2009.)
———. (2009). "'Une perspective trahissant un piètre sens de la religiosité': Émotion et Orient dans l'historiographie religieuse romaine de l'époque moderne." *Trivium*, 4: https://journals.openedition.org/trivium/3377. (French translation of Bendlin 2006.)
Bentham, J. (1825). *A Treatise on Judicial Evidence*. London: J. W. Paget.
Benveniste, É., and J. Lallot. (1973). *Indo-European Language and Society*. Coral Gables, FL: University of Miami Press.
Ben-Ze'ev, A. (2000). *The Subtlety of Emotions*. Cambridge, MA: MIT Press.
Berger, A. (1953). *Encyclopedic Dictionary of Roman Law*. Philadelphia: American Philosophical Society.
Berger, C. R., and R. J. Calabrese. (1975). "Some Exploration in Initial Interaction and Beyond: Toward a Developmental Theory of Communication." *Human Communication Research*, 1: 99–112.
Bergstrom, B., B. Moehlmann, and P. Boyer. (2006). "Extending the Testimony Problem: Evaluating the Truth, Scope, and Source of Cultural Information." *ChildDev*, 77.3: 531–38.
Bernstein, F. (2007). "Pompeian Women." In *The World of Pompeii*, ed. J. J. Dobbins and P. W. Foss, 526–37. New York: Routledge.
Bett, R. (1997). *Sextus Empiricus: Against the Ethicists (Adversus mathematicos XI)*. Oxford: Oxford University Press.
Bettini, M. (2011). "Mos, Mores, and Mos Maiorum: The Invention of Morality in Roman Culture." In *The Ears of Hermes: Communication, Images, and Identity in the Classical World* (trans. W. Short), 87–130. Columbus: Ohio State University Press.
Bicchieri, C. (2006). *The Grammar of Society: The Nature and Dynamics of Social Norms*. Cambridge: Cambridge University Press.
———. (2016). *Norms in the Wild: How to Diagnose, Measure, and Change Social Norms*. New York: Oxford University Press.
Birks, P. (2014). *The Roman Law of Obligations*. Oxford: Oxford University Press.

Blake, R., and M. Shiffrar. (2007). "Perception of Human Motion." *AnnuRevPsychol*, 58: 47–73.

Blake, R., L. M. Turner, M. J. Smoski, S. L. Pozdol, and W. L. Stone. (2003). "Visual Recognition of Biological Motion Is Impaired in Children with Autism." *PsycholSci*, 14.2: 151–57.

Bloch, M. (1989). *Ritual, History and Power: Selected Papers in Anthropology*. London: Athlone.

Bloom, P. (2000). *How Children Learn the Meaning of Words*. Cambridge, MA: MIT Press.

Bloomer, M. (2011). *The School of Rome: Latin Studies and the Origins of Liberal Education*. Berkeley: University of California Press.

Bodel, J. (2008). "Cicero's Minerva, *Penates*, and the Mother of the *Lares*: An Outline of Roman Domestic Religion." In *Household and Family Religion in Antiquity*, ed. J. Bodel and S. M. Olyan, 248–75. Oxford: Blackwell.

Boden, M. A. (2006). *Mind as Machine: A History of Cognitive Science* (2 vols.). Oxford: Clarendon.

Boghossian, P. A. (2001). "What Is Social Construction?" *TLS*, 23 February: 6–8.

———. (2006). *Fear of Knowledge: Against Relativism and Constructivism*. Oxford: Oxford University Press.

Bonner, S. F. (1977). *Education in Ancient Rome: From the Elder Cato to the Younger Pliny*. Berkeley: University of California Press.

Borgeaud, P. (ed.). (1988). *La mémoire des religions*. Geneva: Editions Labor et Fide.

Boudry, M., and J. De Smedt. (2011). "In Mysterious Ways: On Petitionary Prayer and Subtle Forms of Supernatural Causation." *Religion*, 41.3: 449–69.

Bourdieu, P. (1980). *The Logic of Practice*. Stanford, CA: Stanford University Press.

Bowden, H. (2010). *Mystery Cults of the Ancient World*. Princeton, NJ: Princeton University Press.

Bowersock, G. W. (1989). "The Later Momigliano." *Grand Street*, 9.1: 197–209.

Boyce, A. A. (1937). "The Expiatory Rites of 207 B.C." *TAPA*, 68: 151–71.

Boyce, G. K. (1937). *Corpus of the Lararia of Pompeii*. Rome: American Academy in Rome.

———. (1942). "Significance of the Serpents on Pompeian House Shrines." *AJA*, 46.1: 13–22.

Boyd, R., and P. J. Richerson. (2005a). *Not by Genes Alone: How Culture Transformed Human Evolution*. Chicago: University of Chicago Press.

———. (2005b). *The Origin and Evolution of Cultures*. Oxford: Oxford University Press.

Boyer, P. (1992a). "Causal Thinking and Its Anthropological Misrepresentation." *PhilosSocSci*, 22.2: 187–213.

———. (1992b). "Explaining Religious Ideas: Elements of a Cognitive Approach." *Numen*, 39: 26–57.

———. (1994a). "Cognitive Constraints on Cultural Representations: Natural Ontologies and Religious Ideas." In *Mapping the Mind: Domain Specificity in Cognition and Culture*, ed. L. A. Hirschfeld and S. A. Gelman, 391–411. Cambridge: Cambridge University Press.

———. (1994b). *The Naturalness of Religious Ideas: A Cognitive Theory of Religion*. Berkeley: University of California Press.

———. (1996). "What Makes Anthropomorphism Natural: Intuitive Ontology and Cultural Representations." *JRoyAnthropolInst*, 2: 83–97.

———. (1998). "Cognitive Tracks of Cultural Inheritance: How Evolved Intuitive Ontology Governs Cultural Transmission." *AmAnthropol*, 100.4: 876–89.

———. (2000). "Functional Origins of Religious Concepts: Ontological and Strategic Selection in Evolved Minds." *JRoyAnthropolInst*, 6: 195–214.
———. (2001). *Religion Explained: The Evolutionary Origins of Religious Thought*. New York: Basic Books.
———. (2003). "Religious Thought and Behaviour as By-Products of Brain Function." *TrendsCognSci*, 7: 119–24.
Boyer, P., and P. Liénard. (2006). "Why Ritualized Behavior? Precaution Systems and Action Parsing in Developmental, Pathological and Cultural Rituals." *BehavBrainSci*, 29: 1–56.
Boyer, P., and C. Ramble. (2001). "Cognitive Templates for Religious Concepts: Cross-Cultural Evidence for Recall of Counter-intuitive Representations." *CognitiveSci*, 25: 535–64.
Boyer, P., and S. Walker. (2000). "Intuitive Ontology and Cultural Input in the Acquisition of Religious Concepts." In *Imagining the Impossible: Magical, Scientific, and Religious Thinking in Children*, ed. K. S. Rosengren, C. N. Johnson, and P. L. Harris, 130–56. Cambridge: Cambridge University Press.
Bradley, K. R. (1986). "Wetnursing at Rome: A Study in Social Relations." In *The Family in Ancient Rome: New Perspectives*, ed. B. Rawson, 201–29. London: Croom Helm.
———. (1991). "The Social Role of the Nurse in the Roman World." In *Discovering the Roman Family: Studies in Roman Social History*, 13–36. Oxford: Oxford University Press.
———. (1994). "The Nurse and the Child at Rome: Duty, Affect and Socialisation." *Thamyris*, 1.2: 137–56.
Brandom, R. B. (2014). "Intentionality and Language: A Normative, Pragmatist, Inferentialist Approach." In *The Cambridge Handbook of Linguistic Anthropology*, ed. N. J. Enfield, P. Kockelman, and J. Sidnell, 347–63. Cambridge: Cambridge University Press.
Bratman, M. (1987). *Intention, Plans, and Practical Reason*. Cambridge, MA: Harvard University Press.
———. (1992). "Shared Cooperative Activity." *PhilosRev*, 101: 327–41.
———. (1993). "Shared Intention." *Ethics*, 104: 97–113.
———. (2014). *Shared Agency: A Planning Theory of Acting Together*. Oxford: Oxford University Press.
Braund, S. M. (1988). *Beyond Anger: A Study of Juvenal's Third Book of Satires*. Cambridge: Cambridge University Press.
Braund, S. M., and C. Gill. (1997). *The Passions in Roman Thought and Literature*. Cambridge: Cambridge University Press.
Braund, S. M., and G. W. Most. (2003). *Ancient Anger: Perspectives from Homer to Galen*. Cambridge: Cambridge University Press.
Bremer, J. M. (1981). "Greek Hymns." In *Faith, Hope and Worship: Aspects of Religious Mentality in the Ancient World*, ed. H. S. Versnel, 193–203. Leiden: Brill.
Bremmer, J. N. (1995). "The Family and Other Centres of Religious Learning in Antiquity." In *Centres of Learning: Learning and Location in Pre-modern Europe and the Near East*, ed. J. W. Drijvers and A. A. MacDonald, 29–38. Leiden: Brill.
———. (1998). "'Religion,' 'Ritual' and the Opposition 'Sacred vs. Profane': Notes toward a Terminological Genealogy." In *Ansichten griechischer Rituale: Geburtstags-Symposium für Walter Burkert*, ed. F. Graf, 9–32. Stuttgart: Teubner.

———. (2013). "The Agency of Greek and Roman Statues: From Homer to Constantine." *Opuscula: Annual of the Swedish Institutes at Athens and Rome*, 6: 7–21.
———. (2019). *The World of Greek Religion and Mythology*. Tubingen: Mohr Siebeck.
Brennan, G., L. Eriksson, R. E. Goodin, and N. Southwood. (2013). *Explaining Norms*. Oxford: Oxford University Press.
Brennan, T. (2005). *The Stoic Life: Emotions, Duties, and Fate*. Oxford: Clarendon.
Brentano, F. (1874). *Psychologie vom empirischen Standpunkte*. Leipzig: Duncker und Humblot.
Buekens, F. (2014). "Searlean Reflections on Sacred Mountains." In Ziv and Schmid 2014, 33–51.
Bulbulia, J. (2013). "Why 'Costly Signalling' Models of Religion Require Cognitive Psychology." In *Origins of Religion, Cognition and Culture*, ed A. W. Geertz, 71–81. London: Routledge.
Bulbulia, J., and R. Sosis. (2011). "Signalling Theory and the Evolution of Religious Cooperation." *Religion*, 41.3: 363–88.
Burge, T. (1993). "Content Preservation." *PhilosRev*, 102.4: 457–88.
———. (2010). *Origins of Objectivity*. Oxford: Oxford University Press.
Burkert, W. (1984). *Die Anthropologie des religiösen Opfers: Die Sakralisierung der Gewalt*. C. F. von Siemens Stiftung Themen, 40. Munich: Siemens-Stiftung.
Burnet, J. (1924). *Plato's Euthyphro, Apology of Socrates and Crito*. Oxford: Clarendon.
Burns, P. C. (2001). "Augustine's Use of Varro's *Antiquitates Rerum Divinarum* in His *De Civitate Dei*." *AugStud*, 32: 37–65.
Cairns, D. (1993). *Aidos: The Psychology and Ethics of Honour and Shame in Ancient Greek Literature*. Oxford: Clarendon.
———. (2008). "Look Both Ways: Studying Emotion in Ancient Greek." *CritQuart*, 50: 43–63.
Cairns, D., and L. Fulkerson. (2015a). *Emotions between Greece and Rome*. BICS, suppl. 125. London: Institute of Classical Studies.
———. (2015b). "Introduction." In D. Cairns and Fulkerson 2015a, 1–22.
Callaghan, T., H. Moll, H. Rakoczy, F. Warneken, U. Liszkowski, T. Behne, and M. Tomasello. (2011). *Early Social Cognition in Three Cultural Contexts*. Boston: Wiley-Blackwell.
Callaghan, T., P. Rochat, A. Lillard, M. L. Claux, H. Odden, S. Itakura, S. Tapanya, and S. Singh. (2005). "Synchrony in the Onset of Mental-State Reasoning: Evidence from Five Cultures." *PsycholSci*, 16.5: 378–84.
Cancik, H. (2008). "'Parallels'—How the Ancients Compared Their Religions." In *Römische Religion im Kontext*, 395–409. Gesammelte Aufsätze, 1. Tübingen: Mohr Siebeck.
Candea, M. (ed.). (2010). *The Social after Gabriel Tarde: Debates and Assessments*. London: Routledge.
Cardauns, B. (1976). *M. Terentius Varro: Antiquitates Rerum Divinarum*. Wiesbaden: Steiner.
———. (2001). *Marcus Terentius Varro: Einführung in sein Werk*. Heidelberg: Universitätsverlag C. Winter.
Carpenter, M. (2006). "Instrumental, Social, and Shared Goals and Intentions in Imitation." In *Imitation and the Social Mind: Autism and Typical Development*, ed. S. J. Rogers and J.H.G. Williams, 48–70. New York: Guilford.
———. (2011). "Social Cognition and Social Motivations in Infancy." In Goswami 2011, 106–28.

Carpenter, M., N. Akhtar, and M. Tomasello. (1998). "Fourteen- through Eighteen-Month-Old Infants Differentially Imitate Intentional and Accidental Actions." *InfantBehavDev*, 21.2: 315–30.

Carpenter, M., J. Call, and M. Tomasello. (2005). "Twelve- and 18-Month-Olds Copy Actions in Terms of Goals." *DevelopmentalSci*, 8: F13–F20.

Carpenter, M., and K. Liebal. (2012). "Joint Attention, Communication, and Knowing Together in Infancy." In Seemann 2012, 159–81.

Carpenter, M., M. Tomasello, and T. Striano. (2005). "Role Reversal Imitation and Language in Typically-Developing Infants and Children with Autism." *Infancy*, 8: 253–78.

Cartledge, P. (1985). "The Greek Religious Festivals." In *Greek Religion and Society*, ed. P. E. Easterling and J. V. Muir, 98–127. Cambridge: Cambridge University Press.

Casadio, G. (2010). "*Religio* versus Religion." In *Myths, Martyrs, and Modernity: Studies in the History of Religions in Honour of Jan N. Bremmer*, ed. J. Dijkstra, J. Kroesen, and Y. Kuiper, 301–26. Leiden: Brill.

Cascione, C. (2003). *Consensus: Problemi di origine, tutela processuale, prospettive sistematiche*. Naples: Editoriale Scientifica.

Casler, K., and D. Kelemen. (2005). "Young Children's Rapid Learning about Artifacts." *DevelopmentalSci*, 8: 472–80.

Castner, C. J. (1988). *Prosopography of Roman Epicureans from the Second Century B.C. to the Second Century A.D*. Studien zur klassischen Philologie, 34. Frankfurt: P. Lang.

Caston, R. R. (2012). *The Elegiac Passion: Jealousy in Roman Love Elegy*. Oxford: Oxford University Press.

Caston, R. R., and R. A. Kaster. (2016). *Hope, Joy, and Affection in the Classical World*. Oxford: Oxford University Press.

Caston, V. (1993). "Towards a History of the Problem of Intentionality among the Greeks." *PBostonA*, 9: 213–65.

———. (1998). "Aristotle and the Problem of Intentionality." *PhilosPhenomenRes*, 58.2: 249–98.

———. (2001). "Connecting Traditions: Augustine and the Greeks on Intentionality." In Perler 2001, 23–48.

———. (2002). "Gorgias on Thought and Its Objects." In *Presocratic Philosophy: Essays in Honour of Alexander Mourelatos*, ed. V. Caston and D. W. Graham, 205–32. Aldershot: Ashgate.

———. (2008). "Intentionality in Ancient Philosophy." *The Stanford Encyclopedia of Philosophy* (Fall 2008 ed.), ed. E. N. Zalta. http://plato.stanford.edu/archives/fall2008/entries/intentionality-ancient/.

Catalano, P. (1960). *Contributi allo studio del diritto augurale*. Turin: G. Giappichelli.

Chalmers, D. J. (1995). "Facing Up to the Problem of Consciousness." *JConsciousnessStud*, 2: 200–219.

Champion, C. B. (2017). *The Peace of the Gods: Elite Religious Practices in the Middle Roman Republic*. Princeton, NJ: Princeton University Press.

Chan, T. (ed.). (2014). *The Aim of Belief*. Oxford: Oxford University Press.

Chaniotis, A. (2006). "Rituals between Norms and Emotions: Rituals as Shared Experience and Memory." In *Rituals and Communication in the Graeco-Roman World*, ed.

E. Stavrianopoulou. *Kernos*, suppl. 16: 211–38. Liège: Centre international d'étude de la religion grecque antique.

———. (2010). "Dynamic of Emotions and Dynamic of Rituals: Do Emotions Change Ritual Norms?" In *Ritual Matters: Dynamic Dimensions in Practice*, ed. C. Brosius and U. Hüsken, 208–33. New Delhi: Routledge.

———. (2011). "Emotional Community through Ritual: Initiates, Citizens, and Pilgrims as Emotional Communities in the Greek World." In *Ritual Dynamics in the Ancient Mediterranean: Agency, Emotion, Gender, Representation*, ed. A. Chaniotis, 264–90. Stuttgart: Steiner.

———. (ed.). (2012). *Unveiling Emotions: Sources and Methods for the Study of Emotions in the Greek World*. Stuttgart: Steiner.

Chaniotis, A., and P. Ducrey (eds.). (2013). *Unveiling Emotions II: Emotions in Greece and Rome: Texts, Images, Material Culture*. Stuttgart: Steiner.

Chant, S. R., F. Hindriks, and G. Preyer (eds.). (2014). *From Individual to Collective Intentionality: New Essays*. Oxford: Oxford University Press.

Chapot, F., and B. Laurot. (2001). *Corpus de prières grecques et romaines*. Turnhout, Belgium: Brepols.

Cherniak, C. (1981). "Minimal Rationality." *Mind*, 90: 161–83.

Christensen, W., J. Sutton, and D. J. McIlwain. (2016). "Cognition in Skilled Action: Meshed Control and the Varieties of Skill Experience." *MindLang*, 31.1: 37–66.

Chudek, M., S. Heller, S. Birch, and J. Henrich. (2012). "Prestige-Biased Cultural Learning: Bystander's Differential Attention to Potential Models Influences Children's Learning." *EvolHumBehav*, 33: 46–56.

Chudek, M., and J. Henrich. (2011). "Culture-Gene Coevolution, Norm-Psychology and the Emergence of Human Prosociality." *TrendsCognSci*, 15.5: 218–26.

Chudek, M., W. Zhao, and J. Henrich. (2013). "Culture-Gene Coevolution, Large-Scale Cooperation, and the Shaping of Human Social Psychology." In *Cooperation and Its Evolution*, ed. K. Sterelny, R. Joyce, B. Calcott, and B. Fraser, 425–58. Cambridge, MA: MIT Press.

Chudnoff, E. (2011). "What Intuitions Are Like." *PhilosPhenomenolRes*, 82.3: 625–54.

———. (2013). *Intuition*. Oxford: Oxford University Press.

Chwe, M. (2001). *Rational Ritual: Culture, Coordination, and Common Knowledge*. Princeton, NJ: Princeton University Press.

Clark, Andy. (1997). *Being There: Putting Brain, Body, and World Together Again*. Cambridge, MA: MIT Press.

———. (2016). *Surfing Uncertainty: Prediction, Action, and the Embodied Mind*. Oxford: Oxford University Press.

Clark, Anna. (2007). *Divine Qualities: Cult and Community in Republican Rome*. Oxford: Oxford University Press.

Clark, D. L. (1951). "Imitation: Theory and Practice in Roman Rhetoric." *QJSpeech*, 37.1: 11–22.

Clark, G. (2010). "Augustine's Varro and Pagan Monotheism." In Mitchell and Van Nuffelen 2010a, 181–201.

Clark, H. H. (1996). *Using Language*. Cambridge: Cambridge University Press.

Clark, H. H., and T. B. Carlson. (1982). "Hearers and Speech Acts." *Language*, 58.2: 332–73.

Clarke, J. R. (2003). *Art in the Lives of Ordinary Romans: Visual Representation and Non-elite Viewers in Italy, 100 B.C.–A.D. 315*. Berkeley: University of California Press.

———. (2007). *Roman Life: 100 B.C. to A.D. 200*. New York: Abrams.
Clay, D. (1973). "Epicurus' Last Will and Testament." *ArchGeschPhilos*, 55: 252–80.
———. (1986). "The Cults of Epicurus." *CErc*, 16: 12–28.
———. (1998). *Paradosis and Survival: Three Chapters in the History of Epicurean Philosophy*. Ann Arbor: University of Michigan Press.
Coarelli, F. (2003). "Remoria." In *Myth, History and Culture in Republican Rome: Studies in Honour of T. P. Wiseman*, ed. D. Braund and C. Gill, 41–55. Exeter: University of Exeter Press.
———. (2007). *Rome and Environs*. Berkeley: University of California Press.
Cohee, P. (1994). "Instauratio Sacrorum." *Hermes*, 122.4: 451–68.
Cole, T. (1967). *Democritus and the Sources of Greek Anthropology*. Cleveland, OH: Press of Western Reserve University.
Coleman, K. (1998). "'The Contagion of the Throng': Absorbing Violence in the Roman World." *Hermathena*, 164: 65–88.
Collar, A. (2013). *Religious Networks in the Roman Empire: The Spread of New Ideas*. Cambridge: Cambridge University Press.
Comotti, G. (1989). *Music in Greek and Roman Culture* (trans. R. V. Munson). Baltimore: Johns Hopkins University Press.
Congiu, S., A. Schlottmann, and E. Ray. (2009). "Unimpaired Perception of Social and Physical Causality, but Impaired Perception of Animacy in High Functioning Children with Autism." *JAutismDevDisord*, 40: 39–53.
Corbeill, A. (2001). "Education in the Roman Republic: Creating Traditions." In *Education in Greek and Roman Antiquity*, ed. Y. L. Too, 261–87. Leiden: Brill.
———. (2004). *Nature Embodied: Gesture in Ancient Rome*. Princeton, NJ: Princeton University Press.
———. (2010). "The Function of a Divinely Inspired Text in Cicero's *De haruspicum responsis*." In *Form and Function in Roman Oratory*, ed. D. H. Berry and A. Erskine, 139–54. Cambridge: Cambridge University Press.
Courtney, E. (1995). *Musa Lapidaria: A Selection of Latin Verse Inscriptions*. American Classical Studies, 36. Atlanta: Scholars.
Crane, T. (2001a). *Elements of Mind*. Oxford: Oxford University Press.
———. (2001b). "Intentional Objects." *Ratio*, 14.4: 336–49.
———. (2006). "Is There a Perceptual Relation?" In *Perceptual Experience*, ed. T. Gendler and J. Hawthorne, 126–46. Oxford: Clarendon.
———. (2009). "Intentionalism." In *The Oxford Handbook of Philosophy of Mind*, ed. A. Beckermann, B. P. McLaughlin, and S. Walter, 474–93. Oxford: Clarendon.
———. (2013). *The Objects of Thought*. Oxford: Oxford University Press.
Crook, J. (1967). *Law and Life of Rome*. Ithaca, NY: Cornell University Press.
Csibra, G., and G. Gergely. (2006). "Social Learning and Social Cognition: The Case for Pedagogy." In *Processes of Change in Brain and Cognitive Development*, ed. Y. Munakata and M. H. Johnson, 249–74. Attention and Performance, 21. Oxford: Oxford University Press.
———. (2009). "Natural Pedagogy." *TrendsCognSci*, 13.4: 148–53.
———. (2011). "Natural Pedagogy as Evolutionary Adaptation." *PhilTransRSocB*, 366: 1149–57.
Cumont, F. (1906). *Les religions orientales dans le paganisme romaine*. Paris: Leroux.

———. (1909). *Les religions orientales dans le paganisme romaine* (2nd ed.). Paris: Leroux.

Curran, A. (2016). *Routledge Philosophy Guidebook to Aristotle and the Poetics*. New York: Routledge.

Cusumano, N., V. Gasparini, A. Mastrocinque, and J. Rüpke (eds.). (2013). *Memory and Religious Experience in the Greco-Roman World*. Potsdamer Altertumswissenschaftlice Beitrage. Stuttgart: Franz Steiner Verlag.

Damasio, A. R. (1994). *Descartes' Error: Emotion, Reason, and the Human Brain*. New York: Putnam.

Dasen, V. (2009). "Roman Birth Rites of Passage Revisited." *JRA*, 22: 199–214.

———. (2011). "Childbirth and Infancy in Greek and Roman Antiquity." In Rawson 2011, 291–314.

Daube, D. (1938). "*Societas* as Consensual Contract." *CambLawJ*, 6.3: 381–403.

Dautenhahn, K., and C. Nehaniv. (2002). "The Agent-Based Perspective on Imitation." In *Imitation in Animals and Artifacts*, ed. K. Dautenhahn and C. Nehaniv, 1–40. Cambridge, MA: MIT Press.

Davidson, D. (1963). "Actions, Reasons, and Causes." *JPh*, 60: 685–700.

———. (1970). "Mental Events." In *Experience and Theory*, ed. L. Foster and J. W. Swanson, 79–101. Amherst: University of Massachusetts Press.

———. (2005). "Aristotle's Action." In *Truth, Language, and History*, 277–94. Oxford: Clarendon.

Davies, J. P. (2004). *Rome's Religious History: Livy, Tacitus and Ammianus on Their Gods*. Cambridge: Cambridge University Press.

———. (2011). "Believing the Evidence." In *Evidence, Inference and Enquiry*, ed. P. Dawid, W. Twining, and M. Vasilaki, 395–434. Proceedings of the British Academy, 171. Oxford: Oxford University Press.

Davies, M. (2013). "Delusion: Cognitive Approaches—Bayesian Inference and Compartmentalisation." In *The Oxford Handbook of Philosophy and Psychiatry*, ed. M. Davies, K.W.M. Fulford, R.G.T. Gipps, G. Graham, J. Sadler, G. Stanghellini, and T. Thornton, 689–727. Oxford: Oxford University Press.

Davies, M., and A. Egan. (2013). "Delusion: Cognitive Approaches—Bayesian Inference and Compartmentalisation." In *The Oxford Handbook of Philosophy and Psychiatry*, ed. K.W.M. Fulford et al., 689–727. Oxford: Oxford University Press.

De Ciutiis, M. (2007). "Dissensus." PhD diss., Università degli Studi di Napoli Federico II, Naples.

Dein, S. (2013). "How Useful Is 'Religious Belief' in the Anthropology of Religion?" *Anthropology*, 2.1: e116. doi:10.4172/2332-0915.1000e116.

De Lacy, P. H., and E. A. De Lacy. (1978). *Philodemus: On Methods of Inference* (rev. ed.). Naples: Bibliopolis.

De Leersnyder, J., M. Boiger, and B. Mesquita. (2015). "Cultural Differences in Emotions." In *Emerging Trends in the Social and Behavioral Sciences: An Interdisciplinary, Searchable, and Linkable Resource*, ed. R. A. Scott and S. M. Kosslyn, 1–15. New York: J. Wiley.

Dennett, D. C. (1978). "Beliefs about Beliefs." *BehavBrainSci*, 1: 568–70.

———. (1987). *The Intentional Stance*. Cambridge, MA: MIT Press.

———. (1998). *Brainchildren: Essays on Designing Minds*. Cambridge, MA: MIT Press.

———. (2006). *Breaking the Spell: Religion as a Natural Phenomenon.* New York: Viking.
Dennison, W. (1898). "Some New Inscriptions from Puteoli, Baiae, Misenum, and Cumae." *AJA,* 2: 373–98.
Deregowski, J. B. (1989). "Real Space and Represented Space: Cross-Cultural Perspectives." *BehavBrainSci,* 12.1: 51–74.
De Sanctis, G. (2007). "Solco, muro, pomerio." *MEFRA,* 119.2: 503–26.
———. (2009). "Il salto proibito: La morte di Remo e il primo comandamento della città." *SMSR,* 75.1: 65–88.
Develin, R. (1979). "The Political Position of C. Flaminius." *RhM,* 122: 268–77.
De Waal, F. (2013). *The Bonobo and the Atheist: In Search of Humanism among the Primates.* New York: W. W. Norton.
De Waal, F., J. Ober, R. Wright, and S. Macedo. (2006). *Primates and Philosophers: How Morality Evolved.* Princeton, NJ: Princeton University Press.
Dickey, E. (2007). *Latin Forms of Address: From Plautus to Apuleius.* Oxford: Oxford University Press.
Dihle, A. (1996). "Die *theologia tripertita* bei Augustin." In *Geschichte, Tradition, Reflexion: Festschrift für Martin Hengel zum 70. Geburtstag,* ed. M. Hengel, H. Cancik, H. Lichtenberger, and P. Schäfer (vol. 2), 183–202. Tübingen: Mohr Siebeck.
Dixon, S. (1988). *The Roman Mother.* Norman: University of Oklahoma Press.
Döring, S. A. (2003). "Explaining Action by Emotion." *PhilosQuart,* 53.211: 214–30.
———. (2007). "Seeing What to Do: Affective Perception and Rational Motivation." *Dialectica,* 61.3: 363–94.
Dowden, K. (1992). *Religion and the Romans.* London: Bristol Classical.
Driediger-Murphy, L. G., and E. Eidinow (eds.). (2019). *Ancient Divination and Experience.* Oxford: Oxford University Press.
Drummond, J. J. (2012). "Intentionality without Representationalism." In *The Oxford Handbook of Contemporary Phenomenology,* ed. D. Zahavi, 115–33. Oxford: Oxford University Press.
DuBreuil, B. (2010). *Human Evolution and the Origins of Hierarchies: The State of Nature.* Cambridge: Cambridge University Press.
Duff, P. W. (1938). *Personality in Roman Private Law.* New York: Augustus M. Kelley.
Dumézil, G. (1970). *Archaic Roman Religion* (2 vols., trans. P. Krapp). Chicago: University of Chicago Press.
Dunbar, R. (1998). "The Social Brain Hypothesis." *EvolAnthropol,* 6: 178–90.
Dunham, S. B. (1995). "Caesar's Perception of Gallic Social Structures." In *Celtic Chiefdom, Celtic State,* ed. B. Arnold and D. B. Gibson, 110–15. Cambridge: Cambridge University Press.
Durkheim, É. (1897). *Le suicide: Étude de sociologie.* Paris: Alcan.
———. (1889). "Représentations individuelles et représentations collectives." *RevMétaphysMorale,* 6: 273–302
———. ([1895] 1901). *Les Règles de la méthode sociologique: 2e édition revue et augmentee.* Paris: F. Alcan.
———. (1974). "Individual and Collective Representations." In *Sociology and Philosophy,* 1–34. New York: Free Press. (Originally published as Durkheim 1889.)
———. (1982). *The Rules of Sociological Method* (edited with an introduction by S. Lukes, trans. W. D. Halls). New York: Free Press. (Originally published as Durkheim [1895] 1901.)

Dyck, A. R. (1996). *A Commentary on Cicero, De officiis*. Ann Arbor: University of Michigan Press.

———. (2004). *A Commentary on Cicero, De legibus*. Ann Arbor: University of Michigan Press.

Edmondson, J., and A. Keith (eds.). (2008). *Roman Dress and the Fabrics of Roman Culture*. Toronto: University of Toronto Press.

Egan, A. (2008). "Seeing and Believing: Perception, Belief Formation, and the Divided Mind." *Philosophical Studies*, 140.1: 47–63.

Ehrman, B. D. (2003). *Lost Christianities: The Battle for Scripture and the Faiths We Never Knew*. Oxford: Oxford University Press.

Eilan, N., C. Hoerl, T. McCormack, and J. Roessler (eds.). (2005). *Joint Attention: Communication and Other Minds*. Oxford: Clarendon.

Ekman, P. (1999a). "Basic Emotions." In *Handbook of Cognition and Emotion*, ed. T. Dalgleish and M. Power, 45–60. New York: Wiley.

———. (1999b). "Facial Expressions." In *Handbook of Cognition and Emotion*, ed. T. Dalgleish and M. Power, 301–20. New York: Wiley.

Elder-Vass, D. (2010). *The Causal Power of Social Structures: Emergence, Structure and Agency*. Cambridge: Cambridge University Press.

———. (2012). *The Reality of Social Construction*. Cambridge: Cambridge University Press.

Emirbayer, M., and A. Mische. (1998). "What Is Agency?" *AmJSociol*, 103.4: 962–1023.

Erler, M. (1994). "Epikur—Die Schule Epikurs—Lukrez." In *Die Philosophie der Antike*, vol. 4, *Die hellenistische Philosophie*, Part 1, ed. H. Flashar, 29–490. Grundriss der Geschichte der Philosophie, 4.1. Basel: Schwabe.

———. (1997). "Philosophie in Rom." In *Einleitung in die lateinische Philologie*, ed. F. Graf, 537–98. Stuttgart: Teubner.

———. (2002). "Epicurus as *deus mortalis*: Homoiosis theoi and Epicurean Self-Cultivation." In *Traditions of Theology: Studies in Hellenistic Theology, Its Background and Aftermath*, ed. D. Frede and A. Laks, 159–81. Philosophia Antiqua, 89. Leiden: Brill.

Essler, H. (2011). *Glückselig und unsterblich: epikureische Theologie bei Cicero und Philodem (mit einer Edition von PHerc. 152/157, Kol. 8–10)*. Schwabe Epicurea, 2. Basel: Schwabe Verlag.

Evans, J. St. B. T., and K. E. Stanovich. (2013). "Dual-Process Theories of Higher Cognition: Advancing the Debate." *PerspectPsycholSci*, 8.3: 223–41.

Evans, N. (2010). *Civic Rites: Democracy and Religion in Ancient Athens*. Berkeley: University of California Press.

Everson, S. (1990). "Epicurus on the Truth of the Senses." In *Epistemology*, ed. S. Everson, 161–83. Cambridge: Cambridge University Press.

Fagan, G. G. (2011). *The Lure of the Arena: Social Psychology and the Crowd at the Roman Games*. Cambridge: Cambridge University Press.

Falk, D. (2009). *Finding Our Tongues: Mothers, Infants, and the Origins of Language*. New York: Basic Books.

Fantham, E. (1995). "The Concept of Nature and Human Nature in Quintilian's Psychology and Theory of Instruction." *Rhetorica*, 13.2: 125–36.

———. (1998). *Ovid: Fasti, Book IV*. Cambridge Greek and Latin Classics. Cambridge: Cambridge University Press.

———. (2004). *The Roman World of Cicero's De oratore*. Oxford: Oxford University Press.

Farney, G. D. (2007). *Ethnic Identity and Aristocratic Competition in Republican Rome*. Cambridge: Cambridge University Press.
Feeney, D. C. (1998). *Religion and Literature at Rome: Cultures, Contexts, and Beliefs*. Cambridge: Cambridge University Press.
———. (2016). *Beyond Greek: The Beginnings of Latin Literature*. Cambridge, MA: Harvard University Press.
———. (2020). "*Forma manet facti* (Ov. *Fast.* 2.379): Aetiologies of Myth and Ritual in Ovid's *Fasti* and *Metamorphoses*." *CJ*, 115.3–4: 339–66.
Feil, E. (1986). *Religio: Die Geschichte eines neuzeitlichen Grundbegriffs vom Frühchristentum bis zur Reformation*. Göttingen: Vandenhoeck und Ruprecht.
Feinman, S., D. Roberts, K.-F. Hsieh, D. Sawyer, and D. Swanson. (1992). "A Critical Review of Social Referencing in Infancy." In *Social Referencing and the Social Construction of Reality in Infancy*, ed. S. Feinman, 15–54. New York: Plenum.
Festugière, A. J. (1955). *Epicurus and His Gods* (trans. C. W. Chilton). Oxford: Blackwell.
Fichtl, S. (2005). "Murus et pomerium: Réflexions sur la fonction des remparts protohistoriques." *RACF*, 44. http://racf.revues.org/515.
Fiebich, A. (2014). "Perceiving Affordances and Social Cognition." In Gallotti and Michael 2014, 149–66.
Fiebich, A., and S. Gallagher. (2013). "Joint Attention in Joint Action." *PhilosPsychol*, 26: 571–87.
Fiori, R. (2012). "The Roman Conception of Contract." In *Obligations in Roman Law: Past, Present, and Future*, ed. T.A.J. McGinn, 40–75. Ann Arbor: University of Michigan Press.
Fisher, J. (2014). "Spoken Prayers and Written Instructions in the Central Italian Cultural *Koinē* and Beyond." In *Between Orality and Literacy: Communication and Adaptation in Antiquity*, ed. R. Scodel, 197–217. Leiden: Brill.
Fishwick, D. (1986). Review of Price 1984. *Phoenix*, 40: 225–30.
Fiske, S. T., and S. E. Taylor. (2013). *Social Cognition: From Brains to Culture*. Los Angeles: Sage.
Fitzgerald, J. T. (ed.). (2008). *Passions and Moral Progress in Greco-Roman Thought*. London: Routledge.
Flaig, E. (2003). *Ritualisierte Politik. Zeichen, Gesten und Herrschaft im alten Rom*. Historische Semantik, 1. Göttingen: Vandenhoeck und Ruprecht.
Fleckner, A. M. (2015). "Roman Business Associations." *Max Planck Institute for Tax Law and Public Finance Working Paper*, 2015-10 / *Max Planck Private Law Research Paper*, 16/10. Forthcoming in *Roman Law and Economics*. Oxford: Oxford University Press. https://papers.ssrn.com/sol3/papers.cfm?abstract_id=2472598.
Fletcher, G. E., F. Warneken, and M. Tomasello. (2012). "Differences in Cognitive Processes Underlying the Collaborative Activities of Children and Chimpanzees." *CognitiveDev*, 27: 136–53.
Flower, H. I. (2017). *The Dancing Lares and the Serpent in the Garden: Religion at the Roman Street Corner*. Princeton, NJ, Princeton University Press.
Flynn, E., and K. Smith. (2012). "Investigating the Mechanisms of Cultural Acquisition: How Pervasive Is Overimitation in Adults?" *Social Psychology*, 43.4: 185–95.
Flynn, M. B. (2012). "A Realer Institutional Reality: Deepening Searle's (De)Ontology of Civilization," *International Journal of Philosophical Studies*, 20.1: 43–67.

Fogagnolo, S. (2012). "Per una Rilettura del Mosaico con Scena Conviviale e del Cosiddetto Mosaico del "Coro Sacro" dal Museo Provinciale Campano." *Atlante Tematico di Topografia Antica*, 15.6: 231–40.

Fögen, T. (2009a). "*Sermo corporis*: Ancient Reflections on *gestus, vultus* and *vox*." In *Bodies and Boundaries in Graeco-Roman Antiquity*, ed. T. Fögen and M. M. Lee, 15–43. Berlin: De Gruyter.

———. (ed.). (2009b). *Tears in the Graeco-Roman World*. Berlin: De Gruyter.

Fong S. S., P. Paholpak, M. Daianu, M. B. Deutsch, B. C. Riedel, A. R. Carr, E. E. Jimenez, M. M. Mather, P. M. Thompson, and M. F. Mendez. (2017). "The Attribution of Animacy and Agency in Frontotemporal Dementia versus Alzheimer's Disease." *Cortex*, 92: 81–94.

Fontenelle, B. de. (1687). *Histoire des oracles*. Amsterdam: Pierre Mortier.

Forsythe, G. (2012). *Time in Roman Religion*. New York: Routledge.

Fortenbaugh, W. W. (2002). *Aristotle on Emotion: A Contribution to Philosophical Psychology, Rhetoric, Poetics, Politics, and Ethics* (2nd ed.). London: Duckworth.

Fowler, W. W. (1896). "On the Toga Praetexta of Roman Children." *CR*, 10.7: 317–19.

———. (1899). *The Roman Festivals of the Period of the Republic: An Introduction to the Study of the Religion of the Romans*. London: Macmillan.

———. (1908). "The Latin History of the Word 'Religio.'" *Transactions of the Third Congress for the History of Religion*, 2: 169–75.

———. (1911). *The Religious Experience of the Roman People from the Earliest Times to the Age of Augustus: The Gifford Lectures for 1909–10*. London: Macmillan.

———. (1914). *Roman Ideas of Deity in the Last Century before the Christian Era*. London: Macmillan.

Foxe, J. (1570). *Actes and Monuments of the English Martyrs* (2nd ed., 2 vols.). London: John Day.

Freyburger, G. (2001). "Prière silencieuse et prière murmurée dans la religion romaine." *REL*, 79: 26–36.

Freyburger, G., and L. Pernot. (2000). *Bibliographie analytique de la prière grecque et romaine, 1898–1998*. Turnhout, Belgium: Brepols.

Frijda, N. H. (1986). *The Emotions*. Cambridge: Cambridge University Press.

———. (2007). *The Laws of Emotion*. Mahwah, NJ: Erlbaum.

Frijda, N. H., A.S.R. Manstead, and S. Bem. (2000). "The Influence of Emotions on Beliefs." In *Emotions and Beliefs: How Feelings Influence Thoughts*, ed. N. H. Frijda, A.S.R. Manstead, and S. Bem, 1–10. Cambridge: Cambridge University Press.

Frijda, N. H., and B. Mesquita. (1998). "The Analysis of Emotions: Dimensions of Variation." In *What Develops in Emotional Development?*, ed. M. F. Mascolo and S. Griffin, 273–95. New York: Plenum.

Frith, C. D. (2008). "Social Cognition." *PhilosTRoySocB*, 363.1499: 2033–39.

———. (2012). "The Role of Metacognition in Human Social Interactions." *PhilosTRoySocB*, 367: 2213–23.

Frith, C. D., and U. Frith. (2012). "Mechanisms of Social Cognition." *AnnuRevPsychol*, 63: 287–313.

Fröhlich, T. (1991). *Lararien- und Fassadenbilder in den Vesuvstädten: Untersuchungen zur "volkstümlichen" pompejanischen Malerei*. Mainz: Philipp von Zabern.

Fuchs, M. (2015). "Processes of Religious Individualisation: Stocktaking and Issues for the Future." *Religion*, 45.3: 330–43.
Fuchs, M., and J. Rüpke. (2015). "Religious Individualisation in Historical Perspective." *Religion*, 45.3: 323–29.
Fulkerson, L. (2013). *No Regrets: Remorse in Classical Antiquity*. Oxford: Oxford University Press.
Furley, W. D., and J. M. Bremer. (2001). *Greek Hymns: Selected Cult Songs from the Archaic to the Hellenistic Period* (2 vols.). Tübingen: Mohr Siebeck.
Gabba, E. (1991). *Dionysius and the History of Archaic Rome*. Berkeley: University of California Press.
Gager, J. G. (1992). *Curse Tablets and Binding Spells from the Ancient World*. Oxford: Oxford University Press.
Gagné, R. (2013). *Ancestral Fault in Ancient Greece*. Cambridge: Cambridge University Press.
Gaillard-Seux, Patricia. (2014). "Magical Formulas in Pliny's Natural History: Origins, Sources, Parallels." In *"Greek" and "Roman" in Latin Medical Texts: Studies in Cultural Change and Exchange in Ancient Medicine*, ed. B. Maire, 201–23. Leiden: Brill.
Gale, M. (1994). *Myth and Poetry in Lucretius*. Cambridge: Cambridge University Press.
Gallagher, S. (2008a). "Direct Perception in the Intersubjective Context." *ConsciousCogn*, 17: 535–43.
———. (2008b). "Inference or Interaction: Social Cognition without Precursors." *PhilosExplor*, 11.3: 163–74.
———. (2008c). "Intersubjectivity in Perception." *ContPhilosRev.*, 41: 163–78.
———. (2011). "Interpretations of Embodied Cognition." In *The Implications of Embodiment: Cognition and Communication*, ed. W. Tschacher and C. Bergomi, 59–70. Charlottesville, VA: Imprint Academic.
Gallagher, S., and D. Zahavi. (2008). *The Phenomenological Mind: An Introduction to Philosophy of Mind and Cognitive Science*. London: Routledge.
Gallese, V. (2009). "Motor Abstraction: A Neuroscientific Account of How Action Goals and Intentions Are Mapped and Understood." *PsycholRes-PsychFo*, 73.4: 486–98.
Gallese, V., and T. Metzinger. (2003). "Motor Ontology: The Representational Reality of Goals, Actions and Selves." *PhilosPsychol*, 16.3: 365–88.
Gallese, V., and C. Sinigaglia. (2011). "What Is So Special about Embodied Simulation?" *TrendsCognSci*, 15.11: 512–19.
Gallotti, M., and C. D. Frith. (2013). "Social Cognition in the We-Mode." *TrendsCognSci*, 17.4: 160–65.
Gallotti, M., and J. Michael (eds.). (2014). *Perspectives on Social Ontology and Social Cognition*. Dordrecht: Springer.
Gargiulo, T. (1983). "Epicureismo romano." In *SUZHTHSIS: Studi sull'epicureismo greco e romano offerti a Marcello Gigante*, 635–48. Naples: G. Macchiaroli.
Gargola, D. (1995). *Lands, Laws, and Gods: Magistrates and Ceremony in the Regulation of Public Lands in Republican Rome*. Chapel Hill: University of North Carolina Press.
Garrels, S. R. (2011a). "Human Imitation: Historical, Philosophical, and Scientific Perspectives." In Garrels 2011b, 1–38.

———. (ed.). (2011b). *Mimesis and Science: Empirical Research on Imitation and the Mimetic Theory of Culture and Religion.* East Lansing: Michigan State University Press.
Gaselee, Sir S. (1913). "The Common People of the Early Roman Empire." *Edinburgh Review*, 218: 82–101.
Gasparini, V., M. Patzelt, R. Raja, A.-K. Rieger, J. Rüpke, and E. Urciuoli (eds.). (2020). *Lived Religion in the Ancient Mediterranean World: Approaching Religious Transformations from Archaeology, History and Classics.* Berlin: De Gruyter.
Geertz, C. (1973). *The Interpretation of Cultures.* Basic Books.
Gergely, G. (2011). "Kinds of Agents: The Origins of Understanding Instrumental and Communicative Agency." In Goswami 2011, 76–105.
Gergely, G., H. Bekkering, and I. Király. (2002). "Rational Imitation in Preverbal Infants." *Nature*, 415: 755.
Gergely, G., and G. Csibra. (2003). "Teleological Reasoning in Infancy: The Naïve Theory of Rational Action." *TrendsCognSci*, 7.7: 287–92.
———. (2005). "The Social Construction of the Cultural Mind: Imitative Learning as a Mechanism of Human Pedagogy." *InteractStud*, 6.3: 463–81.
———. (2006). "Sylvia's Recipe: The Role of Imitation and Pedagogy in the Transmission of Cultural Knowledge." In *Roots of Human Sociality: Culture, Cognition, and Human Interaction*, ed. N. J. Enfield and S. C. Levenson, 229–55. New York: Berg.
———. (2013). "Natural Pedagogy." In *Navigating the Social World: What Infants, Children, and Other Species Can Teach Us*, ed. M. R. Banaji and S. A. Gelman, 127–32. Oxford: Oxford University Press.
Gergely G., Z. Nádasdy, G. Csibra, and S. Bíró. (1995). "Taking the Intentional Stance at 12 Months of Age." *Cognition*, 56.2: 165–93.
Gervais, W. M., and J. Henrich. (2010). "The Zeus Problem: Why Representational Content Biases Cannot Explain Faith in Gods." *JCognCult*, 10: 383–89.
Gervais, W. M., A. K. Willard, A. Norenzayan, and J. Henrich. (2011). "The Cultural Transmission of Faith: Why Innate Intuitions Are Necessary, but Insufficient, to Explain Religious Belief." *Religion*, 41.3: 389–410.
Giacobello, F. (2008). *Larari pompeiani: Iconografia e culto dei Lari in ambito domestico.* Milan: LED Edizioni Universitarie di Lettere Economia Diritto.
Gibson, J. J. (1986). *The Ecological Approach to Visual Perception.* New York: Psychology Press.
Giddens, A. (1984). *The Constitution of Society: Outline of the Theory of Structuration.* Berkeley: University of California Press.
Gigante, M. (1995). *Philodemus in Italy: The Books from Herculaneum* (trans. D. D. Obbink). Ann Arbor: University of Michigan Press.
Gilbert, M. (1989). *On Social Facts.* London: Routledge.
———. (1990). "Walking Together: A Paradigmatic Social Phenomenon." *MidwestStudPhilos*, 15: 1–14.
———. (2013). *Joint Commitment: How We Make the Social World.* Oxford: Oxford University Press.
Gilhus, I. S. (2006). *Animals, Gods and Humans: Changing Attitudes to Animals in Greek, Roman and Early Christian Ideas.* London: Routledge.

Gill, C. (2009). "Psychology." In *The Cambridge Companion to Epicureanism*, ed. J. Warren, 125–41. Cambridge: Cambridge University Press.

Giordano-Zecharya, M. (2005). "As Socrates Shows, the Athenians Did Not Believe in Gods." *Numen*, 52: 325–55.

Gladhill, B. (2016). *Rethinking Roman Alliance: A Study in Poetics and Society*. Cambridge: Cambridge University Press.

Gladman, K. R., and P. Mitsis. (1997). "Lucretius and the Unconscious." In Algra et al. 1997, 215–24.

Goldberg, S. C. (2015). *Assertion: On the Philosophical Significance of Assertoric Speech*. Oxford: Oxford University Press.

Goldie, P. (2000). *The Emotions: A Philosophical Exploration*. Oxford: Oxford University Press.

———. (2002). "Emotions, Feelings and Intentionality." *PhenomenolCognSci*, 1: 235–54.

Goldman, A. I. (2005). "Imitation, Mind Reading, and Simulation." In Hurley and Chater 2005, 2.79–93.

———. (2006). *Simulating Minds*. Oxford: Oxford University Press.

Goody, E. (1995). "Social Intelligence and Prayer as Dialogue." In *Social Intelligence and Interaction: Expressions and Implications of the Social Bias in Human Intelligence*, ed. E. Goody, 206–20. Cambridge: Cambridge University Press.

Gordon, B., and G. Theiner. (2015). "Scaffolded Joint Action as a Micro-foundation of Organizational Learning." In *Contextualizing Human Memory: An Interdisciplinary Approach to Understanding How Individuals and Groups Remember the Past*, ed. C. B. Stone and L. M. Bietti, 154–86. London: Psychology Press.

Gordon, R. (1990). "The Veil of Power: Emperors, Sacrificers and Benefactors." In Beard and North 1990, 201–31.

———. (2008). "*Superstitio*, Superstition and Religious Repression in the Late Roman Republic and Principate (100 BCE–300 CE)." In *The Religion of Fools? Superstition Past and Present*, ed. S. A. Smith and A. Knight, 72–94. Oxford: Oxford University Press.

Goswami, U. (ed.). (2011). *The Wiley-Blackwell Handbook of Childhood Cognitive Development* (2nd ed.). Oxford: Blackwell.

Gradel, I. (2002). *Emperor Worship and Roman Religion*. Oxford: Clarendon.

Graf, F. (1991). "Prayer in Magical and Religious Ritual." In *Magika Hiera: Ancient Greek Magic and Religion*, ed. C. A. Faraone and D. Obbink, 188–213. Oxford: Oxford University Press.

———. (1997). *Magic in the Ancient World* (trans. F. Philip). Cambridge, MA.: Harvard University Press.

Graf, F., and S. I. Johnston. (2007). *Ritual Texts for the Afterlife: Orpheus and the Bacchic Gold Tablets*. New York: Routledge.

Gräfenhain, M., T. Behne, M. Carpenter, and M. Tomasello. (2009). "Young Children's Understanding of Joint Commitments." *DevPsychol*, 45: 1430–43.

Gragg, D. L. (2004). "Old and New in Roman Religion: A Cognitive Account." In Whitehouse and Martin 2004, 69–86.

———. (2011). "Do the Multiple Initiations of Lucius in Apuleius' Metamorphoses Falsify the Ritual Form Hypothesis?" In *Past Minds: Studies in Cognitive Historiography*, ed. J. Sørensen and L. H. Martin, 125–30. London: Routledge.

Graser, E. R. (1940). "The Edict of Diocletian on Maximum Prices." In *Economic Survey of Ancient Rome*, ed. T. Frank (vol. 5), 305–421. Baltimore: Johns Hopkins University Press.
Graver, M. R. (2002). *Cicero on the Emotions: Tusculan Disputations 3 and 4*. Chicago: University of Chicago Press.
———. (2007). *Stoicism and Emotion*. Chicago: University of Chicago Press.
Green, C.M.C. (2007). *Roman Religion and the Cult of Diana at Aricia*. Cambridge: Cambridge University Press.
Gregory, A. (2012). "Changing Direction on Direction of Fit." *EthicalTheoryMoralPract*, 15.5: 603–14.
Gregory, J. P., and J. L. Barrett. (2009). "Epistemology and Counterintuitiveness: Role and Relationship in Epidemiology of Cultural Representations." *JCognCult*, 9: 289–314.
Grice, H. P. (1975). "Logic and Conversation." In *Syntax and Semantics*, vol. 3, *Speech Acts*, ed. P. Cole and J. Morgan, 41–58. New York: Academic.
———. (1989). *Studies in the Way of Words*. Cambridge, MA: Harvard University Press.
Grzankowski, A. (2015). "Not All Attitudes Are Propositional." *EurJPhilos*, 23.3: 374–91.
Guala, F. (2016). *Understanding Institutions: The Science and Philosophy of Living Together*. Princeton, NJ: Princeton University Press.
Guerrero, S., I. Enesco, and P. L. Harris. (2010). "Oxygen and the Soul: Children's Conception of Invisible Entities." *Journal of Cognition and Culture*, 10: 123–51.
Guittard, C. (1987). "Pline et la classification des prières dans la religion romaine." In *Pline l'Ancien, témoin de son temps*, ed. J. Pigeaud and J. Oroz Reta, 475–86, Salamanca: Universidad Pontificia de Salamanca.
———. (1998). "Invocations et structures théologiques dans la prière à Rome." *REL*, 76: 71–92.
———. (2007). *Carmen et prophéties à Rome*. Turnhout: Brepols.
Guthrie, S. E. (1993). *Faces in the Clouds: A New Theory of Religion*. Oxford: Oxford University Press.
Hacking, I. (1999). *The Social Construction of What?* Cambridge, MA: Harvard University Press.
Haensch, R. (2007). "Inscriptions as Sources of Knowledge for Religions and Cults in the Roman World of Imperial Times." In *A Companion to Roman Religion*, ed. J. Rüpke, 176–87. Oxford: Blackwell.
Hagendahl, H. (1967). *Augustine and the Latin Classics*. Vol. 1, *Testimonia*; vol. 2, *Augustine's Attitude*. Studia Graeca et Latina Gothoburgensia, 20. Gothenburg: Acta Universitatis Gothoburgensis.
Halliwell, S. (2008). *Greek Laughter: A Study of Cultural Psychology from Homer to Early Christianity*. Cambridge: Cambridge University Press.
Hamann, K., F. Warneken, and M. Tomasello. (2012). "Children's Developing Commitments to Joint Goals." *ChildDev*, 83.1: 137–45.
Hammer, D. (2014). *Roman Political Thought: From Cicero to Augustine*. Cambridge: Cambridge University Press.
Hankinson, R. J. (2013). "Lucretius, Epicurus, and the Logic of Multiple Explanations." In *Lucretius: Poetry, Philosophy, Science*, ed. D. Lehoux, A. C. Morrison, and A. Sharrock, 69–97. Oxford: Oxford University Press.

Harders, A.-C. (2010). "Roman Patchwork Families: Surrogate Parenting, Socialization, and the Shaping of Tradition." In *Children, Memory, and Family Identity in Roman Culture*, ed. V. Dasen and T. Späth, 49–72. Oxford: Oxford University Press.

Hardie, P. (1986). *Virgil's Aeneid: Cosmos and Imperium*. Oxford: Oxford University Press.

Harmon-Jones, E. (2000). "A Cognitive Dissonance Theory Perspective on the Role of Emotion in the Maintenance and Change of Beliefs and Attitudes." In *Emotions and Beliefs*, ed. N. H Frijda, A.R.S. Manstead, and S. Bem, 185–211. Cambridge: Cambridge University Press.

Harré, R. (1981). "Psychological Variety." In *Indigenous Psychologies: The Anthropology of the Self*, ed. P. Heelas and A. Lock, 79–103. London: Academic.

Harries, J. (1999). *Law and Empire in Late Antiquity*. Cambridge: Cambridge University Press.

Harris, G. W. (1999). *Agent-Centered Morality: An Aristotelian Alternative to Kantian Internalism*. Berkeley: University of California Press.

Harris, P. L. (2012). *Trusting What You're Told: How Children Learn from Others*. Cambridge, MA: Belknap Press of Harvard University Press.

Harris, P. L., and M. A. Koenig. (2006). "Trust in Testimony: How Children Learn about Science and Religion." *ChildDev*, 77.3: 505–24.

Harris, P. L., E. S. Pasquini, S. Duke, J. J. Asscher, and F. Pons. (2006). "Germs and Angels: The Role of Testimony in Young Children's Ontology." *DevSci*, 9.1: 76–96.

Harris, W. V. (2009). *Dreams and Experience in Classical Antiquity*. Cambridge, MA: Harvard University Press.

Harrison, T. (2000). *Divinity and History: The Religion of Herodotus*. Oxford: Clarendon.

———. (2007). "Greek Religion and Literature." In *A Companion to Greek Religion*, ed. D. Ogden, 373–84. Malden, MA: Blackwell.

———. (2015a). "Belief vs. Practice." In *The Oxford Handbook of Ancient Greek Religion*, ed. E. Eidinow and J. Kindt, 21–28. Oxford: Oxford University Press.

———. (2015b). "Review Article: New Approaches to Greek Religion." *JHS*, 135: 165–80.

Hartung, J. A. (1836). *Die Religion der Römer* (2 vols.). Erlangen: J. J. Palm und E. Enke.

Hayashi, M., G. Raymond, and J. Sidnell. (2013). "Conversational Repair and Human Understanding: An Introduction." In *Conversational Repair and Human Understanding*, ed. M. Hayashi, G. Raymond, and J. Sidnell, 1–40. Cambridge: Cambridge University Press.

Heath, J. (2011). "Women's Work: Female Transmission of Mythical Narrative." *TAPA*, 141.1: 69–104.

Heider, F., and M. Simmel. (1944). "An Experimental Study of Apparent Behavior." *AmJPsychol*, 57: 243–59.

Henig, M. (1995). *Religion in Roman Britain*. New York: St. Martin's.

Henrich, J. (2009). "The Evolution of Costly Displays, Cooperation and Religion: Credibility Enhancing Displays and Their Implications for Cultural Evolution." *EvolHumBehav*, 30: 244–60.

———. (2015). *The Secret of Our Success: How Culture Is Driving Human Evolution, Domesticating Our Species, and Making Us Smarter*. Princeton, NJ: Princeton University Press.

———. (2020). *The WEIRDest People in the World: How the West Became Psychologically Peculiar and Particularly Prosperous*. New York: Farrar, Straus and Giroux.

Henrich, J., and J. Ensminger. (2014). "Theoretical Foundations: The Coevolution of Social Norms, Intrinsic Motivation, Markets, and the Institutions of Complex Societies." In

Experimenting with Social Norms: Fairness and Punishment in Cross-Cultural Perspective, ed. J. Ensminger and J. Henrich, 19–44. New York: Russell Sage Foundation.

Henrich, J., and F. Gil-White. (2001). "The Evolution of Prestige: Freely Conferred Deference as a Mechanism for Enhancing the Benefits of Cultural Transmission." *EvolHumBehav*, 22.3: 165–96.

Henrich, N., and J. Henrich. (2007). *Why Humans Cooperate: A Cultural and Evolutionary Explanation*. Oxford: Oxford University Press.

Henrichs, A. (2010). "What Is a Greek God?" In *The Gods of Ancient Greece: Identities and Transformations*, ed. J. Bremmer and A. Erskine, 19–39. Edinburgh University Press.

Heraeus, W. (1904). "Die Sprache der römischen Kinderstube." *ALL*, 13: 149–72.

Herrmann, E., J. Call, M. V. Hernández-Lloreda, B. Hare, and M. Tomasello. (2007). "Humans Have Evolved Specialized Skills of Social Cognition: The Cultural Intelligence Hypothesis." *Science*, 317: 1360–66.

Herrmann, E., and M. Tomasello. (2012). "Human Cultural Cognition." In *The Evolution of Primate Societies*, ed. J. C. Mitani, J. Call, P. M. Kappeler, R. A. Palombit, and J. B. Silk, 701–12. Chicago: University of Chicago Press.

Herrmann, P. A., C. H. Legare, P. L. Harris, and H. Whitehouse. (2013). "Stick to the Script: The Effect of Witnessing Multiple Actors on Children's Imitation." *Cognition*, 129: 536–43.

Heyes, C. (2016). "Imitation: Not in Our Genes." *Current Biology*, 26.10: 412–14.

Hickson, F. V. (1993). *Roman Prayer Language: Livy and the Aneid [sic] of Vergil*. Stuttgart: Teubner.

Hickson-Hahn, F. V. (2004). "Ut diis immortalibus honos habeatur: Livy's Representation of Gratitude to the Gods." In *Rituals in Ink: A Conference on Religion and Literary Production in Ancient Rome, Held at Stanford University in February 2002*, ed. A. Barchiesi, J. Rüpke, and S. Stephens, 57–75. Stuttgart: Steiner.

———. (2007). "Performing the Sacred: Prayers and Hymns." In Rüpke 2007a, 235–48.

Hobson, P., and J. Hobson. (2012). "Joint Attention or Joint Engagement? Insights from Autism." Seemann 2012, 115–35.

Hölkeskamp, K. J. (1993). "Conquest, Competition and Consensus: Roman Expansion in Italy and the Rise of the *Nobilitas*." *Historia*, 42: 12–39.

Hoppitt, W., and K. N. Laland. (2013). *Social Learning: An Introduction to Mechanisms, Methods, and Models*. Princeton, NJ: Princeton University Press.

Horn, C. B., and J. W. Martens. (2009). *"Let the Little Children Come to Me": Childhood and Children in Early Christianity*. Washington, DC: Catholic University of America Press.

Horsfall, N. (2003). *The Culture of the Roman Plebs*. London: Bristol Classical.

———. (2006). *Virgil, Aeneid 3: A Commentary*. Leiden: Brill.

Horst, S. (2013). "Notions of Intuition in the Cognitive Science of Religion." *Monist*, 96.3: 377–98.

Howe, H. M. (1951). "Amafinius, Lucretius, and Cicero." *AJP*, 72: 57–62.

Hrdy, S. (2009). *Mothers and Others: The Evolutionary Origins of Mutual Understanding*. Cambridge, MA: Harvard University Press.

Humphrey, C., and J. Laidlaw. (1994). *The Archetypal Actions of Ritual: A Theory of Ritual Illustrated by the Jain Rite of Worship*. Oxford: Clarendon.

Hunt, A. (2016). *Reviving Roman Religion: Sacred Trees in the Roman World*. Cambridge: Cambridge University Press.

Hurley, S., and N. Chater (eds.). (2005). *Perspectives on Imitation: From Neuroscience to Social Science.* Vol. 1, *Mechanisms of Imitation and Imitation in Animals*; vol. 2, *Imitation, Human Development, and Culture.* Cambridge, MA: MIT Press.

Hutto, D. (2008). *Folk Psychological Narratives: The Sociocultural Basis of Understanding Reasons.* Cambridge, MA: MIT Press.

Hutto, D., and E. Myin. (2017). *Evolving Enactivism: Basic Minds Meet Content.* Cambridge, MA: MIT Press.

Ikäheimo, H., and A. Laitinen (eds.). (2011). *Recognition and Social Ontology.* Leiden: Brill.

Instinsky, H. U. (1940). "Consensus Universorum." *Hermes*, 75.3: 265–78.

Inwood, B. (1985). *Ethics and Human Action in Early Stoicism.* Oxford: Clarendon.

Irons, W. (2001). "Religion as a Hard-to-Fake Sign of Commitment." In *Evolution and the Capacity for Commitment*, ed. R. Nesse, 292–309. New York: Russell Sage Foundation.

Jacob, P., and M. Jeannerod. (2003). *Ways of Seeing: The Scope and Limits of Visual Cognition.* Oxford: Oxford University Press.

Jary, M. (2010). *Assertion.* Houndmills: Palgrave Macmillan.

Jehne, M. (ed.). (1995). *Demokratie in Rom? Die Rolle des Volkes in der Politik der römischen Republik.* Stuttgart: Steiner.

Jensen, J. S. (2010). "Doing It the Other Way Round: Religion as a Basic Case of 'Normative Cognition.'" *MethTheoryStudRel*, 22.4: 314–21.

———. (2013). "Normative Cognition in Culture and Religion." *Journal for the Cognitive Science of Religion*, 1.1: 47–70.

Johnson, C.V.M., S. W. Kelly, and P. Bishop. (2010). "Measuring the Mnemonic Advantage of Counter-intuitive and Counter-schematic Concepts." *JCognCult*, 10: 109–21.

Johnson, D. (2015). *God Is Watching You: How the Fear of God Makes Us Human.* Oxford: Oxford University Press.

———. (2018). "The Wrath of the Academics: Criticisms, Applications, and Extensions of the Supernatural Punishment Hypothesis." *ReligionBrainBehav*, 8.3: 320–50.

Johnson, D. M. (1987). "The Greek Origins of Belief." *AmPhilosQuart*, 24.4: 319–27.

Johnson, M. E. (2007). *The Rites of Christian Initiation: Their Evolution and Interpretation.* Collegeville, MN: Liturgical.

Johnson, M. J. (2007). "The Pontifical Law of the Roman Republic." PhD diss., Rutgers University.

———. (forthcoming). *The Pontifical Law: Religion and Religious Power in Ancient Rome.* Berlin: De Gruyter.

Johnson-Laird, P. N. (2006). *How We Reason.* Oxford: Oxford University Press.

Johnston, S. I. (2016). "How Myths and Other Stories Help to Create and Sustain Beliefs." In *Narrating Religion*, ed. S. I. Johnston, 141–56. Farmington Hills, MI: Macmillan.

Kahneman, D. (2011). *Thinking, Fast and Slow.* New York: Farrar, Straus and Giroux.

Kant, E. (1784). "Beantwortung der Frage: Was ist Aufklärung?" *Berliner Monatsschrift*, 4: 494.

Kapitány, R., and M. Nielsen. (2017). "The Ritual Stance and the Precaution System: The Role of Goal-Demotion and Opacity in Ritual and Everyday Actions." *ReligionBrainBehav*, 7: 27–42.

Kaster, R. A. (2005). *Emotion, Restraint, and Community in Ancient Rome.* Oxford: Oxford University Press.

———. (2006). *Marcus Tullius Cicero: Speech on Behalf of Publius Sestius*. Oxford: Oxford University Press.

Katajala-Peltomaa, S., and V. Vuolanto. (2011). "Children and Agency: Religion as Socialisation in Late Antiquity and the Late Medieval West." *Childhood in the Past* 4.1: 79–99.

Keith, A. (2006). "Critical Trends in Interpreting Sulpicia." *CW*, 100.1: 3–10.

Kelemen, D., and S. Carey. (2007). "The Essence of Artifacts: Developing the Design Stance." In *Creations of the Mind: Theories of Artifacts and Their Representation*, ed. S. Laurence and E. Margolis, 212–30. Oxford: Oxford University Press.

Kelemen, D., R. Seston, and L. St. Georges. (2012). "The Designing Mind: Children's Reasoning about Intended Function and Artifact Structure." *JCognDev*, 4: 439–53.

Kelly, D., and T. Davis. (2018). "Social Norms and Human Normative Psychology." *SocPhilosPolicy*, 35.1: 54–76.

Kendon, A. (2004). *Gesture: Visible Action as Utterance*. Cambridge: Cambridge University Press.

———. (2017). "Reflections on the 'Gesture-First' Hypothesis of Language Origins." *PsychonBullRev*, 24: 163–70.

Kenward, B. (2012). "Over-imitating Preschoolers Believe Unnecessary Actions Are Normative and Enforce Their Performance by a Third Party." *JExpChildPsychol*, 112: 195–207.

Keupp, S., T. Behne, and H. Rakoczy. (2013). "Why Do Children Overimitate? Normativity Is Crucial." *JExpChildPsychol*, 116.2: 392–406.

Kindt, J. (2012). *Rethinking Greek Religion*. Cambridge: Cambridge University Press.

King, A. (2004). *The Structure of Social Theory*. London: Routledge.

King, C. W. (1998). "The Living and the Dead: Ancient Roman Conceptions of the Afterlife." PhD diss., University of Chicago.

———. (2003). "The Organization of Roman Religious Beliefs." *ClAnt*, 22: 275–312.

———. (2009). "The Roman Manes: The Dead as Gods." In *Rethinking Ghosts in World Religions*, ed. Mu-chou Poo, 95–114. Leiden: Brill.

———. (2020). *The Ancient Roman Afterlife: Di Manes, Belief, and the Cult of the Dead*. Austin: University of Texas Press.

Kinzler, K. D., and E. S. Spelke. (2007). "Core Systems in Human Cognition." *ProgBrainRes*, 164: 257–64.

Kleve, K. (1963). *Gnosis theon: Die Lehre von der natürlichen Gotteserkenntnis in der epikureischen Theologie*. Symbolae Osloenses, fasc. suppl. 19. Oslo: Universitetsforlaget.

Klinghardt, M. (1999). "Prayer Formularies for Public Recitation: Their Use and Function in Ancient Religion." *Numen*, 46: 1–52.

Kloppenborg, J. S., and S. G. Wilson. (1996). *Voluntary Associations in the Graeco-Roman World*. London: Routledge.

Knapp, S., and W. B. Michaels. (1982). "Against Theory." *CritInquiry*, 8.4: 723–42.

Knoblich, G., S. Butterfill, and N. Sebanz. (2011). "Psychological Research on Joint Action: Theory and Data." In *The Psychology of Learning and Motivation: Advances in Research and Theory* (vol. 54), ed. B. H. Ross, 59–101. San Diego, CA: Elsevier Academic.

Knoblich, G., and N. Sebanz. (2008). "Evolving Intentions for Social Interaction: From Entrainment to Joint Action." *PhilosTRoySocB*, 363: 2021–31.

Knuuttila, S. (2004). *Emotions in Ancient and Medieval Philosophy*. Oxford: Clarendon.

Koch, R. (2005). *Comment peut-on être dieu? La secte d'Épicure.* Paris: Belin.
Koenen, M. (1999). "Lucretius' Explanation of Hearing in *De rerum natura* IV 524–562." *Mnemosyne*, 52.4: 434–63.
———. (2004). "*Loca loquuntur*: Lucretius' Explanation of the Echo and Other Acoustic Phenomena in *DRN* 4.563–614." *Mnemosyne*, 57.6: 698–724.
Konstan, D. (1973). *Some Aspects of Epicurean Psychology.* Leiden: Brill.
———. (2006). *The Emotions of the Ancient Greeks: Studies in Aristotle and Classical Literature.* Toronto: University of Toronto Press.
———. (2009). "Y a-t-il une histoire des émotions?" In *Violentes émotions: Approches comparatistes*, ed. P. Borgeaud and A.-C. Rendu-Loisel, 15–28. Geneva: Droz.
———. (2011). "Epicurus on the Gods." In *Epicurus and the Epicurean Tradition*, ed. J. Fish and K. Sanders, 53–71. Cambridge: Cambridge University Press.
———. (2019). "One Soul in Two Bodies: Distributed Cognition and Ancient Greek Friendship." In *Distributed Cognition in Classical Antiquity*, ed. M. Anderson, D. Cairns, and M. Sprevak, 209–24. Edinburgh: Edinburgh University Press.
Korsgaard, C. M. (2014). "The Normative Constitution of Agency." In *Rational and Social Agency: The Philosophy of Michael Bratman*, ed. M. Vargas and G. Yaffe, 190–214. Oxford: Oxford University Press.
Krauter, S. (2004). *Bürgerrecht und Kultteilnahme: Politische und kultische Rechte und Pflichten in griechischen Poleis, Rom und antikem Judentum.* Berlin: De Gruyter.
Kreinath, J. (2007). "Semiotics." In Kreinath et al. 2007, 1.429–70.
Kreinath, J., J. Snoek, and M. Stausberg (eds.). (2007). *Theorizing Rituals.* Vol. 1, *Issues, Topics, Approaches, Concepts*; vol. 2, *Annotated Bibliography of Ritual Theory 1966–2005.* Leiden: Brill.
Kropp, A. (2010). "How Does Magical Language Work? The Spells and *Formulae* of the Latin *Defixionum Tabellae*." In *Magical Practice in the Latin West*, ed. R. L. Gordon and F. M. Simón, 357–80. Leiden: Brill.
Kruger, A. C. (2011). "Imitation, Communion, and Culture." In Garrels 2011b, 111–27.
Kruger, A. C., and M. Tomasello. (1996). "Cultural Learning and Learning Culture." In *The Handbook of Education and Human Development*, ed. D. R. Olson and N. Torrance, 369–87. Cambridge, MA: Blackwell.
Kunda, Z. (1990). "The Case for Motivated Reasoning." *PsycholBull*, 108: 480–98.
Laes, C. (2011). *Children in the Roman Empire: Outsiders Within.* Cambridge: Cambridge University Press.
Laes, C., and V. Vuolanto. (2016). "A New Paradigm for the Social History of Childhood and Children in Antiquity." In *Children and Everyday Life in the Roman and Late Antique World*, ed. C. Laes and V. Vuolanto, 1–10. New York: Routledge.
Laitinen, A. (2014). "Against Representations with Two Directions of Fit." *PhenomCognSci*, 13: 179–99.
Lanman, J. A. (2008). "In Defence of 'Belief': A Cognitive Response to Behaviourism, Eliminativism, and Social Constructivism." *Issues in Ethnology and Anthropology*, 3.3: 49–62.
Larson, J. (2016). *Understanding Greek Religion.* New York: Routledge.
Latour, B. (1998). "Ramses II est-il mort de la tuberculose?" *La Recherche*, 307 (March): 84–85.
———. (2004). "Why Has Critique Run Out of Steam? From Matters of Fact to Matters of Concern." *CritInquiry*, 30: 225–48.

Latte, K. (1960). *Römische Religionsgeschichte*. Munich: Beck.
Lawson, E. T. (2001). "Psychological Perspectives on Agency." In *Religion in Mind: Cognitive Perspectives on Religious Belief, Ritual, and Experience*, ed. J. Andresen, 141–72. Cambridge: Cambridge University Press.
———. (2007). "Cognition." In Kreinath et al. 2007, 1.1.307–19.
Lawson, E. T., and R. N. McCauley. (1990). *Rethinking Religion: Connecting Cognition and Culture*. Cambridge: Cambridge University Press.
Lawson, T. (2012). "Ontology and the Study of Social Reality: Emergence, Organisation, Community, Power, Social Relations, Corporations, Artefacts and Money." *CambJEcon*, 36.2: 345–85.
———. (2016). "Comparing Conceptions of Social Ontology: Emergent Social Entities and/or Institutional Facts?" *JTheorSocBehav*, 46.4: 359–99.
Le Bon, G. (1895). *The Crowd: A Study of the Popular Mind*. New York: Macmillan.
Legare, C., and N. Wen. (2014). "The Effects of Ritual on the Development of Social Group Cognition." *IntJBehavDev*, 2: 9–12.
Legare, C., N. Wen, P. Herrmann, H. Whitehouse. (2015). "Imitative Flexibility and the Development of Cultural Learning." *Cognition*, 142: 351–61.
Lehmann, Y. (1997). *Varron théologien et philosophe romain*. Collection Latomus, 237. Brussels: REL.
Lenaghan, J. O. (1969). *A Commentary on Cicero's Oration De haruspicum responso*. The Hague: Mouton.
Lennon, J. (2015). "*Victimarii* in Roman Religion and Society." *PapBrSchRome*, 83: 65–89.
Leslie, A. M. (1994). "ToMM, ToBy, and Agency: Core Architecture and Domain Specificity." In *Mapping the Mind: Domain Specificity in Cognition and Culture*, ed. L. A. Hirschfeld and S. A. Gelman, 119–48. Cambridge: Cambridge University Press.
Levene, D. S. (1993). *Religion in Livy*. Leiden: Brill.
Levinson, S. (1983). *Pragmatics*. Cambridge: Cambridge University Press.
Lewis, D. (1969). *Convention: A Philosophical Study*. Cambridge, MA: Harvard University Press.
———. (1979). "Scorekeeping in a Language Game." *JPhilosLog*, 8: 339–59.
Lieberg, G. (1973). "Die 'theologia tripertita' in Forschung und Bezeugung." *ANRW*, 1.4: 63–115.
———. (1982). "Die theologia tripertita als Formprinzip antiken Denkens." *RhM*, 125.1: 25–53.
Liebeschuetz, J.H.W.G. (1979). *Continuity and Change in Roman Religion*. Oxford: Clarendon.
Linder, M., and J. Scheid. (1993). "Quand croire c'est faire: Le problème de la croyance dans la Rome ancienne." *Archives de Sciences Sociales des Religions*, 81: 47–62.
Linderski, J. (1972). "The Aedileship of Favonius, Curio the Younger and Cicero's Election to the Augurate." *HSCP*, 76: 181–200.
———. (1982). "Cicero and Roman Divination." *PP*, 202: 12–38.
———. (1986a). "The Augural Law." *ANRW*, 2.16.3: 2146–312.
———. (1986b). "Religious Aspects of the Conflict of the Orders: The Case of *confarreatio*." In *Social Struggles in Archaic Rome: New Perspectives on the Conflict of the Orders*, ed. K. A. Raaflaub, 244–61. Berkeley: University of California Press.
———. (1986c). "Watching the Birds: Cicero the Augur and the Augural *templa*." *CPh*, 81: 330–40.

―――. (1990). "The Auspices and the Struggle of the Orders." In *Staat und Staatlichkeit in der frühen römischen Republik*, ed. W. Eder, 34–48. Stuttgart: Steiner.

―――. (1993). "Roman Religion in Livy." In *Livius: Aspekte seines Werkes*, ed. W. Schuller, 53–70. Constance: Universitätsverlag Konstanz.

―――. (2000). "Beard, North, and Price, Religions of Rome." *JRA*, 13: 453–63.

―――. (2006). "Founding the City." In *Ten Years of the Agnes Kirsopp Michels Lectures at Bryn Mawr College*, ed. S. B. Faris and L. E. Lundeen, 88–107. Bryn Mawr, PA: Bryn Mawr College. (Reprinted with revisions as Linderski 2007.)

―――. (2007). "Founding the City: Ennius and Romulus on the Site of Rome." In *Roman Questions* (vol. 2), 3–19. Stuttgart: Steiner.

Lindquist, G., and S. Coleman. (2008). "Introduction: Against Belief?" *Social Analysis: The International Journal of Social and Cultural Practice*, 52.1: 1–18.

Ling, R. (1977). "Studius and the Beginnings of Roman Landscape Painting." *JRS*, 67: 1–16.

Lintott, A. (1999). *The Constitution of the Roman Republic*. Oxford: Clarendon.

Lipka, M. (2009). *Roman Gods: A Conceptual Approach*. Leiden: Brill.

Lisdorf, A. (2004). "The Spread of Non-natural Concepts: Evidence from the Roman Prodigy Lists." *Journal of Cognition and Culture*, 4: 151–73.

―――. (2005). "The Conflict over Cicero's House: An Analysis of the Ritual Element in *De domo sua*." *Numen*, 52: 445–64.

―――. (2011). "Prisons of the Longue Durée: The Circulation and Acceptance of *Prodigia* in Roman Antiquity." In *Past Minds: Studies in Cognitive Historiography*, ed. L. H. Martin and J. Sørensen, 89–106. London: Equinox.

List, C. (2014). "Three Kinds of Collective Attitudes." *Erkenntnis*, 79: 1601–22.

List, C., and P. Pettit. (2011). *Group Agency: The Possibility, Design, and Status of Corporate Agents*. Oxford: Oxford University Press.

Liszkowski, U., P. Brown, T. Callaghan, A. Takada, and C. de Vos. (2012). "A Prelinguistic Gestural Universal of Human Communication." *CognitiveSci*, 36: 698–713.

Liu, D., H. M. Wellman, T. Tardif, and M. A. Sabbagh. (2008). "Theory of Mind Development in Chinese Children: A Meta-analysis of False-Belief Understanding across Cultures and Languages." *DevPsychol*, 44.2: 523–31.

Liu, J. (2009). *Collegia Centonariorum: The Guilds of Textile Dealers in the Roman West*. Leiden: Brill.

Lobur, J. A. (2008). *Consensus, Concordia, and the Formation of Roman Imperial Ideology*. New York: Routledge.

Luther, M. (1520). *Von der Freiheit eines Christenmenschen*. Wittenberg.

Lyons, D. E., and F. C. Keil. (2013). "Overimitation and the Development of Causal Understanding." In *Navigating the Social World: What Infants, Children, and Other Species Can Teach Us*, ed. M. Banaji and S. Gelman, 145–49. Oxford: Oxford University Press.

Lyons, D. E., A. G. Young, and F. C. Keil. (2007). "The Hidden Structure of Overimitation." *PNatlAcadSciUSA*, 104: 19751–56.

MacBain, B. (1982). *Prodigy and Expiation: A Study in Religion and Politics in Republican Rome*. Bruxelles: Latomus, Revue d'Études latines.

MacFarlane, J. (2011). "What Is Assertion?" In *Assertion: New Philosophical Essays*, ed. J. Brown and H. Cappelen, 79–96. Oxford: Oxford University Press.

Mackey, J. L. (2015). "New Evidence for the Epicurean Theory of the Origin of Language: Philodemus, *On Poems* 5 (*PHerc.* 403, fr. 5, col. i)." *CErc*, 45: 67–84.

———. (2016). "Roman Children as Religious Agents: The Cognitive Foundations of Cult." In *Children and Everyday Life in the Roman and Late Antique World*, ed. C. Laes and V. Vuolanto, 179–97. New York: Routledge.

———. (2017). "Das Erlöschen des Glaubens: The Fate of 'Belief' in the Study of Roman Religion." *Phasis*, 20: 83–150.

———. (2018a). "Roman Ritual Orthopraxy and Overimitation." In *The Routledge Handbook of Classics and Cognitive Theory*, ed. P. Meineck, W. Short, and J. Devereaux, 253–69. New York: Routledge.

———. (2018b). "'Textualizing' Roman Religious Practices." *JRA*, 31: 618–25.

———. (2019). "Developmental Psychologies in the Roman World: Change and Continuity." *History of Psychology*, 22.2: 113–29.

———. (2021). "Saving the Appearances: The Phenomenology of Epiphany in Atomist Theology." *Invigilata Lucernis*, 43: 99–128.

MacRae, D. (2016). *Legible Religion: Books, Gods, and Rituals in Roman Culture*. Cambridge, MA: Harvard University Press.

Magdelain, A. (1969). "L'Auguraculum de l'arx à Rome et dans d'autres villes." *REL*, 47: 253–69.

Mair, J. (2013). "Cultures of Belief." *Anthropological Theory*, 12.4: 448–66.

Malinowski, B. (1935). *Coral Gardens and Their Magic* (vol. 2). London: George Allen and Unwin.

Malle, B. F. (2004). *How the Mind Explains Behavior: Folk Explanations, Meaning, and Social Interaction*. Cambridge, MA: MIT Press.

———. (2008). "The Fundamental Tools, and Possibly Universals, of Human Social Cognition." In *Handbook of Motivation and Cognition Across Cultures*, ed. R. M. Sorrentino and S. Yamaguchi, 267–96. Amsterdam: Elsevier.

Malley, B., and J. L. Barrett. (2003). "Can Ritual Form Be Predicted from Religious Belief? A Test of the Lawson-McCauley Hypotheses." *JRitualStud*, 17: 1–14.

Maltby, R. (1991). *A Lexicon of Ancient Latin Etymologies*. Leeds: Cairns.

Mantle, I. C. (2002). "The Roles of Children in Roman Religion." *G&R*, 49.1: 85–106.

Marrou, H. I. (1956). *A History of Education in Antiquity* (trans. G. Lamb). London: Sheed and Ward.

Martin, L. H. (2004). "Petitionary Prayer: Cognitive Considerations." In *Religion in Cultural Discourse: Essays in Honor of Hans G. Kippenberg on the Occasion of His 65th Birthday*, ed. B. Luchesi and K. von Stuckrad, 115–26. Berlin: De Gruyter.

Massaro, M. (1977). "Aniles fabellae." *Studi italiani di filologia classica: Firenze*, 49.1–2: 104–35.

Matthews, G. (2003). "Aristotle: Psychology." In *The Blackwell Guide to Ancient Philosophy*, ed. C. J. Shields, 211–27. Malden, MA: Blackwell.

McCauley, R. N. (2011). *Why Religion Is Natural and Science Is Not*. Oxford: Oxford University Press.

McCauley, R. N., and E. T. Lawson. (2002). *Bringing Ritual to Mind: Psychological Foundations of Cultural Forms*. Cambridge: Cambridge University Press.

———. (2007). "Cognition, Religious Ritual, and Archaeology." In *The Archaeology of Ritual*, ed. E. Kyriakidis, 209–54. Los Angeles: Cotsen Institute of Archaeology, University of California.

McElreath, R., R. Boyd, and P. J. Richerson. (2003). "Shared Norms and the Evolution of Ethnic Markers." *CurrAnthropol*, 44.1: 122–30.

McGuigan, N., J. Makinson, and A. Whiten. (2011). "From Over-imitation to Super-copying: Adults Imitate Causally Irrelevant Aspects of Tool Use with Higher Fidelity Than Young Children." *BrJPsychol*, 102: 1–18.

McKay, R., and H. Whitehouse. (2015). "Religion and Morality." *PsycholBull*, 141.2: 447–73.

Meijers, A. (2007). "Collective Speech Acts." In *Intentional Acts and Institutional Facts: Essays on John Searle's Social Ontology*, ed. S. L. Tsohatzidis, 93–110. Dordrecht: Springer.

Meineck, P. (2011). "The Neuroscience of the Tragic Mask." *Arion* 19.1: 113–58.

———. (2018). *Theatrocracy: Greek Drama, Cognition, and the Imperative for Theatre*. New York: Routledge.

Meltzoff, A. N. (1988). "Infant Imitation after a 1-Week Delay: Long-Term Memory for Novel Acts and Multiple Stimuli." *DevPsychol*, 24: 470–76.

———. (1995). "Understanding the Intentions of Others: Re-enactment of Intended Acts by 18-Month-Old Children." *DevPsychol*, 31: 838–50.

———. (2007a). "'Like Me': A Foundation for Social Cognition." *DevelopmentalSci*, 10.1: 126–34.

———. (2007b). "The 'Like Me' Framework for Recognizing and Becoming an Intentional Agent." *ActaPsychol*, 124: 26–43.

———. (2011a). "Out of the Mouths of Babes: Imitation, Gaze, and Intentions in Infant Research—the 'Like Me' Framework." In Garrels 2011b, 55–74.

———. (2011b). "Social Cognition and the Origins of Imitation, Empathy, and Theory of Mind." In Goswami 2011, 49–75.

Meltzoff, A. N., and R. Brooks. (2007a). "Eyes Wide Shut: The Importance of Eyes in Infant Gaze Following and Understanding Other Minds." In *Gaze Following: Its Development and Significance*, ed. R. Flom, K. Lee, and D. Muir, 217–41. Mahwah, NJ: Erlbaum.

———. (2007b). "Intersubjectivity before Language: Three Windows on Preverbal Sharing." In *On Being Moved: From Mirror Neurons to Empathy*, ed. S. Bråten, 149–74. Philadelphia: John Benjamins.

Meltzoff, A. N., and M. K. Moore. (1977). "Imitation of Facial and Manual Gestures by Human Neonates." *Science*, 198: 75–78.

———. (1983). "Newborn Infants Imitate Adult Facial Gestures." *ChildDev*, 54: 702–9.

Mercier, H. (2020). *Not Born Yesterday: The Science of Who We Trust and What We Believe*. Princeton, NJ: Princeton University Press.

Mercier, H., and D. Sperber. (2009). "Intuitive and Reflective Inferences." In *In Two Minds: Dual Processes and Beyond*, ed. K. Frankish and J. St. B. T. Evans, 149–70. Oxford: Oxford University Press.

———. (2017). *The Enigma of Reason*. Cambridge, MA: Harvard University Press.

Merrill, W. A. (1907). *T. Lucreti Cari De rerum natura libri sex*. New York: American Book.

Mesquita, B., and P. C. Ellsworth. (2001). "The Role of Culture in Appraisal." In *Appraisal Processes in Emotion: Theory, Methods, Research*, ed. K. R. Scherer, A. Schorr, and T. Johnstone, 233–48. Oxford: Oxford University Press.

Metcalfe, J., and H. S. Terrace (eds.). (2013). *Agency and Joint Attention*. Oxford: Oxford University Press.

Meyer, E. A. (2004). *Legitimacy and Law in the Roman World: Tabulae in Roman Belief and Practice*. Cambridge: Cambridge University Press.

Michael, J. (2011). "Shared Emotions and Joint Action." *RevPhilosPsychol*, 2.2: 355–73.
Michael, J. A., and A. Szigeti. (2018). "'The Group Knobe Effect': Evidence That People Intuitively Attribute Agency and Responsibility to Groups." *PhilosExplor*, 2018: 1–18.
Michotte, A. (1963). *The Perception of Causality*. Andover, Hants: Methuen.
Middleton, C. (1729). *A Letter from Rome, Shewing an Exact Conformity between Popery and Paganism*. London: W. Innys.
Millar, F. (2002). *Rome, the Greek World, and the East*. Vol. 1, *The Roman Republic and the Augustan Revolution*, ed. H. M. Cotton and G. M. Rogers. Chapel Hill: University of North Carolina Press.
Miller, K. (2006). "Social Obligation as Reason for Action." *CognSystRes*, 7: 273–85.
Mills, M., and E. Melhuish. (1974). "Recognition of Mother's Voice in Early Infancy." *Nature*, 252: 123–24.
Minyard, J. D. (1985). *Lucretius and the Late Republic: An Essay in Roman Intellectual History*. Leiden: Brill.
Mitchell, S., and P. Van Nuffelen (eds.). (2010a). *Monotheism between Pagans and Christians in Late Antiquity*. Leuven: Peeters.
———. (eds.). (2010b). *One God: Pagan Monotheism in the Roman Empire*. Cambridge: Cambridge University Press.
Moll, H., M. Carpenter, and M. Tomasello. (2010) "Social Engagement Leads 2-Year-Olds to Overestimate Others' Knowledge." *Infancy*, 1–18.
Moll, H., and A. N. Meltzoff. (2011). "Perspective-Taking and Its Foundation in Joint Attention." In *Perception, Causation, and Objectivity*, ed. J. Roessler, H. Lerman, and N. Eilan, 286–304. Oxford: Oxford University Press.
Moll, H., and M. Tomasello. (2007). "Cooperation and Human Cognition: The Vygotskian Intelligence Hypothesis." *PhilosTRoySocB*, 362: 639–48.
Momigliano, A. (1941). "Epicureans in Revolt." *JRS*, 31: 149–57.
———. (1984). "The Theological Efforts of the Roman Upper Classes in the First Century B.C." *CPh*, 79.3: 199–211.
———. (1987). "Religion in Athens, Rome, and Jerusalem in the First Century B.C." In *On Pagans, Jews, and Christians*, 74–91. Middletown, CT: Wesleyan University Press.
Mommsen, T. (1856). *Römische Geschichte. Erster Band: Bis zur Schlacht von Pydna* (2nd ed.). Berlin: Weidmann.
———. (1857). *Römische Geschichte. Zweiter Band: Von der Schlacht von Pydna bis auf Sullas Tod* (2nd ed.). Berlin: Weidmann.
———. (1862–66). *The History of Rome* (4 vols., trans. W. P. Dickson). London: R. Bentley and Son. (Originally published as *Römische Geschichte* [3 vols.], 1854–56, Leipzig: Weidmann.)
Montague, M. (2007). "Against Propositionalism." *Noûs*, 41.3: 503–18.
Montero, S. (2007). "Del silencio augural al silencio ante el prodigio." *'Ilu. Revista de Ciencias de las Religiones*, 29: 165–74.
Moon, C., H. Lagercrantz, and P. K Kuhl. (2013). "Language Experienced *in utero* Affects Vowel Perception after Birth: A Two-Country Study." *Acta Paediatrica*, 102.2: 156–60.
Morello, A. (2008). *Prorae: La prima prua di nave sulle monete della Repubblica romana; Origine di un simbolo imperituro del potere di Roma; Un inno a Caio Duilio*. Cassino: Diana.
Morgan, T. (1998). *Literate Education in the Hellenistic and Roman Worlds*. Cambridge: Cambridge University Press.

———. (2007). *Popular Morality in the Early Roman Empire*. Cambridge: Cambridge University Press.
———. (2015). *Roman Faith and Christian Faith: Pistis and Fides in the Early Roman Empire and Early Churches*. Oxford: Oxford University Press.
Morgan, T.J.H., and K. N. Laland. (2012). "The Biological Bases of Conformity." *FrontNeurosci*, 6: 87.
Morley, N. (2004). *Theories, Models and Concepts in Ancient History*. London: Routledge.
Morrison, T., and W. A. Conaway. (2006). *Kiss, Bow, or Shake Hands* (2nd ed.). Avon, MA: Adams Media.
Mousourakis, G. (2012). *Fundamentals of Roman Private Law*. Berlin: Springer.
Mueller, H.-F. (2002). *Roman Religion in Valerius Maximus*. London: Routledge.
Mulligan, K. (ed.). (1987). *Speech Act and Sachverhalt: Reinach and the Foundations of Realist Phenomenology*. Dordrecht: Nijhoff.
———. (2013). "Acceptance, Acknowledgment, Affirmation, Agreement, Assertion, Belief, Certainty, Conviction, Denial, Judgment, Refusal and Rejection." In *Judgement and Truth in Early Analytic Philosophy and Phenomenology*, ed. M. Textor, 97–136. London: Palgrave.
Mulligan, K., and K. R. Scherer. (2012). "Toward a Working Definition of Emotion." *Emotion Review*, 4.4: 345–57.
Murphy, T. (1998). "Cicero's First Readers: Epistolary Evidence for the Dissemination of His Works." *CQ*, 48: 492–505.
Murray, P. (1996). *Plato on Poetry*. Cambridge: Cambridge University Press.
Muth, R. (1978). "Vom Wesen römischer 'religio.'" *ANRW*, 2.16.1: 290–354.
Muthukrishna, M., T.J.H. Morgan, and J. Henrich. (2016). "The When and Who of Social Learning and Conformist Transmission." *EvolHumBehav*, 37: 10–20.
Needham, R. (1972). *Belief, Language, and Experience*. Oxford: Oxford University Press.
———. (1990). Review of Veyne 1988. *Man*, 25.1: 157–58.
Néraudau, J.-P. (1979). *La jeunesse dans la litterature et les institutions de la Rome republicaine*. Paris: Belles Lettres.
———. (1984). *Être enfant à Rome*. Paris: Belles Lettres.
Nettleship, H. (1885). *Lectures and Essays on Subjects Connected with Latin Literature and Scholarship*. Oxford: Clarendon.
Nielsen, M. (2009). "The Imitative Behaviour of Children and Chimpanzees: A Window on the Transmission of Cultural Traditions." *Revue de Primatologie*, 1. doi:10.4000/primatologie.254.
Nielsen, M., and K. Tomaselli. (2010). "Over-imitation in Kalahari Bushman Children and the Origins of Human Cultural Cognition." *PsycholSci*, 21: 729–36.
Nock, A. D. (1933). *Conversion: The Old and the New in Religion from Alexander the Great to Augustine of Hippo*. Oxford: Oxford University Press.
———. (1934). "Religion." *The Cambridge Ancient History* (vol. 10, 2nd ed.): 465–511.
———. (1939). "A Feature of Roman Religion." *HarvardTheolRev*, 32.1: 83–96.
Nongbri, B. (2008). "Dislodging 'Embedded' Religion: A Brief Note on a Scholarly Trope." *Numen* 55: 440–60.
Norden, E. (1939). *Aus altrömischen Priesterbüchern*. Lund: C.W.K. Gleerup.
Norenzayan, A. (2013). *Big Gods: How Religion Transformed Cooperation and Conflict*. Princeton, NJ: Princeton University Press.

Norenzayan, A., S. Atran, J. Faulkner, and M. Schaller. (2006). "Memory and Mystery: The Cultural Selection of Minimally Counterintuitive Narratives." *CognSci*, 30: 531–53.

Norenzayan, A., A. F. Shariff, W. M. Gervais, A. K. Willard, R. A. McNamara, E. Slingerland, and J. Henrich. (2016). "The Cultural Evolution of Prosocial Religions." *Behavioral and Brain Sciences*, 39: 1–19.

North, J. A. (1976). "Conservatism and Change in Roman Religion." *Papers of the British School at Rome*, 44: 1–12.

———. (1989). "Religion in Republican Rome." *The Cambridge Ancient History* (vol. 7.2, 2nd ed.): 573–624.

———. (1998). "The Books of the Pontifices." In *La mémoire perdue: Recherches sur l'administration romaine*, 45–63. Collection de l'École française de Rome, 243. Rome: École française de Rome.

———. (2000a). *Roman Religion*. Oxford: Oxford University Press.

———. (2000b). "Prophet and Text in the Third Century B.C." In *Religion in Archaic and Republican Rome and Italy*, ed. E. Bispham and C. Smith, 92–107. Edinburgh: Edinburgh University Press.

———. (2003). "Réflexions autour des communautés religieuses du monde gréco-romain." In *Les communautés religieuses dans le monde gréco-romain: Essais de définition*, ed. N. Belayche and S. C. Mimouni, 337–47. Turnhout, Belgium: Brepols.

———. (2007). "Arnobius on Sacrifice." In *Wolf Liebeschuetz Reflected: Essays Presented by Colleagues, Friends, and Pupils*, ed. J. Drinkwater and B. Salway, 27–36. London: Institute of Classical Studies.

———. (2008). "Action and Ritual in Roman Historians; or How Horatius Held the Door-Post." In *Religion and Society: Rituals, Resources and Identity in the Ancient Graeco-Roman World*, ed. A. H. Rasmussen and S. W. Rasmussen, 23–36. Rome: Quasar.

Nozick, R. (1969). "Coercion." In *Philosophy, Science, and Method: Essays in Honor of Ernest Nagel*, ed. S. Morgenbesser, P. Suppes, and M. White, 440–72. New York: St. Martin's.

Nussbaum, M. C. (1978). *Aristotle's "De Motu Animalium": Text with Translation, Commentary, and Interpretive Essays*. Princeton, NJ: Princeton University Press.

———. (1994). *The Therapy of Desire: Theory and Practice in Hellenistic Ethics*. Princeton, NJ: Princeton University Press.

———. (2001). *Upheavals of Thought: The Intelligence of Emotions*. Cambridge: Cambridge University Press.

Obbink, D. D. (1984). "*P.Oxy*. 215 and Epicurean Religious *Theoria*." In *Atti del XVII Congresso Internazionale di Papirologia* (vol. 2), 607–19. Naples: Centro internazionale per lo studio dei papiri ercolanesi.

———. 1988. "The Origin of Greek Sacrifice: Theophrastus on Religion and Cultural History." In *Theophrastean Studies*, ed. W. W. Fortenbaugh and R. W. Sharples, 272–95. New Brunswick, NJ: Transaction Books.

———. (1996). *Philodemus On Piety, Part 1*. Oxford: Clarendon.

Ober, J. (2008). *Democratic Knowledge: Innovation and Learning in Classical Athens*. Princeton, NJ: Princeton University Press.

Oberle, E. (2009). "The Development of Theory of Mind Reasoning in Micronesian Children." *Journal of Cognition and Culture*, 9: 39–56.

O'Connor, T., and C. Sandis. (2010). *A Companion to the Philosophy of Action*. Malden, MA: Wiley-Blackwell.
O'Daly, G.J.P. (1996). "Augustine's Critique of Varro on Roman Religion." In *Religion and Superstition in Latin Literature*, ed. A. H. Sommerstein, 65–75. Nottingham Classical Literature Studies, 3. Bari, Italy: Levante.
O'Donnell, J. J. (1992). *Augustine "Confessions": Introduction, Text, and Commentary* (3 vols.). Oxford: Clarendon.
Ogilvie, R. M. (1965). *A Commentary on Livy, Books 1–5*. Oxford: Clarendon.
Öhman, A. (2000). "Distinguishing Unconscious from Conscious Emotional Processes: Methodological Considerations and Theoretical Implications." In *The Handbook of Cognition and Emotion*, ed. T. Dalgleish and M. J. Power, 321–52. Oxford: Oxford University Press.
O'Keefe, T. S. (1997). "Epicurus on Reductionism, Determinism and Freedom." PhD diss., University of Texas at Austin.
———. (2005). *Epicurus on Freedom*. Cambridge: Cambridge University Press.
Oostenbroek, J., and H. Over. (2016). "The Cultural Transmission of Social Information." In *Shared Representations: Sensorimotor Foundations of Social Life*, ed. S. S. Obhi and E. S. Cross, 136–50. Cambridge: Cambridge University Press.
Oostenbroek, J., T. Suddendorf, M. Nielsen, J. Redshaw, S. Kennedy-Costantini, J. Davis, S. Clark, V. Slaughter. (2016). "Comprehensive Longitudinal Study Challenges the Existence of Neonatal Imitation in Humans." *CurrBiol*, 26.10: 1334–38.
Opfer, J. E., and S. A. Gelman. (2011). "Development of the Animate-Inanimate Distinction." In Goswami 2011, 213–38.
Ossa-Richardson, A. (2013). *The Devil's Tabernacle: The Pagan Oracles in Early Modern Thought*. Princeton, NJ: Princeton University Press.
O'Sullivan, T. M. (2011). *Walking in Roman Culture*. Cambridge: Cambridge University Press.
Oswald, M. E., and S. Grosjean. (2004). "Confirmation Bias." In *Cognitive Illusions: A Handbook on Fallacies and Biases in Thinking, Judgement and Memory*, ed. R. F. Pohl, 79–96. New York: Psychology Press.
Over, H., and M. Carpenter. (2012a). "Putting the Social into Social Learning: Explaining Both Selectivity and Fidelity in Children's Copying Behavior." *JCompPsychol*, 126: 182–92.
———. (2012b). "The Social Side of Imitation." *Child Development Perspectives*, 7.1: 6–11.
Pacherie, É. (2002). "The Role of Emotions in the Explanation of Action." *European Review of Philosophy*, 5: 53–91.
———. (2013). "Intentional Joint Agency: Shared Intention Lite." *Synthese*, 190.10: 1817–39.
Pagán, V. E. (2004). *Conspiracy Narratives in Roman History*. Austin: University of Texas Press.
Pandey, N. (2018). *The Poetics of Power in Augustan Rome: Latin Poetic Responses to Early Imperial Iconography*. Cambridge: Cambridge University Press.
Parker, R. (1996). *Athenian Religion: A History*. Oxford: Clarendon.
———. (2011). *On Greek Religion*. Ithaca, NY: Cornell University Press.
Pax, E. (1955). *Epiphaneia: Ein religionsgeschichtlicher Beitrag zur biblischen Theologie*. Munich: Zink.
———. (1962). "Epiphanie." In *Reallexikon für Antike und Christentum* (vol. 5), 832–909. Stuttgart: A. Hiersemann.
Pease, A. S. (1955–58). *M. Tulli Ciceronis De natura deorum* (2 vols.). Cambridge, MA: Harvard University Press.

Pelling, C.B.R. (ed.). (1988). *Plutarch: Life of Antony*. Cambridge: Cambridge University Press.
Pépin, J. (1956). "La 'théologie tripartite' de Varron." *REAug*, 2: 265–94.
Perfigli, M. (2004). *Indigitamenta: Divinità funzionali e funzionalità divina nella religione romana*. Pisa: ETS.
Perler, D. (ed.). (2001). *Ancient and Medieval Theories of Intentionality*. Leiden: Brill.
Petrovic, A., and I. Petrovic. (2016). *Inner Purity and Pollution in Greek Religion*. Vol. 1, *Early Greek Religion*. Oxford: Oxford University Press.
Pfister, F. (1924). "Epiphanie." *RE*, suppl. 4: 277–323.
Phillips, C. R., III. (1986). "The Sociology of Religious Knowledge." *ANRW*, 2.16.3: 2677–773.
———. (2007). "Approaching Roman Religion: The Case for *Wissenschaftsgeschichte*." In Rüpke 2007a, 10–28.
Picavet, F. (1888). *De Epicuro novae religionis auctore*. Paris: F. Alcan.
Platt, V. J. (2011). *Facing the Gods: Epiphany and Representation in Graeco-Roman Art, Literature and Religion*. Cambridge: Cambridge University Press.
Pongratz-Leisten, B., and K. Sonik. (2015). "Between Cognition and Culture: Theorizing the Materiality of Divine Agency in Cross-Cultural Perspective." In *The Materiality of Divine Agency*, ed. B. Pongratz-Leisten and K. Sonik, 3–69. Berlin: De Gruyter.
Pouillon, J. (1982). "Remarks on the Verb 'To Believe.'" In *Between Belief and Transgression: Structuralist Essays in Religion, History, and Myth*, ed. M. Izard and P. Smith, 1–8. Chicago: University of Chicago Press.
Preller, L. (1858). *Römische Mythologie*. Berlin: Weidmann.
Premack, D., and G. Woodruff. (1978). "Does the Chimpanzee Have a 'Theory of Mind'?" *BehavBrainSci*, 1: 515–26.
Prescendi, F. (2007). *Décrire et comprendre le sacrifice: Les réflexions des Romains sur leur propre religion à partir de la littérature antiquaire*. Stuttgart: Steiner.
———. (2010). "Children and the Transmission of Religious Knowledge." In *Children, Memory, and Family Identity in Roman Culture*, ed. V. Dasen and T. Späth, 73–93. Oxford: Oxford University Press.
Price, H. H. (1965). "Belief 'In' and Belief 'That.'" *ReligStud*, 1.1: 5–27.
———. (1969). *Belief*. London: Allen and Unwin.
Price, S.R.F. (1984). *Rituals and Power: The Roman Imperial Cult in Asia Minor*. Cambridge: Cambridge University Press.
———. (1999). *Religions of the Ancient Greeks*. Cambridge: Cambridge University Press.
Prinz, J. (2004a). "Embodied Emotions." In *Thinking about Feeling*, ed. R. C. Solomon, 44–58. Oxford: Oxford University Press.
———. (2004b). *Gut Reactions: A Perceptual Theory of the Emotions*. Oxford: Oxford University Press.
Proust, J. (2013). *The Philosophy of Metacognition: Mental Agency and Self-Awareness*. Oxford: Oxford University Press.
Purcell, N. (1995). "Literate Games: Roman Urban Society and the Game of Alea." *Past and Present*, 147: 3–37.
Purzycki, B. G., D. N. Finkel, J. Shaver, N. Wales, A. B. Cohen, and R. Sosis. (2012). "What Does God Know? Supernatural Agents' Access to Socially Strategic and Non-strategic Information." *CognSci*, 36: 846–69.

Purzycki, B. G., J. Henrich, C. Apicella, Q. D. Atkinson, A. Baimel, E. Cohen, R. A. McNamara, A. K. Willard, D. Xygalatas, and A. Norenzayan. (2018). "The Evolution of Religion and Morality: A Synthesis of Ethnographic and Experimental Evidence from Eight Societies." *ReligionBrainBehav*, 8.2: 101–32.

Purzycki, B. G., and A. K. Willard. (2016). "MCI Theory: A Critical Discussion." *ReligionBrainBehav*, 6.3: 207–48.

Pust, J. (2019). "Intuition." *The Stanford Encyclopedia of Philosophy* (Summer 2019 ed.), ed. Edward N. Zalta. https://plato.stanford.edu/archives/sum2019/entries/intuition/.

Pyysiäinen, I. (2004). "Intuitive and Explicit in Religious Thought." *JCognCult*, 4.1: 123–50.

———. (2009). *Supernatural Agents: Why We Believe in Souls, Gods, and Buddhas*. Oxford: Oxford University Press.

Quasten, J. (1983). *Music and Worship in Pagan and Christian Antiquity* (trans. B. Ramsey, OP). Washington, DC: National Association of Pastoral Musicians.

Raja, R., and J. Rüpke (eds.). (2015). *A Companion to the Archaeology of Religion in the Ancient World*. Hoboken, NJ: Wiley-Blackwell.

Rakoczy, H. (2007). "Play, Games, and the Development of Collective Intentionality." *NewDirChildAdolescDev*, 115: 53–67.

Rakoczy, H., and M.F.H. Schmidt. (2013). "The Early Ontogeny of Social Norms." *ChildDevPerspect*, 7.1: 17–21.

Rakoczy, H., and M. Tomasello. (2007). "The Ontogeny of Social Ontology: Steps to Shared Intentionality and Status Functions." In *Intentional Acts and Institutional Facts: Essays on John Searle's Social Ontology*, ed. S. L. Tsohatzidis, 113–37. Dordrecht: Springer.

Rakoczy, H., F. Warneken, and M. Tomasello. (2008). "The Sources of Normativity: Young Children's Awareness of the Normative Structure of Games." *DevPsychol*, 44.3: 875–81.

Ramstead, M.J.D., S.P.L. Veissière, and L. J. Kirmayer. (2016). "Cultural Affordances: Scaffolding Local Worlds through Shared Intentionality and Regimes of Attention." *Frontiers in Psychology*, 7: article 1090.

Randazzo, S. (2005). "The Nature of Partnership in Roman Law." *AustJLegHist*, 9: 119–29.

Rasmussen, S. W. (2002). "*Ars haruspicina* and *ars nesciendi*—Some Reflections on a Sheep's Liver." In *Ancient History Matters: Studies Presented to Jens Erik Skydsgaard on His Seventieth Birthday*, ed. K. Ascani. Analecta Romana Instituti Danici, suppl. 30, 165–71. Rome: "L'Erma" di Bretschneider.

———. (2003). *Public portents in republican Rome*. Rome: "L'Erma" di Bretschneider.

Raubitschek, A. E. (1949). "Phaidros and His Roman Pupils." *Hesperia*, 18: 96–103.

Ravenna, G. (2007–8). "Per il testo e l'esegesi di Aug. *civ*. VI 5 (p. 254, 16s. Dombart-Kalb)." *Incontri triestini di filologia classica*, 7: 117–29.

Rawson, B. (2003). *Children and Childhood in Roman Italy*. Oxford: Oxford University Press.

———. (ed.). (2011). *A Companion to Families in the Greek and Roman Worlds*. Malden, MA: Wiley-Blackwell.

Rebillard, E. (2015). "Late Antique Limits of Christianness." In Rebillard and Rüpke 2015, 293–317.

Rebillard, E., and J. Rüpke. (2015). *Group Identity and Religious Individuality in Late Antiquity* Washington, DC: Catholic University Press of America.

Reeve, C.D.C. (2012). *Action, Contemplation, and Happiness: An Essay on Aristotle*. Cambridge, MA: Harvard University Press.

Regell, P. (1878). *De augurum publicorum libris*. Bratislava: Schottlaenderi. (Reprinted as W. R. Connor and R.E.A. Palmer, eds., 1975, *Roman Augury and Etruscan Divination*, New York: Arno.)

Renberg, G. (2003). "'Commanded by Gods': An Epigraphical Study of Dreams and Visions in Greek and Roman Religious Life." PhD diss., Duke University.

———. (2017). *Where Dreams May Come: Incubation Sanctuaries in the Greco-Roman World*. (2 vols.). Religions in the Graeco-Roman World, 184. Leiden: Brill.

Revell, L. (2013). "Gods, Worshippers and Temples in the Roman West." In *Cities and Gods: Religious Space in Transition*, ed. T. Kaizer, A. Leone, E. Thomas, and R. Witcher, 21–30. Leuven: Peeters.

Réville, J. (1886). *La religion à Rome sous les Sévères*. Paris: E. Leroux.

Rich, J. (2011). "The *Fetiales* and Roman International Relations." In *Priests and State in the Roman World*, ed. J. H. Richardson and F. Santangelo, 187–242. Stuttgart: Steiner.

———. (2015). "Consensus Rituals and the Origins of the Principate." In *Il princeps romano: Autocrate o magistrato? Fattori giuridici e fattori sociali del potere imperiale da Augusto a Commodo*, ed. J.-L. Ferrary and J. Scheid, 101–38. Pavia: IUSS.

Rieger, R. (2007). *Von der Freiheit eines Christenmenschen: De libertate christiana*. Kommentare zu Schriften Luthers, 1. Tübingen: Mohr Siebeck.

Rives, J. B. (1992). "The *Iuno Feminae* in Roman Society." *EMC*, 11: 33–49.

———. (2000). "Religion in the Roman World." In *Experiencing Rome: Culture, Identity and Power in the Roman Empire*, ed. J. Huskinson, 245–76. London: Routledge.

———. (2007). *Religion in the Roman Empire*. Malden, MA: Blackwell.

———. (2010). "Graeco-Roman Religion in the Roman Empire: Old Assumptions and New Approaches." *CurrBiblicRes*, 8: 240–99.

———. (2012). "Control of the Sacred in Roman Law." In Tellegen-Couperus 2012, 165–80.

Robbins, J., and A. Rumsey. (2008). "Introduction: Cultural and Linguistic Anthropology and the Opacity of Other Minds." *AnthropolQuart*, 81.2: 407–20.

Robinson, M. (2011). *A Commentary on Ovid's Fasti, Book 2*. Oxford: Oxford University Press.

Rochat, P. (2001). *The Infant's World*. Cambridge, MA: Harvard University Press.

Rochat, P., T. Striano, and R. Morgan. (2004). "Who Is Doing What to Whom? Young Infants' Developing Sense of Social Causality in Animated Displays." *Perception*, 33.3: 355–69.

Rogoff, B., R. Paradise, R. Mejía Arauz, M. Correa-Chávez, and C. Angelillo. (2003). "Firsthand Learning through Intent Participation." *AnnuRevPsychol*, 54: 175–203.

Roller, M. B. (2018). *Models from the Past in Roman Culture: A World of Exempla*. Cambridge: Cambridge University Press.

Roubekas, Nickolas P. (2015). "Belief in Belief and Divine Kingship in Early Ptolemaic Egypt: The Case of Ptolemy II Philadelphus and Arsinoe II." *Religio: Revue pro religionistiku*, 23.1: 3–23

Ruffle, B. J., and R. Sosis. (2007). "Does It Pay to Pray? Costly Ritual and Cooperation." *B.E. Journal of Economic Analysis and Policy*, 7.1: article 18.

Runciman, D. (1997). *Pluralism and the Personality of the State*. Cambridge: Cambridge University Press.

Rüpke, J. (1990). *Domi militiae: Die religiöse Konstruktion des Krieges in Rom*. Stuttgart: Franz Steiner Verlag.

———. (ed.). (2007a). *A Companion to Roman Religion*. Malden, MA: Blackwell.
———. (ed.). (2007b). *Gruppenreligionen im römischen Reich: Sozialformen, Grenzziehungen und Leistungen*. Tübingen: Mohr Siebeck.
———. (2007c). "*Religio* and *religiones* in Roman Thinking." *LEC*, 75: 67–78.
———. (2007d). *Religion of the Romans* (trans. and ed. R. Gordon). Cambridge, MA: Polity.
———. (2008). *Fasti Sacerdotum: A Prosopography of Pagan, Jewish, and Christian Religious Officials in the City of Rome, 300 BC to AD 499; Biographies of Christian Officials by A. Glock* (trans. D.M.B. Richardson). Oxford: Oxford University Press.
———. (2010). "Representation or Presence? Picturing the Divine in Ancient Rome." *Archiv für Religionsgeschichte*, 12.1: 181–96.
———. (2012). *Religion in Republican Rome: Rationalization and Ritual Change*. Philadelphia: University of Pennsylvania Press.
———. (2013). "Individualization and Individuation as Concepts for Historical Research." In *The Individual in the Religions of the Ancient Mediterranean*, ed. J. Rüpke, 3–38. Oxford: Oxford University Press.
———. (2014). "Historicizing Religion: Varro's *Antiquitates* and History of Religion in the Late Roman Republic." *HR*, 53.3: 246–68.
———. (2015). "Religious Agency, Identity, and Communication: Reflections on History and Theory of Religion." *Religion*, 45.3: 344–66.
———. (2016). *Religious Deviance in the Roman World: Superstition or Individuality?* (trans. D.M.B. Richardson). Cambridge: Cambridge University Press.
———. (2019). *On Roman Religion: Lived Religion and the Individual in Ancient Rome*. Cornell Studies in Classical Philology, 67. Ithaca, NY: Cornell University Press.
Rüpke, J., and W. Spickermann. (2012). "Introduction." In *Reflections on Religious Individuality: Greco-Roman and Judaeo-Christian Texts and Practices*, ed. J. Rüpke and W. Spickermann, 1–7. Berlin: De Gruyter.
Sacks, O. (1984). *A Leg to Stand On*. New York: Simon and Schuster.
Saler, B. (2001). "On What We May Believe about Beliefs." In *Religion in Mind: Cognitive Perspectives on Religious Belief, Ritual, and Experience*, ed. J. Andresen, 47–69. Cambridge: Cambridge University Press.
Salmela, M. (2012). "Shared Emotions." *PhilosExplor*, 15.1: 33–46.
———. (2014a). *True Emotions*. Philadelphia: John Benjamins.
———. (2014b). "The Functions of Collective Emotions in Social Groups." In Ziv and Schmid 2014, 159–76.
Sanders, K. R. (2011). "Philodemus and the Fear of Premature Death." In *Epicurus and the Epicurean Tradition*, ed. J. Fish and K. R. Sanders, 211–34. Cambridge: Cambridge University Press.
Santangelo, F. (2013). *Divination, Prediction and the End of the Roman Republic*. Cambridge: Cambridge University Press.
Satterfield, S. (2012). "Livy and the Timing of Expiation in the Roman Year." *Histos*, 6: 67–90.
———. (2015). "Prodigies, the *Pax Deum* and the *Ira Deum*." *CJ*, 110.4: 431–45.
Schacter, D. L. (2012). "Adaptive Constructive Processes and the Future of Memory." *AmPsychol*, 67.8: 603–13.

Scheid, J. (1981). "Le délit religieux dans la Rome tardo-républicaine." In *Le délit religieux dans la cité antique*, ed. M. Torelli, C. Guittard, G. Piccaluga, T. Cornell, B. Santalucia, A. Fraschetti, J. Scheid, D. Sabbatucci, and G. Crifò, 117–71. Rome: École française de Rome.
———. (1987). "Polytheism Impossible; or, The Empty Gods: Reasons behind a Void in the History of Roman Religion." *HistAnthropol*, 3: 303–25.
———. (1987–89). "La parole des dieux: L'originalité du dialogue des Romains avec leurs dieux." *Opus*, 6–8: 125–36.
———. (1990). *Romulus et ses frères: Le collège des frères arvales, modèle du culte public dans la Rome des empereurs*. Rome: École française de Rome.
———. (1999). "The Expiation of Impieties Committed without Intention and the Formation of Roman Theology." In *Transformations of the Inner Self in Ancient Religions*, ed. J. Assmann and G. Stroumsa, 331–47. Leiden: Brill.
———. (2003a). *An Introduction to Roman Religion* (trans. J. Lloyd). Edinburgh: Edinburgh University Press.
———. (2003b). "Religion romaine et spiritualité." *ARG*, 1: 198–209.
———. (2003c). "Hierarchy and Structure in Roman Polytheism: Roman Methods of Conceiving Action." In Ando 2003, 164–89.
———. (2005). *Quand faire, c'est croire: Les rites sacrificiels des Romains*. Paris: Aubier.
———. (2006). "Oral Tradition and Written Tradition in the Formation of Sacred Law in Rome." In Ando and Rüpke 2006, 14–33.
———. (2007a). "Carmen et prière: Les hymnes dans le culte public de Rome." In *L'hymne antique et son public*, ed. Y. Lehmann, 439–50. Turnhout, Belgium: Brepols.
———. (2007b). "Les sens des rites: L'exemple romain." In *Rites et croyances dans les religions du monde romain*, ed. J. Scheid, 39–63. Geneva: Fondation Hardt.
———. (2008). "Le *carmen* dans la religion romaine." *Mythos: Revista di Storia delle Religioni*, n.s., 2: 17–24.
———. (2011). "Les émotions dans la religion romaine." In *Dans le laboratoire de l'historien des religions: Mélanges offerts à Philippe Borgeaud*, ed. F. Prescendi and Y. Volokhine, 406–15. Geneva: Editions Labor et Fides.
———. (2012). "Roman Animal Sacrifice and the System of Being." In *Greek and Roman Animal Sacrifice: Ancient Victims, Modern Observers*, ed. C. Faraone and F. S. Naiden, 84–95. Cambridge: Cambridge University Press.
———. (2016). *The Gods, the State, and the Individual: Reflections on Civic Religion in Rome* (trans. C. Ando). Philadelphia: University of Pennsylvania Press.
Scheid, J., and E. Wirbelauer. (2008). "La correspondance entre Georg Wissowa et Theodor Mommsen (1883–1901)." In *S'écrire et écrire sur l'antiquité*, ed. C. Bonnet and V. Krings, 155–212. Grenoble: Éditions Jérôme Millon.
Scherer, K. R., E. Clark-Polner, and M. Mortillaro. (2011). "In the Eye of the Beholder? Universality and Cultural Specificity in the Expression and Perception of Emotion." *IntJPsychol*, 46: 401–35.
Schermaier, M. J. (2000). "*Bona fides* in Roman Contract Law." In *Good Faith in European Contract Law*, ed. R. Zimmermann and S. Whittaker, 63–92. Cambridge: Cambridge University Press.
Schiller, A. A. (1978). *Roman Law: Mechanisms of Development*. The Hague: Mouton.

Schleiermacher, F.D.E. (2003). *Der christliche Glaube nach den Grundsätzen der evangelischen Kirche im Zusammenhange dargestellt* (critical ed. of the 2nd ed. of 1830/31). Kritische Gesamtausgabe. Erste Abteilung, Schriften und Entwürfe, 13, ed. R. Schäfer. Berlin: De Gruyter.

Schlottmann, A., and L. Surian. (1999). "Do 9-Month-Olds Perceive Causation-at-a-Distance?" *Perception*, 28: 1105–13.

Schlottmann, A., L. Surian, and E. D. Ray. (2009). "Causal Perception of Action-and-Reaction Sequences in 8- to 10-Month-Olds." *JExpChildPsychol*, 103.1: 87–107.

Schmid, H. B. (2009). *Plural Action: Essays in Philosophy and Social Science*. Dordrecht: Springer.

———. (2014). "Plural Self-Awareness." *PhenomCognSci*, 13: 7–24.

———. (2017). "Collective Emotions." In *The Routledge Handbook of Collective Intentionality*, ed. K. Ludwig and M. Jankovic, 152–61. New York: Routledge.

Schmidt, H. (1907). *Veteres philosophi quomodo iudicaverint de precibus*. Giessen: Töpelmann.

Schmidt, M.F.H., L. P. Butler, J. Heinz, and M. Tomasello. (2016). "Young Children See a Single Action and Infer a Social Norm: Promiscuous Normativity in 3-Year-Olds." *Psychological Science*, 27.10: 1360–70.

Schmidt, M.F.H., and H. Rakoczy. (2018). "Developing an Understanding of Normativity." In *Oxford Handbook of Cognition: Embodied, Embedded, Enactive and Extended*, ed. A. Newen, L. D. Bruin, and S. Gallagher, 685–706. Oxford: Oxford University Press.

Schmitz, M., B. Kobow, and H. B. Schmid (eds.). (2013). *The Background of Social Reality*. Dordrecht: Springer.

Scholl, B. J., and T. Gao. (2013). "Perceiving Animacy and Intentionality: Visual Processing or Higher-Level Judgment?" In *Social Perception: Detection and Interpretation of Animacy, Agency, and Intention*, ed. M. Rutherford and V. Kuhlmeier, 197–229. Cambridge, MA: MIT Press.

Scholl, B. J., and P. D. Tremoulet. (2000). "Perceptual Causality and Animacy." *TrendsCognSci*, 4: 299–309.

Schrijvers, P. H. (1999). *Lucrèce et les sciences de la vie*. Leiden: Brill.

Schultz, C. E. (2006). *Women's Religious Activity in the Roman Republic*. Chapel Hill: University of North Carolina Press.

Schwartz, D. L. (2013). *Paideia and Cult: Christian Initiation in Theodore of Mopsuestia*. Washington, DC: Center for Hellenic Studies.

Schweikard, D. P., and H. B. Schmid. (2013). "Collective Intentionality." In *The Stanford Encyclopedia of Philosophy* (Summer 2013 ed.), ed. E. N. Zalta. http://plato.stanford.edu/archives/sum2013/entries/collective-intentionality/.

Scullard, H. H. (1981). *Festivals and Ceremonies of the Roman Republic*. Ithaca, NY: Cornell University Press.

Searle, J. R. (1969). *Speech Acts*. Cambridge: Cambridge University Press.

———. (1979a). "A Taxonomy of Illocutionary Acts." In *Expression and Meaning: Studies in the Theory of Speech Acts*, 1–29. Cambridge: Cambridge University Press.

———. (1979b). "Indirect Speech Acts." In *Expression and Meaning: Studies in the Theory of Speech Acts*, 30–57. Cambridge: Cambridge University Press.

———. (1983a). *Intentionality: An Essay in the Philosophy of Mind*. Cambridge: Cambridge University Press.

———. (1983b). "The Word Turned Upside Down" [Review of *On Deconstruction: Theory and Criticism after Structuralism*, by J. Culler, 1982, Ithaca, NY: Cornell University Press]. *NewYorkRevBooks*, 27 October, 74–79.

———. (1990). "Collective Intentions and Actions." In *Intentions in Communication*, ed. P. Cohen, J. Morgan, and M. Pollack, 401–15. Cambridge, MA: MIT Press. (Reprinted in Searle 2002, 90–105.)

———. (1991). "Intentionalistic Explanations in the Social Sciences." *PhilosSocSci*, 21: 332–44.

———. (1992). *The Rediscovery of the Mind*. Cambridge, MA: MIT Press.

———. (1994). "Literary Theory and Its Discontents." *NewLiteraryHist*, 25.3: 637–67.

———. (1995). *The Construction of Social Reality*. New York: Free Press.

———. (2001). *Rationality in Action*. Cambridge, MA: MIT Press.

———. (2002). *Consciousness and Language*. Cambridge: Cambridge University Press.

———. (2004). *Mind: A Brief Introduction*. Oxford: Oxford University Press.

———. (2005a). "Desire, Deliberation and Action." In *Logic, Thought and Action*, ed. D. Vanderveken, 49–78. Dordrecht: Springer.

———. (2005b). "What Is an Institution?" *Journal of Institutional Economics*, 1: 1–22.

———. (2007). "What Is Language: Some Preliminary Remarks." In *John Searle's Philosophy of Language: Force, Meaning, and Mind*, ed. S. L. Tsohatzidis, 15–45. Cambridge: Cambridge University Press.

———. (2008a). "Language and Social Ontology." *TheorSoc*, 37: 443–59.

———. (2008b). "The Unity of the Proposition." In *Philosophy in a New Century*, 181–96. Cambridge: Cambridge University Press.

———. (2009) "What Is Language? Some Preliminary Remarks." *Etica and Politica / Ethics and Politics*, 11.1: 173–202.

———. (2010). *Making the Social World: The Structure of Human Civilization*. Oxford: Oxford University Press.

———. (2015). *Seeing Things as They Are: A Theory of Perception*. Oxford: Oxford University Press.

———. (2016). "Human Social Reality and Language." *Phenomenology and Mind*, 2: 24–33.

Searle, J. R., and D. Vanderveken. (1985). *Foundations of Illocutionary Logic*. Cambridge: Cambridge University Press.

Sebanz, N., H. Bekkering, G. Knoblich. (2006). "Joint Action: Bodies and Minds Moving Together." *TrendsCognSci*, 10: 70–76.

Sedley, D. (1989). "Philosophical Allegiance in the Greco-Roman World." In *Philosophia Togata: Essays on Philosophy and Roman Society*, ed. M. Griffin and J. Barnes, 97–119. Oxford: Clarendon.

———. (1998). *Lucretius and the Transformation of Greek Wisdom*. Cambridge: Cambridge University Press.

———. (2009). "Epicureanism in the Roman Republic." In *The Cambridge Companion to Epicureanism*, ed. J. Warren, 29–45. Cambridge: Cambridge University Press.

———. (2011). "Epicurus' Theological Innatism." In *Epicurus and the Epicurean Tradition*, ed. J. Fish and K. R. Sanders, 29–52. Cambridge: Cambridge University Press.

Seebaß, G., M. Schmitz, and P. M. Gollwitzer. (2013). "Introduction." In *Acting Intentionally and Its Limits: Individuals, Groups, Institutions*, ed. G. Seebass, M. Schmitz, and P. M. Gollwitzer, 1–46. Berlin: De Gruyter.

Seemann, A. (ed.). (2012). *Joint Attention: New Developments in Psychology, Philosophy of Mind, and Social Neuroscience*. Cambridge, MA: MIT Press.
Senft, G. (2014). *Understanding Pragmatics*. New York: Routledge.
Seuren, P.A.M. (2009). *Language in Cognition*. Oxford: Oxford University Press.
Shagan, E. (2018). *The Birth of Modern Belief: Faith and Judgement from the Middle Ages to the Enlightenment*. Princeton, NJ: Princeton University Press.
Shahaeian, A., C. Peterson, V. Slaughter, and H. M. Wellman. (2011). "Culture and the Sequence of Steps in Theory of Mind Development." *DevPsychol*, 47.5: 1239–47.
Sharp, S. (2012). "For a Social Psychology of Prayer." *Sociol. Compass* 6/7: 570–80.
Shaw, B. D. (1987). "The Age of Roman Girls at Marriage: Some Reconsiderations." *JRS*, 77: 30–46.
Short, W. M. (2012). "A Roman Folk Model of the Mind." *Arethusa*, 45: 109–47.
Shwe, H. I., and E. M. Markman. (1997). "Young Children's Appreciation of the Mental Impact of Their Communicative Signals." *DevPsychol*, 33.4: 630–36.
Simler, K., and R. Hanson. (2018). *The Elephant in the Brain: Hidden Motives in Everyday Life*. Oxford: Oxford University Press.
Simmons, M. B. (1995). *Arnobius of Sicca: Religious Conflict and Competition in the Age of Diocletian*. Oxford: Clarendon.
Sinhababu, N. (2016). "Imagination and Belief." In *The Routledge Handbook of Philosophy of Imagination*, ed. A. Kind, 111–23. New York: Routledge.
Slone, D. J. (2004). *Theological Incorrectness: Why Religious People Believe What They Shouldn't*. Oxford: Oxford University Press.
Smith, B. (1990). "Towards a History of Speech Act Theory." In *Speech Acts, Meanings and Intentions: Critical Approaches to the Philosophy of John R. Searle*, ed. A. Burkhardt, 29–61. Berlin: De Gruyter.
Smith, J. A. (2011). *Music in Ancient Judaism and Early Christianity*. Farnham: Ashgate.
Smith, J. Z. (1987). *To Take Place: Toward Theory in Ritual*. Chicago: University of Chicago Press.
———. (1990). *Drudgery Divine: On the Comparison of Early Christianities and the Religions of Late Antiquity*. Chicago: University of Chicago Press.
———. (2002). "Great Scott! Thought and Action One More Time." In *Magic and Ritual in the Ancient World*, ed. P. Mirecki and M. Meyer, 73–91. Leiden: Brill.
Smith, M. F. (1993). *The Epicurean Inscription: Diogenes of Oinoanda; Edited with Introduction, Translation and Notes*. Naples: Bibliopolis.
Smith, W. R. (1889). *Lectures on the Religion of the Semites*. London: Black.
Sobocinski, M. G. (2006). "Visualizing Ceremony: The Design and Audience of the *Ludi Saeculares* Coinage of Domitian." *AJA*, 110.4: 581–602.
Sorabji, R. (1991). "From Aristotle to Brentano: The Development of the Concept of Intentionality." *OSAPh*, suppl.: 227–59.
———. (1992). "Intentionality and Physiological Processes: Aristotle's Theory of Sense-Perception." In *Essays on Aristotle's de Anima*, ed. M. C. Nussbaum and A. O. Rorty, 195–225. Oxford: Clarendon.
———. (2000). *Emotion and Peace of Mind: From Stoic Agitation to Christian Temptation*. Oxford: Oxford University Press.

Sosis, R. (2003). "Why Aren't We All Hutterites? Costly Signaling Theory and Religious Behavior." *Human Nature*, 14.2: 91–127.
Sourvinou-Inwood, C. (1990). "What Is Polis Religion?" In *The Greek City from Homer to Alexander*, ed. O. Murray and S.R.F. Price, 295–322. Oxford: Clarendon.
Spaulding, L. C. (1911). *The "Camillus"-Type in Sculpture*. Lancaster, PA: New Era.
Spelke, E. S., E. P. Bernier, and A. E. Skerry. (2013). "Core Social Cognition." In *Navigating the Social World: What Infants, Children, and Other Species Can Teach Us*, ed. M. R. Banaji and S. A. Gelman, 11–16. Oxford: Oxford University Press.
Spelke, E. S., and K. D. Kinzler. (2007). "Core Knowledge." *DevSci*, 10.1: 89–96.
Spelke, E. S., A. Phillips, and A. L. Woodward. (1995). "Infants' Knowledge of Object Motion and Human Action." In *Causal Cognition: A Multidisciplinary Debate*, ed. D. Sperber, D. Premack, and A. J. Premack, 44–78. Oxford: Clarendon.
Sperber, D. (1975). *Rethinking Symbolism* (trans. A. L. Morton). Cambridge: Cambridge University Press.
———. (1996). *Explaining Culture: A Naturalistic Approach*. Oxford: Blackwell.
———. (1997). "Intuitive and Reflective Beliefs." *MindLang*, 12: 67–83.
Sperber, D., F. Clément, C. Heintz, O. Mascaro, H. Mercier, G. Origgi, and D. Wilson. (2010). "Epistemic Vigilance." *MindLang*, 25: 359–93.
Sperber, D., and D. Wilson. (1995). *Relevance: Communication and Cognition* (2nd ed.). Oxford: Blackwell.
Sripada, C. S., and S. Stich. (2006). "A Framework for the Psychology of Norms." In *The Innate Mind*, vol. 2, *Culture and Cognition*, ed. P. Carruthers, S. Laurence, and S. Stich, 280–301. New York: Oxford University Press.
Stalnaker, R. (2014). *Context*. Oxford: Oxford University Press.
Sterelny, K. (2012a). *The Evolved Apprentice: How Evolution Made Humans Unique*. Cambridge, MA: MIT Press.
———. (2012b). "Language, Gesture, Skill: The Co-evolutionary Foundations of Language." *PhilTransRSocB*, 367: 2141–51.
Stevens, W., and M. J. Bates. (1990). *Opus Posthumous*. New York: Vintage Books.
Stevenson, T. R. (1996). "Social and Psychological Interpretations of Graeco-Roman Religion: Some Thoughts on the Ideal Benefactor." *Antichthon*, 30: 1–18.
Stewart, R. (1998). *Public Office in Early Rome: Ritual Procedure and Political Practice*. Ann Arbor: University of Michigan Press.
Stone, J., J. Perthen, and A. J. Carson. (2012). "'A Leg to Stand On' by Oliver Sacks: A Unique Autobiographical Account of Functional Paralysis." *JNeurolNeurosurPs*, 83: 864–67.
Straumann, B. (2016). *Crisis and Constitutionalism: Roman Political Thought from the Fall of the Republic to the Age of Revolution*. Oxford: Oxford University Press.
Streeter, J. (2020). "Should We Worry about Belief?" *AnthropolTheory*, 20.2: 133–56.
———. n.d. "Does Belief Have a History?" Unpublished manuscript.
Stroumsa, G. G. (2002). "Enlightenment Perceptions of Roman Religion." In *Epitomê tês oikoumenês: Studien zur römischen Religion in Antike und Neuzeit für Hubert Cancik und Hildegard Cancik-Lindemaier*, ed. A. Auffarth and J. Rüpke, 193–202. Stuttgart: Steiner.
Summers, K. (1995). "Lucretius and the Epicurean Tradition of Piety." *CPh*, 90: 32–57.

Sutton, J., D. McIlwain, W. Christensen, and A. Geeves (2011). "Applying Intelligence to the Reflexes: Embodied Skills and Habits between Dreyfus and Descartes." *JBSP*, 42.1: 78–103.
Syme, R. (1989). "A Dozen Early Priesthoods." *ZPE*, 77: 241–59.
Szábó, Z. (2003). "Believing in Things." *PhilosPhenomenRes*, 66: 584–611.
Tarde, G. (1895). *Les lois de l'imitation: Étude sociologique* (2nd ed.). Paris: Germier Baillière.
Tardif, T., and H. M. Wellman. (2000). "Acquisition of Mental State Language in Mandarin- and Cantonese-Speaking Children." *DevPsychol*, 36: 25–43.
Tatum, W. J. (1993). "Ritual and Personal Morality in Roman Religion." *SyllClass*, 4: 13–20.
———. (1999). "Roman Religion: Fragments and Further Questions." In *Veritatis Amicitiaeque Causa: Essays in Honor of Anna Lydia Motto and John R. Clark*, ed. S. N. Byrne and E. P. Cueva, 273–91. Wauconda, IL: Bolchazy-Carducci.
Taylor, C.C.W. (1980). "'All Perceptions Are True.'" In *Doubt and Dogmatism*, ed. M. Schofield, J. Barnes, and M. Burnyeat, 105–24. Oxford: Clarendon.
Taylor, L. R. (1913). "The Cults of Ostia." PhD diss., Bryn Mawr College.
———. (1949). *Party Politics in the Age of Caesar*. Berkeley: University of California Press.
Teegarden, D. (2013). *Death to Tyrants! Ancient Greek Democracy and the Struggle against Tyranny*. Princeton, NJ: Princeton University Press.
Tellegen-Couperus, O. (ed.). (2012). *Law and Religion in the Roman Republic*. Leiden: Brill.
Tennie, C., J. Call, and M. Tomasello. (2009). "Ratcheting Up the Ratchet: On the Evolution of Cumulative Culture." *PhilosTRoySocB*, 364: 2405–15.
Thagard, P. (2005). "Testimony, Credibility, and Explanatory Coherence." *Erkenntnis*, 63: 295–316.
Tollefsen, D. (2015). *Groups as Agents*. Malden, MA: Polity.
Tollefsen, D., and R. Dale. (2012). "Naturalizing Joint Action: A Process-Based Approach." *PhilosPsychol*, 25.3: 385–407.
Tomasello, M. (1996). "Do Apes Ape?" In *Social Learning in Animals: The Roots of Culture*, ed. C. Heyes and B. Galef Jr., 319–46. New York: Academic.
———. (1999a). *The Cultural Origins of Human Cognition*. Cambridge, MA: Harvard University Press.
———. (1999b). "The Cultural Ecology of Young Children's Interactions with Objects and Artifacts." In *Ecological Approaches to Cognition: Essays in Honor of Ulric Neisser*, ed. E. Winograd, R. Fivush, and W. Hirst, 153–70. Mahwah, NJ: Erlbaum.
———. (2001). "Cultural Transmission: A View from Chimpanzees and Human Infants." *JCrossCultPsychol*, 32: 135–46.
———. (2008). *Origins of Human Communication*. Cambridge, MA: MIT Press.
———. (2009). *Why We Cooperate*. Cambridge, MA: MIT Press.
———. (2014). *A Natural History of Human Thinking*. Cambridge, MA: Harvard University Press.
———. (2016). *A Natural History of Human Morality*. Cambridge, MA: Harvard University Press.
———. (2019). *Becoming Human: A Theory of Ontogeny*. Cambridge, MA: Harvard University Press.

———. (2021). "Response to: Rethinking Human Development and the Shared Intentionality Hypothesis." *RevPhilosPsychol*, 12: 465–68.
Tomasello, M., and M. Carpenter. (2005). "Intention Reading and Imitative Learning." In Hurley and Chater 2005, 2.133–48.
———. (2007). "Shared Intentionality." *DevelopmentalSci*, 10.1: 121–25.
Tomasello, M., M. Carpenter, J. Call, T. Behne, and H. Moll. (2005). "Understanding and Sharing Intentions: The Origins of Cultural Cognition." *BehavBrainSci*, 28: 675–735.
Tomasello, M., M. Carpenter, and U. Liszkowski. (2007). "A New Look at Infant Pointing." *ChildDev*, 78.3: 705–22.
Tomasello, M., and K. Hamann. (2012). "Collaboration in Young Children." *QJExpPsychol*, 65: 1–12.
Tomasello, M., A. C. Kruger, and H. H. Ratner. (1993). "Cultural Learning." *BehavBrainSci*, 16: 495–552.
Tomasello, M., A. P. Melis, C. Tennie, E. Wyman, and E. Herrmann. (2012). "Two Key Steps in the Evolution of Human Cooperation: The Interdependence Hypothesis." *CurrAnthropol*, 53.6: 673–92.
Tomasello, M., and H. Moll. (2010). "The Gap Is Social: Human Shared Intentionality and Culture." In *Mind the Gap: Tracing the Origins of Human Universals*, ed. P. M. Kappeler and J. B. Silk, 331–49. Berlin: Springer.
Tomasello, M., and H. Rakoczy. (2003). "What Makes Human Cognition Unique? From Individual to Shared to Collective Intentionality." *MindLang*, 18.2: 121–47.
Trevarthen, C. (2012). "The Generation of Human Meaning: How Shared Experience Grows in Infancy." In Seemann 2012, 73–113.
Tsouna, V. (2007). *The Ethics of Philodemus*. Oxford: Oxford University Press.
———. (2009). "Epicurean Therapeutic Strategies." In *The Cambridge Companion to Epicureanism*, ed. J. Warren, 249–65. Cambridge: Cambridge University Press.
Tulloch, J. (2012). "Visual Representations of Children and Ritual in the Early Roman Empire." *StudRelig-SciRelig*, 41.3: 408–38.
Tuomela, R. (2007). *The Philosophy of Sociality: The Shared Point of View*. Oxford: Oxford University Press.
———. (2013). *Social Ontology: Collective Intentionality and Group Agents*. Oxford: Oxford University Press.
Turcan, R. (2000). *The Gods of Ancient Rome: Religion in Everyday Life from Archaic to Imperial Times* (trans. A. Neville). Edinburgh: Edinburgh University Press.
Turner, S. (1994). *The Social Theory of Practices: Tradition, Tacit Knowledge and Presuppositions*. Cambridge, MA: Polity.
———. (1998). "The Limits of Social Constructionism." In *The Politics of Constructionism*, ed. I. Velody and R. Williams, 109–20. London: SAGE.
———. (2002). *Brains/Practices/Relativism: Social Theory after Cognitive Science*. Chicago: University of Chicago Press.
———. (2014). *Understanding the Tacit*. New York: Routledge.
Ullucci, D. C. (2012). *The Christian Rejection of Animal Sacrifice*. Oxford: Oxford University Press.
Usener, H. (1896). *Götternamen*. Bonn: Friedrich Cohen.

Vaahtera, J. (2001). *Roman Augural Lore in Greek Historiography: A Study of the Theory and Terminology*. Stuttgart: Steiner.

Valeton, I.M.J. (1889). "De modis auspicandi Romanorum." *Mnemosyne*, 17: 275–325, 418–52.

———. (1890). "De modis auspicandi Romanorum." *Mnemosyne*, 18: 208–63, 406–56.

———. (1891a). "De inaugurationibus Romanis caerimoniarum et sacerdotum." *Mnemosyne*, 19: 405–60.

———. (1891b). "De iure obnuntiandi comitiis et conciliis." *Mnemosyne*, 19: 75–113, 229–70.

———. (1892). "De templis Romanis." *Mnemosyne*, 20: 338–90.

Valette-Cagnac, E. (1997). *La lecture à Rome: Rites et pratiques*. Paris: Belin.

van Dale, A. (1683). *De oraculis ethnicorum dissertationes duae*. Amsterdam: Henricus en Boom.

Van der Horst, P. W. (1994). "Silent Prayer in Antiquity." *Numen*, 41.1: 1–25.

van der Leeuw, G. (1939). *Virginibus Puerisque: A Study on the Service of Children in Worship*. Mededeelingen der Koninklijke Nederlandsche Akademie van Wetenschappen, AFD Letterkunde, Nieuwe Reeks, 2.12, 443–85. Amsterdam: Maatschappij.

Vanderveken, D. (1990). *Meaning and Speech Acts*. Vol. 1, *Principles of Language Use*. Cambridge: Cambridge University Press.

———. (1991). *Meaning and Speech Acts*. Vol. 2, *Formal Semantics of Success and Satisfaction*. Cambridge: Cambridge University Press.

———. (2004). "Success, Satisfaction, and Truth in the Logic of Speech Acts and Formal Semantics." *Semantics: A Reader*, ed. S. Davis and B. S. Gillon, 710–34. Oxford: Oxford University Press.

Vanggaard, J. H. (1988). *The Flamen: A Study in the History and Sociology of Roman Religion*. Copenhagen: Museum Tusculanum Press.

Van Leeuwen, N., and M. van Elk. (2019). "Seeking the Supernatural: The Interactive Religious Experience Model." *ReligionBrainBehav*, 9.3: 221–51.

Van Nuffelen, P. (2010). "Varro's *Divine Antiquities*: Roman Religion as an Image of Truth." *CPh*, 105.2: 162–88.

Vaquero, M., S. Alonso, S. García-Catalán, A. García-Hernández, B. Gómez de Soler, D. Rettig, and M. Soto. (2012). "Temporal Nature and Recycling of Upper Paleolithic Artifacts: The Burned Tools from the Molí del Salt Site (Vimbodí i Poblet, Northeastern Spain)." *JArchaeolSci*, 39.8: 2785–96.

Várhelyi, Z. (2007). "The Specters of Roman Imperialism: The Live Burials of Gauls and Greeks at Rome." *ClAnt*, 26: 277–304.

Väterlein, J. (1976). *Roma ludens: Kinder und Erwachsene beim Spiel im antiken Rom*. Amsterdam: Grüner.

Versnel, H. S. (1981). "Religious Mentality in Ancient Prayer." In *Faith, Hope and Worship: Aspects of Religious Mentality in the Ancient World*, ed. H. S. Versnel 1–64. Leiden: Brill.

———. (1987). "What Did Ancient Man See When He Saw a God? Some Reflections on Greco-Roman Epiphany." In *Effigies Dei: Essays on the History of Religions*, ed. D. van der Plas, 42–55. Leiden: Brill.

———. (1990). *Inconsistencies in Greek and Roman Religion*. Vol. 1, *Ter Unus: Isis, Dionysus, Hermes: Three Studies in Henotheism*. Leiden: Brill.

———. (2002) "The Poetics of the Magical Charm: An Essay in the Power of Words." In *Magic and Ritual in the Ancient World*, ed. P. Mirecki and M. Meyer, 105–58. Leiden: Brill.

———. (2011). *Coping with the Gods: Wayward Readings in Greek Theology.* Leiden: Brill.

Vesper, C., S. Butterfill, G. Knoblich, and N. Sebanz. (2010). "A Minimal Architecture for Joint Action." *NeuralNetworks*, 23: 998–1003.

Veyne, P. (1983). "'Titulus praelatus': Offrande, solennisation et publicité dans les ex-voto gréco-romains." *RA*, 2: 281–300.

———. (1988). *Did the Greeks Believe in Their Myths?* (trans. P. Wissing). Chicago: University of Chicago Press.

Von Scheve, C. (2012). "Collective Emotions in Rituals: Elicitation, Transmission, and a 'Matthew-Effect.'" In *Emotions in Rituals and Performances*, ed. A. Michaels and C. Wulf, 55–77. New Delhi: Routledge.

Von Scheve, C., and S. Ismer. (2013). "Towards a Theory of Collective Emotions." *Emotion Review*, 5.4: 406–13.

Vuolanto, V. (2010). "Faith and Religion." In *A Cultural History of Childhood and Family in Antiquity*, ed. M. Harlow and R. Laurence, 133–51. Oxford: Berg.

———. (2016). "Experience, Agency, and the Children in the Past: The Case of Roman Childhood." In *Children and Everyday Life in the Roman and Late Antique World*, ed. C. Laes and V. Vuolanto, 11–24. New York: Routledge.

———. (2018). "Children in the Ancient World and the Early Middle Ages: A Bibliography (9th Edition)." Accessed 3 June 2021. https://www.hf.uio.no/ifikk/english/research/projects/childhood/bibliography.pdf.

Wallinga, H. T. (1956). *The Boarding-Bridge of the Romans: Its Construction and Its Function in the Naval Tactics of the First Punic War.* Groningen: Wolters.

Waltzing, J.-P. (1895). *Étude historique sur les corporations professionnelles chez les Romains* (vol. 1). Brussels: Hayez.

———. (1900). *Étude historique sur les corporations professionnelles chez les Romains* (vol. 4). Louvain: Peeters.

Wardle, D. (2009). "Caesar and Religion." In *A Companion to Julius Caesar*, ed. M. Griffin, 100–111. Malden, MA: Wiley-Blackwell.

Warmington, E. H. (ed.). (1940). *Remains of Old Latin "IV": Archaic Inscriptions.* Cambridge, MA: Harvard University Press.

Warneken, F., F. Chen, and M. Tomasello. (2006). "Cooperative Activities in Young Children and Chimpanzees." *ChildDev*, 77: 640–63.

Warren, J. (2009). "Removing Fear." In *The Cambridge Companion to Epicureanism*, ed. J. Warren, 234–48. Cambridge: Cambridge University Press.

Warrior, V. M. (2006). *Roman Religion.* Cambridge: Cambridge University Press.

Watson, A. (1992). *The State, Law, and Religion: Pagan Rome.* Athens: University of Georgia Press.

———. (1993). *International Law in Archaic Rome: War and Religion.* Baltimore: Johns Hopkins University Press.

Weinstock, S. (1971). *Divus Julius.* Oxford: Clarendon.

Wellman, H. M. (1998). "Culture, Variation, and Levels of Analysis in Our Folk Psychologies." *PsycholBull*, 123: 33–36.

———. (2011). "Developing a Theory of Mind." In Goswami 2011, 258–84.

———. (2014). *Making Minds: How Theory of Mind Develops.* Oxford: Oxford University Press.

Wellman, H. M., F. Fang, D. Liu, L. Zhu, and G. Liu. (2006). "Scaling of Theory-of-Mind Understandings in Chinese Children." *PsycholSci*, 17.12: 1075–81.
Whitehouse, H. (2004). *Modes of Religiosity: A Cognitive Theory of Religious Transmission*. Walnut Creek, CA: AltaMira.
———. (2012). "Ritual, Cognition, and Evolution." In *Grounding Social Sciences in Cognitive Sciences*, ed. R. Sun, 265–84. Cambridge, MA: MIT Press.
Whitehouse, H., P. François, P. E. Savage, T. E. Currie, K. C. Feeney, E. Cioni, R. Purcell, R. M. Ross, J. Larson, J. Baines, B. ter Haar, A. Covey, and P. Turchin. (2019). "Complex Societies Precede Moralizing Gods throughout World History." *Nature*, 568: 226–29.
Whitehouse, H., and J. A. Lanman. (2014). "The Ties That Bind Us: Ritual, Fusion, and Identification." *CurrAnthropol*, 55.6: 1–22.
Whitehouse, H., and L. H. Martin (eds.). (2004). *Theorizing Religions Past: Archaeology, History, and Cognition*. Walnut Creek, CA: AltaMira.
Whiten, A., G. Allan, S. Devlin, N. Kseib, N. Raw, and N. McGuigan. (2016). "Social Learning in the Real-World: 'Over-imitation' Occurs in Both Children and Adults Unaware of Participation in an Experiment and Independently of Social Interaction." *PLoS One*, 11.7. doi:10.1371/journal.pone.0159920.
Whiten, A., N. McGuigan, S. Marshall-Pescini, and L. M. Hopper. (2009). "Emulation, Imitation, Over-imitation and the Scope of Culture for Child and Chimpanzee." *PhilosTRoySocB*, 364: 2417–28.
Wiebe, D. (1999). *The Politics of Religious Studies: The Continuing Conflict with Theology in the Academy*. New York: St. Martin's.
Wiedemann, T. (1989). *Adults and Children in the Roman Empire*. New Haven, CT: Yale University Press.
Wille, G. (1962). "Rhythmisch-musikalische Heilpädagogik in der Antike." *Jahrbuch des Orff-Instituts*, 1: 41–52.
———. (1967). *Musica Romana: Die Bedeutung der Musik im Leben der Römer*. Amsterdam: P. Schippers.
Williamson, C. G. (2013). "As God Is My Witness: Civic Oaths in Ritual Space as a Means towards Rational Cooperation in the Hellenistic *polis*." In *Cults, Creeds and Identities in the Greek City after the Classical Age*, ed. R. Alston, O. M. van Nijf, and C. G. Williamson, 119–74. Leuven: Peeters.
Wilson, E. O. (1998). *Consilience: The Unity of Knowledge*. New York: Knopf.
Wimmer, H., and J. Perner. (1983). "Beliefs about Beliefs: Representation and Constraining Function of Wrong Beliefs in Young Children's Understanding of Deception." *Cognition*, 13: 103–28.
Wiseman, T. P. (1994). *Historiography and Imagination: Eight Essays on Roman Culture*. Exeter: University of Exeter Press.
———. (1995). *Remus: A Roman Myth*. Cambridge: Cambridge University Press.
Wissowa, G. (1902). *Religion und Kultus der Römer*. Munich: Beck.
———. (1912). *Religion und Kultus der Römer* (2nd ed.). Munich: Beck.
Woolf, G. (1997). "*Polis*-Religion and Its Alternatives in the Roman Provinces." In *Römische Reichsreligion und Provinzialreligion*, ed. H. Cancik and J. Rüpke, 71–84. Tübingen: Mohr Siebeck.

———. (2013). "Ritual and the Individual in Roman Religion." In *The Individual in the Religions of the Ancient Mediterranean*, ed. J. Rüpke, 136–60. Oxford: Oxford University Press.

Wyman, E., and H. Rakoczy. (2011). "Social Conventions, Institutions, and Human Uniqueness: Lessons from Children and Chimpanzees." In *Interdisciplinary Anthropology*, ed. W. Welsch, W. Singer, A. Wunder, 131–56. Berlin: Springer.

Yule, G. (1996). *Pragmatics*. Oxford: Oxford University Press.

Zahavi, D., and P. Rochat. (2015). "Empathy ≠ Sharing: Perspectives from Phenomenology and Developmental Psychology." *ConsciousCogn*, 36: 543–53.

Zarecki, J. (2014). *Cicero's Ideal Statesman in Theory and Practice*. London: Bloomsbury.

Zetzel, J.E.G. (ed.). (1995). *Cicero, De re publica: Selections*. Cambridge: Cambridge University Press.

Zimmerman, R. (1990). *The Law of Obligations: Roman Foundations of the Civilian Tradition*. Oxford: Oxford University Press.

Ziółkowski, A. (1992). *The Temples of Mid-republican Rome and Their Historical and Topographical Context*. Rome: "L'Erma" di Bretschneider.

Ziv, A. K., and H. B. Schmid. (2014). *Institutions, Emotions, and Group Agents: Contributions to Social Ontology*. Dordrecht: Springer.

Zufferey, S. (2010). *Lexical Pragmatics and Theory of Mind: The Acquisition of Connectives*. Amsterdam: Benjamins.

INDEX LOCORUM

1 Cor.
    10:20, 158n90

Acts
    19:23–41, 82n88

Amm. Marc.
    21.9, 351

Apul.
  Met.
    11.13, 81, 106, 314n73
    11.15, 107n33
    11.17, 13n30, 90n120
    11.23, 82n87

Arist.
  de An.
    433a–b, 115n61
  E.N.
    1147a–b, 115n61
  Int.
    1, 76
    17a1–5, 296
  M.A.
    700b15–16, 114
    700b17–19, 114–15
    701a16, 115n63
    701a30–36, 115n63, 213n20
    701a32–33, 115n62, 213n19
    701a–702a, 115n61

Arn.
  Adv. nat., 376
    1.39, 377
    1.40, 377
    1.42, 377
    7.3.1, 377
    7.3.3, 377
    7.4.1, 378
    7.5.1, 378
    7.36.3, 378
    7.37.1, 378
    7.37.2, 379

Augustine
  Civ.
    2.4, 117
    4.22, 128nn115–16, 308n56
    4.23, 119n79, 129n122
    4.31, 124n101, 125n102, 128n120, 130n128
    6.2, 119n79, 124n101, 129n121, 129n121, 129n123
    6.4, 128n119
    6.5, 86n105, 127nn110–12, 128n117
    6.6, 128n117
    6.10, 91n125
    6.12, 86n105
    7.5, 125n102, 130n128, 310n62
    7.6, 127n112
    7.17, 21
    7.34–35, 277n150
    8–10, 158n90
    14.15, 14n31
    22.8.7, 56n122
    22.8.8, 56n123
    22.8.14, 56n125
    22.8.16, 56n124
    22.8.21, 56n126
  Conf., 48, 251, 254n49
    1.6.7, 249n21
    1.6.8, 249n22, 252nn39–40
    1.6.10, 252n41
    1.7.11, 252n39
    1.7.12, 252n39

Augustine *Conf.* (*continued*)
 1.8.13, 252, 252n139, 252n42, 254n45,
  263n97–98
 1.9.14, 259n78
 1.14.23, 245n5, 255n50
 1.16.25, 255n49
 1.18.28, 255n49
 1.19.30, 255n49
Doct. Chr.
 4.3.5, 254n49
Ep.
 91.4–5, 299n25
Lib. arb. 86
Mus.
 1.4.6ff, 255n49
Serm.
 144.2.2, 78–79
Aur. Vict.
 Vir. ill.
  3.2, 277n150

Caes.
 B.G. 381
  6.11–29, 381
  6.16, 381
  6.17, 382
Cato
 Agr.
  134, 307
  141, 328
  143.1, 153n72
  160, 274n137, 299n27
 Orig.
  1, fr. 24 (Peter), 359
Cat.
 34, 284n173
 61.212–16, 249n25
 62.12–14, 286
 64.171, 327n110
Cic.
 Acad. post.
  1.2.6, 212n16
 Am.
  15, 140n17

  80, 140n19
  81, 140n19
Brut. 354n49
 1, 349nn39–40
 211, 259n79
 247, 212n14
Div. 369
 1.2, 342n11
 1.5, 342
 1.12, 342n11, 350
 1.17.30–33, 184n53
 1.31, 353n44
 1.72, 342n11, 345n25
 1.84, 342n11
 1.109, 342n11
 1.120, 351
 1.128, 342n11
 1.129, 323n98
 2, 123n96, 130n127, 368n80
 2.26, 342n11
 2.27, 342n11
 2.28, 342n11
 2.42, 342n11
 2.42–43, 345n25
 2.79, 342n11
 2.146, 342n11
 2.148, 368n80
Dom.
 107, 40n58
 139, 304n44
Fam.
 15.16, 212n16
 15.19.2, 212n16
Fin.
 2.45, 113n56
 3.16–71, 113n56
 3.64, 200n118
 3.66, 283n168
 5.24–74, 113n56
 5.42, 245n5, 249nn21–22, 279n156
Flac.
 69, xvii
Har. resp.
 9–10, 93n136

9.19, 293n6
10, 94n139
14, 371n2
18, 123n96
19, 128n119
20, 92n133, 93n136
21, 275n144
23, 129n121, 275nn145–46
62, 94n140, 225–26
63, 94n140
62–63, 93n137, 226

Inv.
2.65–66, 129n124
2.66, 101n14
2.160–61, 129n124
2.161, 101n14

Leg.
1.4, 41n64
1.24, 1, 129n124
1.26–27, 15
1.30, 72n48
1.47, 72
2.15, 200
2.15–16, 48n92
2.16, 40n60, 130n126, 200–201, 325
2.19, 281n163
2.20, 354n48
2.20–21, 180n32, 345
2.21, 369n84
2.26, 201n120
2.27, 129n124
2.30, 371n2
2.31, 180n32, 369n84
2.47–53, 122n93
3.43, 180n32
22.13, 121n92

N.D.
1.2, 129n124
1.3–4, 128n118
1.4, 126n106, 142n36
1.29.81, 299n25
1.43–45, 218
1.48, 309n62
1.49, 217
1.116, 21
2.168, 122
2.2, 122
2.4, 223n49
2.5–6, 222
2.6, 221
2.8, 128n119, 293n6
2.11, 157n82, 345n25
2.153, 126n107
2.160, 351n43
2.168, 122
3.5, xvii, 21, 40n59, 122, 357n52, 371n1
3.6, 122

Off.
1.11, 113, 113n56
1.26, 200–201, 201n121
1.50, 139n14, 139n16, 142n34, 254n47, 283n168
1.51–52, 195n94
1.53, 151n65, 195, 199
1.54, 195n92, 280n161
1.55, 280n162
1.56, 140n19
1.57–58, 195n94
1.78, 257n67
1.116, 257n67
1.118, 257n67
1.121, 257n67
1.124, 314n74
1.133, 257n67
1.140, 257n67
1.146, 257n67
1.153, 127n108, 142n35, 200n118
1.157, 139
1.160, 195n94
2.11, 126n107, 142n36, 157n82
3.43ff, 301n35
3.58ff, 301n35
3.60, 324n101
3.102–10, 301n35
3.108, 301
56, 140n18

Phil.
2.81, 347

Cic. Phil. (continued)
    2.110, 347, 347n35, 369
    13.12, 354n48
    13.41, 347n35
De or.
    2.16.68, 284n170
    3.221, 14n33, 253n44
    3.222, 14n33
    3.223, 15, 254n47, 276n148
Pis.
    1.1, 14n33, 276n147
Sest.
    91, 196n 98
    106, 149n58
    Rosc. Am.
    131, 323n96
Rep.
    1.29, 92n128
    1.39, 196, 196n98, 199
    1.49, 201n121
    2.16, 357n51
    2.17, 357n52
    2.17–20, 41n63
    2.26, 40n62
    3.45, 196n97
    4.3, 265n100
    6.13, 196n97
    6.28, 11, 112
Tusc.
    1.30, 129n124
    3.24, 103
    3.52–62, 103n21
    3.61–63, 105
    4.3.6–7, 212n13
CIL
    I^2 581 13–14, 141n24
    III 01614, 225n58
    III 08044, 225n58
    V 05597 (B), 223n52
    VI 1978, 359n59
    VI 2104a 31–38, 305n49
    XIII 06415, 225n59
    XIII 11729, 224n53

Colum.
    Rust.
    10.342, 137n8
    10.342–43, 157n82
Dessau, *ILS*
    3392 (2), 223n51
    4289 (5), 224n54
Dig.
    1.3.32, 258n72
    1.3.32.1, 117n70, 188n72, 193
    1.3.35, 193n86
    1.3.36, 117n71
    1.5.4.1, 182n39
    1.8.9.3, 179n28
    2.14.1.3, 140n23, 264n99
    3.4.1.1, 196n95, 314–15n74
    3.4.7.1, 197n102
    4.3.1.2, 324n101
    17.2.3, 324n101
    17.2.4.1, 142n31
    17.2.5*pr*, 141n27, 195n93
    17.2.31, 141n30
    17.2.63.10, 142n31
    17.2.64, 142n33
    17.2.65.3, 142n31
    46.3.80, 140n22, 142n31
    50.12.3, 140n23
    50.17.35, 142n32
Dio Cass.
    Dig.
    42.51.4, 345n24
    44.6.4, 347n35
    59.7.1, 284n171
    75.4.5 284n171
Diog. Laert.
    10.9, 212n13
    10.32, 216n31, 216n33, 232n83
    10.33, 218n40
    11, 228n61
    31–34, 229n69
Diog. Oen.
    fr. 34.VII (Smith), 213n17

Dion. Hal.
  Ant. Rom. 373
    1.72–75, 360n62
    2.6.1–3, 364n69
    2.22.3, 357n51
    2.67.2, 284n172
    3.69, 359n61
    7.70–71.1, 374n11
    7.70.3, 374
    7.71.1, 374
    7.72.1–4, 374
    7.72.5–12, 374
    7.72.13, 374
    7.72.13–14, 374
    7.72.15, 375, 390
    7.72.16, 391
    7.72.16–17, 375n12
    7.72.18, 374

Enn.
  Ann.
    fr. 47 (Skutsch), 357n53
    fr. 155 (Skutsch), 357n53
Epicur.
  Nat.
    12, 214n28, 231
  Ep. Men.
    123–24, 218n37, 233n85
    124, 218n37, 218n39, 228n64, 240n107
    127, 241n111
    128, 214n22
    129, 214n23
    132, 214n25
    132–135, 214n26
  Ep. Pyth.
    97, 228n61, 228n66
    113, 228n66
    115–16, 228n66
  Ep. Hdt.
    38–39, 217n35
    46–50, 215n29
    49–52, 229n69
    75–76, 229n68
    76–77, 228n61
    77, 228n65, 228n67, 240n106
    81, 228n61, 228n67
    82, 218n40
  Sent. Vat.
    41, 212n13
  KD
    1, 213n17, 228n67, 233n85
    11, 228n61
    15, 214n24
    29, 241n111
Eur.
  Hipp.
    612, 301
Fest.
  Gloss. Lat.
    316–17 (Lindsay), 347n33
    326–9 (Lindsay), 360n62
Flor.
    1.1.7.8, 359n61
Gai.
  Ep.
    2.9.17, 142n31, 195n93
  Inst.
    1.130, 354n47
    2.2–2.9, 188n71
    2.4, 203n125
    2.7, 192n82
    2.8, 179n28, 366n75
    3.92–93, 186n62, 301n34
    3.135, 142n32, 280n157
    3.136, 142n32
    3.151, 142n31
    3.154, 141n30, 195n93
    3.194, 192n83
Gell.
  N.A.
    1.12.15–16, 354n47
    2.28, 94n146
    2.28.2–3, 21
    2.28.3, 94n142, 95n147

Gell. N.A. (continued)
    7.7.4, 359n59
    13.23.1, 305n45
    15.27.3, 122n93

Hist. Aug.
    19.6, 284n171
    20.3, 284n171

Hor.
    C.S. 284n171
        45, 288
        75, 288
    C.
        1.21, 284n173
        4.3.22, 250n29
        4.6.41–44, 287
    Ep.
        1.16.57–62, 301n31
        2.1.132–37, 288
        2.1.134, 308n58
        2.1.139–44, 153n70, 268n108
    Sat.
        1.3.48, 255n52

Isid.
    Orig.
        3.15, 287n178

Juv.
    Sat.
        2.65ff., 101n13

Lact.
    Div. Inst.
        1.22, 277n150
        1.22.13, 12n27, 88, 88n116, 260n84
        1.22.14, 13n28, 89nn117–18
        4.3.1, 33
        6.10.13–14, 250n32

Liv.
    1.6.4, 9n12, 357n53
    1.7.2, 179n27
    1.16.8, 40n61
    1.18.6, 357n51, 357n53
    1.18.6–10, 349, 351–52
    1.18.7, 317n80
    1.18.8, 318n83
    1.18.9, 318n85
    1.18.10, 186n65, 327n108
    1.19–21, 371n1
    1.19.4–5, 40n62
    1.20.6, 371
    1.24.4, 315n77
    1.24.5–6, 315n75
    1.24.7–8, 315
    1.24.9, 316
    1.31.8, 274n141
    1.36.6, 353n44
    1.55.2–4, 359n60
    1.55.3, 353n44
    1.56.10–12, 65n20
    2.2.23, 149n59
    2.5, 124n99
    2.36.1, 374n10
    3.20.5, 301n35
    4.1.14–18, 2n1
    5.22.3–8, 90n124
    5.46.1–4, 112n50, 281n164
    5.50.1, 53n110
    5.50.2l 53n110
    5.52.2, 357n53
    5.52.9, 129n121, 275n143
    5.54.7, 359n61
    7.3.1, 81n84, 108n37
    9.1, 326n106
    9.1.4, 329n114
    9.1.7, 326n104
    9.5.1, 315n76
    9.40.21, 186n66
    9.46.4–7, 296n14
    10.6, 345n24
    10.9, 345n24
    10.19.17, 309n59
    10.19.17–18, 313–14
    10.19.21, 327n112
    21.62.1, 81n83, 81n84, 100n8, 107, 108
    21.62.2–5, 107
    21.62.11, 81n84, 108

22.9–10, 334n124
22.10.1, 194n89
22.10.2, 69n39, 189n74
22.10.4, 190, 190n75
22.57.6, 382n19
23.31.13, 364n69
24.10.6, 81n83
25.1.6, 81
25.1.8, 81, 81n85
25.1.10, 81
25.1.11, 81n84, 108n37
27.8.4, 354n47
27.8.5, 354n47
27.16.15, 353n44
27.37.5, 81n84, 108n37
27.37.7, 284
27.37.12, 286n176
27.37.14, 287n179
29.14.2, 81n83
31.12.9, 284n171
34.44, 334n125
37.3.6, 284n171
39.13.14, 141n26
40.29.7, 277n150
40.42.8–11, 349n39
41.14–18, 2n1

Per.
  89, 345n24

Lucil.
  7.172–73, 100n8
  15.526–27, 260n84
  15.526–28, 12n27, 88–89

Lucr.
  DRN, 212, 237
  1.62ff, 213n17
  1.80–101, 237
  1.83, 237n95
  1.100, 237n96
  1.101, 237n97
  1.102–3, 236n93
  2.352–66, 232n82
  2.622–23, 235n88
  2.919–22, 213n21
  3.28–29, 241

3.41–44, 238n101
3.51–58, 238
4.524–62, 231
4.563–94, 231
5.73–75, 234
5.229–30, 255n51
5.580–83, 231
5.1019–23, 184n50, 250n32
5.1019–27, 143n39
5.1030–32, 250n29, 265n103
5.1059–86, 232n82
5.1161, 214, 218n41, 235
5.1162–63, 233n84
5.1164–67, 234, 241
5.1165, 235n87
5.1169–71, 214
5.1170–1202, 235
5.1175–76, 215
5.1179–80, 215
5.1181–82, 236n91
5.1183–95, 227
5.1194–95, 233
5.1196–97, 236
5.1198–202, 233
5.1198–203, 158n89
5.1226–35, 237n98
5.1229–30, 238n99
5.1233–40, 234n86
5.1240, 233n85
5.1446–47, 217n34
6.75–78, 242
6.76–77, 217n36
6.535–607, 94n141

Macr.
  Sat.
  1.6.14, 284n171
  1.7.34–36, 191n80, 278n155
  3.8.8–14, 257n71
  3.8.9, 257n70, 258n74
  3.8.10, 257n71
  3.8.12, 257n71
  3.9.12, 309n59
  3.13.11, 354n47

Mart.
    9.97.4, 250n29

Non.
    848 (Lindsay), 161n94

Obseq.
    27a, 284n171
    34, 284n171
    36, 284n171
    43, 284n171
    46, 284n171
    48, 284n171
    53, 284n171

Ov.
  Am.
    3.1.1–4, 7
  F. 278
    1.446, 353
    1.631–33, 138n9
    2.533ff, 118n74
    2.639, 269n111
    2.641–42, 268n110
    2.645–58, 153n70, 267
    2.679–82, 266
    4.829, 310
    4.837–48, 179n28
    4.905–9, 137
    4.907, 157n83
    4.911, 157n83
    4.911–32, 138n9
    4.921–22, 137n8
    4.934–35, 156n79
    4.936–37, 164n106
    4.937, 138
    4.937–42, 138n10
    5.444, 363n67
    6.251, 289n185, 300, 308n58
    911, 157n83
  Met.
    1.154, 327n110
    4.516–17, 249n25
    10.250–51, 13n30

Pers.
    1.26, 250n29

Petron.
  Sat.
    29, 104n29
    52.1, 13n30, 90n120
    72, 104n29

Phld.
  Piet. 231, 240, 241n111
    col. 49, 240n108
    col. 8 225–318, 231n76
    col. 8 230–31, 231n77
    col. 9 232–33, 232n80
    col. 9 233–34, 232n79
    col. 9 236, 232
    col. 9 236–38, 232n81
    col. 9 236–237, 232
    col. 11 307, 232
    col. 26 737–40, 242n113
    col. 27 758–61, 242n112
    col. 765–70, 242n114
  Sign.
    XV.21, 218n40
    XXXVII, 216n32

Pl.
  Tht., 21

Plaut.
  Asin.
    259, 353n44
    259–61, 350
  Aul.
    23–25, 270n113
  Capt.
    922–23, 298n23
    922–27, 313
  Mil.
    1.1.39, 140n21
    1219ff, 299n28
  Most.
    84–156, 245n3
    120, 245n3
    135–36, 245n4
  Poen.
    282, 67n32, 79

Plin.
   H.N.
      318n87
      2.140, 274nn139–40
      7 pr. 2, 249n25
      10.6.15, 65n23
      13.84–87, 277n150
      18.2, 358n57
      28.3.10, 303nn37–38
      28.3.11, 273n135, 303n39, 304
      28.3.12, 305n47
      28.3.13, 305n47
      28.4.20–21, 307n52
      28.5.25, 272n127, 273n136
      30.3.12, 382n18
      35.95, 13n30, 90n120
      35.116–17, 182n43

Plin.
   Ep.
      3.6.2, 13n30, 90n120
   Pan.
      3, 158n88

Plut.
   Ant.
      33.1, 348n37
   Cic.
      13.3, 149n58
   Num.
      10.1, 284n172
      15.6, 191n80
      22, 277n150
   Quaest. Rom. 277–78
      93, 278n152
   Rom.
      1–2, 360n62
      11.3, 179n28

Polyb.
   1.22–23, 178n23
   6.4, 220n45
   6.56, 29
   6.56.6, 368

Prud.
   C. Symm. 258
      1.154, 258n 75
      1.197–244, 259
      1.198, 260n81
      1.198–99, 263n93
      1.205–11, 259
      1.213–14, 263n92
      1.244, 258n75
      215, 332
      223–25, 332
      226–40, 332

Psa.
   44:21, 326n107

Quint.
   Inst.
      1.1.5, 255n53
      1.2.9, 258n72
      1.2.20, 284n170
      1.2.21, 256n60
      1.2.29, 256n61
      1.3.1, 255n54
      1.6.40, 299n26
      1.11.2, 256n59
      1.11.3, 256n58
      10.1.88, 112n55
      10.2.1, 255n56
      10.2.2, 256n57
      10.2.4, 256n64
      10.2.8, 256n64
      11.3.66, 15n36
      12.1.1, 257n65
      12.3.6, 196n97

Rom.
   xv, 39

Sen.
   Ben.
      1.6.3, 158n88
   Clem.
      1.24.1, 149n60
   Ep.
      5.4, 284n170
      41.1, 299n25
      41.3, 8n11, 112n55

Sen. Ep. (continued)
    95.50, 40n58
    113.18, 103n21
  Ira
    2.1.3–2.2, 103n21
    2.26.2–3, 14n31
    3.2.2ff, 157n85
    3.8, 257n67
    3.16.2, 157n85
  Ot.
    2.2, 284n172
  Superst.
    fr. 36 (Haase [= fr. 69 (Vottero)]), 91n125
  Q.N.
    6, 94n141
Serv.
  ad Aen.
    1.92, 317n79
    1.273, 360n62
    1.446, 188n70, 203n125
    2.116, 191n79
    3.20, 345n22
    7.120, 304n43
    7.601, 258n72
    8.652, 73n50
    10.76, 161n94
    11.558, 270n113
  ad Ecl.
    4.62, 161n94
    5.73, 287n180
Sext. Emp.
  Math.
    7.216, 218n40
    9.45, 216
    9.54, 220n45
    11.250, 216
    11.250–51, 216
Suet.
  Iul. 347, 365n71

Tac.
  Ann.
    2.24, 100n8
    4.16.2, 354n47
  Dial.
    28.4, 259n79
    7.4, 250n29
  Ger.
    43.4, 382n20
Ter.
  Phorm.
    454, 257n69
Tert.
  Ad nat.
    39, 161n94
Tib.
    1.10.19, 267n106
    1.10.19–24, 153n70, 266n105
    2.1.83–84, 301n31
    3.11.19–20, 324n99
    3.12.15–16, 258n77, 300n30
Ulp.
  Reg. 1.4, 258n72
Val. Max.
    1.1.1, 277n150, 293n6, 303n40
    1.1.9, 293n6
    1.1.12, 277n150
    1.6.12, 327n110
    1.8.6, 221
    4.1.10, 300n29
Varro
  Ant. Div., 118
    fr. 2A (Cardauns), 119n79, 124n101, 129n121, 129n123
    fr. 3 (Cardauns), 128n116, 308n56
    fr. 5 (Cardauns), 128n119
    fr. 6 (Cardauns), 86n105, 127n110
    fr. 7 (Cardauns), 127n111
    fr. 8 (Cardauns), 127n112
    fr. 9 (Cardauns), 127
    fr. 11 (Cardauns), 128n117
    fr. 12 (Cardauns), 124n101, 125n103, 128n120
    fr. 18 (Cardauns), 125n102, 130n128
    fr. 42 (Cardauns), 119n79, 129n122
    fr. 225 (Cardauns), 310n62
    fr. 226 (Cardauns), 127n112

Curio
    fr. 3 (Cardauns), 277n150
L.L.
    5.15.86, 325n103
    5.85, 306
    6.16, 137n8
    7.6, 317n79
    7.8, 317
    7.9, 318n84
    7.9ff, 317n82
    7.26, 299n25
Logist.
    fr. 74 (Bolisani), 257n70
R.R.
    1.6.0, 157n83

Verg.
    Aen.
        6.376, 301n32
        6.847–48, 13n30, 90n120
        8.349, 203
        8.349–50, 7
        8.351–54, 8
    Ecl.
        4.60, 249n25
    G.
        3.34, 13n30, 90n120
Vitr.
    Arch.
        2.1.1, 250n32
        3, 188n69

GENERAL INDEX

action: actors' reasons for, 202; and agency, 111–15, 198, 320; of agents, 57, 129, 132–33, 162, 194, 261, 353; of animals, 366; and belief, 37, 86, 110, 132, 154, 163, 239, 372, 379; and cognition, 113–15, 135, 139, 209–10, 269, 339, 341–43, 378; collective, 136–37, 197, 270, 280, 389; constitutive, 361; constraints on, 247; and cult, 91–116, 127–37, 151–58, 209–14, 225–46, 268–81, 292–93, 334–41, 379–90; cultural, 277; deontic, 129; and direction of fit, 132; divine, 230, 327, 368; Epicurean theory of, 236–37; evaluative, 155–56; Gallic, 385; goals of, 99, 195; of gods/goddesses, 92, 97, 223; high intensity, 81–82; human, 369; imitation of, 263–64, 273; individual, 38, 136; insignificant, 370; instrumental, 262; intentional, 113, 131; Intentional, 96, 134, 213, 260; joint, 145–65, 209, 247, 264–82, 330, 389; and learning, 274; as movement, 11; mundane, 340, 343–44, 359; normative, 275, 365; and norms, 120; as opposed to belief, 27, 31–32, 43, 59, 63; potential, 179; prior, 343–44, 354; purpose of, 278; in pursuit of pleasure, 214; religious, 90, 98, 108, 125, 223, 233, 238, 307, 343–44, 376; restrictions on, 77; as ritual, 28, 31, 42, 238, 248, 262–81, 337–60, 392–93; roles, 147, 342–43, 351; Roman, 205, 392; sacrificial, 372; social, 182; and speech acts, 302, 314; success in, 198; teleological, 115; tendencies, 106–7; as a term, 105; theory of, 109, 133–34, 213; theory of (Aristotelian), 114; theory of (Ciceronian), 113; theory of (Epicurean), 210; toward gods/goddesses, 126

"action representation system" (Lawson & McCauley), 340
action roles: agent, 344, 353–56, 358; patient, 353–54, 356, 359. *See also* action
Acts and Monuments (Foxe), 33
Adversus nationes (Arnobius), 376–77
aedes, 187–89
aetiology, 7–9, 210–17, 229–36, 277–79, 357–58, 360–68, 385–87, 389–92
affordances, 178–80, 261–62
afterlife, 238–39
agency: and action, 110–15, 129, 136, 198, 320, 343; aggregate, 150; of ancestors, 239; animal, 327, 353; augural, 368; and autonomy, 289; beliefs about, 97, 112, 116, 118; causal, 327; causes of, 228, 233–34; celestial, 235; children's, 245–46, 249, 263, 286, 288, 290; cognitive, 244, 288; collective, 150; and communication, 111–13; definition of, 6; and discrimination, 256; divine, 211, 236, 238, 304, 309, 326–28, 344, 351, 355, 359, 367–69; false, 231; human, 11, 14; imitative, 251; and inference, 82; inferential, 289; and Intentionality, 248, 264–65, 282; and intuition, 10–13, 89–90, 92, 95, 327, 340; intuitions about, 261; mundane, 227; and objects, 260; omnipotent, 56, 67, 85, 327; and Roman children, 282; of the Roman senate, 199; sensitivity to, 230; shared, 11, 138–40, 145–46, 148–49, 151–53, 159, 164, 166, 195, 209, 213, 247, 264, 269–70, 281, 389
agents: and action, 129, 131–32, 162, 343, 352; animal, 353; anthropomorphic, 85–87, 336,

459

agents (*continued*)
384; assumptions about, 322; autobiographic, 133; and belief, 52, 82, 99, 111–21, 361; causal relations of, 323; child, 263, 282; and cognition, 342; collective, 314; collectives of, 199; definition of, 5–17; divine, 87, 128, 133, 230, 248, 293, 304, 319, 328, 330, 337, 343, 353–54, 360, 362, 364, 370, 384; expectations about, 329; false, 231; goals of, 272; human, 320, 361; intentions of, 152, 160; interaction among, 249; and intuition, 327, 340; intuitions about, 229; intuitions of, 157; jointly acting, 147; mortal, 364; mundane, 310; normative, 361; norms of, 162; and objects, 92–94; others as, 247, 264; perspectives of, 146; properties of, 320; psychology of, 324; reasoning of, 194; relationalities of, 126, 134, 156, 165, 170; and ritual, 355; roles of, 145; Roman, 294, 315; social, 173, 243–44, 319; unmarked, 370
ager Latiniensis, 92
Amores (Ovid), 7
analogy, 216–17, 231–33, 232n82
Ancestral Fault in Ancient Greece (Gagné), 168
animals, 15, 351–53, 363n66, 367, 373–75, 378–79, 382–83, 386, 388, 391
anthropomorphization, 17, 86, 215, 229–39, 260–61, 309–10, 319–20, 330–36, 377–84
antibelief positions, 27–40, 42. *See also* belief
Antiquitates Romanae (Dionysius of Halicarnassus), 373–74
Antony, Mark, 339, 347–49, 354–55, 360–62, 364–65, 367–69
apprentice model of learning (Sterelny), 244–45
apprenticeship, religious, 248, 263–65, 270, 282–83, 290
Apuleius, 81, 135
Aquinas, Thomas, 17
Aristotle, 20, 114–15, 133–34, 213, 239, 296, 337, 388
Arnobius of Sicca, 372, 376–80, 382–87, 391–92

atheism, 67n30
Atomists, 213
Augustine, 14, 21, 48–57, 78–86, 117, 124, 245–63, 281
Ausfeld, Carl, 308, 311–12, 316, 318
auspicatio (auspication), 344–45, 347, 350, 352, 357, 362, 366
autism, 11n18

Balbus, 40, 122–23, 221–23, 225, 229
Barrett, Justin, 85–86, 310, 332
belief: about behaviors, 202; about institutions, 205; about representations, 180; and action, 37, 86, 110, 132, 154, 163, 239, 372, 379; and agency, 97, 112, 116, 118; and agents, 52, 82, 99, 111–21, 361; as an attitude, 68–69, 187, 388; ancient, 53–54; centrality of, 4, 22, 40, 80n80, 164, 166, 220; of children, 332; Christian, 48; and cognition, 42, 114; collective, 168–69, 364–65, 367; as a concept, 3–4, 7, 17, 27, 34–37, 40, 44–52, 61–63, xv, xvii; and conformity, 245; constitutive, 203–4, 338, 365, 367, 369–70; content of, 18, 65–68, 99, 108, 330; as conviction, 80; counterintuitive, 353; and cult, 236, 263, 300, 330; cultural, 230, 237; and culture learning, 334; deontic, 118–19, 126–35, 155–63, 184–88, 246, 338–39, 360–62, 365, 390; dependency on, 173; and desire, 384; and direction of fit, 71; dispositional, 63–64, 83; doxastic, 20–22, 41, 47–48, 68–69, 192–205, 226, 239–46, 268–70, 281, 292–98, 330, 338, 362, 387; and emotion, 100, 104, 135; and empirical evidence, 221; empty, 214, 260; Epicurean theory of, 217, 219–20; epiphanic, 226, 232–33; etic and emic, 22; false, 16, 72, 217, 228–29, 231, 233, 235–36, 239–42; features of, 75; first-order, 166, 194; Gallic, 383, 387; in gods/goddesses, 39, 123, 123–25, 210–15, 215–16, 216, 227, 227–42, 228–42, 268, 290, 290–93, 291–93, 325, 335, 362, 383–89, 389; horizontal transmission of, 236, 263, 293; imitation

GENERAL INDEX 461

of, 260; -in, 77–79; inconsistent, 74; individual, 168–69; intensity of, 61, 80–82, 97, 295; Intentional, 19–20, 60–61, 68, 102, 247, 262; and intentions, 325; from intuition, 84; learned, 106; as a linguistic practice, 49–51; as a mental state, 77, 175; in miracles, 109; mutual, 144, 147–49, 166, 184; nonconstitutive, 203–4, 367–70, 390; nonreflective, 82–104, 112–13, 157, 200, 293, 302–9, 330–37, 369; normative, 365; and norms, 73n52, 74, 129; objects of, 67, 72; occurrent, 64, 83; as opposed to action, 27, 31–32, 43, 59, 63; pagan, 80, 378; and perception, 133; personal, 380; positive theory of, 59; practical states of, 22, 68, 154, 268–70, 281, 292, 338; and prayer, 305; prestige-based, 332; in pursuit of pleasure, 214; reflective, 82–83, 87–92, 95–97, 104, 113, 157, 293, 321, 337; religious, 23, 35, 43n72, 54–60, 107, 210–19, 234–41, 291–92, 364, 379–85; representative, 18; and ritual, 37, 265, 361, 393; Roman, 5, 22–53, 62, 97, 108–9, 121–23, 150, 283–93, 351–76, 383; second-order, 107, 166, 194; shared, 146–73, 187–92, 200–201, 269, 281–83, 298, 324, 363–64; sociocultural, 72; sources of, 9, 62; and speech acts, 297, 299, 319; and structuralism, 50; of subjects, 177; -that, 77–79; theological, 8–13, 204, 217–18, 227–40, 282, 290, 316–21, 390; traditional, 122, 125; triggers of, 333; unshared, 200; vertical transmission of, 236, 263, 293
Belief, Language, and Experience (Needham), 34, 61
belief-action dichotomy, 27, 31, 42–43, 59, 99, 130, 133. *See also* action; belief
belief-behavior dichotomy, 209. *See also* belief
Bicchieri, Cristina, 118, 160, 162
Boyer, Pascal, 321–23
Brentano, Franz, 19–20, 66

caerimonia, 107–8
Caesar, Julius, 339, 347–48, 354, 364n71, 365, 369, 372, 380, 382–88, 391–93

Capitoline Hill, 1, 7–9, 18, 203, 317, 359
Carmen Arvale, 306–8, 310
catechism, 137, 288–90, 292
Catholicism, 28, 32–33
Cato the Elder, 307–10, 312, 319, 323, 328, 359
causal opacity, 272–74, 276–79, 304, 331, 341
Christian antipagan polemic, 27–28, 385
Christianity, 3–4, 27–48, 242–46, 369–77, 379–80, 383, 385
Cicero, 11–31, 40–41, 91–93, 101–51, 180–200, 225–30, 254–58, 275–83, 323–26, 339–67
civitas (city-state), 196, 198–200
cognition: 4E, 17–18; about action, 113–15, 209, 269, 339, 341–43, 360, 378; about practice, 338, 360–63, 370; about speech acts, 366; in action, 339; affective-behavioral episode of, 108; and agency, 286, 288, 342; aspects of, 66, 83; attunement of, 269; automatic, 84; and autonomy, 31, 138, 289–90, 302; and belief, 42, 114; and biases, 302; child, 286; Christian, 40; collective, 135–36; and common ground, 281; and conformity, 31, 41, 130, 138, 204; constitutive, 189; context of, 22; core competencies of, 248; and cult, 28, 110, 213, 243; cultural, 51, 250–52, 254, 264–65, 281, 290; deontic, 127; developmentally natural, 11n19; development of, 89; doxastic, 176; embedded, 18; embodied, 18; features of, 229; of god/goddesses, 219; human, 181, 338–39, 388; hypothesis of, 359; and Intentionality, 18, 56, 59, 100n5, 104, 143; latent zone of, 279; meta, 4, 40, 47–48, 51–52, 80, 88; natural, 220, 342, 359–60; normativity of, 73, 118, 131; and norms, 129, 271; practical, 337; in practice, 338, 361–62, 365, 370; processes of, 42, 48, 83, 96, 282, 302, 322; purposive, 19; religious, 4, 75, 82, 86, 92–93; and representations, 188, 338; resources of, 343; and ritual, 36, 168, 243, 246, 338–42; Roman, 89–90, 92–93; in Roman cult, 9; shared, 254; skills of, 139; social, 5–6, 10n15–10n16, 11–17, 83–95, 135, 145, 160–64, 199–202,

cognition (*continued*)
247–64, 281, 290, 310–11, 332–42; speech acts as, 187, 192; subjective, 189; System 1, 83–86; System 2, 83–91, 97, 104, 117; theological, 218; theory of, 43n72, 169, 243, 339–40, 358

cognitive optimum, 322–23

cognitive science of religion (CSR), 6, 10, 12, 22, 82, 229

collective acceptance theory, 177n21

collegia, 197–99, 345, 348

commitment, 330

common ground, 151–52, 254, 281, 283, 290, 298. *See also* belief; Intentionality; we-intention

communia, 151

Confessions (Augustine), 48, 251

confirmation bias, 74

congressus naturalis (natural sociability), 283

consensus, 138–43, 148, 195, 199–201, 218, 258. *See also* common ground; we-intention

constitutive attitudes, 338n3

constitutive rules, 180–84, 186–87, 190–92, 202–3, 355–57

consuetudo, 257–58

content, 331–32, 334–36

context, 330–32, 335–36

"coordination problem," 149

core knowledge, 11n19. *See also* knowledge

counterintuitiveness, 331, 353, 388. *See also* intuition

credibility enhancing displays (CREDs), 302, 333–35

credo, 41, 46–47, 66, 78–79

cult: action, 91–116, 127–37, 151–58, 209–14, 225–46, 268–81, 292–93, 330–41, 379–90; aetiology of, 210; ancient, 133; apprentices in, 244, 290; of Bacchus, 140–41; barbarian, 371; and belief, 236, 263, 300, 330; cause of, 214; Christian, 80, 385; cognition of, 28, 135, 137, 213, 243; collective, 136–37, 264, 280; and conformity, 204; context of, 290, 292; domestic, 153, 263, 281; Epicurean, 212; explanations of, 229; family, 263, 281; and gods/goddesses, 42, 122, 130, 293, 302; Greek, 390; images, 13, 90, 94; intensity of, 81; of *manes*, 238; non-Roman, 30; norms of, 118, 122, 125, 129–30; objects, 154, 261, 377; obligations, 121; pagan, 88; performance of, 246; and *pietas*, 200; practices, 68, 129, 203, 234–42, 277–79, 327, 362, 372; psychological effects of, 108, 279; ritual, 270; Roman, 2–31, 40, 59, 95–129, 157–69, 186, 199–210, 245, 265, 283–91, 385, 390, xvii; scenes of, 271; singing and dancing in, 287; and social learning, 272; theory of, 237; traditional practices of, 2–4, 10, 81, 124, 241, 259; transmission through, 87; without belief, 31

cultural learning, 251, 277, 282, 298, 302, 309, 330, 332–36

cultural transmission, 283. *See also* cultural learning

Cumont, Franz, 30

De bello Gallico (Caesar), 381

De divinatione (Cicero), 341, 369

de Fontenelle, Bernard, 31, 31n20, 32, 39

De haruspicum responsis (Cicero), 92–93

de iure pontificum (Numa), 277

De legibus (Cicero), 71, 121

De natura deorum (Cicero), 17, 40, 122, 217–18, 222, xvii

deontic powers, 178–94, 200, 202–3, 337, 348, 354, 357, 363, 369

deontology, 77, 99, 110–35, 155–63, 171–202, 262–65, 354–69, 388, 390–91. *See also* norms; ontology

De pietate (Philodemus), 231

De republica (Cicero), 40

De rerum natura (Lucretius), 212, 214, 231, 237

de Vaca, Cabeza, 183

Die Religion der Römer (Hartung), 28

Dionysius of Halicarnassus, 372–76, 380, 385–93

direction of causation: double, 77; word-to-world, 76–77, 96–99, 104–6; world-to-word, 76, 312

direction of fit: mind-to-world, 69–77, 96–97, 131–33; world-to-mind, 69–77, 96–97, 131–33
dispositions, 184
Durkheim, Émile, 158, 166–70, 196, 198n108, 199, 262, 280, 363–64, 368
dyadic relations, 248, 250. *See also* triadic relations

Elder-Vass, Dave, 177
embodied appraisal, 103n26, 104–7, 389
emergent social entities, 197–99
emic perspectives, 5, 21–22, 52, 209, 372, 387–88, xvi
emotion, 19, 96–110, 119, 135, 157–58, 209, 236, 389
emotional turn (in classical scholarship), 99n2
empiricism, 341–42, 362
Empiricus, Sextus, 216–17, 219, 224, 232–33
Epicurean therapeutic program, 213, 239, 241
Epicurus, 214, 216, 218, 228–29, 231, 234, 236, 239–40, 242, 388–90
epiphany, 210–11, 215–27, 229–30, 232–33, 242, 289
epistemology: empiricist, 362; objective, 68, 174, 189, 205, 367; subjective, 174
Epistles (Horace), 289
etic perspectives, 5, 21–22, 52, 209, 372, 388, 392, xvi
etiology, 63, 209, 362, 388
evaluative judgements, 309, 338, 361
exauguratio, 359
expectation, 161–63, 322, 328–29
experience, 53n111, 54

faith, 34, 37–42, 45–47, 78, 292, 325, xv
Fasti (Ovid), 137, 278, 363n67
Feeney, Denis, 38, 211, 282, 335, 340, 358
fides, 47, 78–79, 325
folk psychology, 10n15, 14, 51, 134, 143, 148, 310, 320–22, 383, 388
folk sociology, 164
folk theology, 17, 86–87, 200, 268–70, 282, 290–93, 307–11, 320–35

force, 76, 294
Foxe, John, 33
friendship (Ciceronian), 140

Gagné, Renaud, 168
gods/goddesses: acts of, 21, 33, 81–82, 92–97, 219–29, 279, 299–304, 351–53; acts toward, 7, 102, 126–29, 234–35, 258–63, 267–69, 303, 319–24, 378–83, xvi, xvii; agency of, 355, 367, 369; as agents, 17, 85, 337; agricultural, 306; anthropomorphic, 86, 239, 261, 320, 377; Apollo, 278, 289, 382; as arbiters of norms, 201; Bacchus, 141; belief in, 123–25, 215–16, 227–42, 268, 290–93, 325, 335, 362, 383–89; Christian, 80; chthonic, 373; commands of, 224; common notion of, 218–19, 227–28, 236, 241–42; communication with, 307; consultation of, 9; and counterintuitivness, 327; and cult, 42, 122, 130, 293, 302; cult images of, 12–13, 42, 88–90; cult of, 122, 293; dispositions of, 232; effigies of, 281; epiphanies of, 7, 92–94, 215–26; existence of, 38, 62, 203, 222, 230, 240; experiences of, 225; Gallic, 382, 384; Greek, 320, 329, 374; happiness of, 217; hierarchies of, 268; and human relationships, 142; inferences about, 236; intuitions about, 15; Juno, 90–91, 286; Jupiter, 2–4, 18, 91–94, 194, 286, 308–29, 345–55, 357–59, 364–68, 382; Mars, 328, 348, 382; Mercury, 382; minds of, 16, 276; Minerva, 382; narratives about, 127; nature of, 210; and norms, 282; pagan, 259; personified, 32; pleasure of, 277, 378; power of, 112, 326; and prayer, 305, 309–10, 323; representations of, 320–21; Roman, 124, 291, 323, 330; of Rome, xvii; sacrifice to, 1–2, 93–95, 153; in *societas*, 200; Terminus, 178–87, 192–93, 203, 266–67, 269, 282, 314, 359; of war, 313
Greeks, ancient, 3, 36–39, 211–13, 306, 308, 374, 385, 390–92
group mind, 199. *See also* common ground; consensus; Intentionality; we-intention

Hartung, Johann Adam, 28–30, 34
Hellenism, 29, 211
Histoire des Oracles (Fontenelle), 31
historical empathy, 55
Horace, 287–89, 300
horror, 234–35, 241–42, 293, 389. See also Lucretius
House of C. Julius Polybius at Pompeii, 153–54
House of Sutoria Primigenia at Pompeii, 269
House of the Arches at Pompeii, 266
House of the Tragic Poet at Pompeii, 104
Hypersensitive Agency Detection Device (HADD), 12–14, 16, 229–30, 331

identity markers, 164
imitatio, 255
imitation, 170, 251, 255–60, 262–65, 271–72, 274, 276, 290, 332. See also overimitation
inauguratio, 337, 339, 341, 345–50, 352–65, 367
inference, 82–97, 126, 215–36, 248, 261, 271–77, 290, 302–9, 321–32, 341–44
Innocentius, 55–57, 63, 105–6, 112
instauratio, 2, 275–77, 334, 373
Institutes (Gaius), 191
institutional facts, 182–83, 204, 367
institutions, 6–9, 120–23, 172–205, 315–19, 331–38, 360–69, 377, 390
intention, 68–69, 110–33, 178–89, 236–52, 262–65, 281–88, 299–307, 324–25, 337, 389
Intentionality: and action, 96, 134, 213, 265; and agency, 248, 264–65, 282; of agents, 133; aggregate, 149–50, 162; of belief, 19–20, 60; causation of, 131, 134; and cognition, 18, 56, 59, 100n5, 143; collective, 22, 150–52, 162–66, 186, 265, 270, 298; content of, 65–76, 87, 96, 102–7, 116, 132, 144–47, 204, 235, 251–54; of cult, 137; cultural, 270, 282; deontic, 390; and direction of causation, 98–99, 102, 104, 106; discursive, 75, 292–93, 302, 330; doxastic states of, 20–22, 41–52, 68–73, 80–87, 98–102, 115–23, 133, 154, 169, 214, 389–90; of emotion, 135; episodes of, 64–65, 99, 146–47, 150, 246, 252; evaluative, 108–9; faculty of, 247; first-order, 147; forms of, 165, 265; individual, 147, 159; joint, 147, 151–53, 163, 186, 270, 298; levels/orders of, 384; linguistic, 75; of mental states, 20–22; normativity of, 73, 101; objects of, 64–67, 104, 107, 144, 251; ontological dependence on, 176; of others, 253, 327; philosophy of, 19n47; practical states of, 169; and prayer, 259; property of, 60; psychological, 75, 302; relations of, 198; religious, 141; Roman, 132; second-order, 147, 384; shared, 9, 22–23, 136–78, 189–205, 248–54, 263–64, 281–90, 330; of speakers, 76; of speech acts, 75, 185; as a state, 17; states of, 57, 63, 67–69, 75, 96–97, 118–19, 260, 300, 319, 337, 362, 387; study of, 73; theory of, 95; third-order, 384; we-, 145, 194
intuition, 5–19, 82–103, 126, 157, 203–10, 221–30, 260–61, 320–27, 338–43, 353–64
invocatio, 308–10, 312, 314, 316, 318
Italy, 2, 32, 212

joint attention, 155, 250–51, 265, 280–82
joint commitment, 279

knowledge, 21–22, 205, 246, 263, 304, 325, 340–41. See also core knowledge

Lactantius, 12–14, 33, 88–90
language, 75, 77, 185, 248–56, 260, 263, 276, 294, 318, 333. See also speech act
Latin, 41, 48, 52, 212–13
Latin literature, 7
Latour, Bruno, 47
Lawson, E. T., 339–41, 343–44, 358, 364
Lawson, Tony, 177, 194
legalistic paradigm (Mommsen's), 29–30
Levinas, 10
litatio, 1–2, 4
Livy, 80–82, 100–112, 135–41, 157–58, 179–86, 274–75, 286–88, 313–28, 349–66, 382–86
Lucilius, 12–14, 88–90, 261
Lucretius, 116, 209–55, 265, 293, 380, 389
Luther, Martin, 32–33

magic, 273, 275, 318. *See also* superstition
Maximus, Valerius, 303
McCauley, R. N., 339–41, 343–44, 358, 364
memory, 69n37, 99, 119, 153n69, 287, 322
mental episode, 16–17, 19–22, 58, 60, 96, 102, 177, 292
Metamorphoses (Apuleius), 81, 106, 314
mindreading, 14n32
minimally counterintuitive (MCI) representations, 320–23, 327, 330, 337, 343–44
Momigliano, Arnaldo, 136–37
Mommsen, Theodor, 29–34, 38, 100
mores, 257, 262
mos, 257–58
Müller-Lyer illusion, 84–86

Needham, Rodney, 34–37, 42, 46, 49–56, 60–61, 168, 175
neuro-atypical development, 11n18
neuropathology, 11n18
Nock, Darby, 30–37
norms: and action, 120; activities governed by, 390; and agents, 162; of belief, 74; circle, 163–64; and conformity, 198; of consistency, 131; and conventions, 120 (*see also* deontology); cooperative, 159, 280; of cult, 118–19, 122, 125, 129–30; cultural, 129, 153; deontic, 338; divine, 201; external, 131; and gods/goddesses, 282; internal, 131, 148, 159, 278; and language, 276; legal, 110, 126; liturgical, 265, 268; local, 121; natural, 129, 159, 271; performative, 281–83, 389–90; political, 199; predictive, 156; ritual, 155, 270, 275–77, 281; Roman, 124; and rules, 272; of satisfaction, 131; shared, 138, 156, 269, 282; social, 99, 110, 117–20, 130–31, 135, 159–63, 166, 209; systems of, 127; universal, 162
Numa, 40, 88, 122, 186–87, 274, 277, 349, 371
the numinous, 8–10
Nussbaum, Martha, 102–3, 238–39

objects: and agents, 92–94; animate, 11–13, 89–90, 229, 249; of attention, 252; of belief, 67, 72; cult, 154, 261, 377; cultural, 262; inanimate, 11, 14, 260; Intentional, 64–67, 104, 107, 144, 251; material, 197; meanings of, 261; mind-independent, 181; perspectives on, 253; physical, 323; properties of, 320–21; repurposed, 178; of sacrifice, 391; social, 180; of speech acts, 76
observation, 341–42, 349–55, 360–61, 363, 390
Oedipus, 65–66
ontogeny: of community, 281; cultural, 249, 253, 262, 264; individual, 271; of infants, 250; perspective of, 282; of social cognition, 89, 248–51, 253
ontology: of *aedes*, 188; and commitment, 191; concept—(*also* cognition-, belief-, mind-, *and* subject) dependent, 49, 57, 63, 173–75, 181, 202, 338, 363, 391; intuitive, 320–22; of objective entities, 63–64; objectivity, 174, 177; possibilities of, 356; of ritual, 190; and rules, 191; social, 22, 172–78, 186–89, 195–97, 262–65, 296, 339, 369, 390, xv, xvi; subjective, 68, 96, 177, 189, 204–5, 338, 367–68, 391. *See also* deontology
opinio, 21, 40–52, 71, 80, 103–6, 122–25, 201, 325, 379–87, xvii
"Oriental religions" (Cumont), 30
orthodoxy, 279, 288
orthopraxy, 248, 272, 273n130, 274, 277–79, 288, 306, 348
overimitation, 273–75, 277–79. *See also* imitation
Ovid, 7–8, 55, 137–38, 156–57, 164, 204–5, 266–84, 310–14, 353

Pagan Priests (Beard & North), 363
pagans, 27–46, 79, 88–89, 136, 332, 380, 393. *See also* polytheism
pars epica, 308, 310, 312, 314, 316, 318
pedagogy, 248, 283–84, 288. *See also* cultural learning; religious education

perception: and action, 113, 115, 131; and belief, 133; cause of, 215; experience of, 71; intellectual, 8; and Intentionality, 17, 60, 64, 71, 99, 103–4; intention and, 281; norms of, 73n52; physics of, 219; sensory, 6–14, 72, 153, 213

performance, 339–41, 348, 363, 389–90

perspective: adopting of, 254; of agents, 264; of others, 60, 250–51, 253, 262, 265, 282; shared, 281

pietas, 118–29, 142, 159–71, 200, 212, 233–35, 265–69, 280–82, 292–93

Plato, 21, 91–92

Plutarch, 277

polydoxy, 278

polytheism, 376–80, 382–83, 385, 393. *See also* pagans

populus, 196, 199–200

Pouillon, Jean, 50–52

practical syllogism (Aristotle), 115

praefatio, 373

prayer, 239–43, 251, 258–63, 272–73, 283–336, 388, 391

preces, 308–9, 312–14, 316, 318

Prescendi, Francesca, 372

presuppositions, 297n19, 298–302, 309, 313, 317, 319, 324, 328, 388, 390

Price, Simon, 37–38, 44–46, 49, 167–68, 245–46, 376, 379

prodigium, 2, 80, 93–94, 100, 107–8, 136, 198, 284

prolēpsis, 218–19

Protestant anti-Catholic polemic, 32–33. *See also* Catholicism; Christianity

Protestantism, 32–33

Prudentius, 251, 258–63, 281, 283, 332

psychological hedonism, 214, 219

psychological mode: attitude, 68–76, 96–102, 123, 144–58, 187–209, 236, 250–81, 293, 362; belief, 68–69; content of, 147; desire, 16, 69–73, 96–99, 114–21, 135, 209–14, 237–47, 289–301, 384, 388; fear, 376; intention, 68–69; of Intentionality, 144; and satisfaction, 73, 75–76, 131, 296–97

Quintilian, 255–58, 262, 283

reasoning: motivated, 74; practical, 131, 194, 205; deontic, 127, 134–35; desire-based, 134

the Reformation, 32–33

The Relation of Álvar Núñez Cabeza de Vaca (de Vaca), 183

religio, 7–8, 38, 81, 101, 107–8, 112, 129n124, 287, 349, 379. *See also* religion

religion: and action, 344, 376; ancient, 35, 39, 82, 209; anthropological study of, 35; in antiquity, 212; and belief, 35, 107, 219, 364, 379–80, 385; cognition of, 75; cognitive science of, 6, 12, 82, 210–11; concept of, xv–xvii; creed-based, 289; domestic, 259n79; and education, 137; experience of, 380; Gallic, 381, 393; Greek, 43, 80; as a human invention, 220; institutions of, 68, 390; learning of, 244–46, 248, 283, 288; orthodox, 278–79; orthoprax, 278–79; phenomena of, 211; practices of, 177, 338, 349, 365, 369, 382; rituals of, 343–44; Roman, 36–77, 93–101, 110–17, 130–38, 165–73, 191, 263, 277–78, 290–306, 327–49, 359–82; shared, 270; social-cognitive accounts of, 258; study of, 36–39, 44

Religion und Kultus der Römer (Wissowa), 29

religious education, 137, 283. *See also* cultural learning; pedagogy

religious transmission. *See* cultural learning

Remus, 9

representations, 153, 177–89, 203–4, 213, 254, 320–21, 329–67

res publica (Cicero), 196

ritual: acts, 3–5, 28–32, 42–43, 55, 238, 248, 262–81, 337–44, 346–60, 392–93; agent, 355; agricultural, 306; of ancient Greeks, 36; augural, 353, 357, 362–63, 365, 370; authority, 355; and belief, 37, 166, 265, 361, 393; Catholic, 28; causally opaque, 278; and cognition, 36, 168, 243, 246, 338–42; collective, 157, 282; commitment to, 282; contexts of, 293, 335–36; cult, 270; empty, 30–33; enabling, 355, 358; failure, 273;

fetial, 326; general discussion of, 36, 188–89, 205, 273, 338, 342, 348, 389; Greek, 39; group, 158–59; high-fidelity, 277, 279; history, 364; and hymn singing, 290; hypothetical, 344, 358; and imitation, 274, 277, 290; of *inauguratio*, 317, 355; incorrect, 276; and intuition, 343; meaning of, 33, 292, 340; norms of, 155, 270, 275–77, 281; ontology of, 190; opaque, 278–79, 303–4; performance, 282; practices, 271–72, 341, 348, 367; and prayer, 290, 298–99, 303; priestly, 346; rational, 324–25; and *religio*, 38; religious, 243, 343–44; Roman, 36, 174, 205, 338, 342, 348, 389; sacralizing, 188; sacrificial, 371; superrational, 325; technologies of, 278–79; as a term, 33; theory of, 364; thesis of, 3

Rituals and Power (Price), 36, 167

Roman Questions (Plutarch), 277–78

Roman religion: and action, 205, 392; agents of, 13, 17, 294, 315; auspices of, 339, 344, 346, 352–55; behaviors of, 57–58; and belief, 5–10, 22–62, 97, 108–9, 121–25, 150, 283–93, 350–70, 376, 383; choral hymns of, 283–89, 303, 318; and cognition, 89–90, 92–93; and cult, 2–31, 40, 59, 95–129, 157–69, 186, 199–210, 245, 265, 283–91, 385, xvii; domestic, 259n79; education in, 137; and epiphany, 220, 225; and faith, 78; general discussion of, 3–77, 93–101, 110–17, 130–38, 165–73, 191, 203–11, 263–78, 290, 299–306, 327–32, 349, 359–82, xv–xvii; gods/ goddesses of, 128, 291, 330, 335–36, xvii; and Intentionality, 132; mythical figures of, 88; norms of, 124, 126; and omnipotence, 327; and orthopraxy, 277; polytheism of, 376; and prayer, 243, 289–334; priests of, 363; psychological states of, 58; and ritual, 36, 188–89, 205, 273, 338–48, 389; and sacrifice, 375–86; and social life, 366; speech acts and, 186; worshippers of, 164, 175, 330

Roman society: adults of, 244; architecture of, 189; children of, 16, 148n54, 243–48, 251, 259, 263–65, 270, 279–82, 284–90, 332; collectives in, 199; consuls of, 1–4; culinary traditions of, 391; culture of, 3, 230; daily life of, 238, 292; elites of, 212, 231; history of, 380; jurists of, 140; law of, 30, 189, 193, 197; politics of, 143; regal period of, 65; republic of, 143, 363; senate of, 2, 197–99, 332; singing in, 283–85, 287, 289–90; slaves of, 116; social reality of, 68, 171, 181–82, 185–86, 189, 191–92, 194, 197, 202–4, 368–69; theories of, 209, 211; traditional, 48, 257, 278

Romulus, 9, 40, 179–80, 310, 349, 357–58, 368, 371

sacra, 233, 280, 371, xvii. *See also* sacrifice

sacrifice, 1–2, 93–95, 153–58, 190–92, 237–38, 266–69, 304–7, 328–35, 371–79, 381–92. *See also sacra*

sacrum, 190–92

schola cantorum, 284

the Scholastics, 20

Searle, John, 77, 143, 177, 186–87, 192

Second Philippic (Cicero), 347

Second Samnite War, 329n114

Seneca the Younger, 8, 40, 149, 170

shared intentionality, 9, 22–23, 136–78, 189–205, 248–54, 263–64, 281–90, 330

Sisyphus, 220

social-cognitive tool, 12, 17, 229. *See also* cognition

social death, 129

social learning, 245, 248, 261, 264–65, 271–72, 290, 299. *See also* cultural learning; cultural transmission; religious education

societas, 142–43, 195–97, 199–201, 254, 276

speech act, 22; about objects, 76; and action, 302, 314; addressees, 294; assertion, 51–52, 64, 76–77, 112, 186, 239, 289, 294–98, 302, 312–19; belief and, 297, 299, 319; and cognition, 176, 187, 192, 366; collective, 194, 314; commissives, 76–77, 187, 294–96, 301, 313, 316, 319, 335; conditions of satisfaction, 296; declarations, 77, 183–92, 294–97, 314, 318–19, 335, 352, 356, 363, 366;

speech act (*continued*)
dedication, 295–96; directives, 76, 187, 261, 294–97, 312–13, 318–19, 328, 388; expressives, 187, 294, 313, 319; hearers of, 294, 297–99, 302, 309–10, 316, 319, 327, 330, 334–35; illocutionary forces of, 76, 294–95, 297, 311, 313, 319; imperative, 318; Intentional, 57–59, 76; oaths as, 200–201, 301, 314–16, 325, 335; as *oratio*, 139, 141; overhearers of, 294, 297–98; as performance, 334–36; performative, 185, 311; perlocutionary aspect of, 297; petitionary, 312–13, 320; prayers as, 292–93, 330, 334, 336; of promise, 185–86, 295, 301, 316, 319; propositions, 289, 301, 307, 312–13, 316; and psychological states, 311–12; Roman religion and, 185; semantic, 185; sincerity conditions of, 295; as socially binding, 186, 316, 335; speakers of, 297–300, 302, 309–10, 313, 316, 319, 327, 330, 334–35; spoken, 294; symbolic, 185; theory of, 185, 311; unsuccessful, 295; vow, 334–35; written, 294
Status Function, 180–84, 186–87, 190–92, 202, 338–39, 366, 391
Sterelny, Kim, 244
Stoics, 103–6, 113–14, 139, 200, 222
subject-object dichotomy, 174–77. *See also* objects
Summa theologiae (Aquinas), 17
superperception, 326. *See also* perception
superstition, 260n81. *See also* magic

Tarde, Gabriel, 170
template of Roman Sacrifice (Prescendi), 372–73. *See also* sacrifice
testimony, 10, 71, 230, 291, 302, 331
Theaetetus (Plato), 21
theologia tripertita (Varro), 86–87, 127–30
"theological correctness" (Barrett), 85
theology: civic, 127–29; natural, 127. *See also theologia tripertita* (Varro)
Theory of Mind (ToM), 14, 16, 331, 383
triadic relations, 249–50. *See also* dyadic relations
Tusculan Disputations (Cicero), 103

universitas, 197

Varro, 21, 86, 94–95, 118–19, 124–30, 258, 306, 308, 317–18
Vergil, 7–8, 10
votum, 319

we-intention, 145, 148–49, 154–55, 159, 247, 264. *See also* common ground; group mind; intention; shared intentionality
Wissowa, Georg, 29–30

Xenophanes, 86

A NOTE ON THE TYPE

This book has been composed in Arno, an Old-style serif typeface in the classic Venetian tradition, designed by Robert Slimbach at Adobe.

GPSR Authorized Representative: Easy Access System Europe - Mustamäe tee 50, 10621 Tallinn, Estonia, gpsr.requests@easproject.com

www.ingramcontent.com/pod-product-compliance
Lightning Source LLC
Chambersburg PA
CBHW030559230426
43661CB00053B/1779